SUSPENDED MUSIC

Lothar von Falkenhausen

# SUSPENDED MUSIC

*Chime-Bells in the Culture of Bronze Age China*

UNIVERSITY OF CALIFORNIA PRESS   BERKELEY   LOS ANGELES   OXFORD

善待問者如撞鐘
叩之以小者則小鳴
叩之以大者則大鳴
待其從容然後盡其聲……
此皆進學之道也

*To my teacher*
*K. C. Chang*

*He who is good at entertaining questions*
*is like a bell when struck:*
*When knocked gently, it merely emits a faint ring;*
*but when knocked forcefully, it resounds loudly.*
*Responding as amply as appropriate,*
*it rings to the fullest and then stops. . . .*
*This is the true way to foster learning.*

*Li Ji* "xueji"

Calligraphy by Zhang Zhenglang

University of California Press
Berkeley and Los Angeles, California

University of California Press, Ltd.
Oxford, England

© 1993 by
The Regents of the University of California

Library of Congress
Cataloging-in-Publication Data

Falkenhausen, Lothar von.
    Suspended music: chime-bells in the
culture of Bronze Age China /
Lothar von Falkenhausen.
        p.   cm.
    Includes bibliographical references
    (p.    ) and index.
    ISBN 0-520-07378-9
    (cloth : alk. paper)
    1. Bells—China.   2. Bronze age—
China.   3. Chimes.   4. China—
Antiquities.   I. Title.
    CC250.C6F35   1993
    786.8'848'0931—dc20            91-34554
                                    CIP

Printed in the United States of America
1   2   3   4   5   6   7   8   9

# CONTENTS

qingtongqi, pl. 77; rubbing from *Shou Xian Cai Hou-mu*, 52–53. / 70

29. *Zheng* excavated in 1987 from tomb no. 2 at Baoshan, Jingmen (Hubei). From *Zhongguo Hubei chutu wenwu*, fig. 66. / 71

30. Set of seven *goudiao* excavated in 1958 at Yancheng, Wujin (Jiangsu). From *Jiangsu chutu wenwu*, pl. 94. / 71

31. *Chunyu* excavated in 1956 at Changde (Hunan). From *Zhongguo meishu quanji, Gongyi meishu-bian*, vol. 5 (Bronzes II), pl. 152. / 72

32. Nomenclature of the constituent parts of *zhong* family bells. After Hayashi 1964, 261 (modified). Calligraphy by Dr. Wang Youqin. / 73

33. Nangong Hu–*yongzhong* excavated in 1979 at Baozigou, Fufeng (Shaanxi) (with inscription rubbing). From *Shaanxi chutu Shang Zhou qingtongqi*, vol. 3, pl. 140. / 74

34. Profile of a European church-bell. After Konrad Bund, *Deutsches Glockenmuseum auf Burg Greifenstein: Eine Einführung*, Greifenstein (1987), 21. / 75

35. Buddhist temple-bell at the Dazhongsi bell museum, Beijing. Photo by the author, 1981. / 76

36. The vibration patterns of a Chinese chime-bell. From Rossing 1989b, 248, fig. 13. / 77

37. Sound spectra showing the relative strengths of the partials of a Chinese chime-bell. From Takahashi 1984, 101. / 78

38. Interferogram showing the nodal pattern (mode 2,0) for the A- and B-tones of a Chinese chime-bell. From Ma Chengyuan 1981, pls. 21–25. / 81

39. The nodal pattern of a Western church-bell. From Rossing 1989b, 248, fig. 13(b). / 82

40. Cross-section of a Chinese chime-bell showing the different vibration patterns of the A- and B-tones at mode (2,0). After Ma Chengyuan 1981, 133. / 83

41. Modulation of wall thickness on the inside of several Zeng *yongzhong*. From *Zeng Hou Yi-mu*, vol. 1, 93–94, figs. 48–49. / 84

42. The standard proportions of a *yongzhong* according to the *Kaogongji*, as reconstructed by Cheng Yaotian. From *Kaogong chuangwu xiaoji*, 538: 21a/b. / 86

43. Scaling proportions of the Jingli-*niuzhong* from Changtaiguan, Xinyang (Henan) (see fig. 104), as charted by André Lehr. From Lehr 1985, 102–3. / 94

44. Qing dynasty chime of sixteen bells, displayed at the former Imperial Palace, Beijing. From *Kokyū Hakubutsuin-ten: Shikinjō-no kyūtei geijutsu tsuroku*, Tōkyō: Seibu Museum of Art, 1985. / 95

qingtongqi-xuan, pl. 78. / 188

# TABLES

# ACKNOWLEDGMENTS

This book was written at Stanford University, where I spent two happy and fruitful years (1988–1990) as an Andrew W. Mellon Postdoctoral Fellow. Besides acknowledging my gratitude to the Mellon Foundation for its generous sponsorship, I would like to express my thanks to my colleagues in the Asian Languages department, especially to professors Albert E. Dien and David S. Nivison, for providing a most agreeable as well as intellectually stimulating working environment.

This book has also benefited from my frequent interaction with colleagues across the bay at Berkeley, and elsewhere in the United States. Professor David N. Keightley provided an extraordinarily careful and thoughtful reading of the manuscript. Chapters 3 and 5 were substantially improved as a result of Professor Robert W. Bagley's generous and timely advice. I am grateful to Dr. Norman E. Cima, Professor Philip J. Ivanhoe, Professor Michael Nylan, Dr. Lisa A. Raphals, Mr. Scott E. Rose, and Professor Edward L. Shaughnessy, all of whom read the book in manuscript form and provided helpful comments. I wish to express my thanks again to those who offered comments at the dissertation stage, for much of their input remained useful in writing this book. Needless to say, any shortcomings that remain are my own responsibility.

I am very grateful to the staff at the University of California Press for their help in producing this book; special thanks to Sheila Levine for serving as the sponsoring editor, and to Amy Klatzkin for seeing this book through press. I wish to extend my heartfelt thanks to Ellen Stein for her insightful editing, which greatly enhanced the readability of my prose. Many thanks are also due to Deborah Rudolph, who did a superb job of proofreading the galleys. At the stage of producing the final version of the manuscript in the summer of 1990, I was capably assisted by Messrs. Claudio Wolfring and Christof Maciejczyk, who produced the drawings, and by Ms. Ingeborg L. Klinger of the Art History Institute at the University of Heidelberg, who took a number of photographs for the book. Thanks to the kind assistance of Dr. Pott, Dr. Behrendes, and Mr. Händler, I was able to produce the manuscript on a laser printer at the Thyssen Hauptverwaltung in Duisburg. Professor Lothar Ledderose put at my disposal the resources of the East Asian Art History Library at Heidelberg, and Ms. Sybille Girmond helped me in locating illustration material. Dr. Thomas Lawton (Washington, D.C.) took an enthusiastic interest in my work on ancient Chinese music and was helpful in procuring a number of professional photographs much superior to my own efforts. The following individuals and institutions have graciously granted permission to reproduce artwork in this book: the Trustees of the British Museum, London (Ms. Jessica Rawson and Ms. Jane Portal); Professor K.C. Chang; the Art Institute of Chicago (Ms. Eleanor Perlstein); the Museum of East Asian Antiquities, Stockholm (Dr. Mette Siggstedt); Professor Hayashi Minao; the Institute of History and Philology, Academia Sinica, Taipei (Dr. Tsang Cheng-hwa); the Hunan Provincial Museum, Changsha (Professor Gao Zhixi); the Metropolitan Museum of Art, New York (Dr. James C.Y. Watt); Dr. André Lehr; Professor Thomas D. Rossing; the Arthur M. Sackler Gallery, Smithsonian Institution, Washington, D.C. (Dr. Thomas Lawton); and the Sen'oku Hakkokan (Sumitomo Collection), Kyōto (Professor Higuchi Takayasu and Ms. Kohno Keiko). Professor Zhang Zhenglang (Institute of History, Chinese Academy of Social Sciences) kindly produced the calligraphy for the jacket of the book. My sincere and cordial thanks to them all.

I dedicate this book to my teacher, Professor K.C. Chang of Harvard University, whose continuing advice, support, cooperation, and friendship I treasure.

Although this book was prefigured by a lengthy dissertation submitted to the Department of Anthropology at Harvard University in 1988 (quoted below as "Falkenhausen 1988"), *Suspended Music* is a new piece of work, incorporating substantial further research. I hope it will make a central, yet so far understudied, aspect of ancient Chinese civilization accessible to a varied interdisciplinary audience. Readers interested in more detailed documentation and further information on ancient Chinese musical theory may wish to consult the now somewhat outdated dissertation, which remains available through University Microfilms.

This book is constructed in a cumulative manner, with later chapters presupposing an understanding of earlier ones. Because the subject matter required development of some new terminology, I have provided a glossary to explain potentially unfamiliar terms from all parts of the book.

After the manuscript was completed I received a copy of the final report on the tomb of Marquis Yi of Zeng at Leigudun, Suizhou (Hubei), *Zeng Hou Yimu*, 2 vols. (Beijing: Wenwu, 1989). Fortunately, in light of the importance of this site to my endeavor in this book, parts of the report had already been communicated, including the sections on the Zeng chime-bells and their inscriptions, which were distributed to participants in the international symposium on the chime-bells of Marquis Yi of Zeng at Wuhan in 1988 and which are frequently referred to in the following pages as "Tan and Feng 1988" and "Qiu and Li 1988."

The documentation in the Appendixes of this book covers evidence reported through the end of 1990. The Bibliography comprises four parts: (1) classical Chinese texts, their editions and translations; (2) Chinese works of premodern scholarship; (3) works quoted by title, such as archaeological reports and exhibition catalogs; and (4) works quoted by author, including all other references. I adhere to the Hanyu Pinyin transcription system in transcribing Chinese, and to the Hepburn transcription (as used in the fourth edition of *Kenkyūsha's New Japanese-English Dictionary* [1974]) for Japanese.

All dates in this book are B.C. unless otherwise indicated.

In ancient China, the art of music was strictly regulated. The most impressive musical performances were embedded in ritual celebrations, to which was attributed the power to keep the cosmos in harmony; music, properly executed, defined and periodically reaffirmed the social order. When the classical texts discuss the subject of music, it is to this peculiarly empowering ceremonial music that they refer. Archaeological remains of musical instruments, commonly found associated with sacrificial vessels and other ritual paraphernalia, also hint at an underlying politico-religious significance. The purpose of this book is to explore the role and nature of early Chinese ritual music within its cultural matrix.[1]

## Some Preconceptions

Texts transmitted from antiquity describe the exercise of music as intimately bound up with rulership. "Government is modeled upon music," says the *Guo Yu* 國語 (Narratives of the states), a fourth-century B.C. compilation,[2] explaining that a ruler's actions should strive to imitate musical harmony. In other texts, rulers are exhorted to use music to regulate the feelings as well as the behavior of their subjects. The *Yue Ji* 樂記 (Records on music, ca. third century B.C.) states:

> The former kings paid close attention to what aroused the feelings [of the people]; they used ceremonies to guide [the people's] intentions, music to

---

1. See Merriam's (1960) definition of ethnomusicology.
2. *Guo Yu* "Zhou Yu-*xia*" (Tiansheng Mingdao ed., 3:14a).

harmonize their sounds, regulations to unify their actions, and punishments to prevent conflict among them. Ceremonies and music, punishments and regulations—their ultimate aim is one: they are that by which the hearts-and-minds of the people are unified and the Way of order is produced.[3]

Here we find music portrayed as a government institution, along with ceremonies, regulations, and punishments. A virtuous ruler could employ music as an instrument in the exercise of power to induce social harmony. The *Zhou Li* 周禮 (Ritual system of the Zhou), an important ritual text probably dating to the third century B.C., therefore assigns the following duty to a "Minister of Rites" (*Dazongbo* 大宗伯):

> With rites and music, he adjusts the transformations of Heaven and Earth
> and the production of all the material things, so as to serve the ghosts and
> spirits, to harmonize the multitudinous people, and to bring all the material
> things to perfection.[4]

But the *Yue Ji*, immediately after the passage quoted above, offers a second, somewhat divergent definition of music:

> All musical tones are born in the hearts-and-minds of humans. The senti-
> ments stir within and thereupon take shape as sounds, and when the sounds
> assume a pattern, they are called musical tones. Therefore, the musical tones
> of a well-ordered age are calm and full of joy about the harmony of its
> government. But the musical tones of an age in disorder are resentful and
> full of anger about the perversity of its government. The musical tones of a
> state that is doomed to perish are mournful and full of anxiety about the
> dire straits of its people. Truly, the Way of the sounds and musical tones
> is intimately linked to government.[5]

According to this view, music operates in a spontaneous manner, objectively expressing the condition of the body politic.[6] In times of good government, music will be harmonizing in and of itself, thus compounding the positive effects of the ruler's actions, but dissolute rulership will always be accompanied

---

3. *Li Ji* "Yueji" (*Li Ji Zhushu* 37:2a–3a, Couvreur, 47–48); identically in *Shi Ji* "Yueshu" (Zhonghua ed., 1179).
4. *Zhou Li: Chun'guan* "Dazongbo" (*Zhou Li Zhengyi* 35:12a/b).
5. *Li Ji* "Yueji" (*Li Ji Zhushu* 37:2a–3a; Couvreur, 47–48); identically in *Shi Ji* "Yueshu" (Zhonghua ed., 1179).
6. See Henderson 1984, 23.

by disorderly music. In this sense, music may serve the sensitive ruler, or an outside observer, as a barometer for assessing the public morale. The *Yue Ji* elaborates:

> The accomplished man, . . . therefore, by scrutinizing sounds, comes to know musical tones. By scrutinizing musical tones, he comes to know music; by scrutinizing music, he comes to know government. With this, his knowledge of the Way is complete.[7]

The *Yue Ji*'s somewhat ambivalent descriptions of how music and government interrelate may reflect different strata of Chinese musical thought. In a general way, however, the conception of music as a moral-political entity pervades the earliest textual sources on ancient Chinese musical theory, which date from the fourth to the second centuries B.C.[8] Their authors imputed a far-reaching cosmic effect to ritual music, whether conceived of as subject to a ruler's administration or as a political agent in itself. In the words of the *Yue Ji*,

> Music has its being in the harmony between Heaven and Earth. Ceremonies have their being in the hierarchical gradations between Heaven and Earth. When based on harmony, all material things will undergo their natural transformations [undisturbed]; when based on hierarchical gradations, the multitude of material things will have their [proper] distinctions. Music-making starts from Heaven, and the ceremonies are fixed by means of the Earth. If the fixing is faulty, disorder will ensue. If the [music-]making is faulty, disruption will ensue. Only after having become enlightened about Heaven and Earth can one make ritual and music prosper.[9]

Following such principles, most early Chinese literature on musical theory consists of attempts to integrate music into an intricate system of correlative cosmology.[10] The texts explain how music expresses the emanations of *yin* 陰 and *yang* 陽. They relate the Five Musical Tones (*yin* 音) to the Five Pro-

---

7. *Li Ji* "Yueji" (*Li Ji Zhushu* 37:4b–5a; Couvreur, 50); identically in *Shi Ji* "Yueshu" (Zhong-hua ed., 1184).

8. In addition to *Guo Yu, Yue Ji* (which is included in both the *Li Ji* and the "Yueshu" of Sima Qian's *Shi Ji*), and the *Zhou Li*, these sources include the *Li Ji* 禮記, the *Guan Zi* 管子, the *Xun Zi* 旬子, the *Lüshi Chunqiu* 呂氏春秋, and the *Huainan Zi* 淮南子. For more information about these texts and the editions used for this study, see the Bibliography. The most comprehensive study of ancient Chinese musical thought is Kurihara 1978. For a brief general introduction in English, see DeWoskin 1982, 29–98.

9. *Li Ji* "Yueji" (*Li Ji Zhushu* 37:9a/b; Couvreur, 60–61); identically in *Shi Ji* "Yueshu" (Zhong-hua ed., 1191).

10. On correlative cosmology, see Eberhard 1933, Henderson 1984, Schwartz 1985, 350–82, Graham 1986a and 1989, 313–56.

cesses,[11] the Five Directions, the Five Tastes, the Five Colors, and so forth; and they match the Twelve Pitch Standards (*lü* 律) to the Twelve Months, the Twelve Terrestrial Branches,[12] and so forth. Even the musical instruments of the court orchestra, classified according to their eight different kinds of materials (metal, stone, clay, leather, silk, wood, gourd, and bamboo), are forced into a numerological straitjacket. In such a system, the potential impact of playing a single tone is immense, and the player's responsibility is enormous. Through its links with aesthetic, calendrical, astronomical, and geographical phenomena, musical performance embraces the entire universe. A ruler's use of music becomes an aspect of his role as a mediator between human society and the impersonal forces of the cosmos.

Such concepts have been basic to the received perceptions of ancient Chinese musical theory, both in China and abroad.[13] Many scholars have assumed that the post–fourth-century B.C. sources present a digest of knowledge accumulated over many centuries. But this assumption is questionable. The grandiose philosophical and cosmological ideas with which we find musical lore intertwined in those texts are clearly specific to one circumscribed period of Chinese intellectual history.[14] Correlative cosmology, in particular, became current during the century preceding the founding of the Chinese empire by the First Emperor of Qin 秦始皇 in 221 B.C. and continued to reign supreme during the Han dynasty (206 B.C.–A.D. 220). There is no reason to believe that it should have been applied to music before it entered the general discourse.[15] Although earlier classical texts—the *Shi Jing* 詩經 (Classic of poetry, ca. 900–700 B.C.) and the *Lunyu* 論語 (Analects of Confucius, fifth century B.C.), for instance—confirm that ritual music was of extraordinary importance in pre-Imperial China, they never even touch upon musical cosmology. Opinions of the late Eastern Zhou thinkers on music appear to have been highly diverse (see Chapter 9); correlative cosmology seems to have been, at first, only one of many acceptable ways of conceptualizing music.

For their ideal of music, the writers of the last centuries B.C. looked back to antiquity. What was it that they so esteemed about the glorious music of the Former Kings? Can we know anything about such early music beyond a few vague lines in the *Shi Jing*? Our chances would appear slim were it not for

11. The Five Processes (*wuxing* 五行), formerly known as the Five Elements, or Five Phases, are wood, fire, soil, metal, and water.

12. The Twelve Terrestrial Branches (*dizhi* 地支) are cyclical elements that, paired individually with the Ten Heavenly Stems (*Tian'gan* 天干), form the Cycle of Sixty, by which days are counted in the most ancient Chinese calendar systems. Good explanations and tables may be found in *Dictionnaire français de la langue chinoise*, appendix pp. 23–25.

13. See, for instance, Yang Yinliu 1980, van Aalst 1884, Laloy 1909, Picken 1957, Needham and Robinson 1962.

14. Henderson 1984, 30–46.

15. *Pace* Graham 1986a, 8 and 91.

archaeological discoveries of a large number of musical instruments—flutes, mouth-organs, ocarinas, zithers, bell-chimes, lithophones, and drums—that have been excavated during the last four decades all over China. These finds make it possible to reconstruct the composition of ritual orchestras from Neolithic down to Imperial times, and thus to infer the timbre of ancient Chinese music. Archaeological context, moreover, confirms the notion of a highly politicized context of musical practice in Chinese antiquity (see Chapter 1). But in and of themselves, the excavated musical instruments can tell us little about the intellectual dimension of music in their time—or so it appeared, until recently.

## An Archaeological Sensation

In 1978, the discovery of the bells of Marquis Yi of Zeng 曾侯乙 (d. ca. 433 B.C.) thoroughly upset previously cherished preconceptions regarding pre-Imperial Chinese music (fig. 1). Totally unprecedented and still virtually unparalleled in the archaeological record, the inscriptions on these bells provide a full and systemically coherent record of musical theory. The impact of this spectacular archaeological find on contemporary scholarship on early Chinese music has been revolutionary.

Marquis Yi's tomb is located at Leigudun, Suizhou (formerly Sui Xian, Hubei). It was found accidentally in September 1977 and excavated in the spring of the following year. A large bell found in the tomb, the Chu Wang Xiong Zhang–*bo* (see fig. 20), a gift (in some scholars' opinion, a posthumous gift) to Marquis Yi from Hui Wang of Chu 楚惠王 (personal name: Xiong Zhang 酓章, r. 488–432), is dated by inscription to the fifty-sixth year in the reign of that king (433 B.C.).[16] About Marquis Yi, who, to judge from his skeletal remains, died at around 45 years of age, we know nothing whatever from other sources. Even his state of Zeng is unattested in the historical records,[17] though it is now

16. The inscription is translated in Thorp 1981–82, 68. Two bells with exactly the same inscription were found in Anlu (Hubei) in the twelfth century (Xue Shanggong 薛尚功, *Lidai zhongding yiqi kuanzhi* j. 6:53a/b; a rubbing of unclear provenance is depicted in Wu Zhao 1980). These bells, long since lost, also featured tone-naming inscriptions similar to those seen on Marquis Yi's bells (with the curious exception of the Chu Wang Xiong Zhang–*bo*). For a long time, these inscribed tone names appeared enigmatic; Tang Lan 唐蘭 (1933, 78) could do no more than to take them as proof that the tone names mentioned in the classical texts were actually used in pre-Qin music. It is now evident that they must have designated the two tones that could be produced on these bells. The two bells from Anlu almost certainly were part of a larger assemblage of musical instruments, some of which were buried in Marquis Yi's tomb.

17. There were several states called Zeng (曾～鄫) in Bronze Age China; as a place name, Zeng 凼 is first attested in a late Shang oracle bone inscription (Chen Pan 1969, vol. 4, 298b–299a; see also Li Xiandeng 1986). The only possible references in the transmitted textual sources to a Zeng in Hubei are the Zeng 繒 in *Zuo Zhuan* 左傳 Ai 4 (HYI ed., 471) and *Guo Yu* "Zheng Yu" (Tiansheng Mingdao ed., 16:6a).

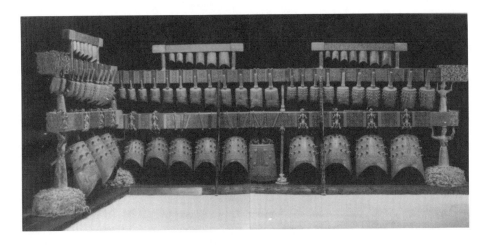

FIGURE 1. Comprehensive view of the Zeng bells, excavated in
1978 from tomb no. 1 at Leigudun, Suizhou (Hubei). Early
Warring States period (ca. 433 B.C.).

quite well known through inscriptions on archaeologically excavated bronzes. It
seems likely that a state named Zeng existed in the vicinity of Suizhou throughout much of the first millennium B.C.[18] Its geopolitical situation will be discussed in Chapter 1.[19]

Though less famous outside China than, for example, the terracotta army of
the First Emperor of Qin near Xi'an (Shaanxi), Marquis Yi's tomb must rank as
one of this century's most significant archaeological discoveries on a world-

18. By far the most, as well as the earliest, Zeng relics have been found within a 200-km radius
of Suizhou. The Zeng Taibao 曾大保 -gui, probably a late Western Zhou piece, was excavated in
1976 at Zhoujiagang, Suizhou; it is mentioned in passing in *Jianghan Kaogu* 1985 (1):106–7, 105 (inscription quoted in n. 4, p. 105). Rong Geng 容庚 (1941, vol. 1, 474; vol. 2, pl. 880) records an unprovenienced Zeng Taibao–*pen*, which, judging by its style, may date to about the same period.
Springs and Autumns period Zeng bronzes have been found at Lianyuzui, Suizhou, in 1975
(*Jianghan Kaogu* 1980 [1]:97 and [2]:pl. 1; Zeng and Li 1980, 72 and 76–77) and, in association
with objects of Chen 陳, at Jishiliang, Suizhou, in 1979 (*Wenwu* 1980 [1]:34–41). The Zeng Zi
Zhongqi 曾子仲淒 –*yan* was discovered at Xiaoxiguan, Xinye (Henan), in 1971 (*Wenwu* 1973
[5]:14–20), and a *ding* inscribed by the same individual was found at nearby Duanying, Zaoyang
(Hubei), in 1972 (*Kaogu* 1975 [4]:222–25). Vessels of Zeng and Huang were excavated together at
Sujialong, Jingshan (Hubei), in 1966 (*Wenwu* 1972 [2]:47–53), and at Xiongjialaowan, Suizhou, in
1970–72 (*Wenwu* 1973 [5]:21–25), perhaps testifying to a tradition of hereditary intermarriage between the ruling families of Zeng and Huang 黄. The mid–Warring States period Zeng Ji Wuxu–*hu*
曾姬無卹 found in the tomb of King You of Chu (r. 237–228 B.C.) at Zhujiaji, Shou Xian (Anhui),
in the 1930s is the latest Zeng bronze vessel on record. Liu Jie (1958, 123) suggests that it may have
been made for another Zeng princess married off to Huang, but this is impossible because Huang
had been extinguished by Chu for more than two centuries before the *hu* was cast. It seems possible
that the vessel in its archaeological context testifies, instead, to a marital alliance between Zeng and
Chu.
19. See Chapter 1 under "The donors of Eastern Zhou bells." Li Xueqin argues that Zeng was
identical with Sui 隨, a well-documented state in the vicinity of Chu (*Guangming Ribao*, October 4,

wide scale. Lavishly furnished and virtually undisturbed, it bears comparison with the tomb of the Pharaoh Tut-ankh-Amun—another historically ephemeral figure owing his fame mainly to archaeology. In its size and wealth, Marquis Yi's tomb exceeds all other known tombs of rulers in pre-Imperial China. The more than seven thousand items of funerary goods allow unprecedented insights into Chinese aristocratic culture in the late fifth century B.C.[20]

In keeping with a practice, quite recent at the time, of fashioning large tombs in analogy with the abodes of the living, the Marquis's tomb (fig. 2) displays the structure of an underground palace.[21] The layout and furnishings of its four chambers recreate the principal parts of a typical ruler's residence.[22] The eastern chamber corresponds to the ruler's private living quarters (qin 寢); Marquis Yi was encoffined there in the company of eight young women, immolated to serve as his attendants in the other world. The northern chamber, the armory, contained a chariot and weapons; in the western chamber, the harem, excavators found the coffins of thirteen more female victims. The large chamber in the center of the tomb corresponds to the public part of the palace, the main hall and its courtyard, where the Marquis would have performed his ritual duties as ruler, offering sacrifices to his ancestors and entertaining guests. Consistent with such a function, this part of the tomb is furnished with ritual vessels and musical instruments.

In this central chamber, during several days following May 22, 1978, archaeologists unearthed the remains of a complete ritual orchestra, including the following instruments:

1978 [not seen]; see Li Xueqin 1985, 181; more references in He Hao 1988). The arguments leveled against this view by Zeng and Li (1980) are unconvincing; nevertheless, Li's identification remains hypothetical.

20. Even before the final archaeological report on Marquis Yi's tomb was published, scholarly articles concerning various aspects of the tomb numbered in the hundreds. Many are listed in this book's bibliography; for a more complete list of Chinese articles relating to the Zeng bells, see Hubei Sheng Bowuguan 1988. The preliminary archaeological report on the tomb (originally published in *Wenwu* 1979 [7]:1–24) has been translated into English in *Chinese Studies in Archaeology* 1 (1979–80), 3:3–45; the same issue of that journal (pp. 46–73) also carries the translation of an article on leather armor excavated in the tomb. Long abstracts of five other articles published at the same time as the preliminary report (including Qiu Xigui 1979 and Huang Xiangpeng 1979a) may be found in Dien, Riegel, and Price 1985, vol. 2, 760–778. Details regarding the discovery of the Zeng bells, as well as size measurements, are available in Tan and Feng 1988. Preliminary sources of illustrations include *Sui Xian Zeng Hou Yi-mu, Hubei Suizhou Leigudun chutu wenwu*, and *Zhan'guo Zeng Hou Yi-mu chutu wenwu tu'an-xuan*. The most comprehensive work on the tomb in a Western language is Thote 1985 (see also Thote 1986). Thorp (1981–82) offers a comprehensive analysis of the art-historical aspects of the Leigudun finds in English. See also Li Xueqin 1985, 175–81.

21. Yu Weichao 1980; Wu Hung 1988. This tendency is doubtless due to changing religious beliefs (Maspero 1950; Dien 1987; Graham 1989).

22. Thorp 1981–82, 75–76; Tanaka 1980.

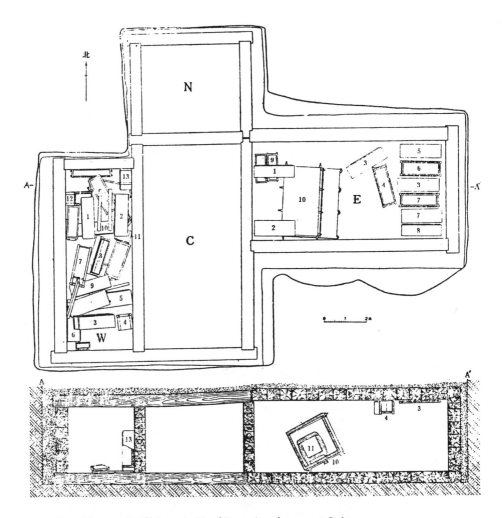

FIGURE 2. The tomb of Marquis Yi of Zeng (tomb no. 1 at Leigudun), plan and cross-section. The plan shows the layout of the four
chambers, including the sarcophagus and coffin of the marquis (east
chamber no. 10), as well as the coffins of his twenty-one con-
cubines (west chamber nos. 1–13 and east chamber nos. 1–8) and
the coffin of his dog (east chamber no. 9).

FIGURE 3. *Se* zither from the tomb of Marquis Yi of Zeng.

- seven large zithers (*se* 瑟) (fig. 3)
- three mouth-organs (*sheng* 笙) (fig. 4)
- two panpipes (*paixiao* 排簫) (fig. 5)
- two transverse flutes (*di* 笛 or *chi* 篪) (fig. 6)
- three drums of different types (figs. 7, 8, and 9)
- one lithophone of thirty-two chimestones (*qing* 磬) (fig. 10),[23] and
- an assemblage of bell-chimes comprising sixty-five bells (see fig. 1).

The composition of this orchestra more or less accords with what had long been known from the *Shi Jing* and other texts, but the prominence of chimestones and bells is somewhat surprising. No other tomb in China has yielded comparable quantities of these two kinds of instruments, which in contemporary writings are referred to as "suspended music" (*yuexuan* 樂縣).[24]

Uniquely, moreover, the Zeng bells and chimestones are covered with inscriptions that record the names of the tones they emitted. These inscriptions constitute an indubitably authentic body of musical theory, predating the late

23. A lithophone is a musical instrument in which a number of tuned flat slabs of stone, usually of oblique L-shape, are suspended from a rack. In their musical role in the orchestra as well as in their playing technique, these instruments have much in common with chime-bells; they will be discussed intermittently throughout this book.

24. The locus classicus of the term *yuexuan* is in *Zhou Li: Chun'guan* "Xiaoxu" (*Zhou Li Zhengyi* 44: 14b–16b).

FIGURE 4. *Upper left:* Mouth-organ (*sheng*) from the tomb of Marquis Yi of Zeng. Only the lacquered body of the instrument is shown; reed pipes were placed into the eighteen holes on each side.

FIGURE 5. *Upper right:* Panflute (*paixiao*) from the tomb of Marquis Yi of Zeng.

FIGURE 6. *Above:* Traverse flute (*di*) from the tomb of Marquis Yi of Zeng.

FIGURE 7. *Opposite, top:* Drum stand from the tomb of Marquis Yi of Zeng, serving to support a pole-drum. Contemporary depictions of such an instrument may be seen in figs. 15 and 22.

FIGURE 8. *Opposite, middle:* Hanging-drum from the tomb of Marquis Yi of Zeng. Alain Thote (1987) has shown that this instrument was suspended from a tall bronze stand in the shape of an antlered bird.

FIGURE 9. *Opposite, bottom:* Hand-drum from the tomb of Marquis Yi of Zeng.

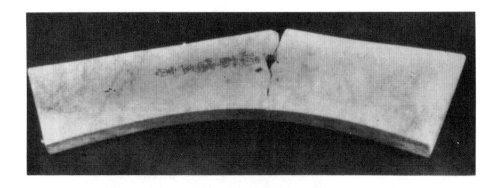

FIGURE 10. One of the chimestones (*qing*) from the tomb of
Marquis Yi of Zeng.

pre-Qin texts by at least one century. They enable us to reconstruct important
aspects of Chinese musical thinking in the fifth century. The sixty-five bells
with their gold-inlaid inscriptions (fig. 11) are of particular interest, for unlike
the musical stones they are well-preserved and can still be played, emitting virtually, if not exactly, the same tones as when they were buried.[25] We can thus
verify the meaning of the theoretical information in the inscriptions by means of
the tones of the bells themselves. When analyzed in conjunction, the bells and
their inscriptions provide an entirely new perspective on the intellectual history
of pre-Imperial Chinese music. They point to new ways of analyzing other
music-related archaeological finds, especially bells. Through them we can gain a
diachronic view of musical history spanning approximately one millennium
before the Qin unification. Truly, using another Egyptian simile, the Zeng bells
have provided the Rosetta Stone for the study of early Chinese music.[26] Now,
for the first time, the study of the material manifestations of music (or musical
archaeology, as it is called by some scholars) can offer a new and different perspective on the transmitted musical lore. This book endeavors to present this
new panorama of music in ancient China.

## The Importance of Bells

Taking the Zeng finds as our point of reference, we shall, for several reasons,
explore ancient Chinese ritual music from the vantage point of bells. Bell-

25. Three sets of tone measurements taken on the Zeng bells have now been published; for
bibliographic information, see Appendix 4.
26. Rossing 1987.

*b*

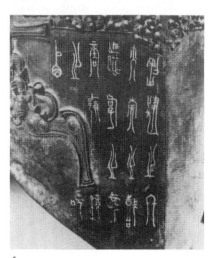

*a*

*c*

FIGURE 11. *Yongzhong* (bell no. M3-6) and details showing inscribed portions, from the tomb of Marquis Yi of Zeng. *a*, recto face of the bell with the name of the Marquis inscribed in the central panel and abbreviated tone names on the striking points of the two tones; *b* and *c*, more extensive tone-naming inscriptions on the verso face: A-tone (*b*); B-tone (*c*). (For details on the inscriptions, see Chapter 8.)

chimes are a unique cultural contribution of the Chinese Bronze Age. Although bells have been made in metal-using cultures the world over,[27] Chinese bell-making traditions are of particularly long standing; the oldest known bell-like metal object in the world seems to be a late Neolithic (ca. 2000 B.C.) specimen from Shanxi province (fig. 12; see Chapter 4). China was also first in the production of tuned sets of bells. The chime-bells of the Chinese Bronze Age have no technological parallel in the ancient world. In Europe, the only other place where tuned sets of bells were used as musical instruments during the pre-industrial age, such cymbals and carillons were not made until the late Middle Ages, and these European bells differ from their ancient Chinese counterparts in all imaginable respects, most notably in bell-shape and manner of playing.[28] Considering their age and the conditions under which they were made, the craftsmanship and acoustical quality of the ancient Chinese bell-chimes, though imperfect, are impressive even by twentieth-century professional standards. Part I of this book (Chapters 1 through 3) presents the basic cultural and technological facts about those instruments.

One reason bell-chimes merit our particular attention is that they occupied a prominent position in the ancient Chinese ritual orchestra. More reliably than other kinds of musical instruments, bells can serve as an indicator of the social context of musical activity, for many bear inscriptions documenting important historical details about their owners. (The Zeng bells are so far unique in furnishing music-related information.) Alone among musical instruments, furthermore, bell-chimes and lithophones—"suspended music"—were subject to sumptuary regulations; consequently, even uninscribed bells, viewed in their archaeological contexts, embody significant social information. Bells appear frequently in the classical texts, sometimes as a synecdoche for music, and these textual loci can furnish additional clues to the cultural role of bells. Chapter 1 will establish the social and economic context of bells within the elite sphere of the early Chinese monarchic states.[29]

We shall see that, during much of the Bronze Age, bells were status-defining luxury objects par excellence. More specifically than other instruments, bell-chimes represented the ritual music of the aristocracy during the Shang and Zhou dynasties, the music of the Former Kings so much regretted by later

27. Price 1983; Lehr 1987a.
28. Cymbals were used from the tenth through the fifteenth centuries, after which they were displaced by carillons (Price 1983; this book is authoritative on the history of Western bells, though weak in its coverage of Chinese bells). For technological comparisons of Chinese and Western bells, see Rossing 1989a and b.
29. Lithophones, which share some technological properties with bells, are far less frequently encountered in the archaeological record than chime-bells and are usually less well preserved. Inscribed specimens are rare.

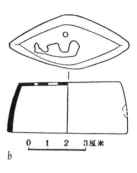

*a*

*b*

FIGURE 12. Copper bell-like object (*ling?*) excavated in 1983 at Taosi, Xiangfen (Shanxi). Terminal Neolithic (ca. 2000 B.C.). *a*, photograph; *b*, section drawing.

philosophers—to the extent that such music ever existed. Tied to the political fortunes of its aristocratic patrons, suspended music, unlike other components of the Shang and Zhou ritual orchestra, was never integrated into the new forms of music emerging at the end of the Warring States period; it is hardly an accident, therefore, that bell-chimes fell out of use with the demise of the traditional court music around that time. Given their chronological limitations, bell-chimes may stand as *Leitfossilien* of Bronze Age music. The geographic distributions of the standard bell-types are quite restricted, and the elevated cultural status of bells may explain, at least in part, why local elites in the areas surrounding the realm of the early Chinese dynasties regarded bells as somehow symbolic of civilization.

As a consequence of their high prestige, considerable economic resources and technological acumen were expended on the manufacture of chime-bells. It is no exaggeration to say that they embody some of the highest achievements of science and technology of the Chinese Bronze Age. An approach that synthesizes the technological history of bells with what we know about Chinese musical theory may therefore yield important insights. How was technology put to the service of music? The answer to this question turns out to be unexpectedly complex. There are indications that preexisting musical concerns by no means always determined technological developments in musical-instrument manufac-

FIGURE 13. *Niuzhong* (no. U3-6?) from the tomb of Marquis Yi of Zeng; abbreviated tone names are inscribed on the striking points of the two tones.

ture; on the contrary, thinking about music may have been conditioned by the possibilities and limitations of instruments such as bells. Before we can hope to understand the musical theory documented by the Zeng bell inscriptions, we must investigate the material properties as well as the technological evolution of bells. Chapters 2 through 6 address these issues.

Of particular importance in elucidating the interrelation of technological development and the formation of musical theory is the "two-tone phenomenon," a crucial acoustical feature of ancient Chinese bells. The inscriptions on the Zeng bells (fig. 13) show that each musical bell was designed to produce two distinct tones: the "A-tone," obtained by striking the lower portion (*gu* 鼓) of the bell in the center, and the "B-tone," obtained by striking the right or left side of the *gu*.[30] The two tones are clearly separated acoustically, usually by

30. In the Chinese literature, the "A-tone" is variously designated as *guzhongyin* 鼓中音, *zhengguyin* 正鼓音, or *suiyin* 遂音, and the "B-tone," as *gupangyin* 鼓旁音, *ceguyin* 側鼓音, or *guyin* 鼓音. The "Sui-tone/Gu-tone" nomenclature has been variously adopted by Western and Japanese authors but is misleading in view of the actual meanings of the terms *sui* and *gu* (see Chapter 2).

either a minor or major third. Forgotten for two thousand years, the two-tone phenomenon was rediscovered only as a result of the excavation of the Zeng bells with their inscriptions placed on the respective striking points (fig. 13). This finding came as a somewhat embarrassing surprise to scholars, since testable musical bells had long been available both in China and abroad.[31] The equally astonishing fact that the two-tone phenomenon is mentioned nowhere in the classical texts only illustrates the limited usefulness of these textual records for the study of technological history. The silence of the *Kaogongji* 考工記 (Notes on examining the artisans; now the final chapter of the *Zhou Li* but originally a separate manual itemizing the activities of artisans attached to the Zhou royal palace) is particularly surprising because it does contain a section describing the tasks of bell-casters attached to the royal court. We shall have more to say about the *Kaogongji* in the context of the technological aspects of bells in Chapters 2 and 3; it will become clear that the study of the extant bells yields far richer and more reliable evidence than that text.

Chapter 2 discusses the acoustic properties of the bell-types most commonly used as musical bells during the Chinese Bronze Age; Chapter 3 addresses issues related to manufacture. Both chapters incorporate information gained between 1979 and 1984, when an interdisciplinary team under the auspices of the State Bureau of Cultural Relics and the Hubei Provincial Government cast a replica of the entire Zeng bell assemblage.[32] This project, which must be counted among the major events in the history of experimental archaeology,[33] provided a valuable opportunity for experiments exploring some of the technical issues involved in manufacturing scaleable and tuneable bells.

Before moving on to issues of performance and musical theory, it is necessary to look at bell-chimes from a diachronic perspective. How did they come into being, and how did they develop over time? Typological analysis can answer such questions. The wealth of useable archaeological material constitutes a further, pragmatic reason why bells lend themselves as a basis for the study of

31. *After* the Zeng finds had proved the existence of the "two-tone phenomenon," several scholars asserted that they had been aware of it before. Ma Chengyuan (1981, 133) claimed to have discovered it in 1977 when examining the Qin Gong–*yongzhong*, and Wang Xiang (1981, 68) said it was discovered in the same year by a team of four researchers directed by Lü Ji during research on the Xing bells (see also Jiang Dingsui 1984, 93). Others maintain that the existence of a second tone on ancient bells was discovered by chance as early as 1958, during a performance of "The East is Red" on the Jingli-*niuzhong* on Radio Peking (Shen 1987, 104–05).

32. Participating institutions included the Hubei Provincial Museum, Wuhan; the Research Institute for the History of the Natural Sciences of the Chinese Academy of Sciences, Beijing; the Wuhan Mechanical Technology Research Institute; the Foshan Nodular Cast Iron Research Institute; and the Wuhan Engineering Institute. See Hubei Sheng Bowuguan 1981.

33. Preliminary summaries have been published in the 1981 (1) issue of *Jianghan Kaogu*; several of these articles are also included in Hua Jueming et al. 1986. See also Guan and Liu 1983, Huang Xiangpeng 1983a, Zhong Hui 1983, Anonymous 1984, Wang Yuzhu et al. 1988, Tan and Feng 1988.

ancient Chinese musical history. Unlike most musical instruments, which were made of perishable materials, bronze bells have been preserved in relatively large numbers. The several thousand extant specimens (for a bibliographic listing, see Appendixes 1 and 2) fall into readily definable typological sequences. In Part II of this book (Chapters 4 and 5), we shall trace these sequences and establish their geographic distributions.

Beyond classification and dating, our aim in using the typological method will be to nail down successive steps in the invention of chimes of two-tone bells. Much but not all of this development took place in areas under the direct political control of the early royal dynasties in north China. The important contribution of bell-casters south of the Yangzi River to the invention of the classical two-tone bell is included in the narrative of Chapter 4, which covers the early Bronze Age through the middle of Western Zhou. Chapter 5 treats the emergence of the classical types of chime-bells in mid- to late Western Zhou and the evolution of various regional strains of bell manufacture during the Eastern Zhou period. During the same period, the paraphernalia of Zhou ritual music were also adopted in peripheral areas all around the Zhou cultural sphere; quite possibly, these bells of regional provenience document the gradual acculturation of local elites to the ways of the Zhou. Appendix 3 traces briefly the development of bells in peripheral areas.

Part III of this book (Chapters 6 through 9) tackles the complex issues of musical performance and theory from the perspective of the suspended music. A great advantage of using bells for musicological analysis is that they can still be played. Chapter 6 discusses techniques by which bells were played in antiquity. Moreover, because each bell can produce no more than two tones, there can be no ambiguity as to their intended tones, as there is, for example, on wind and string instruments. Virtually alone among surviving ancient musical instruments, bells provide useable tonal data that allow consideration of Bronze Age Chinese musical theory. In 1922, the distinguished Japanese musicologist Tanabe Hisao 田邊尙雄 (1883–1983) performed the first modern frequency measurements on ten Western and Eastern Zhou bells in the Sumitomo collection;[34] in China, at roughly the same time, the linguist and folklorist Liu Fu 劉復 (1891–1934) measured the tones of both ancient and late Imperial chimestones and bells.[35]

34. Tanabe's results were published as a supplement to Hamada 1924.
35. Only the tone measurements on the bell-chime and lithophone at the Altar of Heaven in Beijing (Liu Fu 1932) were ever published. In 1930, Liu measured the tones of more than 500 bells and chimestones in the former Imperial Palace in Beijing (Jiang Dingsui 1984, 93; a manuscript article is mentioned in a footnote in Liu Fu 1934. Some of this information seems to have been used by Huang Xiangpeng 1978–80). Liu also measured the tones of chimestones newly excavated in the 1930s at Xincun, Xun Xian (Henan) (a manuscript article is mentioned in *Xun Xian Xincun*, 66). It

Since the 1950s, this approach has been extended to many archaeological finds in China. Appendix 4 lists the most important tone measurements so far reported. The tone measurement methods and their validity are discussed in Chapter 6. In Chapter 7, using the evidence from the Zeng bells and their inscriptions, we shall examine the tone distributions on approximately two dozen bell-chimes dating from the thirteenth to the fourth century B.C. in chronological sequence. Through them, we can trace the progress, if not of early Chinese ritual music in general, at least of the sort of music performable on bell-chimes, as well as the development of bell-chimes into fully melodic instruments. While the scope of these preliminary results turns out to be somewhat narrow, the inscriptions on the suspended music of Zeng suggest a number of far-reaching conclusions about the music of the Chinese Bronze Age.

In Chapter 8, the system of tone nomenclature documented in the Zeng inscriptions is introduced. Comparison with the late pre-Qin texts highlights essential differences between musical theory before and after the rise of correlative cosmology. Chapter 9 attempts to mold the information collected in the preceding chapters into a coherent historical account of the development of classical Chinese musical theory during the Bronze Age, intertwined as it was with the rise and fall of dynastic ritual and of bell-manufacturing technology. The chapter emphasizes the importance of bells in the genesis of musical theory. At the end, ancient Chinese ritual music, while undeniably of great political importance, emerges stripped of the ballast of correlative cosmology.

Reconstruction of the music itself, unfortunately, must be postponed until archaeologists discover ancient Chinese musical scores. So far, we do not even know what kind of notation system was used by the ancient Chinese; conceivably, musical pieces were written down using the tone names of the Zeng inscriptions.[36] Today's performances on ancient or reconstructed instruments (see fig. 108) are no more than imaginative re-creations; this book may provide some hints to make them more historically accurate. For the time being, however, the music of the Chinese Bronze Age remains suspended in the depths of history.

---

appears that there are still plans to publish these seminal studies posthumously (Wang Zichu, personal communication 1990).

36. That some notational system may have existed during late pre-Imperial times is suggested by the Bibliographical Treatise of the *Han Shu*, which mentions the texts and "tone compositions" (*shengqu* 聲曲) for "seven songs from Henan dating to the Zhou," and "seventy-five folk-ballads dating to the Zhou" in the Han Imperial Library (*Han Shu: Yiwenzhi* "Shifu-lüe," 1955 indexed ed., 48–49). At present, we cannot even begin to speculate about the prevalence of playing from such "sheet music" as opposed to the use of improvisational techniques.

## PART I

Rites, Technology, and Political Matrix

# CHAPTER ONE

# Bells in a Bronze Age Culture

Performed in a temple setting, music in Bronze Age China helped to create an atmosphere in which deities and humans could interact. By giving rhythm to human movements and melody to human speech, music imparted indexical significance to ritual action and translated human intentions into a rhetoric of sound powerful enough to penetrate to the ancestral spirits in heaven and elicit a response. Messages encoded through multiple media enabled humans to act upon and to communicate with the spirits.[1] Ancient Chinese ritual performers, like their counterparts in many other cultures,[2] employed percussion instruments to make audible the transition between the human and the divine spheres. Among those instruments, bell-chimes were foremost.

One aim of this book is to show how bells functioned in performance and how musical theory informed that function. In this chapter, I offer an outline of the cultural and socioeconomic environment of bell music: the ritual contexts of bell usage; the social framework in which these instruments were meaningful; historical detail on prominent owners of bells and on changes in bell usage over time; and economic aspects of bells as commodities of status. I conclude with some remarks on the status of bell-players and attached personnel. This background information allows us to assess the significance of the technological, typological, and musicological analyses in the later chapters.

I use the term *Bronze Age* to refer to the roughly two millennia from the first emergence of monarchic states on the north China plain to the founding of the

---

1. My views on Chinese ritual in general have been influenced by Tambiah 1985 (especially pp. 123–66), who builds on Austin 1967. The "performative approach" to ritual has also influenced my reading of the poems quoted below.

2. R. Needham 1967.

TABLE I.    Dynasties and Epochs of Early Chinese History

*Historical Chronology*

| | |
|---|---|
| 2205–1767 B.C. (trad.) | Xia dynasty (semi-legendary) |
| 1766–1123 (trad.) | Shang dynasty |
| 1122–249 | Zhou dynasty |
|   1122–771 | Western Zhou |
|   770–249 | Eastern Zhou |
|     721–468 | Springs and Autumns period |
|     403–221 | Warring States period |
| 221–208 | Qin dynasty |
| 206 B.C.–A.D. 220 | Han dynasty |
|   206 B.C.–A.D. 8 | Western Han |
|   9–22 | Xin (Wang Mang interregnum) |
|   23–220 | Eastern Han |

*Archaeological Chronology*

| | |
|---|---|
| ca. 7000–2000 B.C. | Neolithic period |
| ca. 2000–1600 | Erlitou Culture (Xia period?) |
| ca. 1600–1300 | Erligang (early/middle Shang) period |
| ca. 1300–1050 | Anyang (late Shang) period |
| ca. 1050–770 | Western Zhou period |
| ca. 770–450 | Springs and Autumns period |
| ca. 450–221 | Warring States period |
| 221 B.C.–A.D. 220 | Qin/Han period |

Chinese empire by the First Emperor of Qin in 221 B.C.[3] According to traditional historiography, this was the age of China's first three royal dynasties, from the semi-legendary Xia 夏 through the fully historical Shang 商 and Zhou 周 (for dates and period subdivisions, see table 1). From a techno-historical point of view, this time span was not exclusively a "bronze" age, for copper and bronze had been in use in China for several centuries, and the final centuries of the pre-Qin period witnessed the rise of an iron industry of major proportions. Yet bronze reigned supreme, culturally and politically, throughout the Three Dynasties. Both the social and the cosmic orders revolved around that material. The elites defined their political power and social ranks in terms of access to, and possession of, ritual paraphernalia made of bronze, such as vessels, weapons, chariots, and bells. The centrality of bronze undoubtedly accounts for astounding technological innovations and feats of artistic creativity in the realm

---

3. See Guo Baojun 1963, 3.

of bronze manufacture. During the Bronze Age as defined here, bronze was more than an archaeological indicator of technological development: it occupied a preeminent position in all aspects of Chinese culture.[4]

## Main Functions of Bells
### Ancestral Ritual

Bells loom large among the bronze objects cast during the Shang and Zhou dynasties. The vast majority of them have been excavated from tombs, and from earliest times their distribution was restricted to the wealthiest. A small number of specimens have been found in hoards of bronze vessels that are believed to constitute the inventories of former ancestral temples of aristocratic kin-groups (fig. 14). Both kinds of contexts—burial and temple—attest to the role of bells in ritual.

Throughout the Zhou dynasty, bells served primarily in the context of the ancestral cult. They formed part of an orchestra that provided the musical accompaniment to ritual dances and singing. Such ensembles, comprising string, wind, and percussion instruments, have been excavated archaeologically; the one found in Marquis Yi's tomb is the most complete. Glimpses of Zhou ancestral ritual may be found in the *Shi Jing* (Classic of poetry), a collection of songs and ritual hymns of Western and early Eastern Zhou date. The following stanza describes the musicians and dancers in action:

> They strike the bells solemnly,
> They play their *se* and *qin* zithers,
> The reed-organs and the musical stones blend their sounds;
> Accompanied by them they perform the *Ya* and *Nan* [dances],
> They wield their flutes without error.[5]

These performances accompanied a ceremonial repast to which a kin-group invited its ancestors, who were represented in the temple by impersonators (*shi* 尸). Ostensibly, ritual music served to entertain and humor the heavenly guests,

---

4. This picture of the Chinese Bronze Age is laid out succinctly in K. C. Chang 1983. For further general information, the following works in Western languages are recommended: on Chinese archaeology, Chang 1986 and 1977, 296–470; on Shang culture, Chang 1980 and Keightley 1978; on Western Zhou, Creel 1970, Hsu and Linduff 1988, and Shaughnessy forthcoming; on Eastern Zhou, Hsu 1965 and Li Xueqin 1985. Maspero 1927, Vandermeersch 1977–1980 and Keightley 1983 are also useful. As a compelling anthropological portrait of early Chinese culture, Granet 1929, though based entirely on textual evidence, remains unsuperseded; it should be used in conjunction with Chang 1976.

5. *Shi Jing* Ode 208 "Guzhong" (HYI ed., 50; Karlgren, 159–61). *Ya* 雅 and *Nan* 南 were the names of ceremonial dances with instrumental accompaniment.

FIGURE 14. View of a hoard of Western Zhou bronzes interred ca. 771 B.C. at Zhuangbai, Fufeng (Shaanxi) (Zhuangbai hoard no. 1). Some of the Xing-*yongzhong* (see figs. 19 and 74) are prominently visible.

from whom the living hoped to obtain supernatural blessings, as is evident in the following hymn of the Zhou royal house, which mentions three early Western Zhou kings who may well have been assumed to be present, their spirits having descended into impersonators:

Terrifying and strong is Wu Wang.
Is it not strong, his ardor!
Greatly manifest Cheng [Wang 成王] and Kang [Wang 康王],
God on High made them sovereign.

From the time of their achievements [*cheng* 成] and peacefulness [*kang* 康],
We have extensively held onto the Four Quarters,
Clear-sighted is their splendor.

Bells and drums sound magnificently [*huanghuang* 喤喤],
Musical stones and flutes chime in [*jiangjiang* 將將];
[The former kings] send down blessings that are abundant.

They send down blessings that are great;
Their awe-inspiring demeanor is grand;
They are drunk, they are full,
Blessings and happiness come again and again.[6]


Like the *Shi Jing* poems, the Western Zhou bronze inscriptions—including bell inscriptions—show a strong concern with making the ancestral spirits happy. Reading through the text inscribed on an important Western Zhou bell, the First Xing–*yongzhong*, which is translated in full below,[7] we may imagine ourselves at the scene of a sacrifice, where the bell music has enticed the spirits to descend from heaven; bells were to be used "so as to please and make exalted" the ancestral spirits as they were arriving in the temple and "so as to let the accomplished men of the former generations rejoice." In return for a successful performance, the descendants expected blessings and enduring prosperity, expectations communicated to their heavenly visitors by means of a carefully worded prayer-message during the ceremony. Much of the First Xing–*yongzhong* inscription reads like such a text:[8]

Richly and abundantly, forever let me enjoy at ease evermore ample and manifold good fortune. May you broadly open up my awareness, helping me to obtain an eternal life-mandate; may you personally bestow upon me that multi-colored good fortune of yours. May I live for ten thousand years.


The ancestors, in turn, replied through an oracle. Ode 209 in the *Shi Jing*, excerpted below, describes such an exchange of messages. A priest, the "officiating invocator" (*gongzhu* 工祝), had a pivotal role in this process of communication; bells and drums indicated crucial points of the sequence. First, the setting:

The visitors and guests
Offer toasts and pledges to each other.
The ceremonies are entirely according to rule;
The laughter and talk are entirely to the point.


6. *Shi Jing* Ode 274 "Zhijing" (HYI ed., 75); my interpretation differs decisively from that of Karlgren (pp. 242–43), whose wording I follow whenever feasible.
   7. See below under "The Donors of Western Zhou Bells."
   8. Such a connection between bronze inscriptions and messages offered during ceremonies was first pointed out by Xu Zhongshu 1936.

There follows the offering of the ritual message:

"The divine protectors have arrived.
May they bestow on us increased felicity,
May we be rewarded with longevity of ten thousand years."

We are very respectful,
Our rules and rites have no error.
The officiating invocator proffers the announcement,
He goes and presents it to the pious descendant.

The spirits reply as follows:

"Fragrant is the pious sacrifice,
The spirits enjoy the wine and food,
The oracle predicts for you a hundred blessings.
According to the proper quantities, according to the proper rules,
You have brought sacrificial grain, you have brought millet;
You have brought baskets, you have arranged them;
We will forever give you the utmost blessings, ten-thousandfold, myriad-
    fold."

Immediately afterward, the ritual draws to a close:

The ceremonies are now completed,
The bells and drums have given their signal;
The pious descendant goes to his place,
The officiating invocator makes his announcement:
"The spirits are all drunk."
The august impersonator then rises,
The drums and bells escort away the impersonator.
The divine protectors then leave the temple.[9]

Such, then, was the basic dynamic of Zhou ancestral ritual: humans offered food and performances in exchange for blessings and assistance. In a transaction paralleled and complemented by an exchange of verbal messages, the sustaining role of music can hardly be exaggerated.

9. *Shi Jing* Ode 209 "Chuci" (HYI ed., 50–51; Karlgren 1950, 161–63, *mod. auct.*).

Following the ancestral sacrifice, in which every word and movement was minutely regulated, a feast (*yan* 燕) took place in the temple, an occasion for the assembled male kinfolk to become roaring drunk. *Shi Jing* Ode 209 indicates that here, too, bells and other instruments provided musical accompaniment. The *Zhou Li*, though a far less reliable source than the *Shi Jing* on the authentic ritual customs of the early Zhou, stresses the near-identity of the ritual sequence at royal sacrifices (*jisi* 祭祀) and banquets (*xiang* 饗)[10] and specifies that the same "feasting music" (*yanyue* 燕樂) was to be performed at both occasions.[11]

*Shi Jing* poems also mention bells in the contexts of weddings,[12] ritual archery contests,[13] entertainment of visitors,[14] and ceremonies at ritual structures outside the royal palace.[15] Scenes of such ceremonial activity are depicted on some early Warring States period bronzes with figurative decoration.[16] Figure 15, the detail of a *hu* 壺 vessel, shows bells and chimestones aligned on a single rack below (i.e., *in front of*, according to the pictorial conventions of this decoration style) a temple building atop an elevated platform. In the temple, humans in ceremonial robes have assembled for a ritual; from *hu* vessels displayed on an altar, attendants ladle wine into drinking cups while musicians perform in the courtyard.

Figure 16a shows a shooting ritual at a large temple. The architecture in the center of the composition, though it resembles a two-storied building, probably represents two buildings, one located behind the other and separated by a courtyard (see fig. 16b). Here, musical instruments are suspended on two sides of the temple compound, bells on the left and chimestones on the right, probably indicating two sides of the courtyard between the two buildings. The shooting target is positioned outside the temple. Wine is offered, the musicians play, and the participants show off their archery skills.

References to bells in later Zhou texts by and large corroborate the range of functions to be gleaned from the *Shi Jing*. This is especially true of the *Zhou Li*, perhaps because the scholarly compilers of that text relied on the *Shi Jing* as one of their main sources.[17] The *Zuo Zhuan* 左傳, a fourth-century B.C. historical

---

10. According to *Zhou Li: Chun'guan* "Dasiyue" (*Zhou Li Zhengyi* 43:12b–13a), the sole difference between the two is that the sequence of leading a living sacrificial animal into the temple was dispensed with during banquets.

11. *Zhou Li: Chun'guan* "Zhongshi" (*Zhou Li Zhengyi* 26:10b).

12. *Shi Jing* Ode 1 "Guanju" (HYI ed., 1; Karlgren, 2).

13. *Shi Jing* Ode 220 "Bin zhi chuyan" (HYI ed., 54; Karlgren, 172–74); compare also *Yi Li* "Dasheyi" (*Yi Li Zhengyi* 13:6b–9a and 15:19b–20a).

14. *Shi Jing* Ode 175 "Tonggong" (HYI ed., 35; Karlgren, 118–19).

15. *Shi Jing* Ode 242 "Lingtai" (HYI ed., 61; Karlgren, 196–97).

16. Hayashi 1961–62; C. D. Weber 1968.

17. *Zhou Li: Chun'guan* "Dasiyue" (*Zhou Li Zhengyi* 43:14a/b); "Yueshi" (44:3a–9b); "Shiliao" (45:19b–20a); "Zhongshi" (46:7a–10b); "Shengshi" (46:13b); "Dazhu" (49:18b–19b).

FIGURE 15. Pictorial representation of a ritual performance on an unprovenienced *hu* in the Musée Guimet, Paris. Mid-fifth century B.C. A sacrifice is offered in a temple situated atop an elevated platform. The musicians are placed in the courtyard in front of the building; in addition to a bell-chime and a lithophone, a pole-drum and a pellet-drum are shown.

commentary, informs us that bells were de rigueur at the capping ceremonies of princes.[18] At that time, some people rang a bell before and after meals[19] and when receiving guests.[20] One ruler of Zheng 鄭 had a subterranean chamber dug in his palace, where he would retire to drink wine and listen to the sound of bells.[21] Listening to bell music was proscribed in times of mourning.[22] Although "bells and drums" are occasionally mentioned in connection with warfare,[23] it appears unlikely that the leaders of military expeditions took chime-bells into the field; the bells used in later Eastern Zhou times as signal-giving instruments in battle are typologically distinct from the chimed musical bells of the ritual orchestra.[24]

Although the ceremonies in which bells were used underwent some modification during Eastern Zhou times (as we shall see shortly), the available sources

18. *Zuo Zhuan* Xiang 9 (HYI ed., 268).
19. *Zuo Zhuan* Ai 14 (HYI ed., 489).
20. *Zuo Zhuan* Zhao 11 (HYI ed., 355).
21. *Zuo Zhuan* Xiang 30 (HYI ed., 331).
22. *Zuo Zhuan* Xiang 29 (HYI ed., 327); *Zuo Zhuan* Ding 9 (HYI ed., 453); *Li Ji* "Tan'gong-xia" (*Li Ji Zhushu* 9:17a–18a). *Li Ji* "Quli-*xia*" (*Li Ji Zhushu* 4:9b–10a) seems to stipulate that magnates were *obliged* to listen to bell music when not in mourning.
23. *Zuo Zhuan* Zhuang 29 (HYI ed., 76); *Guo Yu* "Wu Yu" (Tiansheng Mingdao ed., 7b).
24. Falkenhausen 1989a.

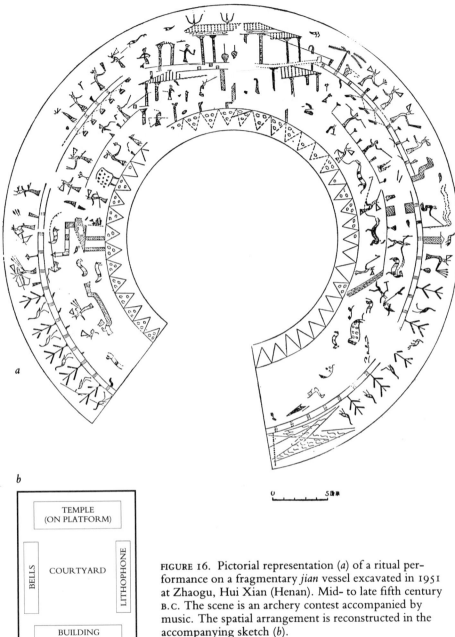

FIGURE 16. Pictorial representation (a) of a ritual performance on a fragmentary *jian* vessel excavated in 1951 at Zhaogu, Hui Xian (Henan). Mid- to late fifth century B.C. The scene is an archery contest accompanied by music. The spatial arrangement is reconstructed in the accompanying sketch (b).

abundantly confirm that the setting in which bells were played and heard was primarily a ritual one. Even at the time of the final decline of the Zhou ritual tradition during the Warring States period, a sacred aura continued to linger about these instruments. Mencius alludes to the custom of ceremonially anointing (*xin* 釁) a newly cast bell with the blood of a sacrificial ox.[25] And the Warring States text *Yan Zi Chunqiu* 晏子春秋 reports how a wise minister admonished his ruler who had just cast a new bell: "To use it in feasting before having sacrificed to the former rulers is against the rules of propriety [*li* 禮]."[26] Such regulations probably did not exist for most other kinds of musical instruments.

## The Social Framework
### Sumptuary Regulations

The rituals and performances involving bells were the privilege of aristocratic kin-groups; ordinary folk had no part in them. Indeed, few people living during the Bronze Age are likely ever to have heard bells in performance. Within the highest echelons of society, however, bell-chimes played a tremendously important role in defining and iteratively reaffirming relationships of power. Although the material value of chime-bells was presumably high enough to put them beyond the reach of most segments of Bronze Age society, including low-ranking nobles, their ownership was even further restricted by sumptuary rules.

To throw some light on such regulations, directly as well as circumstantially, we may refer to both textual and archaeological information, most of which dates from the final centuries of the Bronze Age. Textual records emphasize not the number of bells but their deployment about the ritual space. The *Zhou Li*, for instance, which purports to describe the structure of government during the early Zhou period, stipulates that

> the Zhou king (*wang* 王) was entitled to "palace suspension" (*gong-xuan* 宮縣): sets of bells and musical stones on all four sides of the courtyard of the ancestral temple;

---

25. *Meng Zi* "Liang Hui Wang-*shang*" (HYI ed., 3). *Han Fei Zi* "Shuilin" (23.27) mentions using a human victim for anointing a battle drum (Zhonghua Index ed., 775–76).

26. *Yan Zi Chunqiu* "Neipian, Jian-*xia*" 2:12 (*Yan Zi Chunqiu Jishi* ed., 124). A similar episode in *Yan Zi Chunqiu* "Waipian" 8:9 (*Yan Zi Chunqiu Jishi* ed., 507), is translated in Chapter 3, below. Alleged to have occurred in the Springs and Autumns period, the events described may well be Warring States period historical fiction; they do show that the primacy of the ritual function of bells was still recognized even at a relatively late date.

- the Many Lords (*zhuhou* 諸侯) governing the states surrounding the royal domain were entitled to "awning suspension" (*xuanxuan* 軒縣): bells and musical stones on three sides of the courtyard;[27]
- the ministers (*qing* 鄉) and magnates (*daifu* 大夫) were entitled to "divided suspension" (*panxuan* 判縣): sets of bells and musical stones on two facing sides of the courtyard; and
- the noblemen (*shi* 士) were entitled to "single suspension" (*texuan* 特縣): bells and musical stones suspended from a single rack on one side of the courtyard.[28]

A certain amount of skepticism is in order with such idealizing constructions. And when we further scrutinize the classical literature, we find, not surprisingly, that the early Han scholar Jia Yi 賈誼 (200–168 B.C.) recorded a different rule. Jia is in agreement with the *Zhou Li* when stipulating palace suspension and awning suspension for the Son of Heaven and the Many Lords, respectively, but according to him, magnates (*daifu*) merely had the right to "straight suspension" (*zhixuan* 直縣), which is probably synonymous with single suspension; and noblemen (*shi*) were to have zithers but no bells.[29]

Even though it is difficult to decide which of the above alternatives is closer to historical fact, the archaeological discoveries of the last forty years have confirmed that regulations of this sort existed in China at least since the middle of the Western Zhou (see table 2). For instance, the different arrangements of "suspended" musical instruments in figures 15 and 16 may represent, respectively, single and divided suspension, indicating a difference in rank between participants in the two scenes. Moreover, it is hardly accidental that in the central chamber of Marquis Yi's tomb at Leigudun (fig. 17), the bells on their L-shaped rack together with the lithophone surround the other musical instruments on three sides in an awning-suspension formation corresponding to the Marquis's *zhuhou* rank. This find, however, is so far almost unique. In Zhou period tombs, musical instruments were not usually displayed in the same way as in a palace courtyard. Customarily, bells and chimestones were interred without their racks. According to the *Li Ji* (a heterogeneous ritual text incorporating mostly late pre-Qin material), this practice intentionally marked the distinctions

27. With the term "awning suspension," the underlying image is that of the awning or canopy of a two-wheel chariot, which enclosed the chariot-box on three sides.

28. *Zhou Li: Chun'guan* "Xiaoxu" (*Zhou Li Zhengyi* 44:14b–16b).

29. *Xin Shu* "Shenwei-pian" (*Sibu Beiyao* ed. 2:4a). Sun Yirang, in his commentary on the *Zhou Li* (*Zhou Li Zhengyi* 44:15a), expresses no preference for either of the two systematizations.

TABLE 2.    Archaeological Evidence for the Zhou Sumptuary System

| *First Category*<br>*Nine ding, eight gui, bells, and chimestones* | *Second Category*<br>*Seven ding, six gui, bells, and chimestones* |
|---|---|
| Late Western Zhou through Early Springs and Autumns<br>  Zhuangbai, Fufeng (Shaanxi), hoard no. 1 (YG38, W1)<br>    Owners: House of Wei | Late Western Zhou through Early Springs and Autumns<br>  Ke bronzes (including Ke-*yongzhong*, Ke-*bo*) (YG44, W5)<br>    Donor: Shanfu/Taishi Ke<br>  Liangqi bronzes (including Liangqi-*yongzhong*) (W6)<br>    Donor: Bo Liangqi (office unknown)<br>  Xi bronzes (including Xi-*yongzhong*) (W7)<br>    Donor: Xi Jia (office unknown)<br>  Fu Fu–*xu* inscription (paraphernalia mentioned in text)<br>    Owner: Zheng Ji (house unknown)<br>  Shangcunling, Sanmenxia (Henan) (YG45, W8)<br>    Owner: Crown Prince of Guo |
| Mid–Springs and Autumns through Early Warring States<br>  Lijialou, Xinzheng (Henan), tomb no. 1 (YG91)<br>    Owner: Ruler of Zheng<br>  Liujiadianzi, Yishui (Shandong), tomb no. 1<br>    Owner: Ruler of Ju<br>  Ximennei, Shou Xian (Anhui), tomb no. 1 (YG94, W13)<br>    Owner: Marquis Shen of Cai<br>  Hougudui, Gushi (Henan), tomb no. 1<br>    Owner: Lord of Fan<br>  Liulige, Hui Xian (Henan), tomb *jia* (YG92)<br>    Owner: Ruler of Wei<br>  Liulige, Hui Xian (Henan), tomb no. 60 (YG93)<br>    Owner: Ruler of Wei<br>  Shanbiaozhen, Ji Xian (Henan), tomb no. 1 (YG96)<br>    Owner: Ruler of Wei<br>  Leigudun, Suizhou (Hubei), tomb no. 1 (W12)<br>    Owner: Marquis Yi of Zeng<br>  Leigudun, Suizhou (Hubei), tomb no. 1<br>    Owner: Ruler or consort of Zeng | Mid–Springs and Autumns through Early Warring States<br>  Xiasi, Xichuan (Henan), tomb no. 2 (W14)<br>    Owner: unidentified Chu aristocrat<br>  Dadian, Junan (Shandong), tomb no. 1 (YG100, W15)<br>    Owner: Ju aristocrat (branch of ruling family?)<br>  Dadian, Junan (Shandong), tomb no. 2 (YG101, W15)<br>    Owner: junior member of the Ju ruling family<br>  Fenshuiling, Changzhi (Shanxi), tomb no. 14 (YG102)<br>    Owner: Jin aristocrat (identity unknown)<br>  Jinshengcun, Taiyuan (Shanxi), tomb no. 251<br>    Owner: unidentified Jin(?) aristocrat<br>  Liulige, Hui Xian (Henan), tomb no. 60 (YG97)<br>    Owner: member of the ruling family of Wei<br>  Liulige, Hui Xian (Henan), tomb no. 75 (YG99)<br>    Owner: member of the ruling family of Wei<br>  Luhe, Lucheng (Shanxi), tomb no. 7<br>    Owner: unidentified aristocrat of Han<br>  Houchuan, Sanmenxia (Henan), tomb no. 2040 (YG151)<br>    Owner: unidentified aristocrat of Wei |
| Middle to Late Warring States<br>  Changtaiguan, Xinyang (Henan), tomb no. 1 (YG148)<br>    Owner: unknown Chu aristocrat<br>  Yan Xiadu, Yi Xian (Hebei), tomb no. 16 (YG149)<br>    Owner: member of Yan royal family? (*mingqi* only)<br>  Sanxi, Pingshan (Hebei), tomb no. 1<br>    Owner: King of Zhongshan<br>  Pingliangtai, Huaiyang (Anhui), tomb no. 16<br>    Owner: unclear | Middle to Late Warring States<br>  No instances reported |

NOTE. Finds of vessel sets without bells are not listed. *Ding* and *gui* do not both occur in all cases. Examples discussed by Yu and Gao 1978–79 (YG) and Wang Shimin 1986 (W; see also Wang Shimin 1988) are identified by the numbers used in the respective articles. Some datings and donor ascriptions have been slightly modified in accordance with Li Xueqin 1986.

TABLE 2. *(continued)*

| *Third Category* | *Fourth Category* |
|---|---|
| *Five* ding, *four* gui, *bells, and chimestones* | *Three* ding, *two* gui, *bells [chimestones?]* |

Late Western Zhou through Early Springs and Autumns
   No instances reported

Late Western Zhou through Early Springs and Autumns
   No instances reported

Mid–Springs and Autumns through Early Warring States
   Shangmacun, Houma (Shanxi), tomb no. 13 (YG105)
      Owner: aristocrat of Jin
   Miaoqiancun, Wanrong (Shanxi), large tomb (YG106)
      Owner: aristocrat of Jin
   Fenshuiling, Changzhi (Shanxi), tomb no. 270 (YG109)
      Owner: aristocrat of Jin
   Fenshuiling, Changzhi (Shanxi), tomb no. 269 (YG110)
      Owner: aristocrat of Jin
   Chengcun, Linyi (Shanxi) (details unknown)
      Owner: aristocrat of Jin
   Taijingwang, Linyi (Shandong) (details unknown)
      Owner: aristocrat of Qi
   Shanzhuang, Linqu (Shandong) (details unknown)
      Owner: aristocrat of Qi

Mid–Springs and Autumns through Early Warring States
   Ezhuangqu Huayuan, Linyi (Shandong) (YG122)
      Owner: unidentified Qi aristocrat

Middle to Late Warring States
   Fenshuiling, Changzhi (Shanxi), tomb no. 25
      Owner: aristocrat of Jin
   Zangjiazhuang, Zhucheng (Shandong)
      Owner: Ju Gongsun Chao Zi (Qi administrator)

Middle to Late Warring States
   No instances reported

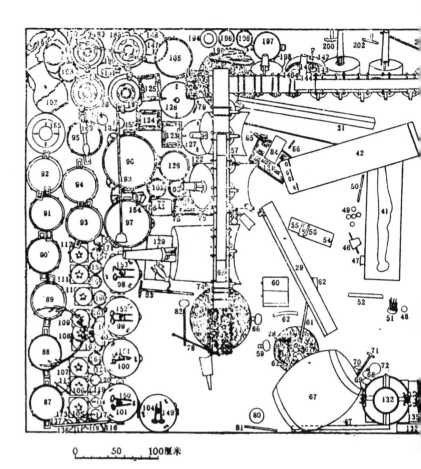

FIGURE 17. Arrangement of musical instruments in the ritual chamber of Marquis Yi's tomb, with other objects also found at the bottom of the chamber at the time of excavation. Musical instruments: *se* zithers (16, 29, 31, 32, 37, 41, 42), *se* bridges in a bamboo basket (131), mouth-organs (3, 51, 57), flute (79), panpipes (28, 85), pole-drum (67), pole-drum mallets (61, 78), hanging-drum (62), hand-drum (77), drum mallet (81), bell-chime (65), bell mallets (6, 50, 73, 83, 200–202), bell striking-bars (63, 64), lithophone (53), lithophone mallets (71, 204). Bronze sacrificial vessels: flat-bottomed large *ding* (87–95), other large *ding* (96–97), covered *ding* (98–104), small-mouthed *ding* (185), *ding* suspension hooks (149–155), tripod-shaped vessels (113–121, 136), spouted tripod (142), *li* (126, 156–164), *yan* (165), *gui* (105–112), covered *dou* (194), *dou* (195, 196), *fu* (122–125), *jian* (127, 128), large *hu* (132, 133), chained *hu* (182, 184), *fou* (141, 186–189), *yi* (147, 190), *yi* suspension hook (191), *pan* (148), "*zun* and *pan*" assemblage (38), ladles (138, 140, 230), spoons (169, 171–181, 183), scoop (170). Lacquered objects: box with wine-drinking utensils (10), boxes (224–228), ladles (82,

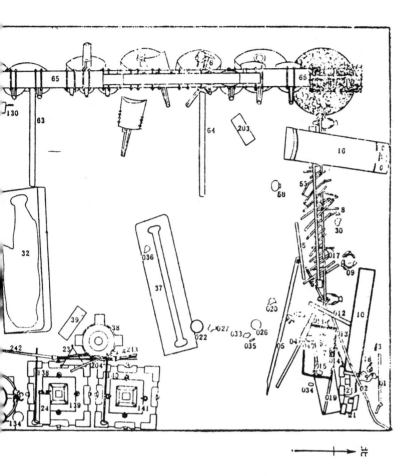

207), *dou* (30, 48, 72, 80, 134, 143–145), cups (46, 58, 146, 208–223), mounted cups (47, 59, 68, 70). Other equipment: bamboo baskets (7, 199), baskets with eating utensils (60, 129), bamboo-stem cups (66, 69, 86), ceramic *fou* (192, 193), chicken head (8), animal bones (sacrificial offerings) (55). Sacrificial furniture: bronze altar (135), lacquered wooden sacrificial altar (21), lacquered stand (75), bamboo mat (76), bronze censer (24), coal-burning basin with shovel and rake (166–168), coal-burning basin (197), lacquered wooden tables (39, 44, 54, 55), lacquered wooden stag (40), fish-shaped ornament (45), hemp fragment (244). (The objects numbered 01 through 043 were left behind by looters.)

between the living and the dead, but that explanation may be nothing more than posterior rationalization.[30]

Nevertheless, there is considerable archaeological evidence bearing upon the issue of elite ranking in Bronze Age China. Although it is difficult to secure direct documentation of the four types of suspension detailed in the *Zhou Li*, one may glean information about the sumptuary role of bells from their association with other ritual bronzes subject to similar regulations. From the mid–Western Zhou period onward, *ding* 鼎 "tripods" and *gui* 殷 "tureens" were the most important bronze vessels used in sacrifice. The sumptuary rule that assigned different numbers of these vessels to different aristocratic ranks has been reconstructed in varying ways;[31] it may have undergone some change over the course of the Zhou period, and it may have varied geographically.[32] Moreover, the extent to which the system was actually followed in practice is debatable. But the basic facts are clear: each rank was entitled to an odd number of *ding* complemented by the next lower even number of *gui*.

To correlate these sumptuary ranks with archaeological finds of bells, let us look at a list of all presently known assemblages of bronzes that comprise bells as well as *ding* and/or *gui* (table 2). It is apparent, first of all, that chime-bells were restricted to the highest ranks. They have not been found to be associated with aristocrats possessing fewer than three *ding*, and even in that lowest category there is so far only one somewhat uncertain instance.[33] Most of the entries in table 2, which accounts for only a small fraction of the bells so far excavated in China, were found with members of the nobility entitled to nine or seven *ding*, that is, with individuals of the two highest ranks.[34]

Moreover, the data in table 2 suggest that the exact number of bells was far less strictly regulated than that of ritual vessels; in the context of sumptuary arrangements, differences among bells of specific types (see Chapter 2) seem to have been unimportant. It does not seem to have mattered, for example,

30. *Li Ji* "Tan'gong-shang" (*Li Ji Zhushu* 8:3b; Couvreur 1:163–64). Zhao Shigang (1988) has postulated that the *Li Ji* injunction to bury bells and chimestones without their racks was commonly followed in north China, whereas the incidence of bell-racks in some large tombs located within the Chu sphere of influence (see Chapter 6) testifies to a specifically southern sumptuary regulation; this, however, would seem to be contradicted by the recent discovery of a set of *niuzhong* on a rack at Liugezhuang, Penglai (Shandong) (for reference, see Appendix 1).

31. Guo Baojun in *Shanbiaozhen yu Liulige*: 41–47, and Guo Baojun 1981; Du Naisong 1976; Yu and Gao 1978–79; Li Xueqin 1985, 460–64; Wang Shimin 1986, Wang Fei 1987, and, with specific reference to bells, Wang Shimin 1988.

32. See, e.g., Guo Dewei 1983 on the Chu sumptuary system.

33. The case in question, a tomb at Ezhuangqu Huayuan, Linyi (Shandong) (Yu and Gao 1978–79, example no. 122), has never been fully reported on (for preliminary references, see Appendix 1).

34. As no assemblages of royal bronzes have so far been excavated, it is unclear whether these two ranks included the royal person. Yu and Gao (1978–79) believe that nine *ding* were originally the prerogative of the king but were usurped by high-ranking aristocrats as early as late Western Zhou times; by contrast, Li Xueqin (1985, 460–64) holds that throughout the Zhou dynasty the king was entitled to twelve *ding* (see also Wang Shimin 1986).

whether a *zhuhou*'s "awning suspension" consisted of *yongzhong, niuzhong*, or *bo*-bells, or, when several types were represented, what the respective proportions were. (The larger the bell assemblage, the greater the room, of course, for typological variety.) We may tentatively conclude from table 2 that in the late Western Zhou and early Springs and Autumns periods, the nine-*ding* rank conferred the right to possess multiple sets of musical bells, while holders of the seven-*ding* rank had to make do with one chime of bells plus a single bell, a distinction which, if real, is no longer apparent in later Eastern Zhou archaeological contexts.

At any rate, the data in table 2 suggest that the accounts from the *Zhou Li* and by Jia Yi, as summarized above, may be accurate in recording that sumptuary distinctions were based on the mode of deployment rather than on the absolute number of bells. Such a deployment-based sumptuary rule contained a loophole for aristocrats intent on outdoing their peers in luxurious display: size and shape of the respective suspension racks remained unspecified. Marquis Yi's three-tiered bell assemblage, for instance, though it conforms to the principle of awning suspension, may be said to have observed the letter but not the spirit of the Zhou sumptuary code. Signs of a tendency to manipulate the ritual rules in the service of all-out conspicuous consumption abound in the Eastern Zhou archaeological record.[35] As we look at individual cases, we may frequently detect a subtle tension between the self-conception of Bronze Age society— something like a Freudian ego-ideal expressed in its ritual forms—and the socioeconomic reality. Through the following examples we shall encounter some of the individuals who enjoyed bell music in ancient China.

## The Donors of Shang and Western Zhou Bells

Some bell-owning aristocrats have left epigraphic records. The earliest bell inscriptions appear on late Shang dynasty (Anyang period) *nao*-bells; they indicate a name and/or a lineage marker (see fig. 56). Such inscriptions may help us to link some sets of *nao* with other bronzes of the period that bear identical inscriptions. In those cases, we may assume that the owners were wealthy and socially prominent, an assumption that accords with the conspicuous richness of the funerary contexts in which Shang bells occur archaeologically.[36] Five *nao* of this type, the largest number ever found at any one place, came from the tomb of a royal consort, Fu Zi (or Fu Hao 婦好), at Yinxu, Anyang (Henan) (see fig. 56).[37] That no specimens have been found in the Shang royal tombs must be due to looting before excavation. The archaeological distribution of chimed

35. See Yang Yubin 1985, 189, translated in Falkenhausen 1988, 1115–16.
36. See, e.g., Yin Zhiyi 1977.
37. References in Appendix 1.

sets of *nao* is heavily concentrated upon the vicinity of the Anyang metropolis, suggesting that royal relatives may have virtually monopolized these bells.

Shang bell inscriptions do not, on the whole, tell us much about the historical context of the inscribed objects. But because many of the social, ritual, and economic institutions of the Zhou may have earlier origins,[38] the following analysis may enhance our understanding of Shang and, perhaps, pre-Shang bells.

Western Zhou bell inscriptions are both more informative and more plentiful than those of the Shang. Almost without exception, they are grammatically coherent texts. In their simplest form, they state little more than an individual's name with a prayer-like final formula attached; the late Western Zhou period Zhong Yi–*yongzhong* inscription (fig. 18) reads: "I, Zhong Yi 中義, made these harmonizing bells; may I for ten thousand years eternally treasure them." Although Zhong Yi and other aristocrats always claimed to have "made" the bells in question, such making must surely be understood in a causative sense. Because I wish to reserve the term *maker* for craftsmen actually involved in the manufacturing process, and because the term *owner* connotes an anachronistic Western sense of property (and because bronzes passed through the hands of many generations of "owners"), I refer to the subjects of the Zhou bronze inscriptions as *donors*. This term acknowledges that ritual bronzes were not held by the individuals who had originally "made" them: they were placed in ancestral temples serving an extended kin-group.

What occasioned the manufacture of inscribed bronzes? First of all, a certain number of ritual objects, apparently including bells (see below), was given to a new lineage when it split off from its main lineage. Inscribed bronzes could also be obtained in recognition of particular merits, or by favor from one's superior, though only a small minority of inscriptions record the events leading to such acts of investiture. When we look at the transmitted pre-Qin texts, we find that several of them claim, using a recurrent, standardized formulation, that the Zhou dynasty elites inscribed bells and tripods to immortalize their donors' exploits in warfare.[39] A martial character, however, is notably absent from most surviving bronze inscriptions, which instead are primarily preoccupied with the cult of the donors' ancestors. For the most part, they celebrate the donors' piety and virtue, and they end with prayers to the ancestral spirits for blessings and long life. Couched in a specialized ritual language, their formulation makes use of such poetic devices as metric regularity and rhyme. To indicate the diction and message of a typical lengthy Western Zhou bell inscription, I offer below a complete translation of the inscription on the First Xing 癲–*yongzhong* (fig. 19);

---

38. See Keightley 1978b; Vandermeersch 1977–80.

39. *Zuo Zhuan* Xiang 19 (HYI ed., 289; Legge 483); *Guo Yu* "Jin Yu" (Tiansheng Mingdao ed. 7:2b); *Mo Zi* "Lu Wen" (HYI ed., 89); *Han Fei Zi* "Waichushui *zuo-shang*" 3 (Zhonghua index ed., 797).

FIGURE 18. One of the eight Zhong Yi–*yongzhong* (with inscription rubbing), excavated in 1960 at Qijiacun, Fufeng (Shaanxi). Later part of late Western Zhou (late ninth–early eighth century B.C.).

this early ninth-century B.C. bell was excavated in 1976 from a spectacular hoard of more than one hundred bronzes at Zhuangbai, Fufeng (Shaanxi), in the area of the first royal Zhou capital.

> I, Xing, am fearful and ceaselessly active from morning to night, always mindful of not losing [my mandate]; striving to practice filial piety toward my High Ancestor Xin Gong 辛公, my Accomplished Ancestor Yi Gong 乙公, and my august deceased father Ding Gong 丁公, [I made] this set of harmonically tuned chime-bells.

> May [these bells] be used so as to please and make exalted those who splendidly arrive [i.e. the ancestral spirits] and so as to let the accomplished men of the former generations rejoice. May they be used to pray for long life,

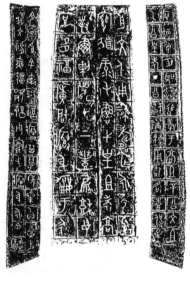

FIGURE 19. Photo and inscription rubbing of the First Xing–
*yongzhong* excavated in 1976 from hoard no. 1 at Zhuangbai,
Fufeng (Shaanxi). (For a view of their excavation context, see fig.
14.) Early part of late Western Zhou (mid-ninth century B.C.).

to beg for an eternal life-mandate, so that I may extensively command a
position of high emolument in respected old age, and enjoy unadulterated
happiness.

My venerable august ancestors, I am facing your brilliant appearance on
high, you who are looking on sternly from your positions above. Richly and
abundantly, forever let me enjoy at ease evermore ample and manifold good
fortune. May you broadly open up my awareness, helping me to obtain an
eternal life-mandate; may you personally bestow upon me that multi-colored
good fortune of yours.

May I live for ten thousand years. [My sacrificial bull] has even horns, he
is well-fattened, and his skin is glistening; sacrificing to the Accomplished

Spirits according to propriety, may I without limit manifest my good fortune.

May [this set of bells] be used to make me radiate with glory, forever shall I treasure it.[40]

At the beginning of this chapter, we pointed out how the contents of this inscription relate directly to ancestral ritual, and especially how closely the final, prayer-like paragraphs resemble an announcement to the spirits offered during an ancestral sacrifice. What do we know about the donor on whose behalf this text was composed? Xing (full name: Wei Bo Xing 微伯廥) was the head of the House of Wei, a territorially based patrilineal kin-group (*shi* 氏);[41] senior members of the Wei *shi*, including Xing himself, hereditarily served as record-keeping officials (*zuoce* 作冊) or as scribes (*shi* 史) at the Zhou court. The Zhuangbai hoard probably constitutes part of the inventory of the Wei ancestral sanctuary. Besides an impressive array of sacrificial vessels (curiously lacking *ding* tripods, which must have been disposed of otherwise), it yielded a total of twenty-seven bells belonging to seven different chimes—the largest single find of Western Zhou bells to date. From Xing's set of eight *gui* vessels, found in the same hoard, we can infer that his *shi* must have been entitled to nine *ding* (see table 2). The founder of the House of Wei—"my High Ancestor Xin Gong" in the inscription—apparently came to Zhou from the Shang court at the time of the overthrow of Shang.[42] Royal Shang descent might explain the exceptionally high rank of the House of Wei, whose sumptuary privileges (see table 3), seem to have exceeded those of other office-holding families of the period.

Xing, therefore, may not be a typical Western Zhou bell-owning aristocrat. Table 3 lists all other epigraphically documented Western Zhou bell-donors of whom something is known beyond their names.[43] The most prominent among them is the Zhou king, Li Wang 厲王 (personal name: Hu 𤱯 ~ 胡), who "made" bells on several occasions during his reign (878 [trad.]–827 B.C.). Two

40. For the text of this inscription see *Shaanxi Chutu Shang Zhou Qingtongqi* 2:77–79 (no. 54). Further references in Appendix 1. Extensive commentary on the inscription may be found in Falkenhausen 1988, 966–71.

41. From the many bronze inscriptions found in the Zhuangbai hoard (see fig. 14), we can piece together the genealogy of one principal Wei lineage throughout most of the Western Zhou period (Li Xueqin 1979).

42. A scion of the Shang royal house, Xin Gong may have been the same person as Wei Zi Qi 微子啓, who was established by the Zhou as the first ruler of the state of Song to perpetuate the ancestral cult to the Shang kings. Following the royal Shang custom of fraternal succession, Wei Zi Qi's younger brother became the second ruler of Song (see *Shi Ji* "Wei Zi Shijia," Zhonghua ed., 1621); the donors of the Zhuangbai bronzes may have been his lineal descendants, who remained in Zhou.

43. Due to inconsistencies in the formulation of the inscriptions, available information varies from individual to individual. In particular, a donor's personal name is not always indicated, but in

of these bells (undoubtedly once parts of chimed sets) are now preserved: the Hu-*yongzhong* (better-known as "Zongzhou-*zhong*" 宗周鐘), now in the National Palace Museum, Taibei, and the Fifth Year (Wusi 五祀) Hu-*yongzhong* recently found in Shaanxi.[44] Other donors included individuals in charge of some of the nominally subordinate polities surrounding the royal domain.[45] The ruling houses of many of these polities were junior branches of the royal lineage belonging to the same exogamous clan, Ji 姬. Non-Ji houses were integrated into the kinship-based power structure by exchanging brides with the royal Zhou and other Ji houses. Remarkably, with the exception of Chu 楚, the polities appearing in table 3 (Bi 畢, Guo 虢, Rui 芮, Shan 單, and Ying 應) were all ruled by branches of the Ji clan; the fief-holders among the Western Zhou bell-donors thus appear to have been, for the most part, relatives of the royal house.

Other bell-donors known through inscriptions were officials in the royal Zhou administration. They occupied offices with such titles as *Situ* 嗣徒 "Intendant of the Multitude," *Yulin* 虞林 "Inspector of Forests," *Taishi* 大師 "Grand Instructor," and *Shanfu* 膳夫 "Master of Viands." Identical or very similar titles appear in the description of the royal Zhou government in the *Zhou Li*, although the attached job descriptions are sometimes fanciful (in the *Zhou Li*, for example, the *Taishi* is the chief music instructor, but from epigraphic contexts he appears to have been a military official).[46] The hierarchical relationships of the bell-donors' offices are unclear; by all indications the Western Zhou administrative apparatus was structured far more loosely than the *Zhou Li* would suggest.

Given the unsystematized setup of the Western Zhou administration, it is almost impossible to establish the relative status of individual offices or fiefs. In particular, we cannot in most cases correlate official titles with specific sumptuary ranks. One of the reasons for this difficulty is the lack of pertinent archaeological context. Little of the material in table 3 can be cross-referenced with the archaeological evidence in table 2; the only exceptions are Xing of Wei, discussed above, and Elder Ke 伯克 (*shi* unknown, fl. late ninth–early eight century B.C.). Ke's career was unusual in that he seems to have occupied succes-

---

most cases we know his *shi*, and often we also know his rank of seniority within the *shi*. The terms *bo* 伯 "Elder," *zhong* 仲 "Second-born," *shu* 叔 "Younger," and *ji* 季 "Youngest" can denote either an individual's seniority among his brothers, or a lineage's genealogical seniority within a *shi*: unfortunately, it is seldom clear which is meant. The subject urgently needs further study.

44. For references, see Appendix 1 (Wusi Hu-*yongzhong*) and Appendix 2 (Hu-*yongzhong*).

45. Late pre-Qin texts mention a five-tiered hierarchy of titles for such rulers: *gong* 公 "Duke," *hou* 侯 "Marquis," *bo* 伯 "Viscount," *zi* 子 "Lord," and *nan* 男 "Baron" (see *Li Ji* "Wangzhi," *Li Ji Zhushu* 11:1a; *Zhou Li: Chun'guan* "Dazongbo," *Zhou Li Zhengyi* 35:1a–2b); it seems, however, that this nomenclature was not consistently employed during most of the Zhou period.

46. Creel 1970, 304; see *Zhou Li: Chun'guan* "Dashi" (*Zhou Li Zhengyi* 45:1a–12b).

TABLE 3.   Donors of Western Zhou Bells

| | House (shi) | Branch seniority | Donor's name | Official position | Investiture by |
|---|---|---|---|---|---|
| Hu–*yongzhong* (1) | Royal Zhou | [eldest] | Hu | King (Li Wang) | – |
| Wusi Hu–*yongzhong* (1) | Royal Zhou | [eldest] | Hu | King (Li Wang) | – |
| Bi Di–*yongzhong* (1) | Bi | ? | Di | ? | ? |
| Xian–*yongzhong* (1) | Bi? | Bo | Xian | ? | King? |
| Chu Gong Jia?–*yongzhong* (3) | Chu | [eldest] | Wei | ruler of Chu | ? |
| Mai–*yongzhong* (5 or more) | Gong | Shu | Mai | Yulin | King |
| Guo Shu Lü–*yongzhong* (7) | Guo | Shu | Lü | ? | King |
| Shu Yufu–*yongzhong* (1) | Guo | Shu | (son of Yufu) | ? | ? |
| Shi Cheng–*yongzhong* (1) | Guo | Ji | Cheng | Shi | ? |
| First Zha–*yongzhong* (5 or more) | Ji? | Bo? | Zha | Taishi? | King |
| Second Zha–*yongzhong* (1) | Ji? | Bo? | Zha | Taishi? | King |
| Nangong Hu–*yongzhong* (1) | Nangong | Zhong? | Hu | Situ | King |
| Rui Gong–*yongzhong* (2) | Rui | [eldest] | ? | ruler of Rui | ? |
| Shan Bo–*yongzhong* (1) | Shan | Bo | ? | ? | King |
| Shan Bo Yisheng–*yongzhong* fragment (1) | Shan | Bo | Yisheng | ? | King |
| First Xing–*yongzhong* (1) | Wei | Bo | Xing | Shi, Zuoce | King |
| Second Xing–*yongzhong* (7) | Wei | Bo | Xing | Shi, Zuoce | King |
| Third Xing–*yongzhong* (6) | Wei | Bo | Xing | Shi, Zuoce | King |
| Xi Zhong–*yongzhong* (6) | Xi | Zhong | ? | ? | ? |
| Zheng Xing Shu–*yongzhong* (1) | Xing | Shu | ? | residing at Zheng | ? |
| Xing Shu–*yongzhong* (3) | Xing | Shu | ? | ? | ? |
| Ying Hou–*yongzhong* (2) | Ying | [eldest] | Jian'gong | ruler of Ying | King |
| Ke–*yongzhong* (7) and –*bo* (1) | ? | Bo | Ke | Taishi, Shanfu | King |
| Liangqi–*yongzhong* (4 or more) | ? | Bo? | Liangqi | Shanfu | [King] |
| Zhong Yi–*yongzhong* (8) | Hua? | Zhong? | Zhong Yi | ? | ? |
| Zuo–*yongzhong* (8) | ? | Zhong? | Zuo | ? | Zhong Dashi |
| Ni–*yongzhong* (4) | ? | Shu? | Ni | "Majordomus" | Shushi |

NOTE. The conventional designation of each chime and the number of extant bells are indicated in the first column of each entry. The other columns summarize what is known about the respective donors. Some of the information in this table is derived from other bronze inscriptions that can be connected with the same individuals; for detailed discussion, see the *yongzhong* section in Falkenhausen 1988, ch. 2.

sively two different offices: "Grand Instructor" and "Master of Viands."[47] His bells (seven *yongzhong* and one *bo* have been preserved) were complemented by a set of seven *ding*, a number that suggests that Ke, though evidently a high-ranking official, occupied a sumptuary position one degree below that of Xing, the royal record-keeper.

All the high court officials documented through Western Zhou bell inscriptions appear to have resided in the Zhou metropolitan area. Moreover, the polities ruled by bell-donors all seem to have been located in the vicinity of the royal capital (though some, notably Chu, were later relocated). Conceivably, bell-chimes in Western Zhou were accessible only to members of a small number of aristocratic houses immediately surrounding the king. This tallies with the archaeological observation that sophisticated chimes of bells of the types used at the royal court in late Western Zhou times (see Chapter 5) have not been found outside of Shaanxi, whereas inscribed Western Zhou bronzes of other kinds have been excavated all over the Zhou cultural sphere.[48]

### The Donors of Eastern Zhou Bells

The identities of Eastern Zhou bell-donors reflect political changes after 771 B.C., when "barbarian" invasions from the north and west forced the Zhou court to move east to Luoyang. With the royal authority greatly weakened, the surrounding *zhuhou* states came to dominate the political scene, and not surprisingly, the rulers of such states appear prominently among the epigraphically documented bell-donors listed in table 4. Two of them, the marquises of Zeng 曾 and Cai 蔡, also appear as holders of nine-*ding* rank in table 2.

Other Eastern Zhou bell-donors listed in table 4 are offspring or other relatives of such rulers, including two aristocrats of seven-*ding* rank (table 2): Wangsun Gao 王孫誥, a mid–Springs and Autumns period descendant of a king of Chu (see fig. 21);[49] and Ju Shu Zhong Zi Ping 莒叔仲子平, a junior member

47. The Ke inscriptions are discussed by Shirakawa in *Kinbun Tsūshaku*, vol. 28. Ke's many bronzes are said to have been found together in a hoard at Famensi, Fufeng (Shaanxi). For references to the Ke bells, see Appendix 2.

48. *Xin Zhongguo de Kaogu Faxian he Yanjiu*, 257–64. It must be cautioned in making this argument that the majority of inscribed Zhou bronzes found in areas far from the metropolitan region (such as Hebei, Liaoning, Shandong, Jiangsu) seem to date to the early part of Western Zhou, when sophisticated chime-bells were not yet manufactured in Zhou. The fact remains that all Western Zhou chime-bells that have turned up in those areas belong to earlier and/or technically somewhat inferior types than those used in the metropolitan area in late Western Zhou (see Chapter 5). The relative dearth of mid- to late–Western Zhou bronzes (including bells) in the outlying areas of the Zhou cultural sphere may require a historical explanation.

49. The identity of the individual buried in tomb no. 2 at Xiasi, Xichuan (Henan), where the Wangsun Gao–bells were excavated (for references, see Appendix 1), has been the subject of some debate; in the past, I have largely agreed with Zhang Yachu's (1985) identifications (Falkenhausen 1988, 1076–1116), but I am now convinced that no sensible discussion of these finds is possible

of the ruling house of Ju 莒 (early fifth century B.C.).[50] Both donors apparently were fairly close relatives of their respective rulers.

The only bell-donor of five-*ding* rank known by name was Ju Gongsun Chao Zi 鄌公孫朝子, a local administrator in Qi 齊 in the early fourth century B.C.[51] He and other bell-owning members of lower sumptuary ranks presumably belonged to aristocratic houses that were further removed genealogically from the centers of power and whose members held hereditary offices as ministers (*qing*) and magnates (*daifu*). Their official titles, when recorded, are essentially identical to those in the Western Zhou records, even though their functions may have changed as administrative practice underwent significant development during the Eastern Zhou period.

A typical Eastern Zhou bell inscription is recorded on the bells of Marquis Shen of Cai 蔡侯申 (r. 519–491 B.C.) (see figs. 26–28), found in his richly furnished tomb at Ximen-nei, Shou Xian (Anhui).

> Given on the first *geng* 庚 day [in the sixty-day cycle] in the first quarter of the regular fifth month [i.e., the fifth month according to the Zhou calendar]. I, Shen, marquis of Cai, proclaim: "I am only the last-born small child. I dare not be complacent and forgetful. Possessed of reverence, everunflagging, I am in the entourage of the king of Chu.
>
> "Punctiliously I carry out the policies. It is the mandate of Heaven that I implement with rectitude. Having pacified and balanced the multitude of polities, I enjoy perfect felicity. Already I am wise in my mind, and in setting it forth I concentrate my virtue. Treating them with equity, I protect the magnates: thus I build up my polity and territory. In carrying out the mandate ever-respectfully, I am not excessive and make no mistakes."
>
> For myself I make these singing bells. May they beautifully resound without end, may sons and grandsons strike them.[52]

When we compare this text to the First Xing–*yongzhong* inscription, we cannot help noticing that the emphasis on ancestral sacrifice is significantly reduced. Instead, the rhetoric reflects on the political rift between north and south that

---

until they have been completely published. It still seems to me that Wangsun Gao was most likely the son of the Chu royal prince and prime minister Wangzi Wu 王子午 (d. 550 B.C.).

50. Ju Shu Zhong Zi Ping's tomb was found at Dadian, Junan (Shandong); references in Appendix 1. He was the second son in a junior line of the ruling house.

51. Ju Gongsun Chao Zi's tomb was found at Zangjiazhuang, Zhucheng (Shandong); references in Appendix 1. The donor may have been a descendant from the former ruling house of Ju, which in his time had been absorbed by Qi.

52. The text of the inscription may be found in Xu Zhongshu 1984, 462–65. Further references in Appendix 1; the inscription is discussed at length in Falkenhausen 1988, 1124–47.

TABLE 4.     Donors of Eastern Zhou Bells

|  | State | Donor's Name | Official Position |
|---|---|---|---|
| **I. Rulers of States** | | | |
| Cai Hou–bells (12 *yongzhong*, 8 *bo*, 9+ *niuzhong*) | Cai | Cai Hou Shen (Zhao Hou) | |
| Chu Gong Ni–*zhong* (1 bell, type unclear) | Chu | Chu Gong Ni | |
| Chu Wang Gan–*niuzhong* (1) | Chu | Chu Wang Gan | |
| Chu Wang–*niuzhong* (1) | Chu | Chu Wang | |
| Chu Wang Xiongzhang–bells (1 *bo*, 2 lost bells) | Chu | Chu Wang Xiongzhang (made for Marquis Yi of Zeng) | |
| Fan Zi–bells (8 *bo*, 9 *niuzhong*) | Fan? | Fan Zi (secondarily inscribed) | |
| Qin Gong–bells (5 *yongzhong*, 3 *bo*) | Qin | Qin Gong (probably Wu Gong) | |
| Ruo Gong–*yongzhong* (1?) | Ruo | Ruo Gong | |
| Song Gong–*bo* (6) | Song | Song Ping Gong | |
| Zi Zhang–*niuzhong* (3 or more) | Xu | Zi Zhang (= king Zhangyu?) | |
| Xu zi–*bo* (1) | Xu | Xu Zi | |
| Yue Wang–*niuzhong* (1 fragment) | Yue | Yue Wang | |
| Zeng Hou Yi–bells (45 *yongzhong*) | Zeng | Zeng Hou Yi | |
| Zhu Gong Le–*yongzhong* (1) | Zhu | Zhu Gong Le | |
| Zhu Gong Keng–*yongzhong* (4) | Zhu | Zhu Gong Keng | |
| Zhu Gong Hua–*yongzhong* (1) | Zhu | Zhu Gong Hua | |
| Zhu Hou–bell (1?) | Zhu | Zhu Hou | |
| **II. Members of Ruling Families** | | | |
| Wangsun Gao–*yongzhong* (26) | Chu | Wangsun Gao | military/ administrative |
| Wangsun Yizhe–*yongzhong* (1) | Chu | Wangsun Yizhe | military/ administrative |
| Ju Shu Zhong Zi Ping–*niuzhong* (9) | Ju | Ju Shu Zhong Zi Ping | |
| Lu Bei?–*yongzhong* (1?) | Lu | Lu Bei? | |
| Chifu-bell (1? bell of unknown type) | Qi | Chifu (bell made for his Jiang clan wife) | |
| Zhejian–*yongzhong* (4) | Wu | Zhejian | |
| Pei'er–*goudiao* (2) | Wu | Pei'er | |
| Gongwu Zangsun–*niuzhong* (9) | Wu | Gongwu Zangsun | |
| Zheshang-bells (5 *bo*, 7 *niuzhong*) | Wu | Zheshang | |
| Yun'er–*bo* (1) | Xu | Yun'er | |
| Shenliu-bells (5 *bo*, 7 *niuzhong*) | Xu | Shenliu | |

TABLE 4. *(continued)*

| | State | Donor's Name | Official Position |
|---|---|---|---|
| **II. Members of Ruling Families *(continued)*** | | | |
| Xu Wangzi Zhan–*niuzhong* (1) | Xu | Wangzi Zhan | |
| Xu Song [?] Jun–*zheng* (1) | Xu | Song [?] Jun (made for the ruler of Xu) | |
| Zhu Gongsun Ban–*bo* (1?) | Zhu | Zhu Gongsun Ban | |
| **III. Office-holding Aristocrats** | | | |
| Chen Dasangshi–*niuzhong* (9) | Chen | Zhong Gao | Dasangshi |
| Jingli–*niuzhong* (13) | Chu | ? | military |
| Jing–*zhong* (1) | Chu | ? | military |
| Biao–*niuzhong* (14) | Han | Biao | military |
| Lü–*yongzhong* (13) | Jin | Lü (House of Wei) | military |
| Ling–*bo* (13) | Qi | Ling | |
| Baoshi–*zhong* (1?) | Qi | Baoshi (House of Bao) | Dagong, Dashi, Datu, Dazai |
| Shu Yi–*zhong* and *bo* (16?) | Qi | Shu Yi | general, chief minister |
| Teng Sima Mao–bells (4 *bo*, 9 *niuzhong*) | Teng | Mao | Sima |
| Xu yang[?]yin–*zheng* | Xu | Yang[?]yin? | Yang[?]yin? |
| Chou[?]'er–*niuzhong* (4) | Xu | Chou[?]'er | "good servant" of Xu king |
| Zhediao–*niuzhong* (12+) | Yue | Zhediao | administrative? |
| Zhu Dazai–*niuzhong* (1) | Zhu | Zi Su | Dazai |

pervaded the Zhou realm during much of the Springs and Autumns period. From the mid-seventh century onward, Chu, by then a powerful southern kingdom surrounded by a growing number of client-states, contended for hegemony with a shifting federation of polities in north China that were allied with the royal Zhou.[53] By the Springs and Autumns period, Chu probably considered the marquises of Cai as retainers under its hegemony. From the northern alliance's point of view, however, as members of a Ji lineage, they remained legitimate *zhuhou* rulers comparable in rank with the king of Chu. Marquis Shen, who is well known from historical texts, attempted to assert a modicum

53. For a convenient summary of Chu northward expansion in the Springs and Autumns period, see Li Xueqin 1985, 170–88. Cai, ruled by an offshoot of the Zhou royal house, had originally been founded as a Zhou stronghold in the area of present-day southern Henan and Anhui, but by the Springs and Autumns period it had come under the sway of Chu, which temporarily extinguished Cai in 531 but reconstituted it in 528.

FIGURE 20. Chu Wang Xiong Zhang–*bo* from the tomb of Marquis Yi of Zeng. Workshop of Chu. The inscription records the donation of this bell to Marquis Yi by Hui Wang of Chu in the fifty-sixth year of Hui Wang's reign (433 B.C.).

of independence by manipulating Cai's traditional ties to other states;[54] even so, Cai remained under a constant Chu threat.

The bell inscription reflects this uneasy political situation. Although it affirms Cai subservience to the king of Chu, it also sustains the mandate of Heaven vested in the Zhou kings. Significantly, the inscription gives the date employing Zhou rather than Chu calendrical terms. In a parallel vein, the set of nine *ding* found in Marquis Shen's tomb comprises seven large vessels of equal size and two smaller specimens of the same type, allowing us to interpret it either as a nine-part set (marking the marquis as one of the *zhuhou* of the northern alliance) or as a set of seven (reflecting that he was subject to Chu suzerainty). It was by such means that Marquis Shen ritually "pacified and balanced the multitude of states." But Cai's "perfect felicity" was of brief duration; in 491 B.C.,

54. Marquis Shen's marriage alliance with the kingdom of Wu 吳 to the southeast (whose rulers, in an attempt to ally themselves with the Zhou, laid a probably fictional claim to Ji clan affiliation) led to a successful military campaign into Chu in 504 B.C.

the *daifu* magnates rebelled and Marquis Shen was murdered. Chu annihilated Cai less than fifty years later.

The political situation in Marquis Yi's state of Zeng, closer to Chu, must have been similar in many ways. Marquis Yi was probably descended from a ruling house of the Ji clan that had imposed Zhou rule in northern Hubei during the Western Zhou period;[55] by late Eastern Zhou times, however, Zeng was bound in a close allegiance with Chu that was probably cemented by marital ties.[56] The inscription of the Chu Wang Xiong Zhang–*bo* (fig. 20), to which I referred in the Introduction, records that Hui Wang of Chu presented Marquis Yi with the full array of ritual paraphernalia (*zongyi* 宗彝), surely indicating a close political relationship. The inscribed bamboo slips found in Marquis Yi's tomb show, moreover, that Zeng used Chu administrative terminology.[57] The musical implications of these dual claims on Marquis Yi's loyalty will become apparent in Chapter 9. Although Zeng seems to have been more fully integrated into the Chu alliance than Cai, it, too, was eventually extinguished by Chu.

*Eastern Zhou Developments in Bell Usage*

The gradual breakdown of the traditional Zhou socio-political framework during Eastern Zhou times is apparent when we look at bell usage in that period. In Eastern Zhou bell inscriptions such as the Cai examples just translated, the focus has shifted from ancestral spirits to their human worshippers. Now the most important function of the bells is to bring happiness to the donor's relatives and distinguished guests, the human participants in the celebrations during which the bells were played. An excerpt from the Wangsun Gao–*yongzhong* inscription (third quarter of the sixth century B.C.) (fig. 21) enumerates such beneficiaries of bell music:

> Glistening are the harmonizing bells. With them feast in order to please and
> make happy the king of Chu, the lords of the states and the fine guests, as
> well as my fathers [i.e. father and paternal uncles] and brothers and the
> various noblemen. How blissful and brightly joyous! For ten thousand
> years without end, forever preserve and strike them.[58]

55. That the Zeng rulers belonged to the Ji clan is known from several Springs and Autumns period bronze inscriptions (Zeng and Li 1980). It is of course possible that Zeng (like Wu) was an autochthonous polity whose rulers claimed fictional kinship with the Zhou kings. Conceivably, moreover, by the early Warring States period Zeng was no longer governed by its indigenous ruling house but had become the appanage of a junior branch of the Chu royal family (see Thorp 1981– 82:72). But Gu Tiefu (1980) has drawn attention to various features of Marquis Yi's tomb that suggest genuine ritual and cultural connections with the Ji states of north China.

56. See Introduction, n. 18.

57. Qiu Xigui 1979, 26–27.

58. The text of this document may be found in Xu Zhongshu 1984, 66–71. See also n. 49 above.

FIGURE 21. Wangsun Gao–
*yongzhong* excavated in 1979
from tomb no. 2 at Xiasi,
Xichuan (Henan). Workshop of
Chu, third quarter of the sixth
century B.C.

The categories of individuals listed were situated at different degrees of genealogical distance from the donor (the host of the ceremony), as well as from one another. In an almost proto-Confucian vein, the Eastern Zhou elites may have perceived ritual as capable, when properly performed, of establishing concord among these different categories of people. The time-honored ritual music remained important as a means of achieving such harmony.

Yet as a consequence of the shift away from the spirits, traditional ancestral ritual was humanized, and in Eastern Zhou times, the distinction between highly prescriptive ceremonial music and musical entertainment widened. Feasts and banquets originally linked to such ritual occasions as ancestral sacrifices and archery contests gradually assumed an independent existence; in the process, novel forms of musical entertainment emerged. Archaeological assemblages of musical instruments reflect this disjuncture. In Marquis Yi's tomb, in addition to the trappings of ritual music in the central chamber, a smaller group of instruments (five large *se* zithers, two small *qin* zithers, two mouth organs, and one tambourine) was found in the eastern chamber. We remember that this part of the tomb corresponded to the Marquis's private quarters in his palace, where women of the harem and singing-girls would have entertained him while he was alive. Their music was probably quite distinct from the ritual music performed in the temple; for one thing, they did not use chime-bells.

We do not know exactly how the Eastern Zhou "new music" differed from traditional ritual music, but it seems to have been more exciting and sensuous. In the *Yue Ji*, the following comments are ascribed to Zi Xia 子夏, a pupil of Confucius:

> In the old-style music, the [musicians and dancers] enter and leave the stage in a well-ordered formation. Using the correct harmonies, [this music] flows magnificently. String instruments as well as bottle-gourd mouth organs with their blowing reeds all together wait for the drum [to start]. The performance begins with the music of King Wen, to which is added the stirring music of King Wu. Order is given to the stirring with the *xiang* 相 [rhythms], and the fast tempo is controlled with the *ya* 雅 [movements]. Having attended such a performance, the accomplished man will talk about it; inspired by it, he will follow the ways of antiquity. He will cultivate his own person as well as his family, and he will establish peace throughout the world. Such are the effects of the old music.

> In new music, the [musicians and dancers] enter and leave the stage with their bodies bent over. Using dishonest tones, [this music] is reckless, and it goes on and on in a debauched manner. Like monkeys, the fools and dwarfs commingle males and females and do not acknowledge the distinction between fathers and sons. When such music has ended, one cannot properly talk about it; one cannot take it as an inspiration to follow the ways of antiquity. This is the effect of the new music.[59]

The new musical styles emerging in Eastern Zhou are known to posterity under the label "Airs of Zheng and Wei."[60] Despite the Confucian scholars' disapproval, they became widely popular, supplanting traditional ritual music. When, in 336 B.C., Mencius broached the subject of music with Hui Wang of Liang (=Wei) 梁 (魏) 惠王 (r. 370–319 B.C.), "the king blushed and said: 'It is not

---

59. *Li Ji* "Yueji" (*Li Ji Zhushu* 38:11a–b and 39:1a; Couvreur 2:86–88); the same text with slight variants in *Shi Ji* "Yueshu" (Zhonghua ed., 1222).

60. For a brief treatment of the Music of Zheng, which quotes most of the relevant loci classici, see DeWoskin 1982, 92–94.

the music of the Former Kings that I am capable of appreciating. I am merely fond of popular music [*shisu zhi yue* 世俗之樂].'"[61]

During the Eastern Zhou period, each of the different regions within the Zhou realm developed its own style of music and dance, some of which may have had roots in local folk traditions. At large-scale entertainments, the musics of many states were performed in mixed programs. An excerpt from a poem in the *Chu Ci* anthology vividly conveys the exuberance of a banquet at the court of Chu in ca. mid–Warring States times.

> Before the dainties have left the tables,
>   girl musicians take up their places.
> They set up the bells and fasten the drums
>   and sing the latest songs:
> "Crossing the River," "Gathering Caltrops"
>   and "Sunny Bank."
> The lovely girls are drunk with wine,
>   their faces are flushed.
> With amorous glances and flirting looks,
>   their eyes like wavelets sparkle;
> Dressed in embroideries, clad in finest silks,
>   splendid but not showy;
> Their long hair, falling from high chignons,
>   hangs low in lovely tresses.
> Two rows of eight, in perfect time,
>   perform a dance of Zheng;
> Their *xi-bi* buckles of Jin workmanship
>   glitter like bright suns.
> Bells clash in their swaying frames;
>   the catalpa-wood zither's strings are swept
> Their sleeves rise like crossed bamboo stems,
>   then slowly shimmer downwards.
> Pipes and zithers rise in wild harmonies,
>   the sounding drums thunderously roll;
> And the courts of the palace quake and tremble
>   as they throw themselves into the Whirling Chu.
> Then they sing songs of Wu and ballads of Cai
>   and play the DALÜ music.
> Men and women now sit together,
>   mingling freely without distinction;
> Hat-strings and fastenings come untied:
>   the revel turns to wild disorder.
> The singing-girls of Zheng and Wei
>   come to take their places among the guests;

---

61. *Meng Zi* "Liang Hui Wang-*xia*" (HYI ed., 5; translation after Lau, 60, *mod. auct.*).

But the dancers of the Whirling Chu
find favour over all the others.[62]

At these spectacles, bells could be used to accompany the dramatic singing and dancing of professional entertainers, though they do not seem to have been essential to the success of the performance.[63] While many Warring States period aristocratic tombs of Chu have yielded well-preserved remains of zithers, drums, and wind instruments, chime-bells are absent in most cases.[64] (Whether the situation was similar in north China is difficult to gauge because of the lack of preserved organic materials in tombs of comparable size, but there, too, the archaeological prominence of bell-chimes decreases notably in the Warring States period.)[65]

Associated almost exclusively with the ritual music played in connection with the ancestral cult of the old aristocracy, bell-chimes went into permanent decline as the traditional Zhou order broke down in the Warring States period and rulers lost interest in traditional musical paraphernalia (see Chapter 9). Until that time, however, they had been status symbols for some of the highest-ranking and most powerful individuals of the times.

62. *Chu Ci: Zhao Hun*, 1.106–23 (*Chu Ci Buzhu* j. 9:10b–12a); Hawkes, 228–29.

63. In view of their exclusivity, it seems unlikely that bells were originally part of any of the folk musical traditions informing the local Warring States musical styles; however, the local musics may have been adapted to the instruments of the traditional ritual orchestra, with the result that bell-chimes, when available, could have been used in court performances of local musics, as described in the *Chu Ci*.

64. For example, at the cemetery at Yutaishan, Jiangling (Hubei), close to the Chu capital, 25 of 1,158 tombs yielded musical instruments, but no chime-bells were found (*Jiangling Yutaishan Chumu*: 105). The only Warring States period Chu chime-bells (including chime-bell replicas) so far known are those from Changtaiguan, Tianxingguan, and Yangmei (references in Appendix 1). Other Warring States tombs in the Middle Yangzi region that have yielded musical instruments (or *mingqi* replicas thereof) but no bells include tombs no. 3 and 4 at Baizifan, Echeng (Hubei) (*Kaogu Xuebao* 1983 [2]: 248); tomb no. 1 at Baoshan, Jingmen (Hubei) (*Wenwu* 1988 [5]:1–14); tomb no. 12 at Caipo, Xinyang (Hubei) (*Wenwu* 1976 [11]:69); tomb no. 47 at Deshan, Changde (Hunan) (*Kaogu* 1963 [9]:461–73, 479); tomb no. 34 at Gebeisi, Jiangling (Hubei) (*Wenwu* 1964 [9]:27–30); tomb no. 1 at Liuchengqiao, Changsha (Hunan) (*Kaogu Xuebao* 1972 [1]:59–72); six tombs at Paimashan, Jiangling (Hubei) (*Wenwu* 1964 [9]:30–32 and *Kaogu* 1973 [3]:151–61); tomb no. 1 at Tengdian, Jiangling (Hubei) (*Kaogu Xuebao* 1982 [1]:71–116); tombs no. 1 and 2 at Wangshan, Jiangling (Hubei) (*Wenwu* 1966 [5]:33–55); tomb no. 48 at Wulidun, Echeng (Hubei) (*Kaogu Xuebao* 1983 [2]:240–41); tomb no. 3 at Wulipai, Changsha (Hunan) (*Hunan Kaogu Jikan* 1 [1981]:32–36, 38); tomb no. 6 at Yangjiawan, Changsha (Hunan) (*Kaogu Xuebao* 1957 [1]:96–99); and tomb no. 3 at Yangwuling, Yiyang (Hunan) (*Hunan Kaogu Jikan* 2 [1984]:70–77). Some of these tombs, e.g., those at Baoshan and Tengdian, are very large in scale; if they had been robbed, one would expect, given the favorable preservation conditions, that at least the remains of chime-bell racks without bells would have been found (as was indeed the case in the large tomb at Jiuli, Linli [Hubei], reference in Appendix 1). Hence it seems likely that the absence of bells in Warring States Chu aristocratic tombs is culturally significant.

65. See Appendix 2, pt. VII.A and passim.

Chinese Bronze Age bells were held in family sanctuaries, and only people of certain aristocratic ranks were entitled to own them. Because they were not items of commercial trade, occasions for their acquisition were very limited. Following a suggestion by Igor Kopytoff, let us trace the putative economic "life history" of chime-bells.[66]

Very little is known about the workshops where bells first saw the light of day. It appears that in Shang and Western Zhou, such workshops were attached to the royal court and to some of the principal aristocratic houses;[67] in later times, they were run by the ruling houses of the individual states.[68] These were not capitalistic enterprises; bronzes were produced here only for the kin-group's own needs and those of its subordinates. For anyone without a workshop, gift-giving rituals provided the only chance to acquire bells.

Bells were, in Kopytoff's words, "terminal" commodities:[69] they were deposited in temples, where, in principle, they were to remain forever. For aristocratic houses above a certain rank, bells seem to have constituted part of the basic equipment of their ancestral sanctuaries. They figure among the ceremonial gifts received by Zhou junior princes when the king enfeoffed them as rulers of territorial states.[70] Bells are listed too in the Shu Fufu–*xu* inscription, which appears to record the initial endowment of a junior aristocratic house that was about to split off and establish itself as a separate ritual and economic unit:

> Given in the king's first year, when the king was in Chengzhou, on the day *Ding-Hai* in the first quarter of the sixth month. Shu Fufu 叔專父 made for Zheng Ji 鄭季 six bells and of metal venerable [ancestral vessels], four *xu* and seven *ding*. May Zheng Ji's sons and grandsons forever treasure and use them.[71]

66. Kopytoff 1986; Appadurai 1986, 16–29.

67. Various bronze workshops have been excavated around the Shang capitals at Zhengzhou and Anyang. For Zhengzhou, see Liao Yongmin 1957 and *Kaogu Xuebao* 1957 (1):56–57; for Anyang, Shi Zhangru 1955, Chang 1980, 233–34, and *Yinxu Fajue Baogao* 1958–1961:11–60. On Western Zhou bronze workshops see Mochii 1980 and Matsumaru 1980.

68. The bronze foundry of the state of Jin has been found at Houma (Shanxi); preliminary reports in *Wenwu* 1960 (8/9):7–14, 1961 (10):31–34, and *Kaogu* 1962 (2):55–62. See also Li Xueqin 1985, 43–46. Although in the Warring States period, at least in some states, bronze manufacture may have undergone a certain degree of commercialization (and "depoliticization"), attempts to elucidate this process have thus far been limited to the study of weapons (Miyamoto 1985).

69. Kopytoff 1986, 75; Appadurai 1986, 23.

70. The *Zuo Zhuan* (Ding 4, HYI ed., 441–42) relates that Kang Shu 康叔, the first ruler of Wei 衛, received DALÜ 大呂, and Tang Shu 唐叔, the first ruler of Jin, received GUXIAN 姑洗; both are names of bells or bell-chimes tuned to particular pitches (see Chapter 9).

71. Four *xu* bearing this inscription were excavated at Zhangjiapo, Chang'an (Shaanxi) (*Kaogu* 1965 (9):447–50). The donor Shu Fufu seems to have been the head of the Junior (*Shu*) lineage of his

These sacrificial bronzes were to constitute the core of Zheng Ji's family holdings, the new *shi*'s means of communication with its ancestral spirits. Possibly, as in some parts of China today, temples, their furniture, and other holdings of a kin-group were considered the "property" of the ancestors to whom they were dedicated.[72]

Besides such cases of initial investiture, legitimate gifts of bells mainly fall into two categories: *gong* 供 "tribute" offered by subordinates to their superiors, and *ci* 賜, presents bestowed in the opposite direction.[73] Both kinds of gifts were exchanged during periodic audiences at the patron's palace.[74] The *Li Ji* specifies that bells (or, according to the commentary, metals fit for the manufacture of bells) were to be part of a *zhuhou* ruler's standard tribute offerings to the Zhou king.[75] The receiver of such tribute would reciprocate amply. Even though from an economic standpoint court audiences were redistributive in nature (and could be highly lucrative for the guest), their ritual process was designed at every moment to reinforce the social distance between the participants. In later Eastern Zhou times, the symmetry of such exchanges was lost: rulers now one-sidedly exacted contributions from their subjects via the anonymous, bureaucratic method of taxation. Zhuang Zi alludes to a case in which Ling Gong of Wei 衛靈公 (r. 534–493 B.C.) levied a special tax for the purpose of casting a set of bells.[76]

The only epigraphic record documenting the upward movement of bells through tribute or taxation is inscribed on the mid-sixth century B.C. Huan Zi Meng Jiang 洹子孟姜–*hu*. The inscription records a mission dispatched by the ruler of Qi 齊 to the Zhou king. A set of bells figures in the long list of gifts offered to various dignitaries at the royal court:

> The Marquis of Qi paid reverence for the fine mandate to the Son of Heaven
> above, offering [*yong* 用] a set of *bi* 璧 [jade discs] and one *si* 笥 [box of jade];
> to the Great Shaman Master of Oaths and the Great Master of Investitures,
> he offered *bi* [jade discs], two *hu* vessels and eight *ding* tripods; to Lord Nan-

---

*shi*, the name of which remains unstated; the receiver of the bronzes was the head of the Youngest (*Ji*) lineage of that *shi* (possibly a junior branch of Shu Fufu's own lineage), which was enfeoffed in Zheng 鄭. In theory, splitting was to occur every five generations (*Li Ji* "Sangfu Xiaoji," *Li Ji Zhushu* 32:4b–5b, and "Dazhuan," ibid. 34:6a–7a; K. C. Chang 1976, 72–78).

72. James L. Watson 1977, 167–168.

73. The following remarks echo some ideas by Mauss 1923–24, Sahlins 1972, Douglas and Isherwood 1981, and Douglas 1982; for the specifics of the Chinese case, see K. C. Chang 1975. An interesting discussion of West Asian parallels may be found in Zaccagnini 1987.

74. The protocol of such an audience ritual is described in *Yi Li* "Jin Li" (*Yi Li Zhengyi* 20; Couvreur, 373–83).

75. *Li Ji* "Jiaotesheng" (*Li Ji Zhushu* 25:7a/b; Couvreur 1:578); the commentary is by Zheng Xuan 鄭玄 (A.D. 127–200).

76. *Zhuang Zi* "Shanmu" (HYI ed, 52; Watson, 212–13).

gong 南宮子, he offered two sets of *bi* [jade discs], two *si* [boxes of jade], and one set [*si* 肆] of striking-bells.[77]

The presentation of gifts to the king's officials constituted an integral part of an audience ritual. Such gifts acknowledged the role of the officials in facilitating access to the royal person.[78] Among the various officials mentioned in the inscription, Lord Nangong was especially honored with the gift of a set of chime-bells. Although as a magnate (*daifu*) at the royal court, Lord Nangong, who may be identical to an individual mentioned in the *Zuo Zhuan*,[79] was equal in rank to a *zhuhou* ruler, his position as an agent for the king made him the marquis's ritual superior for the duration of the audience sequence. The bells presented to Lord Nangong had presumably been manufactured at the Qi court workshops.

Movement of bells from the top down is more amply documented. Inscriptions on non-royal Western Zhou bells habitually emphasize that their donors obtained them as a result of their superiors' favor, often as a reward for virtuous service. The Western Zhou Ying Hou–*yongzhong* inscription, for instance, records a gift-giving ceremony as follows:

> In the first quarter of the regular second month, when the king returned from [the eastern capital] Chengzhou, Jian'gong Marquis of Ying 應侯見工 delivered [*yi* 遺] [tribute] to the king in Zhou. On day *Xin-Wei*, the king went to [the temple of] Kang [Wang]. Rong Bo 榮伯 escorted Jian'gong Marquis of Ying [into the court] and assisted him [in performing obeisance to the king]. [The king] bestowed [*ci* 易 = 賜] on him [Jian'gong] one red-lacquered bow, one hundred red-lacquered arrows, and four horses.
>
> I, Jian'gong, dare in response to praise the Son of Heaven's munificence. With it, I made for my august ancestors, the Marquises of Ying, a great set of chime-bells. Let them be used so that [the ancestors] bestow [*ci* 易 (!)] longevity and an eternal life-mandate. May sons and grandsons forever treasure and use them.[80]

77. Guo Moruo, 1958 186/225–26/212; Shirakawa, *Kinbun Tsūshaku* 38:388–403. Shirakawa dates the *hu* to 532 B.C. For the translation of the official titles see Doty 1982, 407–44. It should be noted, however, that my interpretation differs from that proposed by Doty, who, following Shirakawa, regards the High Son of Heaven as well as Lord Nangong as Qi deities. The ruler of Qi referred to is Jing Gong 景公 (r. 547–490 B.C.); the Zhou king at the time was Jing Wang 景王 (r. 544–520 B.C.).
78. *Yi Li* "Jin Li," see n. 74 above.
79. See Falkenhausen 1988, 1006–35.
80. The text of this inscription may be found in Xu Zhongshu 1984, 316–17. One of the two surviving bells of this chime was excavated at Hongxing Commune, Lantian (Shaanxi); the other is in the Shodō Hakubutsukan (Museum of Calligraphy) in Tōkyō (references in Appendix 1). The first paragraph of this inscription appears to have been copied from an official document, to which the donor appended his own prayer (see Falkenhausen 1988, ch. 3).

The significance of the royal presents here listed far exceeded their material value: they legitimized the recipient's elite status, and they were fundamental to his exercise of power.[81] By means of a bronze inscription, the recipient would formally announce his newly won prestige to the ancestral spirits, thus gaining supernatural validation of his investiture. On bells perhaps more frequently than on other bronzes, inscriptions mention the king himself as the grantor of an investiture (as in the case of the Marquis of Ying); a non-royal patron, however, could also assume that role (see table 3).

Perplexingly, in the Ying Hou–*yongzhong* inscription the bells themselves are not listed among royal gifts to the marquis. Here and elsewhere in the epigraphic records, it appears that the gift actually received was not the bronze objects themselves but merely the privilege of having them cast in commemoration of the investiture. For beneficiaries not in possession of their own bronze-manufacturing workshops, this gift may have entailed access to a patron's workshop facilities, though it seems that donors were ordinarily expected to finance the casting themselves.[82]

Of the exceptional cases of Western Zhou inscriptions that do mention bells in the context of a list of presents, none is actually on a bell. The Duo You 多友–*ding* inscription records that Duo You was given by his lord "one tessera, one set [*si* 肆] of bells, and one hundred catties of *qiaoyou* 鐈鋚 bronze."[83] Likewise, the Shi Hui[?] 師戫–*gui* inscription specifies, at the end of a long list of presents: "I bestow on you one bell, five chimestones, and metal";[84] and in the Gongchen 工臣–*gui* inscription, the donor's patron states: "I bestow on you a horse-drawn chariot, five bells, and metal."[85] The co-occurrence of bells and metal in the inscriptions is curious. It is likely that in some of these contexts, the term *zhong* 鐘 (literally "bell") refers to the players of bells, not to the instruments themselves; the metal may have been intended for casting bells on which the players could perform.[86] Such an interpretation was first proposed by Si Weizhi 斯維至 in connection with the Large Ke (Da Ke 大克)–*ding* inscription, where "winds

81. Keightley 1981; Kane 1982–83; see also Huang Ranwei 1978.
82. In Western Zhou, cowrie shells may have been used as tokens in these transactions; they are mentioned in some bronze inscriptions as part of investiture gifts but (perhaps significantly) are not mentioned in any known bell inscription. From the mid–Springs and Autumns period onward, metallic currencies were available. But the role of such "moneys" in the exchange of ritual paraphernalia may be assumed to be limited; they may have served as "coupons," in Mary Douglas's (1967) sense, that had validity only when used by members of specific social groups for a highly restricted array of transactions.
83. This vessel was reported by Tian and Luo 1981. The translation largely follows that by Shaughnessy (1983–1985, 58), who dates the *ding* to ca. 816 B.C.
84. Shirakawa, *Kinbun Tsūshaku* 31:740–50. This vessel has been lost since the Song dynasty.
85. Shirakawa, *Kinbun Tsūshaku* 49:277–80.
86. If so, the counter *si* 肆 in the Duo You–*ding* inscription would have to be interpreted as a counter for bell-players. This was not its meaning in Eastern Zhou texts (see below, Chapter 6).— For a discussion of this issue, see Keightley 1969, 206 n. 2.

[*linglun* 靈侖 ] and drums and bells [or 'strikers of bells,' *guzhong* 鼓鐘 ]" are enumerated in one breath with "scribes and lesser servants [*shi xiaochen* 史小臣 ]" and other retainers presented by the king to the donor, Ke 克.[87] Because a set of bells was useless if one did not have skilled players, and because players were hereditarily attached to bell-owning aristocratic houses (see below), it is plausible that performers would have been presented jointly with musical instruments. Such exchanges of musicians may have contributed to the spread of regional musical styles during the Eastern Zhou period.[88]

In Eastern Zhou, bells are recorded to have been presented by hegemonial rulers to the rulers of less powerful allied states (such as the large *bo* from Marquis Yi's tomb),[89] and by rulers to their aristocratic subordinates as reward for exceptionally able service.[90] Gifts of bells emphasized social relationships in a vertical hierarchy; they were rarely if ever exchanged across kin-groups of equal social standing. Bells rarely figured among the dowry bronzes given to aristocratic brides (and presumably deposited in their husbands' family sanctuaries).[91] The provenience of the very few known bridal bells suggests that they may have been limited to the eastern portion of the Zhou realm.

### Irregular Events in the Life of Bells

Giving away sanctified heirlooms, and specifically bells, was sacrilegious and would only have occurred in situations of emergency. The *Zuo Zhuan* records two such transactions between the states of Zheng and Jin 晉 . In the first instance, Cheng Gong 成公 of Zheng (r. 584–571), who had been exiled by an internal rebellion, presented to the ruler of Jin a bell dedicated by (or to?) his father Xiang Gong 襄公 (r. 604–587); Jin troops thereupon reinstated Cheng Gong.[92] In the second instance, Zheng, for some time an ally of Chu, had been

87. Si Weizhi 1947, 17. For the text of the Da Ke–*ding* inscription, see Shirakawa, *Kinbun Tsū-shaku* 28:490–509, esp. 504, 508. Ke was probably the same individual mentioned above as a Western Zhou bell-donor.

88. Feng Jiexuan 1984, 77–78.

89. Another case in point is a gift of bronze, later used for casting three bells, given by Chu to Zheng at the occasion of their first alliance (*Zuo Zhuan* Xi 18, HYI ed., 113).

90. The *Zuo Zhuan* (Xiang 11) recounts how Dao Gong of Jin 晉悼公 (r. 572–558 B.C.) gave half the bells and female musicians he had received as a "bribe" from Zheng (see below) to the meritorious minister Wei Jiang 魏絳 (HYI ed., 274; see also *Guo Yu* "Jin Yu," Tiansheng Mingdao ed., Jin 7:6b).

91. The only extant specimen of a bridal bell is the Ling-*bo* in the Museum of Chinese History, Beijing (formerly Shanghai Museum) (reference in Appendix 2); two additional examples, the Chifu–*zhong* from Qi (Doty 1982, 114–24) and the Zhù Hou–*zhong* (Luo Zhenyu 1936, j. 1:9, 1–2), both from the Springs and Autumns period, are lost; the authenticity of the latter piece is questionable.

92. *Zuo Zhuan* Cheng 10 (HYI ed., 230). Common sense dictates that the objects presented by Zheng to Jin at this and the next mentioned occasion were not especially manufactured for the purpose. Apart from the fact that the state had been under siege and thus was hardly in a position to

defeated by the troops of a northern alliance led by Jin; the ruler of Zheng offered lavish presents to the victors to persuade them to spare his state from punishment. Three music masters headed the list of gifts; they were followed by state chariots, war chariots, and weaponry, as well as "two sets of singing bells together with the appropriate number of bo 鎛 bells and chimestones, as well as two teams of eight female musicians."[93] The ruler of Jin accepted the presents, and Zheng was left in peace.

There was something illicit about such gifts, which are referred to as lu 賂, "bribe, corrupt." The giver expected favors that either were not his due or that should have been rendered, according to the rules of propriety (li 禮), without compensation. Giving up one's ancestors' heirlooms meant parting with the tokens of legitimate rulership. In offering lu, the giver thus incurred a serious loss of prestige: he literally sold out to the receiving side. On the other hand, gifts of this category could be offered as a strategic ploy. Chinese historical legend relates several instances in which the weaker side, hoping to induce an adversary to debauchery and loss of strength, would present as lu beautiful women and musicians with their instruments. Under certain circumstances, accepting a bell as a gift or bribe could, therefore, be dangerous.[94]

Ordinarily, bells were kept in storehouses[95] and taken out for display in the temple courtyard when needed. On exceptional occasions, they might be lent to members of related kin-groups.[96] The institutional mechanism by which temple furniture was discarded and eventually consigned to tombs is as yet incompletely understood, but the custom of burying musical instruments and specifically bells with the dead is amply attested in the Zhou Li.[97] Looting of tombs for their metal grave goods appears to have been a problem even in antiquity;[98] it was probably common for bells to be dug up and converted to other uses.

Bells might also leave their temple setting as war booty. To protect them from such a fate, their keepers sometimes buried them underground during emergencies, as evidenced by the caches of Western Zhou bronzes in the Western Zhou capital area in Shaanxi, dating to the time of the "barbarian" in-

---

engage in the manufacture of luxury goods, the fact that the Zheng bell in the present instance is specified as that of Xiang Gong seems to show beyond doubt that it was already extant.

93. *Zuo Zhuan* Xiang 11 (HYI ed., 274; Legge, 453). The same story is told, with a slightly different list of presents, in *Guo Yu* "Jin Yu" (Tiansheng Mingdao ed., Jin 7:6b).

94. A story in which the gift of a bell led to the downfall of an aristocratic *shi* is told in *Han Fei Zi* "Shuilin" 28 (Zhonghua index ed., 776).

95. The *Zhou Li* mentions an official in charge of the storage of these items, the "Registrar of Meritorious Implements" *Dianyongqi* 典庸器 (*Zhou Li Zhengyi* 47:1b–2a).

96. *Zuo Zhuan* Xiang 9 (HYI ed., 268)

97. *Zhou Li: Chun'guan* "Dasiyue" (*Zhou Li Zhengyi* 43:18b–19a) and passim.

98. *Lüshi Chunqiu* "Jiesang" (Sibu Congkan ed., 10:5a/b).

cursions of the late 770s B.C. When bells did fall into enemy hands, they might enter the conqueror's treasury as permanent tokens of his superiority over the donors and their descendants;[99] occasionally the taker would erase the original donor's name from the inscription, sometimes incising his own instead.[100] But captivity, for a bell, could just as likely mean annihilation. The bells of Yun 鄆, taken away by the troops of Lu 魯, were melted down and re-cast into a water-basin ("the lord's *pan* 公盤").[101] On the other hand, new bells might be born from such re-casting of captured bronze, as was the case when a Lu general made a bell from a large number of weapons taken in a campaign against Qi.[102] Later, the First Emperor of Qin did the same thing on a much larger scale when he "collected the weapons of the whole empire, which he assembled in Xianyang. He melted them down and made from them bells, bell-racks, and twelve brazen human figures, each weighing a thousand *dan*; these he had set up in the palace."[103] Nothing could better symbolize a policy of general disarmament than the First Emperor's casting of bells from weapons (the Chinese equivalent of swords into plowshares). Yet above all, Qin asserted sovereignty over its new empire by casting these bells; musical considerations were probably secondary.

## Personnel

Something should be said, finally, about the people professionally in charge of bells. Bells could not ordinarily have been played by their owners, who were otherwise occupied during rituals and banquets. Therefore, whoever possessed a set of bells had to support a staff of specialist musicians as well as additional personnel to help with the difficult task of setting up the bell-rack prior to a cere-

---

99. This seems to have been the case, for instance, with the Chen Dasangshi–*niuzhong*, which were made by a *daifu* in the state of Chen but found in the tomb of a ruler of Ju at Liujiadianzi, Yishui (Shandong) (reference in Appendix 1).

100. On the *yongzhong* from tomb no. 1 at Liujiadianzi, Yishui (Shandong), one can still see traces of inscriptions that appear to have been deliberately erased (Luo Xunzhang, personal communication, 1986). On the *niuzhong* from tomb no. 1 at Xiasi, Xichuan (Henan), only the donor's name has been erased. On the *niuzhong* and *bo* from tomb no. 1 at Hougudui, Gushi (Henan), the original donor's name has been replaced with that of another (references in Appendix 1). On most of the Cai Hou–bells (see above), the Marquis's personal name has been erased, though they were found in an unquestionably Cai context. Had these bells been taken to another state as war booty and later been returned? See Li Chunyi 1973. Or was their original donor not Marquis Shen but perhaps his half-brother Zhu 朱, who had been ousted and sent into exile in 521 B.C.?

101. *Zuo Zhuan* Xiang 12 (HYI ed., 275).

102. *Zuo Zhuan* Xiang 19 (HYI ed., 289).

103. *Shi Ji* "Qin Shihuang Benji" (Zhonghua ed., 239). A thousand *dan* is equivalent to ca. 29.5 metric tons (see Bodde 1986, 56). Worldwide, at present, only about seventeen bells are known to exceed this weight (see table in Williams 1986, 181–83); Sima Qian's figures are either grossly inflated or do not refer to the bells. Zhang Zhenxin (1980) speculates that the "brazen human figures" were caryatids supporting the bell-racks, similar to those found in Marquis Yi's tomb.

mony.[104] Ownership of bells was predicated upon control over human beings. That it is sometimes impossible to tell whether the word *zhong* 鐘 means "bell" or "bell-player" in Western Zhou epigraphic records may illustrate how closely the instruments and their performers were linked conceptually.

Bell-players at the royal and princely courts of the Zhou dynasty were hereditary specialists. The *Zhou Li* enumerates twelve Masters of the Bells (*Zhongshi* 鐘師) among the musicians of the royal Zhou court orchestra. Four of them supposedly held the rank of "middle-level noblemen" (*zhongshi* 中士) and eight that of "junior-level noblemen" (*xiaoshi* 小士); they were supported by an administrative staff of two accountants (*fu* 府), two scribes (*shi* 史), two menial aides (*xu* 胥), and sixty runners (*tu* 徒).[105] While the historical accuracy of these details is open to question, other sources seem to confirm that bell-players were members of the administrative hierarchy. Evidence about their social position is somewhat contradictory: the possibility that players were given away along with their bells invites speculation about low slave-like status, yet people with the surname Zhong 鐘 ～ 鍾 (Bell) occur in the pre-Qin sources as musicians of aristocratic rank. One early example from Chu was Zhong Yi, the lord of Yun 鄖公鐘儀, who lived in the beginning of the sixth century B.C.; he identified himself proudly as the scion of a family of professional musicians (*lingren* 伶人). But he played the zither, not the bell-chime.[106] Zhong Yi's alleged descendant Zhong Zi Qi 鐘子期 became a stock figure in Chinese musical legend as the archetypical good listener.[107] According to a later genealogical compendium, the House of Zhong in Chu derived its surname from its fief of Zhongli 鍾離 (in present-day Anhui);[108] families of musicians who named themselves "Bell" after their occupation may have existed, however, in various states.[109] A considerable number of people in China still bear the family name Zhong. Some of the many place names in China that contain the element *zhong* may originate in fiefs granted to hereditary houses of bell-players.[110]

104. This may have been true very early on. Keightley has speculated (1970, 26–27) that the term *gong* 工 "artisan" (which also occurs in some Eastern Zhou sources in the meaning of "musician") originally denoted "bell-strikers," and that the oracle bone graph *gong* 舌 is the pictograph of a bell-striking mallet.

105. *Zhou Li: Chun'guan* "Liguan zhi shu" (*Zhou Li Zhengyi* 32:14b–15a). In *Yi Li* "Dashe" (*Yi Li Zhengyi* 15:19b–20a), the same officials are referred to as *Zhongren* 鐘人, "bell people."

106. *Zuo Zhuan* Cheng 7 and 9 (HYI ed., 224, 228–29; Legge, 363, 371).

107. The story of the virtuoso Bo Ya 伯牙, who destroyed his zither when Zhong Zi Qi died, appears in numerous late pre-Qin and Han sources (see DeWoskin 1982, 105); another story about Zhong Zi Qi is in *Lüshi Chunqiu* "Jingtong" (Sibu Congkan ed. 9:10a/b).

108. Zheng Qiao (1104–1162) *Tongzhi-lüe: Shizu* "Yi yi wei shi: Chu-yi" (Sibu Beiyao ed. 3:6b).

109. "Bell" also occurs as a personal name, as in the case of Wang Zhong 王鐘 mentioned in the inscription of the early Warring States period Chu Qu Shu Chi Qu X Zhi sun-*ge* (Li Ling 1986, 379).

110. *Zhongguo Gujin Diming Dacidian*, 1303–4 and 1373.

FIGURE 22. Two sides of a lacquered wooden duck from the tomb of Marquis Yi of Zeng, with representations of musical performances: *a*, sword dancer, with a pole-drum being played in the background; *b*, combined bell-chimestone rack with player.

Pictorial representations occasionally show one player handling both bells and chimestones (fig. 22), but according to the *Zhou Li*, a great many officials were involved in bell music in addition to the *Zhongshi*. The "Masters of the Chimestones" (Qingshi 磬師), for example, would have been responsible for giving instruction in bell-playing technique, the task of the *Zhongshi* being effectively limited to performing nine important musical numbers during great sacrifices and banquets. At minor occasions, the "Seeing-Eye Musicians" (*Shiliao* 眂瞭) or the "Masters of the Mouth-Organs" (*Shengshi* 笙師) would have played the bells. The identity of the official who issued the command to start the performance varied from ritual to ritual, and sometimes from sequence to sequence within a ritual.[111]

The suspension of a set of bells in preparation for a performance required both manpower and dexterity (see Chapter 6). According to the *Zhou Li*, the *Shiliao* lent a hand with that task, which was principally the responsibility of the "Lesser Aides" (*Xiaoxu* 小胥): eight junior-level noblemen and an administrative staff of forty-six,[112] personally supervised, on important occasions, by the "Grand Director of Music" (*Dasiyue* 大司樂).[113]

111. See above, n. 17.

112. *Zhou Li Zhengyi* 44:14b–16b. For other references, see n. 17, above.

113. At the Han court, the *Shengxuangong* 繩鉉工 ("String Suspending Workers") who are mentioned among the musical officials in *Han Shu* "Li yue zhi" (Zhonghua ed., 1073–74), also seem to have been in charge of setting up bells and chimestones. In 14 B.C., their number was cut from six to two.

In addition to musicians and technicians, bell-manufacturing craftsmen must have been attached at least to those larger *shi* who had their own bronze workshops. A vague notion of how these workshops were organized may be gleaned from the *Kaogongji*. From the archaeological remains of the bronze foundry of the state of Jin at Houma (Shanxi),[114] we know that bells were cast at the same workshops as other ritual bronze vessels, but their manufacture presented difficulties of a particular kind. Not surprisingly, the *Kaogongji* lists bell manufacturers apart from such other metal-workers as founders, forgers, and the manufacturers of swords and capacity measures. Their name is given as Fushi 鳧氏 (House of Wild Ducks), which is probably a textual corruption of Zhongshi 鐘氏 (House of Bells).[115] Although the *Kaogongji* says nothing about their number or their status in the official hierarchy, we may assume that, like the bell-players, they held their positions on a hereditary basis. The activities of these specialists were supervised and administered by officials who, to judge from the contents and scope of the *Kaogongji*, possessed no profound technical knowledge or experience.

The preceding discussion of economic aspects refers almost entirely to the Zhou dynasty—more exactly, to the half-millennium preceding the cataclysmic transformations of the Warring States period. Such a focus is inevitable given the limitations of the evidence at hand; it is also justifiable because bell music enjoyed its greatest florescence during this period. Some of the textual evidence in the *Zhou Li* may be fanciful, but there is every reason to believe that Zhou court ritual was fastidious and elaborate.

## Conclusion

We may summarize our findings by declaring bells to be, in the language of Durkheim and Mauss, "total social facts." In short, they are items of the cultural inventory whose analysis can illuminate virtually all aspects of ancient Chinese culture. As luxury objects, bells were, above all, items of conspicuous consumption. They were linked to the definition of social rank and to control

---

114. See above, n. 68.

115. The name *Zhongshi*, "House of Bells," appears in *Kaogongji (Zhou Li Zhengyi* 79:13b–16a) as the name of artisans occupied with coloring feathers. Because official titles in the *Zhou Li*, as a rule, are descriptive of the respective officials' tasks, it seems likely that early on, the names of those artisans were mixed up with those of the bell-makers. In other words, in the hypothetical Urtext of the *Kaogongji*, the *Fushi* may have been feather-coloring artisans, while the bell manufacturers were designated as *Zhongshi*. The *Zhongshi* may be in some way related to the *Zhongguan* 鐘官 ("Bell-official") of the Western Han dynasty, an office in charge of bronze manufacture (including the casting of coins), whose holders are documented through archaeologically excavated seals (see Li Xueqin 1986).

over human and material resources, and they embodied an intimate linkage with the ideological superstructure and its performative enactment through ritual. Bell-casting was a matter of considerable political importance, and bell-owners probably regarded the music performed on these instruments not merely as aesthetically pleasing but as empowering in a very concrete sense. It is even conceivable that the extramusical functions of bells were rated above their musical ones, a possibility we must keep in mind as we proceed to a closer examination of the instruments themselves.

CHAPTER TWO

# Shape and Acoustic Properties of Chinese Musical Bells

*Main Classes of Bells*

According to a now-classic definition by Curt Sachs, "a bell is a vessel-like percussion instrument with a sound-producing rim and a mute apex."[1] The entire vibrating body of the instrument produces a sound; musicologists therefore classify bells as idiophones. Unlike gongs and musical stones, idiophones in which the vibrations are strongest in the center, in a bell "the edge or *sound bow* . . . produces the strongest vibrations while the top is mute."[2] A bell is struck close to the sound bow, whereas musical stones, gongs, and the like are struck at the center.

Bells have been made in metal-using cultures all over the world; they can fulfill a wide variety of functions. The typological and functional ramifications of Chinese Bronze Age bells are particularly complex, and their formal and functional features allow various sorts of classifications. A basic distinction is that between clapper-bells and bells that were struck with a mallet. In this book, we shall be concerned mainly with musical bells: bells that were assembled into chimed sets and played as musical instruments. For reasons that will soon become apparent, all Chinese musical bells belong in the category of mallet-struck bells. But not all mallet-struck bells from China are musical bells: some of them were never more than signal-giving implements whose main function was to produce a noise.

In referring to bells, Chinese archaeologists today use a mixed nomenclature containing both ancient bell-names and new terms invented for the sake of con-

---

1. Sachs 1929, 101 (*trad. auct.*).
2. Sachs 1940, 169 (emphasis in the original); this is Sachs's own paraphrase of his earlier, somewhat different German definition.

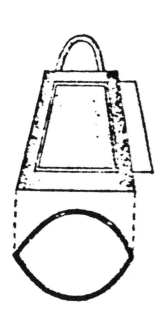

FIGURE 23. *Left: Ling* excavated in 1950 at Wuguancun, Anyang
(Henan). Late Shang period (ca. 1300–1050 B.C.).

FIGURE 24. *Right: Duo* excavated in 1974–75 from tomb no. 1 at
Rujiazhuang, Baoji (Shaanxi). Middle Western Zhou period (tenth
century B.C.).

venience. The ninefold classification proposed in the following paragraphs by
and large represents the current consensus among scholars.

Clapper-bells fall into two classes: those suspended by means of a loop of inverted U-shape (*ling* 鈴) (fig. 23), and those with a massive round shank (*duo* 鐸)
(fig. 24). Evidently, *duo* were used as handbells, whereas *ling* were attached to
moving entities.

Among mallet-struck bells, seven classes may be defined; here, too, the mode
of suspension is a convenient criterion, but the typological distinctions warranted by historical considerations are formally less stringent than in the case of
clapper-bells. Each class can be further subdivided into types and subtypes. The
four most important classes of mallet-struck bells include two types with round
shanks: *nao* 鐃, which were mounted with the face upward (fig. 25), and *yongzhong* 甬鐘, which were suspended obliquely from a ring laterally affixed to the
shank (fig. 26). Mallet-struck bells of two other classes were suspended verti-

FIGURE 25. *Left: Nao* excavated in 1974 at Tangdongcun, Jiangning (Jiangsu). Local culture contemporary to late Shang; probably twelfth century B.C.

FIGURE 26. *Right:* Cai Hou–*yongzhong* excavated in 1955 from the tomb of Marquis Shen of Cai (r. 518–491) at Ximennei, Shou Xian (Anhui). Workshop of Chu(?), late Springs and Autumns period.

cally from loops: *bo* 鎛, with flat rims and sculpturally elaborate suspension devices (fig. 27), and *niuzhong* 鈕鐘, with their rims curved upward and their loops of simple shape (fig. 28). Bells of these four classes often occur in chimed sets. They may be collectively referred to as the *zhong* 鐘 family.

The remaining three classes of mallet-struck bells, *zheng* 鉦 (fig. 29), *goudiao* 句鑃 (fig. 30), and *chunyu* 錞于 (fig. 31), constitute something of a mixed bag, the typological intricacies of which I have treated in a separate article.[3] *Zheng* were signal-giving bells par excellence; they have long shanks and never occur in chimes. *Goudiao*, which are limited to the southeastern region of China, are mounted mouth-up (thus resembling the *nao*) and always occur in chimes. *Chunyu*, with round-oval cross-sections and bulging, often S-shaped profiles,

3. Falkenhausen 1989a.

a

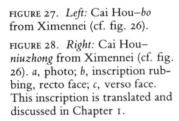

FIGURE 27. *Left:* Cai Hou–*bo* from Ximennei (cf. fig. 26).

FIGURE 28. *Right:* Cai Hou– *niuzhong* from Ximennei (cf. fig. 26). *a*, photo; *b*, inscription rubbing, recto face; *c*, verso face. This inscription is translated and discussed in Chapter 1.

b

c

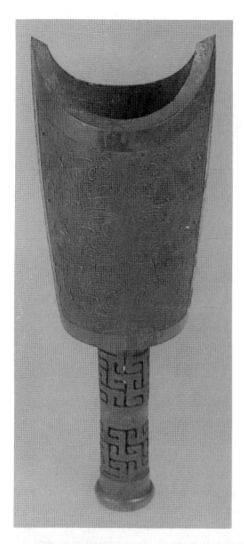

FIGURE 29. *Left: Zheng* excavated in 1987 from tomb no. 2 at Baoshan, Jingmen (Hubei). Mid–Warring States period.

FIGURE 30. *Below:* Set of seven *goudiao* excavated in 1958 at Yancheng, Wujin (Jiangsu). Local culture contemporary to the mid- to late Springs and Autumns period.

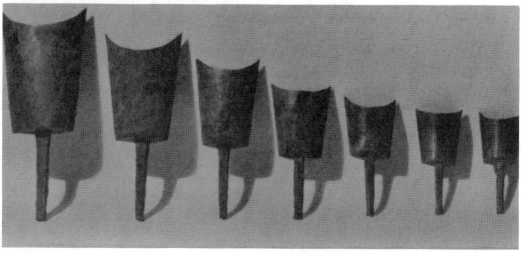

FIGURE 31. *Chunyu* excavated in 1956 at Changde (Hunan). Workshop of Chu(?), early to middle Warring States period.

are oddities among Chinese bells, perhaps originating in pottery vessels or pottery drums. They are mainly distributed in marginal areas and do not usually seem to have served a musical function; chimed sets of *chunyu* have, however, been found in Springs and Autumns period contexts in the southeast.

Bells of these nine classes did not all exist simultaneously, nor did their geographic distributions necessarily overlap at any one time. The historical ("genetic") relationships between them will concern us in Chapters 4 and 5 (see fig. 52). I shall begin by analyzing the overall characteristics shared by Chinese musical bells, stressing their acoustical significance.

## Overall Appearance of Chinese Bells

The traditional nomenclature for parts of Chinese Bronze Age bells, still in use today, is presented in the *Kaogongji*. In the paragraph describing the tasks of the bell-makers, a *yongzhong* bell (fig. 32) is described as follows:

> The "House of Wild Ducks" makes bells. The two vertical sides [*luan* 欒] are called *xian* 銑, what is between the *xian* is called *yu* 于, what is above the *yu*

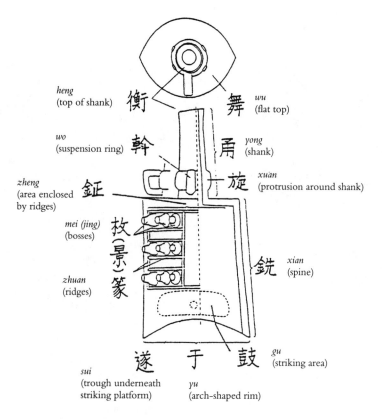

heng
(top of shank) 衡

wu
(flat top) 舞

wo
(suspension ring) 幹

yong
(shank) 甬

zheng
(area enclosed
by ridges) 鉦

xuan
(protrusion around shank) 旋

mei (jing)
(bosses) 枚(景)

zhuan
(ridges) 篆

xian
(spine) 銑

sui
(trough underneath
striking platform) 遂

yu
(arch-shaped rim) 于

gu
(striking area) 鼓

FIGURE 32. Nomenclature of the constituent parts of *zhong* family
bells.

is called *gu* 鼓, what is above the *gu* is called *zheng* 鉦, what is above the
*zheng* is called *wu* 舞, what is above the *wu* is called *yong* 甬, what is above
the *yong* is called *heng* 衡. That from which the bell is suspended is called
*xuan* 旋; the "bug" on the *xuan* is called *wo* 幹.[4]

The first part of the description concerns the resonating body of the bell. *Xian*
refers to the pointed spines bordering the bell-face, and *wu* to the flat top. *Yu*
denotes the bell's curved lips (the sound bow), and *gu* (which means "strike")
the striking-area in the lower third of the bell-face. The *zheng* is the upper part
of the bell-face, which was the visual focus for ornamentation and inscription.
These features are common to all Chinese Bronze Age bells except *chunyu*.

4. *Zhou Li: Kaogongji* "Fushi zuo zhong" (*Zhou Li Zhengyi* 78:11b–12b).

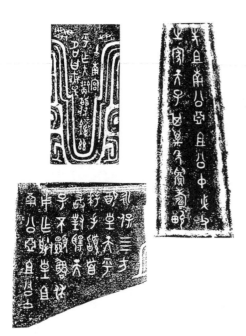

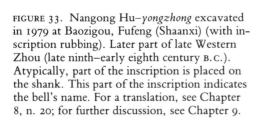

FIGURE 33. Nangong Hu–*yongzhong* excavated in 1979 at Baozigou, Fufeng (Shaanxi) (with inscription rubbing). Later part of late Western Zhou (late ninth–early eighth century B.C.). Atypically, part of the inscription is placed on the shank. This part of the inscription indicates the bell's name. For a translation, see Chapter 8, n. 20; for further discussion, see Chapter 9.

A straight shank (*yong*), which appears massive in proportion to the body of the bell, is seen only on *nao* and *yongzhong*; its flat top is called *heng*. In *yongzhong*, the suspension device consists of the *xuan*, a horizontal bulging ring around the shank, and the *wo*, a vertical ring that is fused laterally to the *xuan* and hence likened to an insect or reptile (the term *chong* 蟲 "vermin" can refer to a variety of animals).[5] On the Nangong Hu–*yongzhong* (fig. 33), the *wo* actually has the shape of a dragon-like animal.

5. In the interpretation of these two terms, I follow Hayashi 1984, 1:92–94. Most Chinese writers invert the meanings of the terms *wo* and *xuan*, a probably mistaken usage that goes back to the Qing dynasty scholar Wang Yinzhi (*Jingyi Shuwen*, Huang Qing Jingjie ed., vol. 263 [j. 1788]: 28a–33a). The character *wo* 斡 is commonly confused with its look-alike, *gan* 幹.

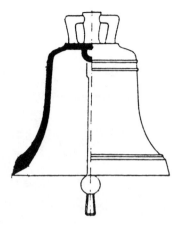

FIGURE 34. Profile of a European church-bell.

The arch- or loop-shaped suspension devices on *niuzhong* and *bo* bells are conventionally referred to as *niu* 鈕 .

Zhou dynasty musical bells are immediately recognizable as such by a peculiar bell-face layout that I shall call the standard *zhong* decoration scheme. This ornamentation may have had some specific iconic significance, now difficult to gauge. The *Kaogongji* names its components as follows: "The bands on the bell[-face] are called *zhuan* 篆 , what is in between the *zhuan* is called *mei* 枚 , the *mei* are called *jing* 景 ."[6] In other words, the *zheng* portion in the upper part of the bell-face is divided into a rectangular grid by means of raised bands or ridges, the *zhuan*. Rows of bosses (*mei*; also referred to as "nipples," *ru* 乳) are placed symmetrically on both sides of a central vertical panel; there are usually three rows of three *mei* on each side. The ornamented horizontal tiers in between rows of *mei* are conventionally called *zhuanjian* 篆間 .

With the exception of *chunyu*, all bells of the Chinese Bronze Age are of almond-shaped (pointed oval) cross-section. The sound bow (*yu*) is enlarged in most of these bells by being curved upward; the spines (*xian*), as a result, are pointed. The bell profile is marked by a flat top and almost vertical sides. An angular quality has been noted as the major difference vis-à-vis European church-bells (fig. 34), which are round in cross-section and have a curved profile.[7] This angularity also distinguishes the bells of the Chinese Bronze Age

6. *Zhou Li: Kaogongji* "Fushi zuo zhong" (*Zhou Li Zhengyi* 78:11b–12b). The last sentence is probably corrupt; it is not clear what the term *jing* really referred to (Hayashi 1984 1:94).

7. Sachs 1929, 67.

FIGURE 35. Buddhist temple-bell at the Dazhongsi bell museum, Beijing. Song dynasty (A.D. 960–1279).

from later Chinese bells, particularly from Buddhist temple-bells (fig. 35), whose shape is of Indian origin. Another difference is that the walls of Chinese Bronze Age bells are noticeably thinner (in proportion to their height) than in Western bells or Buddhist temple-bells, suggesting, among other things, that they must have been struck with considerably less force.

## The Tone

The first Chinese thinker to reflect on the difference between bells with round as opposed to almond-shaped cross-section was the Northern Song polymath Shen Gua 沈括 (1031–1095), who stated that "when a bell is round, its sound is long; when it is flattened, its tone is short. When the tone is short, it is abrupt; when the tone is long, it is undulating."[8] Indeed, the aim in casting a round bell is diametrically opposed to what the makers of Chinese Bronze Age musical

8. *Meng Xi Bitan* "Bubitan" §536 (1957 ed., 293). Hu Daoying's emendations of the text of this paragraph in the 1957 edition indicate philological problems that would decisively influence any interpretation. However one turns it, it seems that beyond the two phrases quoted here, Shen Gua had a rather confused understanding of Bronze Age bells and their historical development.

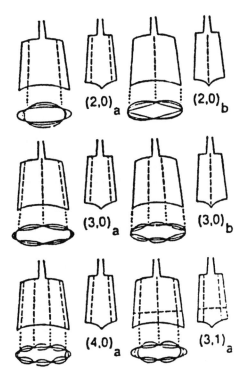

FIGURE 36. The vibration patterns of a Chinese chime-bell. Six modes are charted, with the number of nodal meridians and circles indicated in the conventional way. The subscript letters indicate whether that mode is activated by striking the bell in the center (a) or toward the side (b).

bells had in mind. The caster's objective for a round bell is a rich and harmonic consonance of simultaneously occurring pitches, in contrast to a clearly defined pitch, which was the objective of the ancient Chinese musical bells.[9] Chinese bells were not made singly, but in chimed sets; when played, each individual bell should not vibrate for long, or it would interfere with the others. For most round bells, on the other hand, a long, drawn-out sound is regarded as desirable. To fully appreciate these differences, it is necessary to call to mind some basic facts about the acoustics of bells.

The sound emitted by a bell is complex. What is perceived by the human ear results mainly from flexural vibration, that is, the rapid bending of the bell walls. Whenever a bell is struck, a multitude of flexural vibration patterns, called *modes*, occur simultaneously. Each mode has its own characteristic distribution of vibrating areas, which are separated by non-vibrating lines called *nodes*. The lines of greatest vibrational movement are called *antinodes* (fig. 36). Obviously, those vibration patterns that feature antinodes at the striking point are the most significant.

9. This was perspicaciously realized by Sachs (1929, 168).

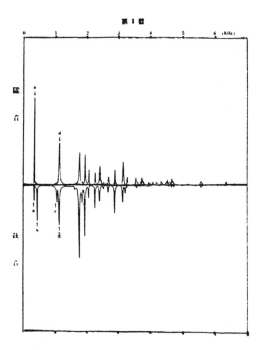

FIGURE 37. Sound spectra showing the relative strengths of the
partials of a Chinese chime-bell.
*Upper half:* A-tone. *Lower half:*
B-tone.

Each vibrational mode produces a certain frequency or pitch; these pitches, termed *partials*, are unequal in strength and duration. A digital measuring device can plot the different co-occurring partials in a graph such as figure 37. One of the partials is usually perceived as the *nominal* tone of a bell, but others will also be audible and influence the sound that is heard.

As with musical instruments in general, the consonance of vibrating partials or overtones determines the timbre of the bell. In stringed instruments, the simultaneously occurring partials of any tone follow the natural overtone scale, including, in descending order of strength, the nominal tone or tonic (expressed by the proportion of 1:1), the octave (1:2), the fifth (2:3), the fourth (3:4), the major third (4:5), the minor third (5:6), and so forth. But in bells (and idiophones in general), the mathematical relationships among the frequencies of the partials do not necessarily follow such a regular succession. Pitches of mathematically complicated relationships to the nominal tone (and thus not expressible as harmonic intervals) often come into play. The mathematical proportions between their frequencies are rather complex and apparently differ from bell to bell, accounting in part for the impression of heterogeneous timbre within many Chinese bell-chimes.

In all idiophones, the frequencies and relative strengths of the partials depend on the shape of the vibrating substance. By manipulating the shape of a bell, therefore, one can emphasize certain partials and mute others, thus influencing both the perceived pitch and the timbre of the instrument. Today, powerful computers allow us to precalculate the shape of bells with a certain constellation of overtones, to a high degree of accuracy;[10] until very recently, however, bell-shape was almost entirely empirically determined. The history of bell-making all over the world is characterized by endless experimentation, involving many discards and few breakthroughs.

That the ancient Chinese casters were aware of a connection between bell-shape and timbre (and, perhaps, pitch) is shown by a possibly corrupt passage from the *Kaogongji*. It begins with what appears to be a mnemonic formula, which is subsequently expounded on in less abstract terms:

> *What is vibrated by thin and thick is that from which the high and low come forth; it is that from which excessiveness and constriction arise.*

There is the following explanation: when a bell is too thick, then [the sound] is [mute like] a stone; when it is too thin, then [the sound] is blasting. When it [the bell's mouth?] is excessive [=of flaring shape?], then [the sound] is bombastic; when it is constricted, then [the sound] is choked. When the shank is [overly] long, then [the sound] is agitated. . . .

If a bell is large and short, then its sound is hasty and heard for only a short time. If a bell is small and long, then its sound is at ease and heard over a long distance.[11]

In spite of such insights, the ancient Chinese musical bells with their complicated, angular shape were not designed from scratch; their casters adopted and perfected a design that had been used previously for non-musical bells (see Chapter 4). In doing so, they strove to define precisely and unambiguously the nominal tone of the bell and to mute the higher partials that might impair the clarity of its pitch. Recent experiments have shown how various features of the characteristic bell-shape are useful in such an endeavor.

In particular, it has been found that the large, flat top (*wu*) of Chinese musical bells is virtually mute and absorbs many of the higher partials; in round bells, by contrast, the non-vibrating area at the apex is deliberately minimized.[12] The often massive suspension devices also cooperate in absorbing some of the higher

---

10. Lehr 1987b.
11. *Zhou Li: Kaogongji* "Fushi zuo zhong" (*Zhou Li Zhengyi* 78:15a–16a). A similar locus, enumerating twelve circumstances of deficient bell-shape (four of which are parallel with those in the *Kaogongji*) is in *Zhou Li: Chun'guan* "Diantong" (*Zhou Li Zhengyi* 46:1b–4a). Imaginative drawings illustrating the various shapes may be found in Dai Nianzu 1986, pl. 6, fig. 30.
12. Lin Rui et al. 1981.

frequencies. The hollow shank (*yong*) of the *yongzhong* often still contains the ceramic core left over from the casting process; it has been suggested that this core was deliberately left in place for acoustic reasons.[13] An acoustic rationale may also account for the bosses (*mei*) on bell-faces decorated according to the standard *zhong* decoration scheme; experiments with bells lacking *mei* suggest that *mei* seem to significantly mute the frequencies of the higher partials and stabilize the two fundamentals.[14] Finally, the comparatively thin walls of ancient Chinese musical bells do not radiate the higher partials effectively;[15] because the mallet strikes with relatively little force, the acoustic impact of the non-musical *Schlagton* (the noise produced by the mallet hitting the metal surface) is much reduced in comparison to European bells. The nominal tone in the ancient Chinese bells is perceived very clearly, and we may conclude that bells of this shape were particularly well suited to function as chime-bells.

## The "Two-Tone Phenomenon"

At some point early in the first millennium B.C., Chinese bell-casters discovered that bells of almond-shaped cross-section can produce two distinct nominal tones. As we noted earlier, this two-tone phenomenon was rediscovered in the wake of the excavation of Marquis Yi's bells. The Zeng inscriptions leave no doubt that it was consciously exploited in making chimed sets of bells. Its physical basis lies in the vibration patterns of bells, which we shall scrutinize closely.

The nodes and antinodes of the vibration pattern of each partial can be made visible by means of time-averaged hologram interferograms. As shown in figure 38, nodes occur as horizontal, ring-shaped nodal circles and as vertical, radiating nodal meridians; they are conventionally notated in the form $(m,n)$, where $m$ is the number of meridians and $n$ the number of circles. Holograms of Chinese Bronze Age bells show partials pertaining to a variety of nodal patterns, including forms of $(2,0)$, $(3,0)$, and $(3,1)$.

The lowest partial, corresponding to the simplest vibration pattern, $(2,0)$, is termed the *fundamental*. While measuring devices record hundreds of partials for each bell, the human ear perceives only the strongest of them—up to about six in large Chinese chime-bells.[16] In round bells, the fundamental is usually

13. Lin Rui et al. 1981, 27. Exactly the opposite is the case in Korean Buddhist temple-bells of the Koryŏ Dynasty, which habitually have a hollow tube sticking out from the flat top, which served to lengthen the sound (three such bells are depicted in *Kungnip Chung'ang Pangmulkwan 84*, figs. 162–64).

14. Lin Rui et al. 1981, 28, fig. 5; Shen 1987, 106, 107.

15. This seems to follow from Rossing 1984.

16. See Ma Chengyuan 1981, 135–36.

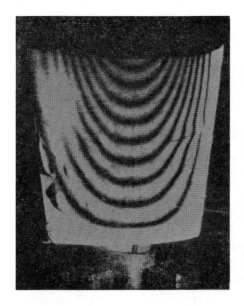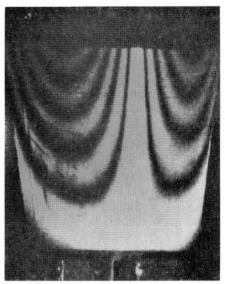

FIGURE 38. Interferogram showing the nodal pattern (mode 2,0) for
the A- and B-tones of a Chinese chime-bell.

perceived as a humming tone lower than the nominal. In the musical bells of the
Chinese Bronze Age, by contrast, the fundamental *is* the nominal tone.[17] The
reason for this is not entirely clear; it must, however, have something to do
with their peculiar, angular shape, and particularly with their almond-shaped
cross-section.

Bell-shape also influences the pattern in which the nodes and antinodes are
distributed on the resonating body. In a round bell, no matter where it is struck,
the same pattern will form spontaneously, symmetrically with respect to the
striking point (fig. 39). Striking a bell of almond-shaped cross-section, by contrast, activates one of two "families" of vibration modes; the distribution of
meridional nodes and antinodes differs depending on where the bell is struck.
The difference is particularly pronounced in the (2,0) mode, which pertains to
the fundamental/nominal tone (see fig. 38); the more complex vibration patterns
do not vary as strongly according to striking point.

The two (2,0) vibration patterns (fig. 40) in a musical bell from the Chinese
Bronze Age may be described as follows:[18] When the bell is struck in the center

17. Lin Rui et al. 1981, 27.
18. Dai Nianzu 1980 and 1986; Ma Chengyuan 1981; Lin Rui et al. 1981; Hua and Jia 1983; Shen
1986–87 and 1987; Rossing and Perrin 1987; Rossing, Hampton et al. 1988, Rossing 1989a and b.

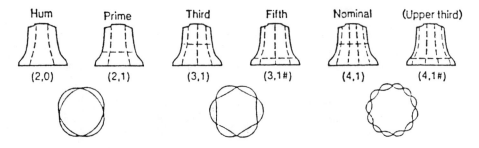

FIGURE 39. The nodal pattern of a Western church-bell.

of the bell-face, antinodes will be located at the center and the spines, whereas nodes will form slightly more than midway from the center toward the spines. By contrast, when the bell is struck midway between the center and one of the spines, nodes form in the center of the bell-face and on the spines; the antinodes are midway between the nodes. Four vibrating zones of equal width and equal shape thus come into being. In the two cases, the shapes of the vibrating zones, the distances between the nodes, and the angles at which they meet all differ. It is intuitively obvious (though mathematically quite difficult to prove) that the resulting sound frequencies will be different as well.[19] Thus Chinese musical bells produce two distinct fundamentals (i.e., nominals), which I call *A-tone* and *B-tone*,[20] the A-tone always being the lower-pitched.[21] In Zhou dynasty chimes, the interval between the two is usually either a minor or a major third, though bells with larger and smaller intervals (ranging from a minor second to a minor sixth) could also be produced. What controls the size of the interval is still unknown; it is possible that it has something to do with the curvature of the arched lip (*yu*) of the bell.[22]

A-tones resound with slightly greater force than B-tones.[23] The higher partials (i.e., those with more complicated nodal patterns) are almost identical

19. For a tentative proof, see Chen and Zheng 1983b.

20. See Introduction, n. 30.

21. Chen and Zheng (1983b, 37) have calculated that in vibrating elliptical truncated cones, the A-tone may be expected to be higher in pitch than the B-tone, provided that wall thickness remains constant throughout. In their view, the ancient Chinese bells behave in the opposite way because the bell walls are of uneven thickness throughout. The main problem with applying Chen and Zheng's calculation to ancient Chinese chime-bells seems to lie in the fact that these idiophones are of almond-shaped, not elliptical, cross-section.

22. In his recent experiments with plaster models of bells, Hirase Takao (1988) was able to achieve a difference of one semitone by modifying the shape of the *yu*.

23. Ma Chengyuan 1981; Takahashi 1984.

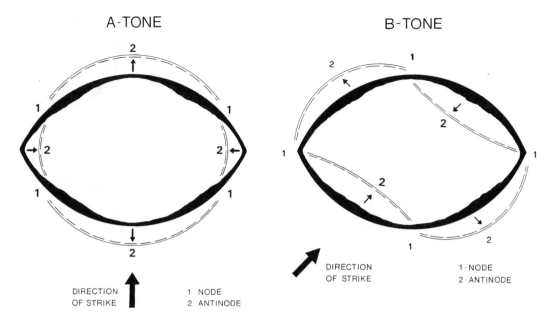

A-TONE

B-TONE

DIRECTION OF STRIKE 1 NODE 2 ANTINODE

DIRECTION OF STRIKE 1-NODE 2 ANTINODE

FIGURE 40. Cross-section of a Chinese chime-bell showing the different vibration patterns of the A- and B-tones at mode (2,0).

with respect to either fundamental, but their relative strengths vary (see fig. 37). Using two mallets, both tones may be produced at the same time. My own experience in striking Chinese musical bells suggests that A- and B-tones are not always completely separate. When one does not hit the respective striking points exactly (and sometimes even when one does), one may hear both tones simultaneously. The B-tone especially is often difficult to produce without the A-tone being audible at the same time.

A key problem in casting a two-pitch bell is thus to keep the two tones separate. The Chinese manufacturers demarcated the respective vibrating areas by varying the thickness of bell walls. In particular, on the inside of many Eastern Zhou bells, the locations of the nodes and antinodes of the A- and B-tones (fig. 41) are marked by rounded troughs. According to the "Fushi" section of *Kaogongji*, "the hollowed-out part above the *yu* is called *sui* 邃."[24] Traditionally, it was believed that *sui* referred to the ornamented portion in the center of the

24. *Zhou Li: Kaogongji* "Fushi zuo zhong" (*Zhou Li Zhengyi* 78:12b–13a).

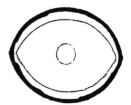

FIGURE 41. Modulation of wall thickness on the inside of several Zeng bells. *Top, yongzhong* from the first middle-tier chime (M1); *middle, yongzhong* from the second middle-tier chime (M2); *bottom, yongzhong* from the third middle-tier chime (M3).

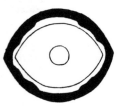

*gu*; but it has recently been shown that the term actually denotes the concave wall portion located beneath the center of the *gu* on the inside of many bells.[25] The elongated shape of the *xian* (which become antinodes when the A-tone is struck) may also have had a certain influence in keeping the two tones separate and approximately equal in strength.[26]

In spite of many efforts, the problem of completely separating the two tones remained a difficult one, and it was never solved to complete satisfaction. Indeed, it seems that after almost a thousand years of experimenting, the Chinese bronze casters finally gave up in frustration; on late Warring States period chime-bells, the two-tone phenomenon was no longer exploited (see Chapters 5 and 7).

25. Li Jinghua and Hua Jueming 1985.
26. Lin Rui et al. 1981.

The two-tone phenomenon is never mentioned in the pre-Qin texts; in the "Fushi" section of the *Kaogongji* we can detect nothing more than some dim awareness of the fact that the sound of an imperfectly shaped bell is cacophonous. Nevertheless, it is clear that the ancient Chinese casters were in full control of the relationship between shape and pitch. The tone–naming inscriptions on the Zeng bells, which were fixed onto the mold before casting, show beyond doubt that their makers knew beforehand what pitch they would sound. What is more, they could also predict the interval between A- and B-tone (which is a minor third in forty-four and a major third in twenty of the Zeng bells). How they did this remains a mystery. One may speculate that intervallic variations were produced by minute adjustments of bell proportions. It seems likely that the corresponding proportions were at first empirically determined; whether and how they were subsequently expressed by mathematical formulas is so far unknown.[27]

The *Kaogongji* provides a set of standard proportions for *yongzhong* bells (fig. 42), but without specifying which pitches or intervals would be produced by bells conforming to the given specifications. The question of whether the

27. The mathematical formula for vibrating plates has been modified to derive the frequency ($F$) of a Chinese bell from its measurements, accounting for such variables as wall thickness ($D$), length of *xian* ($L$) (which in accordance with the *Kaogongji* is taken as the main module of measurement), elasticity, density, a rigidity coefficient, and a constant ($K$). Controlling for material and shape of a bell, the formula can be simplified to read

$$F = K \cdot D/L^{1 + 0.71}$$

As given by Chen and Zheng 1983b (see also Hua and Jia 1983; Takahashi 1986, 54), the formula runs:

$$F = K \cdot D/L^2$$

The exponential factor of $L$ is actually 1 plus a constant determined by the overtone composition of the bell tone; this constant, in accordance with simple vibration theory, is here taken as 1 but empirically, results have been shown to be more exact if it is set at 0.71 (Lehr 1985, 97–98).

To account for the "two-tone phenomenon," the constant $K$ in the above formula must be changed. Chen and Zheng (1983b) arrive at empirical formulas for the relation of shape and pitch in the fourth-century Gengli-*niuzhong*; they are, for the A-tones and B-tones, respectively:

$$F \cong 15.2L^{-1.6}$$

and

$$F \cong 18.6L^{-1.6}$$

In Chen and Zheng 1983a, the same formula is given as:

$$F \cong 15.2 \times 10^4 L^{-1.6}$$

and

$$F \cong 18.6 \times 10^4 L^{-1.6}$$

Takahashi's (1986, 55) corresponding formulas for the slightly earlier Biao-*niuzhong* (turn of the fourth century) are:

$$F = 113 \ L^{-2}$$

and

$$F = 137 \ L^{-2}$$

(The frequency is expressed in KHz, the length in centimeters.)

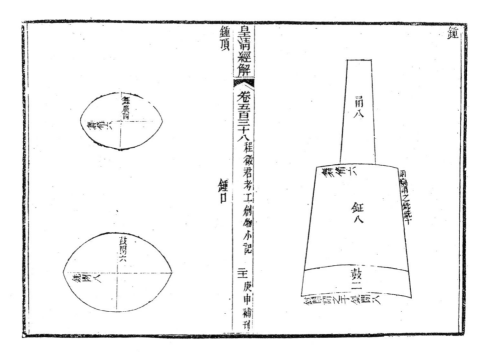

FIGURE 42. Double page from Cheng Yaotian's *Kaogongji chuangwu xiaoji*, showing his reconstruction of the standard proportions of a *yongzhong* according to the *Kaogongji*: *right*, body of the bell with the proportions of the face and shank indicated as numbers; *left*, cross-sections at top and bottom indicating the proportions of the respective diameters.

*Kaogongji* standards (or anything like them) were known to bell-casters in pre-Qin times has been the subject of considerable discussion.

For the resonating body of the bell, which is of prime importance acoustically, the *Kaogongji* stipulates:

When one divides the *xian* into ten parts and takes away two, this is the [height of the] *zheng*. The *zheng* equals the distance between the two [lower end-points of the] *xian*. If one takes away two parts, this is the distance between the two [center-points of the] *gu*; the distance between the two *gu* equals the [lateral] length of the *wu*. If one takes two parts away, the result is the width of the *wu*.[28]

28. *Zhou Li: Kaogongji* "Fushi zuo zhong" (*Zhou Li Zhengyi* 78:13a–14b).

The thickness of the walls is specified as follows:

> In large bells, the distance between the [center-points of the] *gu* is divided
> into ten parts, and one of them is taken as the thickness [of the bell]. In small
> bells, the distance between the [center-points of the] *zheng* is divided into ten
> parts, and one of them is taken as the thickness [of the bell].[29]

Furthermore,

> When making the *sui*, one divides the thickness [of the bell's walls] into six
> parts, taking one [part] to be the depth [of the *sui*], and one makes it
> rounded.[30]

For the suspension device of the *yongzhong* the standard proportions are:

> The length of the *zheng* equals that of the *yong*. The length of the *yong* equals
> its circumference [at the bottom]. If one divides the circumference into three
> parts and takes one away, this is the circumference of the *heng*. If one divides
> the length of the *yong* into three parts, two are above and one below; this is
> where one affixes the *xuan*.[31]

Our understanding of these difficult passages is in large measure due to the
labor of Qing dynasty philologists such as Dai Zhen 戴震 (1724–1777),[32] Cheng
Yaotian 程瑤田 (1725–1814),[33] and Wang Yinzhi 王引之 (1766–1834).[34] Cheng
Yaotian's contributions are particularly significant; his interpretation is still
generally accepted. Taking into account a couple of more recent insights, this
traditional interpretation may be summarized as follows (compare figs. 32 and
42):

1. The height of the lateral spines (*xian*, henceforth abbreviated as *L*) is
   the basic unit of measurement, to which the other dimensions of the
   bell are related by simple fractions.

---

29. *Zhou Li: Kaogongji* "Fushi zuo zhong" (*Zhou Li Zhengyi* 78:15b–16a).
30. *Zhou Li: Kaogongji* "Fushi zuo zhong" (*Zhou Li Zhengyi* 78:17b).
31. *Zhou Li: Kaogongji* "Fushi zuo zhong" (*Zhou Li Zhengyi* 78:14b–15a).
32. Dai Zhen, *Kaogongji-tu* (Huang Qing Jingjie ed., vol. 132 [j. 563]:37a–40a). Qing dynasty
bell reconstructions are summarized and illustrated in Kondō 1955; see also Elman 1984, 182–84.
33. Cheng Yaotian, *Kaogong Chuangwu Xiaoji* (Huang Qing Jingjie ed., vol. 126 [j. 538]:18a–
22b).
34. Wang Yinzhi, *Jingyi Shuwen* (Huang Qing Jingjie ed., vol. 263 [j. 1788]:28a–33a).

2. The diameter between the end-points of the spines at the bottom $(B_1)$ is set as 0.8 times $L$; it equals the height of the *zheng* in the center of the bell-face.

3. The diameter between the midpoints of the bell-faces at the bottom $(B_2)$ is set as 0.6 times $L$.

4. The diameter between the end-points of the spines at the top $(T_1)$ equals $B_2$ (=0.6 $L$); and

5. the diameter between the midpoints of the bell-face at the top $(T_2)$ is set as 0.4 times $L$.

6. Moreover, wall thickness is set as 0.06 times $L$ in large bells, and 0.04 times $L$ in small bells, and

7. the depth of the concave portions on the inside of the bells (*sui*) amounts to 0.01 times $L$ in large bells and two-thirds of that (0.0067 $L$) in small bells.

The dimensions of the resonating body of the bell can be expressed by the following proportions:

$B_1$:L $\approx$ 8:10 (0.80)  $B_2$:L $\approx$ 6:10 (0.60)

$B_2$:$B_1$ $\approx$ 6:8  (0.75)  $T_1$:L $\approx$ 6:10 (0.60)

$T_2$:$T_1$ $\approx$ 4:6  (0.67)  $T_2$:L $\approx$ 4.10 (0.40)

A somewhat different reading has been proposed recently by Okamura Hidenori 岡村秀典.[35] In his opinion, the phrase "one takes away two parts [of ten]" refers not to the length of the *xian* ($L$) but to the immediately antecedent measurement.[36] Thus,

> the *zheng* equals the distance between the two [lower end-points of the] *xian*.
> **If one [divides it into ten parts and] takes away two**, this is the distance between the two [center-points of the] *gu*.

35. Okamura 1986b.
36. Okamura also suggests convincingly that "length of *zheng*" should be taken as the height of the resonating body in the center of the bell-face, starting from the edge of the bell and not from the onset of the *zhuan* bands. This interpretation makes the *zheng* more compatible with the other dimensions that figure in the *Kaogongji*, as well as seeming to accord more closely with what may be observed on actual specimens (see also Feng Guangsheng 1988a, 7–8). The proportion of the height of the *zhuan*-enclosed area to the height of the *gu* apparently never did conform to the ratio 4:1 (as implied by Cheng Yaotian's reconstruction of the *Kaogongji* bell); instead, between the Western Zhou and Warring States periods, this proportion gradually changed from ca. 2:1 to almost 1:1. Ma Chengyuan (1979, 64) takes this as a criterion for dating bells.

And immediately afterwards:

> The distance between the two *gu* equals the [lateral] length of the *wu*. If one [divides it into ten parts and] takes two parts away, the result is the width of the *wu*.

The standard proportions for the vibrating body of a bell that one arrives at as a result are the following:

$B_1{:}L \approx 8{:}10 \ (0.80)$ $\qquad$ $B_2{:}L \approx 8^2{:}10^2 \ (0.64)$

$B_2{:}B_1 \approx 8{:}10 \ (0.80)$ $\qquad$ $T_1{:}L \approx 8^2{:}10^2 \ (0.64)$

$T_2{:}T_1 \approx 8{:}10 \ (0.80)$ $\qquad$ $T_2{:}L \approx 8^3{:}10^3 \ (0.512)$

Philologically, I see little problem in either interpretation of the *Kaogongji* passage under discussion. If we are to assume, however, that the *Kaogongji* size standards bear some relation to the practice of bell-casting, we must put the two sets of figures to the test by juxtaposing them with the size measurements of actual specimens, which, it turns out, do not unequivocally support either Cheng's or Okamura's reading (table 5). Overall, the size proportions of the existing bells are somewhat closer to Okamura's figures than to Cheng Yaotian's, but not in every case, and curiously, the dimensions of the top portions of the bells tend to neatly fit the proportions proposed by Okamura, whereas the measurements of the bottom parts more closely approximate Cheng's ratios. In the *yongzhong* from Marquis Yi's tomb (ca. 433 B.C.), for example, the actual proportions of *L* to the two diameters at the mouth differ from proportions predicted by Cheng's approach by only 4% and 8%.[37] In the same chime of bells, however, the proportions of *L* to the diameters at the top depart from Cheng's standards by 15% and 30% but are far closer to Okamura's ratios.

In a noteworthy departure from either interpretation of the *Kaogongji*, the narrow diameter at the bottom $(B_2)$ has rarely been found to be identical to the wide diameter at the top $(T_1)$ in measured specimens; instead, the proportion $T_1{:}B_2$ usually approximates 0.85 (ca. 6:7). Moreover, the proportions of the two bell diameters at the bottom $(B_2{:}B_1)$ and of those at the top $(T_2{:}T_1)$ are almost always nearly identical, at variance with Cheng Yaotian's interpretation but corresponding to Okamura's. However, the proportions in question are not, *pace* Okamura, equal to the proportion $B_1{:}L$ (10:8 = 5:4); they are closer to 4:3.

Although the figures in table 5 are insufficient for discerning major trends over time, it seems possible that bell proportions eventually came to approxi-

---

37. Hua and Jia 1983 and Lin Rui et al. 1981, 29.

# TABLE 5.   Measured Proportions of Chinese Musical Bells

| | $B_1/H$ | $B_2/B_1$ | $T_2/T_1$ | $B_2/B_1$ | $T_1/H$ | $T_2/H$ |
|---|---|---|---|---|---|---|
| **I. Western Zhou Chimes** | | | | | | |
| First Zha–*yongzhong* (1 bell) | 0.83 | 0.73 | 0.81 | 0.61 | 0.72 | 0.58 |
| Second Zha–*yongzhong* (1 bell) | 0.85 | 0.72 | 0.74 | 0.61 | 0.74 | 0.55 |
| Chu Gong Wei–*yongzhong* (3 bells) | 0.84 | 0.74 | 0.75 | 0.62 | 0.74 | 0.55 |
| Ning–*yongzhong* (part of set) (2 bells) | 0.86 | 0.71 | 0.79 | 0.61 | 0.70 | 0.55 |
| Guo Shu Lü–*yongzhong* (part of set) (2 bells) | 0.81 | 0.71 | 0.69 | 0.57 | 0.69 | 0.47 |
| **II. Eastern Zhou Chimes** | | | | | | |
| Unprovenienced *yongzhong* in the Sen'oku Hakkokan | 0.83 | 0.79 | 0.78 | 0.66 | 0.71 | 0.55 |
| Zheshang–*niuzhong* (7 bells) | 0.79 | 0.71 | 0.75 | 0.56 | 0.66 | 0.50 |
| Cai Hou–*yongzhong* (part of set) (4 bells) | 0.83 | 0.72 | 0.74 | 0.60 | 0.68 | 0.52 |
| Zeng Hou Yi–*yongzhong*, second middle-tier chime (10 bells) | 0.81 | 0.75 | 0.74 | 0.60 | 0.70 | 0.52 |
| *Yongzhong* from tomb no. 2 at Leigudun (28 bells) | 0.73 | 0.77 | 0.75 | 0.56 | 0.66 | 0.50 |
| Biao–*niuzhong* (14 bells) | 0.81 | 0.80 | 0.78 | 0.65 | 0.65 | 0.51 |
| Unprovenienced *niuzhong* set in the Royal Ontario Museum (9 bells) | 0.80 | 0.71 | 0.71 | 0.56 | 0.71 | 0.50 |
| Jingli–*niuzhong* (13 bells) | 0.74 | 0.76 | 0.76 | 0.56 | 0.67 | 0.51 |
| Average ratios | 0.81 | 0.74 | 0.75 | 0.60 | 0.69 | 0.52 |
| **Expected Kaogongji ratios** | | | | | | |
| Per Cheng Yaotian | 0.80 | 0.75 | 0.67 | 0.60 | 0.60 | 0.40 |
| Per Okamura Hidenori | 0.80 | 0.80 | 0.80 | 0.64 | 0.64 | 0.51 |

NOTE. H = height of *xian* spine; $B_1$ = wide diameter at bottom; $B_2$ = narrow diameter at bottom; $T_1$ = wide diameter at top; $T_2$ = narrow diameter at top. The average proportions were computed on the basis of Okamura 1986b, tables 1 and 2 (entries I-a–e, II-a and f), Lin Rui et al. 1981, tables 1 and 11 (entry II-d), and Lehr 1985 (entries II-b, c, e, g, h).

mate those proposed by Okamura.[38] The dimensions of the Biao-*niuzhong* of the mid–Warring States period, for instance, almost exactly conform to Okamura's specifications. In such a case, one would have to conclude that the formulas enshrined in the *Kaogongji* may have come into being long after the onset of bell-casting in China. Conceivably, the *Kaogongji* may contain remnants of late pre-Qin casters' lore, but its author seems to have had very little first-hand knowledge of the subject and relatively more interest in its numerology.

Hirase Takao 平瀬隆郎 has recently proposed that the wider diameter at the bottom of the bell ($B_1$) was the point of departure in designing a bell. Scrutinizing the size measurements of many Shang and Zhou bells, Hirase found that that dimension often equals one foot (*chi* 尺), though the length of the foot in the archaeologically and historically known measurement systems of ancient China was highly variable.[39] If this is true, the Shang and Zhou bell-casters may have used a bell proportioning system quite different from that of the *Kaogongji*. In any case, it seems fair to conclude that casters in Zhou times did not adhere consistently to whatever standards may have existed at that time. Although the overall shape of musical bells remained astonishingly constant over time, there was room for great variation in detail. Rather than following a precise model and producing copies of basically the same standard set of bells, the casters seem to have worked out each new chime individually, producing bells with striking stylistic as well as acoustic differences, even among chimes from the same manufacturing traditions.

## Designing a Chime

This book is mainly concerned with chimed sets of bells of graduated sizes. Since late Eastern Zhou times, such chimes have been known as *bianzhong* 編鐘 "ordered bells";[40] in Western Zhou bronze inscriptions, they are referred to by the synonymous term *linzhong* 鑅鐘.[41] In Eastern Zhou inscriptions, an empha-

38. The authors of the report on the mid–Western Zhou tombs at Baoji, in juxtaposing the actual measurements of two chimes of *yongzhong* and one *nao*-bell with the *Kaogongji* figures in Cheng Yaotian's interpretation, arrive at a similar conclusion (*Baoji Yu-guo mudi*, 558–59 and 608, table 8). Their finding that the proportions of the earlier *nao*-bells show much greater divergence from the *Kaogongji* standards than do those of the *yongzhong* is hardly surprising.

39. Hirase 1988. For archaeological specimens of pre-Qin *chi* measures, see *Zhongguo gudai duliangheng tuji*, pl. 1–3.

40. The locus classicus for *bianzhong* is in *Zhou Li: Chun'guan* "Qingshi" (*Zhou Li Zhengyi* 46:5a).

41. The character *lin* is unknown from the transmitted texts; it consists of the metal radical as a signific, and the two elements 林 *gliəm < lin* ("forest") and 靣 *pliəm, *bliəm < lin* (original meaning unclear; usually glossed as 稟 *pin, lin* "grain bestowed by Heaven < fortunes, emolument"). This is one of a group of characters containing two or more components of roughly the same phonetic

sis on an orderly arrangement of sound-producing bodies is apparent from such bell epithets as *hangzhong* 行鍾 "aligned bells."[42]

The scaling of the chimes presents a number of difficult problems, which must have troubled casters in antiquity just as much as they vex the archaeologist today. *Scaling* means designing a set of bells so that they constitute a tuned chime. The relative sizes of the bells in each chime were of course determined, first of all, by the desired pitches (and their distribution in the chime, which will occupy us in Chapter 7). The ancient Chinese bell-chimes differ from Western keyboard instruments in that the pitches of successive bells are not always at the same interval from one another. Consequently, the relative proportions of successive bells in a chime may vary. For example, the relative sizes of two bells whose A-tones are a fifth apart is different from that of two bells that are only a major third apart. In scaling chimes, the bell-casters of the Chinese Bronze Age must have been aware of a correlation between tonal intervals and relative bell size. But how did they express the corresponding proportions mathematically?[43] The *Kaogongji* does not address this issue.

André Lehr has noted that the bells in Chinese chimes are of different sizes but with the same proportions overall except for wall thickness, which remains virtually constant in all bells of a chime, small or large.[44] From the standpoint of modern physics, this practice was problematic, for in order to create a series of vibrating bodies of regularly varying frequencies, all dimensions, including thickness, should be varied according to a constant proportion. Although using an appropriate scaling formula, one could conceivably assemble an accurately tuned chime from bells of unvarying wall thickness, the timbre would turn out somewhat heterogeneous.

It is clear that the ancient Chinese casters could not possibly have known the physically correct scaling formula; the relations between pitches according to the laws of physics involve exponential factors, which were beyond the reach of Shang and Zhou mathematics. In theory, all dimensions of any two bells of identical shape and material but sounding different tones should be related by an

---

value that at the same time express to some degree the significance of the word (Asahara 1988a). The term *linzhong* 林鍾 is probably ancestral to the name of one of the twelve standard pitches (*lü*) attested in later Zhou texts (see Chapter 8).

42. This epithet is seen in the inscription of the Cai Hou–*niuzhong* (*Shou Xian Cai Hou-mu*, pl. 52–59).

43. Calculating back from the proportions of the Zeng bells, the following equation was empirically inferred by Lin Rui et al. (1981, 29):

$$F_n \cdot L_n{}^a \leftrightharpoons F_n \pm 1 \cdot L_n \pm 1^a$$

$F_n$ is the frequency of a given bell in the series, $L_n$ is the length of the *xian* of that bell, and $a$ is an index number, normally between 1.6 and 2.2.

44. Lehr 1985, 100–101 and tables 20–25. This is also the conclusion of Lin Rui et al. 1981 and Hua and Jia 1983.

exponential coefficient $(C)$; according to simple vibration theory, this coefficient can be determined by the formula

$$C = R^{\frac{1}{2}},$$

where $R$ is the mathematical proportion of the frequencies of the two bells.[45] In a more refined version, substantiated by recent experiments, the coefficient would amount to

$$C = R^{\frac{1}{1.71}}.$$

The ancient Chinese casters, who probably lacked even the concept of frequency, certainly did not know such formulas. They did, however, have to deal with the concrete manifestations of the facts expressed therein, understanding that in large bells, for example, a rather great difference in size may have a neglegible impact on the frequency emitted, while in small bells, even a tiny difference in proportions will significantly influence the sound.[46]

Measurements of excavated bell-chimes indicate that the Chinese casters approximated the "correct" exponential scaling factor by a simple linear factor (fig. 43). In Lehr's words,

> the final conclusion thus appears evident. The Chinese caster from antiquity did not work with more or less abstract proportions from which to determine the dimensions of succeeding bells. . . . On the contrary, he, the bell-caster, seems to have forgotten all existing theories, inasmuch as he had any knowledge of them around 400 BC, and he chose the fundamentally unjust method of equidistant distribution in which each successive bell was derived from the preceding by way of diminishing the measurements of the last bell by a fixed figure. Thus the differential in the dimensions between corresponding parts of a C and a Cis bell, for instance, was as large as that between a C and a Cis bell one octave above.[47]

The arithmetic scaling factor by which the size and pitch of bells in each chime were correlated appears to have differed somewhat in the various sets tested by Lehr. It was presumably experimentally grounded and led to more or less satisfying results within a limited size range. However, the fact remains that any linear scaling factor was but an approximate and fundamentally inaccurate rendering of a mathematically more complex reality.

45. Lehr 1985, 99–100.
46. Lin Rui et al. 1981, 29–30.
47. Lehr 1985, 101–105 (*trad. auct.*).

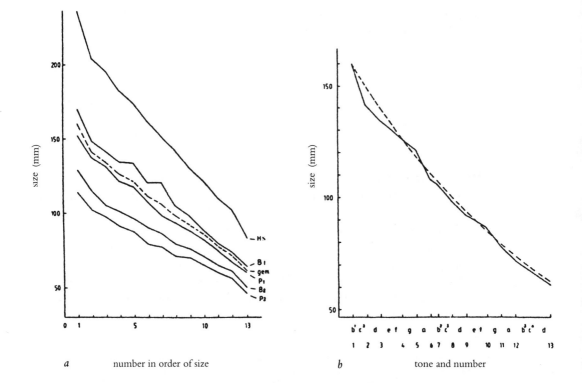

a          number in order of size              b          tone and number

FIGURE 43. Scaling proportions of the Jingli-*niuzhong* from Chang-taiguan, Xinyang (Henan) (see fig. 104), as charted by André Lehr. *a*, measurements for various dimensions of the bells plotted in order of size (Hs = size of the bell; B1 = wide diameter at top; B2 = narrow diameter at top; P1 = wide diameter at bottom; P2 = narrow diameter at bottom; gem = average); *b*, average size-measurement figures from graph *a* correlated with A-tones emitted by the thirteen bells in the chime (bell numbers indicated at appropriate places on a scale of notes; cf. fig. 129 and Appendix 4). Both graphs show a roughly linear progression from large to small bells, and from low to high tones.

FIGURE 44. Qing dynasty chime of sixteen bells, displayed at the former Imperial Palace, Beijing. Dated to the twenty-ninth year of the Qianlong reign period (A.D. 1764) of the Qing dynasty (A.D. 1644–1911).

A chime designed according to such a procedure could not yield an accurately tuned sequence of tones.[48] What might work in one octave could not possibly be replicated in a higher or lower octave if one adhered to the same linear scaling factor. The considerable deviations of measured tones in Chinese chimes from any conceivable tuning system (see Chapter 7) is thus not surprising. The listeners to music performed on these chimes had to have a certain tolerance to inaccuracy. Tuning individual bells (see Chapter 3) could not completely solve the problem. Likening the ancient Chinese bell-casters to their counterparts in late medieval Europe, Lehr suggests, therefore, that the pitch of individual bells may have been improved by slight piecemeal modifications of the shape, which were based on experience rather than calculation.[49] This seems indeed likely.

Recent experiments have confirmed that wall thickness was in fact the acoustically most sensitive dimension of a bell.[50] This was evidently realized as early as the time of the *Kaogongji*, which sets different size standards for wall thickness in small and large bells (see above). Incidentally, pre-Qin chimes contrast most markedly with those of late Imperial China (fig. 44) in terms of wall thickness,

48. See Lehr 1988.
49. Lehr 1985, 99; 110–16.
50. See Hirase 1988.

which in the earlier chimes is held constant throughout while bell-size changes in a graduated chime. Later chimes usually consist of sixteen round bells, all of identical shape and size but differing in thickness; the thicker and heavier the bell, the higher the pitch. The timbre in such chimes is extremely uneven; acoustically, they are far inferior to those of the Bronze Age. Listening to the higher-pitched bells in such chimes, in particular, makes us remember the *Kaogongji* warning that bells too thick for their size sound "stone-like."

## Conclusions

Our consideration of ancient Chinese musical bells has so far led us to realize that the shape of individual bells is exceptionally well suited to their intended function as chime-bells. We shall see in Chapter 4 how this shape was gradually optimized so as to produce two distinct pitches, the acoustical separation of which remained something of a problem throughout the Bronze Age. Over the course of the Zhou dynasty, perfection was ever more closely approximated (Chapter 5), though the bell manufacturers were not completely successful in combining these bells into accurately tuned chimes of uniform timbre. The acoustical imperfections were inevitable in light of the limited mathematical knowledge available. Indeed, the pitches of Chinese Bronze Age chime-bells, which we shall examine below in more detail, are astonishingly accurate considering their technological limitations.

The preceding discussion illustrates a dilemma typical for archaeological research: among the conclusions that can be drawn on the basis of modern physical and technical knowledge, what could possibly have been known in antiquity? Our consideration of the *Kaogongji* throughout this chapter has led us to the perhaps healthy realization that texts do not always hold the answer to such a question. We cannot escape the conclusion that the bell-casters of the Chinese Bronze Age, who may have been illiterate, knew more than the author of the *Kaogongji*, who was probably (in Étienne Balázs's felicitous phrase) an official writing for other officials. Although the text may reflect a certain amount of technological awareness, most of its main points do not hold up in the face of the material evidence.

Some of what was obviously well known to bell manufacturers in antiquity remains a mystery today. How did they determine the interval between A- and B-tones before casting? According to what formula did they design the relative proportions of succeeding bells in the same chime? How, in particular, did they express the concept of pitch, which must have been included as one of the mathematical components of that formula? Takahashi Junji has cautioned:

One cannot exclude the possibility of imagining that the manufacturers [of antiquity] had a more refined understanding of the relation between size and pitch than that expressed though our empirically derived formula.[51]

As interdisciplinary testing and experimenting progress, we may be hopeful that many currently mysterious problems will some day be solved to the satisfaction of the modern technician. But the much more challenging question of how to reconstruct the ideas held by the ancient casters will probably remain open much longer.

51. Takahashi 1986, 58 (*trad. auct.*).

# CHAPTER THREE

# Chime-Bell Manufacture and
# Its Connotations

*Casters' Priorities*

Through the objective examination of Chinese Bronze Age chime-bells in the light of modern science, we have, in the preceding chapter, reconstructed what amounts to one set of manufacturing priorities. At the same time we have noted the difficulty of assessing exactly what went on in the casters' minds when they produced the bells we can see today. Before turning to a consideration of the actual bell-manufacturing process, it is instructive, therefore, to look at some "emic" evidence, such as the inscriptions on bells. What do these inscriptions tell us about the objects on which they are placed?

As objects made of metal, bells were, first of all, objects of value. The epithet *bao* 寶 "precious" frequently appears as an attribute of bells, as it does in other bronzes.[1] The inscribed texts routinely exhort future descendants to treasure (*bao* 寶) or preserve (*bao* 保) them forever.[2] How splendidly the suspended music impressed onlookers at the time we may imagine by looking at the Zeng bells (see fig. 1) or at the depictions of bells on Warring States period pictorial bronzes (see figs. 15 and 16). When displayed for a ceremony, such instruments must have seemed the peak of luxury; they truly deserved the epithet "great" (*da* 大), found in many bell inscriptions.[3] As institutionalized status-markers, chime-bells were inherently desirable.

---

1. I am aware of eight Western Zhou and three Eastern Zhou bronze inscriptions where *bao* appears as an epithet (or part of an epithet) of the inscribed bell. See Falkenhausen 1988, table 16 and appendix 2.

2. The two words were already homophones (*pôg) in Archaic Chinese; *bao* "to treasure" is more frequent in Western Zhou bell inscriptions (19 instances as opposed to 8 from Eastern Zhou), whereas *bao* "to preserve" predominates in Eastern Zhou inscriptions (19 instances as opposed to 1 from Western Zhou). See ibid., table 17 and appendix 2.

3. *Da* appears as an epithet 11 times in Western Zhou and twice in Eastern Zhou bell inscriptions. See ibid., table 16 and appendix 2.

Predictably, therefore, bell inscriptions (again, much like those on other bronzes) tend to stress the outward appearance of the inscribed objects. The inscription of the Zhejian-*yongzhong* (first quarter of the fifth century), for example, runs in part:

> I, Zhejian 者減, the son of King Pinan of Gongyu [= Wu] 工獻 [= 吳] 王皮難, have selected my auspicious metals and for myself made these ringing bells. They are greatly white, greatly red, greatly polished, greatly ornamented. They resound in unison with our divine flutes. They cause everyone to be in harmony and to have confidence in one another.[4]

The material from which ceremonial bronzes were made is here called *jijin* 吉金 "auspicious metals." This expression, which is not attested in the non-epigraphic texts of the period, may allude to cultic practices surrounding the manufacture as well as the use of the cast objects.[5] The phrase "I selected my auspicious metals," ubiquitous in Eastern Zhou bronze inscriptions, probably indicates also that only metal of the highest quality was deemed fit for ritual use. Zhejian's bells are described as glistening in hues of white and red; the inscribed text also seems to mention their ornamentation.[6] At the time of manufacture, they must have looked quite different from today's patina-covered specimens.

What, precisely, were the "auspicious metals"? I do not believe that this term could possibly refer to the chemical components of bronze, such as copper, tin, and other deliberately added constituents or trace metals (see below). Instead, I would link the expression *jijin* to some binominal metal-names that are enumerated in a number of Springs and Autumns period bronze inscriptions.[7] The Ju Shu Zhong Zi Ping–*niuzhong* inscription specifies, for example: "They are made

---

4. Shirakawa, *Kinbun Tsūshaku* 40:596–601.

5. Morohashi 1956 2:806 suggests that, because it was used in auspicious rituals, the material itself was considered auspicious.

6. My translation of the phrase 不帛不騂不濼不鋪 follows Guo Moruo (1958: *kao* 153–54). The character 不, which occurs four times as an adverbial modifier, is taken as *pei* 丕 "greatly," as is normal in bronze inscriptions. The characteristics enumerated are thus all positive ones: *bai* 白 "white," in the sense of "glistening"; *xing* 騂 "red" (elsewhere written as 羍 > 騂, an allograph of *xing*) as "brightly colored"; the following *le* 濼 as "polished" (濼); and the final 鋪 as *diao* 彫 "carved > elaborately ornamented" (*le* 濼 might alternatively be read as "joyful" [樂], and the final character as *tiao* 調 "harmonic, harmonized"). (Reading 不 as *bu* "not" would result in an enumeration of negative traits absent from these bells. To wit: "they are not [ugly] white [e.g., as a result of the usage of some inferior alloy?], they are not [ugly] red [e.g., as the result of corrosion], they have not been scrubbed off [鑠], they have not suffered breakage [*diao* 凋]." Such a reading, though favored by Wen Tingjing [1934–35] and Shirakawa [loc. cit.], seems alien to the spirit of *jinwen*.)

7. Eleven instances of this standard enumeration—8 from bell inscriptions—have been assembled in Falkenhausen 1988, table 18. They all date to the sixth and early fifth centuries. The following discussion (notes 8–9, 12–13) is in large part based on *Jinwen Gulin*, 2751; *fulu*, 3517, *bu*, 1016, character *lü*.

of dark shiny metal [*xuanliu* 玄鏐],[8] of polished hard metal [*shangfu* 鋿鏞];[9] this is what makes their sound: '*tuotuo-yongyong*!'"[10] The most extensive enumeration of this kind may be found in the Shu Yi–*zhong* inscription,[11] which mentions *fuqiao* 鈇鐈 (smooth greenish metal?),[12] *xuanliu* (dark shiny metal), and *xunlü* 鐥鉛 (gray? hard metal).[13] Even though the metals in these expressions cannot be identified with absolute certainty, scrutiny of their attributes reveals an emphasis on shininess, smoothness, and purity. Moreover, metal color was evidently regarded as important: dark (*xuan* 玄), red (*chi* 赤), yellow (*huang* 黄), as well as, perhaps, greenish-white (*qiao* 鐈) and steel-colored gray (*xun* 鐥) hues are mentioned. It appears likely that the various metal-names all denote subtly different bronze alloys that may have been mixed according to various proportions.

What made the metals auspicious was, first and foremost, their fiery brilliance. This quality enhanced the sound of a bronze bell, as may be gleaned from the Ju Shu Zhong Zi Ping–*niuzhong* inscription (above) as well as from the phrase *lanlan hezhong* 爛々和鐘 "glistening are the harmonizing bells," found in the inscriptions of several mid-sixth-century B.C. Chu bells.[14] It seems that the

8. The metal-name *liu* 鏐 is glossed in *Shuowen* as "yellow metal (*huangjin* 黄金) of the most excellent quality" (*Shuowen*, entry *liu*; similarly in *Erya* "Shi Qi" 31, HYI ed., 17). Although *huangjin* usually means "gold" in ancient and modern Chinese, *liu* in the present context cannot have this meaning, as Shang and Zhou bronzes have never been found to contain traces of that metal. Chen Mengjia has proposed that *liu* might refer to surface gilding, but this, too, is virtually never seen on bronzes before the Han dynasty. I believe that *liu* in the present context hyperbolically refers to the glistening quality of a bronze alloy. It is always preceded by *xuan* 玄 "dark."

9. In the various versions of the standard enumeration, the metal-name *lü* 鉛 occurs alternately with *fu* 鏞. Despite a voluminous literature, the meaning of these two characters remains obscure. It would be easiest to assume that the two stand for one and the same word; but they co-occur in the Ju(?)zhong–*fu* inscription (*Kaogutu* 3:42), which shows that there must be a difference between them. I think that both terms may have referred to hard varieties of bronze, e.g., *lou* 鏤, a metal-name ordinarily glossed as "steel." Complicating matters further, the same character *fu* also occurs quite frequently as an adjectival attribute qualifying *lü* (see below). *Fu* 鏞 as a metal-name is preceded by *shang* 鋿 "polished," *pu* 鏷 "[raw metal:] pure(?)," and *chi* 赤 "red."

10. *Kaogu Xuebao* 1978 (3):317–36; Shirakawa, *Kinbun Tsūshaku* 52:571–73.

11. Shirakawa, *Kinbun Tsūshaku* 38:352–74; Doty 1982, 262–386. Doty's explanation of this passage differs significantly from mine.

12. The character *qiao* 鐈 does not appear in the classical texts. In *Shuowen*, it is glossed as "a *ding* tripod with high feet," which is inappropriate in the present context. Zhu Fangpu has noted that many objects containing the graphic element *gao/qiao* 高 / 喬 are greenish-white; he argues that as a metal-name, *qiao* must designate an alloy of such color. The attribute *fu* 鈇, occurring jointly with *qiao*, may stand for *bo* 薄 "thin, smooth."

13. On the metal-name *lü*, see n. 9. *Xun* 鐥 is traditionally glossed as a type of iron; the meaning in the present context is unclear—possibly a color? In other inscriptions, *lü* is seen preceded by the characters *bo* 薄 "thin, smooth," *fu* 鏞 (perhaps a loan for *bo*), *yuan* 元 "good," and *huang* 黄 "yellow."

14. These are the Wangsun Yizhe–*yongzhong* (Shirakawa, *Kinbun Tsūshaku* 40:578–82) and the Wangsun Gao–*yongzhong* (Xu Zhongshu 1984, 66–71). The expression *lanlan* is also seen in the inscription of the Wangsun Wu–*ding* (Xu Zhongshu 1984, 72–74), found in the same tomb as the Wangsun Gao-bells; because it is not limited to bells, it cannot refer to the bell's sound (for parallels, see *Chu Ci: Jiuge* "Yunzhongjun," *Chu Ci Buzhu* 2:4a and passim).

polished metal was seen as the cause of the peculiar sound quality of the bells. In this connection, one cannot help thinking of the traditional classification of musical instruments according to the eight sonorous substances (metal, stone, clay, leather, silk, wood, gourd, and bamboo), found in some late pre-Qin texts,[15] in which bells are identified with the "sound of metal." Although this eightfold systematization probably originated no earlier than the end of Eastern Zhou, the conceptual linkage of bell and metal must date back at least to the time of the earliest bell inscriptions.

That "metal" would have entered into any native definition of the musical instrument "bell" is evident also from the graphs used for writing various words denoting bells, both in the inscriptions and in the pre-Qin texts. They all contain the metal radical (*jin* 金).[16] The most prominent bell-names occurring epigraphically—*ling* 鈴 (archaic pronunciation: \*lįeng), *zhong* 鐘 (\*d'ung), and *zhengsheng* 鉦盛 (\*tįeng-źįeng, i.e. *zheng*),[17] each consist of the metal radical combined with an onomatopoeic component.[18] Most of the words used in rendering the sound of bells are written with characters of the same structure. In a number of Western Zhou bell inscriptions four such words appear jointly: *cang* 鎗 (\*ts'âng),[19] *cong* 鏓 (\*ts'ûng),[20] *tuo* 鍺 (\*to?),[21] and *yong* 雝 (\*·įung).[22] In the inscriptions, each of these characters is accompanied by ditto marks indicating

15. See *Zhou Li: Chun'guan* "Dashi" (*Zhou Li Zhengyi* 45:1a–6a).
16. The only two exceptions, *biao* 剽 and *zhan* 棧, two bell-names occurring in in the *Erya* glossary (*Erya* "Shi Yue" 7.9; HYI ed., 18) and nowhere else, may well be "lexicographers' ghosts."
17. *Zhengsheng* is a dimidiated "spelling" of an onomatopoeic word, in which the first syllable indicates the *Anlaut* and the second syllable the *Auslaut*. *Zheng* is a monosyllabic rendering of the same word.
18. The phonetic contrast between *ling* (labial *Anlaut* and bright vowel) and *zhong* (dental *Anlaut* and dark vowel) may reflect the difference between clapper-bells of relatively high pitch, and the lower-pitched mallet-struck *zhong* chimes. *Zheng* (dental *Anlaut* and bright vowel) are intermediate between the two. This is a rare correspondence between linguistic categorization by onomatopoeia and archaeological classification by material attributes.
19. *Cang* 鎗 > 倉 (archaic reading \*ts'âng) is glossed in *Shuowen* (entry *cang*) as "sound of a bell."
20. *Yong* 雝 (\*·įung) means "harmonious."
21. In the inscriptions, each character is accompanied by ditto marks indicating repetition. Different readings have been proposed for this character; in spite of some graphic inconsistency, clearly the same word is intended in all occurrences. Commentators on the Hu-*yongzhong* (Zongzhouzhong; Shirakawa, *Kinbun Tsūshaku* 18:260–85) have identified the character as *yang* 央 (archaic reading \*·įang) "brilliant," which occurs three times in *Shi Jing* (Odes 168, 177, 283; HYI ed., 36, 39, 76) as an onomatopoeia of the waving of a ceremonial banner and, once, for "harmonizing *ling*" played at a ruler's audience. However, the graph in most inscriptions does not resemble *yang*. Neither does it resemble the character *jie* 諸, which has been proposed by Chen Peifen 陳佩芬 (1982) in her article on the Liangqi-*yongzhong*. This character *jie* occurs four times in *Shi Jing* in onomatopoeic renderings, especially of birdsong (Odes 2, 41, 90, 252; HYI ed., 1, 9, 18, 65); it also once describes the sound of ritual bells (Ode 208; HYI ed., 50) and twice that of horse-bells (Odes 168 and 260; HYI ed., 36, 71). I provisionally concur with Wu Shiqian 伍士謙 (1980), who found that all occurrences of the graph seem to contain the element 者, making them part of a word family that contains words pronounced \*tįǎ, \*tįo, \*to, as well as \*t'įak (and their palatalized alternates).
22. *Cong* 鏓 (\*ts'ûng) is not known from the classics in such a meaning but is obviously a phonetic counterpart of *cang*; if not purely onomatopoeic, it probably stands for *cong* 聰 "brilliant, intelligent."

repetition: *cangcang congcong/tuotuo yongyong!*[23] The four characters describe the sounds made by a metallic object; the meanings of their phonetic components all pertain to the semantic field of "brilliant, harmonious."[24] The characters *cang* and *yong* also appear in the *Shi Jing*, where they render the harmonious sound of bells, mostly of chariot-bells (*luan* 鸞 "crotals"), as well as, curiously, the twittering of birds.

These graphs suggest that Curt Sachs's modern, formal definition of "bell," with its stress on the location of vibrating areas, may be useful to us in describing and characterizing ancient Chinese bells but would have been quite irrelevant to the Bronze Age casters and their patrons. Metal is not part of this definition; objects that can be called bells may be made of all kinds of materials. Contrastingly, what seems to have interested the Chinese manufacturers was, above all, the material constitution of bells, which in turn determined their characteristic timbre. In the Chinese Bronze Age, nonmetal bell-like objects are invariably nonfunctional substitutes made in deliberate imitation of bronze bells, usually to serve as grave-goods (*mingqi* 明器).

Quintessentially, then, a bell had to be made of metal, more specifically of bronze, and the status of bronze as an item of conspicuous consumption desirable in its own right (see Chapter 1) was undoubtedly one of the main reasons for the exalted appeal of bells in the culture of the Chinese Bronze Age and their preeminent position in ritual orchestras at the time. Bells were not primarily conceptualized as sound producers, their acoustic effect was not considered in purely functional terms, and their impact transcended the realm of music. Nonmusical considerations were of major concern to the casters; we, too, must keep them in mind when turning now to technical issues surrounding the manufacture of bells.

## The Material

The bronze alloy used in manufacturing bells decisively influenced both their acoustic quality and their external appearance. The *Kaogongji* gives ratios of copper and tin for various kinds of metal objects:

23. This may be a dimidiated "spelling" for "*ts'ung ts'ung/tung tung." Wu Shiqian (1980) has suggested that the ditto marks might call for a repeated reading, not of individual syllables but of two successive syllables (thus: *ts'ângts'ûng ts'ângts'ûng/to·jung to·jung). According to Wu, each of these onomatopoeic binomes should, moreover, be fused into one syllable according to the principle of dimidiation, with the initial (*Anlaut*) of the first syllable and the final (*Auslaut*) of the second (thus: *"ts'+ung ts'+ung/t+ung t+ung").
24. The character *lin* 鐚 in the Western Zhou expression *linzhong*, "a set of bells," also consists of "metal" plus a phonetic component.

In the making of bronze metal there are six formulae; six parts of copper to one of tin is the formula prescribed for *zhong*-bells and *ding*-cauldrons; five parts of copper to one of tin is the formula prescribed for axes [*fu* 斧] and hatchets [*jin* 斤]; four parts of copper to one tin is the formula prescribed for dagger-axes [*ge* 戈] and halberds [*qi* 戚]; three parts of copper to one tin is the formula prescribed for large swords [*daren* 大刃]; five parts of copper to two of tin is the formula prescribed for pen-knives [*xiao* 銷] and hunting-arrows [*shashi* 殺矢]. Equal proportions of copper and tin is the formula pre-scribed for mirrors [*jian* 鑑] and specula [*sui* 燧].[25]

From an archaeological point of view, this passage may be dismissed as irrelevant numerology: metallurgical tests performed on ancient Chinese bronzes of various kinds have not revealed significant adherence to the formulas specified.[26] Those tests do, however, show some differences among alloys used for bronze objects of different intended usage. To add to their hardness, weapons contain more tin than vessels, and to obtain a shiny surface, vastly more tin was used for mirrors than for any other kind of bronzes.[27] The *Kaogongji* shows some awareness of this, though the numbers given in that text are plainly not in accordance with the composition of actual specimens.

Even so, the *Kaogongji* formula for the bronze alloy of bells, six parts of cop-per and one of tin (14.28% tin), is not without resemblance to the actual com-position of analyzed bells from the Eastern Zhou period (table 6). Five bells from Zeng chimes for which analyses have been published contain between 12.5% and 14.6% (averaging 14.2%) tin, very close to the proposed standard. Although published data are still too meager to permit assessment of historical trends, it seems safe to say that the proportions observed in the Zeng specimens are the product of centuries of experience.[28] Interestingly, even in Shang dy-nasty Anyang-type *nao* the copper-tin ratio was already reasonably close to that seen in the much later Eastern Zhou bells, though the data from the intervening period do include one case of enormous disparity in metal composition within a single three-part Western Zhou set of *yongzhong* from Shaanxi. Perhaps due to differences in the local metal resources, Springs and Autumns period musical bells from the Lower Yangzi area (for example, those from Beishanding, Dantu [Jiangsu]) tend to contain slightly more tin and considerably more lead than contemporary specimens from north-central China; the deviations seem to be

25. *Zhou Li: Kaogongji* (*Zhou Li Zhengyi* 78:1b–2a), translated by Noel Barnard 1961, 9–10 (*pinyin* and some transcriptions inserted). This translation reflects Dai Zhen's understanding of the passage, which has been followed by the majority of modern scholars. On other interpretations, see Barnard 1961, 9–12, and Tian Changhu 1985 and Wu Laiming 1986 on scholarship in main-land China.
26. Barnard 1961, 169–98.
27. Wu Laiming 1986.
28. Li Zhongda et al. 1982.

TABLE 6.    Metallic Composition of Chinese Bells

|  | Cu | Sn | Pb | Zn | Fe | As | Ni |
|---|---|---|---|---|---|---|---|
| **I. Pre-Shang** | | | | | | | |
| a. Bell-like object from Taosi, Xiangfen (Shanxi) | 97.86 | trace | 1.54 | 0.16 | trace | | |
| **II. Shang** | | | | | | | |
| a. *Nao* formerly in the possession of C. T. Loo | 68.9 | 11.8 | trace | | 0.29 | 0.15 | |
| b. *Nao* in the Ashmolean Museum, Oxford | 87.3 | 4.9 | 5.1 | | 2.4 | 0.27 | |
| c. *Nao* fragment in the Kyōto University Museum | 73.72 | 12.17 | trace | | 0.45 | 0.1 | |
| d. *Nao* from Shiguzhaishan, Ningxiang (Hunan) | 98.22 | 0.002 | 0.058 | | | | |
| e. *Bo* in the Sackler Gallery | 87.1 | 11.6 | <0.02 | trace | <0.05 | | |
| **III. Western Zhou** | | | | | | | |
| a. "Western Zhou bell" (details unknown, perhaps a jingle) | 81.55 | 10.9 | 2.33 | 0.12 | 0.59 | | 0.01 |
| b. "Western Zhou jingle" (details unknown) | 80.62 | 16.88 | 0.04 | 0.93 | 0.11 | | |
| c. "Western Zhou crotal" (details unknown) | 86.4 | 13.27 | | 0.06 | 0.12 | | 0.05 |
| d. First *yongzhong* from tomb no. 7 at Zhuyuangou, Baoji (Shaanxi) | 92.0 | 3.7 | 1.6 | | 0.29 | | |
| e. Second *yongzhong* from tomb no. 7 at Zhuyuangou | 97.18 | 1.90 | 0.21 | | 0.235 | | trace |
| f. Third *yongzhong* from tomb no. 7 at Zhuyuangou | 61.0 | 13.8 | 10.2 | | 0.17 | | |
| g. Crotal from tomb no. 7 at Zhuyuangou | 73.5 | 11.8 | 12.7 | | 1.05 | | |
| h. Crotal from tomb no. 21 at Zhuyuangou | 73.9 | 11.3 | 12.1 | | 0.34 | | |

TABLE 6. *(continued)*

| | Cu | Sn | Pb | Zn | Fe | As | Ni |
|---|---|---|---|---|---|---|---|
| **IV. Eastern Zhou** | | | | | | | |
| a. First *niuzhong* from Jishiliang, Suizhou (Hubei) | 81.24 | 15.9 | 1.00 | | | | |
| b. Second *niuzhong* from Jishiliang | 85.27 | 12.63 | 0.8 | | | | |
| c. Large *bo* in the Freer Gallery | 82.1 | 16.3 | | | | | |
| d. First of 4 *yongzhong* from among the Zeng bells | 85.08 | 13.76 | 1.31 | | | | |
| e. Second *yongzhong* from among the Zeng bells | 83.66 | 12.49 | 1.29 | | | | |
| f. Third *yongzhong* from among the Zeng bells | 78.25 | 14.6 | 1.77 | | | | |
| g. Fourth *yongzhong* from among the Zeng bells | 81.58 | 13.44 | 1.4 | | | | |
| h. 1 *niuzhong* from among the Zeng bells | 77.54 | 14.46 | 3.19 | | | | |
| i. 1 of 2 chime-bells from Leshan (Sichuan) | 71.88 | 15.31 | 4.0 | | | | |
| j. Second chime-bell from Leshan | 75.56 | 14.12 | | | | | |
| k. "Eastern Zhou (Warring States period?) bell" (details unknown) | 73.26 | 17.72 | 8.53 | 0.07 | 0.03 | | 0.05 |
| l. "Eastern Zhou bell" (details unknown) | 73.73 | 17.45 | 8.45 | 0.08 | 0.02 | | 0.03 |
| m. 1 *niuzhong* from Beishanding | 77.25 | 17.20 | 4.61 | | | | |
| n. 1 *bo* from Beishanding | 71.12 | 14.85 | 9.77 | | 0.01 | | |
| o. First chimed *chunyu* from Beishanding | 76.13 | 16.70 | 4.92 | | 0.59 | | |
| p. Second chimed *chunyu* from Beishanding | 78.49 | 13.99 | 6.18 | | 0.35 | | |
| q. 1 chimed *chunyu* from Wangjiashan | 66.62 | 26.20 | 4.63 | | 0.59 | | |
| r. *Goudiao* from Qiqiao | 84.92 | 6.51 | 7.39 | | 0.11 | | |
| **V. Dian Culture** | | | | | | | |
| a. Beehive-shaped bell from Dabona, Xiangyun (Yunnan) | 79.96 | 16.34 | trace | | | | |
| b. Beehive-shaped bell from Zhuanchangba, Huili (Sichuan) | 92.49 | 7.0 | trace | | trace | | |

SOURCES: I-a: *Kaogu* 1984 (12): 1068; II-a, c: Umehara 1944, 176–78; II-b: Helen Loveday, personal communication (1990); II-d: *Wenwu* 1966 (4): 2; II-e: Bagley 1987, 557; III-a–c and IV-k, l: Liang and Zhang 1950 (not seen), quoted in Barnard 1961, table 13, and Barnard and Satō 1975, 13; III-d–h: *Baoji Yu-guo mudi*, vol. 1, tables 17, 18; IV-a, b, d–h: Ye et al. 1981, 32; IV-c: Gettens 1969, 22; IV-i, j: Tian Changhu 1985 (these bells have never been discussed elsewhere in the archaeological literature); IV-m–r: *Wenwu* 1990 (9): 39, 40, 42, 50; V-a: *Kaogu* 1964 (12): 613; V-b: *Kaogu* 1982 (2): 216–17.

somewhat more pronounced in musical bells of local types (such as *goudiao* and chimed *chunyu*), than in those classes of bells that were used throughout the Zhou cultural sphere. On the whole, however, the impression of uniformity prevails. The greatest deviations from the *Kaogongji* standard occur in specimens that are either very early, such as in the copper bell-like object from Taosi, or from marginal areas, such as in a *nao* excavated in Hunan, contemporary to late Shang, which is made of almost pure copper. Although possibly the result of inaccurate analysis, the last-mentioned case may show a lack of access to tin resources, and/or an attempt by the Hunan manufacturers to imitate the shape but not the tonal properties of their metropolitan Shang model.[29]

Compared to Western bells, the tin content of ancient Chinese bells is relatively low. In the words of André Lehr,

> A bell will possess a truly sonorous and long-sounding tone only if the bronze contains 20–25% tin. Incidentally, this is true first and foremost of thick-walled bells, that is to say, those of European manufacture. The Eastern bell, by contrast, is comparatively thinner and will therefore be able to emit a sound more easily. Formulated differently, the tin content is therefore less critical than for its European sister. But all this cannot detract from the fact that 17% tin for a bell is decidedly on the low side.[30]

Metallurgical experiments performed in the wake of the Zeng discoveries have shown that in Chinese musical bells, with their peculiar shape and thickness, a tin content between 12% and 16% provides optimum hardness for striking. A bell with more tin would become too brittle and would easily burst when struck. If the alloy contained too much copper, on the other hand, the bell would become too soft and prone to deformation by the mallet, which in turn would influence the tone. Furthermore, it has been reported that a tin content of 13% or more leads to a fine consonance of the first, third, and fifth partials, which enhance the fundamental; with less tin than that, the fundamental resounds more weakly and the second partial is relatively strong, resulting in an unpleasantly sharp timbre.[31]

Besides copper and tin, Chinese bells typically contain about 2% lead. When distributed evenly in the alloy, lead hastens sound decay, serving to muffle

29. By contrast, a bell from a Dian culture site in Yunnan is made of a bronze alloy very similar to that of contemporaneous Eastern Zhou bells, even though it is stylistically and typologically completely different. This may conceivably show some measure of south Chinese influence on Dian bell manufacture.

30. Lehr 1985, 141–42 (*trad. auct.*). Lehr unwittingly accepts a now-obsolete interpretation of the above *Kaogongji* locus, according to which the proportion of tin to copper in bells and tripods would have been 1:6 instead of 1:7.

31. Ye Yuxian et al. 1981, 34.

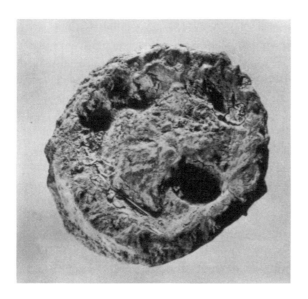

FIGURE 45. Copper ingot from Tonglüshan, Daye (Hubei).

unwanted high partials, though too much of it causes cacophonous flat overtones.[32] Traces of other materials are found in ancient Chinese bells, but these do not seem to influence the sound appreciably. Interestingly, the lead content of the Zeng *niuzhong* is about twice as high as that of the *yongzhong* from the same tomb, perhaps to compensate for the lack of the usual adornment of overtone-damping bosses (*mei*) on those bells.

The disparities in table 6 also indicate that precise control of alloy composition in bronze-casting presented considerable difficulties in the Bronze Age. Metal was supplied to the workshops in the form of ingots made at the mines. Archaeological information on bronze workshops is still insufficient for determining whether the ingots normally consisted of one chemically pure metal (like the copper ingot in figure 45), or of metals that were already composed into an alloy; their composition, of course, was decided at the mines and not at the workshops. Even so, the bronze alloy used in manufacturing Bronze Age musical bells on the whole appears to complement the acoustic goals noted in the previous chapter. Whether it was specifically devised for its acoustic properties, however, is not entirely certain. The *Kaogongji*, for example, states that the same alloy was used for both ceremonial vessels and bells; it seems possible that it was judged fitting primarily on account of other (e.g., visual) qualities.

As an aside, we should note that it was by no means necessary to cast metal bells exclusively from bronze. Iron-casting had become a major industry during

32. Ibid., 38.

the second half of Eastern Zhou. There is some indication that, at the end of the Bronze Age, the core-mold assemblages of bronze bells were at least occasionally made of iron,[33] but actual iron bells were apparently not made before the Northern Song dynasty. (The only known pre-Song iron bells are Han dynasty *mingqi*.)[34] Actually, perfectly feasible bells can be manufactured from white cast iron, which was produced in China at least as early as the Han dynasty and probably earlier.[35] Even though shifting from bronze to iron chimes would have necessitated certain technological adjustments, it should have been worthwhile economically in view of the much lower material cost. The major Western objection to iron bells—that their sonorous qualities are inferior to those of bronze—should actually have come as a boon to ancient Chinese casters; after all, their chime-bells are notable, in comparison to European bells, for their reduced sonority, a characteristic that may have been musically valuable.

The absence of iron bell-chimes from the archaeological record of the Chinese Bronze Age must, I submit, be understood in social terms. Musical bells, unlike agricultural tools, were status items of the old aristocracy; their possession was regulated, in theory at least, by sumptuary laws. There was no incentive for producing them cheaply or in great quantity. The same may be true of other categories of prestige items, such as display weapons. It seems likely in the case of bells that the lackluster appearance of iron was considered unsuitable for ritual objects.

## Casting

Throughout the Bronze Age, the casting of bells did not differ in any major respect from that of other bronzes. To say that the ancient chime-bells were cast in the "piece-mold technique" then current amounts to stating the obvious. The term *piece-mold technique* is an abstraction covering a vast range of casting possibilities that changed considerably over the centuries. To date, not enough bells have been examined to be certain about all the details of the procedure as it was

33. Remnants of an iron core have been reported to be on the inside of a single *zheng* found at Liyang (Jiangsu) in 1972; moreover, the handles of two smaller handbells collected at the same time are reported to still contain an iron core (*Wenwu Ziliao Congkan* 5 [1981]:108–09; unfortunately, the photos on pls. 9.2 and 3 do not show these phenomena). All three items probably date no earlier than Western Han. One wonders how far back in time this peculiar casting technique of manufacture was used in bell-making, and what the advantages were. Perhaps there is a connection with the Warring States period iron molds found at Xinglong (Hebei) (*Kaogu Tongxun* 1956 [1]:29–35, pl. 10); in contrast to the original report, which surmises that they were intended for iron objects (see also Yang Kuan 1982, 28–29), Gu Tiefu (1958, 8) believes that they were used for casting bronze coins and tools. This problem seems to remain unsolved at present.

34. One such piece was excavated at Luoyang (*Kaogu Xuebao* 1963 [2]:34); a similar, but larger object is in the Field Museum in Chicago.

35. Rostoker et al. 1984. Cast iron of other than the white variety does not seem viable for the production of sound-generators.

applied to bells at specific times. Yet we may distinguish roughly between the casting procedure practiced during the Shang and Western Zhou, on the one hand, and that of mid- to late Eastern Zhou on the other.

## Basic Casting Techniques of Shang and Western Zhou

Because they have been described many times,[36] we can afford to be brief in recapitulating the basic steps in Shang and Western Zhou bronze-casting. A massive core model of the intended bell was fashioned in clay and fired. This model served as the imprint for the outer molds, which were produced by applying a layer of clay to the model surface. For convenience of assemblage and handling, the outer molds were removed from the model in sections of regular size, which were then fired. Afterward, the outside of the core model was scraped down to leave a gap of the desired thickness of the bell between the outer mold and what would then serve as an interior core. (This step, incidentally, departs strikingly from traditional Western bell manufacture, where, to this day, a model ["false bell"] is always made separately from the core and removed after the mold has been prepared.)[37]

In the next step, the outer section molds were reassembled around the core for casting, the hollow space in between corresponding exactly to the shape of the intended bell. The seams between the section molds remain distinguishable on the finished object; from such information, Noel Barnard has reconstructed the core-mold assemblage of a large *yongzhong*, in which eight mold pieces are placed symmetrically on two tiers on each side (fig. 46).[38] Care was taken in the placement of sprues through which the metal would be cast into the hollow space, and of vents through which the air displaced by the metal could escape. Casting could now begin. The constituent metals, mixed according to the proper proportions, were molten in crucibles. The core-mold assemblage was heated to avoid sudden cooling of the metal at the time of casting; then the molten metal was poured in. The assemblage would be left to cool down before the molds were taken off and the core painstakingly chiseled out. Later work included retooling the decorated portions and polishing the inside and outside of the bell.

36. Important contributions on this topic include the studies by Karlbeck 1935; Shi Zhangru 1955; Barnard 1961; Guo Baojun 1963; Wan Jiabao in Li Ji 1964–1973, esp. vol. 1; Fairbank 1972 (originally published 1962 and 1965); Gettens 1969; Barnard and Satō 1975; Bagley 1987 (esp. pp. 37–45).
37. Lehr 1976, 6–15.
38. Barnard 1961, 139; 142–43. The authors of the report on the important Western Zhou tombs at Baoji reconstruct a generally similar technique for the manufacture of the *nao* and *yongzhong* excavated there (*Baoji Yu-guo mudi*, 558–61).

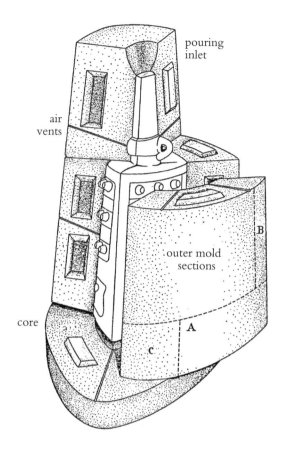

FIGURE 46. Setup of casting molds for a *yongzhong*, as reconstructed by Noel Barnard. In some details, this reconstruction has been superseded by more recent research (cf. fig. 48).

*Eastern Zhou Innovations*

The piece-mold casting technique of mid- to late Eastern Zhou times differed from that of Shang and Western Zhou in the manner by which the decoration was applied. Now the core was left plain and decoration was applied in a secondary step to the mold pieces. This procedure, called the *pattern-block technique*, has been reconstructed by careful examination of actual bronzes[39] and of piece-mold fragments excavated in 1959 at the early fifth-century B.C. casting workshop outside the capital city of Jin at Houma (Shanxi).[40] A single unit of a decoration pattern was sculpted in positive relief onto a flat block of clay, which was fired. Numerous negative impressions could subsequently be made from such a pattern block, and these impressions, made in soft clay, would be fitted

39. Keyser 1979.
40. See Chapter 1, n. 68.

a

b

FIGURE 47. Bell-casting molds excavated ca. 1959 near Niucun, Houma (Shanxi). *a*, suspension device of a *bo*; *b*, *bo* face.

into designated portions of the mold,[41] adapted to the rounded shape of the object and cut off at the edges as dictated by the space available. As a result, an entire face of a bell could be impressed into one mold piece, as seen in one instance from Houma (fig. 47).[42] This technique is at the root of the somewhat standardized appearance of the banded decor usually seen on mid- to late Eastern Zhou bronzes. Yet it allowed ample room for variety, as numerous pattern blocks

41. Conceivably, this technique, which seems conceptually antecedent to woodblock printing, was first used in placing bronze inscriptions: fired clay dies with the imprint of written characters seem to have been placed into designated spaces in the mold at least as early as Western Zhou times.

42. Barnard (1961, 144–45) proposed that the ornaments on Chinese bronzes (even those of Shang and Western Zhou) were produced as ready-made blocks in positive relief that were second-

TABLE 7.    Core and Mold Components Used in Manufacturing One *Yongzhong* from the
            Tomb of Marquis Yi of Zeng

---

*Yong* (shank), core (1 piece)
*Yong* (shank), outer mold (1 piece), with the following components inserted:
  *Heng* (top) section-mold (1 piece)
  Section-molds for the shank (2 pieces), containing:
    Pattern-blocks for each of the eight sides of the shank (8 pieces)
  *Wo* (suspension ring) molds (3 pieces)
  *Wu* (flat top of the bell body) pattern-blocks (4 pieces)
Core of the resonating body of the bell (1 piece)
Piece-mold assemblage of the resonating body of the bell (2 pieces), with the following components
      inserted:
  Pattern-blocks for the ornamented margins of the upper part of the bell-face (*zheng*) (9 pieces)
  Section-molds for the rows of *mei* (bosses) (12 pieces), containing:
    Individual pattern-blocks for all bosses (72 pieces)
  Pattern-blocks for the *zhuanjian* (ornamented areas between the rows of bosses) (8 pieces)
  Section-molds for the *gu* (striking area) (2 pieces)

Total: 126 pieces

---

NOTE. This is an adapted translation of a table by Hua Jueming (1981, 18). For an illustration, see fig. 48.

with different designs could be used in making one object. Hua Jueming has demonstrated, for example, that in manufacturing Marquis Yi's *yongzhong* more than one hundred separate components per bell were used (table 7; fig. 48).[43]

Appearing suddenly shortly before the middle of the sixth century B.C., the pattern-block technique seems to have been adopted immediately by all major Eastern Zhou bronze-manufacturing centers. Compared to the bronze-casting methods current in Shang and Western Zhou, the new technique offered striking economic advantages. Although each core-mold assemblage could still be used only once, it could now be prepared in much less time. Formerly, enormous efforts had had to be expended in decorating each core model individually, a process now greatly speeded up thanks to the repeated use of impres-

---

arily fixed onto the model before the outer mold was obtained; it is now clear, however, that no pattern-block technique of any kind was used before the mid–Springs and Autumns period. Hua Jueming (1981) came up with a model similar to Barnard's in reconstructing the manufacture of the Zeng bells. Keyser's (1979) painstaking observations, however, show beyond doubt that the pattern-blocks had to be inserted as negatives into the outer mold pieces. I am grateful to Robert W. Bagley for patiently explaining all this to me (personal communication, December 1989), and I hope that the results of Bagley's research on this topic will soon be published.

    43. Hua Jueming 1981.

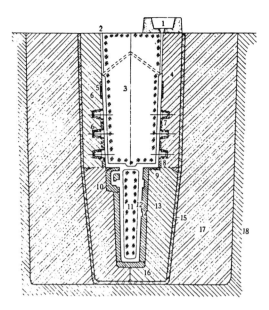

FIGURE 48. Core-mold assemblage of one of the Zeng *yong-zhong*, as reconstructed by Hua Jueming and Jia Yunfu.

sions from the same pattern block. Moreover, the process allowed for greater division of labor, requiring only a few specialist carvers to produce the decorated pattern blocks. Each production step could now be assigned to a different individual. In short, the pattern-block technique enabled bureaucrats to run bronze workshops almost like modern industrial operations, which was certainly a major factor accounting for the considerably increased output of decorated bronzes (including a profusion of bells) observable in the archaeological record around the middle of Eastern Zhou (see Appendix 2).

### Chaplets and Spacers

In order to keep the core and the molds separated from one another during the casting, founders used *chaplets*, which became part of the cast object, and core-extension *spacers*, which were removed after casting. Chaplets are small scraps of bronze, placed at certain intervals into the space between core and mold. They stand out in the rubbings of many a Western Zhou bronze inscription. On bells, however, due to acoustic considerations, chaplets had to be used with caution; for such extraneous pieces of metal do not fuse with the hot metal that is poured into the mold but are locked into place mechanically.[44] Their presence in

44. Gettens 1969, 131–34.

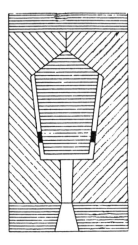

FIGURE 49. Position of core-extension spacers.

the vibrating parts of the bell-body might have impaired the sound quality, perhaps explaining why chaplets are virtually absent from Eastern Zhou bells.

Spacers had the advantage that they could be removed after casting. Holes in the walls of the bells indicate their position (especially large and conspicuous holes occur on some provincial pieces; see fig. 153). What the spacers consisted of is unknown; the most likely material is clay, but some may have been made of iron, a material that gradually came to play a role in bronze-casting in Eastern Zhou times.[45] Except on bells, evidence for such spacers is rarely seen on Eastern Zhou bronzes. Casters had to be careful about their placement; they could not be too close to the sound-bow, where they would have impacted the vibration patterns of the fundamentals. Typically, spacers were placed in portions of the bell in which they would be inconspicuous, and they were kept very small.[46]

Two or three spacers are usually seen in the upper part (*zheng*) of the faces of bells, between the bosses (*mei*) (fig. 49); two additional spacers are frequently encountered on the flat top. Sometimes attempts seem to have been made to fill these holes after casting, though filling might have influenced the sound. In modern steel and aluminum bells, slot-shaped holes like these (though usually much larger) are often intentionally placed into the walls to improve sound radiation. Whether the spacer holes on Zhou chime-bells were intended to serve a similar purpose has not been experimentally tested,[47] but it seems doubtful.

45. See n. 33 above.
46. There are exceptions to this, usually on bells that appear to be of poor quality; frequently, these may be addressed as *mingqi*.
47. Conversation with T. Rossing and A. Lehr, January 1989.

In the Zeng bells, nonmetallic inclusions and "blowholes" (remnants of gaseous inclusions) are concentrated around the sound-bows, features indicating that these bells were cast with the mouths facing upward, as shown in figure 48.[48] Many bells, especially large ones, were not cast in one piece; protruding parts, such as suspension devices, flanges, and possibly large bosses, could be precast and incorporated into the mold, or they could be secondarily soldered to the bell-body. In the Zeng bells, low-tin bronze (Sn = 3%) was used as a solder.[49] An analysis of their microstructure has led to the conclusion that quenching (sudden cooling) was not performed on the Zeng bells; the metal was allowed to cool gradually after casting.[50]

After casting, it was vital to remove all traces of the core and mold from both the inside and the outside of the vibrating body of a bell. As noted above, however, remnants of the core can still be found inside the shanks of many *yongzhong* bells, where they serve to dampen the higher partials. This acoustically desirable effect may have quite fortuitously resulted from ancient casters' customs long predating the invention of that type of bell, for in other types of bronzes (e.g., the legs of *ding* tripods), the core was also not usually removed from narrow tubular portions.

## Alternative Techniques

A few bells show evidence of the use of other techniques. Metal inlay, for example, a favorite mode of decoration in late Eastern Zhou bronzework, is rarely encountered on bells, though it does appear on a few late Warring States, Qin, and Han specimens (see fig. 97).[51] The earliest known instances are the gold-inlaid inscribed characters on the Zeng bells. On the molds of bells decorated in this way, the areas to be inlaid were fashioned as shallow recesses in the bell surface, to be filled in at a later stage in the manufacturing process. In general, inlaid decoration on bells does not seem to differ in any important respect from that seen on contemporary bronzes of other types. Whether it had any acoustical impact is unknown.

Some highly ornate Eastern Zhou bronzes, such as the famous "*zun* and *pan*" from Marquis Yi's tomb (fig. 50) with their openwork lacery wildly bending into all directions, could not feasibly have been produced by the usual piece-mold technology. It has been suggested that their protruding ornamented por-

48. Hua Jueming 1981; Tan and Feng 1988, 16.
49. Tan and Feng 1988, 16.
50. Ye Xuexian et al. 1981, 32–33.
51. So 1980b.

tions were precast by the lost-wax (*cire perdue*) method, in which a wax model of the entire object to be cast was first coated with clay; the wax subsequently melted and poured out as the external clay mold was fired.[52] This method, which was widely used in medieval China (and from very early on in West Asia and Europe), seems to have been known in China since around the middle of the sixth century B.C., arising about the same time as the pattern-block technique described above. In the pre-Qin period, lost-wax and related casting methods were probably employed alongside the traditional piece-mold technology; ordinarily, use of the newer techniques was probably limited to the three-dimensionally ornamented parts of bronzes.[53]

There is so far no proof that lost-wax casting played much of a role in Eastern Zhou bell manufacture. When the sixty-five Zeng bells were replicated in the early 1980s, some of them were reproduced, with excellent results, in a traditional lost-wax casting process.[54] (The majority of the Zeng bells were replicated by means of silicone rubber molds made from the original specimens.)[55] While nobody pretended at the time that such a method had been used by the original manufacturers, a related technique has recently been mentioned in connection with the Zeng bells. Li Zhiwei 李志偉, inspired by the lead *mingqi* vessels found in various Shang and Zhou tombs, proposed that bells might have been manufactured by a "lost-lead" method,[56] in which molds would have been obtained by coating lead models with clay; when fired, the lead would have melted down much like the wax models used in the lost-wax method. This idea remains experimentally untested.[57]

In a similar, somewhat imaginative vein, Noel Barnard has speculated that the many portions of ancient Chinese bronzes that appear to imitate the shapes of rope or cord were cast from molds produced by coating actual pieces of cord with clay, removing the cord, and then firing the clay. In particular, the *wo* (suspension rings) of many of the earliest *yongzhong* may conceivably have been produced in such a way.[58] If there is any reality to Barnard's proposed "lost-cord" casting, it must have been limited to small portions of bronzes otherwise produced by the piece-mold technique.

52. Hua and Guo 1979.
53. Bagley 1987, 44–45; Barnard 1987.
54. Guan and Luo 1983.
55. Hu Jiaxi et al. 1981.
56. Li Zhiwei 1984.
57. Barnard, commenting (1987, 22–25) surprisingly favorably on Li's idea, suggests that the "lost-lead" technique may have been limited to pre-formed panels of relieved decoration that were incorporated into a traditional piece-mold assemblage.
58. Barnard 1987, 25–48, especially p. 44 and fig. 13. Barnard's observations of cord-shaped *wo* extend only to Warring States period bells from Guangdong; in fact, however, this feature may be seen even in some of the earliest *yongzhong*, made in the Middle Yangzi area in a period contempo-

FIGURE 50. Set of two vessels, conventionally labeled "*zun* and *pan*," from the tomb of Marquis Yi of Zeng. For a view of their excavation context, see fig. 17 (no. 38).

## The Technical Rationale for the Almond-Shaped Cross-Section

The almond-shaped cross-section characteristic of most Bronze Age chime-bells is a vestige of a very early stage in the evolution of metal casting. At first, only flat items such as weapons and button-shaped objects were cast in open molds. Subsequently, solid objects with two molded sides were obtained by casting metal into the space between two identical molds, one placed on top of the other. The first hollow items were produced by introducing a core between two such outer molds. At this early stage the casting process may have started not with the preparation of a model, as it did later, but with the two outer molds, from which a model (or core) was secondarily obtained. This method intrinsically favors objects of almond-shaped cross-section.

Interestingly, such a shape is characteristic not only of the earliest small clapper-bells of the Chinese archaeological record, dating back to the turn of the second millennium (see fig. 12) but also of the earliest ritual vessels, the *jue* from Erlitou.[59] In later times, use of a larger number of mold pieces permitted pro-

---

raneous with early and middle Western Zhou (see Chapter 4). Quite apart from their possible casting method, cord-shaped *wo* may represent a reminiscence of primitive methods of suspending such bells from ropes. The casting of *wo* by means of the ordinary piece-mold technique current in Western Zhou is well illustrated in *Baoji Yu-guo mudi*, 561, fig. 24.

59. For some convenient illustrations, see *The great Bronze Age of China*, 69–75.

duction of round vessels, but even when the number of mold pieces was increased for bell-casting, the primeval flattened shape was preserved throughout the Bronze Age and beyond. It seems that, in order to obtain two clearly separated tones on a bell of almond-shaped cross-section, the bell must be of a certain size. As we shall see in Chapter 4, bells of such a shape were manufactured in China for centuries before the "two-tone phenomenon" was first realized and musically exploited.

In addition to being technically simple, the almond-shaped cross-section is functionally advantageous even in non-musical bells. Bells of this shape are distributed in many areas of the world: simple clapper-bells, such as those from the Ban Chiang culture in northern Thailand and from present-day sub-Saharan Africa, tend to be of flattened cross-section, quite irrespective of their method of manufacture (the African bells, for example, consist of two bent sheets welded together).[60] In China, an almond-shaped cross-section is characteristic even of the Neolithic pottery bells, which may predate the earliest metal specimens by several centuries. For small clapper-bells, this shape is acoustically superior; two joined bent plates, with just enough space between them for a clapper to move back and forth, vibrate at wider amplitudes (and thus create a stronger noise when rung) than a round cylinder with the same amount of wall surface.

*Tuning*

As we have seen in Chapter 2, the design of Chinese chime-bells did not (and could not at the time) conform to a physically correct scaling formula; it is likely, therefore, that most bells were acoustically imperfect when removed from their molds. Such a situation is alluded to in an episode from the *Lüshi Chunqiu* (mid-third century B.C.):

> Ping Gong of Jin 晉平公 cast a Great Bell. He ordered the officiating [musicians] to listen to it; they all pronounced it to be in tune. But Music Master Kuang 師曠 said: "It is not in tune. I request that it be re-cast."[61]

In cases of serious deviation from desired tuning, re-casting is the only way to correct acoustic deficiencies. In European carillon foundries, a large proportion of bells cast were failures that were either melted down or sold off for inferior

60. Sachs 1929; Price 1983. Bells from all over the world may be seen at the National Carillon Museum in Asten, The Netherlands (Lehr 1987a).

61. *Lüshi Chunqiu* "Zhongdongji" (Sibu Congkan ed., 11:10a). This was part of a collection of stories about the blind Music Master Kuang, fragments of which are dispersed among various ancient texts. The same story is in *Huainan Zi* (Lu Wenhui 1985, 43–44).

uses (e.g., as ship-bells);[62] we have no idea what the corresponding turnaround might have been in the Chinese Bronze Age. Small acoustic alterations, however, could be achieved by altering the shape of a bell.

The intonation system (or systems) to which the ancient bell-chimes may have been tuned will occupy us later on in this book; what concerns us here is merely how the ancient craftsmen modified the perceived tone of a bell after casting. Polishing, for example, both enhances a bell's appearance and affects (and usually improves) a bell's acoustic quality, by flattening and regularizing the shape of the vibrating substance. Experiments undertaken during the replication of the Zeng bells have shown, moreover, that tempering (reheating the object after it had first cooled down) has the effect of raising the pitch of a bell.[63] Conceivably, this technique might have been used for tuning purposes.

That the pitches of individual bells can be modified by retooling the bell surfaces was apparently realized by Chinese bell-makers from Western Zhou times onward. The two-tone phenomenon, however, imposed narrow limits on the tuning of bells, for whenever the nodes of one vibration pattern are modified, those of all others will also be affected. Hence, adjusting the A-tone could not fail to change the B-tone as well, and vice versa. Utmost caution was required, and it is likely that tuning was on the whole less important in the Chinese Bronze Age than in European workshops. Nevertheless, traces of posterior retooling may be observed on the inside of many Zhou dynasty chime-bells. Like their medieval European counterparts, the ancient Chinese bell-tuners avoided affecting the bell-face, so as to leave the decoration and smooth shiny surfaces intact.[64]

Vibration frequency in a bell is determined primarily by wall thickness. The thickness of a bell, once cast, could not be increased,[65] but by thinning the

62. Price 1983.
63. Ye Xuexian et al. 1981, 39–40.
64. There is some dissent among Chinese scholars as to the degree to which the tones of Bronze Age chime-bells could be modified. Where Ma Chengyuan (1981) and Huang Xiangpeng (1983a) emphasize the narrow limits of tuning, Feng Guangsheng, who has fine-tuned several sets of replicas of the Zeng bells, is confident that he can get both tones of any bell with almond-shaped cross-section to sound within 10 cents of the desired frequencies (personal communication, 1990). Feng admitted that he relied on his intuition and experience, not mathematical or physical knowledge in tuning bells. If such exact tuning was within reach of the Bronze Age bell manufacturers, this would throw open the question why all known bell-chimes from the Chinese Bronze Age show significant deviations from any conceivable tuning system (see Chapters 6 and 7). Feng suggested that sets of bells found in tombs might have been deliberately left untuned in order to emphasize the distinction between the living and the dead. But this smacks of ad-hoc speculation. True enough, a *Li Ji* locus, alluded to in Chapter 1, which stipulates that bell-chimes should be buried without their racks ("Tan'gong-*shang*," *Li Ji Zhushu* 8:3b) does state that zithers, when buried, should be left untuned, and mouth organs should be equipped with non-harmonizing pipes; but it does not refer to the tuning of bells. Anyway, being a relatively late work of systematization, the *Li Ji* is hardly a reliable basis for a hypothesis of such scope.
65. Although theoretically, metal could have been soldered onto the sound-bow, that seems never actually to have been done in Bronze Age China.

FIGURE 51. Modulation of wall thickness on the inside of one of Marquis Yi's chime-bells (*yongzhong* no. 12 in the second middle-tier chime).

walls, the pitch could be lowered. On the inside of some Eastern Zhou bells examined by Ma Chengyuan 馬承源, wedge-shaped protuberances may be seen in strategic places along the sound-bow; these wedges could be chiseled off in order to modify the tone.[66] In other bells, parts of the sound-bow were removed for similar reasons. Thinning the walls of a bell seems to have been the principal technique employed in ancient Chinese bell-tuning.

The acoustic effect is especially pronounced when matter is removed from the areas where the vibrational nodes and antinodes are located; as this affects the elasticity of the vibrating substance, the effect may sometimes be a slight raise in pitch, which, however, will be at least partly offset by lowering due to loss of thickness (the mathematical relationships involved are complex because mass is related to the first power of thickness, whereas it is inversely related to the second power of elasticity). The Zhou bell manufacturers presumably honed their tuning skills through assiduous experimentation. We can tell that they must somehow have realized the locations of the principal nodes and antinodes, as well as their importance, from the fact that they positioned the rounded

66. Ma Chengyuan 1981.

troughs (*sui*) at those exact points on the inside of the bell-body (fig. 51). Although the *sui* must not penetrate too far into the wall, lest a warbling sound be produced, on most specimens I have seen they are considerably deeper than the one-sixth of wall thickness stipulated by the *Kaogongji*. Before the two-tone phenomenon was rediscovered, scholars had generally assumed that the *sui* were "tuning grooves" carved into the bells after casting.[67] Although one frequently does find evidence of posterior tuning activity on or around the nodal and anti-nodal areas, it is now realized that the *sui* themselves were part of the cast object, their main function being to keep the A- and B-tones separate.[68]

I have not seen any clear physical evidence that early Chinese casters attempted to raise the pitch of a bell already cast. But they may have had some dim idea about how it could be done; the *Kaogongji*, though silent about bell-tuning, does describe how a musical stone could be tuned: "If it is too high, then one rubs away at the sides. If it is too low, then one rubs away at the ends."[69] This exactly accords with physical principles: by abrading the faces of the stones in the center, one diminishes their mass, lowering the audible partials. The principal nodes of a musical stone converge at its pointed ends; by filing them off, one increases the elasticity, thus raising the pitch.[70] Experience gained on the less sophisticated musical stones may have contributed to the practice of bell-tuning.[71]

## The Finished Product

The feature of ancient Chinese chime-bells that most amazes a modern observer—their (relatively) exact pitch, which made them useable as fully musical instruments—may have been accorded surprisingly little emphasis in

67. *Wenwu Cankao Ziliao* 1958 (1):15–23.

68. The *sui* first appears on the inside of late Western Zhou chimed *yongzhong* (see Appendix 2, Early *yongzhong* II); diagrams of different distributions of troughs on bells from different chimes are given by Li Chunyi (1990). Li concludes from the absence of *sui* on earlier types of *yongzhong* that the two-tone phenomenon was not realized until late Western Zhou; but this is doubtful because B-tone markers appear even on some of the earliest *yongzhong* known. It seems much more likely that the *sui* represents a secondary step towards acoustically more sophisticated two-tone bells; it must have come into being as a result of experimentation at the Western Zhou court workshops.

69. *Zhou Li: Kaogongji* "Qingshi" (*Zhou Li Zhengyi* 80:16b–17a).

70. Lithophones are technologically simpler than bell-chimes because they lack the complications brought about by the two-tone phenomenon. Some chimestones of the characteristic *qing* shape can, however, emit more than one tone depending on the striking point (as I found to be the case in the largest chimestone in a modern replica of the Zeng lithophone at the Hubei Provincial Museum). Such an effect is probably caused by impurities in the stone material and cannot be easily expressed through a designing formula. If the two-tone phenomenon ever occurred on Bronze Age chimestones, it was almost certainly unintentional. Inscribed specimens naming their tones (such as the Zeng chimestones and some unprovenienced specimens discussed by Fang Jianjun 1990) only ever indicate one tone per stone.

71. Kuttner 1953.

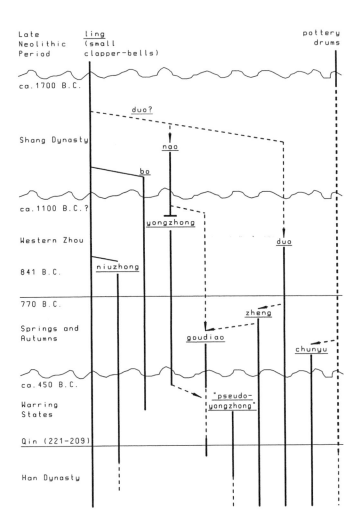

FIGURE 52. Development of early Chinese bell-types.

the native concept of "bell" at the time. Bells were to be seen just as much as they were to be heard. This is not to say that the musical functionality of chime-bells was considered unimportant; it merely seems to have been taken for granted. Bell inscriptions (with the exception of those on the Zeng bells), if they refer at all to acoustical aspects, do not dwell on music-related matters but merely refer to the bells as sound-emitters. As such, each bell was endowed with a singing voice of its own.[72] The inscription on the mid-sixth century B.C. Yun'er-*bo* characterizes that bell's tone as follows:

> Strike them for their long-resounding tone that heightens your elation; let their perfect sound come forth very loudly; greatly rejoice in this epitome of perfection.[73]

We have seen that some inscriptions render bell sound by way of onomato-poeia, using characters that show concern with the bells' metallic timbre. It is curious that inscriptions and texts (especially the *Shi Jing*) use identical expressions to describe both the sound of bells and birdsong.[74] The word *ming* 鳴, commonly seen in the Odes in association with bells, where it means "to sound, ring," also means, primarily, "to twitter, cry, sing" (of birds). An affinity of birds and bells is apparent in parts of the iconography of bell decoration (see Chapters 4 and 5). That bells were conceived of as reproducing birdsong (if not actually manufactured with such intention) shows again how the definition of

---

72. This idea is shown by the occasional epithet *gezhong* 歌鐘 "singing bells," found both in *Zuo Zhuan* Xiang 11 (HYI ed., 274) and in the inscription of the Cai Hou Shen bells. Related is the epithet 鶚 (found in the Zhejian-*yongzhong*), transcribed by Guo Moruo as *yaozhong* 瑤鐘 "singing bell." Three Eastern Zhou bells (the Chu Wang Jin–*niuzhong*, the Xu Zi–*bo*, and the Chen Dasangshi–*niuzhong*) contain the epithet *lingzhong* 鈴鐘 (*ling* is reduplicated in the case of the Chen Dasangshi–*niuzhong*), best translated as "ringing bell."

73. The Chinese text runs: *Zhong han zha yang / yuan ming kong huang / kong jia yuan cheng* 中翰叔煬元鳴孔諻孔嘉元成. The first eight characters of the phrase also appear in several contemporaneous inscriptions on bells that are probably all, like the Yun'er-*bo*, of Chu manufacture. They include the Wangsun Gao–*yongzhong* from tomb no. 2 at Xiasi, Xichuan (Henan), and the unprovenienced Wangsun Yizhe–*yongzhong*, Xu Zi–*bo*, and Xu Wangzi Jiong–*niuzhong*; shorter portions of the phrase may be seen in the inscriptions of the Cai Hou–*niuzhong* and the Qin Gong II–*bo* (for references, see Appendix 2; the textual variants are tabulated in Falkenhausen 1988, table 20). My translation differs from that of previous commentators in that I divide the text into rhyming parallel four-word phrases. *Zhong* 中 is taken verbally in the meaning "to hit, strike (a bell)"; *han* 翰 as "long, extended sound" (*Li Ji* "Qu Li-*xia*," *Li Ji Zhushu* 5:11b); *zha* 叔 as an untranslatable particle similar to *qi* 其; and *yang* 煬 as an allograph of *yang* 揚 "elated." *Yuan* 元 (archaic reading: *ngịwan) may be taken in its sense of "good, perfect" (or it may be amended, in a phonetically unproblematic loan, to its semantic cognate *wan* [*ngwan] 玩 "to play," a common word in pre-Qin texts). *Yuan* is linked to *ming* 鳴 "to sound/emit a sound." *Kong* 孔 means, as it always does in such a position, "very"; *huang* 諻 doubtless stands for *huang* 喤 "forceful, loud [sound]," as in *Shi Jing* (Odes 274 and 280, HYI ed., 75, 76), where it renders the sound of court music.

74. E.g., *cang* 鎗, *cong* 鏓, *yang* 央, *yong* 雝, *jie* 諧; see nn. 19–22.

"bell" centered on the sound, not on the music; albeit aesthetically pleasing, birdsong cannot, strictly speaking, be called a musical phenomenon. The *Shi Jing* contexts help to establish the intended connotations: both birds and bells were conceived of as peaceful, loving, orderly, and harmonic.

The extensive extramusical meanings of bells hark back to the extravagant conception of music in the late pre-Qin and early Han texts, briefly outlined above in the Introduction. Unlike birds, of course, bells constituted a component of material culture under human control and able to induce artificially a state of harmony among humans comparable or analogous to that of singing birds in nature. In Western and especially Eastern Zhou inscriptions, such a function is made explicit by the common bell epithet *he* 和 "harmonizing."[75] The music performed on the bells was to have a beneficial effect on the relations between the living and the ancestral spirits (see Chapter 1); such music stood for peaceful and well-ordered social relations.

Eastern Zhou and early Han texts, when mentioning bells, often dwell on these socio-moral implications,[76] sometimes extending them into the cosmological realm. The *Yan Zi Chunqiu*, for example, contains an episode in which the Qi statesman Yan Zi, Confucius, and the magician Bochang Qian 柏常騫 (all three reduced to stock figures representing particular philosophical viewpoints) each pronounce a verdict on a bell newly cast by Jing Gong of Qi 齊景公 (r. 547–490 B.C.):

> Jing Gong made a Great Bell. When it was about to be suspended, Yan Zi, Confucius, and Bochang Qian came to court and jointly said: "The bell will break." And indeed, when [the bell] was struck, it broke. [Jing] Gong summoned the three sages to inquire [the reason]. Yan Zi replied: "The bell was large. To use it in feasting without having sacrificed to the former lords was against the rules of propriety; hence I said that the bell would break." Confucius said: "The bell was large, yet it was suspended [facing] downwards, so when it was stuck, its emanations [*qi* 氣] were sinuous at the bottom and thinned-out at the top. Hence I said that the bell would break." Bochang Qian said: "Today is a *geng-shen* day, a day [governed by] thunder.

---

75. See Falkenhausen 1988, table 16 and appendix 2. The epithet *he* is not usually seen on bronzes of other kinds.

76. The most grandiose expression of such views may be found in two long discourses in *Guo Yu* "Zhou Yu-*xia*" (Tiansheng Mingdao ed., 3:12a–18b). They also consistently underlie Xun Zi's views on music (*Xun Zi* "Fuguo," HYI ed., 32–34; "Lilun," ibid., 70–75; "Yuelun," ibid., 77–78), as well as those of the *Yue Ji* (*Li Ji* "Yueji," *Li Ji Zhushu* 37:6b–9b and 39:3a–4a; identically in *Shi Ji* "Yueshu," Zhonghua ed., 1186–89, 1224–25 and passim).

[The bell's] tone was not superior to that of thunder; hence I said that it would break."[77]

At the end of the Bronze Age, bells seem to have been commonly viewed as one material means by which humans could imitate nature and act upon nature. If this was done unwisely or at the wrong time, disaster could result; the breaking of Jing Gong's bell, for example, was a highly inauspicious omen for the fate of the ruling lineage (which, at that time, was being pushed from power, eventually to be replaced on the throne of Qi by the House of Chen 陳 [or Tian 田]).[78] The potential impact of bell-casting was thus considerable and could not be undertaken lightly.

In summary, bell manufacture rested on complex motifs and a comprehensive sort of knowledge that was hardly akin to the mindset of modern engineering.[79] A one-sided view restricted to technological or musical issues would omit important cultural factors. We should not be too surprised when occasionally in the archaelogical record we encounter cases where the visual aspect of bells appears to have taken precedence over the acoustic ones (as occurred especially frequently in areas that were but marginally touched by the culture and ritual of the Shang and Zhou courts; see Appendix 3). Bell-chimes were sound-producers, but they were more; their significance was many-layered.

77. *Yan Zi Chunqiu* "Waipian" (*Yan Zi Chunqiu Jishi*, 507). The idea that the sound of bells imitated that of thunder may also be found in *Huainan Zi* (Sibu Congkan ed. 8:4a).

78. Written in Qi during the Warring States period, one aspect of the *Yan Zi Chunqiu*'s agenda seems to be legitimation of Chen dynastic rule.

79. See Franklin et al. 1985.

PART II  The History of Chinese Musical Bells

# CHAPTER FOUR

# Origins and Early Development

Unlike other great inventions of ancient China (such as silk, porcelain, and the much-touted "paper, printing, compass, and gunpowder"), chimes of two-tone bells are limited to a single historical period, the Bronze Age. They have not survived as part of living Chinese culture, and they have not been imitated abroad. It might be argued, therefore, that they are not worth spilling much ink on. But from another perspective, the fact that the chime-bells died out after the end of the Bronze Age would seem to make them all the more interesting. We know from both texts and archaeological finds that chime-bells were for a time of great political and intellectual significance, and it is no exaggeration to say that they embody the highest technical skills of Shang and Zhou civilization. Why did they fall into disuse? How could their sophisticated technology be so completely forgotten? In making us reflect about such questions, the ancient Chinese chime-bells make palpable the inseparability of inventions from their cultural and social context. To make such connections explicit is an overarching concern of this book. The technological basics having been explained in Part I, we can now explore the historical development of ancient Chinese chime-bells as it can be traced through surviving material evidence.

## Typology and the History of Inventions

Archaeology helps us realize that the great inventions of the past, upon which our modern technology rests, rarely arose from a single flash of genius.[1] Aptly, the etymological meaning of "to invent" is "to come upon." Through most of

---

1. E.g., White 1962.

human history, innovation came about in a haphazard and often fortuitous manner, occurring slowly and cumulatively over long periods of time. Craftsmen typically did not devise new inventions deliberately but quite literally stumbled upon them. Rather than proceeding in a straight line, therefore, the history of science and technology is riddled with curious back alleys, culs-de-sac, and turnabouts.

The objective of this and the following chapter goes beyond straight art history, to which much of their contents inevitably bear some resemblance. It is important to realize that the evidence presented here embodies the history of the technology under discussion. Through continuous archaeological sequences, we can retrace, step by step, the "invention" of ancient Chinese chime-bells, using typology as a research tool indispensable not only to archaeology but also to some aspects of intellectual history. The fuller historical implications will be made explicit in Chapter 9.

For present purposes, it is useful to distinguish between two levels of typological analysis: the morphological and the stylistic. At the morphological level, objects are classified according to their overall shape and their external attributes, such as handles, bosses, and the presence or absence of decoration, whereas at the stylistic level, typological distinctions are based on the details (as well as the execution) of surface ornamentation. Both morphology and stylistics are useful as dating devices, to be used in conjunction with epigraphic analysis and other methods, such as stratigraphy and carbon-14 dating. Additionally, the study of morphological features can enlighten us about intellectual processes.[2]

Figure 52 presents the genealogy of Chinese bell-types and their temporal range. The six principal steps in the history of chimes of two-tone bells may be enumerated as follows:

1. *Use of metal for sound-generating bodies.* The first metal bells are seen in the archaeological record of the late third millennium; as discussed in the preceding chapter, they already feature the characteristic almond-shaped cross-section.

2. *Manufacture of chimes of bells of graduated sizes.* This development apparently first occurred in the late Shang period (second half of second millennium), perhaps after the invention of bells with round shanks.

---

2. These brief methodological considerations take up on Montelius 1903. It should be noted that Montelius continues to be of great influence on Chinese archaeologists (see Yu Weichao and Zhang Zhongpei in Su Bingqi 1984, 306–19).

3. *Realization of the two-tone phenomenon.* This important discovery took place sometime after 1000 B.C.; concomitantly, the mode of installation of bells underwent an important change.

4. *Utilization of the two-tone phenomenon in the manufacture of chimed sets of bells.* This important step occurred separately from and subsequent to the invention of two-pitch bells.

5. *Emergence of complex chime-bell assemblages.* From the ninth to the mid-fourth centuries, two-pitch bells of a variety of types were produced in multiple chimes, which could be played simultaneously. This was the time of the greatest florescence of Chinese musical bells, the culmination of which is represented by the Zeng bells.

6. *Abandonment of the two-tone phenomenon.* This regression in technological sophistication coincided with the demise of most types of chime-bells during the late Warring States period (mid-fourth to third centuries). The bell-making tradition of the Chinese Bronze Age came to an end sometime during the Han dynasty.

Archaeology also reveals an important geographic dimension to these developments. Although the chronological steps were each based on the preceding ones, they took place at different locations and under different cultural conditions.

The multiplicity of regional traditions in early Chinese civilization has emerged as one of the main themes of recent archaeological research and theory-building. K. C. Chang has characterized ancient China as an "interaction sphere" in which influences and stimuli were exchanged among a variety of coexisting cultures.[3] Cultural diffusion, albeit rightly discredited as a universal explanatory device, prevailed in Neolithic and Bronze Age China, especially at the elite cultural level.[4] Chime-bells were among the symbolically charged status items by which regional elites in and around the areas dominated by the early Chinese dynasties asserted themselves as such and made themselves compatible with one another. Their evolution derives much of its dynamics from a dialectic of transregional standard-emulation and local innovation. While embodying the achievements of regional or local workshop traditions, bells also exemplify centripetal trends in the long-term cultural development of the Chinese Bronze Age. In short, the evolution of chime-bells is in many ways representative of ancient Chinese cultural processes.

3. Chang 1986, ch. 5.
4. See Keightley 1987.

China seems to have produced the earliest bells anywhere in the world.[5] We have noted in Chapter 3 that the earliest metal bells may have been derived from pottery prototypes, which seem to go back in time to the late stage of the Yangshao culture (early third millennium B.C.) (fig. 53).[6] The first metal bells date to the late third millennium B.C., being among the earliest metal artifacts in the Chinese archaeological record. By contrast, in West Asia, where metallurgy was practiced far earlier than in China, bells were not made until ca. 1000 B.C.[7] On the other hand, the primacy of bells in the autochthonous development of metallurgy is not limited to China; west Mexico during the late first millennium A.D. offers an interesting parallel to the Chinese case.[8]

At present we can trace the modest origins of Chinese metal bells to one fairly circumscribed region along the middle reaches of the Yellow River, comprising parts of present-day Shanxi, Henan, and Anhui provinces. The time and area of origin coincide with those assigned by the traditional sources to the Xia, the legendary first dynasty of Chinese history (trad. dates: 2207–1766 B.C.). An incompletely preserved copper specimen (see fig. 12) from the late Neolithic cemetery at Taosi in Xiangfen (Shanxi) (ca. 2000 B.C.), already referred to several times in passing, appears to resemble a suspended clapper-bell (*ling*).[9] This "bell-like object" is important not only as the earliest hollow cast-metal object so far found in China but also for its co-occurrence with the earliest indicators of the classical Chinese musical-ritual complex. Taosi and other contemporary sites in the same area have yielded remains of musical instruments apparently prefiguring those of the ritual orchestra of the later Bronze Age: chimestones (*qing*), ceramic drums, and alligator-skin drums.[10]

5. *Lüshi Chunqiu* "Guyue" mentions bells cast by the first sovereigns of the Three Dynasties, as well as by even earlier mythical rulers. For a synopsis of legends ascribing the invention of bells to various pre-dynastic heroes, see Feng Guangsheng 1988b.

6. Two Late Yangshao–period (early third millennium) gray "pottery bells" were excavated at Dahecun, Zhengzhou (Henan). Two similar objects were found at the late-third-millennium site of Taosi, Xiangfen (Shanxi). Other bell-like objects have turned up at the sites of Liulin and Dadunzi, Pi Xian (Jiangsu), Miaodigou, Sanmenxia (Henan), Keshengzhuang, Chang'an (Shaanxi), and Shijiahe, Tianmen (Hubei). References in Appendix 1. See also Chen Xingcan 1990.

7. Price 1983. Despite their later date, diffusion from China seems to have played no role in the origin of these bells.

8. Hosler 1988.

9. References to archaeologically excavated bells may be found (in alphabetical order by site name) in Appendix 1.

10. All these musical-instrument types are mentioned in *Zhou Li*. For the Taosi drums see *Kaogu* 1983 (1):30–42; large chimestones were excavated at Taosi as well as the nearby sites of Dagudui, Xiangfen (Shanxi) (*Kaogu* 1988 [12]:1137), Nansongcun, Wenxi (Shanxi) (*Kaogu yu Wenwu* 1986 [2]:94, 60; *Kōga bunmei-no nagare*:61 [cat. no. 31]) and Dongxiafeng, Xia Xian (*Kaogu* 1980 [2]:97–107; photo p. 100, fig. 7.19). See also Fang Jianjun 1989. On a possible relationship between Taosi and the Xia dynasty see Zhang Changshou 1987.

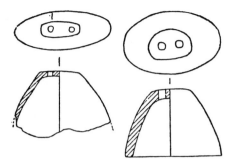

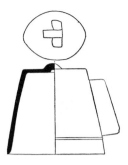

FIGURE 53. Pottery bells excavated in 1972–75 at Dahecun, Zhengzhou (Henan). Late Neolithic (third millennium B.C.).

FIGURE 54. Bronze *ling* excavated in 1982 from Area IX, tomb no. 4, at Erlitou, Yanshi (Henan). Late Erlitou culture (ca. 1800–1600 B.C.).

The Taosi "bell" remains an isolated find in the archaeological record of its period, but during the second millennium B.C., *ling* clapper-bells gradually became ubiquitous. The earliest bronze specimens were excavated in tombs of the Erlitou culture (early second millennium).[11] Virtually unornamented, they are remarkably uniform in shape and feature one lateral flange (fig. 54); later *ling* have two such flanges, perhaps left over from the bivalve casting process. The clappers (mod. Chin. *she* 舌 "tongue") are not preserved; they were probably made of perishable materials such as wood or bone, and they seem to have been connected, through a hole in the top, to the suspension loop by means of a piece of string.

*Ling* have been found at virtually every Bronze Age cemetery in the country.[12] In general, they are comparatively small in size (height below 10 cm). In late Shang dynasty pieces, a ring and a moveable metal clapper are cast onto the inside of *ling* (fig. 55). Those bells do not seem to be designed to be directly and purposefully manipulated by human beings; their small suspension loops are inconvenient for holding them in hand. They were agitated by virtue of being attached to other moving substances. Although considerable numbers of *ling* have been excavated together, these clapper-bells were never, as far as we know, assembled into tuned sets.[13]

11. References in Appendix 1. For a list of typologically related specimens, see Appendix 2.
12. For an article-length treatment of *ling*, see An Jiayao 1987.
13. The so-called "chimed *ling*" from Zhuangbai, Fufeng (Shaanxi) are discussed with the earliest *niuzhong* in Chapter 5, below, although they do not seem to have been made as a chimed set (Fang Jianjun, personal communication).

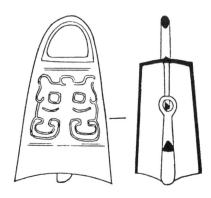

FIGURE 55. *Ling* excavated in 1965–66 from tomb no. 1 at Subutun, Yidu (now Qingzhou) (Shandong). Late Shang period (ca. 1300–1050 B.C.).

The Neolithic and Erlitou *ling* occur as single pieces directly associated with human individuals. *Ling* function as noise-producers. When dangling, for example, from a shaman's belt, as may have been the case with the Taosi *ling*, which was found near the tomb-occupant's pelvis, their tinkling would have acoustically underlined the bearer's body movements. The distribution of these earliest specimens is limited to some of the richest tombs. Being associated with individuals of authority, their symbolic function appears to be analogous to that of the later musical bells. The early *ling* thus not only have an important role in the evolution of metal sound generators but arguably played a much more prominent cultural role than was ever true thereafter for clapper-bells of this sort. With the emergence of other kinds of bells during the Shang period, *ling* were relegated to subservient functions; at Shang and Zhou sites, they are habitually found not in immediate association with their owners but as part of the horse-and-chariot gear and as collar-bells of dogs. In later times, *ling* were also suspended from canopy curtains, to be agitated by the wind.[14]

## The Emergence of Musical Bells

The Erligang period of Shang civilization (ca. 1500–1350 B.C.) is still a blank spot in our typological sequence. Because no Erligang bells have so far been excavated, we can only conjecture that during this period, significant developments must have taken place; in the subsequent Anyang period (ca. 1350–1045 B.C.), we find, in addition to *ling* of various types, a new kind of clapperless bell with a round, hollow shank (figs. 56 and 57). These bells, which present-day

14. Examples documenting such a use in the Eastern Zhou and Late Han period have been reported from tomb no. 75 in the Shaoshan Guanqu project (Hunan) (*Wenwu* 1977 [3]:36–54, photo p. 48), dating to Eastern Zhou, and at Xiaoyancun, Shijiazhuang (Hebei) (*Kaogu* 1980 [1]:52–54,

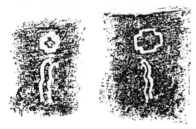

FIGURE 56. Enlarged set of five *nao* excavated in 1976 from tomb no. 5 ("Fu Hao's tomb") at Yin-xu, Anyang (Henan). The inscription "Ya Gong" (see rubbing) is found only on two of the five bells. Late Shang period (probably early to mid-twelfth century B.C.).

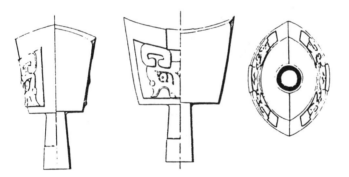

FIGURE 57. One of an enlarged set of four *nao* excavated in 1935 from tomb no. 1083 at Xibeigang, Anyang (Henan). Late Shang period (twelfth–eleventh century B.C.).

photo p. 54 figs. 5.6 and 5.7), dating to Western Han. At Xiaoyancun, the bells were suspended from arch-shaped arms in a mobile-like arrangement.

archaeologists in China commonly call *nao*,[15] were produced in sets of three. They were mounted on wooden stands with their mouths pointing upward. *Nao* are the earliest chime-bells of the Chinese Bronze Age and, for that matter, anywhere in the world.

The resonating bodies of *nao* and *ling* are sufficiently similar in shape to suggest that the two kinds of bells are genetically related.[16] Nonetheless, *nao* may not have been derived directly from *ling*; it has been hypothesized that *nao* may have been preceded by clapper-bells with cylindrical shanks (*duo*),[17] which makes logical sense, although archaeological proof is still lacking. *Duo* clapper-handbells were common in the later part of the Bronze Age, but the earliest mainstream specimen so far excavated (see fig. 24) dates only to mid–Western Zhou times.[18]

At the Late Shang metropolis of Anyang, three-part chimed sets have been found not only of *nao* but of chimestones as well. They formed part of ritual orchestras that also included various wind and possibly stringed instruments.[19] *Nao* chimes were occasionally enlarged by inserting additional bells of ex-

---

15. Most Japanese scholars prefer the term *zheng* (pron. *shō* in Japanese), which is also seen in some older Chinese works; the original name for bells of this class is unknown.

16. Li Chunyi 1957b; Zhang Yachu 1985; Wu Hung n.d., sec. 1. In both *nao* and *ling* the rim may be either level or curved upwards (as in later *yongzhong* and *niuzhong*). This lack of uniformity with regard to the shape of the rim may be a technologically primitive feature. The exact acoustic impact of rim shape has not yet been clarified by experiments.

17. Hayashi Minao (1984 2:392, *taku* 1) has classified a set of early-looking *nao* from tomb no. 51 at Dasikongcun, Anyang (Henan) (references in Appendix 1), whose elongated proportions seem to resemble those of contemporary clapper-bells, such as *duo*. However, because the published report does not mention the existence of a clapper, this identification must remain speculative; we may also wonder how a three-piece set of clapper-bells could have been played as a chime. In the absence of archaeological data from the crucial Erligang period, we cannot determine with certainty when and how bells were first assembled into graduated sets.

18. This earliest mainstream *duo* was excavated at tomb no. 1 at Rujiazhuang, Baoji (Shaanxi) (*Baoji Yu-guo mudi*, 1: 281; drawing, p. 310, fig. 217. 2; photo, v. 2, pl. 155. 2; *Shaanxi Chutu Shang Zhou Qingtongqi* 4:64 [photo]). Another early bronze *duo* excavated at Caojiayuan, Shilou (Shanxi) may date back to Shang times, but it is extraordinary in many ways (*Shanxi chutu wenwu*, cat. no. 57 [photo]; *Zhongguo kaoguxue yanjiu lunji*, 218; photo, p. 216, fig. 3.3). This bell is rung by means of a multitude of loose 8-shaped bronze elements affixed to the handle and the bell-body, which hit the metal surface when the object is shaken. Some of these jingling elements appear to end in tiny crotals. Whether the bell has a clapper is not clear; it would hardly seem to need one. Other unusual features include slot-shaped holes in the resonating body paralleling the vertical rows of jingling elements, as well as bands of hatched raised-line decoration suggesting northern (Siberian and northeast Asian) derivation. While the overall shape of the resonating body (including its almond-shaped cross-section) speaks for a Chinese connection, this unique specimen clearly emanates from a peripheral manufacturing tradition and hardly fits into the developmental sequence of the *zhong* family bells in the central and southern regions of China. At best, it is a distant reflection of the putative clapper-handbells of Shang. The origins of the *duo* may go back even further: Li Chunyi (1957a) and Wu Zhao (1983, 4) illustrate an otherwise unreported pottery object allegedly excavated at Keshengzhuang, Chang'an (Shaanxi), perhaps dating to the late Neolithic. It is difficult to imagine a function for it, but the shape vaguely prefigures that of a bell with a handle. If this object was in fact a musical instrument, it might suggest that independent typological lineages of bells with shanks go back to pre–Bronze Age times, but this is highly speculative.

19. Tong Kin-woon 1983–84; Pratt 1986.

traneous origin. The five pieces found in the famous tomb no. 5 ("Fu Hao's tomb") at Xiaotun, probably the resting place of a consort of King Wu Ding (trad. dates: 1324–1266), constitute such a composite set (fig. 56). Their sizes are not evenly graduated, and the second and third bells in the set are conspicuously close to one another in size. Moreover, only two bells in the set (nos. 1 and 2) bear the inscription "Ya Gong[?]" 亞弜,[20] which points to an origin different from that of the three uninscribed ones. Likewise, the four *nao* from tomb no. 1083 at Xibeigang (fig. 57), with two specimens similarly close to one another in size, seem to have been jumbled together from two different chimes, an impression confirmed by tone measurements (see Chapter 7 and fig. 112).[21]

In most Anyang *nao*, the striking point for the A-tone is clearly demarcated as a thickened portion in the center of the sound-bow. This morphological feature seems to indicate that the two-tone phenomenon was probably not recognized at the time. We recall from Chapter 2 that later Zhou bell-casters deliberately thinned the nodal area in that part of the bell by fashioning the hollow *sui* on the inside; doing so assured optimal separation of the A- and B-tones. A thickened wall portion in this part of the bell would have had a contrary effect. Tone measurements corroborate that B-tones were not yet used in Shang times (see Chapter 7).

In the Anyang period, we for the first time see decoration on bells, perhaps reflecting the increasing importance of such musical instruments in the pursuit of conspicuous consumption. While the five *nao* from "Fu Hao's tomb" (fig. 56) are unornamented save for a raised line defining an empty central field, on many other Anyang *nao* the entire bell-face is covered by a mask motif. This mask is sometimes executed in raised lines (as in the unprovenienced Ya-Wan Fu Ji–*nao* in the Palace Museum, Taibei),[22] but much more frequently it is rendered in high relief (e.g., fig. 57). Mask iconography and style resemble those on other types of late Shang bronzes, though the ubiquitous background decor of "cloud-pattern" spirals is never seen on the *nao*. The mask faces the viewer when the bell is installed with the mouth facing upward.

Exactly the same two modes of bell-face layout—simple enclosed field and central mask motif—may be observed on Anyang period *ling*.[23] On *ling* decorated with masks (see fig. 55), that motif is invariably executed in raised lines; interestingly, moreover, it always faces upside down when the bell is

20. These two characters probably designate a clan or lineage name.
21. References in Appendix 1. For a list of typologically related specimens, see Appendix 2.
22. For references see Appendix 2.
23. At Anyang, *ling* with simple decoration were found, for example, in the royal tomb no. 1001 at Xibeigang (one piece, *Houjiazhuang*, vol. 2 [1962], fasc. 1:313, illustrations: fasc. 2:pls. 244.3 and 247.1), in the large tomb at Wuguancun (one piece [H. 8.8 cm], *Kaogu Xuebao* 5 [1951]:19–21, drawing: p. 40 fig. 8), and in tomb no. 20 at Xiaotun (two pieces, *Xiaotun*, 1st ser., pt. 3, vol. 1 [1970], fasc. 1:144–45, illustrations: fasc. 2:pl. 121). This list is not complete.

suspended.[24] Evidently, the motif was transferred from *nao* onto *ling* without considering *ling*'s different mode of installation. The fact that both *ling* and *nao* feature basically identical, and identically displayed, ornamentation motifs may show that both were perceived as pertaining to the same category of objects. They were probably made in the same workshops. But it is the *ling* that, despite their greater antiquity, are decorated in imitation of the *nao*; hence it would seem that by the time of the Anyang period, nonmusical clapper-bells were considered secondary to musical chime-bells.

Sets of *nao* are virtually limited to the immediate surroundings of Anyang, with outliers in northern and central Shandong.[25] They occur exclusively in tombs of considerable wealth. By contrast, *ling* very much like those from Anyang have been found in tombs hundreds of kilometers away from the metropolis.[26] Both *ling* and *nao* continue virtually unchanged into the Western Zhou period, where their stylistic development appears to have stagnated for almost two centuries after the end of Shang.

## The Nao Bells of Southern China
### Northern versus Southern Nao

During the Anyang period, the regions along the Yangzi River (see map 1) were probably beyond the realm of the Shang kings. The various local Bronze Age cultures produced a characteristic hard-fired patterned pottery, which was exported to Anyang. Conversely, metallurgy had apparently been transplanted into the area from the north during the Erligang period; stylistically distinctive

24. Pieces with this sort of decoration found at Xiaotun, Anyang, include two from tomb no. 20 (*Xiaotun*, 1st ser., pt. 3, vol. 1 [1970], fasc. 1:144–45, illustrations: fasc. 2:pl. 122) and one from tomb no. 164 (*Xiaotun* 1st ser., pt. 3, vol. 2 [1972]:30–31, illustration: pl. 6.8). This enumeration is not exhaustive.

25. A chime of three *nao* with mask decoration in the Anyang style was excavated from tomb no. 8 at Subutun, Qingzhou (Shandong); that tomb was part of a necropolis of local rulers who virtually equalled the Shang kings in prestige and wealth. The Ya Chou 亞醜–*nao* in the Shanghai Museum (photo in Ma Chengyuan 1981, pl. 23.1) may have been looted, together with many other bronzes all featuring the same clan marker, from one of the large tombs at Subutun in the early part of the twentieth century; other bronzes with Ya Chou inscriptions have since turned up in controlled excavations at that site (Yin Zhiyi 1977). Another *nao* (possibly a set) was excavated at Daguo, Huimin (Shandong); unfortunately, the only published photograph is so blurred that it is impossible to assess its similarity to Anyang pieces. References in Appendix 1.

26. Random examples of ornate Shang–period *ling* from outside the Anyang metropolitan area include the following: five pieces (H. 7–9.7 cm) from tomb no. 1 at Subutun, Qingzhou (formerly Yidu, Shandong) (*Wenwu* 1972 [8]:17–30, photo: p. 26 fig. 20, drawing: p. 30 figs. 38.4,5,8); six pieces (H. 5.5 and 6.5 cm) from a tomb at Yiduhoucheng, Shouguang (Shandong) (*Wenwu* 1985 [3]:1–11, photo, p. 8 fig. 29, drawing: p. 7 fig. 28); three (H. 8.5 cm) from tomb no. 1 at Jingjiecun, Lingshi (Shanxi) (*Wenwu* 1986 [11]:1–18, photo, p. 8, fig. 16; drawing, p. 9 fig. 20.2). The following are some examples from Western Zhou tombs in Shaanxi: one piece (H. 9.4 cm) from the early Western Zhou tomb no. 77M1 at Keshengzhuang, Chang'an (*Kaogu* 1981 [1]:13–18, 76; photo, pl. 3.3); and one (H. 8 cm) from a middle Western Zhou tomb at Nanluo, Lintong (*Wenwu* 1982

bronzes loosely patterned on northern models were manufactured locally.[27] In particular, the bronze-casters in the Yangzi River region imitated *nao* of the Anyang types just described; specimens of these appear to have been diffused here sometime during the Anyang period—or, possibly, somewhat earlier. In the period corresponding to late Shang and early Western Zhou, the southern casters transformed these *nao* into much larger bells with elaborate decoration.

Although similar in shape to northern *nao*, the *nao* from the Yangzi region may have served a quite different ritual function. As Robert W. Bagley has pointed out: "In northern ritual the central role of the bronze vessel was unchallenged, but in the south vessels were clearly far less important than bells."[28] In spite of the evident prominence of bells, the idea of manufacturing them in chimed sets does not seem to have occurred to the southern bronze casters. All *nao* found in south China are single specimens; even when several are found together,[29] they never constitute a chimed set.[30] There are no indications that the ritual orchestra of the Shang and Zhou courts was known in the south at that time; it has been observed, for example, that in the Yangzi region, bells were not associated with chimestones (*qing*), as they were in the north.[31] The fact that most specimens have been discovered in isolated mountainous areas has given rise to the speculation that they played a role in mountain cults of some kind.[32] They may have been used for convoking the populace or for conjuring the spirits, or bells may have been thought of as emitting the voices of deities. Rather than serving as musical instruments in an orchestra, the southern *nao* thus resembled later European church-bells or Buddhist temple-bells in their function.

Unlike their northern counterparts, none of the southern *nao* has been found in tombs; they were apparently buried at the sites where they had been used, usually without any accompanying artifacts. The lack of archaeological context makes it difficult to periodize them, much less determine their absolute dates. Various sequences have been proposed on the basis of decoration style. What

---

[1]:87–89; photo, p. 88 fig. 3, rubbing: ibid., fig. 4). The middle Western Zhou tomb no. 21 at Xincun, Xun Xian (Henan), as well as several later tombs at the same site, also yielded similar pieces of different sizes (*Xun Xian Xincun*, 58, photos: pls. 5.12,13; rubbings: pls. 96 and 97).

27. Kane 1974–75, Hayashi 1980, Bagley 1987.

28. Bagley 1987, 34.

29. For example, the groups of five and two *nao* excavated, respectively, at Shiguzhaishan and Beifengtan. References in Appendix 1. For a list of typologically related specimens, see Appendix 2.

30. The only possible exception to this is the set of two *nao* excavated at Nanya, Jian'ou (Fujian), probably dating to the late Western Zhou dynasty, which appear to be provincial survivals in a time when *nao* were no longer generally produced anywhere else. The decoration of these specimens (especially their studded *zhuan*) betrays some secondary influence from contemporary *yongzhong* types. Reference in Appendix 1.

31. Chen Zhenyu 1988a.

32. Gao Zhixi 1984b.

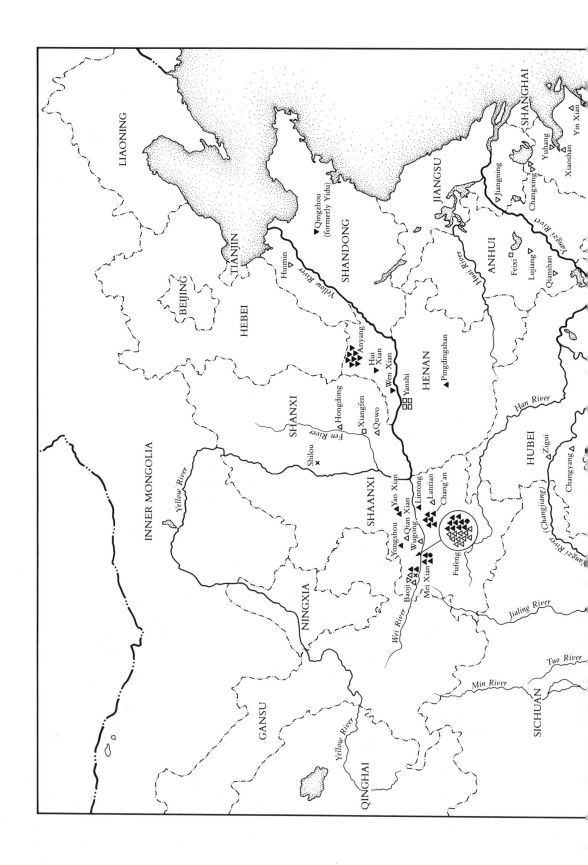

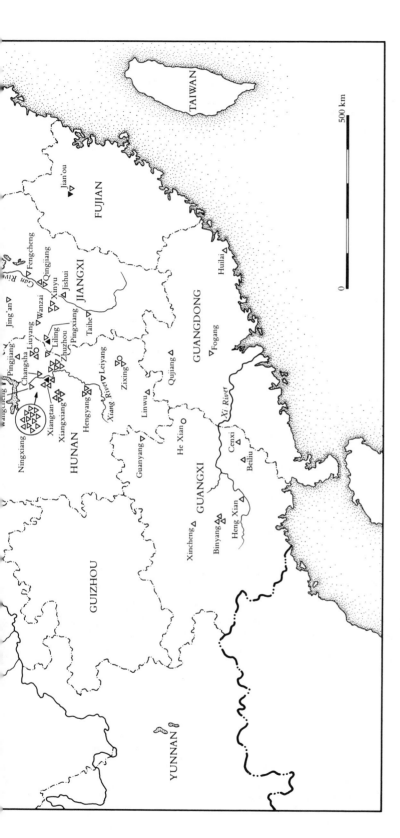

MAP 1. Geographical distribution of archaeologically provenienced Chinese musical bells dating from ca. 2000–771 B.C. (early Bronze Age–Western Zhou and contemporary regional cultures).

A symbol executed in outline indicates the find of a single bell; a solid symbol indicates a set comprising several bells.

Only the names of cities and county seats are given. For site names, consult Place Names in Geographical Arrangement and Appendixes 1 and 2.

EXPLANATION OF SYMBOLS

- ■ early clapper-bells (prehistoric–Erlitou)
- ▽ nao
- ◁ yongzhong
- ○ bo
- ◇ niuzhong
- ◆ other kinds of bells, or cases where information is
- ✕ insufficient for classification

TAIWAN

FUJIAN
Jian'ou ▼

JIANGXI
Fengcheng ▽
Qingjiang ▽
Xinyu ✕
Jishui △
Taihe ◁
Huilai △

GUANGDONG
Fogang ◁
Qujiang △

HUNAN
Wangcheng
Pingjiang
Jing'an ▽
Liuyang ○
Wanzai ▽
Liling ▽
Zhuzhou
Pingxiang ▽
Changsha
Xiangtan ▽
Xiangxiang ▽
Ningxiang
Hengyang ✕✕
Leiyang ▽
Zixing ◇
Xiang River
Linwu △
He Xian ○
Guanyang △

GUIZHOU

GUANGXI
Xincheng △
Binyang △△
Heng Xian ◁
Cenxi △
Beiliu ◁
Xi River

YUNNAN

Gan River

500 km
0

makes the matter complicated is that several southern workshops seem to have been involved in the casting of *nao* at different times. Because morphological innovations spread with amazing rapidity, it is difficult to relegate individual specimens to particular workshops or sub-areas. The two most important new features that emerged in the course of two centuries or so of sustained development of bell-making in the south are the *xuan* and the standard *zhong* ornamentation scheme.

## The Emergence of the Xuan

Southern *nao* are considerably larger and heavier than those from Anyang. The enlarged size required some modifications in the way in which these bells were installed. Although we do not know exactly what the *nao*-racks looked like, wood remains inside the shanks (*yong*) of *nao* found at Anyang show that these bells were impaled onto vertical sticks.[33] For the much larger southern specimens, this method would not have provided enough stability. It appears that the *yong* of southern *nao* were, instead, stuck into a cavity or through a hole in a rack that reached almost to the flat bottom of the bell's resonating body.[34] In order to maintain the *nao* in position and prevent them from sliding too far into the rack (which would have impaired the sound), a bulging protrusion, the *xuan*, was introduced onto the *yong* (see figs. 32 and 58). Large *nao* seem to have been additionally secured by ropes, which could be conveniently tied around the notch between the *xuan* and the resonating body. Undoubtedly, these more sophisticated mounting devices were engendered by increased bell size: in the earliest southern *nao*, dating to the time before the *xuan* became a universal feature, size strongly correlates with the presence or absence of a *xuan*.

## Some Large Specimens

The largest *nao* known to date was excavated at Yueshanpu, Ningxiang (Hunan) (fig. 58).[35] Measuring 103 cm in height and weighing 225 kg, it is one of the largest known Chinese bronzes. The Yueshanpu *nao* is representative of a conspicuous group of about twenty known large pieces (average height ca. 70 cm) with stylistically similar decoration. They all have a *xuan*, and they all feature the same three-dimensionally molded mask motif, which is placed in a recessed central panel. Although oriented in the same way as on the *nao* from

---

33. Traces of wood were found in the shanks of the *nao* from tomb no. 5 at Xiaotun, Anyang (*Yinxu Fu Hao-mu*, 100), and of the *nao* excavated at Jiazhuang, Anyang (*Zhongyuan Wenwu* 1986 [3]:12).
34. Various kinds of stands have been reconstructed by Tong Kin-woon 1983–84 pt. 2:136–42.
35. References in Appendix 1. For a list of typologically related specimens, see Appendix 2.

FIGURE 58. *Nao* from Yueshanpu, Ningxiang (Hunan). Photo and rubbings of the zoomorphic decoration on the sound-bow (two facing elephants) and on the *xuan* (two-bodied dragon). Local culture contemporary to late Shang, probably twelfth–eleventh century B.C.

Anyang (see fig. 57), this mask does not otherwise resemble its comparatively "naturalistic" Anyang counterpart. The eyes are separated from the surrounding parts of the face, which may be described as a highly abstracted configuration of molded ridges. The broad central ridge ("nose") has a fork-shaped top ("forehead") and ends in two hooked bends at the bottom ("muzzle"). Two symmetrical T-shaped "cheeks" branch off in the center of the central ridge; the arms of the T in turn branch out into hooked bends filling the space around the eyes and forming the "fangs" in the lower portion of the decoration panel. One wonders about the iconographic significance of this motif and whether it was even still perceived as a mask.[36]

36. Kane 1974–75, 88–89.

FIGURE 59. *Nao* from Nihequ, Lujiang (Anhui). Local culture contemporary to late Shang, probably twelfth–eleventh century B.C.

The thickened portion in the center of the sound-bow of these bells (and of southern *nao* in general) is highlighted by special ornamentation. On the Yue-shanpu *nao*, two symmetrical elephants are depicted in high relief (the *xuan* of that bell, moreover, features a pair of converging snakes, executed in a similar way). Such relieved decoration, for which there is no parallel on northern bells, can be found on some, though not all, of the large *nao* of this group of large pieces. Others, such as the one from Nihequ, Lujiang (Anhui) (fig. 59),[37] are wholly covered by "abstract" sunken-line volute decoration; here the decoration motif in the center of the sound-bow takes the form of a smaller mask-like configuration of scrolls.

Almost all archaeologically excavated specimens of this group have been found in Hunan, though the one depicted in figure 59 was discovered further down the Yangzi in Anhui. They are all so similar to one another that it seems safe to assume that they represent a distinct workshop tradition. Although Gao Zhixi 高至喜 places them at the beginning of his sequence of southern *nao*,[38] I would concur with Wu Hung 巫鴻 in that these large specimens constitute by

37. References in Appendix 1.
38. Gao Zhixi 1984b (English translation, 277–84).

no means the earliest southern *nao*.[39] They seem to represent a local strain, secondary to other filiations that we shall review below. Perhaps on account of their excessive size, this group of *nao* constitute an evolutionary cul-de-sac.

*Genesis of the Standard* Zhong *Ornamentation Scheme*

The majority of southern *nao* can be placed on a continuum leading from the earliest Anyang pieces to the *yongzhong* of mid- to late Western Zhou. The evolution of their surface design is coterminous with the genesis of the standard *zhong* ornamentation scheme, which was initially demonstrated by Chen Mengjia 陳夢家,[40] though Virginia Kane was the first to call attention to the underlying geographic dimension of that development.[41] Hayashi Minao 林巳奈夫 and Wu Hung, among others, have since refined the sequence.[42] In my own research, I have found that the evolution of the bell's morphological features by and large supports the stylistic periodization proposed by Wu Hung: the southern *nao* that he regards as the earliest lack *xuan* (as do the ones from Anyang), whereas *xuan* are present on all the stylistically later ones. I also believe that the adoption of the peculiar "standard" decor may reflect the casters' attempts to control the bells' acoustic properties (as discussed in Chapter 2). In time, the casters' experiments led to the discovery of the two-tone phenomenon.

*Nao* of the principal southern typological filiations have been found from Hunan and Hubei downstream to Jiangxi, Jiangsu, Zhejiang, and northern Fujian; later pieces have also been reported from Guangxi and, apparently, Guangdong.[43] Their sites of manufacture have not yet been identified. The decoration style, however, with its abundant scroll motifs, generally accords with that of locally produced bronzes of other kinds.

Following Wu Hung, we may take as our starting point a *nao* (no. 1) excavated at Liurongshan, Yangxin (Hubei) (fig. 60); though larger than any known Anyang specimens, it is one of the smallest found so far in the south.[44] This bell bears a certain resemblance to those from Anyang. The bell-face is completely flat save for the bulging pupils of a central mask motif, which has been disassembled into five separate parts, each covered with hooked sunken lines. A second, rudimentary mask is delineated on the small raised portion in the central part of the rim.

39. Wu Hung n.d.
40. Chen Mengjia 1955–56, pt. 5, 124–27.
41. Kane 1974–75, esp. 88–93.
42. Hayashi 1980; Wu Hung n.d.
43. Enumerated in Appendix 2; for references to provenienced specimens see Appendix 1. Distribution maps in Bagley 1987, 33, and Wu Hung n.d.
44. References in Appendix 1. For a list of typologically related specimens, see Appendix 2.

a

b

FIGURE 60. *Above:* First *nao* excavated in 1974 at Liurongshan,
Yangxin (Hubei). *a*, rubbing of
the bell-face; *b*, photo. Local culture contemporary to late Shang,
probably twelfth century B.C. or
earlier.

FIGURE 61. *Right: Nao* excavated
in 1963 at Xujiafan, Yuhang
(Zhejiang). Local culture contemporary to late Shang, probably
twelfth–eleventh century B.C.

b

FIGURE 62. Second *nao* from
Liurongshan (see fig. 61): *a*,
photo; *b*, rubbing of the bell-face.
Local culture contemporary to
late Shang, probably twelfth–
eleventh century B.C.

a

The next step in the stylistic development of *nao* decoration may be seen in
the *nao* from Xujiafan, Yuhang (Zhejiang) (fig. 61).[45] The flat, disassembled
mask is similar to that on bell no. 1 from Liurongshan, except that the simple
sunken-line decoration now extends over the entirety of the bell's surface. The
central mask motif is, moreover, surrounded by a pattern of small circlets in
raised thread relief. The Xujiafan *nao* is ancestral to two filiations of *nao* on
which the central ornamentation motif becomes less and less similar to the erstwhile mask.[46] *Nao* of the first group feature raised-line decor and lack *xuan*;
those of the second group are ornamented with sunken lines and have *xuan*. It
appears that these two groups represent different workshop traditions.

*Nao* no. 2 from Liurongshan (fig. 62) represents the first stylistic group of
specimens, characterized by raised-line decoration (figs. 62 and 63; see also fig.

45. The importance of this bell was stressed by Hayashi Minao (1980, 20).

46. The Xujiafan bell also appears to be ancestral to the group of large *nao* exemplified by the
piece from Yueshanpu, reviewed above. A partially molded mask design, which may link the
Xujiafan *nao* and the bells of that group, may be seen on an unprovenienced *nao* in the Portland
(Oregon) Art Museum (Kane 1974–75, 89, fig. 26; Hayashi 1984 2:380 *shō* 6).

FIGURE 63. *Nao* in the Museum of Far Eastern Antiquities, Stockholm. Local Middle Yangzi culture contemporary to late Shang, probably twelfth–eleventh century B.C.

25). Here the former mask is reduced to a filigree of relieved ridges.[47] The nose has become a thin line running down the full height of the ornamentation panel. Unlike thread-relief decoration in north China (as seen on the *ling* in fig. 55), the mask's contours are not emphasized. The spaces between the constituent ridges are entirely filled with raised circlets. In the much larger specimen from Tangdongcun, Jiangning (Jiangsu) (fig. 25),[48] the central mask is divided into two symmetrical receding panels separated by a broad ridge. Each panel contains one-half of a dissolved mask motif in raised-line decor. The raised lines of the mask expand outward, forming roughly three horizontal tiers; circlets fill the spaces in between. The same motif is seen in an unprovenienced *nao* in the Museum of Far Eastern Antiquities, Stockholm (fig. 63), but instead of two eyes, each of the two symmetrical panels features a group of nine nipple-shaped bosses.[49] They prefigure the *mei* characteristic of the standard *zhong* decoration scheme. Although the scrolls between the bosses are, evolutionarily speaking, components of a mask, any similarity with such a motif is gone.

47. References in Appendix 1.
48. Ibid. For a list of typologically related specimens, see Appendix 2.
49. Karlgren 1949, pl. 37.

In the second stylistic group of southern *nao* descended from the Xujiafan bell, all decoration is executed as sunken lines on the same plane. Yet we may observe the same stylistic progression as in the first group: from the mask-like motif of the Xujiafan *nao*, via symmetrical tiers of spirals with two bulging eyes in the center, as on the bell from Sanmudi, Ningxiang (Hunan) (fig. 64),[50] to a scroll pattern with two symmetrical groups of bosses (*mei*), as on the *nao* from Yangze, Jian'ou (Fujian) (fig. 65).[51] Curiously, at the final stage represented by the Yangze *nao*, two groups of nine bosses have again appeared on each side of the bell, no more and no less.[52] How this number was determined and whether it has any particular significance is unknown.[53]

The bells of the second group (average height 63.7 cm) are, on the whole, much larger in size than those of the first (average height 37.4 cm), though the stylistically more advanced pieces in the first group also show a marked increase in size. This size difference between the bells of the two groups seems to correlate with the presence or absence of *xuan*: none of the specimens in the first group has a *xuan*,[54] whereas all of those in the second group do.[55] Given their smaller size and the absence of *xuan*, the first group may be considered somewhat more conservative than the second and also, perhaps, a little earlier in date.

As the *xuan* became a universal feature on south Chinese *nao*, *xuan*-less *nao* with raised-line ornaments disappeared; *nao* with *xuan* and sunken-line decoration, on the other hand, feed into later *nao* sequences and ultimately into *yong-zhong*.

---

50. References in Appendix 1. For a list of typologically related specimens, see Appendix 2.

51. References in Appendix 1.

52. The only exception is an unprovenienced *nao* in the Hunan Provincial Museum, Changsha (photo in Gao Zhixi 1984a, pl. 91), which, on each face, features two panels with four rows of bosses (two rows of two and two of three). This highly atypical effort seems to be the product of a far-removed local workshop.

53. According to Chen Mengjia, the bosses developed out of the bulging eyes of earlier mask motifs, which were filled with geometrical ornaments and distorted in shape. The ubiquitous two groups of nine bosses may have arisen from a fan-like arrangement of three groups of three spliced-up masks that were laid atop one another along a central axis of symmetry. The tendency to multiply the mask motifs in the central panel can also be observed on early southern *bo* bells. As an alternative theory, Gao Zhixi (1984b, 132 [English translation p. 293]) has proposed that the predecessors of the *mei* bosses may be found in rows of minuscule round protrusions adorned with sunken-line whorls (*jiongwen*), which may be seen placed around the central decorative panel of some southern *nao* and *bo* bells (see fig. 77). Both ideas have some plausibility.

54. This holds true not only for now-extant *nao* but also for specimens of comparable decor (formerly in the Song imperial collection) depicted in *Bogutulu* (reference in Appendix 2). All other *nao* in *Bogutulu* have *xuan*.

55. The only exception to the apparent correlation of raised-line decoration and lack of *xuan* is the *xuan*-less *nao* from Huangmasai, Xiangxiang (Hunan) (references in Appendix 1), which is ornamented by sunken-line volutes; the arrangement of these spirals, however, significantly differs from that on other specimens with sunken-line ornamentation, such as that in fig. 65. Perhaps this transitional piece is an early local effort.

a                                                 b

FIGURE 64. *Above: Nao* excavated
in 1973 at Sanmudi, Ningxiang
(Hunan). Local culture contemporary to late Shang, probably
twelfth–eleventh century B.C. *a,*
frontal view; *b,* side view.

FIGURE 65. *Right: Nao* excavated
in 1978 at Yangze, Jian'ou (Fujian). Local culture contemporary
to late Shang, probably twelfth–
eleventh century B.C.

## The Invention of Yongzhong

By pursuing the typological sequence of *nao* bells somewhat further, we shall be able to pinpoint the time and place where the two-tone phenomenon was initially realized and the major chime-bell type of the Zhou dynasty, the *yongzhong*, came into being.

### Changes in Nao *Shape and Ornamentation*

We may now turn to a group of *nao* that on a stylistic basis clearly appears to be posterior to those described above. The vast majority of these, as well as the earliest *yongzhong*, have been excavated in the Xiang River valley of Hunan and adjacent parts of Jiangxi. After the peak in size and massiveness represented by such pieces as those in figures 58 and 64, the size of *nao* decreased considerably to an average height of ca. 30–40 cm. At the same time, the proportions of the resonating bodies of *nao* became somewhat more elongated, and the surface decoration changed. While on the face of the bells in figures 63–65, spirals and bosses (*mei*) are arranged in seven rows, they are reduced to five rows on later specimens, such as the *nao* from Liling (Hunan) (fig. 66):[56] three rows of bosses with two intervening horizontal *zhuanjian* tiers. The bosses consequently increased both in size and in visual prominence, assuming the "round hammer" shape characteristic for bosses on *yongzhong*. The five horizontal registers were marked off by low ridges prefiguring the *zhuan* in the standard *zhong* decoration scheme. Later, these ridges became wider and more massive or were replaced by wide sunken lines of a similar visual effect.

In the center of the bell-face of *nao*, between the two symmetric fields of bosses separated by *zhuanjian* tiers, a vertical ornamentation panel came into its own. The central ridge between the two ornamental panels (which was the location of a casting seam) was first emphasized as three parallel raised lines, as on the *nao* from Liling (fig. 66). Subsequently, it was transformed into a molded, tongue-shaped motif, as on the *nao* from Xiajiashan, Leiyang (Hunan) (fig. 67).[57] Still later, this part of the bell-face was cleared of all decorative elements, remaining as an empty field in the center of the bell, as on the *nao* excavated at Huangzhu, Zhuzhou (Hunan) (fig. 68);[58] on late Western Zhou *yongzhong* from the metropolitan workshops, this central panel was to become the preferred location of inscriptions.

The ornamentation of the last-mentioned *nao* thus virtually conforms to the standard *zhong* decoration scheme, except that the *gu*, the portion between the

---

56. In my treatment of the latest *nao*, I basically follow Gao Zhixi's proposed stylistic sequence. For a list of all typologically related specimens, see Appendix 2.

57. References in Appendix 1.

58. Ibid.

FIGURE 66. *Above, left: Nao* from Liling (Hunan) (exact locus of excavation unknown). Local culture contemporary to late Shang and early Western Zhou, probably eleventh–tenth century B.C.

FIGURE 67. *Above, right: Nao* excavated in 1980 at Xiajiashan, Leiyang (Hunan). Local culture contemporary to late Shang and early Western Zhou, probably eleventh–tenth century B.C.

FIGURE 68. *Right: Nao* excavated in 1981 at Huangzhu, Zhuzhou (Hunan). Local culture contemporary to early Western Zhou, probably tenth century B.C.

sound-bow and the area enclosed by *zhuan*, is still considerably narrower than in *yongzhong* (see fig. 69). We can see, however, that the small secondary mask motif seen on the thickened striking platforms of southern *nao* is the forerunner of the *gu* ornamentation in *yongzhong*. In the *nao* from Liling, for example (fig. 66), the ornamentation in the center of the *gu* has been reduced to an abstract configuration of spirals in two tiers, identical to what is seen in the earliest *yongzhong* (see figs. 69, 71–72). As the proportions of the bell-body became more elongated, the visual importance of the *gu* portion increased.

On the *nao* in figures 67 and 68, the striking platform in the center of the sound-bow is no longer thickened. This, in accordance with the physical principles discussed in Chapter 2, very probably indicates that the existence of the two-tone phenomenon was already known to the casters of the last southern *nao*.

## The Transition from Nao to Yongzhong

*Nao* grade into *yongzhong*. The only morphological difference lies in the presence, in *yongzhong*, of a small suspension ring, the *wo*, which was laterally affixed to the *xuan*. This innovation decisively altered the mode in which the bells were installed: instead of standing on their *yong* with the mouth facing upward, they were now suspended obliquely with the mouth facing down.

It is possible that, before the *wo* was invented, *nao* had been hung in a similar fashion by means of ropes slung around the *xuan*, as is indeed suggested by the fact that in early *yongzhong*, the shape of the *wo* often imitates a piece of rope or cord, which perhaps, as proposed by Barnard, is the remnant of an actual piece of rope used in fashioning the mold.[59] In any case, such a manner of hanging must have been somewhat precarious; a fixed *wo* of metal was an undeniable improvement,[60] which may explain why, with the transition to *yongzhong*, the fabrication of *nao* abruptly ended.[61] Later kinds of chime-bells mounted with the mouth facing upward (the *goudiao* of the Lower Yangzi region and the far

59. Barnard 1987 (see Chapter 3, above).
60. Various kinds of suspension modes have been reconstructed by Tong Kin-woon 1983–84 pt. 2:136–42.
61. Wu Hung (n. d., sec. 5) suggests that *nao* and *yongzhong* were produced side by side with each other for some time in the south. He takes the *yongzhong* from Datang, Xincheng (Guangxi) (references in Appendix 1), which seems to have had its *wo* deliberately removed, as showing a lingering preference for *nao* in the more remote regions. We have noted above (n. 30) that the *nao* from Nanya is a clear instance of such a phenomenon. Nevertheless, it appears highly unlikely that *nao* continued to be manufactured in the same workshops that produced *yongzhong*. Wu Hung also believes that southern *nao* with faint, raised-line decor came into being as a result of re-diffusion of similarly ornamented *yongzhong* from the north. This belief apparently stems from the impression, justifiable at the time of Wu's writing, that *yongzhong* with this type of decoration do not occur in the south, a misconception that should have been laid to rest by the publication of the Chang'anxiang *yongzhong* in 1985 (references in Appendix 1).

southern provinces) are not descended directly from the southern *nao* of Shang and early Western Zhou.

The invention of the *wo* was probably triggered by the discovery of the two-tone phenomenon. As we have discussed previously (Chapter 2), it was crucial for the player of a two-tone bell to hit the exact striking points of the A- and B-tones to obtain acoustically optimal results. In a *nao* mounted with the mouth facing upward, the player will find it somewhat difficult to see the bell-face because of the bell's upward-tapering resonating body (unless we suppose that *nao* players were positioned *underneath* the bells, which seems unlikely). Contrastingly, when a bell of the same shape is suspended from a *wo*, the bell-face is tilted toward the performer, who then has much better control over where the mallet hits the bell surface.

That both A- and B-tones were used musically even in the earliest *yongzhong* is corroborated by markers designating the striking point of the B-tone. These markers are usually in the shape of a bird; occasionally a round whorl, a dragon, or a small elephant appears instead. From the player's point of view, they were placed to the right side (very rarely to the left) of the central *gu* ornament.

Designed to fully bring out the peculiar acoustic properties of bells of almond-shaped cross-section, *yongzhong* became the quintessential musical bells of ancient China. In their earliest archaeological contexts in the south, however, the newly invented *yongzhong* do not seem to have served a function different from that of their *nao* predecessors. They, too, are usually found in caches, for the most part as single bells without any accompanying artifacts; they almost never occur in southern funerary contexts.[62]

Stylistic similarities between the latest *nao* and the earliest *yongzhong* types are so considerable that it is tempting to perceive the two as a single class of bells.[63] Two slightly different types of southern *nao* developed into two types of *yongzhong*, which apparently coexisted in the period (perhaps produced by different workshops). In the first type, the principal ornamentation is executed in sunken lines, as in the *nao* from Huangzhu introduced above (see fig. 68). The decoration on the corresponding *yongzhong* type, as on the piece from Pingru, Xiangxiang (Hunan) (fig. 69),[64] differs from that of the *nao* prototypes in but one respect: instead of preserving the formerly arched and pointed contours of the

---

62. The *yongzhong* from Lianhua (reference in Appendix 1) is the only early southern bell to have been unearthed from a tomb; but that tomb dates only to the later part of Eastern Zhou. The bell's archaic decoration style makes it appear likely that it is an heirloom of much earlier date.

63. In taking the presence of the *wo* in defining a major typological break, I follow Chen Mengjia 1955–56, pt. 5 and Hayashi 1980. In his most recent work, Hayashi (1984) has classified the small Shang metropolitan *nao* (*shō* [*zheng*] 鉦) apart from the class of *shō* (*zhong* 鐘) that includes large southern *nao* as well as *yongzhong*.

64. References in Appendix 1.

FIGURE 69. *Yongzhong* excavated in 1982 at Pingru, Xiangxiang (Hunan). Local culture contemporary to early Western Zhou, probably tenth century B.C.

FIGURE 70. *Nao* in the Arthur M. Sackler Gallery, Smithsonian Institution, Washington, D.C., acc. no. S1987.278. Local Middle Yangzi culture contemporary to early Western Zhou, probably tenth century B.C.

central vertical panel of the *zheng*, the panel is enclosed by straight-line *zhuan* ridges on all four sides.

In the second type of *nao* that grades into an equivalent *yongzhong* type, essentially the same design is reduced to patterns of faint raised lines (fig. 70). The pronounced *zhuan* ridges are replaced by bands of dotted circlets. The *zhuanjian* are filled with elegant spirals. On the *nao* of this group, only the flat bottom (in *yongzhong*, the flat top [*wu*]) is ornamented with scrollwork in deep sunken lines. As in the *nao* from Huangzhu (see fig. 68), the central portion of the sound-bow is no longer thickened, though the raised-line decoration on that part of the bells is delineated by faint ridges. The erstwhile mask motif decorating this portion of the bell seems to have developed into two symmetrically

FIGURE 71. *Yongzhong* from Cheng-tan, Liuyang (Hunan). Local culture contemporary to early Western Zhou, probably tenth century B.C.

arranged groups of large volutes.[65] The corresponding *yongzhong* type is represented in the south by the bell from Chang'anxiang, Hengyang (Hunan).[66]

On a group of similar *yongzhong*, for example in a specimen from Dengtan, Liuyang (Hunan) (fig. 71),[67] the dotted circlets surrounding the ornamented parts of the *zheng* were transformed into small protruding studs. This stylistic feature, which is never seen on *nao* from this region, was probably introduced after the transition from *nao* to *yongzhong*. *Yongzhong* of this type are considerably more common in the south than specimens featuring bands of faint circlets.

These three earliest types of *yongzhong* must date to a time approximately corresponding to middle Western Zhou in north China, the period when quantities of these three types of *yongzhong* suddenly show up archaeologically in Shaanxi. Their typically southern geometrical decoration style contrasts with the animal-derived ornamentation characteristic of the metropolitan Zhou bronze workshops of that period. This southern ornamentation, as well as the apparent

65. To date, this type is best documented by unprovenienced *nao* in art-historical publications, e.g., one in the Zhang Naiji collection, one in a private collection in New York, and one in the Sackler Collections. These and recently excavated specimens that probably belong to this type are listed and referenced in Appendix 2.

66. References in Appendix 1. For a list of typologically related specimens, see Appendix 2. The Chang'anxiang bell much resembles the First Xing–*yongzhong* (fig. 19), though lacking, of course, an inscription.

67. References in Appendix 1. For a list of typologically related specimens, see Appendix 2.

nonexistence, in that part of north China, of the antecedent *nao* types (contrasting with their abundance in the archaeologically much less well-known Yangzi region), makes it appear certain that *yongzhong* were diffused northward after the transformation of *nao* into *yongzhong* had been completed in the south.[68] Although we still know very little about the local cultures of the Yangzi River region, all the available evidence indicates that this was where the *yongzhong* was invented and the two-tone phenomenon discovered.

## Intermezzo

We have followed the evolution of Chinese chime-bell types through the first three steps in the sequence outlined at the beginning of this chapter. The path from the first use of metal in making bells to the first useable two-pitch bells was a circuitous one. Slowly, and by no means purposefully, the morphological characteristics of the classical Zhou dynasty chime-bell types emerged over several centuries. The oldest of these characteristics is the almond-shaped cross-section, which goes back at least to the first Neolithic attempts at casting bells. The round, hollow shank appeared next, but without the *xuan* and the *wo*, which were added in sequence later. The standard *zhong* decoration scheme seems ultimately derived from the mask motif seen on Anyang *nao*, though that mask appears changed beyond recognition in the Zhou dynasty *yongzhong*. It may be doubted whether in Zhou times this decor was still conceived of as a mask; if so, one might have to look for an explanation as to why it was positioned upside down on the *yongzhong*, just as it was on the Anyang period *ling* discussed at the beginning of this chapter.

In tracing the above typological developments, we have traveled from Shanxi and Henan to southern China, straddling two quite different cultural traditions that put bells to different uses. The first *yongzhong*, though indirectly derived from chime-bells (namely, from the Anyang *nao*), do not appear to have been chime-bells themselves; like their antecedent southern *nao*, they were apparently always produced as single pieces.[69] In the following chapter, the stage shifts northward again: to Shaanxi, where *yongzhong* were first manufactured as chimed sets.

68. Hayashi 1980, 28.

69. Two southern sites have each yielded two *yongzhong*: Hongjiaqiao, Xiangtan (Hunan), and Pengjiaqiao, Pingxiang (Jiangxi); three *yongzhong* of different types were found at Huaibiaoshan, Zigui (Hubei) (references in Appendix 1). Otherwise, there is no evidence for early southern attempts at grouping bells of this kind into sets. The only known southern set of three *yongzhong*, found at Jishui (Jiangxi), seems to be late in date (perhaps as late as a time corresponding to the Springs and Autumns period), judging by the very long *mei*, in spite of its deceptively early-looking studded *zhuan*. (Compare the *yongzhong* from Pengshan, Lianping [Guangdong].) References in Appendix 1.

# CHAPTER FIVE

# Perfection and Decline

## Chime-Bells of the Zhou Dynasty

The vast majority of mainstream Zhou dynasty musical bells dates to two distinct periods: the late Western Zhou (ca. 885–771 B.C.) and the transition from the Springs and Autumns to the Warring States (ca. 550–400 B.C.). The relative lack of evidence from the intervening two centuries may be due in part to accidents of archaeological discovery, but it is also possible that political and economic circumstances in the early Springs and Autumns period caused a temporary decline in (or a decrease in the scale of) the Zhou bronze industry (including bell manufacture)—a trend that was reversed with the emergence of new technologies during the sixth century B.C. (see Chapter 3). Eastern Zhou court orchestras contained chimed sets of bells of three classes: *yongzhong*, *bo*, and *niuzhong* (see figs. 26–28).[1] These different kinds of bells have quite heterogeneous roots. *Yongzhong* originated from southern *nao*, as detailed in the preceding chapter. Both *bo* and *niuzhong*, on the other hand, were enlarged and clapperless versions of *ling* clapper-bells.[2] Like the *yongzhong*, *bo* came into being in the area south of the Yangzi in the time corresponding to the late Shang and early Western Zhou. *Niuzhong*, however, were of north Chinese origin and did not emerge until the very end of Western Zhou. In their decoration, the earliest *yongzhong*, *bo*, and *niuzhong* were completely distinct from one another. During

---

1. Besides these three kinds, some late Springs and Autumns to early Warring States period tombs (Liulige tomb no. 60, Liulige tomb *jia*, and Shanbiaozhen tomb no. 1 [references in Appendix 1]) yielded separate sets of a fourth kind of bell, intermediate between *niuzhong* and *bo* (see n. 45). Moreover, some Springs and Autumns period tombs in eastern China have yielded one each of *chunyu* and *zheng* in association with complete sets of other types of musical bells (see Appendix 3).

2. Another analogous process of *ling*-like clapper bells evolving into much larger clapperless bells occurred in Japan during the Yayoi period (ca. 250 B.C.–A.D 250): the transformation of small

the first half of Eastern Zhou, however, the standard *zhong* decoration scheme, formerly restricted to *yongzhong*, was gradually adopted on *bo* and *niuzhong*, so that bells of the three classes came to look more and more alike. In time, that mode of layout itself became an icon by which bells could be recognized as such; it appears even on some kinds of nonmusical bells and on nonfunctional *mingqi* bells.

In the following, we shall take up each of the three principal classes of Zhou musical bells in turn, discussing their development in the Western Zhou and early Springs and Autumns period. We shall then trace later Eastern Zhou developments jointly for all three kinds of bells, concluding with an analysis of the demise of the Zhou bell-manufacturing tradition after the mid–Warring States period.

## *Western Zhou and Early Eastern Zhou* Yongzhong *in North China*
### *The Northward Diffusion of* Yongzhong

Soon after their invention in the south, *yongzhong* first appeared in the Zhou heartland in Shaanxi. The earliest northern specimens date to the middle Western Zhou, probably to around the end of the tenth century B.C. Before that time, Anyang-type *nao* had apparently been used at the Zhou court; only one of these has so far been found archaeologically in Shaanxi,[3] but Hayashi Minao has classed some unprovenienced *nao* that differ slightly in their proportions from ordinary Anyang pieces as dating to Western Zhou.[4] It thus appears conceivable that the Zhou continued the tradition of Shang court music from the Anyang period, though at present we know too little about early Zhou music to affirm this with certainty.

It is probably no accident that the *yongzhong* entered the metropolitan cultural repertoire at the time of what seems to have been a major restructuring of Zhou ritual. We know frustratingly little about that mid–Western Zhou reform, which is not documented in surviving historical texts, but we can see its reflec-

---

horse-bells of Korean origin (and probably derived from Chinese Bronze Age *ling*) into the *dōtaku*, which, like the Chinese *bo*, were single bells of enormous size with prominent flanges and suspension devices (Umehara 1927).

3. This specimen was discovered at the middle Western Zhou tomb no. 13 at Zhuyuangou, Baoji (Shaanxi) (references in Appendix 1); the original report supposes it to have been an heirloom imported from Anyang in an earlier period.

4. Hayashi 1984 2:391, *shō* 21–28. No musical instruments at all have so far been reported from early- and mid–Western Zhou archaeological contexts. An indicator of continuities from the Shang, however, is the presence of sets of chimestones (*qing*) at some late Western Zhou sites in Shaanxi: Shaochen, Fufeng (*Kaogu yu Wenwu* 1987 [6]:84–86, 65; also in *Chūgoku Sensei-shō Hōkei-shi Shūgen bunbutsuten*: 108–9 [cat. no. 35]), Hejiacun, Qishan (*Kaogu* 1976 [1]:31–38), and Shangguancun, Baoji (*Wenwu* 1982 [2]:53–55; *Wenwu* 1984 [6]:18–20). As far as we known, such instruments were unknown in the southern local cultures, whereas they were a hallmark of dynastic court music in both Shang and Eastern Zhou times.

tions in all aspects of the material record. As will be discussed more fully in Chapter 9, ritual music was one of the facets of Zhou court culture that underwent fundamental change at that time, and the demise of Anyang-type *nao* seems to have been part and parcel of this development.

In Shaanxi, *yongzhong* were employed in ways differing radically from their previous usages in southern cultural contexts. From the start, they were assembled into chimed sets (table 8), analogous to those of the Anyang period *nao* and chimestones (*qing* 磬); they were played as musical instruments in a ritual orchestra. We may speculate that before chimed sets of *yongzhong* were manufactured as such in Shaanxi, bells emitting different tones were haphazardly combined into chimes; in fact, this may already have been done in Shang times (e.g., in the composite set of *nao* found in Fu Hao's tomb, discussed in the previous chapter [fig. 56]).

Arguing from analogy with Eastern Zhou customs, we might assume that, at the time of their diffusion from the south, the *yongzhong* would have been accompanied by their players. On the other hand, because the function of these bells in the south had not been, strictly speaking, a musical one, specialized bell-playing musicians may not have existed. Instead of adopting southern music wholesale, the Zhou immediately and completely adapted the foreign bells to their own preexisting musical tradition. Evidently, these bells catered to a Zhou need; they must have been perceived as superior to whatever had previously fulfilled a comparable function in Zhou court music.

The exact political circumstances of bell diffusion from south to north remain unclear. In any case, the appearance of southern *yongzhong* at the Zhou court emphatically does not prove the conquest of the bell-producing areas by the Zhou.[5] Even though the Zhou undertook several large-scale military campaigns to the south, notably under Zhao Wang 昭王 (trad. r. dates: 1052–1002),[6] the geographic scope of such Zhou forays into southern territory does not seem to have extended beyond the Han and Huai river valleys. The area south of the Yangzi, where most of the southern nao and *yongzhong* have been found, remained far beyond the reach of any direct Western Zhou political impact. Although it appears likely that bells were acquired as tribute or diplomatic gifts (the prevalent form of exchange in ancient China),[7] it is by no means certain that the Zhou received them directly from their original producers.

Sets of *yongzhong* exactly imitating the shape of southern pieces were manufactured in Shaanxi very soon after their first diffusion. One may wonder whether the bronzesmiths at the Zhou court learned the technical know-how of

5. *Pace* Hsu and Linduff 1988, 214–24, whose point was prefigured by Karlgren 1935, 142.
6. Creel 1970, 233–36.
7. Chang 1975.

TABLE 8. The Number of Components in Archaeologically Excavated Bell-Chimes and Lithophones

*I. Numerical Data*

| Number of pieces in chime | Western Zhou yongzhong (N. China) | | Eastern Zhou yongzhong | | Eastern Zhou niuzhong | | Eastern Zhou bo | | Eastern Zhou chimestones | |
|---|---|---|---|---|---|---|---|---|---|---|
| | N | % | N | % | N | % | N | % | N | % |
| 1 | 11 | 32 | 3 | 8 | 1 | 2 | 2 | 8 | | |
| 2 | 9 | 26 | 1 | 3 | 1 | 2 | 1 | 4 | | |
| 3 | 3 | 9 | 1 | 3 | | | 2 | 8 | | |
| 4 | 7 | 21 | 2 | 6 | 3 | 7 | 7 | 29 | | |
| 5 | | | 5 | 14 | 1 | 2 | 3 | 13 | 1 | 4 |
| 6 | 1 | 3 | 1 | 3 | 3 | 7 | 1 | 4 | | |
| 7 | 1 | 3 | 1 | 3 | 3 | 7 | 1 | 4 | | |
| 8 | 2 | 6 | 7 | 19 | 2 | 5 | 3 | 13 | 1 | 4 |
| 9 | | | 7 | 19 | 19 | 46 | 4 | 17 | | |
| 10 | | | 2 | 6 | 2 | 5 | | | 8 | 34 |
| 11 | | | 1 | 3 | 1 | 2 | | | 5 | 22 |
| 12 | | | 3 | 8 | | | | | 3 | 13 |
| 13 | 1 | 3 | | | 1 | 2 | | | 3 | 13 |
| 14 | | | | | 4 | 10 | | | | |
| 15+ | | | 2 | 6 | | | | | 2 | 9 |
| | 34 | | 36 | | 41 | | 24 | | 23 | |

*II. Histogram*

| Number of pieces in chime | Western Zhou yongzhong (N. China) | Eastern Zhou yongzhong | Eastern Zhou niuzhong | Eastern Zhou bo | Eastern Zhou chimestones |
|---|---|---|---|---|---|
| 1 | xxxxxxxxxx | xxx | x | x | |
| 2 | xxxxxxxxx | x | x | x | |
| 3 | xxx | x | | xx | |
| 4 | xxxxxxx | xx | xxx | xxxxxxx | |
| 5 | | xxxxx | x | xxx | x |
| 6 | x | x | xxx | x | |
| 7 | x | x | xxx | x | |
| 8 | xx | xxxxxxx | xx | xxx | x |
| 9 | | xxxxxxx | xxxxxxxxxxxxxxxxxxx | xxxx | |
| 10 | | xx | xx | | xxxxxxxx |
| 11 | | x | x | | xxxxx |
| 12 | | xxx | | | xxx |
| 13 | x | | x | | xxx |
| 14 | | | xxxx | | |
| 15+ | | xx | | | xx |

casting two-tone *yongzhong* from southern craftsmen who traveled to Shaanxi, but in my opinion there would have been little need for that: the whole process may have been triggered by a small number of imported sample bells. Middle Western Zhou bronze manufacture was highly developed. As in many cases of "stimulus diffusion" in world history, the Zhou adapted southern two-pitch bells with little attention to the original cultural context of what they had borrowed.[8] Anyway, "foreign experts" from the south could not have helped their metropolitan colleagues much in their major concern: designing two-tone *yongzhong* in tuned sets. Such scaling may have presented considerable technical difficulties at the beginning, and much experimentation must have preceded the emergence of the Zhou bell-chimes.

### Middle Western Zhou Yongzhong

Middle Western Zhou *yongzhong* from north China comprise specimens of the three earliest southern types described in the preceding chapter, distinguishable, respectively, by (1) sunken-line contours (*zhuan*) around the decorated area in the upper portion of the bell-face (see fig. 69), (2) decoration in faint raised lines and bands of circlets (see figs. 70 and 19), and (3) decoration in faint raised lines and bands of small studs (see fig. 71). In fact, it is virtually impossible to tell whether individual *yongzhong* of these early types found in the Zhou metropolitan area were locally made or imported from the south,[9] though chimes of *yongzhong* may be assumed to be of northern manufacture. Sometimes, on the other hand, chimes may have been assembled initially by combining bells of heterogeneous origins. The earliest archaeologically datable finds in Shaanxi are several three-part sets of bells, all excavated from middle Western Zhou tombs. One such chime was found at Puducun, Chang'an (fig. 72),[10] and two at the important necropolis of the lords of Yu 強 at Baoji.[11] A similar set of three was excavated at Weizhuang, Pingdingshan (Henan);[12] though little is known about the archaeological context, this discovery shows that chimes of mid–Western

8. Kroeber 1940.
9. All inscribed specimens can be connected with the Zhou court aristocracy; moreover, chimed sets of bells of these types are, most probably, of north Chinese manufacture.
10. References in Appendix 1. For a list of typologically related specimens, see Appendix 2.
11. These are the chimes from Rujiazhuang tomb no. 1 and Zhuyuangou tomb no. 7; references in Appendix 1. Interestingly, each of these three-part sets of bells features specimens of two stylistic types, the smallest one in each case being considerably less ornate than the two larger ones. Possibly, these chimes were composed of pieces of heterogeneous origin, an impression that is corroborated in the case of the Zhuyuangou chime by the tone distribution and by the fact that the metal composition varies enormously among the three pieces (see table 6). The Yu bells may be a bit earlier in date than the stylistically more uniform Puducun set (fig. 72).
12. References in Appendix 1.

FIGURE 72. Set of three *yongzhong* excavated in 1954 at Puducun, Chang'an (Shaanxi). Middle Western Zhou period (first half of tenth century B.C.).

Zhou bells were not entirely limited to Shaanxi.[13] The majority of these bells feature the decoration type in which the *zhuan* ridges take the form of rows of small studs. The fact that the number of bells per set is three in each case might prompt speculations about possible continuity with respect to three-part sets of Shang dynasty *nao*; however, several four-part sets of *yongzhong* of the three earliest types have also been excavated from later hoards.[14]

Most archaeologically provenienced Western Zhou *yongzhong* have been found in hoards of ritual bronzes that in all likelihood were hastily buried when the Zhou court moved east in 771 B.C.; they contain temple inventories accumulated over many generations. Frequently, bells of several types are found in the

13. Single specimens of mid–Western Zhou *yongzhong* have also been found in Shanxi province, e.g., at Qucun, Quwo (references in Appendix 1). As noted previously (ch. 1, n. 48), *yongzhong* of later Western Zhou types are, by contrast, curiously absent from the archaeological record in areas outside the metropolitan area.

14. See the list of typologically related specimens in Appendix 2. The great differences in size between the second and third pieces within the Puducun and Rujiazhuang sets, as well as the typological heterogeneity already noted (see n. 11 above), make it appear possible that these three-part sets may not have been complete.

same hoard; the famous hoard no. 1 at Zhuangbai, Fufeng (Shaanxi), for example (see fig. 14), yielded twenty *yongzhong* that belonged to at least six chimed sets, representing four different stylistic types.[15] Because they constituted part of the furnishings of the same temple, such multiple sets of bells of heterogeneous origins and dates may yet have been used jointly during ceremonies (see Chapter 6).

Placing long inscriptions on bells was another Western Zhou innovation. The inscriptions, which ordinarily were placed in the central *zheng* panel and the *gu* portions of the bell-face, were generally similar in form and content to those on ritual vessels. Such inscriptions occur on some *yongzhong* of the earliest types, proving beyond doubt that bells of these types were in fact manufactured in the north.[16] A good example is the First Xing–*yongzhong* from hoard no. 1 at Zhuangbai (see fig. 19), whose inscription we have discussed in Chapter 1.[17] This bell features faint line decoration and *zhuan* of framed bands of circlets. The characters are placed in a grid of faint raised lines—a fairly secure indicator for a mid–Western Zhou date,[18] which in this case can be corroborated by other epigraphic evidence.

## *Late Western Zhou* Yongzhong

The "abstract" decoration of the three early types described above seems to have gone out of fashion toward the end of middle Western Zhou; the *zhuan* henceforth were executed as massive raised ridges. Fairly radical changes in the exterior appearance of Western Zhou *yongzhong* seem to have occurred over a relatively brief period. Late Western Zhou *yongzhong* are decorated with the sorts of zoomorphic designs typical of other Zhou bronzes. Two additional *yongzhong* sets from Zhuangbai, also inscribed by Xing of Wei (see fig. 74), though they represent later Western Zhou types must date to within the same generation as the First Xing–*yongzhong*. It is possible that, for a time, *yongzhong* in the mid–Western Zhou style continued to be manufactured concurrently with specimens of the new types, perhaps in different workshops.[19]

15. The important epigraphic finds in this hoard are partly discussed in Shaughnessy 1991.

16. Perhaps the earliest known *yongzhong* inscriptions are those on the *yongzhong* from Dongjucun, Fufeng (Shaanxi), and on the fourth set of *yongzhong* from Zhuangbai (references in Appendix 1). They consist of illegible marks in a script that may be distinct from Chinese writing as we know it; one may speculate (albeit admittedly with very little basis) that these bells were imported from the south and that their enigmatic characters pertain to an otherwise unknown southern writing system, though it is also possible that the markings had some sort of musical significance.

17. References in Appendix 1.

18. This feature can also be seen on some ritual vessels; it has not been observed on bells other than the First Xing–*yongzhong*.

19. The unprovenienced bells inscribed by the donor Zha 戱 provide another example of the same kind. The First Zha–*yongzhong* is of the early type in which the *zhuan* take the form of rows of

FIGURE 73. Shicheng-*yongzhong* excavated in 1974 at Qiangjiacun, Fufeng (Shaanxi). Early part of late Western Zhou (mid-ninth century B.C.).

Figures 73 and 74 illustrate the two most important late Western Zhou *yongzhong* types (see also figs. 18 and 33). Some of the most impressive chime-bells of the Chinese Bronze Age belong to these two types; almost all of them are inscribed and hence of interest as historical documents. It appears that in late Western Zhou, a chime of *yongzhong* ordinarily consisted of eight pieces (see table 8), the two largest of which always lacked B-tone markers (see fig. 110). Their musical properties will be considered in Chapter 7.

The decoration of the Shi Cheng–*yongzhong* from hoard no. 1 at Qiangjiacun, Fufeng (fig. 73),[20] is still somewhat reminiscent of the earlier type represented by figure 69, especially in its *gu* ornament, which consists of symmetrical groups of four linked volutes. The *zhuan*, however, are executed as raised

---

little studs (see figs. 71 and 72), whereas the Second Zha–*yongzhong*, which was probably cast by the same donor, belongs to a later type (here represented by fig. 73). A *gui* cast by the same individual (Hayashi 1984 2:119, *ki* 319) allows cross-dating these bells to some time in the middle Western Zhou period (Hayashi 1980, 28).

20. References in Appendix 1. For a list of typologically related specimens, see Appendix 2.

FIGURE 74. One of the six bells of the third set of Xing-*yongzhong* from hoard no. 1 at Zhuangbai (see fig. 14). Early part of late Western Zhou (mid- to late ninth century B.C.).

ridges, and the decoration of the *zhuanjian* panels has changed from the abstract configurations of spirals seen in earlier specimens to a two-headed "Z-shaped dragon," a decorative motif similar to those encountered on contemporary ritual bronzes.[21] With a height of 76.5 cm, this is, incidentally, the largest *yongzhong* found in Shaanxi to date; the genealogical information in the inscription suggests a date in the reign of Li Wang (878 [trad.]–827).[22]

The next stage of stylistic development may be observed in figure 74, which shows one of the Third Xing–*yongzhong* from Zhuangbai.[23] Here, figurative decoration has taken possession not merely of the *zhuanjian* (whose decoration noticeably resembles that in figure 73) but also of the *gu*. The identity of the two symmetrical creatures decorating that portion of Western Zhou bells was for a long time enigmatic—they have been compared to birds and to elephants.[24] Recently, Hayashi Minao has convincingly demonstrated that they

21. This follows the nomenclature in Hayashi 1986, pls. 202–3.
22. Li Xueqin 1979, 31–32.
23. References in Appendix 1. For a list of typologically related specimens, see Appendix 2.
24. Rong Geng 1941 1:143–146.

are dragons (in his terminology, "downward-facing L-shaped dragons").[25] On the Third Xing–*yongzhong*, the B-tone marker replicates the shape of the dragons in the *gu* decoration motif. Although the decoration in figure 73 appears manifestly more primitive than that in figure 74, inscriptional evidence demonstrates that there was considerable chronological overlap between these two types of *yongzhong*.[26]

The shift from the abstract decoration characteristic of the south to the typical zoomorphic patterns of the metropolitan Zhou foundries illustrates a further step in the acculturation of the *yongzhong*. Such decoration as seen on the bells shown in figure 74 is ancestral to that of most Eastern Zhou musical bells. Operating within the rigid confines of the standard *zhong* decoration scheme, bell-makers came up with ever-different ways of adorning the resonating body. Notably, toward the end of Western Zhou, the protrusions and extremities of the L-shaped dragons in the *gu* portion tend to develop into little dragon-like creatures of their own, thus gradually multiplying the number of constituent zoomorphs. Ornament could also be applied to other portions of the bells; on the Nangong Hu–*yongzhong* from Baozigou, Fufeng (see fig. 33),[27] the *wo* takes the form of a three-dimensionally sculpted dragon with spiraled horns, and the shank is decorated with the "mountain pattern."

### Early Eastern Zhou Yongzhong

On late Western Zhou and especially on Eastern Zhou *yongzhong*, the *gu* became the principal focus of decoration. Ma Chengyuan has observed that over time the relative proportions of the bell surface occupied by the *gu* increased significantly.[28] Throughout the later history of the standard *zhong* decoration scheme, the iconography of the *gu* ornament is virtually limited to dragons, the ideological significance of which remains unknown.

The Qin Gong–*yongzhong* from Taigongmiao, Baoji (Shaanxi) (see fig. 110), datable by inscription to the first quarter of the seventh century, are the latest known representatives of the orthodox Western Zhou type.[29] On other contem-

---

25. Hayashi 1986, 118–19, pl. 175.

26. For instance, among the two known bells cast by Li Wang of Zhou mentioned in Chapter 1, the Wusi Hu–*yongzhong* resembles fig. 73, while the Hu–*yongzhong* resembles fig. 74.

27. References in Appendix 1. The dragon ornamenting the *gu* of this bell is structured somewhat differently from all others known; see Hayashi 1986, 180, pl. 5/132.

28. Ma Chengyuan 1979, 63–64. Ma includes statistics based on the rich holdings of the Shanghai Museum. One should note that the greatest usefulness of Ma's argument is for dating *yongzhong* of the mainstream Zhou types; it has been somewhat less convincingly employed in some recent archaeological reports (e.g., those on Leijiashan, *Jianghan Kaogu* 1980 [2]:95–96, and Ya'erzhou, *Jianghan Kaogu* 1984 [4]:38–47) dealing with *yongzhong* of southern local types (see Appendix 3).

29. References in Appendix 1. As regards the reason for the stylistic conservatism of these Qin bells, one may speculate about the possibility that metropolitan Zhou workshop traditions survived

porary or even earlier pieces, the dragon ornaments in the *gu* portions can be seen to have undergone considerable change, either becoming so completely attenuated as to lose all zoomorphic resemblance, as in the *yongzhong* from the large tomb at Lijialou, Xinzheng (Henan) (fig. 75),[30] or multiplying in number, as on the unprovenienced Zheng Xing Shu–*yongzhong* (fig. 76).[31] The decoration of later Eastern Zhou bells, with their maze of dragons reduced to nearly geometric patterns, combines these two tendencies.

Whereas the Qin Gong–*yongzhong* seem to have formed, originally, an "orthodox" even-numbered set,[32] other Eastern Zhou sets are comprised of various numbers of bells (see table 8), some ranging to twelve and more pieces. Because not all excavated sets of bells are complete, it is difficult to determine a standard number; quite frequently, chimes seem to have been divided up before burial, and "half-sets" of four or five *yongzhong* may have played a role.[33] As will be discussed in Chapter 7, variation in the number of bells per chime reflects underlying changes in the musical nature of the bell-chimes.

## The Origins and Spread of Bo

In the Bronze Age cultures of the Middle Yangzi valley, small nonmusical *ling*, probably of north Chinese derivation, were adapted and transformed into huge hanging bells known to archaeologists as *bo*.[34] The earliest specimens have been found in Hunan; they show stylistic resemblance to the large *nao* found in the same area, such as the specimen from Yueshanpu (see fig. 58), discussed in the preceding chapter. This resemblance suggests a date corresponding to the Anyang period of Shang.

All known *bo* are clapperless, but the presence of round holes in the center of the flat top in some of the earliest pieces from the south has given rise to the

---

in the area of the former dynastic capital. Alternatively, these bells may simply be copies of Western Zhou pieces, then already ancient, that had either been handed down or excavated locally.

30. References in Appendix 1.

31. This piece was most recently in the Morse Collection, New York (*Spirit and Ritual*, 34).

32. Five pieces are now preserved, the two largest ones lacking B-tone markers; the inscription distribution suggests that the extant set is incomplete.

33. This is strongly suggested by the distribution of inscriptions on Western and early Eastern Zhou bells. The four Ni 逆–*yongzhong* from Haosihe, Yongshou (Shaanxi) (references in Appendix 1), whose inscription appears to render exactly one-half of a document, provide a good example. This subject is treated in detail in Falkenhausen 1988, ch 3.

34. The term *bo* 鎛 (which is often confused with *bo* 鏄, "hoe") is known from two inscriptions, both curiously on bells from the state of Qi: the Shu Yi–*bo*, formerly in the Song imperial collection (Guo Moruo 1958, 237/251/209), and the Ling-*bo*, now in the Museum of Chinese History, Beijing (Rong Geng 1941 2:969). Otherwise, bells of this shape are referred to in their inscriptions as *zhong* 鐘. The exact original meaning of the term *bo* is unknown; Hayashi Minao (1964, 281–86) has suggested that it denoted a subordinate class of *zhong*, which may have been a general term for all musical bells.

FIGURE 75. *Yongzhong* from a set of ten excavated in 1923 at Li-jialou, Xinzheng (Henan). Early Springs and Autumns period (late eighth or early seventh century B.C.).

FIGURE 76. Zheng Xing Shu-*yongzhong*, recently in the Morse Collection, New York. Terminal Western Zhou or early Springs and Autumns period (early to mid-eighth century B.C.).

suggestion that a wooden clapper might have been affixed through such holes to the suspension loop. A thin strut that sometimes connects the two sides of the loop (see fig. 79) may have served for suspending such a clapper.[35] Be that as it may, the *bo* had been assimilated to the clapperless musical bells of northern China by mid–Western Zhou times at the latest. In their early southern cultural contexts, *bo*, like their *nao* counterparts, always occur as single pieces; as far as we know, they were not combined into sets. Early *bo* are more frequently of round-oval than of almond-shaped cross-section; they do not seem to lend themselves to exploitation of the two-tone phenomenon.

Visually, with their elaborate lateral and central flanges and their sculpturally decorated suspension devices, the early south Chinese *bo* are among the most

35. Bagley 1987, 549 n. 5; Bagley credits Wu Hung with this suggestion. If it is correct, the earliest *bo* would have to be reclassified, either as *ling*, or under a special typological heading.

impressive bells of the Chinese Bronze Age. Figure 77 shows what seems to have been an early standard type;[36] perching on its flat top are two birds whose long tail-feathers descend the tapering sides of the resonating body, forming wide lateral flanges. Another, shorter flange in the shape of a long-tailed bird forms the nose of the mask decorating the center of the bell-face. Robert W. Bagley has shown that the northern prototype of this mask can be no later in date than the first half of the Anyang period.[37] A prominent feature of the decoration of many early *bo* are bands of alternating whorls and flowerets (Hayashi Minao's *jiongwen* 囧文),[38] which are a hallmark of the southern bronze-casting tradition.

*Bo* resembling that in figure 78 seem to have been the point of departure for a number of locally created specimens from southern Hunan and northern Guangxi. They all differ from one another in many details, the mask in most cases being rendered more abstractly than in figure 77.[39] The *bo* from Hengyang (fig. 78) also exemplifies a curious duplication of the central mask motif,[40] which goes hand in hand with narrowing bell proportions.

In another early type of *bo*, apparently of Hunan origin, the birds in the lateral flanges have been replaced by tigers (fig. 79).[41] This may have been the first *bo* type imitated in the Zhou heartland. On some specimens the mask motif adorning the bell-face has been transformed in such a way that it can be read as two symmetrically placed dragons, a feature that recurs on some late Western Zhou *bo* found in Shaanxi (see fig. 80). The same iconographic tendency is also observable on early *niuzhong* of north Chinese provenience.[42]

Because *bo* are much rarer than *yongzhong*, it is still difficult to say when they were first diffused into the Zhou metropolitan area. Like *yongzhong*, however, *bo* were locally produced as chimed sets soon after they were introduced into the metropolitan area. So far, the set of three uninscribed *bo* excavated at Yangjiacun, Mei Xian (Shaanxi) (fig. 80), in conjunction with at least ten *yongzhong* belonging to three different sets, is the only archaeologically provenienced such find of Western Zhou date.[43] With their tiger flanges, these *bo* resemble the southern piece in figure 79, but their suspension device is much more elaborate:

36. This bell is in the Sackler Gallery, Washington, D.C. (Bagley 1987, 537–51). No archaeologically provenienced specimens of this type are known so far; a list of related unprovenienced finds may be found in Appendix 2.

37. Bagley 1987, 543.

38. Hayashi 1980; the term *floweret* is from Bagley 1987, 537–51.

39. Gao Zhixi 1986.

40. *Wenwu* 1980 (11):95–96, pl. 8.3. For a list of other related specimens, see Appendix 2.

41. This bell is in the Sackler Gallery, Washington, D.C. (*Art from Ritual*, cat. no. 471). A list of the other specimens is in Appendix 2. Again, there are no archaeologically provenienced specimens; the one in the Hunan Provincial Museum is presumed to have been found within that province.

42. See Falkenhausen 1989b.

43. References in Appendix 1.

FIGURE 77. *Above, left: Bo* in the Arthur M. Sackler Gallery, Smithsonian Institution, Washington, D.C., acc. no. S1987.10. Local culture contemporary to late Shang, probably eleventh century B.C.

FIGURE 78. *Above, right: Bo* from Hengyang, Hunan (exact circumstances of excavation unknown). Local culture contemporary to late Shang and early Zhou, probably eleventh–ninth century B.C.

FIGURE 79. *Left:* "Tiger *bo*" in the Arthur M. Sackler Gallery, Smithsonian Institution, Washington, D.C., acc. no. S1987.36. Local Middle Yangzi culture contemporary with early to mid–Western Zhou, probably tenth–ninth century B.C.

FIGURE 80. One of a set of three *bo* excavated in 1985 at Yang-jiacun, Mei Xian (Shaanxi). *a*, line drawing; *b*, rubbing of the bell-face and the flat top (*wu*). Late Western Zhou (mid-ninth to early eighth century).

the loop emerges from the heads of two bird-like creatures. On later Western Zhou and early Eastern Zhou *bo*, the flanges and suspension devices are merged into an overarching, elaborate openwork crest. Good examples include the un-provenienced Ke-*bo*, which may be dated by inscription to the year 812,[44] and the Qin Gong–*bo* (early seventh century; fig. 81), a three-part set excavated together with the five Qin Gong–*yongzhong* mentioned above (see fig. 110).[45] Both the Ke-*bo* and the Qin Gong–*bo* bear inscriptions identical to those on sets of *yongzhong* commissioned by the same donors, indicating that *bo* and *yongzhong* were considered part of the same bell assemblage and that musicians played them jointly, despite the fact that the two classes of bells differed completely in their ornamentation.

During the mid- to late Springs and Autumns period, *bo* assumed many of the features characteristic of *yongzhong*, especially the standard *zhong* decoration

44. This bell is now in the Tianjin Museum. *Wenwu* 1972 (6):14, photo: pl. 6.
45. References in Appendix 1.

FIGURE 81. One of the three Qin Gong–*bo* (with its suspension hook), excavated in 1978 at Taigongmiao, Baoji (Shaanxi). Workshop of Qin, early Springs and Autumns period (probably reign of Wu Gong, 697–678 B.C.).

scheme. However, while the *mei* of *yongzhong* are cylindrical or "round hammer" shaped, those of *bo* are almost always globular in shape and often elaborately decorated. As one may see in the seventh-century specimens from Lijialou (fig. 82),[46] elaborate sculptural ornamentation is henceforth reserved for the suspension loop. Lateral flanges are no longer encountered after the seventh century; their removal may have been acoustically advantageous. Many later Eastern Zhou *bo* are of almond-shaped cross-section; perhaps it was now possible to produce two tones on *bo*. Later Eastern Zhou sets of *bo* comprise significantly more pieces (up to nine) than the three-piece sets of late Western and early Eastern Zhou (table 8).

## The First Niuzhong

The *niuzhong* emerged in the Zhou heartland at the end of Western Zhou, the result of another process of transformation of *ling* into larger, clapperless musical bells. Like *bo*, *niuzhong* were suspended vertically; the major morphological difference lies in the shape of the rim, which is typically flat in *bo* but curved upward in *niuzhong* (as in *yongzhong*); also, the *bo* generally have an elaborate and sculptural suspension device, whereas the *niuzhong* have simple loops similar to those of *ling*.[47] Unlike *bo*, *niuzhong* were from the outset assembled into chimed sets, in analogy to the metropolitan *yongzhong*; markers on many early pieces show that both A- and B-tones were used musically.

What appears to be the earliest set of *niuzhong* has been found in hoard no. 1 at Zhuangbai.[48] They seem to have originally been nonmusical clapper-bells that were secondarily incorporated into the ritual orchestra as an auxiliary set of chime-bells. Such bells subsequently increased in size, and in time the bell-faces were laid out in accordance with the standard *zhong* decoration scheme (fig. 83).[49] Chimes of nine pieces were the norm for *niuzhong* throughout the Springs and Autumns period (see table 8).

46. Ibid.
47. A few items of mixed *niuzhong* and *bo* attributes do exist, however. Because the few such "hybrid" bells with elaborate suspension devices and curved rims (see n. 1) are extremely close to typologically "pure" *bo*, they may be classed as a subtype of *bo*. The case of typological "hybrids" with simple loops and a level rim, however, is not so simple. Distinguishing on the basis of bell size, I regard as *bo* a number of relatively large bells with simple loops and level rims, dating to the Springs and Autumns period and apparently limited in distribution to the eastern seaboard (see Appendix 3 and fig. 146). This classification seems vindicated by the archaeological contexts: in three of the four tombs in Shandong that yielded such *bo* (Liujiadianzi, Dadian M1, and Fenghuangling [references in Appendix 1]), much smaller typologically "pure" *niuzhong* were also found. On the other hand, some later Eastern Zhou sets of small bells with the same mix of morphological features have been rubricized as variants of *niuzhong* (e.g., the specimens from Miaoqiancun, Wanrong [Shanxi] [reference in Appendix 1]).
48. References in Appendix 1. For a list of typologically related specimens, see Appendix 2.
49. The stylistic sequence of *niuzhong* is treated in some more detail in Falkenhausen 1989b.

FIGURE 82. *Left:* One of a set of four *bo* from Lijialou (see fig. 75).
Early Springs and Autumns period (seventh century B.C.).

FIGURE 83. *Right: Niuzhong* in the Art Institute of Chicago, mid–
Springs and Autumns period (seventh century B.C.).

## Yongzhong, Bo*, and* Niuzhong *in Eastern Zhou Times*
### Overall Trends

In Eastern Zhou it became de rigueur, at least among those of very high rank, to combine chimes—sometimes multiple chimes—of several kinds of musical bells into larger assemblages, which can be found archaeologically in tombs. Table 9 lists the sites in which combinations of two and three kinds of bells have been discovered together. Such bell assemblages seem to bespeak a much-increased sophistication of bell music; their sheer numbers provided a far greater quantity of tones than hitherto available (see Chapter 7). However, as we shall discuss more thoroughly in Chapter 6, no strict rules seem to have governed either the specific combinations chosen or the number of bells per set (see table 8).[50]

50. Wang Shimin 1988 seeks to establish some standards for Eastern Zhou times, but his conclusions still appear vague.

TABLE 9.  Archaeological Assemblages of Bell-Chimes and Lithophones

*First category: three or more chimes of bells, with or without chimestones.*
*Late Western Zhou through early Springs and Autumns*

Yangjiacun, Mei Xian (Shaanxi): 3 sets yongzhong (4/4/2), 3 bo

Zhuangbai, Fufeng (Shaanxi): 6 sets yongzhong (1/4 + 3/6/3/2/2), 7 proto-niuzhong ("chimed ling")

Lijialou, Xinzheng (Henan): 4 bo, 2 sets yongzhong (10/9)

*Second category: two chimes of bells, with or without chimestones.*
*Late Western Zhou through early Springs and Autumns*

Guanyang Gucheng, Haiyang (Shandong): 1 yong-zhong, 4 niuzhong

Shangcunling, Sanmenxia (Henan): 9 niuzhong, 1 zheng

Taigongmiao, Baoji (Shaanxi): 3 bo, 5 yongzhong

Zuiziqiancun, Haiyang (Shandong): 2 bo, 5 yong-zhong

*Third category: one chime of bells plus one or several sets of chimestones.*
*Late Western Zhou through early Springs and Autumns*

Zhangjiapo, Chang'an (Shaanxi), tomb no. 163: 2+ yongzhong, 5+ chimestones

*Mid–Springs and Autumns through early Warring States*

Fenshuiling, Changzhi (Shanxi), tomb no. 25: 4 bo, 5 yongzhong, 9 niuzhong, 10 chimestones

Houchuan, Sanmenxia (Henan), tomb no. 2040: 9 bo, 2 sets niuzhong (10/10)

Leigudun, Suizhou (Hubei), tomb no. 1: 4? sets yongzhong (12/11/12/10), 1 bo, 3 sets niuzhong (6/6/7), 32 chimestones

Liujiadianzi, Yishui (Shandong): 6 bo, 4 sets yong-zhong (9/7/3/1), 1 zheng, 1 chunyu

Liulige, Hui Xian (Henan), tomb no. 60: 4 large bo, 8 small bo, 8 yongzhong, 9 niuzhong, 11 chimestones

Liulige, Hui Xian (Henan), tomb no. 75: 4 bo, 8 yongzhong, 9 niuzhong, 10 chimestones

Liulige, Hui Xian (Henan), tomb jia: 4 large bo, 9 small bo, 8 yongzhong, 9 niuzhong, 11 chimestones

Luhe, Lucheng (Shanxi), tomb no. 7: 4 bo, 2 sets yongzhong (8/8), 8 niuzhong, 10 chimestones

Ximennei, Shou Xian (Anhui): 8 bo, 12 yongzhong, 9+ niuzhong, 1 chunyu, 1 zheng

*Mid–Springs and Autumns through early Warring States*

Beishanding, Dantu (Jiangsu): 5 bo, 7 niuzhong, chunyu, chimestones

Chengqiao, Luhe (Jiangsu), tomb no. 2: 5 bo, 7 niuzhong

Dadian, Junan (Shandong), tomb no. 1: 1 bo, 9 niuzhong

Fenghuangling, Linyi (Shandong): 9 bo, 9 niuzhong, 1 duo

Fenshuiling, Changzhi (Shanxi), tomb no. 14: 2 yongzhong, 8 niuzhong, 2 sets chimestones (11/11)

Fenshuiling, Changzhi (Shanxi), tomb no. 269: 9 yongzhong, 9 niuzhong, 10 chimestones

Fenshuiling, Changzhi (Shanxi), tomb no. 270: 8 yongzhong, 9 niuzhong, 11 chimestones

Hanshan, Leping (Jiangxi): 4 yongzhong, 6 niuzhong

Hougudui, Gushi (Henan): 8 bo, 9 niuzhong

Jinshengcun, Taiyuan (Shanxi), tomb no. 251: 2 sets bo (5/14), 14 chimestones

*Mid–Springs and Autumns through early Warring States:*

Chengcun, Linyi (Shanxi), tomb no. 1: 9 niuzhong, 10 chimestones

Chengcun, Linyi (Shanxi), tomb no. 2: 9 niuzhong, 10 chimestones

Dadian, Junan (Shandong), tomb no. 2: 9 niuzhong, 12 chimestones

Daifuguan, Linzi (Shandong): 9 yongzhong, 8 chimestones

Houchuan, Sanmenxia (Henan), tomb no. 2041: 9 niuzhong, 10 chimestones

Jiefanglu, Luoyang (Henan): 9 bells (type unspecified), 23 chimestones

Jiulidun, Shucheng (Anhui): 4 yongzhong, 5 chimestones

Shangmacun, Houma (Shanxi), tomb no. 13: 9 niuzhong, 10 chimestones

Xiasi, Xichuan (Henan), tomb no. 1: 9 niuzhong, 13 chimestones

Xiasi, Xichuan (Henan), tomb no. 10: 9 niuzhong, 13 chimestones

## Middle to late Warring States

Leigudun, Suizhou (Hubei), tomb no. 2: 2 sets yongzhong (8/28), 12 chimestones

Shanbiaozhen, Ji Xian (Henan), tomb no. 1: 5 large bo, 9 small bo, 10 chimestones

Tianjingwang, Ju Xian (Shandong): 3 bo, 6 zhong (type unclear)

Xiasi, Xichuan (Henan), tomb no. 2: 26 yongzhong, 8 bo?, 13 chimestones

Yangshan, Linqu (Shandong): 5 bo, 5 niuzhong

## Middle to late Warring States

Zangjiazhuang, Zhucheng (Shandong): 7 bo, 9 niuzhong, 13 chimestones

## Middle to late Warring States

Huangjiashan, Haiyan (Zhejiang): 13 yongzhong, 3 niuzhong, 12 goudiao, 2 chunyu, 11 globular bells?, 4 chimestones, many fragments (all ceramic mingqi)

Yan Xiadu, Yi Xian (Hebei), tomb no. 16: 2 sets bo (4/6), 2 sets yongzhong (8/8), 9 niuzhong, 15 chimestones (all ceramic mingqi)

## Middle to late Warring States

Changtaiguan, Xinyang (Henan), tomb no. 2: 13 niuzhong, 2 sets chimestones (9/9) (all wooden mingqi)

Jiuli, Linli (Hunan), tomb no. 1: bell-rack, lithophone-rack

Sanji, Pingshan (Hebei), tomb no. 1: 14 niuzhong, 13 chimestones

Tianxingguan, Jiangling (Hubei): 4 niuzhong (bell-rack has slots for 22 bells), many chimestones

## Han and later periods

Jishan, Linzi (Shandong): 4 yongzhong?, 9 niuzhong (gilt bronze mingqi), chimestones (number unclear)

Shuanggudui, Fuyang (Anhui): 5 bo, 9 yongzhong, 2 sets chimestones (10/10) (all ceramic mingqi)

## Han and later periods

Xianggangshan, Guangzhou (Guangdong): 14 niuzhong, 5 yongzhong, 8 goudiao, 2 sets chimestones

## Han and later periods

Beidongshan, Xuzhou (Jiangsu): 3 niuzhong (mingqi), 13 chimestones

Dazhongyingcun, Ci Xian (Hebei): 12 bianzhong (niuzhong imitations?), 14 chimestones (all ceramic mingqi)

Xianjiahu, Changsha (Hunan): niuzhong (number unclear), 2 sets chimestones (14/14)

NOTE. For references and details, see Appendix 1. Instances of the lowest category of assemblages (one bell-chime or one lithophone) are not listed here.

Stylistic differentiation of bell decoration in Eastern Zhou reflects their widened geographical spread (see map 2). In Western Zhou, chimed sets of musical bells had been virtually restricted to the capital area, their manufacture apparently being a monopoly of the metropolitan workshops. As a consequence of the rise of the princely states after the removal of the Zhou court to Luoyang, the trappings of royal court ritual and music, including bells, came to be manufactured throughout the Zhou realm. Differences among various stylistically distinctive regional workshop traditions in Eastern Zhou times have been the subject of considerable research;[51] only the characteristics specific to Eastern Zhou bells need be treated here. Concurrent centripetal trends should also be stressed, because as we have seen, over the course of the Springs and Autumns period, *yongzhong, bo*, and *niuzhong* became morphologically standardized, with their specific features de-emphasized and their bell-face layout becoming homogeneous. The shapes of their resonating bodies also became more and more uniform, perhaps indicating attempts to unify the timbre of the three kinds of bells. Finally, though the decoration of Eastern Zhou bells exhibited considerable stylistic variation, it was universally executed by means of the pattern-block technique (see Chapter 3), resulting in a preference for repetitive banded motifs. The climax of this homogenizing development is documented by sets of *yongzhong, bo*, and *niuzhong* with matched ornamentation, such as the bells of Marquis Shen of Cai (d. 491 B.C.) from Ximennei, Shou Xian (Anhui) (see figs. 26–28).[52]

Such a tendency toward greater technical and, perhaps, musical uniformity among the different classes of musical bells can be observed more or less throughout the Zhou realm, despite the diverging local workshop traditions. If royal Zhou ceremonial music were to serve the Eastern Zhou local rulers effectively as a symbol of legitimacy, it had to remain recognizable with respect to the Western Zhou original. To some extent, musical bells thus visually and acoustically underscored the overarching unity of Zhou aristocratic culture.

Among the bells dating to the second period of florescence of Zhou dynasty bell-making from the late Springs and Autumns to the early Warring States, one may distinguish two principal stylistic clusters: a northern group and a southern group.[53] The stylistic differences correlate with those observable on other kinds of bronzes; the fact that they are not very conspicuous on bells (probably less so

51. See, for instance, So 1982; Mackenzie 1987.
52. References in Appendix 1.
53. It should be cautioned that the geographical distribution areas of various bell types are by no means necessarily homologous with the areas covered by certain local cultures. Hence in this book (here as well as in Appendix 3), regional grouping of bells follows the archaeologically observable distributions, with no further cultural, historical, or economic ("Skinnerian") significance necessarily implied. Too little is known about local archaeological sequences, especially in outlying areas, to allow firm identification of bells of specific types with specific ethnic or political groups.

than on ceremonial vessels) may have something to do with the rigidity of the standard *zhong* decoration scheme.

## North-Central China

Many Eastern Zhou chime-bells of the northern stylistic cluster, with decoration executed in the pattern-block technique, can be linked to the foundry remains at Houma, near the capitals of the powerful state of Jin.[54] Excavations at this foundry have brought to light the only bell-casting molds so far known (see fig. 47); cast specimens with similar decoration have been excavated at various aristocratic burial grounds in Shanxi and adjacent areas. Formerly known as the "Liyu style," the motifs seen in the sumptuous dragon-derived decoration bands of the Houma bronzes often appear more "naturalistic" than those of earlier styles. Principal pattern blocks were executed in high relief, while in subsidiary areas, the units of decoration are commonly small and flat and their patterns virtually abstract.[55] In time, ever-larger surface areas became covered with patterns of varying density.[56]

On northern specimens dating to around the turn of the fifth century, such as the Lü-*yongzhong*, allegedly from Ronghe (Shanxi) (see fig. 100),[57] the decoration in the striking-area (*gu*) consists of a variety of small reptiles, their backs covered with different patterns. They are grouped in such a way as to circumscribe a roughly trapezoidal area, similar in its contours to the area reserved for ornamentation on the *gu* portions of earlier bells. Together, these various elements form a mask (with the eyes in the upper corners) that faces upside down when the bell is suspended. In the decoration of the *zhuanjian* tiers between the bosses (*mei*), dragon-band motifs have become transformed into "'relieved hooks" of greatly attenuated iconographic significance.

On later, mid-fifth century bells, such as the unprovenienced *bo* in figure 84,[58] the entire *gu* surface is covered with broad interlaced dragon bands of even width. Sometimes, as in figure 85, these bands converge into a central face, harking back to the mask motifs seen in this area close to the sound-bow in much earlier Shang period *nao*. Similar but more densely spaced dragon bands extend upward into the other ornamental portion of the bell-face. The gorgeous suspension devices of many northern *bo* render analogous interlaced dragons in

54. See Chapter 1, n. 68. Of course, not all bells of the northern stylistic cluster were necessarily of Jin manufacture, but it is my impression that the characteristic style of the Houma foundry was widely influential all over north China.

55. For the details of the manufacturing process, see Keyser 1979.

56. Very detailed descriptions of Jin style pieces may be found in Weber 1973.

57. Yetts 1929 1:29–43 and 2:43–49. For a list of other pieces of the same chime, and of typologically related specimens, see Appendix 2.

58. Weber 1973, 48–67. For a list of typologically related specimens, see Appendix 2.

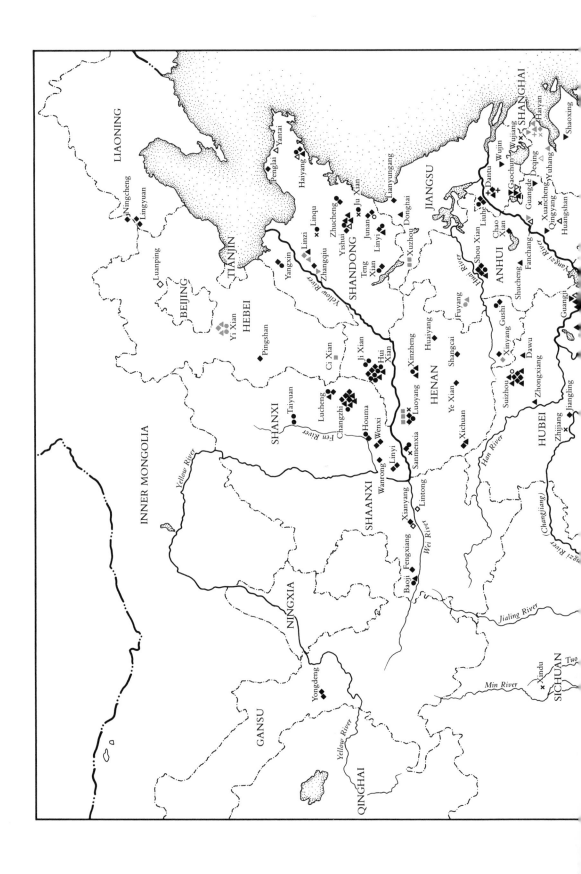

LIAONING

Ningcheng
Lingyuan

Luanping

BEIJING

TIANJIN

Penglai Yantai
Haiyang

Yangxin
Linzi
Linqu
Zhangqiu
Zhucheng
Ju Xian
Yishui
Junan
Lianyungang
Xuzhou Donghai

HEBEI

Yi Xian

Pingshan

SHANDONG
Teng Xian
Linyi

JIANGSU

Ci Xian

Ji Xian
Hui Xian
Xinzheng
Luoyang
Huaiyang
Shangcai

SHANXI

Taiyuan
Lucheng
Changzhi
Houma
Wenxi
Linyi
Sanmenxia
Ye Xian
Xichuan

Shou Xian
Liuhe
Chao Xian
Fanchang

ANHUI

Fuyang

Gushi
Xinyang
Dawu
Zhongxiang

Suizhou

Dantu
Wujin
Gaochun Wujiang
Guangde Deqing
Xuancheng Yuhang
Qingyang
Huangshan

SHANGHAI
Haiyan
Shaoxing

Guangji
Jiangling

HUBEI
Zhijiang

Wanrong

Yellow River
Fen River

Xianyang
Fengxiang
Lintong

Baoji

Wei River

Han River

(Changjiang)
Yangzi River

SHAANXI

Jialing River

NINGXIA

Yongdeng

Yellow River

GANSU

Min River

Xindu
Tuo

SICHUAN

QINGHAI

INNER MONGOLIA

HENAN

Huai River

Yangzi River

Yellow River

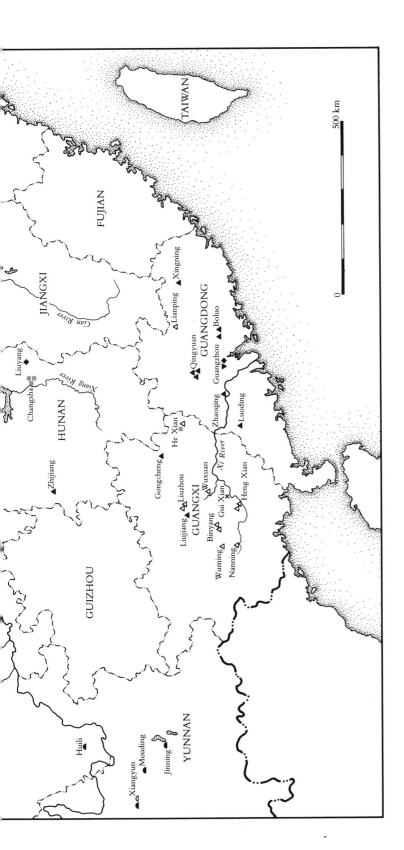

**MAP 2.** Geographical distribution of Chinese musical bells dating after ca. 771 B.C. (Eastern Zhou and later, including regional cultures).

A symbol executed in outline indicates the find of a single bell; a solid symbol indicates a set comprising several bells. *Mingqi* (imitations in miniature and/or inferior materials) are screened.

Only the names of cities and county seats are given. For site names, consult Place Names in Geographical Arrangement and Appendixes 1 and 2.

**EXPLANATION OF SYMBOLS**

| | |
|---|---|
| ▲ △ | *yongzhong* |
| ● ○ | *bo* |
| ◆ ◇ | *niuzhong* |
| ▶ ▷ | *goudiao* |
| + | chimed *chunyu* (single *chunyu* not included) |
| ◖ | "beehive-shaped bells" |
| ■ □ | clapper-bell-like *mingqi* of indeterminate type |
| ✕ | other kinds of bells, or cases where information is insufficient for classification |

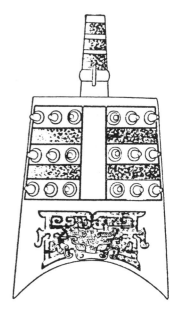

FIGURE 84. *Left: Bo* in the British Museum, London, from a dispersed set of at least five bells. Workshop of Jin, first half of the fifth century B.C.

FIGURE 85. *Right: Yongzhong* excavated in 1983 from tomb no. 7 at Luhe, Lucheng (Shanxi). Workshop of Jin, mid-fifth century B.C.

three dimensions. On the approximately contemporaneous (if visually somewhat disparate) bells from tomb no. 7 at Luhe, Lucheng (Shanxi) (figs. 85–87),[59] the ornamented area in the *gu* is more circumscribed, and geometric patterns are pervasive.

Possibly, the final breakup of Jin in 403 ushered in the decline of that state's bronze-casting industry. On northern pieces dating perhaps to the turn of the fourth century, the decoration is greatly simplified and sometimes takes on archaistic features, as in the bells from tomb no. 75 at Liulige, Hui Xian (Henan) (fig. 88).[60] One may speculate that such deliberate reference to earlier decoration motifs may have been connected to the new regimes' quest for legitimation.

The places of manufacture of Warring States period bells of the northern group are so far unknown. With few exceptions, chime-bell production became virtually restricted to *niuzhong*. On them, the *gu* has been transformed into a recessed panel entirely filled with pattern-block decoration. Reminiscences of a

59. References in Appendix 1.
60. Ibid.

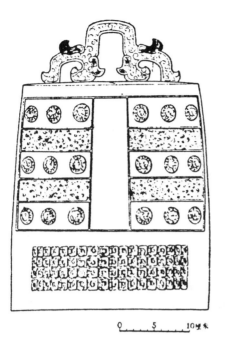

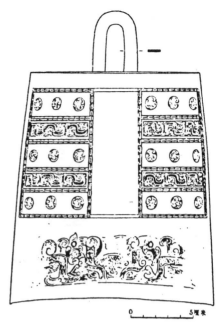

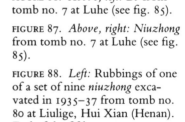

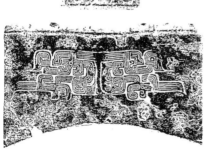

FIGURE 86. *Above, left: Bo* from tomb no. 7 at Luhe (see fig. 85).

FIGURE 87. *Above, right: Niuzhong* from tomb no. 7 at Luhe (see fig. 85).

FIGURE 88. *Left:* Rubbings of one of a set of nine *niuzhong* excavated in 1935–37 from tomb no. 80 at Liulige, Hui Xian (Henan). End of the fifth century B.C. or later.

FIGURE 89. *Upper left:* One of the fourteen Biao-*niuzhong* found ca. 1929 in tomb no. 7 at Jincun, Luoyang (Henan). Ca. 404 B.C.

FIGURE 90. *Upper right:* No. 5 of the nine Ju Gongsun Chao Zi–*niuzhong* excavated in 1970 at Zangjiazhuang, Zhucheng (Shandong). Fourth century B.C.

FIGURE 91. *Above:* The Yuefu-*niuzhong* excavated in 1978 near the tomb of the First Emperor of Qin in Lintong (Shaanxi). Qin dynasty (221–209 B.C.). *a,* exterior view of the bell-face; *b,* section drawings; *c,* interior decoration of the bell.

mask motif may still be seen at the center of the *gu* in the Biao–*niuzhong* from Jincun, Luoyang (Henan), which may be dated to ca. 404 (see fig. 89);[61] in the somewhat later Ju Gongsun Chao Zi–*niuzhong* from Zangjiazhuang, Zhucheng (Shandong) (fig. 90),[62] the entire surface shows a continuous expanse of ornament generated by pattern blocks, with little evident concern for symmetry. On the inlaid Qin dynasty *niuzhong* excavated near the tomb of the First Emperor of Qin in Lintong (Shaanxi), even the inside of the bell is exuberantly decorated (fig. 91). In the last two examples, as in other contemporaneous *niuzhong*, the lateral profile is slightly bent. On bells of such a rounded overall shape, it may have been difficult to exploit the two-tone phenomenon; the evidence suggests a regressive development of the bells' technological complexity.

### South-Central China

The southern group of bells from the late Springs and Autumns to early Warring States period are of somewhat wider geographical distribution than the northern ones. Many of the best specimens have been found in tombs of the state of Chu or can be associated with Chu by inscription. Others pertain to the Lower Yangzi area, where they seem to have replaced bells of a non–Zhou regional tradition that will be discussed in the following chapter. Eastern Zhou bronze workshop sites in the south have not yet been identified.

The bronze decoration style most commonly seen in the south (formerly known as "Huai style") is characterized by a prevalence of "relieved hooks," which are derived from dragon ornament. A fairly early version of this design may be seen in the *gu* of the unprovenienced mid-sixth century Zhu Gong Keng–*yongzhong* (fig. 92),[63] where such hooks accentuate the bends and joints in the bodies of "banked dragons." Some contemporary southern bells, however, feature a "flat" variant of the same decor, on which, in the absence of relieved hooks, the dragon bands are more easily visible; good examples are the *niuzhong* from tomb no. 1 at Xiasi, Xichuan (Henan) (fig. 93).[64]

The *gu* ornament of the somewhat later Wangsun Gao–*yongzhong* from tomb no. 2 at Xiasi (see fig. 21) marks a step toward greater abstraction.[65] The contours of the Western Zhou "L-shaped dragon" motif have been preserved, and animal heads may still be distinguished, but the ubiquitous relieved hooks and

---

61. Ibid.
62. Ibid.
63. *Shanghai Bowuguan-cang Qingtongqi* 1:81, 2:81. For a list of typologically related specimens, see Appendix 2.
64. References in Appendix 1. For a list of typologically related specimens, see Appendix 2. On the difference between "flat" and "relieved" versions of identical patterns, see also Falkenhausen 1989b.
65. References in Appendix 1. For a list of typologically related specimens, see Appendix 2.

FIGURE 92. *Left:* Zhu Gong Keng–*yongzhong* in the Shanghai Museum. Middle Springs and Autumns period (first half of sixth century B.C.).

FIGURE 93. *Right:* One of a set of nine *niuzhong* excavated in 1979 from tomb no. 1 at Xiasi, Xichuan (Henan). Middle Springs and Autumns period (middle of sixth century B.C.).

commas obscure the zoomorphic content and create an abstract overall effect. The subsidiary decorated portions of the bells are covered with unarticulated comma patterns. The decoration on the somewhat later bells of Marquis Shen of Cai (figs. 26–28) illustrates a later stage in the same process of development. Jenny So has observed that, despite the dazzling complexity of the ornament, the intersecting dragon bodies ubiquitous on contemporary northern pieces are largely absent from the southern sequence.[66] Such "interlacery" may nevertheless be observed occasionally, as on the unprovenienced Zhediao-*niuzhong* (fig. 94).[67]

The bells from Leigudun mark the climax of bell evolution in the south. The *yongzhong* found in Marquis Yi's tomb and the adjacent, slightly later tomb no. 2 demonstrate the tendency, present also in the north, toward covering pro-

66. So 1982.
67. References in Appendix 1.

FIGURE 94. *Left:* One of the dispersed chimes of Zhediao-*niuzhong*; this piece now in the Sen'oku Hakkokan (Sumitomo collection), Kyōto. Ca. 478 B.C.

FIGURE 95. *Right:* One of the thirty-six *yongzhong* excavated in 1981 from tomb no. 2 at Leigudun, Suizhou (Hubei). Late fifth century B.C.

gressively larger surface portions with ornament. Those from tomb no. 2 (fig. 95) are especially remarkable for the anthropomorphic design in the *gu* portion, which may represent a demon like those depicted occasionally in Chu lacquer painting. On the Chu Wang Xiong Zhang–*bo*, which is part of the bell assemblage from tomb no. 1 (see fig. 20), the restrictions of the standard *zhong* decoration scheme are partially loosened to create a greater continuous expanse of "relieved hooks": the number of *mei* has been reduced to two symmetrical groups of five, with no intervening *zhuanjian* bands.[68] On some of the middle-tier *yongzhong* from tomb no. 1 (set M2), *mei* are entirely absent. Marquis Yi's *niuzhong* (see fig. 13), finally, are completely unornamented, though musically functional.

68. Some of the Zeng *yongzhong* go even further in the abandonment of the "standard" *zhong* decoration scheme: they have no *mei* whatever, only two panels filled with relieved hooks, with a vertical panel in the center of the *zheng*.

FIGURE 96. *Left:* One of four *niuzhong* excavated in 1978 at Tian-xingguan, Jiangling (Hubei). Workshop of Chu, fourth century B.C.

FIGURE 97. *Right:* One of a set of fourteen *niuzhong* excavated in 1972 from the tomb of a ruler of Ba at Xiaotianxi, Fuling (Sichuan). Workshop of Chu, mid- to late fourth century B.C.

Just as in the north, *yongzhong* and *bo* disappear from the south Chinese archaeological record after the late fifth century B.C. All later Warring States period musical bells from Chu and adjacent areas are *niuzhong*. The tendency toward abandoning the standard *zhong* decoration scheme, noticeable on some of the Zeng bells, is also evident on the *niuzhong* from Tianxingguan, Jiangling (Hubei) (fig. 96):[69] here, the upper portion of the bell-face is devoid of all decoration while the *gu* is ornamented as usual.

Unlike specimens of the northern group, southern Warring States period chime-bells continued to preserve the characteristic trapezoidal contours of the ornamented area in the center of the *gu*; within that portion of the *gu*, however, symmetry was no longer maintained, and the limbs and heads of dragons are no longer articulated with one another. Such dissolved ornaments cover all the

69. References in Appendix 1. For a list of typologically related specimens, see Appendix 2.

space available for ornamentation, as may be seen on the mid-fourth-century Jingli-*niuzhong* from tomb no. 1 at Changtaiguan, Xinyang (Henan) (see fig. 102).[70] On the approximately contemporary fourteen-part set of *niuzhong* from the tomb of a ruler of Ba 巴 at Xiaotianxi, Fuling (Sichuan), the same design is combined with an exuberant inlaid pattern covering all the flat parts of the surface (fig. 97).[71] Although inlaid bronzes are typical for Warring States period Chu, these are the only inlaid pre-Qin bells known. Inlay and gilding is seen on some Qin and Han *niuzhong* (compare fig. 91), but the decoration on those bells seems to have grown out of the northern stylistic tradition. So far, bells showing southern characteristics are unknown after the fourth century.

The tone measurements now available (see Chapter 7) show a correlation between increasingly elaborate bell-decoration and a decline in acoustical sophistication. Even though chime-bells were still valued, the two-tone phenomenon apparently fell into disuse within a century or so after the casting of the Zeng bells.

### The End of the Zhou Bell-Manufacturing Tradition

The Zeng bells mark both the climax and the beginning of the end of Zhou chime-bell making. In late Warring States times, Zhou bell music already seems to have been a thing of the past, of which there existed merely some ossified reminders. For unknown reasons, the manufacture of *yongzhong* and *bo* had virtually ceased in the central states of the Zhou realm after the mid- to late Warring States period.[72] Only *niuzhong* lingered; their archaeological sequence terminates early in the Western Han dynasty. As *niuzhong* had become the only kind of bells in use, the number of pieces in chimed sets of *niuzhong* showed considerable increase in Warring States times (see table 8); due to the disuse of the two-tone phenomenon, however, those later specimens were no longer musically on a par with their antecedents.

In addition to the tangible archaeological evidence of the *niuzhong* depicted in figure 91, there is also some textual indication that chime-bells continued to be made during the Qin dynasty, though whether the bells cast when the unification was completed (see Chapter 1) represented Zhou chime-bell types is unknown. In the official history of the following dynasty, the Han, bell-players

70. References in Appendix 1.
71. Ibid.
72. The stylistically latest *yongzhong* known are probably those from Liulige tomb no. 75 in the north (compare the identical decoration on the *niuzhong* in fig. 88) and those from tomb no. 2 at Leigudun in the south (fig. 95); both date to about the middle of the second half of the fifth century. The latest known *bo* are the fourth-century pieces from Zangjiazhuang (references in Appendix 1).

are listed among the performers of ceremonial music at the imperial court.[73] It is possible that these Han musicians perpetuated some of the traditional lore of Zhou bell music; they may even have played on instruments dating back to Zhou times. Actual specimens of bona fide Han bells are virtually absent from the archaeological record,[74] except for replicas made for funerary purposes (*mingqi*).[75] Executed in inferior materials, most of them tend to be grotesquely deformed and greatly reduced in scale vis-à-vis their Zhou prototypes, though the decoration on most of them is patterned on the standard *zhong* decoration scheme. These objects indicate that the trappings of Zhou court music remained icons of cultivation and status. Access to this form of music, even if merely symbolic, seems to have remained a matter of importance to a person of rank on entering into the other world.

During the turbulent times after the fall of the Han, the hereditary court musicians eventually became separated from their instruments.[76] When the musicians fled to present-day Nanjing with the court of the Jin dynasty after the fall of Luoyang in A.D. 316, the bell-chimes stayed behind in the north, where they were handed from dynasty to dynasty as a mute symbol of dynastic legitimacy. These bells were gradually dispersed and lost, though at least one important Zhou bell still seems to have been around at the time of the Sui reunification in 589.[77] The latest ceramic *mingqi* bell-replicas thus far reported were excavated from the Eastern Wei tomb of the Rouran princess Linhe 鄰和 (A.D. 538–550) at Dazhongyingcun, Ci Xian (Hebei) (fig. 98), demonstrating that such objects had become attractive to at least some members of the non-Chinese warrior aristocracies that at that time were ruling north China.[78]

In the south, circumstances did not permit the reconstitution of the lost bells. Whatever may have still been known of the Zhou art of bell-playing at the beginning of the fourth century A.D. probably died out within one generation after the last musicians arrived in the south without their instruments.

73. *Han Shu* "Li Yue zhi," Zhonghua ed., 1073–74.

74. The only possible exception is set of *niuzhong* found at the early Western Han tomb of the king of Nanyue at Xianggangshan, Guangzhou (Guangdong) (references in Appendix 1), which may, however, be a Warring States period heirloom.

75. Some *mingqi*, such as the gilt sets of *niuzhong* and *yongzhong* from an early Western Han princely tomb at Jishan (references in Appendix 1), are visually extravagant, if musically non-functional, but most are both small and inconspicuous. I suspect that only a fraction of archaeologically found specimens have so far been reported upon. For a comprehensive list of Warring States period and Han *mingqi* bells, see Appendix 2.

76. J. Boltz n.d.

77. This was the WUYI bell cast by Jing Wang of Zhou 周景王 (r. 554–520 B.C.), the subject of learned discourses recorded in *Zuo Zhuan* Zhao 21 (HYI ed., 404) and *Guo Yu* "Zhou Yu-*xia*" (Tiansheng Mingdao ed., 3:12a–18b). Kong Yingda 孔穎達 (A.D. 574–648), in his *Zuo Zhuan* sub-commentary (see Ruan Yuan, ed., *Shisanjing Zhushu* vol. 2:2097), traces its transmission through the Kaihuang period (A.D. 581–600).

78. References in Appendix 1.

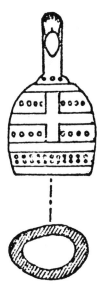

FIGURE 98. *Mingqi* pottery bell
excavated in 1978 from the tomb
of the Rouran princess Linhe
(A.D. 538–50) at Dazhongyingcun, Ci Xian (Hebei).

The chime-bells used in East Asian court music during later dynasties, and, since the Song dynasty, in the annual sacrifices to Confucius, are the outcome of later attempts at musical revival. Some of them resemble Zhou dynasty bells in shape, such as the bells cast at the Northern Song court from 1105 to 1113; their manufacture was triggered by the accidental discovery, then regarded as a highly auspicious omen, of a set of mid–Springs and Autumns period *bo* of the state of Song.[79] Others, such as the Qing bell-chimes that may still be seen in Beijing (see Chapter 2 and fig. 44), are morphologically and technologically novel creations, influenced by the design of Buddhist temple-bells (see fig. 35).[80] Significant innovations in bell manufacture still occurred after the end of the Bronze Age, and the history of bell-casting in East Asia after the Han remains a fertile topic for future study.

79. These are the Song Gong–*bo*, found in 1104 at a site close to the site of the capital of the state of Song of the Zhou dynasty. While the original Springs and Autumns period pieces have long been lost (they are depicted in *Bogutulu* 22:27), some of the Song dynasty recasts still survive (two are in the Royal Ontario Museum, Toronto, at least one in the Palace Museum in Beijing, and one apparently in the Jilin Provincial Museum, Changchun). Their number seems to have been considerable; some of them had colorful histories after they were dispersed at the time of the conquest of the Song capital by the Jurchen in 1125 (Chen Mengjia 1964a; for reports on individual pieces in China, see *Wenwu* 1963 [5]:42–44; *Gugong Bowuyuan Yuankan* 1980 [4]:77ff., and *Wenwu* 1983 [11]:72–73).

80. The earliest Buddhist temple-bell cast in China to have come to my attention is a Chen dynasty (A.D. 557–589) piece on display in the Nara National Museum.

## Conclusion

This chapter has led us through the final three stages of evolution sketched out at the beginning of Chapter 4. The typological filiations of musical bells from the late Neolithic through Eastern Zhou may be roughly summarized as in figure 52. In tracing the development of instrument form and ornament, we recognized that variation among artifacts is never arbitrary: every step taken prefigures and at the same time limits the next. George Kubler's evocation of a "chain" of artistic tradition, though primarily concerned with the fine arts, also applies to the products of Bronze Age craftsmanship:

> The artist is not a free agent obeying only his own will. His situation is
> rigidly bound by a chain of prior events. The chain is invisible to him, and it
> limits his motion. He is not aware of it as a chain, but only as *vis a tergo*, as
> the force of events behind him. The conditions imposed by these prior
> events require of him either that he follow obediently in the path of tradi-
> tion, or that he rebel against the tradition. In either case, his decision is not a
> free one: it is dictated by prior events of which he senses only dimly and in-
> directly the overpowering urgency, and by his own congenital peculiarities
> of temperament.[81]

A conscious rebellion against tradition almost never occurred in premodern manufacturing traditions; stylistic change as observable in the archaeological record was gradual, as is the case in the ancient Chinese chime-bells. The *stylistic* development of bell decoration largely followed its own inherent dynamic.

Matters turn out to be somewhat more complex, however, when we consider the *morphological* features of the bells. In Chapter 4, we traced the gradual crea-tion of the two-tone *yongzhong* by adding *xuan* and *wo* to *nao* bells. In this chap-ter, we have seen how these *yongzhong*, when assembled into large chimed sets, became some of the most splendid and technologically sophisticated symbols manipulated in the context of Western Zhou ritual. Ever larger and more lavish ensembles of bells were created by complementing *yongzhong* chimes with other kinds of musical bells of extraneous origin, which were physically assimilated to the *yongzhong*. These morphological changes over time reflect technological developments, but the *vires a tergo* behind them are largely socio-political. As chime-bells were destined for use in the rituals through which the Zhou polity iteratively defined and established itself, their technological and morphological evolution is in large measure determined by the rise and decline of Zhou

81. Kubler 1962, 50.

ritual.[82] Their perfection from the late Western Zhou through the early Warring States reflects the florescence of Zhou aristocratic society, and their final demise went hand in hand with the disintegration of the Zhou ritual-political system.[83]

## Regionalisms

The history of bells aptly illustrates various forms of cultural interchange between dynastic civilization in north China and the surrounding populations. Influences were traded in both directions and integrated into quite different cultural surroundings.[84] Throughout this and the preceding chapter, we had ample occasion to mention the bronze-manufacturing traditions along the Yangzi River, contemporary with the Shang and Western Zhou, in terms of their important contributions to the invention of the *yongzhong* and *bo*, two kinds of musical bells that later became essential parts of the Zhou "suspended music." In the later part of the Zhou dynasty, the ever-shifting boundaries between the dynastic civilization in north China and the surrounding areas remained eminently permeable; cultural stimuli were incessantly transferred back and forth. Bells figure prominently among the bronze and other Zhou ritual objects that found their way into surrounding areas, no doubt through various forms of trade, and perhaps also through the custom of exchanging bells as diplomatic gifts between allied rulers (discussed in Chapter 1), which may well have extended to the non-Zhou periphery.[85]

In a number of places along the periphery, musical bells of Zhou types were imitated locally, sometimes resulting in highly original and innovative departures from the "mainstream" evolution traced above. In this book, those typological ramifications are treated in detail in Appendix 3. In general, throughout the Bronze Age, musical bells coexisted along the Zhou margins with unchimed bells that were for the most part derived from the same typological roots: *duo*, *nao*, *zheng*, and *chunyu*. Casters in the southerly areas displayed a high degree of originality in the manufacture of such nonmusical bells, which served, for example, as signal-giving instruments in warfare.[86] Musically viable chime-bells remained predominantly characteristic of the dynastic civilization in north

82. On this topic see Bilsky 1975; Pratt 1986; Wu Hung 1988.
83. Hsu Cho-yun 1965, 24–52. Li Xueqin 1985, 460–90.
84. Hsu and Linduff (1988, ch. 6) discuss such developments during Zhou times in crude military-political terms.
85. K. C. Chang 1975. For a recent cross-cultural overview on the role of trade in early states, see Kipp and Schortman 1989.
86. See Falkenhausen 1989a.

China. From Eastern Zhou times onward, sets of such bells made their appearance in the peripheral areas as imports or as local imitations.

Pre–Eastern Zhou finds of bells in the Yangzi region and elsewhere in the south show no indication that chimed sets of musical bells were considered important. By Eastern Zhou times, however, a concern with chimes is clearly apparent from the locally manufactured bells found in areas along the southern fringes of the Zhou realm, possibly indicating major cultural changes. Phenomena in the Lower Yangzi area (which included, at the end of the Springs and Autumns period, the territory of the states of Wu and Yue) are quite fascinating in this respect. Here we find local types of *yongzhong* coexisting with *goudiao* (chimed *zheng*) and chimed *chunyu*, both resulting from attempts at fashioning chimed sets of bells out of common local kinds of nonmusical bells. Whether the mere existence of such chimes shows a significantly enhanced degree of understanding of the musical principles of Zhou court music is debatable, however; locally manufactured sets of bells, in the Lower Yangzi and elsewhere, often seem to imitate merely the outward appearance and not the musical properties of their Zhou models.

Even though many chime-bells of regional manufacture may thus have been designed as showpieces, unable to function in the same way as contemporary northern chimes, it is significant that they imitated not merely the shape of single bells but the appearance of entire chimes. Clearly, in producing such objects, the local elites along the borders of the Zhou realm were consciously emulating the models of the Zhou aristocracy. In manipulating items of Zhou material culture, they strove to make themselves ritually compatible with their Zhou peers. Ironically, as they were drawn into the orbit of Chinese dynastic civilization in the course of the Eastern Zhou period, the position of these local power-holders seems to have become marginalized.

In general, Eastern Zhou texts document a tendency toward a more pronounced distinction between "us" and "them"—between the civilized "Chinese" (Hua Xia 華夏) on the one side, and the "barbarians" of the Four Directions on the other.[87] In the process, it seems, attitudes toward the latter became increasingly judgmental. Although we must be wary of perpetrating Great Han chauvinism, Bronze Age archaeological finds throughout the areas bordering on the Zhou realm make it plain that the regional non-Zhou elites did covet the paraphernalia of the Zhou dynastic rituals as items of conspicuous consumption. Clearly, their fascination with these objects had more than a little to do with the fact that they were of foreign origin. How these imported luxury articles and their local imitations concretely affected individual local societies

87. Okura 1965.

almost certainly differed from area to area. If general parallels to other parts of the world can be applied, we may suggest that the possession of such objects helped certain groups within the local elites assert themselves vis-à-vis other contenders for power.[88] Conceivably, the quest for such power-conferring para-phernalia may have triggered or accelerated indigenous development toward more complex social organization. In the long run, however, the assimilation of local potentates to Zhou elite models appears, ironically, to have facilitated the wholesale absorption of most of the Zhou peripheries into the Chinese cultural and political hegemony in the late third century B.C. In this process, too, bells had their part to play.

88. Wells 1980; Kipp and Schortman 1989.

PART III    Musical Performance and Musical Theory

# CHAPTER SIX

# Playing the Bells

*Prelude*

*Cangcang congcong tuotuo* [?] *yongyong!* Though but imperfectly approximating the instruments' musical quality, the onomatopoeic renderings of their sound in some Western Zhou bell inscriptions quite accurately imitates what happens when a bell is struck: the initial consonants render the *Schlagton* produced by the mallet hitting the bell surface; and the subsequent vocal-nasal clusters suggest the long, drawn-out tone produced by the vibrating bells. Although the harmonizing voice of bells was conventionally likened to the harmonious singing of birds (see Chapter 3), the ancients realized that deliberate human action was necessary to make the bells "sing" in the proper way.[1] How were the bell-chimes played, and how did they sound?

## Arranging the Bell-Chimes
### Archaeological Evidence on the Composition of Chimes

In Shang and Zhou ritual music, single bells were musically meaningless. It was sets of chime-bells rather than individual specimens that constituted the conceptual units, as is clear from the admonition inscribed on the early sixth-century B.C. Zhu Gong Keng–*yongzhong* (see fig. 92): "If you divide up the sacrificial vessels, leave this [set of bells] intact."[2] In the archaeological record, however, numerous instances of incomplete sets, as well as composite sets of bells that did

---

1. Metaphors based on that fact may be found in *Mo Zi* "Feiru" (HYI ed., 27) and "Gong-meng" (ibid., 84), as well as *Li Ji* "Xueji" (*Li Ji Zhushu* 36:9a; see the dedication of this book).
2. Shirakawa, *Kinbun Tsūshaku* 39:478–81.

not originally belong together, show that such injunctions were not always heeded.

How many bells were there to a chime? Our intermittent glances at table 8 throughout Chapter 5 have made us realize that this question has no easy answer. Not only can one rarely be certain whether an archaeologically discovered set of bells is complete, but the ancient music-masters also frequently composed elaborate assemblages by taking bells, seemingly at their own discretion, from many different sets. Such a trend can be observed as early as the Anyang period, when, though the standard number of *nao* in a chime seems to have been three, larger sets were created by combining bells from several sets (see Chapter 4). Such assemblages are also common in the late Western Zhou hoards, which often contain three or more different types of *yongzhong* but seldom one set in its entirety. Similarly, in Eastern Zhou, the sixty-five bells from the tomb of Marquis Yi of Zeng are of heterogeneous origins (see Chapter 7).

There is some indication that in late Western Zhou times, the standard number per set of *yongzhong* may have been eight, and that of *bo*, possibly, three. Even in incomplete chimes of *yongzhong*, even-numbered assemblages appear to have been favored at that time. In Eastern Zhou, by contrast, odd-numbered sets of *yongzhong* occur just as frequently as even-numbered ones, and though there was a high degree of local as well as temporal variety, the overall numbers of bells per set increased considerably. The key to understanding the significance of these changes is technological, having to do with the evolution of bell-scaling principles and the trend to ever-denser tone distributions; this matter will be explored in the following chapter.

The largest known contiguous set of bells from the Chinese Bronze Age is the twenty-eight-part set of small *yongzhong* from the late fifth century B.C. tomb no. 2 at Leigudun (see fig. 95); a close second is the Wangsun Gao–*yongzhong* chime from tomb no. 2 at Xiasi, Xichuan (Henan) (third quarter of the sixth century), which comprises twenty-six pieces. (None of the chimes on Marquis Yi's sixty-five-bell-rack is composed of more than nineteen pieces.) Chimes ranging up to about a dozen pieces are more normal, both for *yongzhong* and for *bo*. As to *niuzhong*, we have noted that Springs and Autumns period chimes of such bells for the most part comprised nine pieces, increasing to as many as fourteen in the Warring States period.

In Eastern Zhou archaeological contexts, sets of *yongzhong*, *bo*, and *niuzhong*, which had formed part of the Chinese cultural inventory since the end of Western Zhou, often occur together. While the sixty-five-part assemblage from the tomb of Marquis Yi remains exceptional, in a dozen or so archaeologically known cases the number of bells excavated in one tomb is in the vicinity of thirty (see table 9). That the respective musical roles of the three kinds of bells may not have been identical is suggested by differences in their numbers and sizes. In general, *bo* are the largest in size and the fewest in number per set. *Yongzhong* occur in far larger numbers and in a wide range of sizes, but they are on the average somewhat smaller than *bo*. *Niuzhong*, throughout their developmental sequence, remained conspicuously smaller in size than *yongzhong* and *bo*. Following Asahara Tatsurō 淺原達郎, we may liken the large *bo* to the bass and the *yongzhong* to the baritone and tenor ranges in a chorus of bells, complemented by the soprano of the *niuzhong*.[3] There were fewer bells emitting tones in the bass range than in the higher ranges, perhaps because large bells are louder and resonate considerably longer than small ones. We may infer that large *bo* (as well as *yongzhong* of comparable size, e.g. those on the lower tier of the Zeng bell-rack) mainly served to provide a "ground layer" to the more complex tonal patterns played by bells of the higher ranges.

Single or multiple chimes of bells are frequently found in association with lithophones; in the late pre-Qin ritual texts, these two kinds of instruments together constitute the category of suspended music, the possession and display of which was regulated by sumptuary laws (see Chapter 1). Although unknown to European musical traditions, chimes of sonorous stones are widespread in South, East, and Southeast Asia.[4] In China, the history of musical stones goes back to Neolithic times;[5] they were mostly manufactured from calcareous stone, which is acoustically favorable on account of its hardness and density.[6] Although lithophones are technologically less sophisticated than chime-bells, the evolutionary histories of the two show certain parallels. In both cases, the earliest known chimed sets date to the Anyang period, and the number of pieces per set increased greatly in Eastern Zhou. Most Eastern Zhou lithophones appear to have consisted of ten to fourteen chimestones (table 8). With thirty-six pieces (originally there were forty-one), the Zeng lithophone from tomb no. 1 at Leigudun (fig. 99) is exceptionally large; it covered a range of three and one-half octaves.

3. Asahara 1984. The additional sets of smaller *bo*-like bells found in some large north Chinese tombs of the fifth century probably served to strengthen the higher register.
4. For some well-known and, for a time, controversial prehistoric finds in Vietnam, see Schaeffner 1951 and Condominas 1952; some recent discoveries in eastern India were reported by Yule and Bemmann 1987.
5. See Chapter 4, n. 10. Large chimestones similar to those from Shanxi have also been found in Lower Xiajiadian cultural contexts to the north of China proper, e.g., at Kalaxinhe East, Jianping (Liaoning) (*Kaogu* 1983 [11]:973–81), and Xishan, Kalaxin Banner (Inner Mongolia) (*Wenwu* 1983 [8]:54).
6. Tong Kin-woon 1983–84, pt. 1:97–100; Chen Zhenyu 1988b. It may be assumed that the lithic material used varied somewhat with the resources available near the place of manufacture. The only polished material documented for ancient Chinese chimestones is marble. Although jade chimestones are sometimes mentioned in the literature, they are so far unknown from the Bronze Age archaeological record; they did exist in later periods. Kuttner (1953) has determined that the acoustic quality of jade is superior to that of other stones, but his theory that the flat jade rings (*bi*

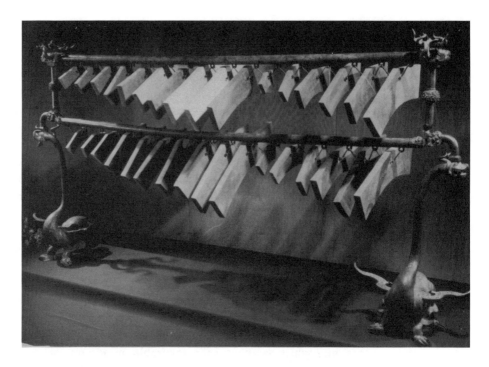

FIGURE 99. Lithophone from the tomb of Marquis Yi of Zeng.


*Textual Records on the Composition of Chimes*

A poetic description of bells and lithophones on their racks may be found in the inscription of the Lü-*yongzhong* from the late Springs and Autumns period (fig. 100):

> The [bells] are of dark shiny metal [*liu*] and of smooth hard metal [*lü*].[7] The great bells [amount to] eight *si* 肆 sets, matching them there are four *du* 堵 sets [of chimestones?]. Proudly, proudly, [the posts and bars of the bell-racks] rear their dragon heads. Now their casting is completed, the rack has been fashioned, and the great bells have been suspended from it. The large jade chimestone and the alligator-skin drum [are also in place].[8]

---

璧) and segments (*yuan* 瑗) of Chinese antiquity were parts of lithophones lacks plausibility. Rather than dating to "around 1000 B.C.," the jade *bi* in the Royal Ontario Museum investigated by Kuttner date to the Warring States period.

7. On these metal-names see Chapter 3 above.

8. My translation follows Yetts (1929 2:43–49) wherever possible; for philological and historical commentary and an analysis of the text's poetic language, see Falkenhausen 1988, 1148–55.

*a*

*b*

FIGURE 100. One of the thirteen Lü-*yongzhong* allegedly excavated in 1870 at Ronghe (Shanxi); this piece (*a*) now in the British Museum, London. Rubbing (*b*) of another member of the set, now in the Shanghai Museum. Workshop of Jin, first quarter of fifth century B.C.

The text mentions the terms *si* and *du*, counters for bells that also appear in the classical literature. The original meaning of *si* is "to deploy [in a row]"; *du* is semantically connected with walls and bulwarks, probably reflecting how, during performances, racks of suspended musical instruments screened off the ritual area from the surrounding space.

The *Zhou Li* states: "In all suspended bells and chimestones, half [a set] is a *du* and a whole [set] is a *si*."[9] The archaeological evidence in table 8 vaguely corroborates the idea that a distinction between whole sets and half-sets may have been important. Exactly how many pieces constituted a *si* or a *du*, however, is not specified anywhere in the pre-Qin sources. The Eastern Han commentary by Zheng Xuan 鄭玄 (A.D. 127–200) on the *Zhou Li* explains:

> When bells and chimestones, eight of each, amounting to sixteen, are suspended in a row on one rack, this is called a *du*. One *du* of bells plus one *du* of chimestones is called a *si*.

9. *Zhou Li: Chun'guan* "Xiaoxu" (*Zhou Li Zhengyi* 44:16b–18b).

Accordingly, a *du* would amount to sixteen, and a *si* to thirty-two pieces. Zheng Xuan's view has not remained uncontested, however. In his commentary on *Zuo Zhuan*, Du Yu 杜預 (4th century A.D.), though accepting that a *du* is half a *si*, takes one *si* as comprising sixteen bells, one *du* thus amounting to eight bells.[10] For centuries, Du Yu's numbers were universally accepted; throughout Imperial times, for instance, Chinese bell-chimes were designed as sets of sixteen (see fig. 44).

More recently, however, Du's interpretation of *si* and *du* has been called into doubt by epigraphers who have noted a number of occurrences of those two terms in bronze inscriptions.[11] The Lü-*yongzhong* inscription is so far the only one referring to both *si* and *du*. The possible meaning of its "eight *si* and four *du*" has elicited considerable discussion. In 1896, Wu Dacheng 吳大澂 (1835–1902) expressed the opinion that eight sets of 16 bells each would amount to an impossibly high number of bells.[12] For the sake of reducing the number to a more "reasonable" one, Wu therefore proposed that *si* and *du* are simply counters for individual bells rather than for sets.[13] Since the discovery of the 65 bells in Marquis Yi's tomb, however, an assemblage of 128 bells, though still enormous, is no longer unimaginable.

As an alternative, Guo Moruo 郭沫若 (1892–1978) suggested that *si* and *du* referred to different instruments: the four *du* were not bells but lithophones.[14] This reading seems possible in the case of the Lü-*yongzhong* inscription, since chimestones are also named in that text; moreover, archaeological finds show that musical assemblages universally comprise fewer musical stones than bells (in Marquis Yi's tomb, the number of slots on the lithophone rack was almost exactly half the number of chime-bells).[15] Other inscriptions, however, use

10. Du Yu on *Zuo Zhuan* Xiang 11 (see Ruan Yuan, *Shisanjing Zhushu* 2:1951).
11. Beside the Lü-*yongzhong*, references to *si* or *du* appear in the following bronze inscriptions: the late-ninth-century Duo You–*ding* (Tian and Luo 1981; Shaughnessy 1983–85), the early- to mid-sixth-century Zhu Gong Keng–*yongzhong* (Shirakawa, *Kinbun Tsūshaku* 39:478–81), the mid- to late-sixth-century Huanzi Meng Jiang–*hu* (Shirakawa, *Kinbun Tsūshaku* 38:388–403).
12. Wu Dacheng, *Kezhai Jigulu*, j. 1:7–11. This opinion, published in 1896, seems to have influenced Sun Yirang's commentary on the *Zhou Li* locus quoted above, in *Zhou Li Zhengyi* 44:16b–18b (preface dated 1899).
13. Wu Dacheng proposed that the difference between *si* and *du* might have been not a numerical but a musical one. According to him, the eight bells of the *si* emitted the tones of a standard scale, whereas the four *du* bells rang intervening chromatic tones; we now know that the Lü-*yongzhong* set comprised at least thirteen pieces that are documented through rubbings, not twelve (8 + 4) pieces, as Wu Dacheng mistakenly believed. Though ingenious, Wu's hypothesis is incompatible with the actual tone distribution in Eastern Zhou bell-chimes (see Chapter 7).
14. Guo Moruo 1958, *Kao* 270–76. Guo believes that the meanings of the terms *si* and *du* were reversed in the Han commentaries: a *si* for him equals half a *du*; accordingly, in the Lü-*yongzhong* context, there would have been identical numbers of chimestones and bells.
15. As each chimestone could emit only one tone, the number of tones on the Zeng lithophone was effectively one-fourth the number playable on the Zeng bells.

both *du* and *si* with unambiguous reference to bells, showing that the two terms cannot always denote a difference between bells and lithophones.

The archaeological data in table 8 suggest that the meaning of such terms as *si* and *du* must have undergone considerable change from Western to Eastern Zhou; the meaning may have differed, moreover, with respect to each of the three principal classes of musical bells. Sets of sixteen or thirty-two musical bells of any kind have not been seen so far. On the other hand, sets of eight and half-sets of four bells seem to have been of some importance in Western Zhou *yongzhong*; hence one may speculate that there may have been eight *yongzhong* to a *si* and four to a *du* at that time, assuming the validity of the *Zhou Li* stipulation that a *du* was half a *si*. If so, eight-part sets of Western Zhou *yongzhong* such as the Zhong Yi- and the Zuo-*yongzhong*, which were excavated together at Qijiacun, Fufeng (Shaanxi), would each constitute a complete *si* of bells, and an incomplete set of four, such as the Ni-*yongzhong* from Haosihe, Yongshou (Shaanxi), might be termed a *du*.[16] In Eastern Zhou, on the other hand, the two terms must have become more flexible in their significance; while retaining the meaning of "set" and "half-set," respectively, they may no longer have denoted a fixed number of chime-bells.

*Suspension*

Much care was expended on the ornamentation of the racks ( *ju*.虡 or 鐻) from which the bells and musical stones were suspended.[17] The two racks excavated in tomb no. 1 at Leigudun are the best preserved specimens. The heavy wooden horizontal beams of the L-shaped bell-rack (see fig. 1) are covered with brightly colored lacquer decoration. The beams of the first and second tiers are supported by massive bronze figures of standing human beings (fig. 101); the third tier rests on cylindrical bronze columns.[18] The lithophone rack from the same tomb is made entirely of bronze and of much more slender proportions than the bell-rack; the vertical supports take the shape of elegant antlered birds, a com-

16. Some idea of the original Western Zhou meaning of these two terms may have been preserved, along with other Western Zhou musical lore, into late Eastern Zhou times. The putative Eastern Zhou or early Han source for Du Yu's figures may have simply mistaken the number of bells in a *si* for that in a *du*, thus doubling the actual numbers; Zheng Xuan in turn redoubled those figures.

17. Zhang Zhenxin 1979 and 1980.

18. Zhao Shigang speculates (1988, 18) that the number of tiers in a bell-rack may reflect Chu sumptuary conventions; thus, the three-tiered rack from Marquis Yi's tomb would have been appropriate to the *zhuhou* rank, while the two-tiered rack reconstructible for the bells from tomb no. 2 at Leigudun, as well as for the Wangsun Gao–*yongzhong* from Xiasi, Xichuan (Henan), corresponded to a lower rank, and so forth. This seems uncertain, however.

FIGURE 101. Detail of the bell-rack from the tomb of
Marquis Yi of Zeng (see fig. 1).

posite animal commonly seen in Chu art.[19] The earliest preserved bell-rack on
record, excavated at Liugezhuang, Penglai (Shandong), and dating to the early to
middle Springs and Autumns period, is of much simpler construction; its single
wooden beam is adorned at both ends by carved dragon heads, just as described
in the Lü-*yongzhong* inscription (see above).[20] Bell-racks with similar dragon-
headed supports are also depicted on the Warring States period pictorial bronzes
(figs. 15, 22), and written records suggest that they may have existed in Chu.[21]
Zhuang Zi tells the story of Wood Carver Qing 梓慶, who carved a bell-rack so
skillfully that "those who saw it were startled, as if it were the work of ghosts
and spirits."[22] A later commentary asserts that the rack in question "resembled

19. Thote 1987.
20. Reference in Appendix 1.
21. Gao You's commentary explains the "Nine-dragon bells" in *Huainan Zi* "Taizu" (Sibu
Congkan ed., 20:13b) as a Chu bell-chime suspended from a dragon-shaped rack.
22. *Zhuang Zi* "Dasheng" (HYI ed., 50).

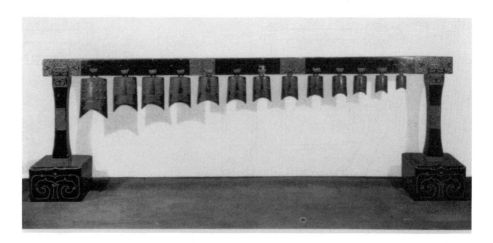

FIGURE 102. Chime of thirteen Jingli-*niuzhong* excavated in 1957
from tomb no. 1 at Changtaiguan, Xinyang (Henan); rack reconstructed after original remains. Workshop of Chu, first half of
fourth century B.C.

the shape of tigers."[23] Lacquer painting and carved wooden portions are also
characteristic of other known Eastern Zhou bell-racks (fig. 102), which lack
both representational decor and the elaborate bronze fittings seen on the one
from Leigudun.[24]

The suspension armature of the Zeng *yongzhong* is highly ornate and of complicated design. Probably in order to prevent the bells from swaying backwards
when struck, the *wo* (suspension rings) rest in fixed U-shaped hooks, which in
turn are connected to clamps that are tightly fastened around beams of the rack
(fig. 103). The clamps of nine *yongzhong* on the lower tier are fashioned in the
shape of fully sculptural crouching tigers (fig. 104) that adorn the front and back
faces of the beams; the tigers' tails and paws are hinged and bolted together on
the top and bottom.[25] On Marquis Yi's bell-rack, the *yongzhong* on the lower
and middle tiers are tilted to opposite sides, in order that the musicians in charge
of the lower- and middle-tier chimes not get in each other's way.

Some surviving bell-hooks (*gou* 鉤), roughly in the shape of a lower-case q,
suggest that a much simpler and less stable way of suspending bells prevailed

23. Guo Qingfan, *Zhuang Zi jishi*. Beijing (Zhonghua) 1979, vol. 3, 658–59.
24. Such racks have been found at the following sites (references in Appendix 1): Changtaiguan, Xinyang (Henan), M1 and M2 (the latter for wooden *mingqi* bells); Hougudui, Gushi (Henan),
Jiuli, Linli (Hunan), and Tianxingguan, Jiangling (Hubei). All these sites are located within the Chu
sphere of influence.
25. Five suspension methods occurring in connection with the Zeng bell assemblage are described by Tan and Feng 1988.

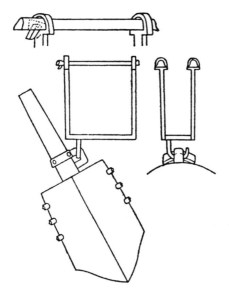

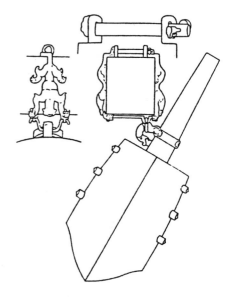

FIGURE 103. The suspension of
the Zeng bells (simple mode).

FIGURE 104. The suspension of
the Zeng bells (elaborate mode,
with tiger clamps).

during earlier times. The only provenienced specimens have been excavated
with the early seventh-century B.C. Qin Gong bells at Taigongmiao, Baoji
(Shaanxi) (see figs. 81 and 110). It seems significant that both the *yongzhong* and
the *bo* were suspended by means of identical hooks. The rounded hook at one
end was inserted into the suspension device (*wo* or *niu*) of a given bell, while the
ring at the other end was somehow connected to its rack, probably by a rope.[26]
This type of *gou* apparently goes back in time to Western Zhou; other preserved
specimens are more ornate than those from Taigongmiao, but of similar basic
shape (fig. 105).[27]

*Niuzhong* were suspended in a less complicated fashion: their suspension loops
were fitted into slots on the bottom side of the rack-beam, where they were

26. If so, it would seem puzzling that a rope was not fastened immediately to the *wo*; possibly,
again, the aim was to limit the swaying of the bell when it was struck.
27. The late Western Zhou specimen in fig. 105 is inscribed as "the *gou* of the *congzhong* 從鐘
(bells for enjoyment, *cong* 縱?) made and cast by the ruler of Rui 芮" (Rong Geng 1941, vol. 2, pl.
976; inscription transcribed in vol. 1, 510); it has a second ring fused to the top. A similar specimen
with somewhat more extravagant sculptural dragon decor (vol. 2, pl. 977) is dated by Rong to
"Springs and Autumns to Warring States." Rong (vol. 1, loc. cit.) also mentions the closed metal
ring inserted in the ox-head–ornamented *wo* of the Ji Hou–*yongzhong* in the Sen'oku Hakkokan,
Kyōto (*Gakki*, 24), but for a number of reasons, that bell may not be genuine.

FIGURE 105. Rui Gong–*zhonggou*
(present whereabouts unknown).
Late Western Zhou period.

kept in place by means of bronze insertion pegs (*chaxiao* 插銷). The peg tops
were visible on the side of the bell-rack, and those excavated with the Jingli-
*niuzhong* (see fig. 102) were ornamented with the typical late Warring States
*pushou* 撲獸 mask (fig. 106).[28] In the case of the Zeng-*niuzhong*, the peg tops are
concealed from the view of those standing in front of the rack.

Setting up the bell- and lithophone-racks in the temple courtyard prior to a
ceremony involved specialized personnel (see Chapter 1). This was a major
operation, which the *Shi Jing* describes as follows:

> We put up the beams, we put up the posts [of the bell-rack],
> With their tusk-shaped ornaments and their upright plumes,
> And the responding small drums, the suspended large drums,
> The hand-drums and the musical stones, the wooden striking-basins and the
> tiger-scrapers.
> All is prepared; now they play.[29]

28. For close-up illustrations, see *Xinyang Chu-mu*, pl. 12.4. Very similar pins were found with
the fourteen inlaid *niuzhong* from Xiaotianxi (*Wenwu* 1974 [5]:63–64, pl. 2.4).

29. *Shi Jing* Ode 280 "Yougu" (HYI ed., 76); *trad. auct. adiuv.* Karlgren 1950, 245–46, Waley
1960, 218.

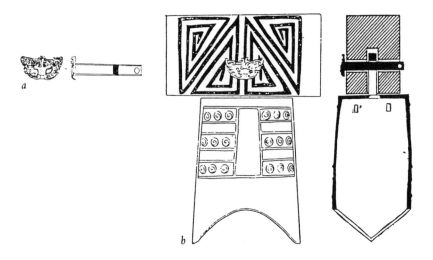

FIGURE 106. Insertion peg of the Jingli-*niuzhong* (see fig. 102). *a*, the peg; *b*, diagram demonstrating the suspension of the *niuzhong*.

## Performance
### Playing Technique

Bells and chimestones were struck by means of mallets. T-shaped specimens of lacquered wood, a little more than one-half meter long, have been excavated in several Eastern Zhou archaeological contexts (fig. 107).[30] Tomb no. 1 at Leigudun yielded six such mallets, and two round lacquered wooden bars measuring 2.15 meters in length;[31] the bars were for striking the large bells on the lower tier of the bell-rack.

The T-shaped mallets extended a player's arm by about half its length, still allowing as much control as necessary to exactly hit the striking point of the A- or B-tone, whichever was intended.[32] It is unclear whether a player handled one or two mallets. This is a matter of importance for reconstructing bell music: if every musician had two mallets rather than one, twice the number of tones could have been played simultaneously, achieving a considerably faster tempo. In today's reenactments (fig. 108), players habitually wield two mallets each,

30. Such mallets have been found, e.g., in tomb no. 1 at Leigudun, at Hougudui, and in tomb no. 1 at Changtaiguan (references in Appendix 1).

31. Tan and Feng 1988, 14–15. The metal butt of a similar bar was found in tomb no. 2 at Xiasi, Xichuan (Henan).

32. My own experiments on Western Zhou bells at the Sen'oku Hakkokan in Kyōto suggest that the B-tone resounds most clearly when the head of the bird- or dragon-shaped marker is hit.

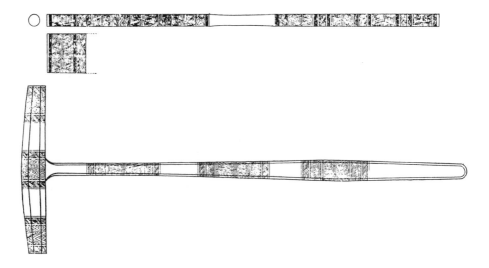

FIGURE 107. T-shaped mallet and round striking-bar excavated in 1978 from the tomb of Marquis Yi of Zeng. The two pieces are drawn to different scales; the bar (L = 215 cm) is actually about four times as long as the mallet (L = 62 cm).

FIGURE 108. Reenactment of performance of Bronze Age music by the Hubei Provincial Folk Music Troupe, using a set of bell replicas tuned to the standard of a Western piano.

FIGURE 109. Pictorial representation of a ritual performance on an unprovenienced *hu* vessel in the Palace
Museum, Beijing. Late fifth century B.C.

which agrees with some depictions on Warring States–period bronzes (see figs.
22 and 23); at least one representation, however, on a *hu* in the Palace Museum,
Beijing (fig. 109), shows several bell-players each holding one mallet with both
hands. In any case, one set of a dozen or so bells was probably the maximum
one player could handle considering the human armspan, even when extended
by two mallets.

The six mallets in Marquis Yi's tomb include two for each of the three chimes
of *yongzhong* on the middle tier of the Marquis's sixty-five-part bell assemblage
(see fig. 1); either one player or a team of two players was in charge of each
chime. From the direction in which the bells were tilted when suspended,
we know that those musicians were positioned behind the rack, facing the audience. Each of the two heavy bars used for striking the lower-tier Zeng bells was
handled by two musicians, whose task was a delicate one: there was some danger that the large bells might break when struck with the relatively forceful
blows required to make them produce a tone. It is possible, moreover, that
the musicians, standing inside the rack, had to keep their faces turned toward
the audience—away from the bells (see fig. 22).[33] This posture must have
made it difficult to hit the striking points of the A- and B-tones with the required
exactitude.

Because of the reduced mobility of these players, the music produced on the
lower-tier Zeng bells was by necessity slow. The time of resonance of those

33. Tan and Feng 1988, 13–14.

FIGURE 110. The five Qin Gong–*yongzhong* (with their suspension hooks), excavated in 1978 at Taigongmiao (see fig. 81). Workshop of Qin, early Springs and Autumns period (probably reign of Wu Gong, 697–678 B.C.).

bells was so much longer that they could not have been played at the same tempo as the smaller *yongzhong* of the middle tier, anyway. We may make the following inference concerning the sort of music played on the Zeng bell assemblage: if the bells on the two tiers were used simultaneously, continuous melodies were probably played only on the middle-tier chimes while the large lower-tier bells provided a bass accompaniment that was melodically much reduced. The vertically suspended *niuzhong* on the third tier could conceivably have been reached by players standing on either side of the rack, but as presently arranged, their musical usefulness may have been quite limited (see Chapter 7).[34]

Because the B-tone markers of early *yongzhong* are habitually placed on the right side of the *gu*, it appears that the bell-chimes of that period were arranged with the deeper tones to the left and the higher tones to the right (fig. 110)—in the same direction as on a modern piano. In most Eastern Zhou bells, B-tone markers are absent, testifying, perhaps, to a higher degree of flexibility in bell arrangements. On the long arm of the Zeng bell-rack, for example, the *yongzhong* on both the middle and lower tiers are positioned in such a way that the

---

34. Players whom I had an opportunity to observe at the Hubei Provincial Museum in 1990 used two mallets each on a set of replicas of the Zeng bells, but only ever struck one note at a time. The players on the rear side of the bell-rack were standing on a low pedestal, from which they could reach both the middle-tier and the upper-tier bells. Being evidently less familiar with the tone distributions in the chimes than the Bronze Age musicians, they had marked the striking points of the A- and B-tones on the bells with large numbers written in chalk (the original tone-naming inscriptions, besides being written in archaic script, are too small to be legible to the naked eye).

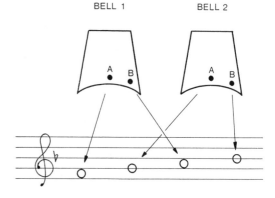

FIGURE 111. Tone distribution on two adjacent bells in a chime. In order to play a scale, it is necessary to move back and forth between the two bells.

largest bell is the furthest on the right from the audience's point of view (see fig. 1); the musicians who played these bells, however, were positioned on both sides of the rack. Thus, from the musician's point of view, in the three sets of *yongzhong* on the middle tier the size gradation proceeds from left to right (as in the Western Zhou bells), but on the long arm of the lower tier it proceeds the other way around. The *yongzhong* performers standing on the two sides of the rack thus played moving in opposite directions. Because the Zeng tone-naming inscriptions are placed on the striking point of the B-tone on both sides of the *gu*, one may suppose that the B-tone was probably produced on whichever side of the bell was convenient to the player. The fact remains that the Zeng virtuosi had to be capable of playing a chime irrespective of whether the bells were arranged from left to right or right to left—a remarkable feat. What modern pianist, or xylophonist, for that matter, would feel comfortable with an instrument on which the order of keys was inverted from the habitual one, or, even worse, on which the order of tones varied in different sections of the instrument?

The two-tone phenomenon was the root of another challenge to the players of Eastern Zhou bell-chimes, making them more difficult in some ways to play than a piano, a Western carillon (where the bell clappers are attached to keys arranged much as on a piano or organ), or indeed a Chinese lithophone. In the other kinds of instruments, adjacent tones are always located next to one another, but in the densely scaled Eastern Zhou bell-chimes, this was not the case. The reason for this lies in the nature of two-tone bells: A- and B-tones are always either a minor or major third apart on the Zhou musical bells. As a result, adjacent tones may be physically far removed from one another in the chime; in the hypothetical example in fig. 111 (two two-tone bells in which the interval between A-tone and B-tone is a major third), to play the simple sequence **do-re-mi**, one had to go from bell 1 to bell 2 and back to bell 1. A player had to memorize exactly on which bell any given tone was to be found, a difficulty that was surely compounded by the lack of any standardized pattern for scaling bell-chimes. As we shall discuss in detail in Chapter 7, the distribution of tones varied from chime to chime, making it necessary for players to familiarize themselves with each chime individually. One of the functions of the tone-naming inscriptions on the Zeng bells may have been to help musicians find their way around that particularly complex assemblage of bells, though, as we shall see, they could not have consulted that information while playing (see Chapter 8).

## The Bells in Concert

Although the classical sources occasionally mention individuals playing on bells or chimestones for their personal enjoyment,[35] we shall do well to remind ourselves that during performances, chimes were not usually played on their own. Their metallic timbre was heard mixed in with the sounds of many other kinds of musical instruments. In a rare Eastern Zhou "concert program" preserved in the *Zuo Zhuan*, two vocal pieces (the *Shi Jing* odes "Wenwang" 文王 and "Luming" 鹿鳴, presented by the "officiating singers" *gong* 工) are preceded by the performance of the ritual dance *Sixia* 肆夏, wherein instrumental accompaniment was provided by bells.[36] This presumably means that the bell-chime had the solo part in a piece performed by a larger ensemble.

What was the position and role of bells in the ancient ritual orchestras? In listing the king's monthly tasks, the *Lüshi Chunqiu* enumerates the instruments of a ritual orchestra as follows:

> In [the fifth] month, [the king] orders the Music Masters to repair the pellet-drums and tambourines [leather] and to harmonize the *qin* 琴 and *se* 瑟 zithers [silk] as well as the pipes and vertical flutes [bamboo]. They hold the shields, halberds, dagger-axes, and plumes,[37] and they tune the *yu* 竽 and *sheng* 笙 mouth-organs [gourd], the ocarinas [clay], and the traverse flutes. They set up the bells [metal], the lithophones [stone], the wooden striking-basin, and the tiger-scraper [wood].[38]

This list includes all the cosmologically relevant Eight Sonorous Substances, among which bells represent metal. But whether the ensemble here listed is a

---

35. *Zuo Zhuan* Xiang 30 (HYI ed., 331); *Lunyu* "Xianwen" par. 39 (HYI ed., 30.)
36. *Zuo Zhuan* Xiang 4 (HYI ed., 257).
37. All these were props used in ritual dances.
38. *Lüshi Chunqiu* "Zhongxia zhi yue" (Sibu Congkan ed., 5:1b–2a); the same text with minor variants may be found in *Li Ji* "Yueling" (*Li Ji Zhushu* 16:10b–11a).

typical one for the late Bronze Age appears questionable. Archaeologically excavated assemblages of musical instruments, especially those from Marquis Yi's tomb (see Introduction), have yielded many of the same instruments, but so far, all Eight Timbres have never been found in any one place.[39] Similarly, in the many *Shi Jing* poems mentioning musical instruments, enumerations stop short of ever providing a complete set of eight, though each of the eight is represented somewhere in the classic.[40] In its very completeness, the *Lüshi Chunqiu* list may reflect a systematizing agenda, motivated by cosmological speculation. As to the actual bell-chimes, apparently they could be used in quite a variety of orchestral settings.

The classical texts provide extremely limited clues that might help us imagine what the actual musical pieces sounded like. Confucius offers the following glimpse:

> This much can be known about music. It begins with playing in unison.
> When it gets into full swing, it is harmonious, clear, and unbroken. In this
> way it reaches the conclusion.[41]

Other snippets from Eastern Zhou texts allude to the role of bells in such musical performances. The *Guo Yu* hints that bells and drums were used to give the impetus at crucial points during the performance, whereupon stringed and wind instruments played the tunes.[42] In several *Shi Jing* odes, a similar succession of musical events may be implied when bells and chimestones are mentioned ahead of other types of melodic instruments.[43] And Mencius builds a metaphor of wisdom and sageness on the image of a piece of music in which metal bells mark the beginning and "jade" chimestones the end.[44] But elsewhere, there are indications that instruments might also have been played in a different order. The *Yue Ji* locus on the "Old Music," for example, which describes how "the performance begins with the music of King Wen, to which is added the stirring music of King Wu,"[45] has traditionally been taken in the sense that the music of Wen consisted of the beating of drums, and that bells

---

39. See Appendix 1.
40. Falkenhausen 1988, 61–69 and table 1.
41. *Lunyu* "Baxian" (HYI ed., 5; Lau, 71).
42. *Guo Yu* "Zhouyu-*xia*" states: "The bells merely impel the tone" (Tiansheng Mingdao ed. 3:12a; d'Hormon, 311), and further on in the same passage: "With metal [bells] and stone [lithophones, the music] is impelled; with silk [zithers] and bamboo [flutes], it is moved on" (Tiansheng Mingdao ed. 3:14a; d'Hormon, 314).
43. *Shi Jing* Odes 208 and 280 (HYI ed., 50 and 76).
44. *Meng Zi* "Wanzhang-*xia*," paragraph 1 (HYI ed., 39).
45. *Li Ji* "Yueji" (*Li Ji Zhushu* 38:11a–b; Couvreur 2:86); *Shi Ji* "Yueshu" (Zhonghua ed., 1222). The entire locus is quoted in Chapter 1.

were struck only during the subsequent music of Wu. And the *Han Fei Zi* says, by way of an extended metaphor for how big troubles can arise from small:

> The *yu* mouth-organ is chief among the [emitters of the] Five Tones. Therefore, when the *yu* plays first, the bells and the *se* zithers all follow suit. When the *yu* sounds, the various instruments are all in harmony.[46]

These bits of information about bells in musical performances are difficult to reconcile; they may refer to different pieces or to regionally different musical practices. They do suggest, however, that bells were viewed as percussion instruments akin to drums; rather than playing melodies, their main function may have been to signal the beginning, the internal subdivisions, and the end of musical pieces. There is no evidence that they marked the time or rhythm of musical pieces, as do some percussion instruments; and, with the possible exception of the "concert program" in *Zuo Zhuan*, mentioned above, there is no indication of a melodic content to what was played on the bell-chimes. Yet their appearance at structurally crucial moments harks back to Rodney Needham's suggestion of a correlation of percussion and transition.[47] We may tentatively conclude that the importance of bell-playing must be evaluated chiefly in terms of the overall process of the ritual action. But our further analysis will reveal that the ancient texts may well not provide the entire story of bell music.

## *The Sound of Bells*

Many extant bronze bells can still be played today. Their tones can be recorded and measured, and this information can be used for reconstructing certain aspects of early Chinese music and musical theory. In this respect, bells are unique among archaeologically known musical instruments from China; even lithophones, made of calcareous stone material that easily disintegrates in the ground (never of jade, *pace* Mencius), are for the most part broken and hence useless for tone measurement.[48] Much of the discussion in the following chapters will be largely concerned with the tone measurements on Bronze Age Chinese chime-bells.

46. *Han Fei Zi* "Jielao" (Zhonghua index ed., 765). On the Five Tones, see Chapter 8.
47. R. Needham 1967.
48. This had happened, e.g., to the Zeng chimestones. Some exceptionally well-preserved lithophones whose measured tones may still tell us something are discussed in Chapter 7. On the acoustical properties of jade, see n. 6, above.

The bell-tones we shall be dealing with are the vibration frequencies of the fundamentals as perceived by the measuring devices used. Frequencies are measured in cycles per second (Hz); for our purposes, however, such figures are more convenient to use when converted into the logarithmic *cent* measurement.[49] In Appendix 4 I have calculated each tone as the distance in cents with respect to $C_0(= 16.352$ Hz), the lowest C the human ear can perceive as a musical tone.[50] ($C_0$ being zero, the standard $A_4$ of 440 Hz, 57 semitones above $C_0$, equals 5700 cents.)

Tone measurements obtained from single bells are of limited musicological interest. What we need are sets of measurements obtained from chimes comprising several bells. How exact do they have to be for us to be able to draw culturally relevant conclusions? This question provokes another: how exact were the instruments under analysis even by their own contemporary standards? We know from Chapter 2 that the tones heard—whether now or in the Bronze Age—could not be exactly identical to those intended by the makers: the mathematically unsound scaling formulas employed by the Zhou casters made it impossible for them to design bell-chimes that would adhere to a single stringent standard of tuning. Under the circumstances, any ideally intended tones could merely be approximated; listeners must have possessed a certain level of tolerance to such inherent inaccuracy. But how much deviation was too much for the Bronze Age connoisseur? Any answer to this question would probably depend on the specific period and place, as well as on the listeners' degree of musical training, which in turn would depend on their social status.

Some reports correlate the measured frequency values with Western tone names (such as C, D, E, etc.) on the equal-tempered scale,[51] with $A_4$ defined as 440 Hz and deviations from the tones on the equal-tempered scale indicated in cents.[52] It should be stressed that, with tone measurements expressed in this

---

49. *Cents* are a logarithmic measuring unit for tonal intervals in a system invented by Alexander Ellis (1814–1890). Each semitonal step in the equal-tempered scale (see below) is assigned a value of 100 cents, the length of an octave being 1200 cents. Whereas raw frequency figures increase exponentially as the pitch becomes higher, intervals expressed in cents are always identical.

50. L. S. Lloyd in *The New Grove* 14: 788.

51. The equal-tempered scale is a series of twelve tones per octave, constructed in such a way that the interval between every two succeeding semitones is mathematically expressed by an exactly equal proportion. This differs from other twelve-tone series that stress simpler mathematical relationships (with the consequence that the intervals between successive semitones differ, sometimes considerably; two examples, the "Pythagorean" and the "Natural" dodecatonic series, are discussed in Chapter 7). The equal-tempered scale has the advantage of consisting of mathematically equal units; the proportion relating every two tones in the scale, however, is a rather complicated mathematical expression.

52. Some authors indicate such equivalencies by means of Western-style musical notation.

manner, the equal-tempered scale is by no means an ideal standard of exactitude against which to evaluate the ancient instruments. It merely serves as a musicological measuring rod; the system of subdividing it by cents was devised as a neutral and relatively simple means for describing the musics of various cultures. No ethnomusicologically known tonal system uses equal tempering in instrument-making. Besides being mathematically difficult to calculate, equal-tempered tone series appear to be cross-culturally regarded as unpleasant to the human ear. It is therefore not at all surprising that the tone series emitted by the ancient Chinese bell-chimes diverge conspicuously from the equal-tempered scale. If, within such a set of measurements, some sort of pattern could be discerned to the deviations of the measured bell-tones from those of the equal-tempered scale, we might be able to reconstruct the system of intonation used in China during the Bronze Age. It is thinkable that, in the future, statistical analysis of a very large amount of such data might reflect prevalent tendencies, though bell-chimes, with their built-in inaccuracy, may not be the best source of for such evidence. This problem will be considered again at the end of Chapter 7.

For us, the main interest of the bell-tone measurements lies in the fact that they indicate the intervals between tones, evidence from which we can reconstruct the tonal framework of ancient Chinese musical practice. In order to obtain such information, we need not pay much attention to the absolute frequency measurements; instead, what is important is the internal consistency of each set of tone measurements. In Chapter 7, therefore, the relationships among the tones, and not their frequencies themselves, are the subject of historical inquiry, and it is my reasoned opinion that the data listed in Appendix 4 can be used for such an analysis. But taking the reported sets of tone measurements to be internally consistent requires certain assumptions; this sort of data presents pitfalls of which we should be clearly aware. Some further discussion here is warranted.

## Tone-Measuring Methods

Bell-tones may be measured in a variety of ways, yielding results of varying accuracy; although it is theoretically safest to combine several methods,[53] this is seldom possible. In the few cases where several sets of measurements are available, one should not expect complete agreement among them; rather, they will illustrate a range of pitch for each tone.

53. Takahashi (1984, 1986) has established and exemplified this method with the Biao-*niuzhong*. Unfortunately, most Chinese sources referred to in Appendix 4 are not explicit as to how the reported frequencies were determined.

The crudest of the most common tone-measurement methods consists of relying simply on aural perception, perhaps aided by a tuning fork.[54] Such a procedure, albeit highly inexact, may not be entirely without value because one's subjective impression might be similar to that of a Bronze Age listener. Since bell-tones are composite tones, the partials picked up by more sophisticated measuring instruments may sometimes differ from the ones most strongly perceived by the human listener.[55] In such cases, the human ear is the ultimate arbiter. However, the exactitude of aural tone measurements is inadequate for the sort of analysis attempted in Chapter 7.[56]

Generally, the exactitude achieved by sophisticated modern equipment is highly dependent on the skill and patience of the user. Stroboscopes, invented some fifty years ago, are still widely used for measuring tones.[57] Although they are commendable for their precision, the margin of error being potentially as little as 1 cent in either direction,[58] these instruments cannot account for changes in frequency occurring after an idiophone has been struck (the tones emitted by most musical instruments are not entirely constant); because the partials of a bell-tone decay at different speeds, the pitch of the fundamental changes to some extent after the idiophone is struck. Comparing stroboscopic measurements with those taken by digital devices, which can do justice to such phenomena, Takahashi has determined the range of difference to amount to ca. 3 cents

54. A list of purely aural values for various sets of bells in the Shaanxi Provincial Museum is given by Ma Chengyuan (1981, 138–39), most of which have since been backed up by more exact measurements (Jiang Dingsui 1984). The tone measurements for the *niuzhong* from tomb no. 1 at Xiasi seem to have been derived entirely by ear; the vibration values indicated are the standard values of the equal-tempered scale with $A_4 = 440$ Hz.

55. This is the case, e.g., in bell no. 22 in the Wangsun Gao–*yongzhong* set from tomb no. 2 at Xiasi, Xichuan (Henan).

56. As a rule, the ear of a well-trained listener can pinpoint tones only to an exactitude of one-half semitone (50 cents), though differences between tones become audible at a threshold of roughly 20 cents. Even under the exacting standards of modern piano-tuning, deviations of up to ca. one-tenth of a semitone (10 cents) are considered inevitable.

57. "The chromatic stroboscope (Stroboconn) [was] invented shortly before World War II by physicists in the laboratories of C. G. Conn Ltd, the American musical instrument makers. In this instrument the frequency of a [tuning] fork whose vibrations are maintained electrically is adjusted by turning a knob that moves a weight along each prong. The vibration of the fork controls the speeds of rotation of patterned discs, there being one disc for each chromatic note in the octave. These discs are illuminated by a gaseous discharge lamp that flashes at the frequency of a sound falling on a microphone. After turning the knob to the right or left, until the pattern on one of the rotating discs appears to stand still, the observer is able to read at once from a graduated scale the deviation of the frequency of the sound from that of the nearest note of the chromatic musical scale at standard pitch ($A_4 = 440$ Hz). The material of the fork is a nickel-chromium-steel alloy that makes the fork's frequency practically independent of the temperature" ("Tuning Fork" entry, by L. S. Lloyd, *The New Grove* 19:256).

58. This at least is the conclusion reached by Wang Xiang (1981, 70) after comparing the strobotuner data taken on the Zeng bells with those determined by a set of tuning forks of German manufacture.

within each tone.[59] This is neglegible; when competently performed, stroboscopic measurements are quite adequate for our present purposes.

Electronic spectrum analyzers, such as the Fast Fourier Transform (FFT) tonometer used by Takahashi, represent a newer generation of technology. They force the vibrations through a digital filter that can determine the pitch and time of decay of every partial with considerable precision. Takahashi does not state the possible margin of error of these measurements, but an apparently similar electronic instrument used by a Shanghai Museum team in testing the Zeng bells had a margin of error of up to 5 cents.[60] Such a margin of error is inevitable because prior to measurement, the machine must be set by its human operator so as to trigger a certain frequency range. Even with repeated measurements triggering slightly different frequency ranges, a probability of some degree of imprecision remains, though not nearly enough to make us hesitate to accept bona fide digital tone measurements for our analysis.

An advantage of digital devices is their ability to produce *sound spectra* for each bell-tone: diagrams plotting the frequencies as well as the relative strengths of all simultaneously occurring partials (fig. 37).[61] Sound spectra constitute useful visual images for each tone, but in the following pages, we shall not use all the information they provide. For our analysis, what we need to know most are the frequencies of the partials that the human ear perceives as the fundamentals. Other variables that may come into play in determining the physical definition of a tone, such as loudness and timbre (i.e., overtone constellation), may be left out of consideration for the time being.

Because almost all sets of tone measurements listed in Appendix 4 were obtained by means of either a stroboscope or some digital device, inaccuracy inherent in the measuring methods need not represent a major source of concern. However, caution is warranted when we proceed to compare different sets of tone measurements obtained under different conditions. Overall, we must take into account two principal sources of inaccuracy: the condition of the instruments measured, and the external circumstances of measurement.

## The Condition of the Instruments

As a general principle, the analysis of tone measurements should be combined with the stylistic examination of the measured specimens, as well as, if possible, an investigation of the archaeological record. Chapter 7, in other words, cannot stand on its own without Chapters 4 and 5 to back it up. Above all, one should

---

59. Takahashi 1984, 94; compare also Takahashi 1986, 51, fig. 1.
60. *Shanghai Bowuguan Jikan* 2 (1982):89.
61. Takahashi 1984, 94–95; Wang Yuzhu et al. 1988; Rossing and Zhou 1989.

ascertain the intended function of the bell or set of bells under analysis. Were they manufactured for musical use, as visual props, or as *mingqi?* In the latter two cases, one would not expect their tones to be musically meaningful. Or, if a set of reported tone measurements does not seem to make musical sense, the possibility that the objects analyzed were not (or not principally) intended for musical use may be considered.

Preservation-related factors may impair the usability of tone measurements. It is true that the bells' age is not in itself a reason to doubt the validity of the frequency figures, for the crystalline structure of cast bronze is not known to undergo any significant long-term transformation that would make itself felt acoustically, even after a timespan of two to three millennia.[62] On the other hand, Chinese bronze bells might well have suffered from excessive use. Referring to Russian church-bells, Edward V. Williams has remarked that "perhaps the most common source of injury to bells in Russia resulted from a breakdown of the microcrystalline structure of the bell metal under repeated blows of the clapper at the same point on the sound-bow."[63] Such a reason for breakage is hard to imagine in the case of the much smaller Chinese chime-bells, except perhaps for large specimens such as the lower-tier Zeng *yongzhong*, which were struck by heavy wooden bars; most bells I have inspected lacked obvious marks of wear.

Being made of bronze, bells are subject to the effects of corrosion. Fortunately, several sets of Chinese chime-bells have been preserved in virtually mint condition, such as the Jingli-*niuzhong* from tomb no. 1 at Changtaiguan, Xinyang, and the two sets of bells from Hougudui, Gushi (both in Henan).[64] Caution may be warranted when dealing with tone measurements from severely corroded bells, whose tone may have been flattened due to loss of substance. How exactly corrosion affects bronze acoustically has yet to be systematically studied. It is generally assumed, however, that a moderate amount of surface corrosion does not significantly affect the tonal qualities of a bell.[65] As long as corrosion is limited to the surface of a bell, the amount of substance lost is insignificant.[66] Pitch frequencies obtained from bells in a less than perfect state of preservation, such as the Biao-*niuzhong* and those from Shangmacun, may hence be accepted with some confidence.

---

62. John Merkel, personal communication, 1986.
63. Williams 1985, 130.
64. For references see Appendix 1.
65. It might be fruitful to test this proposition experimentally.
66. In theory, if each bell in a chime were corroded to an equal extent, the tone distribution within the chime would still remain internally consistent, if generally somewhat flattened due to the loss of substance. But because corrosion also affects the nodal areas, the flattening effect may be at least partially offset by the increased elasticity of the material.

Once broken, on the other hand, an ancient bell is useless for musicological analysis; this remains true even when such a bell has been expertly repaired.[67] Because the mending procedure involves re-casting part of the bell and sometimes adding new metal, it ends up changing the metal structure and uncontrollably altering a bell's vibration frequencies. In cases where retaining the original pitch is not important, a cracked or damaged bell can be reused after welding, as described by Williams for Russian church-bells;[68] but such repair would not have been viable for the ancient Chinese chime-bells.

For similar reasons, replicated bells, even ones that purport to exactly reconstruct a broken original, cannot take the place of the original for tone-measurement purposes. As the production of the replicas of the Zeng bells has shown, it is extremely difficult to cast a bell exactly replicating not only the shape and decoration but also the tone of another.[69] A deviation of at least 50 cents (a quarter-tone) is to be expected even in replicas produced with the most modern technology.[70] Such a deviation is perceptible even to the untrained ear.

On the whole, it is difficult to be precise about the acoustical impact of preservation-related inaccuracy, but as long as we are dealing with measurements taken on original bells in reasonably good condition, what we hear now is probably not too far off from what was heard during the Bronze Age.[71]

*Circumstances of Measurement*

Acoustical frequency measurements are affected by a variety of external factors. The variable that most strongly influences bell frequencies seems to be room temperature. Differences in room temperature at the time of measurement are assumed to have been the principal reason for the considerable and fairly regular differences between the three published sets of tone measurements for the Zeng bells.[72] When comparing his measurements on the Biao-*niuzhong* taken in December 1983 at 17 degrees Celsius with those taken at 29–30 degrees Celsius in August 1985 and August 1986, Takahashi observed an average difference of 8

67. Cases in which tonal data have been taken from repaired bells and are thus no longer useable are those of the middle Western Zhou sets of *yongzhong* from Puducun, Chang'an (Shaanxi), and Rujiazhuang, Baoji (Shaanxi), and apparently also those of the three Chu Gong Wei[?]–*yongzhong* in the Sen'oku Hakkokan (see Appendix 4).

68. Williams 1985, 130–31, see also n. 62 (p. 229).

69. Huang Xiangpeng 1983a.

70. André Lehr, personal communication, 1989.

71. Although excavation reports in most cases are not very explicit about the condition of bronzes, there is no indication of major inaccuracy on account of poor preservation in the chimes singled out for analysis in the following chapters. In Appendix 4, brackets indicate cases in which there is some question as to the validity of the measurement.

72. Tan and Feng 1988, 19–20 and 41–44; for further references see Appendix 4. The only other case in which the temperature at the time of tone measurement was reported is that of the Wangsun Gao–*yongzhong* (Zhao Shigang 1986).

cents per 10 degrees Celsius change in temperature. These deviations are regularly larger for the A-tones (up to 19.8 cents!) than for the B-tones, and they also seem to vary somewhat with the size of the bells.[73] By implication, we may infer that during the Zhou dynasty, too, sets of bells could not have emitted exactly the same tones (or exactly the same set of intervals between tones) at all times of the year. It would have been impossible, moreover, to make sets of bells that were tonally identical to sets of musical stones, if only because of the different behavior of their materials under a change of temperature.

Differences in temperature can become significant in comparing tone-measurement data from different sets. Takahashi is so far alone in adjusting his frequency figures for the Biao-*niuzhong* to the standard temperature of 30 degrees Celsius;[74] most Chinese measurements neglect even to indicate the temperature at the time of measurement. If we are to make any use of such unadjusted measurements, we must make the working assumption that the temperature did not change significantly while the bells of one set were being measured, so that the resulting set of frequency values is at least internally consistent.

Moreover, perceived pitch is amplitude-dependent; in other words, it varies somewhat with the loudness of the tone. This variable is not taken into account in any of the published tone measurements, which do not indicate the amount of force applied in striking the idiophones under analysis.[75] One must make the assumption that the force with which the mallet struck the bells within a set was identical each time. The material of the mallet used for striking the bells at the time of measurement might also have made a difference. An experiment on the Zeng bells with a wooden and a rubber mallet has shown, however, that the tonal differences are infinitesimally small, provided that the strike force remains constant.[76] Even though the subjective impact of the nonmusical *Schlagton* varies greatly with the material of the mallet, the perceived pitch of the fundamentals does not appear affected by a change of materials.

Thus, the concept of pitch is quite relative, and the published tone-measurement data must not be regarded as the non plus ultra.[77] Each of the individual sources of possible error produces deviations that, though virtually neglegible, may cumulatively become significant, especially in cases where we cannot establish with certainty a bell's state of preservation and accuracy of testing. As long as the analysis of tone measurements remains limited to one set,

73. Takahashi 1986, 51–52.
74. Takahashi 1986, 53, table 2.
75. The striking force can be normalized if, instead of using a mallet, a pendulum is placed at a constant distance from the surface to be struck.
76. *Shanghai Bowuguan Jikan* 2 (1982):90.
77. Rossing and Houtsma 1986; Houtsma and Rossing 1987.

some optimism seems justified; ordinarily, published sets of tone measurements may be assumed to be internally consistent. Comparing the measured absolute frequencies of different bell-chimes with one another, on the other hand, raises risks with respect to the lack of standardization of measurements and the generally insufficient information about measurement conditions. In such cases, as long as all external conditions are not accounted for, a margin of tolerance of at least one semitone must probably be allowed, which severely limits the possibility of comparing chimes with one another.

## Summary

During the Bronze Age, bell-chimes developed into more and more versatile instruments, comprising an ever-larger number of components that were assembled in ever more variable arrangements. Because the actual musical compositions are lost, we cannot be entirely certain whether the Zhou dynasty bell-players made full use of the potential of their instruments, but even when looking merely at how the "suspended music" was arranged, it becomes obvious that playing the bell-chimes necessitated an appreciable degree of dexterity and coordination. To some extent, such skills may in the future be regained through practice with imaginative reconstructions.

We have established that chime-bells, when played today, still emit more or less the same tones as they did in the Bronze Age, provided they have been reasonably well preserved. With the techniques now available, these tones can be measured with a high degree of accuracy. The published tone-measurement figures can be accepted with some confidence, though caveats are in order when it comes to comparing data from different sources. The impact of instrument preservation or inaccurate tone measurement on the frequency figures listed in Appendix 4 is trivial compared to the impact of deficiencies inherent in ancient bell manufacture.

# CHAPTER SEVEN

# The Tone Measurements and
# Their Interpretation

*Charting the Tone Distributions*

Being chimed idiophones, bell-chimes and lithophones differ from other ancient musical instruments in that the number of tones one could play on them was quite limited. All playable tones thus were probably musically relevant. On archaeologically excavated wind instruments such as flutes or ocarinas, a large number of tones may still be obtained by various blowing and fingering techniques, yet we cannot know which of these tones were habitually played by the ancient Chinese musicians. The only technique for playing the bell-chimes, on the other hand, is striking with a mallet. Considering the effort and expense involved in manufacturing every single bell, at least one of its two tones must have had a musical rationale. Even though both A- and B-tones played a role in the scaling of Zhou dynasty chimes, we must pay particular attention to A-tones, which resound more strongly and are easier to produce, and which therefore may have been of somewhat greater importance in practice than B-tones. Sometimes, indeed, morphological indications (e.g., the modifications of the sound-bow in Shang *nao* and the absence of B-tone markers in some Western Zhou *yongzhong*) allow us to conclude that only the A-tone was intended to be played.

Our assumption in this chapter, then, is that the observable distributions of tones in Bronze Age bell-chimes are meaningful. Most Chinese bell-chimes emit far fewer tones than, say, modern Western pianos, xylophones, or Glockenspiele, which feature twelve tones per octave. If the distribution of tones in one chime follows a discernible pattern, that pattern should tell us something about ancient Chinese music; and if comparison of such patterns on a number of chimes reveals changes through time, such changes may be assumed to elucidate aspects of the historical development of Chinese music.

Reserving the intricacies of ancient Chinese musical theory for the following chapter, suffice it for now to say that ancient Chinese music, like Western classical music, used discrete notes of definable pitch. Notes separated by an octave (or by multiple octaves) were conceived of as equivalent. In both the Chinese and the Western traditions, one octave contains a gamut of twelve notes.[1] Throughout this chapter, rather than using the ancient Chinese tone nomenclature, I shall employ Western terms such as **do-re-mi** for designating notes within a tonality, and *C-D-E* for indicating tones of absolute pitch.

In rendering the bell-tone measurements musically meaningful, each measured pitch must be defined as a note in a tonality, as is attempted in the charts illustrating this chapter (figs. 112–139). The principle in deciding which notes to assign to each measured tone is to avoid complex designations such as **do**-sharp or **re**-flat. Thus, our first objective is to define one tone in a set of measurements as **do** in such a way that, subsequently, as many other tones within the set as possible can be defined by simple names such as **sol**, **mi**, **la**, and **re**. The validity of this method, which was first applied systematically to an appreciable amount of data by Li Chunyi,[2] has been demonstrated by the Zeng bell inscriptions: the names of notes inscribed on their recto faces exactly correspond to what one would expect from such principles (see Chapter 8). When a chime of bells contains a large number of tones per octave, more than one possibility of defining **do** may suggest itself; but in practice one alternative usually stands out as strikingly superior to all others.

Secondly, when analyzing the tone measurements, we shall look for octavic regularity: we want to see whether certain tonal patterns within a chime are repeated from octave to octave. Such patterns are likely to possess musical relevance. To make it easier to detect octavic regularity, I have charted the tone measurements in superimposed octaves, the numbers 1 to 12 at the top of the

1. Comparison with other musical traditions shows that this is by no means a matter of course. Correspondences between traditional Chinese and Western systems of musical theory (including the associated cosmological thinking) are sufficiently impressive to have prompted repeated claims for a Western origin for ancient Chinese music—be it Greece (Chavannes 1898), Persia (Kuttner 1968), or Babylonia (Major 1978; McClain 1985). As there is so far virtually no reliable archaeological evidence to document direct Sino-Western interaction in pre-Qin times, such arguments have been based exclusively on comparisons of the respective musical systems. I shall not try to disprove such diffusion hypotheses, though it should be pointed out that the mathematical relationships among harmonically related tones are unvarying regardless of space or time and that there is nothing inherently improbable in the notion that they might have been discovered several times in different cultural contexts (see Rao Zongyi 1988b; a sophisticated argument against musical diffusion to China in antiquity, albeit somewhat superseded by new archaeological finds, may be found in Granet 1934, 174–209). In this book, it is my intention to stake out the local time-depth and historical development of musical ideas. Such evidence may eventually be used in evaluating diffusion hypotheses.

2. Li Chunyi 1957a and b, 1964a and b. Yang Yinliu (1959b) also used this method in discussing the tones of the Jingli-*niuzhong*; see also Huang Xiangpeng 1978–80.

chart indicating segments of 100 cents' width. Each measured frequency can be placed in one such segment; with **do** conventionally set as 1, all notes correspond to certain numerical positions (**re** = 3, **mi** = 5, **sol** = 8, **la** = 10). An A-tone is represented by a round mark, a B-tone by a square mark.

In accordance with the cautionary tales on the validity of absolute tone measurement values, spelled out in the preceding chapter, we shall not put much weight on the comparison of absolute frequencies of bells from different chimes. However, the relationships among tones within a chime that become apparent when a set of measurements is charted according to the above principles may be profitably compared to one another. Even though the absolute frequencies of **do** tend to differ from chime to chime, the intervals between the notes are often interestingly similar.

One pervasive phenomenon should be briefly addressed before we scrutinize the tone-measurement charts: tone distributions are usually not uniform throughout the total range of a chime. Within any one chime, the constellations of tones emitted by the larger and lower-pitched bells significantly diverge from those of the smaller, high-pitched ones. Typically, in what I shall refer to as the "higher register," a regular pattern can be seen repeating itself through several octaves. In the "lower register," by contrast, such a pattern is less frequently observable (or less easy to spot).[3] This dichotomy probably reflects the fact that, given their longer time of resonance, the musical functions of large bells differed from those of small ones, an issue already addressed in the previous chapter.

Let us now review the chimes for which relevant tone measurements have been published, following the chronological order of manufacture.

### The Tones of Shang Dynasty Nao

The tone measurements obtained from five late Anyang period chimes of *nao* are charted in figure 112.[4] They fail to show a coherent pattern: no two chimes are alike, and no preference for any interval between successive tones can be detected. As detailed in Appendix 4, the intervals between the A-tones of the largest and smallest bells in each chime vary greatly: they lie between ca. a major third (475 cents) and ca. a major sixth (954 cents), averaging 792 cents. We may observe that in each of the five chimes, all tones fall within the range of a single octave; there is thus no chance for octavic regularity.

---

3. The notion of a "higher register/lower register" dichotomy was first developed by Asahara 1987.

4. With the exception of the bells from tomb no. 1083 at Xibeigang, all these measurements are from Huang Xiangpeng 1978–80. The author's indications as to the identities of the respective sets are so vague that only the set from Xiaonanzhuang, Wen Xian (Henan), can be identified with some certainty. References in Appendix 1.

In figure 112, the lowest tone in each *nao*-chime has been arbitrarily defined as **do**; the pitch of this **do** varies considerably from set to set, ranging from C to E and A, and the additional tones besides **do** differ from chime to chime. But even when a different arrangement is chosen (as in figure 113, where identification of any tone with **do** is renounced),[5] structural parallels between the tone distributions in the different chimes do not emerge.

In the three cases where B-tones have been measured, such measurements only add to the impression of irregularity of the tonal arrangement. The intervals between A- and B-tones on individual bells vary widely, ranging from virtual identity of pitch (bell no. 3 in the chime from Dasikongcun) to a fourth (bells nos. 1 and 3 in the chime from Anyang).[6] This variability corroborates our previous notion, based on morphological evidence—the thickened center portion of the sound-bow (see Chapter 2)—that the two-tone phenomenon was not yet realized by the Anyang bell-players. Moreover, the virtually overlapping tones of the two smallest bells in the four-part chime of *nao* from tomb no. 1083 at Xibeigang, Anyang (Henan), reconfirm our previous impression (see Chapter 4) that one of these two bells probably did not originally belong to that chime.

We are forced to conclude that producing any sort of regular tonal pattern on bell-chimes was apparently not yet a high priority for the Shang bell-casters. Perhaps, at the time, the attractive novelty consisted merely in the idea of having several metallic objects "sing" at different pitches.

## Chimes of Mid–Western Zhou–Type Yongzhong

In the Chinese archaeological record, mid–Western Zhou *yongzhong* sets from Shaanxi are the next type of bells that were manufactured as chimed sets. We have seen in Chapter 4 that the transformation of *nao* into *yongzhong*, which had occurred in the intervening one and one-half centuries or so, was probably triggered by the discovery of the two-tone phenomenon. Although tone measurements have been published for a fair number of individual *yongzhong* of the earliest stylistic types (see Appendix 3), useable data are as yet scarce for

---

5. Huang Xiangpeng (1978–80, pt. 1) endeavors to correlate the tones measured on various kinds of Shang instruments (including bells and chimestones) into a single tonal system; the validity of that attempt is doubtful, first, on account of the difficulty of comparing sets of tone measurements obtained under different conditions, and second, because it is impermissible to jumble together data from different kinds of musical instruments.

6. Such findings accord with Ma Chengyuan's (1981, 134) measurements on eight individual Shang dynasty bells in the Shanghai Museum, where the A–B-tone interval ranges between a minor second and a minor sixth. Ma does not provide any details about the stylistic characteristics of the bells in question, which might permit inference as to whether they are of southern or northern manufacture.

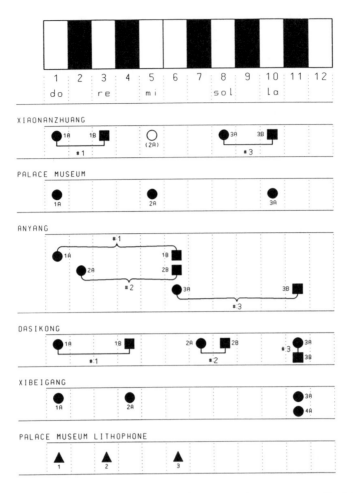

FIGURE 112. Tone distributions in some late Shang chimes. All of the tone-
distribution diagrams in this chapter (figs. 113–140) may be interpreted as follows:
tone distributions are superposed octave by octave. A round marker indicates the
A-tone of a bell, a square marker the B-tone, and a triangular marker a tone played
by a chimestone; filled-in markers indicate considerable confidence in tone-
placement, while outline-only markers reflect hypothetical placement or questionable data. The two tones on each bell are linked by brackets: a square bracket if the
interval between the two tones is a minor third or smaller, and a pointed bracket if
the interval is a major third or larger. The numbering of the bells, which in most
cases follows the original reports, exhibits some inconsistencies. The absolute cent
figures are listed chronologically in Appendix 4 (except for figs. 117, 125, 126,
130–133, 136–140, and the bottom half of fig. 114). In the present diagram, the
lowest tone playable in each chime has been arbitrarily designated as **do**. For two
of the five bell-chimes, B-tone measurements are unavailable.

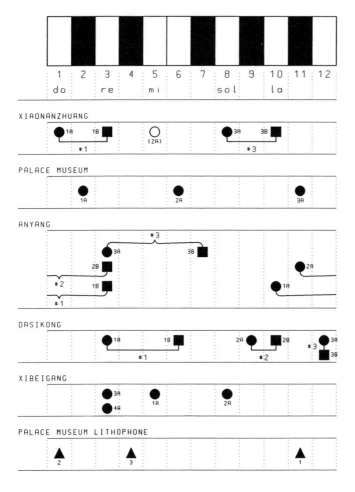

FIGURE 113. Tone distributions in late Shang sets of *nao*. In this diagram, the tone C is arbitrarily designated as **do**, and the measured tones are charted accordingly. All tones are kept within the span of a single octave.

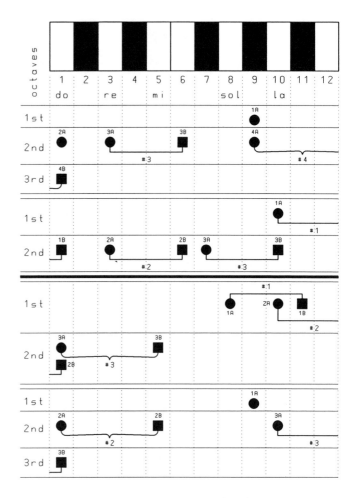

FIGURE 114. Tone distributions in several mid–Western Zhou sets of *yongzhong*. At the top are data from well-preserved chimes: *tier 1*, Mawangcun set no. V; *tier 2*, Zhuangbai set no. V. Below the solid line are data from chimes of repaired bells, to be taken with some caution: *tier 3*, *yongzhong* from Puducun; *tier 4*, *yongzhong* from Rujiazhuang.

bell-chimes. Only two fully valid sets of measurements could be included in figure 115: from the four-piece chime no. 5 from hoard no. 1 at Mawangcun, Chang'an (Shaanxi),[7] and the three-piece chime no. 5 from hoard no. 1 at Zhuangbai, Fufeng (Shaanxi).[8]

In figure 114 we immediately notice a trend to much greater uniformity than in the Anyang period *nao* tones. As the tone distributions range somewhat in excess of one octave, it is possible to spot some overlap of tones from one octave to the next. Moreover, the tendency toward emphasizing tones of the anhemitonic pentatonic gamut (**do-re-mi-sol-la**) is remarkable. In both the Mawangcun and the Zhuangbai chimes, measurements make the best sense when **do** is defined as ca. C or C-sharp; this seems to prefigure later trends.[9]

The two largest bells in the Mawangcun chime did not emit recognizable B-tones. The preferred A–B tone interval in other bells of the three earliest stylistic *yongzhong* types (table 10) for the most part ranges between a minor third and a major third, though the observable variation (236–420 cents) is still quite considerable. These characteristics may prefigure the tonal patterns seen in later Western Zhou chimes, in which the B-tones of the two largest bells appear irrelevant and the interval between A- and B-tones is always either a major or a minor third. Below, I shall term bells in which the A- and B-tones are a major third apart *major-third bells*; *minor-third bells* are bells in which the two tones are separated by a minor third.

7. Reference in Appendix 1. The bells look similar to the ones in figs. 72–73.

8. Reference in Appendix 1. The bells look similar to the inscribed specimen in fig. 73, which was excavated from the same hoard but which, as the tone measurements show, cannot possibly have been part of the same chime originally.

9. The tone measurements on the three-*yongzhong* chime from tomb no. 6 at Zhuyuangou, Baoji (Shaanxi), and the approximate aural equivalents for the tones of the chime from Weizhuang, Pingdingshan (Henan), by and large confirm this picture (references in Appendix 1; the Zhuyuangou data are included in Appendix 4). The tone distribution in the Zhuyuangou chime shows some structural similarity to that of the Mawangcun chime (compare fig. 115): setting 2A as **do** (as proposed in the original report), we arrive at a sequence of **sol-si, do-mi, sol**-sharp–**la**-sharp. It must be noted, however, that the **do** of the Zhuyuangou chime is D-sharp, not C as in the Mawangcun chime. The original report notes that the third Zhuyuangou bell, given its stylistic and acoustic heterogeneity, probably did not originally belong to the same chime as the other two; Li Chunyi (1990) suggests that it may have been combined with the others because its A-tone was the approximate octavic equivalent of *yongzhong* no. 1 (interval: 1275 cents). On the other hand, bells no. 2 and 3 are actually more in tune with each other than with bell no. 1 (cf. tabulation in Appendix 4). The Weizhuang chime shows less regularity; although its tone distribution, too, spans an octave and a half (from $F_3$ to $B_4$), there is no instance of octavic equivalence. Largely similar characteristics can also be observed in the tone measurements on the mid–Western Zhou three-part sets of *yongzhong* from Puducun and Rujiazhuang; here, too, the most suitable **do** is ca. C. The funerary context of excavation for these bells permits a more exact dating than is possible for the Mawangcun and Zhuangbai sets, which were unearthed from terminal Western Zhou hoards. It should be cautioned, however, that the bells in both these sets have undergone repair, so that all the tones emitted may no longer be accurate.

TABLE 10.    A–B Tone Intervals in Mid–Western Zhou *Yongzhong* Chimes

|  | Interval (in cents) | Interval type |
|---|---|---|
| (J23) Zhuangbai set VII, no. 1 | 334 | minor third |
| (J24) Zhuangbai set VII, no. 2 | 353 | Major third |
| (J25) Mawangcun set I, no. 23 | 374 | Major third |
| (J29) Mawangcun set V, no. 3 | 329 | minor third |
| (J30) Mawangcun set V, no. 4 | 420 | Major third |
| (J31) Dongjucun | 338 | minor third |
| (J32) Liujiacun | 314 | minor third |
| (J40) First Xing–*yongzhong* | 278 | minor third |
| (J41) Zhuangbai set V, no. 1 | 297 | minor third |
| (J42) Zhuangbai set V, no. 2 | 236 | Major second |
| (J43) Zhuangbai set V, no. 3 | 363 | Major third |
| (J44) Qijia | 363 | Major third |
| (J45) Qizhen hoard no. 2 | 301 | minor third |
| (J46) Beiqiao no. 2 | 258 | minor third |
| (J47) Mawangcun no. 20 | 312 | minor third |
| (J48) Mawangcun no. 21 | 366 | Major third |
| (SH Yi 121) (uninscribed) | 245 | Major second |
| (SH Chen 2) First Zha | 314 | minor third |
| Zhuyuangou tomb no. 7, no. 1: | 353 | Major third |
| Zhuyuangou tomb no. 7, no. 2: | 382 | Major third |
| Zhuyuangou tomb no. 7, no. 3: | 224 | Major second |
|  |  |  |
| Average interval | 313.9 cents | |
| Average minor third (or smaller, $N = 13$) | 293.8 cents | |
| Average Major third ($N = 8$) | 371.8 cent | |

NOTE. Entries identified with numbers prefixed by *J* are based on raw data from Jiang Dingsui 1984; entry numbers prefixed by *SH* denote bells in the Sen'oku Hakkokan measured by Takahashi and Ueda 1986.

## Late Western Zhou Chimes of Yongzhong

In Chapter 5, it was mentioned that late Western Zhou chimes of *yongzhong* from Shaanxi appear to have consisted, as a rule, of eight bells. Published tone measurements show a high degree of consistency among the tone distributions in all these chimes. The pattern charted in figure 115 reflects what may be observed in the two complete chimes from Qijiacun, Fufeng (Shaanxi) (the Zuo-*yongzhong* and the Zhongyi-*yongzhong*), as well as in partially preserved chimes of the same type, such as the Ni-*yongzhong* from Haosihe, Yongshou (Shaanxi), and the Second and Third Xing–*yongzhong* from Zhuangbai, Fufeng

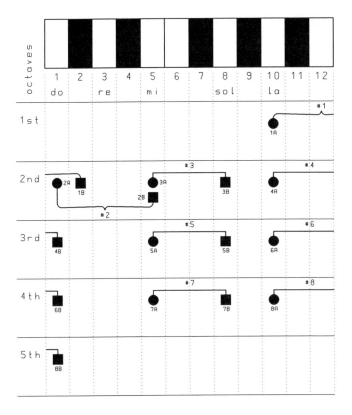

FIGURE 115. Tone distribution in late Western Zhou
eight-part sets of *yongzhong* (e.g., the Zhong Yi–
*yongzhong* chime; see fig. 18). Lower register: bells nos.
1 and 2; higher register: bells nos. 3–8.

(Shaanxi). With the exception of the Ni-*yongzhong*, all these chimes exemplify
the more ornate type of late Western Zhou *yongzhong*, featuring dragon ornamentation in the *gu*.

In late Western Zhou chimes of *yongzhong*, the lower register consists of bells
nos. 1 and 2, the higher register of bells nos. 3 to 8. The A-tones of the two
bells in the lower register were regularly spaced a minor third apart, and they
are best defined as **la** and **do**, respectively. Those lower-register *yongzhong* on
which a B-tone can be produced at all were major-third bells; the already-noted
absence of B-tone markers on the two largest *yongzhong* in these chimes (see fig.
110) suggests that their B-tones had little or no musical relevance.[10]

10. The question of why the largest bells in late Western Zhou chimes were usually major-third
bells (and not minor-third bells like the others) remains obscure.

The six *yongzhong* of the higher register (which do have B-tone markers) are all minor-third bells. They are grouped in pairs, every two bells invariably emitting an identical pattern of four tones: **mi-sol/la-do**. In a complete chime of eight, this pattern is repeated through three octaves.

With the exception of the probably irrelevant B-tone of the largest bell (which corresponds to **do**-sharp), all tones in such a chime are part of the pentatonic gamut. The conspicuous absence of the tone **re** from this tone distribution has led to interesting speculations, to which we shall return later in this chapter. As in the mid–Western Zhou *yongzhong* chimes considered earlier, **do** hovered in the vicinity of C, ranging from A-sharp through C-sharp (table 11). Such a discrepancy probably lay well within the limits of tolerance of Bronze Age listeners.[11]

In table 12, the A–B tone intervals in Western Zhou *yongzhong* have been tabulated separately for different stylistic types of these bells. The statistics show that late Western Zhou bell-casters were able to assert much greater control over the A–B tone interval in *yongzhong* than their mid–Western Zhou predecessors. In mid–Western Zhou, this interval is often close to 350 cents, midway between a minor and a major third. Late Western Zhou bell-casters, by contrast, had evidently learned to manipulate the shape of the bell in such a way as to create distinct minor- and major-third bells. This was a significant technical development. The A–B tone intervals in **mi-sol** bells and **la-do** bells of late Western Zhou chimes of the elaborate stylistic type are, on average, extremely close to the "natural" minor third of 316 cents. The histogram in table 13 shows that Eastern Zhou bell-casters kept up the standards established by their Western Zhou predecessors, slightly improving upon them on occasion.

*Chimes of the Springs and Autumns Period*

The tone-distribution pattern established for the late Western Zhou *yongzhong* chimes remained standard throughout most of Eastern Zhou. The early seventh-century Qin Gong–*yongzhong* from Taigongmiao, Baoji (Shaanxi), virtually reproduce a Western Zhou prototype, which is not surprising given the very conservative shape and ornamentation of those bells.[12] Other Springs and Autumns period chimes, however, show an increased degree of tonal complexity: for example, **re** was now regularly included among the notes playable on a chime. The earliest known instance of such a tendency is a seventh-century B.C. *yongzhong* chime from Lijialou, Xinzheng (Henan). The tones of only six

11. See Asahara 1987, 93 and passim.
12. These bells are illustrated in fig. 111; references in Appendix 1. It must be cautioned that the data published by Ma Chengyuan (1981, 139) are based on aural perception only.

TABLE 11.    The Pitch of **do** in Western and Eastern Zhou Chimes

| | Bell tone producing lowest **do** in chime | Pitch of lowest **do** | |
| --- | --- | --- | --- |
| | | Cents notation | Conventional notation |
| *Western Zhou* | | | |
| Mawangcun chime no. 5 | 2A | 4819 | C$_4$ + 19 |
| Zhuangbai chime no. 5 | 1B | 4775 | C$_4$ − 25 |
| Zhuyuangou tomb no. 7 *yongzhong* | 2A | 6326 | D$\sharp_5$ + 26 |
| Ni-*yongzhong* | 2A | 4803 | C$_4$ + 1 |
| Second Xing–*yongzhong* | 11–2A | 4590 | A$\sharp_3$ − 10 |
| Third Xing–*yongzhong* | 2A | 4598 | A$\sharp_3$ − 2 |
| Zhong Yi–*yongzhong* | 2A | 4700 | B$_3$ +/−0 |
| Zuo-*yongzhong* | 2A | 4764 | C$_4$ − 36 |
| *Eastern Zhou* | | | |
| *Yongzhong* from Lijialou (6 bells from set B[?]) | (4)A | 4600 | A$\sharp_3$ |
| Lithophone from Shangmacun tomb no. 13 | No.4 | 6030 | C$_5$ + 30 |
| *Niuzhong* from Shangmacun tomb no. 13 | 6B | 6042 | C$_5$ + 42 |
| *Niuzhong* from Xiasi tomb no. 1 | 3A | ? | G$_4$? |
| Wangsun Gao–*yongzhong* (higher register only) | 10A | 5249 | E$_4$ + 49 |
| Zeng *niuzhong* chime U2 + 3 | U3–7A | 5377 | F$\sharp_4$ − 23 |
| Zeng *yongzhong* chime M1 | 7A | 5840 | B$_4$ + 40 |
| Zeng *yongzhong* chime M2 | 7A | 5965 | C$_5$ − 35 |
| Zeng *yongzhong* chime M3 | 8A | 4774 | C$_4$ − 26 |
| Zeng *yongzhong* chime L1 + 2 | L1–1A | 2392 | C$_2$ − 8 |
| Lithophone from Sanmenxia (Houchuan tomb no. 2041?) | No.1 | 4656 | B$_3$ − 44 |
| Biao-*niuzhong* | 1A | 5372 | F$\sharp_4$ − 28 |
| Jingli-*niuzhong* | 7A | 7090 | B$_5$ − 10 |
| alternative **do** | 4A | 6576 | F$\sharp_5$ − 24 |

NOTE. The Jingli-*niuzhong* chime includes two possible **do**, either of which may have been considered the principal one, but the first bell in that chime is probably of heterogeneous origin and was therefore omitted from consideration for this table. A similar reason (broken condition of the lower-register bell expected to have originally yielded the lowest **do**) explains the atypically high **do** value in the Shangmacun bell-chime. For the bell-chime from tomb no. 1 at Xiasi, the exact tone measurements have not been reported.

TABLE 11. The Pitch of **do** in Western and Eastern Zhou Chimes (*continued*)

*Histogram*

| No. of occurrences, Western Zhou | Frequency range | No. of occurrences, Eastern Zhou |
|---|---|---|
| | A—A + 50 | |
| xx | A + 50—A♯ | |
| | A♯—A♯ + 50 | x |
| | A♯ + 50—B | xx |
| x | B—B + 50 | x |
| x | B + 50—C | xxx |
| xx | C—C + 50 | xx |
| | C + 50—C♯ | |
| | C♯—C♯ + 50 | |
| | C♯ + 50—D | |
| | D—D + 50 | |
| | D + 50—D♯ | |
| | D♯—D♯ + 50 | |
| | D♯ + 50—E | |
| | E—E + 50 | x |
| | E + 50—F | |
| | F—F + 50 | |
| | F + 50—F♯ | xxx |
| | F♯—F♯ + 50 | |
| | F♯ + 50—G | |
| | G—G + 50 | |
| | G + 50—G♯ | |
| | G♯—G♯ + 50 | |
| | G♯ + 50—A | |

TABLE 12. A–B Tone Intervals in Late Western Zhou *Yongzhong*

| | Interval (in cents) | Interval type |
|---|---|---|
| *Earlier Stylistic Type (Geometric Ornaments in gu)* | | |
| (J33) Beiqiao no. 1 | 361 | Major third |
| (J34) Zhuangbai set V, no. 1 | 348 | minor third |
| (J35) Zhuangbai set V, no. 2 | 355 | Major third |
| (J36) Mawangcun set IV, no. 1 | 338 | minor third |
| (J37) Mawangcun set IV, no. 2 | 358 | Major third |
| (J38) Ying Hou–*yongzhong* | 306 | minor third |
| (J82) Ni-*yongzhong* no. 1 | 0 | ? |
| (J83) Ni-*yongzhong* no. 2 | 0 | ? |
| (J84) Ni-*yongzhong* no. 3 | 306 | minor third |
| (J85) Ni-*yongzhong* no. 4 | 356 | Major third |
| (J62) Yongxiang-*yongzhong* | 329 | minor third |
| (J65) Shi Cheng–*yongzhong* | 308 | minor third |

TABLE 12. *(continued)*

| | Interval<br>(in cents) | Interval type |
|---|---|---|
| *Earlier Stylistic Type (Geometric Ornaments in* gu*) (continued)* | | |
| (SH Chen 10) Second Zha | 329 | minor third |
| (SH Chen 5) Chu Gong Jia?–*yongzhong* no. 1 (repaired?) | 344 | minor third |
| (SH Chen 6) Chu Gong Jia?–*yongzhong* no. 2 (repaired?) | 378 | Major third |
| (SH Chen 7) Chu Gong Jia?–*yongzhong* no. 3 (repaired?) | 347.7 | minor third |
|   Average interval | 335.5 cents | |
|   Average minor third (*N* = 7) | 323 cents | |
|   Average Major third (*N* = 4) | 357.5 cents | |
| *Later Stylistic Type (Animal Ornamentation in* gu*)* | | |
| (J50) Second Xing–*yongzhong* II-2 | 392 | Major third |
| (J51) Second Xing–*yongzhong* II-3 | 318 | minor third |
| (J52) Second Xing–*yongzhong* II-4 | 345 | minor third |
| (J53) Second Xing–*yongzhong* IV-1 | 324 | minor third |
| (J54) Second Xing–*yongzhong* IV-2 | 331 | minor third |
| (J55) Second Xing–*yongzhong* IV-3 | 307 | minor third |
| (J58) Third Xing–*yongzhong* no. 3 | 308 | minor third |
| (J59) Third Xing–*yongzhong* no. 4 | 329 | minor third |
| (J60) Third Xing–*yongzhong* no. 5 | 245 | Major second |
| (J61) Third Xing–*yongzhong* no. 6 | 317 | minor third |
| (J66) Zuo–*yongzhong* no. 1 | 396 | Major third |
| (J67) Zuo–*yongzhong* no. 2 | 400 | Major third |
| (J68) Zuo–*yongzhong* no. 3 | 333 | minor third |
| (J69) Zuo–*yongzhong* no. 4 | 315 | minor third |
| (J70) Zuo–*yongzhong* no. 5 | 342 | minor third |
| (J71) Zuo–*yongzhong* no. 6 | 291 | minor third |
| (J72) Zuo–*yongzhong* no. 7 | 235 | Major second |
| (J73) Zuo–*yongzhong* no. 8 | 309 | minor third |
| (J74) Zhong Yi–*yongzhong* no. 1 | 460 | fourth |
| (J75) Zhong Yi–*yongzhong* no. 2 | ? | ? |
| (J76) Zhong Yi–*yongzhong* no. 3 | 320 | minor third |
| (J77) Zhong Yi–*yongzhong* no. 4 | 343 | minor third |
| (J78) Zhong Yi–*yongzhong* no. 5 | 317 | minor third |
| (J79) Zhong Yi–*yongzhong* no. 6 | 347 | minor third |
| (J80) Zhong Yi–*yongzhong* no. 7 | 310 | minor third |
| (J81) Zhong Yi–*yongzhong* no. 8 | 303 | minor third |
| (J86) Ning–*yongzhong* (Shaanxi) | 348 | minor third |
| (SH Chen 1) Ning–*yongzhong* | 336 | minor third |
| (J87) Nangong Hu–*yongzhong* | 343 | minor third |
| (SH Chen 9) Guo Shu Lü–*yongzhong* | 349 | minor third |
| (SH Chen 3) Xi Zhong–*yongzhong* | 333 | minor third |
|   Average interval | 335 cents | |
|   Average minor third (or smaller) (*N* = 26) | 323 cents | |
|   Average Major third (or larger) (*N* = 4) | 416 cents | |

NOTE. Entries identified with numbers prefixed by *J* are based on raw data from Jiang Dingsui 1984; numbers prefixed by *SH* denote bells in the Sen'oku Hakkokan measured by Takahashi and Ueda 1986.

TABLE 13.    A–B Tone Intervals in Western and Eastern Zhou Bells

*Histogram*

| No. of occurrences, Western Zhou | Range (in cents) | No. of occurrences, Eastern Zhou |
|---|---|---|
| XXX | ≤249 | XXXX |
| X | 250–259 | X |
| XX | 260–269 | X |
| XX | 270–279 | XXX |
|  | 280–289 | XXXXX |
| X | 290–299 | XXXXXXXXXX |
| XXXXXXXXXX | 300–309 | XXXXXXXXX |
| XXXXXXXXXX | 310–319 | XXXXXXXXXXXXXXXXX |
| XXXXXXX | 320–329 | XXXXXXXXXXXXXXX |
| XXXXXX | 330–339 | XXXXXXXX |
| XXXXXXXXXX | 340–349 | XXXXXXXX |
| XXXXX | 350–359 | XXXXXX |
| XXX | 360–369 | XXX |
| X | 370–379 | XXXXX |
|  | 380–389 | XXXXXXX |
| XX | 390–399 | XXXX |
| X | 400–409 | XXX |
|  | 410–419 | XXXXXXX |
| X | 420–429 | XXXX |
|  | 430–439 | XX |
|  | 440–449 | X |
| X | ≥450 | XX |

*Tabulation*

| Range (in cents) | Percentage of Intervals | |
|---|---|---|
|  | Western Zhou | Eastern Zhou |
| ≤249 | 5 | 3 |
| 250–259 | 2 | 1 |
| 260–269 | 3 | 1 |
| 270–279 | 2 | 2 |
| 280–289 | 9 | 4 |
| 290–299 | 2 | 9 |
| 300–309 | 15 | 7 |
| 310–319 | 15 | 13 |
| 320–329 | 11 | 12 |
| 330–339 | 9 | 9 |
| 340–349 | 15 | 6 |
| 350–359 | 8 | 5 |
| 360–369 | 5 | 2 |

TABLE 13.    *(continued)*

Tabulation *(continued)*

| Range (in cents) | Percentage of Intervals | |
| --- | --- | --- |
| | Western Zhou | Eastern Zhou |
| 370–379 | 2 | 4 |
| 380–389 | | 6 |
| 390–399 | 3 | 3 |
| 400–409 | 2 | 2 |
| 410–419 | | 6 |
| 420–429 | 2 | 3 |
| 430–439 | | 2 |
| 440–449 | | 2 |
| ≥450 | 2 | 2 |

bells out of a chime of ten have been measured (fig. 116);[13] each A-tone corresponds to a note of the pentatonic gamut. The distribution of the B-tones is somewhat irregular. As in the higher register of the Western Zhou chimes, figure 116 shows a preference for minor-third bells; but the characteristic **re**-less four-tone pattern of the Western Zhou bells appears to be absent. It is unclear whether the pattern charted in figure 116 extended into another octave.

More complete information is available for two mid-sixth-century chimes of nine *niuzhong* each: from tomb no. 1 at Xiasi, Xichuan (Henan) (fig. 117),[14] and from tomb no. 13 at Shangmacun, Houma (Shanxi) (fig. 118).[15] While the structure of the tone distribution is virtually identical in the two chimes, the pitch of **do** differs significantly: it is close to C in the Shangmacun chime, but close to G in the Xiasi chime. This difference must have been recognized as such at the time; we are dealing here with two chimes scaled in different keys (see table 11).

In scaling these chimes, the objective appears to have been to expand the repertoire of playable tones while leaving intact the structure of the tone distribution characteristic of late Western Zhou chimes. The mid–Springs and Autumns

13. These are probably the six bells exhibited in Montreal in 1986 (*Chine, trésors et splendeurs*, cat. no. 25). I believe that they are nos. 5–10 from the ten-part *yongzhong* set B found at Lijialou (Sun Haibo 1935). No. 4 of the same set is now in the National Museum of History in Taibei (Tan Danjiong 1977, 57–62). One bell of this set is illustrated in fig. 76.

14. For an illustration, see fig. 94. References in Appendix 1. The tonal data provided in the original report are not the frequencies of the actual instruments but the vibrations of the tones of the equal-tempered scale with $A_4 = 440$ Hz. It may be assumed that the measured data are somewhere in the vicinity of these standard figures.

15. References in Appendix 1.

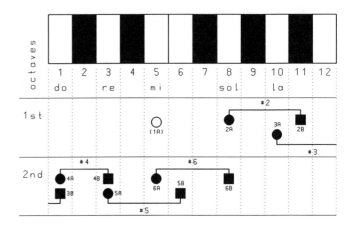

FIGURE 116. Tone distribution in six *yongzhong* from a set of ten from Lijialou (see fig. 75). The numbering of these bells, which appear to constitute part of set B, is provisional.

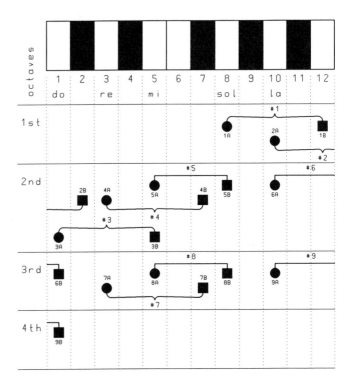

FIGURE 117. Tone distribution in the chime of nine *niuzhong* from tomb no. 1 at Xiasi (see fig. 93). Lower register: bells nos. 1–3; higher register: bells nos. 4–9. The tone measurements reported are approximations.

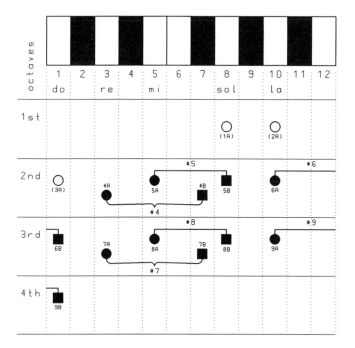

FIGURE 118. Tone distribution in the chime of nine *niuzhong* from tomb no. 13 at Shangmacun, Houma (Shanxi). Lower register: bells nos. 1–3; higher register: bells nos. 4–9. Note the overall similarity to fig. 117, which allowed some reconstruction in the lower register, where bell preservation is poor.

period craftsmen therefore included the note **re** in the higher register by inserting an additional bell per octave; the other bells of the higher register each emit the same two tones as their counterparts in late Western Zhou chimes. In both the Shangmacun and the Xiasi chimes, bells nos. 5, 6, 8, and 9 provide the notes **mi-sol/la-do** through two octaves (as opposed to the three octaves in the eight-part Western Zhou chimes). Into this pattern bells nos. 4 and 7 are inserted, spaced exactly one octave apart: two major-third bells that both have **re** as the A-tone (the B-tone being **fa**-sharp). As far as one can judge from the approximate measurements of the three larger bells in the Xiasi chime (those of the Shangmacun chime are broken or in bad condition), the tone distribution in the lower register resembles that of the late Western Zhou chimes. All three are major-third bells; two of them have **la** and **do** as their A-tones, just as in the late Western Zhou chimes, and the A-tone of the largest bell is **sol**. As in the Lijialou chime, the A-tones of the first five bells in the Xiasi chime thus constitute a pentatonic gamut in its entirety, starting on **sol**; in the higher register, such a gamut can also be produced, but only when also making use of some of the B-tones.

In sum, these two sixth-century chimes, probably produced at workshops in different parts of the Zhou realm, preserve the essential tonal characteristics of their Western Zhou predecessors, but the tone-distribution pattern is denser, with more tones in each octave than before. Although the Springs and Autumns period chimes actually contain more bells, their range (two and a half octaves) is more restricted than the three-plus octaves of the late Western Zhou chimes.

## The Zeng Bells
### The Chimes of the Zeng Bell Assemblage

The earlier bell-chimes help us elucidate the much more complicated tone distributions in the Zeng bells. As indicated previously, Marquis Yi's sixty-five bells (see fig. 1) by no means constitute a single instrument: they represent at least eight different chimes, most of which were not included in their entirety in the bell assemblage. The different constituent units within the Zeng bell assemblage are readily distinguishable on the basis of typology, ornament style, and inscription type (a criterion to which we shall return in the following chapter). They may be briefly enumerated as follows:

### Upper Tier

All the bells on the upper tier are *niuzhong* (see fig. 13). At present, they are displayed in three groups, labeled U1, U2, and U3. The six bells of U2 and the seven bells of U3 originally constituted part of one chime of fourteen (one bell is lost). Tan Weisi and Feng Guangsheng have shown that at an earlier stage in the history of the Zeng bell assemblage, these fourteen *niuzhong* were suspended from what is now the middle-tier bar of the short arm of the bell-rack.[16] The six *niuzhong* of group U1 differ in important respects from those of the U2 + 3 chime. They seem to have been put together from at least two separate *niuzhong* chimes.

16. Tan and Feng 1981; see also Li Chunyi 1985. In the present state, a set of *yongzhong* (M1) is suspended from this bar; but stopped-up vertical slots on the lower side show that it originally served for suspending *niuzhong*. At that stage, the bar in question was not yet in its present position on the Zeng rack, because one of the fourteen *niuzhong* holes (the largest) is now blocked by one of the caryatid stands. When it was put to secondary use in the present rack, the bar was retooled at the sides.

*Middle Tier*

The middle tier of the Zeng bell-rack houses three chimes of *yongzhong*: M1, the eleven-part chime on the short arm of the rack, and M2 and M3 with twelve and ten pieces, respectively. Chimes M1 and M2 are completely identical except for one bell in M2 (M2-10) that has no equivalent in M1. The ten-part chime M3 differs from these two in both tonal range and inscription type; it can be linked to the majority of the *yongzhong* on the lower tier.

*Lower Tier*

The twelve *yongzhong* of the lower tier of the Zeng bell-rack are arranged in two groups, with the largest bells sensibly positioned at the end-points of the rack. The three bells on the short arm of the rack, labeled L1, and the nine pieces on the long arm, L2, seem to jointly constitute a single chime. Closer inspection, however, reveals that three bells, L1-1, L2-10, and L2-9, differ from the rest in their inscription type (see Chapter 8); they must have originally been members of a different chime. These three bells were obviously interspersed with the others according to an overall design, so as to fill certain lacunae. Similarly, the single Chu Wang Xiong Zhang–*bo* (see fig. 20) is apparently suspended on the long arm of the rack between *yongzhong* L2-7 and L2-5 because its tone exactly fits that position in the chime. The heterogeneous nature of the lower-tier bells explains a certain amount of tonal overlap within the chime.[17] An earlier, somewhat different chime may be reconstructed from inscriptions on the bell-rack naming the A-tones of the bells that should be suspended in each position; the actual bell arrangement partially deviates from this order.

*The Tone Distributions in Chimes M1 and M2*

The distribution of tones in the chimes becomes clearest when each constituent chime is first analyzed by itself. In defining the tones emitted by the Zeng bells as musical notes we can rely on the tone-naming inscriptions (see Chapter 8). Given the large number of bells, the overall tone distribution is considerably denser than in the earlier chimes considered above and also includes a significant amount of overlap, especially among the middle-tier chimes. In their tone-distribution pattern, the *yongzhong* chimes M1 and M2 (fig. 119) closely resemble the two mid-sixth-century *niuzhong* chimes from Shangmacun and Xiasi. In

17. Though different in inscription type, the tones of L1-2 and L2-10 exactly overlap. The rationale for this apparent entropy may have to do with the fact that the two bells were physically removed from one another; having two of them on opposite ends of the rack may possibly have facilitated the playing. Also, perhaps for similar technical reasons, the tones of M2-1 (the highest bell on the lower tier) and M3-10 (the lowest bell on the middle tier) are identical.

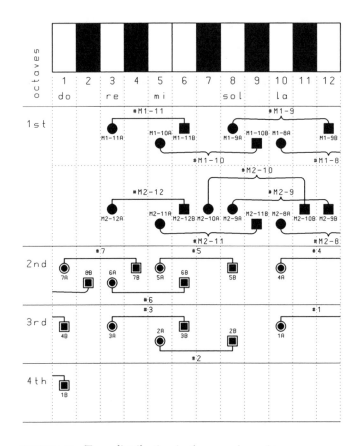

FIGURE 119. Tone distribution in the *yongzhong* chimes
M1 and M2 from the tomb of Marquis Yi of Zeng. The
tone distribution in the two chimes is identical except in
the lowest octave, which is tabulated separately for each
chime. Lower register: bells nos. M1-11 through M1-8
and M2-12 through M2-8; higher register: bells nos. 7
through 1 for chimes M1 and M2.

fact, the higher registers of the four chimes are almost identical. In both M1 and
M2, bells nos. 5, 4, 2, and 1 reproduce the characteristic late Western Zhou
four-tone pattern (**mi-sol/la-do**) through two octaves. This pattern is complemented by bells nos. 6 and 3, one octave apart and with **re** as the A-tone;
these, however, are minor-third bells, not major-third bells as in the Shangmacun and Xiasi chimes.

The lower registers of M1 and M2 comprise five and six bells, respectively,
about twice as many bells as in the lower registers of the *niuzhong* chimes from

Xiasi and Shangmacun, which consist of only three bells each. The array of available tones is correspondingly richer. Moreover, not all of the lower-register bells in M1 and M2 are major-third bells like the ones in the earlier chimes; the largest bells in each, M1-11 and M2-12, are minor-third bells that are octavically identical to nos. 6 and 3 in the higher register. The two chimes also manifest a tendency for the higher- and lower-register tone distributions to interpenetrate.

In the lower registers of both M1 and M2, we find bells with **re**, **mi**, **sol**, **la**, and **do** as A-tones. The major-third bell M2-10 stands out as the only bell that does not have an exact pendant in M1 and the only one in which neither the A- nor the B-tone is part of the pentatonic gamut; the role of this bell will be discussed shortly.

### The Tone Distributions in Chimes L1 + 2 and M3

Although the tone distribution of the lower-tier *yongzhong* links up with that of chime M3 on the middle tier, we must remember that these two chimes were played by different players standing on opposite sides of the rack (fig. 120). M3 can best be interpreted as providing a higher-register-type tone distribution, while the lower-tier *yongzhong* serve as an extended lower register of the same chime. Except for the intrusive major-third bell M3-2, which will be discussed below, the higher-register tone distribution in M3 has exactly the same structure as that of M1 and M2 (though pitched one octave lower). The time-honored **mi-sol/la-do** pattern, ranging through two octaves, is provided by bells M3-1, 3, 5, and 6, which are complemented by M3-4 and 7, two minor-third bells with **re** as the A-tone.

The combined lower register of L1 + 2 and M3, on the other hand, is considerably more complex than anything we have seen so far. At present, the A-tone of the deepest bell (L1-1) is **do**, though an inscription on the bell-rack shows that a "large **la** bell" was originally intended to occupy that position.[18] The range of more than two octaves allows for considerable octavic regularity throughout the lower register: bells L1-1, L1-2 (L2-10), L2-9, and L2-8 in the lowest octave correspond to L2-5, L2-4, L2-3, and L2-1 (L3-10) in the second octave, respectively. The A-tones of these bells all correspond to notes in the pentatonic gamut. In the second octave, additional bells are inserted into this pattern, with the result that A- and B-tones are distributed to cover the entire gamut of twelve tones. This pattern extends into part of the higher-register tone

---

18. Li Chunyi (1985) speculated that such a bell could not be accommodated because it was too large for the rack. Feng Guangsheng (1988a) established that the short arm of the Zeng bell-rack must have been longer originally than it is today. As a consequence of its reduction in length (perhaps at the time of burial), the original bell L1-3 no longer fit into its allotted space and had to be exchanged for a smaller specimen. This, too, may account for the removal of the "large **la** bell."

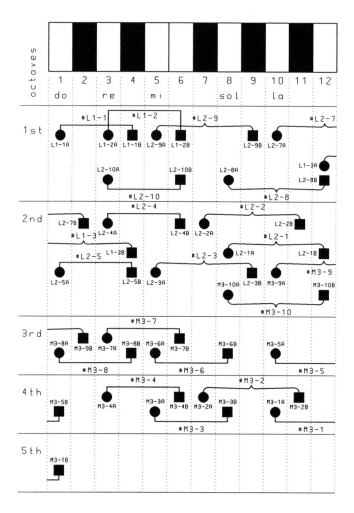

FIGURE 120. Tone distribution in the *yongzhong* chimes
L1 + 2 and M3 from the tomb of Marquis Yi of Zeng.
Lower register: bells nos. L1-1 through M3-9; higher
register: bells nos. M3-8 through M3-1.

distribution, making it possible to produce a continuous chromatic sequence of
tones through one and a half octaves. Even so, this highly complex tone distribution is still accommodated to the time-honored higher-register framework
of late Western Zhou chimes; as a consequence, minor- and major-third bells
are combined in somewhat irregular succession. These chimes must have been
tremendously difficult to play.

*Tone Distributions in the Upper-Tier* Niuzhong

The *niuzhong* on the upper tier of the Zeng bell-rack manifest an interesting contrast to the middle- and lower-tier *yongzhong*. In a total break with the Western Zhou–derived conventions, these chimes were designed with an emphasis on mathematical regularity. They cover the full gamut of twelve tones per octave; moreover, each chime consists exclusively of either minor-third bells or major-third bells.

The case is clearest with the U2 + 3 chime, whose original arrangement can be reconstructed as in figure 121. A succession of six minor-third bells recurs identically in each octave, yielding a tone-distribution pattern of great mathematical elegance. Of course, in such an arrangement there can be no dichotomy between the higher and lower registers. Such a chime must have been much easier to play than the cumbersome *yongzhong* of the middle and lower tiers. Emphasis on mathematical regularity is also evident in the present arrangement of this chime in two groups (figs. 122 and 123) with a succession of three bells per octave,[19] demonstrating the possibility of subdividing an octave into three equal segments, as well as dividing a gamut of twelve tones into two mutually exclusive sets of tones. On the other hand, no pentatonic music can be produced on either of these two groups of *niuzhong*.

The six *niuzhong* now grouped as set U1 are remnants of chimes consisting exclusively of major-third bells. With such bells, it is possible to cover the entire gamut of twelve tones per octave; however, the arrangement is mathematically less elegant than one limited to minor-third bells, since an identical pattern recurs only once every two octaves (see fig. 124). The six U1 bells, whose inscriptions and measured tones are not consistent with any single possible arrangement of major-third bells, appear to be fragments of at least two separate chimes (see fig. 125).

*The Zeng Bell Assemblage as a Whole*

We shall now consider the Zeng bell assemblage as a comprehensive unit. The tone distributions of all the sixty-five bells from Marquis Yi's tomb have been charted in figure 126. Although each of the constituent chimes could function musically by itself, the assemblage on its three-tiered rack is by no means merely a random collection of "all the family silver." Instead, those responsible for the present setup of the Zeng bells purposefully combined elements of preexisting chimes so as to create a musical assemblage that, as a whole, was more comprehensive and versatile than any of its parts.

19. The only exception to this is bell U3-1, which would better fit into the U2 set.

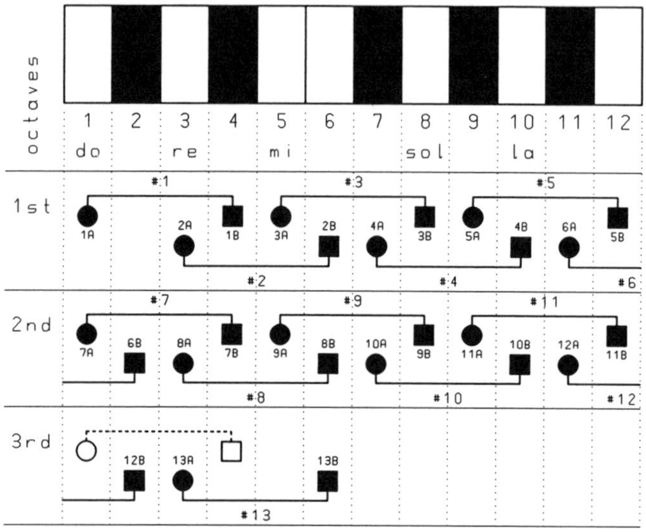

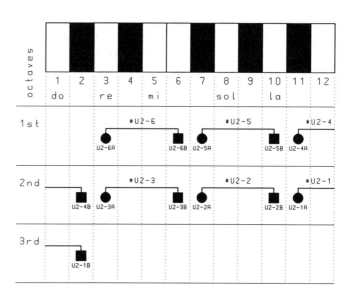

FIGURE 121. Reconstructed original tone distribution in the chime of thirteen (formerly fourteen) *niuzhong* constituting groups U2 and U3 from the tomb of Marquis Yi of Zeng. In this table, the extant bells have been renumbered; for the original numbering, see figs. 122 and 123.

FIGURE 122. Present tone distribution in the six *niuzhong* of group U2 from the tomb of Marquis Yi of Zeng.

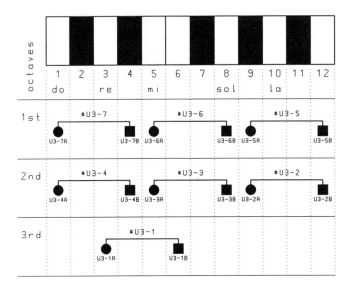

FIGURE 123. Present tone distribution in the seven *niuzhong* of group U3 from the tomb of Marquis Yi of Zeng.

In this connection, we must notice that the three octavically equivalent major-third bells L2-2, M2-10, and M3-2 stand out in the overall tone distribution.[20] They are the only ones in which neither the A- nor the B-tones (**fa**-sharp and **la**-sharp) are members of a pentatonic gamut defined with respect to **do**. M2-10 has little meaning within the lower-register tone distribution of the chime M2 per se; the same is true of M3-2 within the higher-register tone distribution of the chime M3. The function of these bells is to integrate the tone distributions within the lower- and middle-tier bells into a more coherent whole and to stake out a coherent tonal pattern throughout three octaves. This cannot be perceived through the tone-distribution charts of the individual chimes but becomes apparent in the comprehensive chart in figure 126. The tonal pattern thus created comprises all twelve tones in an octave. The bell inscriptions leave no doubt that such full chromatic coverage, as observable especially in the second and third octaves of the overall tone distribution, was a deliberate objective of the Zeng bell-makers. Without **fa**-sharp and **la**-sharp, furnished by the three bells just characterized, full coverage of the twelve-tone gamut would be impossible.

20. Asahara (1987, 78) has pointed this out most clearly.

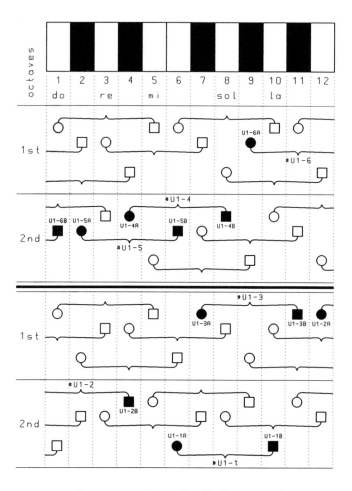

FIGURE 124. Reconstructed tone-distribution pattern in the six *niuzhong* of group U1 from the tomb of Marquis Yi of Zeng. Each half of the diagram charts the design of a chime fitting three of the six bells, as suggested by different **do** implied by their inscriptions. The tones of bell no. U3-1 have been charted a semitone lower than what is actually heard, so that they can be accommodated in the lower part of the diagram. It is conceivable, however, that bell no. U3-1 belonged to a third chime with yet another implied **do**.

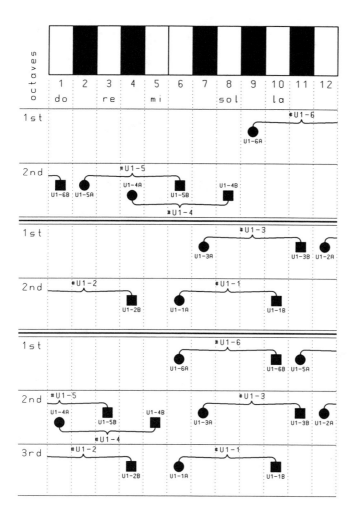

FIGURE 125. Present tone distribution in the six *niuzhong* of group U1 from the tomb of Marquis Yi of Zeng. In the upper and middle tiers, the two groups of three bells each (cf. fig. 125) are charted separately; in the lower tier, they are put together (with the **do** of the second group as the point of reference). Again, bell U1-3 is placed one semitone lower.

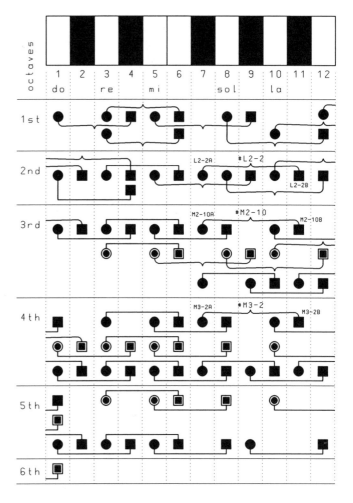

FIGURE 126. Tone distribution in the Zeng bells (comprehensive chart). The important role of bell M2-10, with its octavic counterparts in chimes L2 and M3, is emphasized; the twofold tone distribution in chimes M1 and M2 is indicated by the same symbols as in fig. 120. The first group of *niuzhong* of the upper tier and the Chu Wang Xiong Zhang–*bo* on the lower tier are not included.

Some overall heterogeneity is evident between the principal chimes on the lower and middle tiers and the upper-tier *niuzhong* chimes. In particular, throughout the lower- and middle-tier chimes, **do** is equal to C, while the inscriptions on the upper-tier *niuzhong* relate to quite a variety of **do** pitches. In the U2 + 3 chime, **do** corresponds to F-sharp, a tritone (exactly half an octave) removed from C; and the U1 bells seem to require two **do**: D-sharp and F-sharp (D-sharp being, interestingly, midway between C and F-sharp). The presence of multiple **do** suggests that these instruments were used for playing music in a variety of tonalities, as is also strongly suggested by the inscriptions on the Zeng *yongzhong*, which correlate gamuts of notes defined with respect to a variety of **do** (see Chapter 8). Theoretically, of course, twelve tones per octave are sufficient material for music-making in twelve different tonalities.

Summing up our observations of the Zeng bell assemblage, we cannot help but be impressed by the sheer quantity of tones that it provides, despite the existence of considerable overlap between chimes. We might be tempted to view the Zeng bells as the climax in a straight line of development toward greater tonal complexity in bell-chimes: from the four-tone pattern of the late Western Zhou via the five-tone pattern of the Springs and Autumns period to twelve-tone patterns in early Warring States. However, consideration of other, somewhat later bell-chimes of the Warring States period will show that evolution did not follow such a simple path. In fact, the Zeng bells are so far unique in consciously striving, in a variety of ways, to cover the full gamut of twelve tones per octave, an intent also evident, as we shall see, in the lithophone remains from the same tomb. As will become clear, however, the musicians of the Chinese Bronze Age did not in all probability make full use of the plethora of musical possibilities afforded by these instruments. The reasons for such comprehensiveness, which were apparently extramusical, will occupy us in the following chapter.

## Other Warring States Period Chimes

By comparison to the complexities of the Zeng instruments, other Warring States period *niuzhong* chimes on which tone measurements have been performed suggest a more conservative picture. While they provide a greater variety of tones than the Springs and Autumns period chimes from Xiasi and Shangmacun, the tone distributions in these late-fifth- and fourth-century B.C. cases do not approach the complexity of the Zeng chimes. In particular, the pervasive mathematical regularity characteristic of the tone distribution of the Zeng *niuzhong* chimes has not been observed anywhere else.

In the Biao-*niuzhong* from Jincun, Luoyang (Henan) (fig. 127),[21] which date to about a generation after the Zeng bells, the tendency toward interpenetrating lower and higher registers is particularly evident. The four-tone pattern of the late Western Zhou *yongzhong* chimes (**mi-sol/la-do**) permeates the entire chime through a range of three octaves; in each octave, moreover, two additional minor-third bells sound the notes **re-fa** and **si-re**, respectively. In the lower register, three additional major-third bells enter into this pervasive pattern. Their tones for the most part coincide exactly with those of the higher-register bells.

Although many tones can be produced on more than one bell in the chime, a glance at figure 127 shows that, astonishingly, five positions of the twelve-tone gamut (the second, fourth, seventh, ninth, and eleventh) are not covered at all. The tone distribution in the Biao-*niuzhong* may therefore be called heptatonic, but it could also be interpreted as intended for the production of pentatonic music in three different tonalities, with **do** in positions 1, 6, and 8, respectively.

Similarly, the A-tones playable on the mid-fourth-century Jingli-*niuzhong* from Changtaiguan, Xinyang (Henan), yield a coherent six-tone pattern through two octaves: the pentatonic gamut plus **si** (fig. 128),[22] which would allow for playing pentatonic music with **do** in positions 1 and 6. A separation of lower and higher registers is not apparent; only the smallest bell (no. 13) appears to fall out of the overall arrangement. The B-tones in the Jingli-*niuzhong* chime show no octavically recurrent pattern, suggesting that the players of these bells may not have made use of the two-tone phenomenon. The Western Zhou–derived four-tone pattern no longer seems to have played a role. Such developments, along with other phenomena detailed elsewhere in this book (see Chapters 1, 5, and 9) illustrate the decline of bell-making in the later Warring States period.

## Aberrant Cases

Not all sets of tone measurements so far reported neatly fit the sequence traced above. When charted according to the method delineated in the opening section of this chapter, the tonal data from some Eastern Zhou chimes—in particular, the Wangsun Gao–*yongzhong* from tomb no. 2 at Xiasi, Xichuan (Henan), the unprovenienced Zhediao-*niuzhong*, and the *yongzhong* from tomb no. 2 at Lei-

---

21. For an illustration, see fig. 90. References in Appendix 1.
22. For an illustration, see fig. 103. References in Appendix 1. The A-tone of the lowest bell (no. 1) is somewhat too high; judging from the fact that no. 1 has an (apparently incomplete) inscription while the others are all uninscribed, it seems possible that its origin is different from that of the rest of the set.

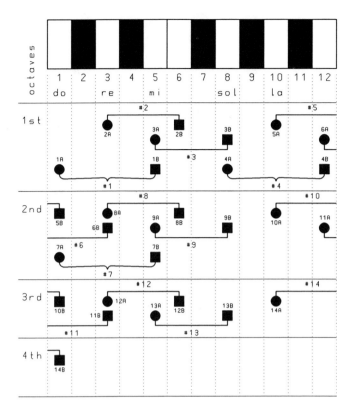

FIGURE 127. Tone distribution in the chime of fourteen Biao-*niuzhong* (see fig. 89). Lower register: bells nos. 1–7; higher register: bells nos. 8–14. The bells have been renumbered for this diagram. Bells nos. 1–3, 5–7, and 9–12 are in the Sen'oku Hakkokan (Sumitomo collection), Kyōto; bells nos. 4 and 8 are in the Royal Ontario Museum, Toronto. Only the tones of the Sen'oku Hakkokan bells have been measured; for the Royal Ontario Museum specimens, the convincing reconstruction by Asahara Tatsurō (1987, 85–87 and tables) is followed.

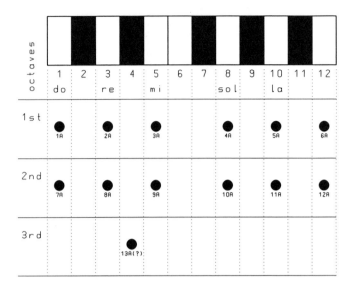

FIGURE 128. Tone distribution in the chime of thirteen Jingli-*niuzhong* (see fig. 102). The wildly irregular B-tones reported by Ma Chengyuan (1981) are omitted from this chart.

gudun, Suizhou (Hubei)—fail to show evidence of stringent octavic regularity,[23] presenting tone distributions that are thus difficult to interpret in a meaningful way. One may wonder if these chimes reflect different kinds of musical thinking that the method of analysis adopted in this chapter may be inadeqate to bring out; I do not believe so. These three chimes do not differ fundamentally from other contemporary chimes: they show such features as a separation of lower and higher registers, the possibility of playing pentatonic music (sometimes in several tonalities), as well as a certain amount of parallelism between different octaves. I therefore consider it likely that the bell-chimes in question were simply less successful attempts at producing chimes similar to those introduced earlier in this chapter. Bad preservation or incompetent handling of tone-measuring devices may in part account for the impression of acoustical insufficiency. But it is also possible to imagine extramusical reasons, such as a lack of

23. Moreover, the A-tone measurements published by Li Chunyi (1973) for the late Springs and Autumns period *niuzhong* from Ximennei, Shou Xian (Anhui), and from tomb no. 14 at Fenshuiling, Changzhi (Shanxi), do not yield an octavic pattern altogether meaningful. This problem may have to do with poor preservation; in any case, the data are difficult to judge in the absence of B-tone measurements.

familiarity with the principles of chime-bell manufacture (a consideration applying especially to regional products such as the Zhediao-*niuzhong*), an exclusive preoccupation with the visual aspects, or an intended function as *mingqi*.

In the mid-sixth-century B.C. Wangsun Gao–*yongzhong* chime,[24] the lower register of eight bells features a significantly sparser distribution of tones than the higher register of eighteen bells (fig. 129). While it is difficult to make any sense of the lower-register tone distribution, the higher register, when **do** is set at E, features bells with A-tones of **do**, **re**, **mi**, and **la** in three octaves; **sol** is also covered by either A- or B-tones in all three octaves. The chime, however, provides considerable tonal material in excess of this, the presence of which cannot easily be accounted for.

Visually, the twenty-six Wangsun Gao–*yongzhong* bells appear to be of outstandingly high quality (see fig. 21), but when listening to a recording of the tones, I noted a lack of separation between the A- and B-tones. The timbre is far less homogeneous than that of the Zeng bells or the Biao-*niuzhong*. Possibly, these bells, which were almost certainly manufactured in Chu, represent an early and as yet unfocused local attempt at creating an all-encompassing chime, similar in principle to the Zeng-*yongzhong* realized a century later within the same workshop tradition. The mid-sixth-century Chu bronze-casters may not yet have obtained sufficient acoustical expertise to realize such an ambitious plan.

The now-dispersed Zhediao-*niuzhong*, another chime of southern manufacture that may be dated to around 478 B.C., present a set of quite different problems. Measurements are available for the tones of only ten bells (two in the Sen'oku Hakkokan [Sumitomo Collection] in Kyōto and eight in the Tōhata Collection, Kōbe) of what must have been a far larger bell assemblage.[25] They seem to belong to several chimes that were tuned to a variety of keys. A further complication is that each bell contains different portions of an inscription text; if these text portions are arranged in order, the last bells in the textual sequence are by no means the highest in pitch. It is possible that the tones of some of the Zhediao-*niuzhong* were altered as the result of post-excavation repairs.[26]

Asahara Tatsurō has proposed a partial reconstruction of the intended tone distribution of the chime (fig. 130), which resembles that of the Biao-*niuzhong*. However, only four of the ten measured bells fit into this scheme (two more can be accommodated if we disregard the inscription sequence). In Asahara's view, the larger of the two Zhediao-*niuzhong* now in the Sen'oku Hakkokan

---

24. References in Appendix 1.

25. Several more bells from the set are extant; references in Appendix 2.

26. The Zhediao-*niuzhong* were apparently dispersed soon after their discovery, and it seems that various art dealers restored them in different ways. Asahara (1988b, 19, fig. 2) depicts one piece, of now-unknown location, that was inadvertently misrepaired into a *yongzhong*.

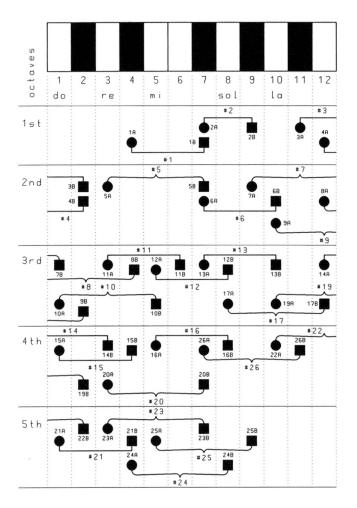

FIGURE 129. Tone distribution in the chime of twenty-six Wangsun Gao–*yongzhong* (see fig. 21). Lower register: bells nos. 1–8; higher register: bells nos. 9–26.

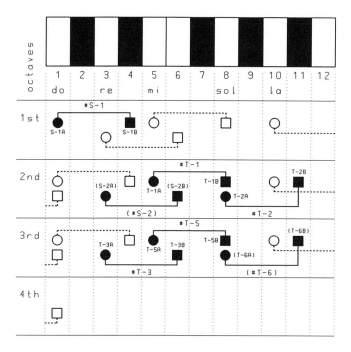

FIGURE 130. Tone distribution in ten of the Zhediao-niuzhong (see fig. 94) as reconstructed by Asahara Tatsurō (1988b). The bells with numbers indicated in brackets fit the tone-distribution pattern, but their inscription texts are out of sequence.

forms part of a hypothetical lower register, with the other bells all belonging to the higher register.

When we look at the tone distribution of all ten bells as charted in figure 131, we notice that the tones of bells S2, T1, and T2 are octavically equivalent to T3, T5, and T6; moreover, T4, T7, and T8 emit the same tonal pattern, but one semitone removed. It must be admitted, however, that such an ordering of bells disregards the arrangement of the inscription text; I know of no parallel case among extant Eastern Zhou chimes that could corroborate such a disjunction of text and tones.

The thirty-six haphazardly numbered *yongzhong* from tomb no. 2 at Leigudun (adjacent to the tomb of Marquis Yi and presumed to be somewhat later in date) also show some puzzling features (fig. 132).[27] Within the tomb, the eight

27. For an illustration, see fig. 96. References in Appendix 1.

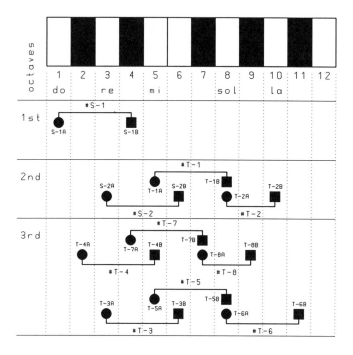

FIGURE 131. Tone distribution in ten bells from the Zhediao-*niuzhong* chime. Bells S-1 and S-2 are in the Sen'oku Hakkokan (Sumitomo collection), Kyōto, the others in the Tōhata collection, Hyōgo. Bell no. S-1 may be part of a lower register, the others of a higher register pattern.

larger bells were found at some distance from the twenty-eight smaller bells. The two groups of bells, which differ in their ornamentation, are separated tonally by a hiatus of about half an octave. Nevertheless, a few instances of octavic identity between them suggest that the larger bells may have functioned as a lower register with respect to the smaller ones. It is difficult to decide which tone to designate as **do**; my own reconstruction, with A as **do**, varies from that of Tong Zhongliang 童忠良, who proposes D-sharp.[28] In many cases throughout the chime, the same tones are playable on several different bells, and several groups of bells have exactly identical tones: nos. 10 and 11; 6 and 32; 7, 8, and 35; and 21 and 22. On account of such entropy, despite the large overall number

28. Possibly, the higher-register bells originally constituted several chimes; in spite of various trials, however, I have not come up with any very convincing combinations.

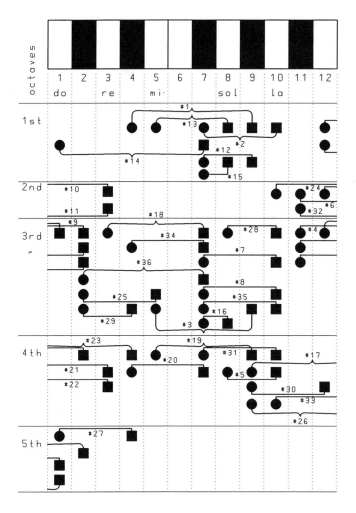

FIGURE 132. Tone distribution in the thirty-six *yongzhong* from tomb no. 2 at Leigudun (see fig. 95). Bells nos. 1, 2, and 10–15 are larger than the others and of another type; they may constitute a lower register.

of bells, the higher-register tone distribution ranges through only two and a half octaves, and the twelve-tone gamut is by no means completely covered. Nevertheless, the tones playable on these thirty-six bells can be defined as notes in a variety of pentatonic gamuts; conceivably, like the Zhediao-*niuzhong*, they formed several complementary chimes. As in the Wangsun Gao–*yongzhong*, the elaborately decorated outside of these bells (see fig. 94) contrasts with their unsatisfactory acoustic quality.[29]

## Interpretation
### Musical versus Technological Evolution

What do these tone-measurement data tell us? Certainly we may conclude that as chime-bells developed from Shang to late Western Zhou and through the Warring States period, they underwent acoustical refinement. A trend toward increased tonal richness and greater control over pitch is manifest. In Western Zhou times, casters discovered the two-tone phenomenon and worked out chimes scaled in such a way as to emphasize octavic regularity. Moreover, the minor- and major-third bells became clearly differentiated from one another. In Eastern Zhou, the lower register was expanded from two bells to more than ten bells in the lower and middle tiers of the Zeng bells. Whereas major-third bells were limited to the lower register and minor-third bells to the higher register in Western Zhou chimes, both kinds of bells could be found in either register in Eastern Zhou chimes. Toward the end of Eastern Zhou, moreover, the tone distributions in the lower and higher registers of bell-chimes grew ever more alike.

Some researchers, such as Huang Xiangpeng 黃翔鵬 and Feng Jiexuan 馮洁軒,[30] have interpreted such trends in bell-tone distributions as reflecting the increased complexity of Chinese music. Given that the Western Zhou chimes emit only the four tones **mi-sol/la-do** (quite rightly discounting the B-tone **do**-sharp of the first bell, which lacks a B-tone marker), they infer that Western Zhou musicians played music with only four tones per octave. In their view, it was only in Eastern Zhou that gamuts of five and then of twelve notes were dis-

---

29. The recently reported tone measurements on the late Springs and Autumns period *bo* and *niuzhong* from Beishanding, Dantu (Jiangsu)—another instance from the southeastern margins of the Zhou cultural sphere—feature a similarly irregular tone distribution, here extending through four octaves. Although a regular pattern is not evident among the eleven bells well-preserved enough to be measured, it is remarkable that there are ten instances of octavic identity. It is interesting, moreover, that the five *bo* evidently served as a lower register to the nine *niuzhong*. That the two sets of bells belonged together is underscored by the fact that they bear identical inscriptions. Composite assemblages where nine *niuzhong* were paired with a smaller number of larger bells (*yongzhong* or *bo*) occur with some frequency in the Eastern Zhou archaeological record (see Appendix 2).

30. Huang Xiangpeng 1978–80; Feng Jiexuan 1984.

covered, apparently presenting a textbook case of evolution from the simple to the complex. The picture is shattered, however, as soon as one includes contemporary musical instruments other than bells. The authors themselves duly note that some ocarinas, for example, permit the playing of five, and sometimes more, tones per octave.[31] Ocarinas of this sort have been found in some quantity at Neolithic and Shang sites, but so far not in Zhou archaeological contexts. The absence of pentatonic material from Western Zhou has prompted Huang and Feng to conclude that the Shang Chinese knew pentatonic music (and perhaps even more complex gamuts of notes), but that the Zhou, on account of their "barbarian" origin, were less sophisticated musically than the Shang. While Huang assumes that pentatonicity was lost at the end of the Shang dynasty and rediscovered in the Eastern Zhou period, Feng believes that it survived among the descendants of the Shang and was reintroduced into Zhou court music after the court moved east (into former Shang territory) in 770 B.C.

In my view, such theories are fundamentally fallacious. Ethnomusicological research has so far failed to establish a correlation between the pentatonic scale and any particular form of social organization anywhere in the world.[32] Moreover, comparing clay flutes to chimes of bronze bells *sans phrase* is methodologically impermissible. The decisive difference between the meanings of tone measurements obtained from musical instruments of different kinds has already been explained. In order to understand what the bell-tone measurements mean, we must reflect again on how the bell-chimes were played in conjunction with the other instruments of the ritual orchestra. When we remember their probable primary function as percussion instruments marking the subdivision of musical pieces (see Chapter 6), an alternative conclusion suggests itself: while Western Zhou music may well have used more than four tones per octave, not all of these tones were necessarily played on bells.[33]

From this perspective, we realize that the bells tell us relatively little about the progress of Chinese music as a whole. They do, however, inform us about the history of bell-chimes and their usage in musical performances. Through this evidence, we can trace the transformation of bell-chimes from percussion-like instruments into instruments capable of playing melodies. This development, which has few parallels in other ethnomusicological traditions, bespeaks an increasing emphasis on the timbre of metal in ancient Chinese music. In view of

31. A bone flute recently discovered at the Yangshao culture site of Jiahu, Wuyang (Henan), also is capable of emitting a considerable number of tones, depending on blowing technique (Huang Xiangpeng 1989).

32. The pentatonic gamut, in particular, appears to be part of the *Ur*-patrimony of all humankind, existing in societies of all conceivable types. Yang Yinliu (1944) even mentions hearing some birds in Sichuan twitter pentatonically.

33. In fact, if bell-chimes were to serve as a standard of tonal richness, we would have to conclude from the three-part Shang *nao*-chimes that Shang music was tritonal.

the preciousness of bronze and the sumptuary restrictions surrounding its use, we may indeed speak of an ever-stronger inclination to express wealth and status through the sound of music.

Let us recapitulate. At the Shang stage, little if any attention seems to have been paid to the pitch of the bell tones. In Western Zhou, some care was taken that the tones were in some fashion harmonically coherent and, presumably, that they fit in with tones played by the other instruments. By the Springs and Autumns period it was possible to play pentatonic melodies on chimes such as the *niuzhong* from Xiasi and Shangmacun. Later on, in the Warring States, other tones not part of the pentatonic gamut were also included, so that pentatonic melodies could be played in multiple tonalities.

The watershed in this development probably occurred sometime during the Springs and Autumns period, when the tone **re** first occurs in the tone distributions of chime-bells. What had happened? In my opinion, the evolution toward a denser tone distribution presupposed a radical break with the conventions underlying the manufacture of Western Zhou chimes. Late Western Zhou chimes were scaled in such a way that musically useful tones were always located next to one another, as on a Western piano or Glockenspiel (see fig. 111). The ranges of two adjacent bells never overlap (except in the case of the two largest bells in the lower register, whose B-tones were most likely not used). But the tonal ranges of adjacent bells do regularly overlap in Eastern Zhou chimes, those from Lijialou (see fig. 116) being the earliest example.

In Zhou dynasty chimes, the A–B tone interval could be no other than a minor or a major third; to the manufacturers at the time, this seems to have been an unchangeable technological given. If, in addition, they were operating under the convention that the tonal ranges of adjacent bells must not overlap (at least not if both A- and B-tones were to be used in music-making), then the tetratonic **mi-sol/la-do** pattern encountered in the higher register of the Western Zhou chimes was the closest possible approximation of a regular pentatonic tone distribution through several octaves. One could not cram in any additional tones unless one were willing to sacrifice the principle of octavic regularity, and even then the outcome would not be the desired pentatonic gamut but a musically quite useless constellation of tones.

Only by inserting additional bells into the Western Zhou four-tone pattern did it become possible to play pentatonic music on chimes of two-tone bells. On the other hand, as we already discussed in the previous chapter, such bell-chimes were considerably more difficult to play than those of late Western Zhou times: players now had to negotiate their way back and forth between bells in complicated ways (see fig. 111). They had to be much more familiar than before with the tone distributions in their chimes. Indirectly, the tone-measurement data thus attest to a considerable increase in the virtuosity of bell-playing musicians during the Zhou period. But it should be stressed that music itself did not necessarily become more complex; the tones and melodies played on bells only became more similar to those produced on wind and stringed instruments.

## Lithophones and the Importance of Pentatonicity

We have seen that the greater richness of tones on Warring States period bell-chimes may be interpreted in two ways. Conceivably, musicians may have played tonally ever more complex music, not only pentatonic melodies but also melodies based on hexatonic (Jingli-*niuzhong*), heptatonic (Biao-*niuzhong*), and dodecatonic (Zeng bell assemblage) gamuts of notes. Alternatively, one may suggest that the additional tones enabled the performer to play pentatonic melodies in different keys (two on the Jingli, three on the Biao, and twelve on part of the Zeng bells). Although these two interpretations are not mutually exclusive, I doubt that melodies exceeding the scope of the pentatonic gamut were important in Zhou music. Most sources on traditional Chinese musical theory describe musical melodies in terms of pentatonic modes with varying central notes.[34] Taken by itself, the fact that most present-day Chinese music continues to be essentially pentatonic (with a few additional or "incidental" tones occurring here and there) would admittedly be a poor basis for any statement regarding music in antiquity. Yet the idea that Zhou ceremonial music was, at least predominantly, pentatonic is also suggested by the evidence from lithophones, which were used in conjunction with bell-chimes.

Made of soft lithic material, chimestones (as we have seen in Chapter 6) tend to decompose or break when buried. Tone measurements therefore have to be treated with caution. Among the many dozens of excavated lithophones, only three have so far been subjected to measurement. The earliest in date is the ten-

34. Levis 1936; Pian 1967; DeWoskin 1982, 43–54. In Harold S. Powers's unmatched definition ("Mode" entry in *The New Grove*, 12:377): "Mode can be defined as either a 'particularized scale' or a 'generalized tune', or both, depending on the particular musical and cultural context. If one thinks of scale and tune as representing the poles of a continuum of melodic pre-determination, then most of the area in between can be designated one way or another as being in the domain of mode. To attribute mode to a musical item implies some hierarchy of pitch relationships, or some restriction on pitch successions; it is more than merely a scale. At the same time, what can be called the mode of a musical item is never so restricted as what is implied by referring to its 'tune'; a mode is always at least a melody type or melody model, never just a fixed melody. . . . When modes (or their equivalents) are construed as primarily scalar, they tend to be used for classifying, for grouping musical entities into ideal categories. When the melodic aspects of modality are its predominant features, the modes are seen as guides and norms for composition or improvisation." An early instance of the use of the mode concept in pre-Qin Chinese musical theory can be seen in *Zhan'guo-ce*. The hero Jing Ke 荆轲, as he was about to embark on his ill-fated attempt to assassinate the king of Qin, moved the courtiers of Yan 燕 to tears by singing first *yu* 羽 and then *bianzhi* 升徵 (*Zhan'guo-ce: Yance* "Yan Taizi Dan Zhiyu Qin," Sibu Congkan ed., j. 9:46a/b). *Yu* and *bianzhi* are the names of musical notes (see Chapter 8); but presumably, what Jing Ke sang were melodies built on modes in which these two notes played an important role.

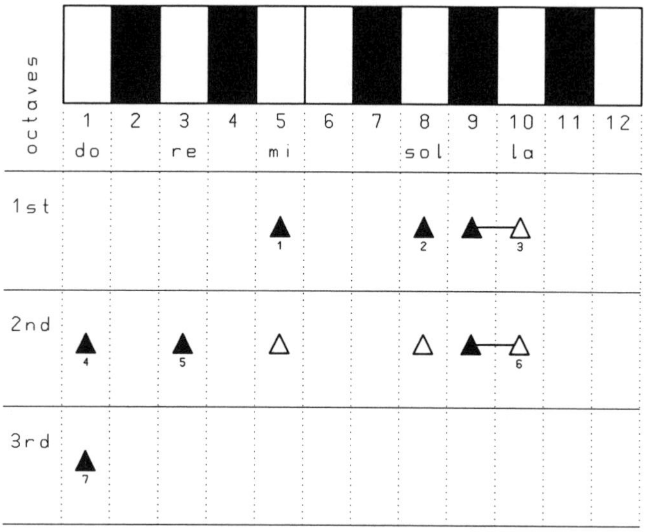

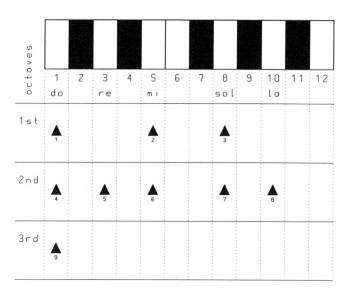

FIGURE 133. Tone distribution in the lithophone from tomb no. 13 at Shangmacun, Houma (Shanxi). The somewhat damaged chimestones nos. 3 and 6 were probably meant to sound a semitone higher, as indicated in the chart.

FIGURE 134. Tone distribution in the lithophone from tomb no. 2040 at Houchuan(?), Sanmenxia (Henan).

part lithophone from the mid-sixth-century tomb no. 13 at Shangmacun, which complemented the *niuzhong* discussed above.[35] Of the seven chimestones that still emit a tone, at least two may be significantly out of tune. From their tone distribution, charted in figure 133, one may tentatively reconstruct an original pentatonic arrangement.

The remaining two measured lithophones both date to the Warring States period. The nine-part lithophone from Sanmenxia (Henan) has not yet been properly reported on (it is probably the one excavated from tomb no. 2040 at Houchuan),[36] but it seems to be exceptionally well preserved. Its tone distribution, charted in figure 134, shows a clearly pentatonic pattern through two octaves. The three stones of the lower octave emit a major chord (**do-mi-sol**), whereas the higher octave contains a full pentatonic gamut. By contrast, the beautifully decorated chimestones of a twenty-five-part lithophone found in the ancient capital of Chu at Jinancheng, Jiangling (Hubei),[37] seem to have been too badly deformed to yield any meaningful tone distribution (fig. 135), though several instances of octavic equivalence may be observed.[38]

Despite the evident pentatonicity of the Sanmenxia lithophone, the information we can glean from these three lithophones is certainly insufficient for far-reaching conclusions. Nevertheless, what we may glean from figures 133–135 is of interest because it points in the same direction as the much more comprehensive evidence available for the lithophone from the tomb of Marquis Yi of Zeng (see fig. 99).[39] From inscriptional information, we can reconstruct a chime of forty-one musical stones, twenty-eight of which have survived. Even though almost without exception the chimestones themselves are broken and can no longer be played, their inscriptions inform us about the originally intended tones. Moreover, each specimen bears a number indicating its position in order of size, the largest piece being no. 1. When not displayed on their rack, the chimestones were placed into three lacquered wooden boxes holding thirteen, fourteen, and fourteen pieces, respectively, in troughs cut to fit each chimestone

35. Huang Xiangpeng 1978–80, pt. 2:147; original report in *Kaogu* 1963 (5):229–45.

36. Huang Xiangpeng 1978–80, pt. 2:147; a preliminary notice on Houchuan may be found in *Kaogu Tongxun* 1956 (11):74–77.

37. *Wenwu* 1972 (1):75; *Kaogu* 1972 (3):41–48 (tone measurements p. 44); color photograph in *Wenhua Dageming Qijian Chutu Wenwu* 1:74.

38. Like the lithophones just mentioned, the stone panflute excavated from the mid-sixth century tomb no. 1 at Xiasi, Xichuan (Henan) (in the same context as the *niuzhong* chime discussed above), has been subjected to measurement (*Kaogu* 1981 [2]:126). The tone distribution shows a marked pentatonic tendency (Falkenhausen 1988, 875 and table 59), but the higher pipes seem to be in a less than perfect state of preservation. Since each pipe in this unusual instrument was presumably designed to emit one single tone, these data may also offer some corroborative value.

39. For references see n. 20 to Introduction. The reconstruction of the chimestones and the elucidation of their tone distribution pattern has been the subject of a number of articles, including Tong Shibu 1981; Xu, Feng, and Chu 1982 and 1983; Xu, Feng, and Zhang 1983; Huang Xiangpeng 1983c; and Li Chengyu 1983 and 1984.

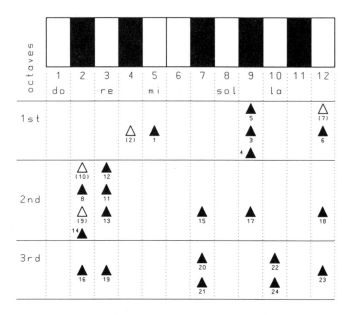

FIGURE 135. Tone distribution in the lithophone from
Jinancheng, Jiangling (Hubei). Many chimestones in this
lithophone are broken, others imperfectly preserved.

exactly; numbers inscribed next to these troughs correspond to the numbers of
the chimestones.

The inscriptions tell us that the forty-one chimestones of Zeng emitted an unbroken chromatic sequence of tones through three and a half octaves (fig. 136).
In covering the entirety of the dodecatonic gamut, this lithophone is similar
to the bell assemblage excavated from the same tomb. What is noteworthy,
however, is the way in which the chimestones were arranged in the three boxes,
as well as the order in which they were suspended from their rack. In each case,
analysis reveals strikingly pentatonic ordering principles.

Let us look at the distribution of chimestones in the three lacquered boxes (fig.
137). The pieces in boxes 1 and 2 form two mutually exclusive pentatonic sets,
with **do** at C and at F-sharp; it is surely not by accident that these two **do**, a tritone (half an octave) apart, are identical to the two principal **do** of the Zeng bell
assemblage.[40] The inscription on box 3 aptly labels its contents as "Intermediate
Tones" (*jianyin* 間音): here we find the chimestones that could be accommo-

40. Each of the two boxes is labeled with the name of the basic pitch according to the Zeng tone
nomenclature (see Chapter 8). The only irregularity is that box no. 2 contains stone no. 40 instead
of no. 39, which has ended up in box no. 3.

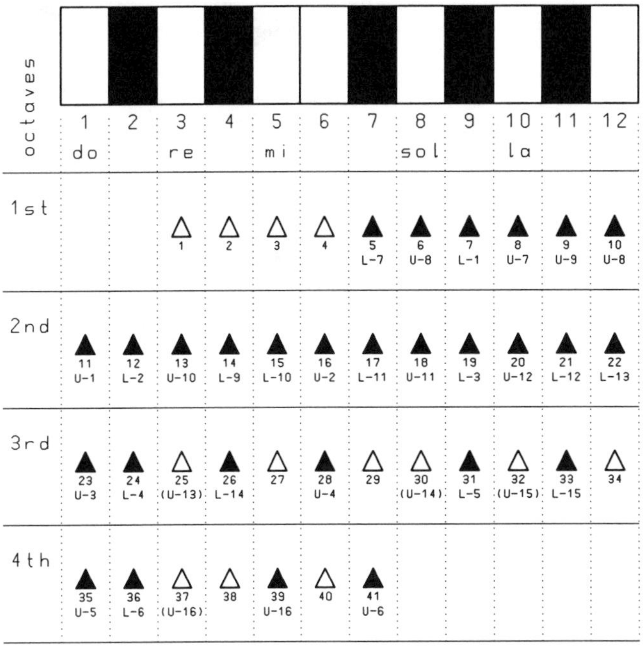

FIGURE 136. Comprehensive tone distribution in the lithophone from the tomb of Marquis Yi of Zeng (see fig. 99).

dated in neither of the above two pentatonic sets (i.e., **fa** and **si** with respect to the two principal **do**). This box also contained some of the larger components of the lithophone, which did not fit into the other two boxes; possibly, these were somehow equivalent to the lower register of the contemporary bell-chimes.

When arranged on the two-tiered lithophone-rack, the Zeng chimestones did not necessarily follow the same order as in the boxes, as is illustrated by the manner in which they were displayed at the time of excavation. As the rack provided space for only thirty-two of the forty-one chimestones, a selection of chimestones had to be made, presumably before each performance; the specimens chosen could have varied with the tonality of the piece to be performed. At excavation, the chimestones on each tier were displayed in two groups, of six and ten pieces, respectively. Figure 138 shows the tone distribution on the upper tier, as evident from inscriptions on the stones displayed there. Altogether, the sixteen chimestones on the upper tier provided the tonal material of a pentatonic gamut through three octaves. Within the upper-tier gamut,

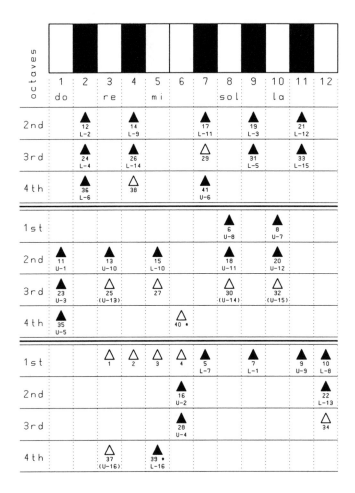

FIGURE 137. Tone distribution in the lithophone boxes from the tomb of Marquis Yi of Zeng. *Top*, the GUXIAN box (thirteen chimestones forming a pentatonic set with respect to the pitch standard [*lü*] GUXIAN); *middle*, the XINZHONG box (fourteen chimestones); *bottom*, the box for the fourteen leftover "intermediary notes" (*jianyin*). An asterisk indicates what appears to be irregularity in placement.

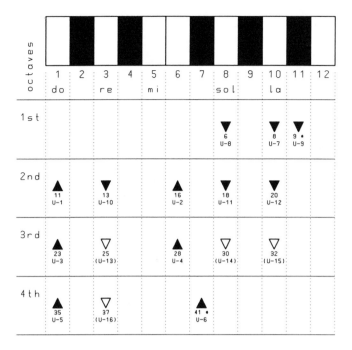

FIGURE 138. Tone distribution among the chimestones on the upper tier of the lithophone from the tomb of Marquis Yi of Zeng. The stones fall into two groups, which are here distinguished by the positions of the triangles.

the **do** and **sol** stones were arranged as one group separated from the **re**, **mi**, and **la** stones.[41] Astonishingly, this gamut is not identical to either of the gamuts defined in the lithophone boxes: **do** is on B.

A similar but somewhat less regular picture emerges from the tone distribution of the sixteen chimestones of the lower tier (fig. 139), where the intended **do** of the pentatonic gamut is G. However, because the pentatonic gamuts with **do** on B and G are not mutually exclusive (B equals **mi** when **do** is on G) and because the set contained only a single chimestone for each tone, several of the intended members of the lower-tier chime had already been preempted for use on the upper tier. Their places in the lower-tier chime were filled by substitutes, for the most part by specimens sounding a semitone higher than the intended

41. There are two small irregularities, such as the presence of U9, which does not fit the pentatonic gamut, and U6, which is a semitone too high.

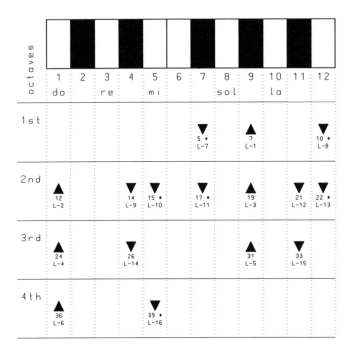

FIGURE 139. Tone distribution among the chimestones on the lower tier of the lithophone from the tomb of Marquis Yi of Zeng. As in fig. 138, there are two groups of chimestones.

tone. Because the preemption involves the note **mi** in each of the three octaves, the **do** and **sol** stones (which again form a group of their own on the lower tier) are complete and accurate; only the second group, comprising the **re, mi,** and **la** stones, is beset with some irregularity.

It is unclear why the **do** and **sol** stones were set apart from **re, mi,** and **la**: perhaps to enable two musicians to play the two groups of stones simultaneously, or to make it possible for one musician to handle each group with a separate mallet. Or the purpose may have been merely to exemplify various systematic arrangements of tones. In any case, it cannot be overlooked that all the various arrangements of chimestones that we can reconstruct on the basis of the Zeng data follow pentatonic principles. The forty-one chromatically numbered chimestones were by no means used to play music with twelve tones; instead, chosen specimens were arranged so as to provide the tonal material for pentatonic gamuts in a variety of tonalities.

Essentially the same conclusions can be applied to chime-bells. Again, chimes were designed to contain more musical material than was required for any one piece. But bells differed from chimestones in that they were probably not rearranged for each performance, which would have been difficult because each bell contained two tones that were not located adjacent to one another on a scale; because of the inseparability of the A- and B-tones on individual bells, the structure of a bell-chime tone distribution is much harder to disentangle than that of a lithophone. Nonetheless, it appears likely that regardless of how many tones *could* be produced on a chime, only a limited number of them *were* used in the performance of any one piece; probably, in any particular tonality, the tones actually used would have been the notes of the respective pentatonic gamut.[42]

Despite the transformation of bell-chimes from merely accompanatory instruments into instruments on which melodies could be played, it is likely that throughout the Zhou period their role in music-making remained somewhat distinct from that of other melodic instruments such as flutes and zithers. They may have mainly provided a harmonic *Grundgerüst*, a tonal basis for the tunes or melodies performed on wind and stringed instruments.[43] If "incidental" tones played a role in Zhou ceremonial music, it is likely that those would have been played on melodic instruments other than bell-chimes and lithophones.

### The "Revolving **Do**"

If Zhou ceremonial music was essentially pentatonic, the bell-tone measurements reviewed earlier in this chapter lead us to a musicologically important insight: the increasing density of tones playable on Eastern Zhou bell-chimes and lithophones must indicate that, as opposed to earlier custom, *music in several tonalities was now performed on these instruments*. In the parlance of traditional Chinese musical theory, this innovation was called the "revolving **do**" (*xuangong* 旋宮).[44] We have traced the emergence of coexisting multiple **do** throughout this chapter; the first clear evidence for such a phenomenon dates to the mid-sixth century, on the two separate chimes from Xiasi and Shangmacun. While the pitch of **do** seems to be close to C in Western Zhou as well as some Eastern Zhou chimes, other Eastern Zhou chimes are clearly outside this range (see table 11).

---

42. This harks back to Curt Sachs's warning: "The series of notes available on an instrument does not necessarily represent its scale; the keyboard of an occidental piano with its twelve semitones within an octave gives the *possibility* of playing scales in twenty-four tonalities, but the scales themselves comprise only seven notes" (Sachs 1940, 167; emphasis as in the original).

43. Harich-Schneider 1955.

44. The term *xuangong* does not actually appear in any pre-Qin text; the earliest locus is in the Tang dynasty subcommentary on *Li Ji*, "Liyun" by Kong Yingda (*Li Ji Zhushu* 3b–6b).

One might suppose that, in the long run, the increased number of tones available through the *xuangong* principle might have resulted in a greater modal complexity of Chinese ritual music. But this does not actually seem to have been the case. The pre-Qin texts uniformly consider tunes of complex tonal structures as unorthodox and morally evil: we have seen in Chapter 1 how Confucius and other Eastern Zhou philosophers battled against the "dishonest tones" used in the popular musical styles that were then finding favor in high places. There is a distinct possibility that the late Eastern Zhou "New Music" was characterized not only by lascivious styles of performance but also by variety of tones greater than in traditional ritual music. While the Zeng bells certainly provide the musical potential for the performance of such "New Music," it appears likely that their principal function remained connected to the performance of ritual music, which in all probability continued to employ pentatonic modes. The *xuangong* principle made it possible, however, to produce pentatonic series in several tonalities. The theoretical and political implications of this innovation will occupy us in the following chapters.

## The Problem of Intonation

Having established which notes and intervals were intended by the casters, we may now briefly digress on the red herring in Chinese musical archaeology: what can the tone measurements tell us about the system (or systems) of intonation used in ancient Chinese music? We remember that, due to the inherent mathematical incorrectness of their scaling principles, the ancient Chinese chimes themselves could not possibly have been, strictly speaking, in tune (see Chapter 2). We may expect them to show considerable deviations from any conceivable regular tuning system because, with a linear scaling formula, no intonation pattern can be consistently replicated through more than one octave. Nevertheless, as conceded in Chapter 6, the analysis of a statistically significant sample of tone measurements might conceivably point to certain tendencies.

Three systems of intonation have been discussed in the literature on ancient Chinese bells: "natural" intonation, tempering, and tuning by the "Spiral of Fifths." Natural (or "just") intonation, which is apparently preferred by the human ear, defines each note as the simplest possible mathematical proportion with respect to **do**. A disadvantage of this method is that tones will differ minutely from tonality to tonality (for example, **mi** on C and **sol** on A are both approximately E, but they are not exactly identical).[45] If a chime of bells was in-

---

45. **Mi** on C equals 532 Hz × 5/4 = 665 Hz; **sol** on A equals 440 Hz × 3/2 = 660 Hz, and so forth.

tended for playing in only one tonality, however, this limitation may not have mattered.

On melodic instruments such as flutes and zithers, it was easy to make the minute adjustments of pitch necessary for playing in a variety of keys, but not on chimed idiophones, with their restricted number of playable tones. It seems likely, therefore, that as soon as the "revolving **do**" principle started to influence the scaling of chimes, the bell tones were subjected to tempering: they were adjusted slightly to make them compatible in pitch with the notes of several keys, if not actually coinciding with any one of them. Theoretically, the ultimate outcome of such tempering would have been the equal-tempered scale mentioned in the preceding chapter, though it is universally agreed that that scale was yet unknown in Bronze Age China.[46] Whether the ancient Chinese bell manufacturers consciously performed tempering at all, and whether such tempering was governed by any mathematical principle, is so far unknown.

A third, mathematical method of intonation determines the pitch of notes according to the "Spiral of Fifths" (also known somewhat inexactly as *Pythagorean tuning*). As will be explained in the following chapter, it seems likely that the method of generating tones through the Spiral of Fifths was known in Eastern Zhou China and may have had some influence on the scaling of chimes; whether that procedure was applied in fine-tuning of bells after casting, however, appears doubtful.

If, for instance, measurements indicate that two tones playable on a chime are about 300 cents apart, we would not hesitate to say that they represent an interval of a minor third; it is virtually impossible, however, to determine whether the manufacturers intended the interval to be either a natural minor third of 316 cents or a Pythagorean minor third of 294 cents, or whether it was the product of intentional tempering. The differences between the frequency figures to be expected by each method are so minute as to fall easily within a bell's usual range of inaccuracy. Various scholars have nevertheless endeavored to juxtapose the tone measurements from ancient instruments to the three sets of "expected" frequencies and, because of differences in the methods used in doing so, have reached a variety of conclusions.[47] Having treated the matter elsewhere,[48] I find it unnecessary to repeat the procedure here; the results are summarized in table 14. In brief, no clear pattern is apparent, though overall, the actually measured tones seem to diverge least from those of the natural intonation system, a finding that confirms the impression that the human ear played a major role,

46. See Chapter 8, n. 44.
47. Huang Xiangpeng 1981, Pan Jianming 1982, Tong Zhongliang 1984, McClain 1985a.
48. Falkenhausen 1988, 917–32; in tables 80–98, the actual and expected values are tabulated in the way I believe to be correct.

TABLE 14. Deviation of Measured Pitches from Expected Intervals in Three Systems of Intonation (in cents)

|  | Spiral of Fifths | Natural | Tempered |
|---|---|---|---|
| **Western Zhou** | | | |
| Zuo-*yongzhong* | 39.3 | 20.3 | 19.3 |
| Zhong Yi–*yongzhong* | 37.1 | 13.7 | 18.0 |
| Third Xing–*yongzhong* | 40.1 | 29.5 | 32.9 |
| Second Xing–*yongzhong* | 16.7 | 32.2 | 31.0 |
| Ni-*yongzhong* | 29.0 | 38.3 | 32.7 |
| Mawangcun chime no. V | 72.5 | 64.3 | 70.0 |
| Average | 39.1 | 33.1 | 34.0 |
| **Eastern Zhou** | | | |
| *Yongzhong* from Lijialou (6 bells from set B?) | 18.6 | 14.6 | 16.4 |
| Lithophone from Shangmacun tomb no. 13 | 10.2 | 7.4 | 9.0 |
| *Niuzhong* from Shangmacun tomb no. 13 | 14.3 | 13.2 | 14.0 |
| Wangsun Gao–*yongzhong* (higher register only) | 84.6 | 61.2 | 61.8 |
| Zeng *niuzhong*, chime U2 + 3 | 33.5 | 40.7 | 37.8 |
| Zeng *yongzhong*, chime M1 | 27.0 | 31.1 | 28.1 |
| Zeng *yongzhong*, chime M2 | 20.3 | 15.2 | 16.2 |
| Zeng *yongzhong*, chime M3 | 23.0 | 11.6 | 10.5 |
| Zeng *yongzhong*, chime L1 + 2 | 54.2 | 41.1 | 42.3 |
| Lithophone from Sanmenxia (Houchuan tomb no. 2041?) | 26.5 | 10.3 | 16.8 |
| Biao-*niuzhong* | 41.4 | 17.1 | 19.2 |
| Jingli-*niuzhong* | 22.4 | 14.8 | 19.1 |
| Average | 31.3 | 23.2 | 24.2 |

NOTE. Average deviations within each chime from the supposed standards are calculated on the basis of the **do** listed in table 11 (for the raw cent figures, see Appendix 4). Natural (or "just") tuning prefers the simplest mathematical relations between frequencies; the tempering system referred to here is equal-tempered intonation. For an explanation of the method of generating notes through the Spiral of Fifths, see Chapter 8.

both in establishing the conventional scaling principles and in tuning individual bells after casting.

Regardless of which intonation system one takes as a standard of reference, we may observe that the overall accuracy of bell-tuning significantly increased from Western to Eastern Zhou, especially in small and medium-sized bells. Table 14 shows that average deviations from the intonation standards in terms of each of the three systems decreased by more than 10 cents. An average deviation of ca. 10–15 cents from natural intonation seems to have been the maximum accuracy realizable by even the most expert Eastern Zhou bell manufacturers; the Shangmacun *niuzhong* and, among the Zeng bells, the third *yongzhong* chime of the middle tier, stand out as particularly successful efforts in this regard. The intonation of large bells presented significant problems, however, as witnessed by the lower-tier Zeng bells. Interestingly, the two lithophones included in table 14 are considerably closer to the three intonation standards than any of the bell-chimes, doubtless because chimestones were easier to tune than two-tone bells (see Chapter 3). Evidently, over the course of the Zhou dynasty, the suspended music of the Chinese Bronze Age not only became richer, more complex, and more musically versatile but also grew ever more pleasant to listen to.

# CHAPTER EIGHT

# Musical Theory through the Zeng Inscriptions

*The Conception of Tone in the Zeng Inscriptions*

The inscriptions on the Zeng bells are unique among the epigraphic remains of the Chinese Bronze Age. All other known bell inscriptions, like inscriptions on other kinds of ritual bronzes, are self-congratulatory messages; they inform the ancestors in Heaven of their earthly descendants' merits and continuing piety. Examples have been quoted in Chapter 1. By contrast, the inscriptions on the Zeng bells and chimestones relate directly to the musical function of the instruments on which they are placed. Among other things, they provide tone definitions, on which we can reconstruct Zeng musical theory in some detail.[1]

We must recognize that the inscriptions have little direct connection to the musical function of the bells. Those on the Zeng *yongzhong* were placed in such a way that the most extensive body of their tone-naming information faced into the rectangular space framed by the bell-rack—that is, toward the audience. The outward-facing sides of the bells all contain a briefer dedicatory inscription and abbreviated names of the tones. Since the *yongzhong* on the lower and middle tiers are tilted in opposite directions, the kind of information found on the recto faces of the lower-tier *yongzhong* appears on the verso of the middle-tier *yongzhong* and vice versa. This, incidentally, proves once again that, at some level, the entire Zeng *yongzhong* assemblage must have been conceived as a unity. The placement of the tone-naming inscription toward the audience must be of key

---

1. Transcriptions of the Zeng bell and lithophone inscriptions may be found in *Yinyue Yanjiu* 1981 (1):3–16; also in Rao and Zeng 1985, 129–48, with an index on pp. 157–79. Tan and Feng (1988) report that the bell inscriptions number 3,755 characters, 187 thereof inscribed on the bell-rack and 740 on the suspension armature. Rubbings and photographs have so far been published only for a small number of the inscriptions.

significance to understanding the inscriptions, but beyond this general insight, the exact underlying rationale remains mysterious. That the viewers were meant to read the tone definitions from a distance is out of the question. Nor could the inscriptions have been intended for the orientation of the performers, because the majority of the music-related information appears on the verso faces of the middle-tier *yongzhong*; when the bells were suspended, that portion of their surface could not be seen without crouching underneath the bell-rack from the side opposite the musicians. It was hence obviously impractical to consult the inscriptions during performances. We shall further consider the problem of the inscriptions' function below.

The recto sides of the middle-tier *yongzhong* (see fig. 11), which, when suspended, tilted toward the player, were inscribed only with one brief phrase: "Marquis Yi of Zeng made [this], preserve [it]!" (*Zeng Hou Yi zuo chi* 曾侯乙作畤 [= 持]), plus rudimentary designations for the A- and B-tones. By contrast, the verso faces of the middle-tier bells usually provide multiple definitions of both tones, which, as on the recto, are placed at the respective striking points. If the bell-players were well versed in musical theory, they may be assumed to have known these definitions by heart. It is possible that the limited tonal information on the recto served to evoke the memory of the more complex tone-naming texts written on the verso face; but this would seem to be contradicted by the reversed placement of the two kinds of inscriptions on the lower-tier bells.

How, then, are tones named in the Zeng inscriptions? Let us consider as an example the verso inscription of the largest *yongzhong* in the second chime on the middle tier, M2-12. The text in the center of the bell-face, on the striking point of the A-tone, runs as follows:

> *Gong* of PINGHUANG 坪皇之宮, *qianshang* of GUXIAN 姑洗之猷商, *jue* of MUZHONG 穆鐘之角, *gongzeng* of XINZHONG 新鐘之宮曾, *zhi* of ZHUO-SHOUZHONG 濁獸鐘之徵.

For the B-tone, which can be produced by striking either to the left or the right of the *gu*, there are two separate inscriptions; on the right side of the *gu*, we read:

> *Yu* of SHOUZHONG 獸鐘之羽, *zhi* of MUZHONG 穆鐘之徵, *yuzeng* of GUXIAN 姑洗之羽曾, *gong* of ZHUO-XINZHONG 濁新鐘之宮;

and on the left side:

*Xi* of YINGZHONG 應鐘之喜, *zhibu* of XINZHONG 新鐘之徵頮, next *jue* of ZHUO-PINGHUANG 濁坪皇之下角, *shang* of ZHUO-WENWANG 濁文王之商.[2]

To the uninitiated, this must sound highly enigmatic. But although much of the terminology used in the Zeng inscriptions was unknown before the discovery of Marquis Yi's tomb in 1978, part of it is familiar from the classical literature.[3] Comparison with the traditional Chinese tone nomenclature provides a key to understanding the system as a whole.

Such terms as *gong* 宮, *shang* 商, *jue* 角, and so forth, are used even in present-day Chinese music: they designate moveable notes (*yin* 音, or *sheng* 聲), comparable to **do**, **re**, **mi**, and so on, as used in the Anglo-American choral-music tradition.[4] Terms such as SHOUZHONG and GUXIAN are known as *lü* 律 (pitch standards); for the time being, we may provisionally liken them to the names of tonalities. In Western musical terminology, we might approximately render the string of terms defining the A-tone of the just-mentioned bell M2-12 (measured as 284.8 Hz = 4947 cents)[5] as "**do** in the key of D, **re** in the key of C, **mi** in the key of B-flat," and so forth. Alternatively, we could also conceptualize the *yin* as intervals between notes, and the *lü* as tones of fixed frequency; in Western terminology, the A-tone of M2-12 might accordingly be expressed as "prime in relation to D, major second in relation to C, major third in relation to B-flat," and so forth. Both attempts at translation, though imperfect, make evident the relational character of tones as conceptualized by the Zeng musical theorists. Any tone can be referred to by many names, its designation at any time depending on its relationships with the other tones in a given piece of music. The Zeng inscriptions indicate a series of such names for each tone; how many terms are indicated for each tone seems to depend primarily on the amount of space available on the bell surface.

The tone-naming inscriptions on the striking points on the recto face of the Zeng middle-tier *yongzhong* differ from the verso in that they do not indicate the pitch standard (*lü*). On the recto of bell M2-12, for example, only the names of the notes (*yin*)—*shang* for the A-tone and *yuzeng* for the B-tone—are indicated. In the verso inscription, translated above, the bell's A-tone is desig-

2. *Yinyue Yanjiu* 1981 (1):10.

3. The following discussion draws on several important philological studies of the Zeng inscriptions: Qiu Xigui 1979, Qiu and Li 1981 and 1988, Rao and Zeng 1985, Feng Shi 1986. From a musical point of view, the inscriptions have been studied by Huang Xiangpeng 1981 and 1983b, Li Chunyi 1981, Pan Jianming 1982, Tong Zhongliang 1984 and 1988, and others.

4. In France and Italy, the terms **do** (**ut**), **re**, **mi**, etc., have for a long time been used to designate notes of fixed pitch, equivalent to C-D-E in the Anglo-American tradition. This is *not* the meaning of the Chinese *yin* names in the present context.

5. This is the measurement published by the Shanghai Museum (*Shanghai Bowuguan Jikan* 2 [1982]:91).

nated as *qianshang* (= lower-octave *shang*) of GUXIAN, and the B-tone is given as *yuzeng* of GUXIAN. The intended pitch standard (*lü*) of the recto inscriptions thus must be GUXIAN. Comprehensive comparison of this sort reveals that GUXIAN is implied by the recto inscriptions on all middle-tier *yongzhong* (as well as by the verso inscriptions on all lower-tier *yongzhong*): it is undoubtedly the main pitch standard of reference for that part of the Zeng bell assemblage. The **do** referred to in analyzing the tone distribution on the Zeng *yongzhong* in Chapter 7 is none other than *gong* of GUXIAN 姑洗之宫, which (as tone measurements on the Zeng bells reveal) is approximately equivalent to C.

The moveable *yin* notes are useful because they can describe melody without regard to pitch. The function of the pitch standards (*lü*) is complementary to that of the notes (*yin*): the *lü* coordinate the pitches of different musical instruments in an ensemble. The musical system documented by the Zeng inscriptions can be distilled into gamuts of twelve *yin* and twelve *lü*; however, considerable complication is introduced by the presence of numerous alternative terms that are synonymous with others. Close analysis reveals that the Zeng inscriptions synthesize fragments of a number of different but related musical systems. As a first step toward elucidating the overall structure of early Warring States period musical theory, we shall scrutinize the note (*yin*) and pitch-standard (*lü*) nomenclatures in the Zeng inscriptions.

## The Yin Notes

Simplifying matters somewhat, we may start out by stating that the *yin* nomenclature in the Zeng inscriptions uses four simple (monosyllabic) and eight complex (binominal) names to designate twelve notes per octave (table 15). The four simple *yin* names are *gong* 宫 (**do**), *shang* 商 (**re**), *zhi* 徵 (**sol**), and *yu* 羽 (**la**). The complex *yin* names are formed by adding the suffixes *jue* 角 and *zeng* 曾 to each of these four. They function as follows:

The element *jue* raises a note by a major third, *gongjue* 宫角 thus being equal to **mi** in Western nomenclature, *shangjue* 商角 to **fa**-sharp, *zhijue* 徵角 to **si**, and *yujue* 羽角 to **do**-sharp. *Jue* is sometimes alternatively rendered as *bu* 頫 (= 補) "altered."

The suffix *zeng* raises a note by two superimposed major thirds: *gongzeng* 宫曾 thus corresponds to **sol**-sharp, *shangzeng* 商曾 to **la**-sharp, *zhizeng* 徵曾 to **re**-sharp, and *yuzeng* 羽曾 to **fa**. Because the interval of an octave equals three superimposed major thirds, one may also conceptualize the four notes named with the suffix *zeng* as situated one major third below the corresponding notes of monosyllabic name, but an interpretation as two major thirds above appears substantiated by etymology (*zeng* 曾 very probably stands for *zeng* 增

TABLE 15.    Nomenclature of Notes (*Yin*) in the Zeng Inscriptions

|  | *Zeng inscriptions* | *Traditional texts* |
|---|---|---|
| 12 | **zhijue** | *biangong* |
| 11 | **shangzeng** | *qingyu* |
| 10 | **yu** | **yu** |
| 9 | **gongzeng** | *bianyu, qingzhi* |
| 8 | **zhi** | **zhi** |
| 7 | **shangjue** | *bianzhi* |
| 6 | **yuzeng** | *qingjue* |
| 5 | **gongjue** | **jue** |
| 4 | **zhizeng** | *bianjue, qingshang* |
| 3 | **shang** | **shang** |
| 2 | **yujue** | *bianshang, qinggong* |
| 1 | **gong** | **gong** |

"augment"), and by the alternative rendering of *zeng* as *buxiajue* 顅下角 "next *jue* after the alteration."[6]

In traditional Chinese musical theory, the term *jue* is well known, but not as a suffix: it is instead the name of the note **mi**. Given that **mi** is a major third above **do**, it is easy to see that this meaning is closely related to the function of *jue* as a suffix modifying other notes by a major third. In the Zeng inscriptions (as, e.g., in the inscription of bell M2-12, quoted above), *gongjue* is often simply rendered as *jue* 角 or *xiajue* 下角 "next jue." Evidently, therefore, designating the note **mi** must have been the primary meaning of *jue* as a musical term even in the fifth century. From this we may infer that the systematically defined gamut of twelve notes (*yin*) in the Zeng inscriptions is secondary to the pentatonic gamut of *gong, shang, jue, zhi,* and *yu.* These "Five Notes" (*wu yin* 五音) have remained the basis of traditional Chinese musical theory throughout its recorded history.

At the stage of the Zeng inscriptions, the "Five Notes" do not yet seem to have formed a closed set; indeed, the *yin* nomenclature throughout the Zeng inscriptions is considerably less regular than might appear from the somewhat idealizing presentation given so far. For almost every note of the pentatonic gamut the inscriptions give variant names, some of which appear to indicate

6. Huang Xiangpeng (1981) has contrived an explanation of *bu* and *buxiajue* as implying a movement upward (a "sharp" major third, so to speak), while *zeng* and *jue* imply a downward ("flat") movement. This view has no philological or musicological basis; the four terms constitute two entirely synonymous pairs, differing primarily with respect to their roles in the two basic tone-naming inscription types explained below.

equivalents in higher or lower octaves.[7] Pitch is also indicated, albeit in a somewhat inconsistent manner, by a variety of affixes specifying whether a tone is "high" or "low,"[8] a system that may hark back to a stage at which octavically identical notes were not yet referred to by the same terms.[9] A related phenomenon, which we will discuss below, may be seen in connection with the pitch standards (lü).

Although the Zeng bells provide the earliest datable occurrence of gong, shang, jue, zhi, and yu as the names of the Five Notes,[10] these names must have had considerably earlier origins. In the Zeng inscriptions, we find them in a state of secondary elaboration: here the original pentatonic set of notes with simple monosyllabic names has been extended to encompass twelve notes per octave. By using major thirds to define additional complex notes, the late Zhou music theoreticians had obtained a closed set of exactly twelve notes in which no two names overlap. This system is unusual in that the complex notes are located four semitones removed from the unprefixed ones, with other, completely unrelated notes in between (table 15). In the traditional Chinese system of yin nomenclature, just as in the West, affixes indicate the semitones immediately adjacent to the basic notes of the gamut. This simpler, though less elegant, principle of extending the pentatonic gamut of notes was also known to the Zeng musicians, as evidenced by the occurrence, in some of the inscriptions, of the prefix bian 弁, which lowers a note by one semitone (e.g., bianzhi 弁徵 = sol-flat). One may suppose that the use of such semitonic prefixes is older than the sophisticated nomenclature involving the suffixes jue and zeng.[11] That nomenclature, which is based on major thirds, appears to have been contrived for systematic purposes; known so far only from the Zeng inscriptions, it may not have enjoyed wide currency in pre-Qin China.

7. Sun [?] 巽 (perhaps pronounced gong) appears as an alternate for gong 宮; jue [?] 鳩, gui 隯, the character 庨 (pronunciation unclear), and wei 鍏 appear as alternates for jue 角 as the name of a note; zhong 終 for zhi 徵; zhu 壴, gu 鼓, and xi 喜 (three terms with similar reconstructed archaic pronunciations) for yu 羽 (which is often written with a double phonetic as 罜). No alternative name is indicated for shang 商.

8. The adjectives da 大 "large" and shao 少 "small" are used to indicate, respectively, lower and higher octavic pitch. Fan 反 "return, overturn" occurs as a suffix with the same meaning as shao; the prefixes jia 珈 (etymologically and semantically related to jia 加 "add to, increase") and qian 昔 (perhaps etymologically related to qian 遣 "transfer, transpose") are synonymous with da.

9. In addition to the terms already mentioned, the Zeng inscriptions record three terms that seem to denote yin in a particular octave: Zhongbo 中鎛, the "Middle bo-bell (L2-3A)," denotes a low-pitched **mi** of GUXIAN (Rao Zongyi in Rao and Zeng 1985, 8); the enigmatic Xi [?] bo 鎮鎛 (L2-1A), a low-pitched **sol** of GUXIAN (Qiu and Li 1981, 20; Rao Zongyi in Rao and Zeng 1985, 10; Huang Xiquan 1988); and Yinhe 音和 "Tonal Harmony (M3-4B)," a high-pitched yuzeng 羽曾 of GUXIAN (Qiu and Li 1981, 21). All three binomes curiously resemble the names of pitch standards (lü) such as HUANGZHONG, presented later on in this chapter.

10. The earliest textual occurrences of these terms are discussed further below.

11. Bian also figures prominently in later traditional Chinese musical theory. Its opposite, the prefix qing 清, which raises a note by one semitone, does not occur in the Zeng inscriptions.

TABLE 16.  Nomenclature of Pitch Standards (*Lü*) in the Zeng Inscriptions

| | *Traditional Texts* Other than *Zhou Li* | *Zhou Li* | *Zeng Inscriptions* "Zeng" set | *Octavic equivalents* | *Zhou set* | *Jin set* | *Qi set* | *Shen set* | *Chu set* |
|---|---|---|---|---|---|---|---|---|---|
| 12 | JIAZHONG | JIAZHONG | | | | | | | zhuo-GUXIAN |
| 11 | TAICOU | TAICOU | TAICOU | MUYIN | LIEYIN | BANZHONG | | | MUZHONG |
| 10 | DALÜ | DALÜ | | | | | | | zhuo-MUZHONG |
| 9 | **HUANGZHONG** | **HUANGZHONG** | **HUANGZHONG** | YINGZHONG | YINGYIN | | | | SHOUZHONG |
| 8 | YINGZHONG | YINGZHONG | | | | | | | zhuo-SHOUZHONG |
| 7 | WUYI | WUYI | WUYI | YINGZI | | | | | XINZHONG |
| 6 | NANLÜ | NANLÜ | HANYIN | | | | **LÜYIN** | | zhuo-XINZHONG |
| 5 | YIZE | YIZE | | | | | | | WENWANG |
| 4 | LINZHONG | HANZHONG | | | | | | | zhuo-WENWANG |
| 3 | SUIBIN | SUIBIN | SUIBIN | | | | | YIZE | PINGHUANG |
| 2 | ZHONGLÜ | XIAOLÜ | | XUANZHONG | | LIUYONG | | | zhuo-PINGHUANG |
| 1 | GUXIAN | GUXIAN | **GUXIAN** | | | | | | LÜZHONG |

NOTE. The principal pitch standards in the various nomenclatures, where known, are in boldface type.

In the inscription on bell M2-12, quoted above, we notice two kinds of *lü* names: binominal names, such as SHOUZHONG and GUXIAN, and names that are prefixed by the term *zhuo* 濁, which means "muddy," or, in a musical sense, "flat." The Zeng inscriptions provide some twenty-two different binominal *lü* names; but *zhuo* appears in conjunction with only six of them: GUXIAN 姑洗, PINGHUANG 坪皇, WENWANG 文王, XINZHONG 新鍾, SHOUZHONG 獸鍾, and MUZHONG 穆鍾 (see table 16). As we shall see, this set of *lü* is closely linked in the Zeng inscriptions with the state of Chu.

When we define the note *gong* (**do**) with respect to each of these six *lü*, we find that the six notes so obtained are spaced at equal intervals,[12] forming the following set: C, D, E, F-sharp, G-sharp, and A-sharp. If these tones were played in succession, the result would be what Western musical theory is wont to call a whole-tone scale, but we must remember that in the musical system documented by the Zeng inscriptions, musically relevant tone sequences or melodies cannot be expressed by a succession of different pitch standards (*lü*), or as *gong* (**do**) defined with reference to different pitch standards (*lü*). (In this system, a whole-tone scale is properly conceptualized as a succession of moveable notes, e.g., as *gong, shang, gongjue, shangjue, gongzeng, shangzeng* [**do, re, mi, fa**-sharp, **sol**-sharp, **la**-sharp], which may be defined in terms of any *lü*.) Abbreviating somewhat, we may say nevertheless that the six *lü* just enumerated form an equidistant hexatonic set.

The six pitch standards that are prefixed by *zhuo* occupy the intermediary positions between those six, where *zhuo* lowers the *gong* (**do**) of the unprefixed pitch standard (*lü*) in question by one semitone. Here again, the six *gong* (**do**) taken together form an equidistant hexatonic set (B, C-sharp, D-sharp, F, G, A). If we combined the two sets and arranged their twelve *gong* in sequence of pitch, the twelve tones amount to a full chromatic set (table 16). The six pitch standards (*lü*) with their "muddy" counterparts thus form an equidistant dodecatonic gamut—the most complete set of pitch standards among the several documented in the Zeng inscriptions.

We may conceive of the "muddy" *lü* in two ways: as subordinate to or complementary to the hexatonic core. That a "muddy" and an unprefixed pitch standard were definitely aspects of one and the same *lü* is suggested by inscriptions on four bamboo pitch-pipes recently discovered at the Chu tomb no. 21 at Yutaishan, Jiangling (Hubei) (fig. 140), in which some of the non-"muddy" *lü*

12. In doing so, we implicitly liken the *lü* to tones of fixed pitches (comparable to the Western C-D-E), which may be conducive to the conceptual muddling of *yin* and *lü* characteristic of later Chinese musical theory (see below).

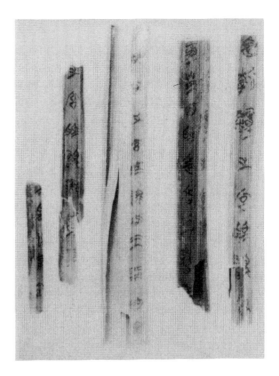

FIGURE 140. Fragments of pitch-pipes (or panflute pipes) excavated in 1986 from tomb no. 21 at Yutaishan, Jiangling (Hubei). Warring States period (fourth century B.C.).

names are prefixed with a character readable as *ding* 定 "determined" (perhaps equivalent to *zheng* 正 "correct"); "muddy" pitch standards also occur.[13] In the Zeng inscriptions, moreover, each of the sixteen *lü* that never occur prefixed by *zhuo* is equivalent to one of the six unprefixed pitch standards just examined. For each of those six principal pitch standards (table 16), the inscriptions provide at least two and as many as five different names; by contrast, the "muddy" *lü* have no additional names. This demonstrates a preference for the hexatonic core set of *lü*, compared to which the "muddy" *lü* are secondary and apparently less important. The term *zhuo* "muddy," perhaps originating in Chu, may have been a new invention at the time of the Zeng inscriptions. Historically, the twelve-part set of pitch standards (*lü*) seems to be have been devised later than the hexatonic core.

Eighteen "equivalency formulas," which are embedded in selected tone-naming inscriptions, coordinate the multiple names of pitch standards.[14] They

13. *Wenwu* 1988 (5):35–38; Tan 1988.
14. Two *lü* names are documented from the inscriptions on the Zeng rack only; it is not known to which pitches they corresponded or to which state they belonged.

correlate the *lü* systems of different states in Eastern Zhou China. For example, the definition for the A-tone of bell L1-2 runs as follows:

> *Gong* of SUIBIN 妥賓之宮. **As to SUIBIN, in Chu it is called PINGHUANG** 妥賓之在楚號爲坪皇; **in Shen it is called YIZE** 其在[illegible] [= 申] 號爲遲 [= 夷] 則. *Jiagui* of TAICOU 太簇之珈歸, *gongzeng* of WUYI 無射之宮曾, *shangjue* of HUANGZHONG 黃鐘之商角.[15]

All in all, the Zeng inscriptions provide equivalents for seven pitch standards with binominal names for Chu 楚, two each for Zhou 周 and Jin 晉, and one each for Qi 齊 and Shen 申. Nine names that are not linked explicitly to any particular state (such as SUIBIN in the example just quoted) are thought to constitute the indigenous Zeng system. It is of particular interest that five of the six *lü* names that possess "muddy" alternates (e.g., PINGHUANG in the above example) are unambiguously linked in the inscriptions with Zeng's powerful neighbor Chu.[16] The political aspects of these *lü* correlations will occupy us in the following chapter.

Like the *yin* names reviewed above, each *lü* name originally seems to have been restricted in its pitch-range to a single octave. For example, six of the nine *lü* names said to be of the state of Zeng form an equidistant hexatonic set; the three supernumerary names have been explained as identifying alternate *lü* pitched an octave higher.[17] Some of the other pitch standards named in the equivalency formulas are also specified as positioned in a higher octave. Part of the definition of the B-tone of bell L2-2, for example, is "*Gong* of TAICOU 太簇之宮, its turnover [*fan* 反] is called BANZHONG in Jin 在晉號爲槃鐘."[18] The expression here rendered as "turnover" also occurs as a suffix of *yin* names, where it indicates the equivalent note one octave above.[19] The nine-part "Zeng" set of pitch standards thus extended its hexatonic coverage over one and one-half octaves.

From the classical texts, we know binominal *lü* names similar, indeed partly identical, to those inscribed on the Zeng bells (see table 16). The earliest occurrence of one of these binominal *lü* names in a musical meaning seems to be that

15. *Yinyue Yanjiu* 1981 (1):4. The "equivalency formula" is highlighted in boldface.

16. Curiously, the *lü* name GUXIAN, which appears prefixed with *zhuo*, is not linked with Chu in the inscriptions; on the other hand, its so-designated Chu equivalents, LÜZHONG 呂鐘 and XUANZHONG 宣鐘, never appear in connection with *zhuo*.

17. Huang Xiangpeng 1981, 24.

18. *Yinyue Yanjiu* 1981 (1):5.

19. Li Chunyi (1981) has read *fan* as *ban* 半 "one-half," implying that if the two notes were produced on a string, the *gong* of BANZHONG would have been half the length of the *gong* of TAICOU.

of WUYI 無射 in the inscription on the late Western Zhou Nangong Hu–*yongzhong*; we shall return to that inscription in the following chapter.[20] In the late pre-Qin texts, the "traditional" pitch standards (*lü*) form closed dodecatonic sets of twelve.[21] Significantly, in these sets of twelve, no inherent philological distinction is made between "ordinary" and "muddy" pitch standards: all *lü* names are "simple" binominal terms of similar form. In emphasizing a central set of six *lü* and defining alternate *lü* beyond the scope of one octave, the system of pitch standards documented by the Zeng inscriptions differs decisively from that of the classical texts.

It is instructive in this connection to look at those *lü* names in the Zeng inscriptions that have equivalents in the "traditional" set of pitch standards; with one exception, all of these belong to the set of nine *lü* assumed to be indigenous to Zeng.[22] Five of them correspond exactly in their relative positions to those of the traditional set: GUXIAN, SUIBIN, WUYI, HUANGZHONG 黃鐘, and TAICOU. The remaining three, YINGZHONG 應鐘,[23] XUANZHONG 宣鐘,[24] and HANYIN 函音,[25] are positioned one semitone above their traditional equivalents; HANYIN is a name for the sixth *lü* of the hexatonic core set above GUXIAN (see table 16); and YINGZHONG and XUANZHONG are alternants to HUANGZHONG and GUXIAN in a higher octave. These three terms appear to have undergone a change in significance between the time of the Zeng inscriptions and the earliest enumerations of pitch standards in the transmitted texts (see below). At some point, the meanings of some preexisting *lü* names designating octavic alternates to the pitch standards in the hexatonic core set were changed to give binominal names to the six pitch standards that are defined as "muddy" in the Zeng inscriptions.

20. This important bell (see fig. 33) was excavated in 1979 at Baozigou, Fufeng (Shaanxi) (reference in Appendix 1). Besides the bell-face, which bears the main inscription, the shank of the Nangong Hu–*yongzhong* features a separate inscription that reads: "The *Situ* official Nangong Hu made a set of harmonically-tuned chime-bells. This bell's name is 'WUYI' 嗣徒南宮呼作大鑄協鐘茲鐘名曰無射." No other bells of the same set have been found so far. For more extensive treatment see Falkenhausen 1988, 906–07, 1000–39 and passim.

21. The *lü* names differ somewhat among different texts. In table 16, the most commonly used names (as seen in *Guo Yu* "Zhou Yu," *Li Ji* "Yueling," *Lüshi Chunqiu* "Yinlü," *Huainan Zi* "Tianwen," *Shi Ji*, "Lüshu," and *Han Shu* "Lüli-zhi") are placed in column 1. Column 2 indicates the variants found in *Zhou Li: Chun'guan* "Dasiyue" and "Dashi." The *Zhou Li* consistently uses HANZHONG 函鐘 instead of LINZHONG 林鐘, and XIAOLÜ 小呂 instead of ZHONGLÜ 仲呂; HUANZHONG 亘鐘 appears as an alternate of JIAZHONG 夾鐘 in only one instance (references below).

22. The only exception is the sole *lü* of Shen mentioned in the Zeng inscriptions, YIZE, which corresponds in name, but not in relative position, to one of the *lü* in the transmitted set.

23. In the so-called Zeng set of *lü*, YINGZHONG is named YINGYIN 應音. However, the same *lü* is designated YINGZHONG in the Zhou set.

24. XUANZHONG is identical to HUANZHONG 亘鐘, which occurs once in the *Zhou Li* as a variant of JIAZHONG (*Zhou Li Zhengyi* 43:1a).

25. HANYIN is identical to HANZHONG 函鐘, which occurs in the *Zhou Li* (Qiu Xigui 1979, 30; Asahara 1987, 117 n.79); in other texts, the same *lü* is named LINZHONG 林鐘.

In summary, the Zeng inscriptions represent a stage at which a full dodecatonic gamut of twelve pitch standards had not yet been defined and at which octavic equivalency could not yet be taken for granted. The nine *lü* names said to pertain to the state of Zeng do not form a closed dodecatonic gamut limited to one octave but an extended hexatonic gamut reaching out into a second octave.

## Tone-Definition Distribution Patterns

Looking again at the inscription quoted above from bell M2-12, we notice that both A-tone and B-tone are defined as notes with respect to GUXIAN, MUZHONG, and XINZHONG. In that inscription, other *lü* names occur only in connection with one or the other of the two tones. Theoretically, with twelve *yin* and twelve *lü*, every tone could be defined in twelve different ways; but there is nowhere near enough space on the surface of any of the bells to accommodate such a twelve-part tone-definition sequence. We may wonder, therefore, whether the inscriptions show any consistent preference for certain *lü*, or for pairing certain *lü* with certain *yin*. By comparing the inscriptions on the three sets of bells in the middle tier, we may in fact discover two such patterns, which will be referred to as System A and System B.[26] The differences between the two, which illustrate the nature of Zeng musical theory as a whole, are noteworthy.

We may recall from Chapter 7 that sets M1 and M2 are virtually identical in their tone distributions except for bell M2-10, which has no equivalent in M1; this near-identity extends to the inscriptions on these bells, M2-10 again being exceptional. The tone definitions in these inscriptions contain the names of both ordinary and "muddy" pitch standards (*lü*). As to *yin* notes, there is a predominance of simple (monosyllabic) names, bespeaking a tendency to define each tone in terms of those *lü* with respect to which it is a note of the pentatonic gamut. In particular, only monosyllabic notes occur in connection with "muddy" *lü* names. Complex (binominal) *yin* names do occur in the M1 and M2 inscriptions, but they are defined only with respect to two *lü*: GUXIAN and XINZHONG, three whole tones (half an octave) apart from one another (fig. 141).

This is significant, for, as we have seen at the beginning of this chapter, GUXIAN is the principal pitch standard in the Zeng *yongzhong*; and the **do** of reference for most of the *niuzhong* on the upper tier of the Zeng bell-rack (set U2 + 3) is half an octave removed from that of the middle- and lower-tier *yongzhong* (see Chapter 7). In addition to defining each tone as a member of various

26. I first discovered this phenomenon in 1985 (Falkenhausen 1985; see also Feng Guangsheng 1988a).

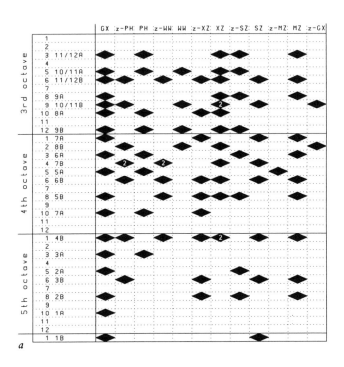

FIGURE 141. *Above and opposite:* Distribution of tone definitions in the Zeng inscriptions, System A. On the vertical axis, the tones playable on each chime are marked on a continuous chromatic scale. On the horizontal axis, abbreviations indicate pitch standards with respect to which tone definitions are provided for tones positioned on the vertical axis (GX = GUXIAN, PH = PINGHUANG, WW = WENWANG, XZ = XINGZHONG, SZ = SHOUZHONG, MZ = MUZHONG; z = *zhuo*, indicating the respective "muddy" pitch standard). Tones defined twice are indicated by the numeral *2*. *a*, bell chimes M1 and M2. The data for bells nos. 2 and 1 and some further definitions apply to set M2 only. Bell no. M2-10, which has a System B inscription, is omitted (see fig. 142). *b*, the Zeng lithophone. *NP* indicates that a chimestone is not preserved; *FR* indicates that the inscription is fragmentary.

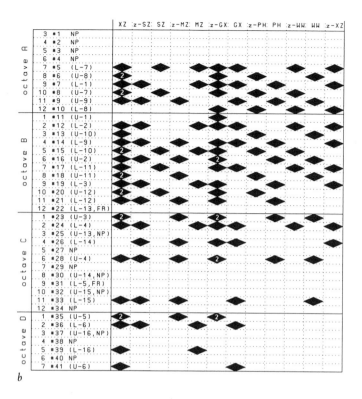

*b*

pentatonic sets of notes, the inscriptions on the M1 and M2 bells thus stress the two principal *lü* in Marquis Yi's bell assemblage. Clearly, in this manner, which I shall designate as System A, the inscriptions serve to integrate the tone distributions of the various components of the Zeng suspended music.

An idea of System B may be gained by looking at the distribution of tone definitions in the third set of bells on the middle tier (M3), which is quite different from the patterns of M1 and M2. "Muddy" *lü* do not occur in the M3 inscriptions at all; on the other hand, complex (binominal) *yin* names are seen just as frequently as simple ones. In these inscriptions, tone is defined only with respect to the six *lü* of the equidistant hexatonic set. Whether or not a given note is a member of a pentatonic gamut of notes with respect to a particular *lü* seems immaterial: the emphasis is entirely on the equidistant spacing of *lü* (fig. 142). Here, too, GUXIAN and XINZHONG play prominent roles, only partly accounted for by the fact that both belong to the basic set of six; many tones are defined twice with respect to each of these two *lü*. Significantly, moreover, only the six binominal *lü* names of Chu (the ones that can be prefixed by *zhuo*) are used in System A. In contrast to this, the *lü* terminology in System B–type inscriptions

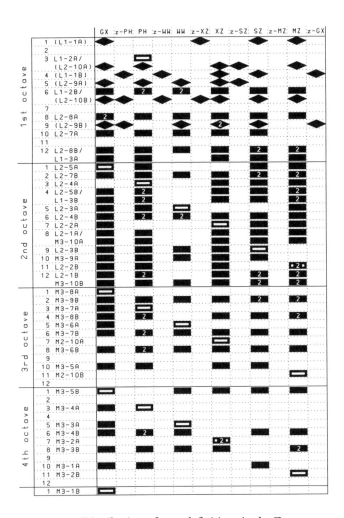

FIGURE 142. Distribution of tone definitions in the Zeng inscriptions, System B: bell-chimes L1 + 2 and M3, plus bell no. M2-10 and several members of chime L1 + 2 that have System B–type inscriptions (marked by symbols used in fig. 141). The structure of the tabulation and abbreviation key are the same as in fig. 141. It should be noted that the pitch standards abbreviated on the horizontal axis are also correlated in the inscriptions to their equivalents in other systems of pitch-standard nomenclature (cf. table 16). The presence of an equivalency formula correlating the pitch standards of different states is indicated by white space within the symbol for a tone; the regularity in the placement of these equivalency expressions throughout the chime is striking.

is far richer, necessitating equivalency formulas that correlate different *lü* nomenclatures. In System A, which has no need for such equivalency inscriptions, they are absent.

There are several other discrepancies between these two systems, principally regarding the details of *yin* nomenclature.[27] In addition to the bell-chimes M1 and M2, System A–type nomenclature prevails on the Zeng lithophone,[28] as well as on three *yongzhong* of the lower-tier assemblage (bells nos. L1-1, L2-9, and L2-10); it is also fundamental to the inscription pattern observable on the recently discovered pitch-pipes from tomb no. 21 at Yutaishan.[29] Inscriptions of System B type, on the other hand, occur on the bell-chime M3 as well as on most of the bells on the lower tier, the tone distribution on which, as noted in Chapter 7, forms a unity with that of M3; the somewhat abbreviated inscriptions on the upper-tier Zeng *niuzhong* also seem to be akin to this type.

The dual tone-definition patterns are systemically complementary. System A stresses the Five Notes (*yin*) in their pristine, monosyllabic form; the pitch standards are adjusted to the *yin*, with the result that both ordinary and "muddy" *lü* occur, whereas complex *yin* are avoided (except with GUXIAN and XINZHONG, as explained above). In System B, by contrast, the six *lü* are primary, and the *yin* are adjusted to the *lü*, requiring, as a consequence, both simple and complex *yin* names, while "muddy" *lü* are absent. The presence of chimes representing both systems among the sixty-five bells from Marquis Yi's tomb is not accidental; on the contrary, their interplay constitutes a central feature in the overall design of the Zeng bell assemblage. That the co-occurrence must have been deliberately intended is indicated, for instance, by the peculiarities of bell M2-10, one of the three bells highlighted in Chapter 7 as overarchingly unifying the tone distribution of the entire Zeng bell assemblage. Alone among the bells in sets M1 and M2, M2-10 has an inscription of the System B type, even though its stylistic

27. In System A inscriptions, the prefix *bian* never occurs; *xiajue* and *bu* are sometimes used instead of *jue*, but never *buxiajue* instead of *zeng*. In inscriptions of System B type, *bian* is used with some frequency; *bu* and *xiajue* never occur instead of *jue*, but *zeng* is sometimes replaced by *buxiajue*. Expressions of the type "*bu* of the unmodified *gong/shang* 素宮 (商) 之頏" (Qiu and Li 1981, 20; Rao Zongyi in Rao and Zeng 1985, 12; Huang Xiquan 1988) are limited to System B. Alternate *yin* names (see n. 7 above) are much more numerous in System A than System B. Octavic differentiation by means of *da* and *shao*, as well as *qian* (see n. 8 above), is frequent in System A; in System B, *shao* occurs seldom and *da* and *qian*, never. Conversely, the usage of *jia* and the three fixed *yin* names is limited to System B.

28. There is one very curious difference within System A between the distributions of tone definitions in the M1 and M2 bells as opposed to the Zeng lithophone. Whereas in the former, as we have seen, complex *yin* names occur in connection with the pitch standards GUXIAN and XINZHONG, the lithophone inscriptions feature, instead, XINZHONG and *zhuo*-GUXIAN. Instead of a tritone, these two *lü* are a fifth apart, an interval also emphasized elsewhere in the lithophone arrangement. By deciding to bring out the fifth in this way, one must sacrifice the emphasis on the equidistant spacing of pitch standards.

29. See n. 13.

attributes correspond exactly to those of the other bells of the M2 chime, which differ externally from the other Zeng *yongzhong* in lacking *mei* bosses. Thus, M2-10 cannot have been secondarily inserted into M2, from, for example, set M3. The only possible conclusion is that the casters and music-masters of Zeng, when manufacturing this assemblage of bells, intended to express a duality of concepts of tone definitions, differentially emphasizing the notes (*yin*) and the pitch standards (*lü*). Because both systems occur on bell-chimes emitting virtually identical tone distributions, the different theoretical conceptualizations of tones cannot have been of much influence on musical practice.

## The Historical Position of the Zeng Musical Terminology
### Complementary Sets of Pitch Standards (Lü)

An overriding concern with musical systematics emerges as the most salient characteristic of the Zeng inscriptions. It is especially evident in their dodeca-tonic *yin* nomenclature, which is based on successive major thirds. As we have seen, this nomenclature seems to be derived from, and proved to be less endur-ing than, the pentatonic *yin* nomenclature in the traditional texts, in which other notes may be indicated by semitonal prefixes. With respect to the notes (*yin*), then, the late pre-Qin texts, such as the *Guo Yu*, *Zhou Li*, and *Lüshi Chunqiu*, seem to preserve the older system, while the Zeng inscriptions, though earlier than those texts, appear to document a specifically Warring States (and perhaps specifically Chu) *yin* nomenclature.

The case of the Zeng *lü* nomenclature, with its complementary hexatonic sets of unprefixed and "muddy" *lü*, appears to be different from that of the *yin*: the twelve *lü* in the late pre-Qin texts, each referred to by a binominal designation, seem clearly posterior in date to the system of pitch-standard nomenclature documented in the Zeng inscriptions. While espousing a twelve-part set of pitch standards, those classical sources ordinarily specify a gamut of "six pitch standards" (*liu lü* 六律) when casually mentioning pitch standards. By comparing the Zeng evidence to various enumerations of *lü* found in various pre-Qin texts, we can trace the evolution from six to twelve *lü*. Part of the significance of the Zeng inscriptions in the context of pre-Qin musical history lies in making possible this historical reconstruction.

The *lü*-names recorded in the *Zhou Li* (third century B.C.) show the greatest similarity to those occurring in some of the Zeng inscriptions (see table 16, column 3). The *Zhou Li* contains two enumerations of pitch standards. In the sec-tion on the Great Instructor (*Taishi* 大師), they are listed as two separate sets: the "six pitch standards" (*liu lü* 六律), HUANGZHONG 黃鐘, TAICOU 太簇, GU-XIAN 姑洗, SUIBIN 妥賓, YIZE 夷則, and WUYI 無射; and the "six identicals" or "accompaniers" (*liu tong* 六同), DALÜ 大呂, YINGZHONG 應鐘, XIAOLÜ 小呂,

HANZHONG 函鐘, NANLÜ 南呂, and JIAZHONG 夾鐘.[30] Both enumerations are arranged as if constituting a scale; but while the *lü* are listed in an ascending order of pitch (or rather, of the pitch of their *gong* [**do**]), the *tong* are listed in descending order. In the section on the Great Director of Music (*Dasiyue* 大司樂), each *lü* on the ascending scale is paired with a *tong* on the descending scale, the interval between the two *gong* thus increasing from pair to pair.

The term *tong* 同, whether translated as "identical" or "accompanier," seems to connote the idea that these six pitch standards might be in some way derived from the six pitch standards designated by the *Zhou Li* as *lü*: each *tong* would seem to have been thought of as linked to one of the *lü*. Based on what we know from the Zeng inscriptions, we may speculate that the original meaning of the term might have been either "octavic equivalent" or "muddy alternate." But such a meaning is evidently no longer implied in the extant *Zhou Li* text, with its series of *lü* and *tong* running in opposite directions. It is telling that elsewhere in the *Zhou Li* the six *lü* and the six *tong* are collectively referred to as the "Twelve *lü*."[31]

A fundamental difference between the concepts of pitch standard (*lü*) in the *Zhou Li* and the Zeng inscriptions is apparent from the fact that the connection between the "real" *lü* of the hexatonic core and the "muddy" *lü* a semitone removed from them has been severed. Nothing in the *Zhou Li* enumerations indicates that, for instance, ZHONGLÜ might have been conceived as an alternate (or an "identical") of the adjacent SUIBIN. In this respect, the pitch-standard nomenclature found in the "Zhou Yu" section of the *Guo Yu*, though probably not much earlier in date than the *Zhou Li*, is closer to that of the Zeng inscriptions.[32] Here, too, the twelve pitch standards are enumerated as two sets: the six pitch standards (*liu lü*), and the "six intermediaries" (*liu jian* 六間), also referred to by the term *lü* 呂.[33] Both are enumerated in an ascending order. That the "intermediaries" (here called DALÜ, JIAZHONG, ZHONGLÜ 仲呂, LINZHONG 林鐘, NANLÜ, and YINGZHONG) occupy the positions in between the six *lü* is implicit in the term *jian* 間. The manner in which the two sets are juxtaposed makes it easy to connect each *lü* of the hexatonic core to its alternate *jian*. Significantly, the *Guo Yu* does not use a term encompassing both the *lü* and the *jian*.

The *Zhou Li*, in the two contexts just alluded to, classifies its six *lü* as *yang* 陽 "male, sunny" etc., and the six *tong* as *yin* 陰 "female, shadowy" etc. Such a

---

30. *Zhou Li: Chun'guan* "Dashi" (*Zhou Li Zhengyi* 45:1a).

31. Ibid. "Diantong" (*Zhou Li Zhengyi* 46:4A).

32. *Guo Yu* "Zhou Yu-*xia*" (Tiansheng Mingdao ed., 3:15a–16b); d'Hormon 1985, 321–22; Hart 1973, 396–97.

33. The original meaning of *lü* 呂 is difficult to establish; in the present case, it undoubtedly means something like "muddy pitch standard (*lü*)." The semantic relationship with *lü* 侶 "accompany" suggested by Wei Zhao's 韋昭 (A.D. 197–278) commentary on *Guo Yu* "Zhou Yu" (loc. cit., 16a) may be etymologically relevant.

TABLE 17.    Order of *Lü* Enumeration in Various Classical Texts

| | 1 | 2 | 3 | 4 | 5 | 6 | 7 | 8 | 9 | 10 | 11 | 12 |
|---|---|---|---|---|---|---|---|---|---|---|---|---|
| **I. Enumeration as two complementary sets** | | | | | | | | | | | | |
| a. *Guo Yu* "Zhou Yu" | HZ | TC | GX | SB | YZE | WY | DL | JZ | ZL | LZ | NL | YZH |
| b. *Zhou Li: Chun'guan* "Dashi" | HZ | TC | GX | SB | YZE | WY | DL | YZH | NL | HAZ | XL | JZ |
| **II. Enumeration in chromatic order** | | | | | | | | | | | | |
| a. *Lüshi Chunqiu* "Yinlü," *Huainan Zi* "Tianwen-xun" (first and second enumerations), *Shi Ji* "Lü Shu" (first enumeration) | HZ | DL | TC | JZ | GX | ZL | SB | LZ | YZE | NL | WY | YZH |
| b. *Huainan Zi* "Tianwen-xun" (third enumeration) | HZ | YZH | WY | NL | YZE | LZ | SB | ZL | GX | JZ | TC | DL |
| c. *Shi Ji* "Lü Shu" (second enumeration) | YZ | HZ | DL | TC | JZ | GX | ZL | SB | LZ | YZE | NL | WY |
| d. *Li Ji* "Yueling" | TC | JZ | GX | ZL | SB | LZ | YZE | NL | WY | YZH | HZ | DL |
| **III. Enumeration according to the Spiral of Fifths:** | | | | | | | | | | | | |
| a. *Lüshi Chunqiu* "Yinlü," *Han Shu* "Lüli Zhi" | HZ | LZ | TC | NL | GX | YZH | SB | DL | YZE | JZ | WY | ZL |

NOTE.   DL = DALÜ,   GX = GUXIAN,   HZ = HUANGZHONG,   HAZ = HANZHONG,   JZ = JIAZHONG,   LZ = LINZHONG, TC = TAICOU,   NL = NANLÜ,   SB = SUIBIN   (or RUIBIN),   WY = WUYI,   XL = XIAOLÜ,   YZE = YIZE,   YZH = YINGZHONG, ZL = ZHONGLÜ.

division has been followed throughout the later history of Chinese musical thought;[34] one may wonder, therefore, whether it applies also to the pitch standards of Zeng, where the complementary sets of "ordinary" and "muddy" *lü* could easily enough be "gendered" in this manner. Yet it must be emphasized that there is no textual evidence for the use of the *yin/yang* dichotomy in any text predating the end of the fourth century.[35] Interestingly, moreover, the *Guo Yu* refrains from specifically labeling its *lü* and *jian* as *yin* and *yang*, in spite of the fact that it discusses each of the twelve pitch standards in terms of sweeping *yin/yang* rhetoric.[36] If it is true that the *Guo Yu* concept of pitch standards is in some respects more conservative than that of the *Zhou Li*, it seems likely that the *lü* in the even-earlier Zeng inscriptions were not yet conceived of in terms of *yin* and *yang* groups. Such classification probably represents merely a late Warring States afterthought.

## Conflation of Yin and Lü

In most classical sources other than *Zhou Li* and *Guo Yu*, the contrast between two complementary sets of six *lü* is not explicit. Instead, the *lü* are listed as a single set of twelve, usually in ascending order of the pitches of their *gong*. A majority of these enumerations start with HUANGZHONG, the principal *lü* of traditional Chinese musical theory (see table 17).[37]

In such enumerations, the Five Notes (*wu yin*) often appear along with the pitch standards in ways suggesting that both were now regarded as notes of fixed pitch similar to C-D-E in present-day Western usage.[38] The earliest passage showing such a tendency is probably a somewhat garbled locus in the *Zhou Li*.[39] In the "Lü shu" chapter of Sima Qian's *Shi Ji* 史記, written around the

---

34. The dichotomy of *yang lü* 律 and *yin lü* 呂 is built into the much-discussed myth of the creation of the pitch-pipes by Music Master Lun 伶倫, recounted in *Lüshi Chunqiu* "Guyue" (Sibu Congkan ed., 5:8b–9a; for a ready translation see DeWoskin 1982, 59–60).

35. Schwartz 1985, 350–82; see also the *Guo Yu* translation by Hart, 77–94.

36. The text assigns the function of "helping along the *yang*" both to a pitch standard (*lü*) of the hexatonic core, TAICOU, and to one of the "intermediate pitches," NANLÜ; this perplexed Wei Zhao, who naturally regarded the "intermediate pitches" as *yin*, rather than as *yang*.

37. The pitch standard (*lü*) enumerations in the following loci start on HUANGZHONG: *Lüshi Chunqiu* "Yinlü" (Sibu Congkan ed., j. 6:3b, second enumeration); *Huainan Zi* "Tianwen-xun" (Sibu Congkan ed., j. 3:10b–12b, three enumerations, one exceptionally in descending order); and *Shi Ji* "Lü Shu" (Zhonghua ed., 1249). A second enumeration in *Shi Ji* "Lü Shu" (Zhoughua ed., 1243–47) begins on YINGZHONG; and the one in *Li Ji* "Yueling," on TAICOU (*Li Ji Zhushu*, j. 14–17 passim; also *Lüshi Chunqiu* passim).

38. The connoisseur of Western music may notice a curious European parallel to this blurring of distinctions between notes and pitch standards. On the European continent, the use of the **do- (ut-) re- mi-** series as a solmization system is now virtually obsolete, having been supplanted by notes designating fixed frequencies. Although in Germany, such notes are referred to as C-D-E, etc., they are referred to as **do- (ut-) re-mi** etc., in Italy and France.

39. *Zhou Li: Chun'guan* "Dasiyue" (*Zhou Li Zhengyi*, j. 45:1a–12a).

turn of the first century B.C., the *lü* are listed as a set of twelve pitch-pipes of specified lengths. The enumeration proceeds according to the following pattern:

> The length of HUANGZHONG is 8 *cun* 寸 1 *fen* 分 ; this is *gong*. The length of DALÜ is 7 *cun* 5-2/3 *fen*. The length of TAICOU is 7 *cun* 2 *fen*, this is *shang*.[40]

As enumerated here, the twelve *lü*-pipes constitute an ascending twelve-tone scale; when appropriate, they are equated to the notes of a pentatonic series. Clearly, this is the series of notes (*yin*) defined with respect to HUANGZHONG, though Sima Qian seems to see no need to say so explicitly.

Such equations of notes and pitch standards would be impractical in the Zeng system of *lü* nomenclature, with its complementary sets of unprefixed and "muddy" *lü*; for when superimposing a pentatonic gamut of *yin* onto the pitch standards documented in the Zeng inscriptions, three *yin* correspond to unprefixed *lü* and two to "muddy" *lü*. The dichotomy is removed only when all twelve pitch standards are assigned binominal *lü* names. The "Tianwen-xun" chapter in *Huainan Zi* 淮南子 (compiled sometime before 122 B.C.), for example, states that "HUANGZHONG is *gong*, TAICOU is *shang*, GUXIAN is *jue*, LINZHONG is *zhi*, NANLÜ is *yu*."[41] Even more directly than in the *Shi Ji*, each *yin* is defined as coinciding with one of the twelve *lü*. Such a conception became possible only as a result of the formation of the traditional set of Twelve *lü*. In the Zeng system, such a phrase as "TAICOU is *shang*" would be meaningless; what the *Huainan Zi* means to express would be expressed, in the parlance of the Zeng inscriptions, as "*gong* on TAICOU is *shang* on HUANGZHONG." Similarly, "GUXIAN is *jue*" would be rendered as "*gong* on GUXIAN is *jue* on HUANGZHONG," and so on.

The Zeng inscriptions consistently keep the functions of notes (*yin*) and pitch standards (*lü*) separate. While *yin* names sometimes do occur without the pitch standard being explicitly stated (e.g., on the recto faces of the middle-tier *yong-zhong*, where the *lü* GUXIAN is implied throughout), *lü names are never seen alone*. The dual pattern of tone-definition distributions in the Zeng inscriptions (expressed through System A and System B–type tone definitions) is built on this very tension between the *yin* and *lü* dimensions of each tone. Comparison with the Zeng inscriptions reveals that the *Shi Ji* and *Huainan Zi* document a fundamental change in the conception of tones, resulting in a situation in which a tone could be defined by stating a pitch standard (*lü*) by itself. This semantic shift, which must have occurred sometime in late Warring States or

---

40. *Shi Ji* "Lü Shu" (Zhonghua ed., 1249). The original text is garbled; I follow the emendations by Chavannes (1895–1910, 3:314), based in part on those by Cai Yuanding 蔡元定 (1135–1198).
41. *Huainan Zi* "Tianwen-xun" (Sibu Congkan ed., j. 3:10b).

early Western Han times, has colored all subsequent understanding of notes and pitch standards.[42]

The consequences of this conceptual conflation are especially evident in the ways in which the *lü* were mathematically calculated throughout the two-thousand-year history of Imperial China. No consideration of pre-Imperial Chinese music would be complete without discussing the methods and principles involved in such calculations and exploring possible points of connection to the Zeng chimes and their musical nomenclature.

## Generation of Notes by "Subtracting or Adding a Third"

In the "Yinlü" chapter of the *Lüshi Chunqiu* 呂氏春秋 (compiled ca. 245 B.C.), pitch standards are for the first time listed according to the Spiral of Fifths principle, well known in Western musical theory. Such a progression can be demonstrated quite elegantly on a string vibrating at a certain frequency, as described by Bell N. Young:

> After the length of the vibrating string, which produces the fundamental note . . . has been determined, the next note is obtained by multiplying the length of this string by a factor of 2:3. . . . The resultant note is a perfect fifth higher in frequency than [the fundamental note]. . . . The next step is to multiply the length of [the second note] by the factor of 4:3, which results in a note a perfect fourth lower than [that note]. . . . By applying the same process repeatedly, . . . a series of twelve notes is obtained.[43]

The note obtained by the twelfth step of generation is 1224 cents removed from the fundamental note, a "Pythagorean Comma" of 24 cents in excess of the just octave. Scholars of many dynasties worked at refining the calculations so as to reconcile them with the just octave of 1200 cents; such efforts led to various systems of temperament. A mathematically exact equal-tempered scale of twelve tones was finally calculated by the Ming dynasty prince Zhu Zaiyu 朱載堉 (1536–ca. 1610).[44]

Even since the time of the *Lüshi Chunqiu*, the method of generating notes through the Spiral of Fifths, which is generally known to Chinese musicologists as the *Sanfen Sunyi-fa* 三分損益法 (roughly, "method of subtracting or adding

---

42. Influenced by the Han texts, many commentators on the Zeng inscriptions have tended to confuse the terms *lü* and *yin*, misunderstanding the musical theory of the inscriptions as a result (e.g., Huang Xiangpeng 1981, Li Chunyi 1981).

43. Young 1980, 261.

44. For treatments of the history of Chinese tuning systems, see Courant 1922, Needham and Robinson 1962, and Wu Nanxun 1964.

the third part"), has remained the cornerstone of Chinese musical theory. Scrutinizing the textual sources as well as the musical-archaeological evidence, we can point to some indications that a method for calculating notes (*yin*) by means of the Spiral of Fifths was known in the Bronze Age, though its application to the pitch standards (*lü*) constitutes a later development incompatible with the principles of the musical theory documented through the Zeng inscriptions.

Because the notes obtained by subtracting or adding the third part—situated, respectively, a fifth above and a fourth below the fundamental note—are octavically identical, a set of twelve notes according to the *Sanfen Sunyi-fa* can be generated by subtracting and adding in any sequence. The various sequences of subtracting and adding in the pitch-standard generation described in different texts are of great interest in tracing the evolution of musical thinking in early Imperial China.

As described in *Lüshi Chunqiu* (fig. 143), the Spiral of Fifths begins on HUANG-ZHONG. It continues through alternating steps of subtracting and adding, producing LINZHONG, TAICOU, NANLÜ, GUXIAN, and YINGZHONG. There follow two successive steps of adding, yielding SUIBIN and DALÜ, after which the alternation of subtracting and adding resumes with YIZE, JIAZHONG, WUYI, and ZHONGLÜ. As a result, when the twelve *lü* are arranged in chromatic order, the first seven are all derived by inferior and the following five by superior generation; the whole set of notes is neatly confined to the range of one octave.

Contrastingly, the *Han Shu* 漢書 (first century A.D.) offers an enumeration of *lü* in which the alternation of superior and inferior generation is unbroken throughout.[45] Thus, after the sixth step of generation, the procedure differs from that in *Lüshi Chunqiu*. The six pitch standards obtained by superior generation and the six obtained by inferior generation form two equidistant hexatonic sets, which are referred to as *lü* 呂 and *lü* 律 and classified as *yin* 陰 and *yang* 陽. But when the *gong* defined with respect to these twelve *lü* are arranged in order of pitch, they do not form a continuous chromatic scale, and the scope of an octave is exceeded by one-half (fig. 144). Chen Qiyou 陳奇猷 has shown that the *Han Shu* list of *lü* originated from tinkering with the *Lüshi Chunqiu* text;[46] the method of *lü* enumeration described in *Lüshi Chunqiu* is clearly earlier than that of the *Han Shu*.

In Greece, the Spiral of Fifths was used by the Pythagoreans in the sixth century B.C., and it may have earlier antecedents in Babylonian musical cosmology. But the Pythagoreans, instead of either subtracting or adding the third part of a vibrating string at each step (and thereby obtaining the fifth above the original tone or its lower octavic equivalent), multiplied the "length" of the original tone

---

45. *Han Shu* "Lüli-zhi" (Zhonghua ed., 958–59).
46. Chen Qiyou 1962b.

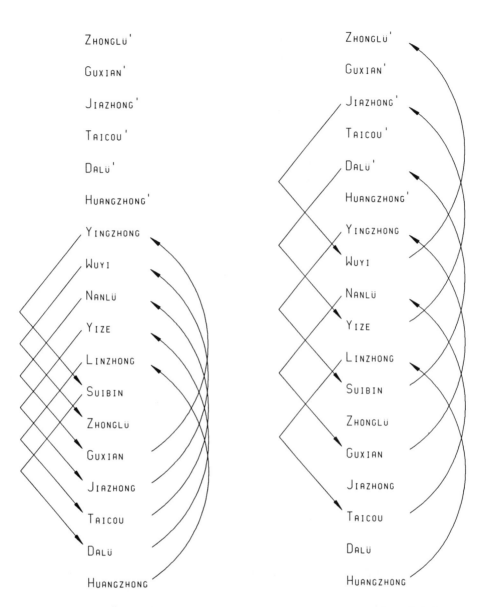

ZHONGLÜ'

GUXIAN'

JIAZHONG'

TAICOU'

DALÜ'

HUANGZHONG'

YINGZHONG

WUYI

NANLÜ

YIZE

LINZHONG

SUIBIN

ZHONGLÜ

GUXIAN

JIAZHONG

TAICOU

DALÜ

HUANGZHONG

FIGURE 143. Generation of pitch
standards according to the *Lüshi
Chunqiu*.

ZHONGLÜ'

GUXIAN'

JIAZHONG'

TAICOU'

DALÜ'

HUANGZHONG'

YINGZHONG

WUYI

NANLÜ

YIZE

LINZHONG

SUIBIN

ZHONGLÜ

GUXIAN

JIAZHONG

TAICOU

DALÜ

HUANGZHONG

FIGURE 144. Generation of pitch
standards according to the *Han
Shu*, "Lüli-zhi."

by 3/2, thereby obtaining a note a fifth deeper than the original. Repeating such a procedure twelve times, they descended downward through seven octaves until regaining an approximate octavic equivalent of the first note. The mathematical differences from the Chinese procedure are evident,[47] casting doubt on the suggestion, brought forward by Chavannes and others, that the Chinese obtained knowledge of the Spiral of Fifths from the West.[48]

The *Sanfen Sunyi-fa* as seen in connection with the twelve *lü* in the *Lüshi Chunqiu* constitutes, at any rate, a highly developed application of "Pythagorean" principles. It must have been known in China for some time previously. But how long? We naturally wonder whether the tone nomenclature in the Zeng inscriptions may reflect an awareness of the Spiral of Fifths. From the vantage point of the *Lüshi Chunqiu*, we may be tempted to look to the pitch standards for clues in this regard. Upon reflection, however, when considering the function of *lü* in Zeng musical theory, we should not expect them to have been derived through the *Sanfen Sunyi-fa*, which is a method of generating a set of notes in certain intervallic relations to one another. Regardless of the absolute pitch of the tone of departure, the mathematical relations between notes always remain the same. But the *lü* in the Zeng inscriptions, as we have seen, are not notes; they are pitch standards, similar to clefs in Western musical notation, which serve as anchoring points in the tonal realm. In the inscriptions, as we have remarked, no tone is expressed by the name of a *lü* alone; a tone is primarily identified as "*yin x* of *lü* M." Similarly, when generating one tone from another, one always primarily generates one *yin* from another *yin*; in such a case, a pitch standard (*lü*) serves merely to determine the absolute pitch of both tones. We may thus conclude that the idea of deriving the *lü* from one another by means of "Pythagorean" principles must have been conceived *after* the conflation of *yin* and *lü*, a phenomenon that, in turn, postdates the Zeng inscriptions.

Such common-sense deliberations can be followed up by analyzing the *lü* in the Zeng inscriptions with their two complementary hexatonic sets: the "hexatonic core" of *lü* with unprefixed binominal names, and the "muddy" *lü*. If we generated the twelve pitch standards by alternately subtracting and adding the third part (i.e., according to the *Sanfen Sunyi-fa*), we would obtain an alternating series of *lü* of the hexatonic core and "muddy" *lü*; each "muddy" *lü* thus generated would correspond to the "muddy" alternate of some core *lü* other than the one generated just before. For example, GUXIAN yields ZHUO-SHOUZHONG, which yields PINGHUANG, and so forth. It cannot be otherwise, because the *Sanfen Sunyi-fa* operates with fifths and fourths, and in an equidistant hexatonic set, no two members are spaced either a fifth or a fourth apart from

47. Needham and Robinson 1962, 172–73.
48. See Chapter 7, n. 1.

one another. In other words, no application of the *Sanfen Sunyi-fa* can conceivably remain only within one of the above-mentioned complementary hexatonic sets; the procedure always oscillates between the two sets of pitch standards. As we have noted earlier in this chapter, the two sets are probably not coeval; the hexatonic core preceded the "muddy" *lü*, perhaps by a considerable span of time. Moreover, the pitch-standard nomenclature of the Zeng inscriptions suggests that "muddy" *lü* were regarded as closely related to their unprefixed counterparts (e.g., ZHUO-SHOUZHONG to SHOUZHONG) and not derived from those a fifth below (in this case, GUXIAN). If generated by "Pythagorean" principles, on the other hand, a *lü* of the hexatonic core and its "muddy" alternate would be five steps of generation apart.

It seems likely, therefore, that in the time of the Zeng inscriptions, the *Sanfen Sunyi-fa* was not yet applied to the pitch standards. This conclusion does not, however, exclude the possibility that the method was used with reference to the notes (*yin*). Indeed, the more we pursue this idea the more likely it appears, though definite proof cannot yet be offered. For example, probably the earliest Chinese textual reference to the *Sanfen Sunyi-fa*, in the "Diyuan" chapter of the *Guan Zi* 管子,[49] concerns the notes (*yin*) and not the pitch standards (*lü*). The first five notes in a *Sanfen Sunyi* sequence constitute a pentatonic gamut of notes: **do-sol-mi-la-re**. In the *Guan Zi* locus, the five notes are derived in that order (the "lengths" of their pitches expressed by convenient ordinal numbers, which may be imagined as the relative lengths of vibrating strings), but the succession of steps of inferior and superior generation results in a set of notes in which **sol** is the deepest note:

$$\textbf{sol} = 108 : \textbf{la} = 96 : \textbf{do} = 81 : \textbf{re} = 72 : \textbf{mi} = 64.$$

This pattern differs from schemes of *yin* generation recorded in later sources, which, by inverting the order of superior and inferior generation, yield a series of notes in which *gong* (**do**) is the deepest tone. All these enumerations, including that in the *Guan Zi*, are limited in scope to the Five *Yin* of the pentatonic gamut.

It is interesting, moreover, that the four "simple" names of notes (*yin*) in the nomenclature documented by the Zeng inscriptions—**do**, **sol**, **re**, and **la**—coincide with the first four notes obtained by the *Sanfen Sunyi-fa*;[50] the generation of the eight remaining notes in the set of twelve *yin* involved steps of a major third, precisely the interval between **do** and **mi**, the next following note

49. *Guan Zi* "Diyuan-pian" (Guoxue Jiben Congshu ed., j. 3:21); the passage in question probably dates to sometime during the Warring States period. Dating problems with respect to the *Guan Zi* are discussed in Rickett 1985, 3–24.

50. The following analysis mainly follows Asahara 1987, 98–110. Similar conclusions were reached independently by Chen Cheng-yih 1987.

obtained by the *Sanfen Sunyi-fa*. It seems possible that the Zeng *yin* nomenclature was mathematically grounded in *Sanfen Sunyi-fa* principles. Theoretically, then, a "Pythagorean" major third of 408 cents, rather than the "natural" major third of 396 cents,[51] would have been intended in designing the Zeng chimes. To what degree the Eastern Zhou music masters and bell casters were aware of the theoretical difference between the two kinds of major thirds, however, is difficult to tell.[52] As we have discussed in Chapter 7, there is little chance of finding a hint along these lines from the measurable tones emitted by the bells themselves.[53]

Asahara Tatsurō has sought additional evidence for an early use of the *Sanfen Sunyi-fa* in the tone distributions in earlier Zhou chime-bells.[54] The five largest bells of the *niuzhong* chime from tomb no. 1 at Xiasi, for example, which we discussed in Chapter 7, have A-tones that can be rendered as **sol, la, do, re,** and **mi** (see fig. 117). This is perhaps not coincidentally the same sequence of notes as found in the *Guan Zi* locus just mentioned. Possibly, the numerical proportions recorded there were of some importance in designing and tuning bells. One may speculate, moreover, that the suffix *jue* as used in the Zeng inscriptions may have originated from makeshift names for the (usually non-pentatonic) B-tones of major-third bells, which are particularly plentiful in these lower-register tone distributions.[55] If so, this would be an interesting instance of an innovation in musical theory that grew out of the musical instruments' technological features.

<br>

51. I.e., the interval obtained by a five-fold application of the *Sanfen Sunyi-fa* (expressible by the proportion $2^5:3^5$ or as 32:243) rather than the "natural" (or just) interval corresponding to the proportion 4:5.

52. Asahara (1987, 99–100) has calculated that two "Pythagorean" major thirds plus one natural major third almost exactly equals the natural octave of 1200 cents. But even if the Zeng music masters did not realize this fact, a succession of two "Pythagorean" major thirds and one natural one would have been quite naturally obtained by deriving "complex" *yin* by means of the "Pythagorean" major third, while at the same time obtaining octavic equivalents by means of the "natural" octave. At any rate, Asahara's idea of superimposing "Pythagorean" and natural thirds is musically and mathematically far superior to Li Chunyi's (1981, 67) schema (also adopted in McClain 1985), which supposes the use of the natural major third in generating the "complex" notes (*yin*). The result would have been a cacophonous enlarged interval between a note with a name containing the suffix *zeng* and the next corresponding note (*yin*) of "simple" name (e.g., between *shangzeng* and *shang*).

53. Predictably, therefore, Asahara failed to find significant corroboration of his ideas in the actual tone measurements from the Zeng bells (1987, 105–09; similarly Chen Cheng-yih 1987, 175–76).

54. Asahara 1987, 74–89.

55. Let us inspect, for instance, the *niuzhong* chime from tomb no. 1 at Xiasi (see fig. 118). The B-tone of the **sol** bell no. 1 is a semitone below **do**; the B-tone of the **la** bell no. 2 is a semitone above **do**; the B-tone of the **re** bell no. 4 is a semitone below **sol**. Such tones, for which there may have been no established *yin* name at first, may therefore have been conceived of as correlates of their A-tones: **sol + mi, la + mi,** and **re + mi**. This may at least explain the origin of the suffix *jue*; the origin of *gongzeng* must have been a secondary phenomenon.

In the Zeng bells, dated to about one century after the Xiasi chime, the lower-register tone distributions among the bells of the lower and middle tiers (figs. 119 and 120) furnish a series of A-tones virtually identical to that in the Xiasi chime; and in the even later Biao- and Jingli-*niuzhong* (figs. 127 and 128), that A-tone series is expanded to include **si**, the sixth note generated by the *Sanfen Sunyi-fa*. The emphasis on fifths in the tone distributions in Warring States chimes, especially in all parts of the Zeng bell assemblage, corroborates the notion that their makers may have designed them according to *Sanfen Sunyi-fa* principles.

An emphasis on the fifth is noticeable even earlier in the tone distributions in late Western Zhou chime-bells, in which the principal four-tone pattern is emitted by two minor-third bells spaced a fifth apart (see fig. 114). What these chimes lack, of course, is a full pentatonic gamut of notes: there is no *shang* (**re**), but as we have seen, this absence probably resulted from overriding conventions of instrument manufacture; the tone **re** was certainly used in Western Zhou music. It is conceivable, therefore, that Chinese musicians generated notes by means of the *Sanfen Sunyi-fa* as early as the Western Zhou period, though at the present state of knowledge, we cannot be sure about this.

## Conclusions

Through the maze of cosmological speculation pervading the late pre-Qin texts we can but dimly perceive the music of the earlier part of the Bronze Age. It has long been suspected, however, that early Eastern Zhou musicological thinking must have differed significantly from that of the late pre-Qin texts.[56] The Zeng inscriptions have enabled us to trace a series of significant changes that occurred from mid- to late Eastern Zhou times.

Precisely when Chinese musicians began to use composite terms to define tones as notes (*yin*) with respect to pitch standards (*lü*) (such as "*shang* of TAICOU"), as in the Zeng inscriptions, is unknown. We may reason, however, that pitch standards are useful whenever music is to be performed by several instruments in concert, and we know, on the basis of archaeological finds, that ensemble music was performed in China at least as early as the Shang period. Hence, the use of *lü* may go back to fairly early times. Individual *lü* names

56. In her dissertation, Babette Becker (1957, 89–90 and passim) was able to reach such a conclusion without the benefit of archaeological evidence, relying entirely on scattered textual references. It is a particular gratification for me, in this book, to provide resounding confirmation of Becker's pioneering insights.

appear in the late Western Zhou epigraphic record,[57] though it is unclear whether these Western Zhou *lü* formed an ordered system of pitch standards comparable to those of later times. At any rate, sets of six equidistantly spaced pitch standards per octave must have come into existence during the Springs and Autumns period at the latest. The principle that *lü* whose *gong* (**do**) were an octave apart are equivalent seems not to have been acknowledged at first, so that these early systems of pitch standards may have contained quite a large number of *lü* names, corresponding to a limited number of positions in the octave (witness the nine-part "Zeng" set of pitch standards in the Zeng inscriptions). The Zeng inscriptions manifest the incipient stage of a process by which these sets of six *lü* per octave were expanded into sets of twelve; this was done by defining "muddy" *lü* that were clearly secondary and subordinate to the former sets of six. During the later part of the Warring States period, these "muddy" *lü* became a six-part set of their own (known as *tong, jian,* or *lü* 呂), complementary to the hexatonic core set of pitch standards and referred to by names previously reserved for the octavic equivalents of the core *lü*. By the mid-third century B.C., these two sets of six had fused into the set of Twelve Pitch Standards (*Shi'er lü* 十二律) that has been in use ever since.[58]

We have seen that the pentatonic set of five notes has been the mainstay of Chinese music since the earliest times. Even though the traditional *gong-shang-jue* nomenclature is not textually documented before the Warring States period, it may have very early origins. The Zeng inscriptions record a variety of names designating equivalent notes (*yin*) in different octaves. Moreover, since at least early Eastern Zhou (and quite possibly earlier) times, the Five Notes (*wu yin*) of the pentatonic gamut appear to have been mathematically conceived in terms of *Sanfen Sunyi-fa* ("Pythagorean") principles. Similarly, the complex dodecatonic *yin* nomenclature in the Zeng inscriptions, in which the non-pentatonic notes are defined by steps of one or two major thirds, is probably grounded in the basic pentatonic set of notes defined according to the *Sanfen Sunyi-fa*. Possibly because of its intricacy, this dodecatonic *yin* nomenclature apparently enjoyed somewhat limited success; instead, a more primitive system defining the non-pentatonic notes as semitones below or above each of the five pentatonic notes remained in use throughout historical times. The early existence of that system is also documented in the Zeng inscriptions.

57. See above, n. 20. I plan to treat the origins and semantics of the pitch standard (*lü*) nomenclature in a separate article; for the time being, see Falkenhausen 1988, 813–29. See also Fang Jianjun 1990.

58. As to why only six pitch standards were used before the Warring States period, Asahara (1987, 93–98) has suggested that earlier standards of intonation were too inexact to allow perception of semitonic distinctions. We have seen in Chapter 7 that Eastern Zhou instrument-builders were able to achieve considerably greater accuracy in tuning bells than their Western Zhou forebears; such technological know-how may indeed have evolved hand in hand with increased sensitivity toward tonal nuances.

The Zeng inscriptions are remarkable for strictly maintaining the distinction between the functions of notes and pitch standards. In all the traditional texts, that difference has already become confused to a certain degree. As a result, the pitch standards (*lü*) came to be defined in terms of the *Sanfen Sunyi-fa*, in analogy to the notes (*yin*). Moreover, many of the terms recorded in the Zeng inscriptions went out of use as the musical terminology was standardized. In the process, both the Five Notes (*wu yin*) and the Twelve Pitch Standards (*Shi'er lü*) came to be looked on as closed sets, which invited interpretation in terms of *yin/yang* and correlative cosmology. The evidence of the Zeng inscriptions strongly suggests that such interpretation was applied to systems of Chinese musical theory not from primordial times, but only during the late Warring States period.

What, then, are the specific features of musical theory in Zeng? With twelve *yin* per octave, and every tone (theoretically) definable in terms of twelve *lü*, the system of tone classification in the inscriptions is supremely versatile, capable of bringing out many different kinds of regular tone arrangements. Throughout the Zeng inscriptions, a preoccupation with arranging the tones in ever-different patterns is manifest, especially in the *yin* and *lü* nomenclature and the dual pattern of tone-definition distribution. A central theme of these ever-shifting (and consciously juxtaposed) tonal arrangements was to render the *lü* mathematically compatible with the *yin*, and vice versa. This thrust of the Zeng tone nomenclature may in some way prefigure the conflation of *yin* and *lü* later on in the Warring States period. The same overarching fascination with pattern is also expressed, to some extent, in the tone distribution of the Zeng instruments; it explains, for instance, the peculiar scaling principle of the *niuzhong* on the upper tier of the Zeng bell-rack, as well as the scaling of the forty-one-part lithophone in its various arrangements.

Measuring these tonal intervals and equivalencies must have been, for the most part, an intellectual rather than an artistic activity. Later developments suggest that this subdividing and correlating a gamut of tones in ever-new ways may have been thought to be imbued with deep cosmological significance.[59] The Zeng bell-chimes and lithophone were more than mere musical instruments; perhaps more importantly, they were tools with which the tonal realm could be measured. It did not matter that the inscriptions were placed out of sight of the musicians; as indications of the far-flung connections and equivalences entailed by producing any tone, they were guideposts in the cosmic realm. The systematizing thrust of the Zeng inscriptions far transcends the scope of music.

59. DeWoskin 1982, 55–83 and passim.

# CHAPTER NINE

# Music Suspended: Tone Theory and
# Its Political Ramifications

When we consider the tone distributions of the Zeng bells in conjunction with their tone-naming inscriptions, we find that musical theory was more or less divorced from musical practice—a phenomenon that has continued to characterize Chinese music throughout its later history. As shown in Chapter 7, the Zeng bell assemblage and lithophone were undoubtedly viable musical instruments: they could be used to play pentatonic music in a variety of keys according to the *xuangong* (revolving **do**) principle. But quite independently of their musical usefulness, these instruments were also repositories of cosmological knowledge: they functioned as a musical tonometer, a device for imposing ever-varying regular patterns onto the tonal realm (see Chapter 8). There seems little inherent connection between the tone-naming inscriptions on the Zeng "suspended music" and the musical potential of those instruments (except, perhaps, in the case of the upper-tier *niuzhong* with their astonishingly regular arrangements of thirds). How are we to explain that somewhat uneasy fusion of musical practice and theory? Why were the inscriptions placed on bells to begin with?

*Pitch-Pipes and Bells in Zhou Musical Theory*

The semantic field of the term *lü* 律, here translated as "pitch standard," is not limited to musicology. As a legal term, *lü* means "regulation," and with reference to tones in music, it also connotes "regulator, measuring standard." A *lü* determined the pitch to which all musical instruments in an orchestra were tuned when they performed in concert. Traditional sources mention two kinds of instruments from which this pitch standard was obtained by the other instruments: bells and pitch-pipes (*lüguan* 律管). A debate about whether "bell pitch standards" (*zhonglü* 鐘律) or "pipe pitch standards" (*guanlü* 管律) were primary has raged throughout much of Chinese musical history.[1]

Although chime-bells and pitch-pipes belong to completely distinct classes of sound generators, they share one feature that makes both viable as tuning standards: they are composed of discrete sound-producing units, each of which emits a distinct tone. Unlike a flute, a pitch-pipe is designed to produce only one tone (though its pitch is somewhat dependent on blowing technique). For tuning purposes, pitch-pipes have an advantage over bells in that their lengths reflect the mathematical proportions of tonal frequencies in a simple way. In the list of pitch-pipes in the "Lü shu" chapter of *Shi Ji*,[2] for instance, the length of the LINZHONG pipe, a fifth above HUANGZHONG, is given as ⅔ the length of the HUANGZHONG pipe.[3] The lengths of the twelve pitch-pipes listed by Sima Qian were determined by the *Sanfen Sunyi-fa*: by alternately subtracting and adding the third part of the length of the previous pipe, starting from HUANGZHONG.

As has been shown in the preceding chapter, the application of the *Sanfen Sunyi-fa* to the Twelve *Lü* is probably a secondary phenomenon, postdating the late Warring States conflation of notes and pitch standards. Even though the *Lüshi Chunqiu* claims that the music master Ling Lun 伶倫 tuned the first standard set of bamboo pitch-pipes in the distant time of the Yellow Emperor,[4] it seems likely that the use of graduated pitch-pipes as pitch standards does not long predate the late pre-Qin texts. This impression is confirmed by archaeological finds. Pitch-pipes probably evolved from panpipes (*paixiao*), which remain part of the Chinese orchestra to this day.[5] An instrument type of uncertain but probably early origin, panpipes have been found in Springs and Autumns period tombs; the earliest ones, from the early seventh-century tomb no. 2 at Shangguan'gang, Guangshan (Henan),[6] are made of bamboo. The unusual stone panpipe from tomb no. 1 at Xiasi (mid-sixth century) seems to have been de-

1. See *Zhongguo Yinyue Cidian*, entries *zhonglü* and *guanlü*.

2. The beginning of this list is quoted in Chapter 8. I follow Chavannes's reconstitution of the text (see Chapter 8, n. 40).

3. This would be exactly correct if the pipe's diameter and the thickness of the body were adjusted in the same way as the length. The respective proportions can be even more elegantly demonstrated on a vibrating string, where the width and thickness can be disregarded. It has therefore been proposed (e.g., by Yang Yinliu 1979) that the actual proportions of the "lengths" of pitches were established not by means of pipes but by a stringed instrument. Of course, what is meant by the HUANGZHONG pipe is, in the parlance of the Zeng inscriptions, a pipe emitting the **do** of HUANGZHONG.

4. *Lüshi Chunqiu* "Guyue" (Sibu Congkan ed., 5:8b–9a; see Chapter 8, n. 34).

5. Zhuang Benli 1963. It may be objected that sets of blowing-tubes of graduated sizes were also used in mouth-organs (*sheng*), but, having finger-holes, they must be classified as flutes. Panpipes are the musical instruments organologically closest to pitch-pipes.

6. *Kaogu* 1984 (4):302–32, 348; drawing, p. 328 fig. 29.3–5.

signed to emit a pentatonic series of notes.[7] Marquis Yi's tomb yielded two well-preserved lacquered bamboo panpipes of thirteen pipes each (see fig. 5), which comprised six tones per octave (the pentatonic series plus **si**), ranging through two octaves. They appear to have been tuned to two different keys.[8] Like their modern-day descendants, the early panpipes were evidently designed to function as melodic instruments, emitting series of *yin* notes.

The function of sets of pitch-pipes, as opposed to panpipes, is not musical in the strict sense; they are useless for playing melodies (to do so, one would have to pick up and play the loose pitch-pipes one by one in quick succession, which is impracticable). The four fragmentary bamboo pipes from the mid–Warring States period tomb no. 21 at Yutaishan, Jiangling (Hubei), mentioned in Chapter 8 (see fig. 140),[9] may be the earliest known remains of a set of pitch-pipes, though the possibility that they may have been part of a panpipe cannot be entirely excluded. Their inscriptions exactly resemble those on Marquis Yi's bells and lithophones in defining each tone (one tone per pipe) by a string of equivalent terms of the type "*yin x* of *lü* M."[10] It should be stressed that none of these pitch-pipes is itself identified as representing one particular *lü*, as one might expect from the *Shi Ji* list of pipes; on the contrary, several *lü* names appear on each pipe. This is exactly where the Yutaishan pitch-pipes differ from Han dynasty specimens, such as the complete set of twelve bamboo pitch-pipes found in the early Western Han tomb no. 1 at Mawangdui, Changsha (Hunan) (fig. 145).[11] Each of the Mawangdui pipes is inscribed with one of the twelve binominal *lü* names known from the classical texts; *yin* names are not specified (in the spirit of the Zeng inscriptions, one may infer *gong* [**do**] each time).[12] The inscription on an unprovenienced bronze pitch-pipe in the Shanghai Museum, dating to the Wang Mang interregnum (A.D. 9–24),[13] also indicates only a single *lü* name, WUYI. In these Han pitch-pipes, a tone is directly identified as a *lü*, just as present-day Western musicians would unhesitatingly identify a tone as C

7. See Chapter 7, n. 37; also Chapter 7, n. 14.
8. Jiang Wujian 1988, 4 and fig. 2; Huang Xiangpeng 1979.
9. See Chapter 8, n. 13.
10. The *lü* nomenclature corresponds to that identified in the Zeng inscriptions with the state of Chu, which is not surprising, considering that the locus of excavation is in the immediate vicinity of the Chu capital. The tone-definition distribution pattern seems to correspond with that in sets M1 and M2 of the Zeng bells.
11. *Changsha Mawangdui Yihao Hanmu* vol. 1:107–10; vol. 2, ill., p. 204; Lü Linlan 1983.
12. These pitch-pipes were likely *mingqi* of purely mortuary function; the report notes that their absolute and relative lengths are at variance with those stipulated in the Han dynasty texts. Their measured tones (*Changsha Mawangdui Yihao Hanmu* 1:110) do not form the expected dodecatonic series, though they must have had considerable symbolic and cosmological significance.
13. Because it is fragmentary, its value in reconstructing the standard pitches of Wang Mang's reign is very limited; the reconstruction of the entire set of *lü* proposed by Ma and Pan (1981) is not convincing.

FIGURE 145. Set of twelve pitch-pipes (with silk pouch) excavated in 1972 from tomb no. 1 at Mawangdui, Changsha (Hunan). Early Western Han (before 168 B.C.).

or D (and not as "**do** on C," etc.); clearly, by this time, the earlier method of defining a tone as a note with respect to a pitch standard had been abandoned.

Pitch-pipes, in other words, may not have been in use before the Warring States period; at any rate, they do not seem to have served to determine the pitch standard in ritual orchestras until then. Throughout most of the Zhou dynasty, such a function was apparently fulfilled by bells,[14] as is suggested, for example, by the fact that the most common type of *lü* name includes the element *zhong* 鍾 "bell": HUANGZHONG 黃鍾 "Yellow Bell," XINZHONG 新鍾 "New Bell," and so forth (see table 16).[15] These names seem to allude to some early connection between the fixation of *lü* and bell-casting.[16] A similar relationship is indicated by the fact that the earliest known occurrence of a *lü* name, in the Nangong Hu–*yongzhong* inscription, is as the name of that bell: "This bell is called WUYI." The idea that bells embodied the pitch standards accords well with their purported musical role of providing the impetus at the beginning of the performance and playing notes that defined a fundamental consonance (see

14. A similar argument is made by Needham and Robinson 1962, 169–71. Even the Ling Lun myth relates that Huang Di ordered the founding of a tuned set of bells immediately after receiving the pitch-pipes (*Lüshi Chunqiu* "Guyue," Sibu Congkan ed., 5:9a).

15. Altogether, eleven known *lü* names belong to this type—more than one-third of those documented in transmitted texts and inscriptions combined (Falkenhausen 1988, 821–24); their etymology will be treated in a separate article.

16. See Chavannes in *Mém. Hist.* 3:628.

Chapter 7). In the words of Kenneth J. DeWoskin, "control over the moment and pitch at which the music began was control over the entire performance."[17] Since the tones of bells and lithophones could not be adjusted (except permanently, by altering the shape of the sonorous substance), it stands to reason that winds and strings should have adjusted their pitches to those of the "suspended music." Thus the tones played by the suspended music, though fewer in number than those of the flutes and stringed instruments, were of special significance: bells and lithopones served as standard-givers for the orchestra.

One may speculate that the concept of pitch standard originated from this basic function of bells. At an early stage of development, the bells embodied the pitch standards: they *were* the *lü*. The standard *yin/lü* nomenclature in the Zeng inscriptions may have come into existence as a result of the realization that the tones emitted by different standard bells were different; the *gong* of the HUANG-ZHONG bell, for instance, was equivalent to *shang* when compared to the *gong* of the WUYI bell. As we have seen in Chapter 8, the diversification of *lü* and the emergence of comprehensive sets of *lü* (first six, then twelve per octave) came about in a gradual, piecemeal way (see table 16).

Chime-bells, then, were of considerable importance in the genesis of classical Chinese musical theory; at an early stage, their theoretical and regulatory function may well have outshone their musical one. This extramusical significance may in part account for the existence of the Zeng inscriptions. Even though chime-bells gradually evolved into melodic instruments, the Zeng inscriptions attest that, in the mid-fifth century B.C., they had not yet lost their early theoretical importance. It was not until the late Warring States period that the conception of tone underwent major changes, with the result that pitch-pipes came into use and eventually replaced bells as standard tonometers. Unlike bell-chimes, pitch-pipes could not double as musical instruments during performances; they served exclusively regulatory purposes. Although technologically far less sophisticated, it must be admitted that pitch-pipes were functionally superior to chime-bells. Not only were they vastly more economical to produce, but, if they were correctly dimensioned, they rendered the intended pitches with potentially greater exactitude than bells with their complex overtone structure. It is no accident, therefore, that the rise of pitch-pipes coincides with the decline of bell manufacture in late Eastern Zhou.

## The Political Role of Pitch Standards

Many classical texts emphasize the relationship of pitch standards (*lü*) with other systems of measurement. In the Han dynasty, the length of the HUANG-

---

17. DeWoskin 1982, 48.

ZHONG pitch-pipe became the basis for all length, weight, and volumetric measurements; the method by which they were correlated is first laid out in the *Han Shu*.[18] Interestingly, probably the earliest textual locus hinting at such an idea, in *Guo Yu* "Zhou yu," occurs in the context of a discussion of bell-making:

> Therefore when the former kings made bells, the size did not transgress the uniform standard, and their weight did not exceed one *dan* 石. The pitch standards, length, volume, and weight measures all took their origin from this.[19]

The suggestion here is that a bell (or set of bells) embodied the "uniform standard" for other systems of measurement. Conceivably, a physical dimension of the bell itself (Hirase points to the *xianjian* as a possible candidate)[20] provided the basis for length, volume, and weight measures. On the other hand, the fundamental unit of measurement as envisaged by the *Guo Yu* passage might equally likely have been a pitch-pipe or a vibrating string that was tuned to the pitch of a bell. The origin of this system is usually ascribed to the sages of high antiquity.[21] I suspect, however, that the idea of grounding all measurements acoustically may have been new in the time of the *Guo Yu*; it may have been triggered by the rise of correlative cosmology in late Warring States times.[22]

The late pre-Qin sources refer to a well-ordered tonal system as a metonym for a well-governed polity, specifying that musical theory was imbued with moral and cosmological significance (see Introduction). In the absence of pertinent textual evidence, it is difficult to trace the roots of conceptions of music. The Zeng inscriptions do not explicitly mention such extramusical connotations. The multiple pitch-standard (*lü*) nomenclatures documented in the Zeng

18. *Han Shu* "Lü Li-zhi" (Zhonghua ed., 966–69); see Dubs 1938–1955 1:276–77.

19. *Guo Yu* "Zhou Yu" (Tiansheng Mingdao ed., j. 3:12b; for a translation of the wider context, see d'Hormon, 311–12; Hart, 387–88). *Dan* 石 is the largest unit of weight measurement (its size in the Zhou dynasty is uncertain). Needham and Robinson (1962, 199) mistakenly take *zhong* 鍾, which here means "bell" (as it usually does in pre-Qin texts), in the meaning of *zhong* 鍾 "a grain vessel"; taking this locus as a point of departure for a fanciful discussion of the origins of the Chinese system of measurements, they go on to follow the absurd theory from *Lie Zi* 列子 that derives the origin of bells from grain scoops (see DeWoskin 1982, 63–64). Needham and Robinson (followed by Hart) also take *jun* 均, which I render literally as "uniform standard," as a "seven-foot tuner," a monochord used to derive pitches according to exact mathematical proportions (see Huang Xiangpeng 1988). However, the existence of such an instrument is attested nowhere in the pre-Qin textual record; the earliest possible locus seems to be in Zhang Heng's 張衡 (A.D. 78–139) "Si-xuan-fu" 思玄賦 (*Wen Xuan*, Sibu Congkan ed., j. 15:21a).

20. Hirase 1988.

21. As in the sequel to the *Guo Yu* passage just quoted. Similar ideas can be seen in *Shu Jing* "Yaodian" (*Shangshu Tongjian*, 1–2) and *Zhou Li: Chun'guan* "Diantong" (*Zhou Li Zhengyi* 46:4a–b).

22. Graham 1986a; Schwartz 1985, 350–82.

inscriptions, however, may in and of themselves possess a far-reaching political significance. For the first time, the "equivalency formulas" embedded in the System B–type inscriptions (see fig. 142) have made us realize that, in Eastern Zhou China, each state had its own system of *lü*, a phenomenon that may indicate deliberate attempts at separation by ritual means, born out of a competitive political situation. In this connection, we may profitably pursue the parallel between pitch standards and other systems of measurements somewhat further.

Later, in Imperial China, the task of establishing a correct measurement system commanded the highest moral and political priority. It was the prerogative, as well as the responsibility, of rulers to establish a unified and internally coherent standard for all aspects of government. The rectification of measurements at the beginning of each dynasty was a supreme assertion of sovereignty. At the latest, this tradition started with the imposition of new measurements at the time of the Qin unification in 221 B.C.[23]

Going back to pre-Imperial times, we find that each of the states in the Zhou realm had its own measurement system. As demonstrated by archaeological and philological research on pre-Qin weights and measures, variations among the different late Zhou measurement systems were quite insignificant.[24] The several systems appear to be variations on a single system of weights and measures; quite possibly, they were all derived from one common ancestral source and then altered.[25] In the course of political reforms in some Eastern Zhou states, such as in Qi in 539 B.C.[26] and Qin in 344 B.C.,[27] weights and measures were redefined, perhaps so as to deliberately assert the independence of the respective states.

The different *lü* systems of the various Eastern Zhou states, documented by the Zeng inscriptions, manifest a curious parallel to this situation. They differ from one another, of course, in the names assigned to the various pitch standards. Each state seems to possess a different series of six (or more) *lü* names, though there is some overlap, both among the different series and between the various regional series and the set of Twelve Pitch Standards (*shi'er lü*) known from the classical texts (see table 16). (There are also cases where the same *lü* name designates different pitches, as in the case of YIZE, whose **do**, in the state

23. *Shi Ji* "Qin Shihuang Benji" (Zhonghua ed., 237–38); Li Xueqin 1985, 240–41.
24. *Zhongguo gudai duliangheng tuji*, 2–3; Yu Weichao and Gao Ming 1973. Similar ideas also apply to the Chinese script; see Karlgren 1936, Barnard 1978.
25. *Shi Ji* "Zhou Benji" (Zhonghua ed., 133) reports a previous unification of measurements under Cheng Wang of Zhou 周成王 (trad. dates: 1115–1078), but one must be cautious in accepting this as historical fact. If it is true that a unified measuring system existed in Western Zhou times, that system probably was not in common use in the outlying parts of the Zhou cultural sphere. It is also likely to have been far less regular or "scientific" than the late pre-Qin and early imperial metrological systems known from the historical texts.
26. *Zuo Zhuan* Zhao 3 (HYI ed., 348).
27. *Shi Ji* "Shang Jun Liezhuan" (Zhonghua ed., 2232).

of Shen, was a whole tone step removed from the **do** of YIZE of the "traditional" Twelve Pitch Standards.) The various *lü* nomenclatures in the Zeng inscriptions also differed as to which pitch standard was regarded as the principal one. We have seen that the principal *lü* in the Zeng *yongzhong*, and thus probably in the state of Zeng, is GUXIAN, with **do** on C. The same pitch standard appears to be the primary one in the nomenclature of Chu, where it is called LÜZHONG 呂鐘, a term that may mean "bell of the principal pitch standard." In the state of Qi, by contrast, LÜYIN 呂音 (essentially synonymous with LÜZHONG) has its **do** on F-sharp, a tritone removed from GUXIAN. In the classical texts, moreover, HUANGZHONG is always given as the principal pitch standard; that *lü* name also appears inscribed on the Zeng bells, where its **do** has been measured to correspond approximately to G-sharp (impressively close to the pitch of the HUANGZHONG pitch-pipe in Han times, which was roughly equivalent to G).[28]

Apart from these two points of distinction, the several musical systems in the Zeng inscriptions are eminently compatible with one another. The method by which tones are defined is the same throughout, and the same set of notes (*yin*) is used regardless of which state's pitch-standard system is used. Moreover, even though the *lü* names differ in detail, they all represent the same type of binomic designations (with additional "muddy" *lü* in the Chu system). They are also fundamentally similar to the system of tone definition in the classical texts, which, as we have discussed in Chapter 8, represents a somewhat later stage of development. On the whole, then, the ritual musics of the various Eastern Zhou states embody the cultural unity of the Zhou realm.

Like the systems of measurement of the Eastern Zhou states, the various pitch-standard systems of that period may, then, all derive from one predecessor and represent variant manifestations of one and the same musical system. It is possible that the differences between them had been deliberately contrived and emphasized for political reasons. Although pitch standards are not mentioned in connection with the pre-Qin and Qin measurement reforms (a fact that may indicate that in actual practice, the *lü* were not linked to other systems of measurement until the Han dynasty), it is probable that the musical system was reformed along with the length, weight, and volume measurements at the time of the Qin unification. The casting of bells from the weapons captured during the preceding military campaigns (see Chapter 1), which, significantly, took place in the same year as the reform of the measurements,[29] may have been connected with the redefinition of pitch standards. After the Han dynasty, when the standard pitch-pipes (*lüguan*) had come to be regarded as the foundation of all other

28. The exact pipe lengths and pitches of the Han dynasty *lü* were calculated by Chen Qiyou (1962a), superseding Liu Fu's (1934) earlier effort.

29. The *Shi Ji* recounts the two events virtually in the same breath (Zhonghua ed., 237–239).

measurement systems, pitch standards were fixed anew by each dynasty down to 1911, altogether more than thirty times.[30]

## International Music

The "equivalency formulas" on the Zeng bells seem to testify to a concern with reconciling the various musical systems current in the mid-fifth century, which had, over the centuries, come to diverge in significant ways from their putative common origin. Because the bells could be used for playing music in a number of different keys, they could serve for performing musics of many countries, and presumably, ensembles of musicians from different parts of the Zhou realm could play the compositions of their own traditions on them. The *Chu Ci*, as quoted in Chapter 1, vividly describes how music and dance from all over the Zhou realm were mixed at Eastern Zhou court banquets. Beyond mere entertainment, international music-making may have had a profound political and even cosmological significance. It denoted connections with distant regions and perhaps suggested a sort of control over the world. By shifting from one **do** to the next, and thus making a transition from the musical system of one state to the next, one could harmonize and integrate various political forces in the Zhou realm. In the course of diplomatic banquets, for example, music played on the Zeng bells might have been capable of musically enacting foreign policy.

We have noted that the nine pitch standards of the so-called Zeng set of *lü* documented in the Zeng inscriptions are by and large homonymous with those in the twelve-part set transmitted in the classical texts (see table 16). Because it is hardly probable that the classical musical nomenclature of China originated in the obscure statelet of Zeng, we may assume that these names, with some variations, were relatively widely used. Possibly, they originated at the Western Zhou court; their usage in Zeng may show the connections of the Zeng ruling house with the Zhou royal family through the Ji clan. The principal pitch standard in the Zeng bell assemblage and in the so-called Zeng set of *lü*, however, is GUXIAN, equivalent to the LÜZHONG of Chu, not HUANGZHONG, the principal *lü* of the traditional texts (and quite probably of Zhou court music), which, though present, does not play a significant role in the inscribed tone definitions.[31] This situation may reflect the Zeng state's political subservi-

30. Yang Yinliu 1980; Qiu Qiongsun 1964; Courant 1922.

31. We cannot be completely certain that HUANGZHONG already was the principal *lü* in the Zhou system. For instance, in the tone distributions of Western Zhou bell-chimes, **do** is invariably located around C, by and large compatible with GUXIAN in the Zeng inscriptions. But the *lü* names in Zhou may not have had the same associated pitches as those in the Zeng inscriptions; in fact, the Nangong

ency to Chu in early Warring States times: although Zeng's *lü* nomenclature harked back to its original Zhou affiliation, its music in the fourth century was keyed to that of its powerful southern neighbor. In this way, the musical systems of Zeng may have expressed a principal theme in Eastern Zhou political history: the struggle for hegemony between the northern and southern alliances.

## The Origins of Zhou Ritual Music

If the various musical nomenclatures of Eastern Zhou all have a common ancestor, where can it be found? It has already been implied that the ritual music of the royal Zhou court in mid- to late Western Zhou times is the most likely candidate. This requires some explanation.

We know very little about ritual music before the Zhou. Although a recent article has advanced the hypothesis that instrumental and vocal music played a relatively insignificant role at the Shang court, where ritual dances were paramount,[32] this is quite uncertain. In any case, Zhou ritual during the early part of Western Zhou still seems to have fairly closely followed Shang models. Archaeological finds attest to what appears to have been a major ritual reform (if not indeed a "cultural revolution"),[33] which may have taken place during the reign of Mu Wang 穆王 (traditional dates 1001–946; actual dates probably ca. one-half century later).[34] The exact nature of that reform remains difficult to gauge, as the historical texts provide frustratingly little information on the mid–Western Zhou period, though assemblages of bronzes in tombs and hoards suggest that the classical Zhou sumptuary system, with its matching sets of *ding* and *gui*, originated at that time,[35] indicating a significant reorganization (or at least standardization) of aristocratic society. Art historians have long noted the significant changes in bronze decoration styles in mid–Western Zhou times: the animal-derived iconography of earlier times was replaced by more abstract patterns,[36] and the shapes of ritual vessels changed considerably.[37] Given the

---

Hu–*yongzhong*, which its inscription identifies as a WUYI bell, emits the tone D, nowhere close to the *gong* of WUYI in the Zeng bells, which is ca. F-sharp.

32. Pratt 1986.

33. Pratt 1986, 38.

34. *Shi Ji* puts the origin of the *Zhou Guan* (a repertory of Zhou officials possibly ancestral to the *Zhou Li*) and the systematization of the Zhou measurement system into the reign of Cheng Wang in the early Western Zhou period ("Zhou Benji," Zhonghua ed., 133); but archaeological evidence indicates major changes in material culture at a somewhat later time.

35. Yu and Gao 1978–79, 86–93, and Guo Baojun 1981, 62–63, point out that, in keeping with the Shang tradition, early Zhou assemblages of ritual vessels comprise mainly drinking vessels. It is possible that, as Yu and Gao claim, a sumptuary system involving *ding* existed before mid–Western Zhou times, but it is far less clear than that of later times.

36. Karlgren 1935, 86–87 and 116–30; Bagley 1980.

37. Hayashi 1984, vol. 2 passim; Rawson 1988.

importance of bronzes in Zhou ritual, such a thorough revamping of the ritual apparatus is likely to bespeak changes in religious ideology.[38]

We have seen, furthermore, that for the history of ritual music, the final century and a half or so of Western Zhou was a period of important innovation. At that time, new musical developments were triggered by the newly imported kinds of chime-bells of southern origin, *yongzhong* and *bo*. Chimes of two-tone bells became common at the Zhou court; they became an integral part of the Zhou sumptuary system. Late Western Zhou eight-part chimes of *yongzhong* for the first time feature octavically regular tone-distribution patterns (ancestral to those of Eastern Zhou chimes), which may be the earliest evidence for the application of *Sanfen Sunyi-fa* principles. These bell-chimes, embodying the tuning standards of Western Zhou music, appear to have given rise to the concept of *lü*; their names evolved into the traditional pitch-standard (*lü*) nomenclature.

From archaeological evidence it appears that this ritual music, centered on the use of bell-chimes, was at first virtually limited to the Zhou metropolitan area in Shaanxi. After 770 B.C., the standards of royal court music were adopted by rulers throughout the Zhou realm. Bells were now manufactured at many different workshops and reflect local stylistic characteristics. Their much wider distribution may in itself indicate that Eastern Zhou local rulers now arrogated the former royal privilege of fixing the principal pitch standard so as to musically legitimize their rule. The Zeng bells with their tone-naming inscriptions mark a final climax in the elaboration of the Western Zhou musical tradition.

### The Demise of Chime-Bell Music in Late Eastern Zhou

As noted in Chapter 1, Eastern Zhou bell inscriptions point to a trend toward secularization (or humanization—either term must be used with a grain of salt) of the ritual forms that had been fixed in the Western Zhou period. Perhaps inevitably, Zhou ritual music became obsolete during the Warring States period, when, partly in response to new intellectual currents surrounding the conception of tones, chime-bells lost their importance in the definition of musical theory. The intellectual and economic resources that had been poured into bell-centered ritual music from the late tenth to the mid-fourth century B.C. were increasingly directed elsewhere.

Underlying these developments was a collapse of the aristocratic order manifested in the traditional Zhou ritual system. The sumptuary regulations could no longer be enforced. The *Li Ji*, for example, apparently referring to conditions in Lu during Confucius's lifetime, inveighs against the use of "palace sus-

---

38. Chang 1976, 174–96, and 1981a.

pension" by *zhuhou* rulers.[39] Occasionally, bells were now found in the possession of persons of lowly status who were not entitled to them.[40] In the texts, several rulers are criticized for "multiplying" (*fan* 繁) or "enlarging" (*da* 大) their sets of bells and drums beyond what was their due.[41] The *Lüshi Chunqiu* enumerates three states that perished for casting new bells (and thereby defining new pitch standards) that exceeded the standard measures,[42] ascribing the same fault to Jie 桀 and Zhou 紂, the wicked last rulers of the Xia and Shang dynasties. And the *Shen Zi* 慎子 (ca. 360–ca. 285 B.C.) reports the following episode:

> When Zhuang Gong of Lu 魯莊公 [r. 693–662] cast a large bell, Cao Han 曹翽 came in for an audience and said: "At present our state is reduced to smallness, yet the bell is so large, how could you not take this into consideration?"[43]

Inevitably, in this period of social transformation, situations were bound to arise in which either the wrong individuals possessed bells or the individuals who were technically entitled to them no longer had the moral worth (and the material means) to keep up anything but an empty pretense to their former status.

As the old elites lost political power, their rituals became ossified. Perhaps, bereft of control over economic resources, they could simply no longer afford the luxury of producing large sets of bells—especially as technological and musical developments called for ever-larger and more sophisticated chimes. For their part, the newly powerful of the Warring States period had different ritual and religious preferences, requiring different musical styles. Inasmuch as they still paid lip service to the ritual traditions of the Zhou, the new elites may have

---

39. *Li Ji* "Jiaotesheng" (*Li Ji Zhushu* 25:9a). According to the *Lunyu* "Baxian" paragraph 1 (HYI ed., 4; Lau, 67), Confucius himself was scandalized at the usurpation of eight rows of dancers by the Ji family, one of the three powerful families in Lu descended from Huan Gong 桓公 (r. 711–694).

40. The *Guan Zi* ("Qi Chen Qi Zhu," Guoxue Jiben Congshu ed., 3:5) has a story about bells made by unruly subjects (*chen* 臣); the *Lüshi Chunqiu* recounts how a member of the ordinary people (*baixing* 百姓) got hold of a bell ("Zizhi," Sibu Congkan ed., 24:5b).

41. The first phrase is from the *Guan Zi* "Sicheng" (Guoxue Jiben Congshu ed., 2:42), the second from the *Lüshi Chunqiu* "Tingyan" (Sibu Congkan ed., 13:7b). This concern is also evident in the first *Guo Yu* discourse on the casting of a WUYI bell by Jing Wang of Zhou ("Zhou Yu," Tiansheng Mingdao ed., 3:11a–15a). The *Xun Zi* ("Zhengming," HYI ed., 84) warns that enlarging the bells does not increase the music (or, in a play on the identity of the words *yue* 樂 "music" and *le* 樂 "joy," the joy to be obtained from music).

42. *Lüshi Chunqiu* "Chiyue" (Sibu Congkan ed., 5a–6b). The states mentioned and the names of their fatal *lü* are Song (QIANZHONG 千鐘 "Thousand Bells"), Qi (DALÜ 大呂, which may be identical to the LÜYIN mentioned in the Zeng inscriptions; see table 18), and Chu (WUYIN 巫音 "Witches' Sound"). Here the three *lü* names undoubtedly represent the evils of excessive quantity, excess in size, and sexual depravity.

43. *Shen Zi*, Fragment no. 95a (Thompson, 285).

emulated the paraphernalia formerly reserved for the aristocracy, though they may also have been reluctant to commit the same amount of resources to such endeavors.

Chimes made from the mid–Warring States period onward materially manifest this slackening of the cultural commitment to suspended music. We have seen in Chapter 5 how multiple chimes of *yongzhong* and other bells were replaced by single chimes of smaller and technologically less sophisticated *niuzhong*, and we have seen how, concomitantly, the two-tone phenomenon was abandoned. When bells were used at all in funerary contexts, they were increasingly replaced by lower-value *mingqi*.

The sentiment that bells and the ritual display associated with them were an unnecessary luxury is pervasive in the writings of the late pre-Qin philosophers and their contemporaries. The Mohists, from the fifth century B.C. onward, proposed to abolish music altogether because it seemed to them to serve no useful purpose.[44] Members of other schools, while refraining from so radical a view, agreed that the essential value of music was not in bell music.[45] It was stressed that a ruler should indulge in such music only when the state is well-ordered and peaceful. Mencius (ca. 372–289 B.C.), for example, warned the king of Qi that indulging in sumptuous display could aggravate his estrangement from the common people.[46] Rulers who listened to bell music rather than attending to the affairs of government were ridiculed,[47] while those who removed their bells and (temporarily, at least) forsook sensual gratification in the single-minded pursuit of strengthening the state were praised as models.[48] In some texts, listening to bell music comes close to being synonymous with a dissolute lifestyle.[49] Xun Zi (ca. 313–238 B.C.) is alone among Warring States thinkers to insist that listening to bell music was not merely pleasurable but part of a ruler's ritual duties[50] (an opinion later elaborated in the *Li Ji*), through the

---

44. *Mo Zi* "Feiyue" (HYI ed., 54–55).

45. *Lunyu* "Yanghuo" (HYI ed., 36); *Zuo Zhuan* Zhao 21 (HYI ed., 404); *Guo Yu* "Zhou Yu" (Tiansheng Mingdao ed., 3:11a–18a passim); *Zhuang Zi* "Tiandao" (HYI ed., 34); *Li Ji* "Zhong Ni yanju" (*Li Ji Zhushu* 50:13a–13b). In a related vein, *Han Fei Zi* "Waichushui *zuo-shang*" (Zhonghua index ed., 797) opines that bell inscriptions are of ephemeral use in the assertion of real political power.

46. *Meng Zi* "Liang Hui Wang-*xia*" (HYI ed., 5; Lau, 60–61).

47. *Mo Zi* loc. cit.; *Zuo Zhuan* Ai 7 (HYI ed. 477); *Han Fei Zi* "Waichushui *zuo-shang*" (Zhonghua index ed., 797); *Shi Ji* "Chu Shijia" (Zhonghua ed., 1700).

48. *Guan Zi* "Baxing" (Guoxue Jiben Congshu ed., 2:2–4) and "Jinzang" (ibid. 3:6); *Lüshi Chunqiu* "Shunmin" (Sibu Congkan ed., 9:4b).

49. *Zuo Zhuan* Xiang 30 (HYI ed., 331) and Zhao 20 (ibid., 402); *Guan Zi* "Sicheng" (Guoxue Jiben Congshu ed., 2:42) and "Qing Zhongding" (ibid., 3:111); *Zhuang Zi* "Dao Zhi" (HYI ed., 84); *Han Fei Zi* "Shuiyi" (Zhonghua index ed., 844).

50. Xun Zi did, however, state that spreading the true doctrine was even "more enjoyable than the music of bells and drums and of zithers and lutes" (*Xun Zi* "Feixiang," HYI ed., 14; Knoblock, 208).

punctilious fulfillment of which he could bring peace and order to his realm.[51] But Xun Zi's eminent pupil Han Fei Zi cynically noted that political skill was all that really mattered. As long as a ruler was attentive to his ministers' advice, he could indulge mindlessly in chariotry and "the sounds of bells and chimestones" and still flourish; an incompetent ruler, even one so sorely afflicted by the plight of his state that he explicitly renounced the pleasures of suspended music, was doomed to perish no matter what, as was the fate of Prince Kuai of Yan 燕君子噲 (r. 320–314 B.C.).[52]

It is curious that in the musical shake-up of the Warring States period, the suspended music fared differently from other kinds of musical instruments. Winds and strings continued to loom large in emerging forms of popular music, but bells and chimestones gradually ceased to be made. Ironically, their demise was due precisely to the exalted position they had occupied during much of the Zhou dynasty, through which they had become too exclusively identified with the old aristocracy and had become too valuable to be readily incorporated into yet unestablished new types of musical ensembles. Players of the late Zhou "popular music" may not have obtained ready access to bells until the new musical styles had already taken shape.

There may have been another, aesthetic reason why chime-bells were ultimately discarded from the orchestras. With the ongoing sophistication and intellectualization of musical theory during the later part of the Warring States period, listeners' requirements as to the accuracy of pitch and intonation may have become more rigorous. As we have observed in Chapter 7, the Warring States period casters were able to significantly improve the tuning accuracy of the bell-chimes, but before long they reached the limits of what was possible when operating with a linear scaling formula (see Chapter 2). As a consequence, bells, despite their prestige, may have been deemed inadequate for their traditional coordinating and standard-giving function within the orchestra, a function now taken over by pitch-pipes.

By the end of the Bronze Age, chime-bells had, in short, lost their musical, ideological, and social significance. Even though specimens were kept at the imperial courts of the Han and later dynasties and bell *mingqi* continued to accompany the high-ranking dead for several centuries, they had become part of the dead weight of the past. For two millennia, the full scope of their erstwhile significance was but dimly perceived; it remained to be rediscovered by late-twentieth-century scholars.

---

51. *Xun Zi* "Fuguo" (HYI ed., 32, 34); "Lilun" (ibid., 70–75); "Yuelun" (ibid., 77–78); "Zhengming"( ibid., 86).
52. *Han Fei Zi* "Shuiyi" (Zhonghua index ed., 844).

*Envoi*

In the preceding chapters we have been able to make some general suggestions about the music involving bell-chimes. Actual compositions, however, have disappeared without a trace. Perhaps, given the fundamental separation of musical practice from theory, the radical changes in the theoretical conceptualization of tones that occurred after the time of the Zeng bells may not have immediately been reflected in starkly different musical styles. Some scholars have suggested that echoes of Zhou music might still be picked up in present-day musical traditions in East Asia, such as Japanese court music (*gagaku* 雅樂),[53] the music of Daoist ritual, Chaozhou ballads, and more generally in East, South, and Southeast Asian folk music,[54] all of which may furnish analogies useful for understanding Zhou ritual music. In connection with the Zeng bells, an especially fruitful ethnomusicological comparison may lie in the gamelan music of Java and Bali, in which chimed idiophones play a major role. Here lies a challenge for future research.

The prominent place of music in ancient Chinese thought is amply attested to by archaeological finds, inscriptions, and classical texts. Our archaeological investigation of bells has emphasized the social and cultural setting of ancient Chinese music, leading to an appreciation of music as a generalized regulative system and means of political coordination. The historical, technological, typological, and musicological analyses presented in this book have invariably shown bells at the focus of power relations. As instruments translating human relationships into ritual, bell-chimes and other paraphernalia of ritual music were emblematic of the aristocratic culture of the Chinese Bronze Age. As testimonies of their time, they manifest a phenomenon that has remained characteristic of Chinese culture:[55] the primacy of politics.

53. Harich-Schneider 1955.
54. Picken 1977, 87–88.
55. See K. C. Chang 1983.

# Bibliographical List of Archaeological Sites[1]

Baijiacun, Fufeng ShX (1981): 1 *yongzhong*★ [WUSI HU].
*Renwen Zazhi* 1983 (2): 118–21 (reduced rubbings on p. 118); 2 photos on back cover.[2]

Baijiacun, Liuyang HuN (1975): 1 *nao*.
*Hunan Wenwu* 1 (1986): 56–57; blurred photo inside front cover; blurred rubbing, p. 56, fig. 1.

Baizhadi, Chao Xian AH (1945?): 11 *niuzhong*.
*Wenwu Cankao Ziliao* 1956 (8): 73.

Bajiaolou, Suizhou HuB (1979): 2 *niuzhong*.
*Wenwu* 1980 (1): 34–41; rubbing, p. 39, fig. 12.

Banqiao, Changsha HuN (1979): 1 *nao*.
*Wenwu Ziliao Congkan* 5 (1981): 103–105; Gao Zhixi 1984b, 130; 1986a, 288; photo, fig. 61.2.

Baozigou, Fufeng ShX (1979): 1 *yongzhong*★ [NANGONG HU].
*Kaogu yu Wenwu* 1980 (4): 6–22, 53; photo, pl. 2.2; *Shaanxi chutu Shang Zhou qingtongqi* 3:145–47, pl. 140 (photo, rubbings). Tone measurements: Jiang Dingsui 1984, 90.

Beidongshan, Xuzhou JS (1986): 3 *niuzhong (mingqi)*.
*Wenwu* 1988 (2): 2–18, 68, esp. p. 16; photo, p. 14, fig. 32.
    Other musical instruments found: 14 chimestones.

---

1. An asterisk indicates the presence of an inscription; the donor's name or another conventional designation is given in brackets. County seats and cities are indicated in maps 1 and 2.
2. Instead of two photos showing the front and back faces of the bell, respectively, the same photo has been reproduced twice.

Beifengtan, Ningxiang HuN (1977): 2 *nao*.

No. 2 only, *Wenwu* 1983 (10): 72–74; *Wenwu* 1978 (6): 42; *The great Bronze Age of China*, 123–25;[3] both pieces: Gao Zhixi 1984b, 129, English translation, 277–79; photos, fig. 58.1,3.

Beiliu GX (location unclear) (year unknown): 1 *yongzhong*.

*Kaogu* 1984 (9): 798–806 (esp. 802–804); photo, p. 804, fig. 8 center.

Beiqiao, Fufeng ShX (1972): 2 *yongzhong*.

*Wenwu* 1974 (11): 85–89; *Shaanxi chutu Shang Zhou qingtongqi* 3:102, photos, pl. 98 (no. 1), pl. 97 (no. 2). Tone measurements: Jiang Dingsui 1984, 88/89.

Beiqishan, Fufeng ShX, hoard no. 1 (1940s): 2 *yongzhong*.

*Wenwu* 1965 (7): 17–22, photos, p. 18, figs. 1 and 2.

Beishanding, Dantu JS (1983): 5 *bo*★, 7 *niuzhong*★ [SHENLIU], 3 *chunyu* (chimed set?), 1 bell mallet.

*Wenwu* 1989 (4): 51–56. *Bo*, photos, pl. 3 and p. 54, fig. 3. *Niuzhong*, rubbings, p. 52, fig. 1, and p. 53, fig. 2. *Dongnan Wenhua* 1988 (3/4): 13–50. *Bo*, photos: pl. 6, 7.2, 3; drawing, p. 24, fig. 12.1; rubbing, p. 25. *Niuzhong*, photo, pl. 5.4, 7.4; drawing, p. 24, fig. 12.2; rubbing, p. 30. *Chunyu*, photo, pl. 7.6; drawing, p. 32, fig. 13.1; rubbings, p. 31. Tone measurements: p. 27.

Other instruments found: 12 chimestones.

Beitang, Hengyang HuN (1978): 1.*nao*.

*Wenwu* 1980 (11): 95–96; photo, pl. 8.4.

Caoloucun, Changxing ZJ (1959): 1 *nao*.

*Wenwu* 1960 (7): 48–49; *Arts of China* 1:43, pl. 59 (photo); Gao Zhixi 1984b, 130, English translation, 287; photo, fig. 63.4.

Cenxi GX (location unclear) (1987): 1 *yongzhong*.

*Guangxi Wenwu* 1987 (2) [not seen]; mentioned in Jiang Tingyu 1989, 30.

Chang'anxiang, Hengyang HuN (1977): 1 *yongzhong*.

*Wenwu* 1985 (6): 83; photo, fig. 1; partial rubbings, figs. 3 and 4.

Changhe, Wanzai JX (1965): 1 *nao*.

*Jiangxi Lishi Wenwu* 1984 (1): 3 (photo).

Changlelu, Luoyang HN (year unknown): 4 *bo*, 9 *niuzhong*.

Unpublished, exhibited by the Institute of Archaeology, Chinese Academy of Social Sciences, at the Palace Museum, Beijing, in 1990.

Changsha HuN, tomb no. 401 (1951–52): 7 *niuzhong* (lead *mingqi*).

*Changsha fajue baogao*, 119, photo, pl. 73.2.

Changtaiguan, Xinyang HN, tomb no. 1 (1957): 13 *niuzhong* (1★: JINGLI).

---

3. The catalog text confuses the Beifengtan bells with those from Shiguzhaishan (q. v.).

*Wenwu Cankao Ziliao* 1957 (9): 21–22; *Wenwu* 1959, 15–23; photos, p. 4, 12, 13; *Xin Zhongguo de kaogu shouhuo*, pl. 70; *Chūka Jinmin Kyōwakoku shutsudo bunbutsu-ten* (1977–78), cat. no. 28–40; *Xinyang Chu-mu*, 21–29 (drawings, rubbings); photos, pls. 6–12. Tone measurements: Yang Yinliu 1959; Chen and Zheng 1980, 1985.

> Other musical instruments found: 3 *se*, 3 drums of different sizes; *yu* and *sheng* mentioned in tomb inventory.

Changtaiguan, Xinyang HN, tomb no. 2 (1958): 13 *niuzhong* (wooden *mingqi*).
*Kaogu Tongxun* 1958 (11): 79–80. *Xinyang Chu-mu*: 86–95; photos, pls. 77–88; drawing, p. 88, fig. 59.

> Other musical instruments found: 5 *se*, 2 drums of different sizes, 2 sets *qing* (9/9; *mingqi*).

Changxing Middle School, Changxing ZJ (1969): 1 *nao*.
*Wenwu* 1973 (1): 62; Gao Zhixi 1984b, 130, English translation, 287, photo, fig. 63.4.

Chengcun, Linyi SX, tomb no. 1 (1987): 9 *niuzhong*.
*Zhongguo kaoguxue nianjian 1988*, 132–33; no illustrations published.
> Other instruments found: 10 chimestones.

Chengcun, Linyi SX, tomb no. 2 (1987): 9 *niuzhong*.
*Zhongguo kaoguxue nianjian 1988*, 132–33; no illustrations published.
> Other instruments found: 10 chimestones.

Chengqiang Xiufu Gongdi (City Wall Repair Site), Shou Xian AH (1950s?): 17 *niuzhong*.
> Mentioned in Ma Chengyuan 1981, 142, table 1; no illustrations published.

Chengqiao, Luhe JS, tomb no. 1 (1964): 9 *niuzhong*★ [GONGWU ZANGSUN].
*Kaogu* 1965 (3): 105–15, photo, pls. 1.3, 6, 11; rubbings, pp. 109–11, figs. 8–10.

Chengqiao, Luhe JS, tomb no. 2 (1973): 5 *bo*, 7 *niuzhong*★ [ZHESHANG].
*Kaogu* 1974 (2): 116–20. *Bo*, photos, pls. 4.2 and 3; rubbing, p. 117, fig. 3.2. *Niuzhong*, photos, pls. 4.1 and 4; rubbing, p. 117, fig. 3.1.

Chengtan, Liuyang HuN (1979): 1 *yongzhong*.
Gao Zhixi 1984a, 29; photo, pl. 7.2.

Chenjiawan, Ningxiang HuN (1974): 1 *nao*.
Gao Zhixi 1984b, 129, pl. 6.3, English translation, 278, photo, fig. 58.4.

Chongxian, Yuhang ZJ, tomb no. 1 (1984): 4 *yongzhong* (pottery *mingqi*).
*Dongnan Wenhua* 1989 (6): 121–25; photo, back cover, 1; drawings, p. 123, figs. 3.1 and 2.

Dabeimiao, Binyang GX (year unknown): 1 *yongzhong*.
*Kaogu* 1984 (9): 798–806 (esp. 802–804); photo, p. 804, fig. 8 left.

Dabona, Xiangyun YN (1964): 1 beehive-shaped bell.
*Kaogu* 1964 (12): 607–14; drawing of bell, p. 612, fig. 9.
Other musical instruments found: 1 bronze *sheng*, 1 bronze drum.

Dadian, Junan SD, tomb no. 1 (1974): 1 *bo*, 9 *niuzhong*.
*Kaogu Xuebao* 1978 (3): 317–36. *Bo*, photo, pl. 4.7; rubbing, p. 324, pl. 8.
*Niuzhong*, photo, pl. 4.8; rubbings, pls. 324–25, figs. 8–9.

Dadian, Junan SD, tomb no. 2 (1975): 9 *niuzhong*★ [JU SHU ZHONGZI PING].
*Kaogu Xuebao* 1978 (3): 317–36, photo, pl. 8.1; rubbings, pp. 331–34, figs. 18–22; *Dai Kōga bunmei-no nagare (Santō-shō bunbutsuten)*, 98–99 (color photos).
Other musical instruments found: 12 *qing*.

Dadunzi, Feixi AH (1972): 1 *ling*.
*Wenwu* 1978 (8): 1–11, esp. 2–3; photo, p. 2; *Anhui Sheng Kaoguxuehui Huikan* 1 (1979): 38–43.

Dadunzi, Pi Xian JS, tomb no. 253 (1966): 1 pottery bell.
*Kaoguxue Jikan* 1 (1981): 27–81; drawing, p. 41, fig. 16.14.

Dadunzi, Pi Xian JS, tomb no. 335 (1966): 1 pottery bell.
*Kaoguxue Jikan* 1 (1981): 27–81; drawing, p. 41, fig. 16.4.

Daguo, Huimin SD (1973): 1? *nao*.
*Kaogu* 1974 (3): 208 (blurred photo).

Dahecun, Zhengzhou HN (1972–1975): 2 pottery bells.
*Kaogu Xuebao* 1979 (3): 332; drawing, p. 330.

Daifuguan, Linzi SD (year unknown): 8 *yongzhong*.
Seen in 1986; unpublished.
Other musical instruments found: 8 *qing*.

Dalingjiao, Pubei GX (1974): 4 *yangjiao*–bells.
*Wenwu* 1984 (5): 66–69.

Dalisanwucun, Boluo GD (1984): 7 *yongzhong*.
*Kaogu yu Wenwu* 1987 (6): 15–16, 24; photos, inside front cover and p. 15, fig. 1; drawings, p. 16, fig. 2; *Guangdong wenwu pucha chengguo tulu*, items 51–57 (photos, drawings).

Dasikongcun, Anyang HN, tomb no. 1 (1983): 3 *nao*★ [GU].
*Kaogu* 1988 (10): 865–74; photos, pl. 1 (inside front cover), p. 15, fig. 1; drawings, p. 16, fig. 2.

Dasikongcun, Anyang HN, tomb no. 51 (1957): 3 *nao*★ (inscription unpublished).
*Kaogu Tongxun* 1958 (10): 51–62, esp. 56; photo, pl. 3.15; Guo Baojun 1981, pl. 28.5 (better photo).

Dasikongcun, Anyang HN, tomb no. 312 (1953): 3 *nao*★ [YA ?–MU PENG].
   *Kaogu Xuebao* 9 (1955): 49–50; photo, pl. 10; Guo Baojun 1981, pls. 28.1–4 (photo).

Datang, Xincheng GX (1976): 1 *yongzhong*.
   *Wenwu* 1978 (10): 93–96; photo, p. 95, fig. 11; *Guangxi chutu wenwu*, pl. 37.

Daxin, Fengxiang SX (pre-1949): 3 *niuzhong*.
   Zhao Congcang 1988, 83–85, photos, rubbings, and drawings, p. 84.
   Other musical instruments found: 2 "flat-handled *zhong*."

Dazhongyingcun, Ci Xian HB (1978): 12 *bianzhong* (ceramic *mingqi*).
   *Wenwu* 1984 (4): 1–9; drawings, p. 5, figs. 6.1,2.
   Other *mingqi* musical instruments found: 9 *qing*.

Dengjiatiancun, Pingxiang JX (1984): 1 *nao*.
   *Jiangxi Lishi Wenwu* 1985 (2): 18 (blurred photo).

Dingjiagou, Yao Xian ShX, hoard no. 1 (1984): 4 *yongzhong* (2 sets).
   *Kaogu yu Wenwu* 1986 (4): 4–5; photo, p. 5, fig. 4 (blurred; 2 pieces only).

Dongjucun, Fufeng ShX (1978): 1 *yongzhong*★ (inscription of enigmatic characters).
   *Kaogu yu Wenwu* 1980 (4): 19; photo, pl. 2.1; rubbing, p. 19, fig. 17. Tone measurements: Jiang Dingsui 1984, 88 (#78.909).

Dujiacun, Xiaoshan ZJ (1981): 1 *yongzhong*.
   *Wenwu* 1985 (4): 90–91; photo, p. 90, fig. 1; rubbing, ibid., fig. 2.

Erlitou, Yanshi HN (context unclear) (1960s): 3 *ling* (1 bronze, 2 pottery).
   *Kaogu* 1965 (5): 215–24; photos, pl. 5.20 (bronze *ling*); pl. 5.4 (pottery *ling*).

Erlitou, Yanshi HN, Area V tomb no. 4 (1981): 1 *ling*.
   *Kaogu* 1984 (1): 37–40; photo, color plate 4.1.

Erlitou, Yanshi HN, Area IX tomb no. 4 (1981): 1 *ling*.
   *Kaogu* 1985 (12): 1085–94; drawing, p. 1091, fig. 7.1.

Erlitou, Yanshi HN, Area VI tomb no. 11 (1982): 1 *ling*.
   *Kaogu* 1986 (4): 318–23; photo, pl. 8.5; drawing, p. 321, fig. 6 lower half.

Ezhuangqu Huayuan, Linyi SD (1966): 9 *yongzhong*.
   *Wenwu* 1972 (5): 12; photo, pl. 8.5 (blurred).

Feijiahe, Yueyang HuN (1971): 1 *nao*.
   *Wenwu Ziliao Congkan* 5 (1981): 103–105; Gao Zhixi 1984b, 129, English translation, 279; photo, fig. 61.1.

Fenghuangling, Linyi SD (1984): 9 *bo*, 9 *niuzhong*.
   *Linyi Fenghuangling Dong-Zhou-mu. Niuzhong*: photo, pl. 8.2, pl. 12; drawing, p. 15, fig. 10; rubbing, p. 16, fig. 11. *Bo*: photo, pl. 13; drawing, p. 19, fig. 14; rubbings, pp. 17–18, figs. 12–13.
   Other kinds of bells found: 1 *duo*.

Fenshuiling, Changzhi SX, tomb no. 14 (1953–54): 2 *yongzhong*, 8 *niuzhong*.
*Kaogu Xuebao* 1957 (1): 111–15. *Yongzhong, Wusheng chutu wenwu zhanlan tulu*, 65 (photo). *Niuzhong*, photo, *Kaogu Xuebao* 1957 (1), pl. 1.2; rubbings, p. 113, fig. 14; *Wusheng chutu wenwu zhanlan tulu*, 65 (photo). Tone measurements (A-tones of seven pieces only): Li Chunyi 1973, 16.

Other music-related finds: 2 sets *qing* (11/11); clay figurines of performers.

Fenshuiling, Changzhi SX, tomb no. 25 (1959–61): 4 *bo*, 5 *yongzhong*, 9 *niuzhong*.
*Kaogu* 1964 (3): 111–37. *Yongzhong*, line drawing, p. 128, fig. 17.1; partial rubbing, p. 127, fig. 16.4. *Bo*, photo, pl. 4.3; rubbing, p. 127, figs. 16.1 and 2. *Niuzhong*, photo, pl. 4.2; drawing, p. 128, fig. 17.2; rubbing, p. 127, fig. 16.5.

Other musical instruments found: 10 *qing*.

Fenshuiling, Changzhi SX, tomb no. 126 (year unknown): 1 set *niuzhong* (number unreported).
Mentioned in Ma Chengyuan 1981, 142, table 1; *Wenwu* 1972 (4): 38 (no illustrations published).

Fenshuiling, Changzhi SX, tomb no. 269 (1972): 9 *yongzhong*, 9 *niuzhong*.
*Kaogu Xuebao* 1974 (2): 63–85. *Yongzhong*, photos, pls. 3.4 and 5; rubbing, pl. 71, fig. 10.1 (also *Shanxi chutu wenwu*, cat. no. 106). *Niuzhong*, rubbing, p. 71, fig. 10 right.

Other musical instruments found: 10 *qing*.

Fenshuiling, Changzhi SX, tomb no. 270 (1972): 8 *yongzhong*, 9 *niuzhong*.
*Kaogu Xuebao* 1974 (2): 63–85. *Niuzhong*, photo, pls. 9.1 and 2 (*yongzhong* not depicted).

Other musical instruments found: 11 *qing*.

Futulongcun, Mouding YN (1978): 6 beehive-shaped bells.
*Wenwu* 1982 (5): 84 (photo, drawing).

Other musical instruments found: 1 bronze drum.

Gao'an, Fanchang AH (1980s): 1 *yongzhong* (?), 1 *niuzhong* (?).
*Xuanzhou Wenwu* 6 (1988): 24–25 (no illustrations published).

Gaochong, Wangcheng HuN (1977): 1 *nao*.
Gao Zhixi 1984b, 129, English translation, 280; photo, fig. 60.3.

Gaotun, Xiangtan HuN (1976): 1 *yongzhong*.
*Hunan Kaogu Jikan* 1 (1981): 21–24; photo, pl. 9.6; rubbings, p. 24, figs. 7 and 8.

Goutouba, Xiangxiang HuN (1964): 1 *nao*.
*Wenwu* 1977 (2): 2; Gao Zhixi 1984b, 129, English translation, 279–80; photo, fig. 60.4.

Goutoushan, Shaoxing ZJ (1977): 2 *goudiao*★ [PEI'ER].
*Kaogu* 1983 (4): 371–72 (photos, drawings, rubbings); *Zhejiang Wenwu*, pl. 59 (photo).

Guangde AH (location unclear) (1986): 3 sets *goudiao* (3/4/2).
*Xuanzhou Wenwu* 5 (1987): 13 (no illustrations published).

Guanwudiaozhuang, Fufeng (?) ShX (1982): 5 *yongzhong*.
Luo Xizhang 1988, 42, fig. 1.6 (photo of hoard; details so far unpublished).

Guanyang Gucheng, Haiyang SD (1950s): 1 *yongzhong*, 4 *niuzhong*.
*Shandong wenwu xuanji*, 47–48 (photos); Hayashi 1984 2:387, *shō* 63 (*niuzhong*).

Guishuwo, Xingning GD (1984): 6 *yongzhong*.
*Guangdong wenwu pucha chengguo tulu*, items 72–77 (photos, drawings).

Guozhen, Baoji ShX (1940s): 1 *yongzhong*.
*Qingtongqi tushi*, pl. 14 (photo, rubbing); *Shaanxi chutu Shang Zhou qingtongqi*, vol. 4, pl. 103 (photo, rubbing). Tone measurements: Jiang Dingsui 1984, 88.

Haosihe, Yongshou ShX (1979): 4 *yongzhong*★ [NI].
*Kaogu yu Wenwu* 1981 (1): 9–11; *Shaanxi chutu Shang Zhou qingtongqi* 4:161–67; photos, entries 185–88. Tone measurements: Jiang Dingsui 1984, 90.

Hengba, Wujiang JS (1960): 1 bell fragment★ [YUE WANG].
*Kaogu* 1961 (7): 390, 394; rubbing, p. 390, fig. 1.1.

Hengshan, Liuzhou GX (1985): 1 *yongzhong*.
*Liuzhou Ribao*, November 23, 1985, p. 2 (not seen); mentioned in Jiang Ting-yu 1989, 30.

Heyatou, Linzi SD (1965): *zhong* (type and number unknown).
*Wenwu* 1972 (5): 8 (no illustrations published).

Hongjiaqiao, Xiangtan HuN (1965): 2 *yongzhong*.
*Wenwu* 1966 (4): 3 (photo, rubbings); *Chūgoku Konan-shō shutsudo bunbutsu*, cat. no. 10 (photo of no. 1 only).

Hongxing (Red Star) Commune, Lantian ShX (1974): 1 *yongzhong*★ [YING HOU].
*Wenwu* 1975 (10): 68–69; photo, p. 68, fig. 1; rubbing, p. 69, fig. 2. Tone measurements: Jiang Dingsui 1984, 88.

Houchuan, Sanmenxia HN, tomb no. 2040 (1957–58): 9 *bo*, 2 sets *niuzhong* (10/10).
*Kaogu Tongxun* 1957 (11): 74–77 (no illustrations); *Bo*, photos in Guo Baojun 1981, pl. 89.3; Wu Zhao 1983, 15.[4]

Houchuan, Sanmenxia HN, tomb no. 2041 (1957–58): 9 *niuzhong*.
Mentioned in Wang Shimin 1988, 6; no illustrations published.

---

4. Wu identifies the site of excavation as Shangcunling.

Other musical instruments found: 10 *qing*; tone measurements: Huang Xiangpeng 1978–80, pt. 2, 147.

Hougudui, Gushi HN (1978): 8 *bo*★, 9 *niuzhong*★ [FAN ZI].
  *Wenwu* 1981 (1) : 1–8. *Bo*, photos, *Wenwu* 1981 (1): pls. 3.2 and 4.3; *Quanguo chutu wenwu zhenpinxuan*, cat. nos. 197–204. *Niuzhong*, photo, *Wenwu* 1981 (1), pl. 4.2; line drawing, *Zhongyuan Wenwu* 1984 (1): 76, fig. 3.
  Other musical instruments found: 6 *se*, 2 *gu*.

Huahu, Huilai GD (1979): 1 *yongzhong*.
  *Guangdong chutu xian-Qin wenwu*, 69, 59, fig. 2 (traditional line drawing).
  *Shantou Wenwu* 6 (1979): 30 (blurred photo).

Huaibaoshicun, Zigui HB (1985): 3 *yongzhong* (different types).
  *Jianghan Kaogu* 1988 (4): 133–34 (blurred photos and rubbings, p. 133).

Huangdui, Fufeng ShX, tombs no. 3 and 4 (1980): 1 *yongzhong* each.
  *Wenwu* 1986 (8): 56–68; line drawing, p. 61, fig. 11.5.

Huanghu, Fanchang AH (year unknown): 2 *goudiao*-like bells (*mingqi*).
  *Xuanzhou Wenwu* 1 (1983): 47–48 (illustration missing).

Huangjiashan, Haiyan ZJ (1983): 13 *yongzhong*, 3 *niuzhong*, 12 *goudiao* (all ceramic *mingqi*).
  *Wenwu* 1985 (8): 66–72; photos, pls. 5.1 and 2.2; p. 69, figs. 8, 9, 11, and p. 71, figs. 14–17; drawings, p. 68, figs. 2–7, and p. 72, figs. 18.1 and 2.
  Additional *mingqi* bells and other musical instruments found: 2 *chunyu*, 11 globular bells(?), 4 *qing*, and many fragments.

Huangjing, Liuyang HuN (year unknown): 1 *bo*.
  Gao Zhixi 1984a, 30; photo, p. 31.4; Gao Zhixi 1984c, 68; photo, fig. 1 (unrestored); *Chūgoku Konan-shō shutsudo bunbutsu*, cat. no. 13 (restored).

Huangmasai, Xiangxiang HuN (1975): 1 *nao*.
  Gao Zhixi 1984a, 29; Gao Zhixi 1984b, 130, English translation, 287; photo, fig. 62.2.

Huangzhu, Zhuzhou HuN (1981): 1 *nao*.
  Gao Zhixi 1984a, 29; photo, pl. 7.3.

Huashan, Zhongxiang HuB (1958): 5 *yongzhong*.
  *Wenwu Cankao Ziliao* 1958 (6): 76 (blurred photo).

Huilongcun, Wugong ShX (1974): 1 *yongzhong*.
  Mentioned in *Shaanxi chutu Shang Zhou qingtongqi* 4:19.

Hui Xian HN (location unclear) (pre-1949?): 3 *nao*.
  Wu Zhao 1983, 6 (photo).

Jiancun, Xiangyun YN (1977): 3 beehive-shaped bells.
  *Wenwu* 1983 (5): 33–41; drawings, p. 39, fig. 23.

Jiangshan, ZJ (location unclear) (1969): 7 bells (*yongzhong* ?).
  *Wenwu* 1972 (3): 75 (no illustrations published).

Jiashan, Xinyu JX (1981): 1 *nao*.
  *Wenwu* 1982 (9): 88–89 (very blurred photo).

Jiazhuang, Anyang HN, tomb no. 269 (1970s): 3 *nao*★ [ZHONG].
  *Zhongyuan Wenwu* 1986 (3): 9–13 (no photos published).

Jiefanglu, Luoyang HN (1982): 9 bells (type unspecified).
  Yang Yubin 1985, 189.
    Other musical instruments found: 23 *qing*.

Jincun, Luoyang HN, tomb no. 7 (1928): 14 *niuzhong*★ [BIAO].
  White 1934, pl. 167–69; Sen'oku Hakkokan, *Gakki*, cat. no. 16; more detailed photos and drawings in Sahara 1984 and Okamura 1986b. Tone measurements: Hamada 1924 supplement volume; Takahashi 1984, 1986.

Jinhua ZJ (location unclear) (1976): 1 *nao*.
  Mentioned in *Dongnan Wenhua* 1989 (6): 107 (no illustration published).

Jinpingshan, Lianyungang JS (1957): 9 *niuzhong*.
  *Kaogu* 1960 (7): 1–11, esp. 4; indistinct photo, pl. 1.5; *Jiangsu chutu wenwu*, pl. 88 (photo).

Jinshengcun, Taiyuan SX, tomb no. 251 (1988): 2 sets *bo* (5/14).
  *Wenwu* 1989 (9): 59–86; photos, pls. 7.1–5, p. 77, fig. 29; drawing, p. 76, fig. 26; rubbings, p. 77, fig. 27.
    Other musical instruments found: 14 *qing*.

Jishan, Linzi SD (1983): 4 *yongzhong*, 9 *niuzhong* (gilt bronze *mingqi*).
  *Dai Kōga bunmei-no nagare*, 124–25 (*niuzhong* only).
    Other *mingqi* musical instruments found: *qing* (number unclear).

Jishiliang, Suizhou HuB (1979): 4 *niuzhong*, 1 small *niuzhong*.
  *Wenwu* 1980 (1): 34–41; photo, p. 40, figs. 16 and 17; rubbing, p. 39, fig. 11.

Jishui JX (location unclear) (1970s): 3 *yongzhong*.
  *Jiangxi Lishi Wenwu* 3 (1980): 50 (blurred photo).

Jiuli, Linli HuN, tomb no. 1 (1980): bell-rack.
  *Chu wenhua kaogu dashiji*, 124 (no illustration published).
    Other music-related finds: lithophone-rack, drum stand.

Jiuliandun, Xindu SC (1980): 5 pseudo-*yongzhong*.
  *Wenwu* 1981 (6): 1–16; photo, p. 16, fig. 49.

Jiulidun, Shucheng AH (1980): 4 *yongzhong*.
  *Kaogu Xuebao* 1982 (2): 229–42; photos, pls. 17.2 and 19.2; *Anhui Sheng Bowuguan-cang qingtongqi*, item 55.
    Other musical instruments found: 5 *qing*, 1 drum stand★.

Jiuxian, Ye Xian HN, tomb no. 1 (1987): 6 *niuzhong* (incomplete set)★ (inscription deliberately effaced).

> *Hua Xia Kaogu* 1988 (3): 1–18; photo, p. 6, fig. 8; drawings, p. 9, figs. 10.1 and 2; rubbing, p. 9, fig. 10.3, and p. 10, fig. 11.
>
> Other musical instruments found: 2 *se*.

Keshengzhuang, Chang'an ShX (1950s): 1 pottery handbell(?).

> Li Chunyi 1957a; Wu Zhao 1983, 4.

Kewang Damiaoxia, Fogang GD (1984): 1 *nao*.

> *Guangdong wenwu pucha chengguo tulu*, item 43 (photo, drawings).

Lanshi, Zixing HuN (1980): 1 *nao*.

> *Hunan Kaogu Jikan* 3 (1986): 29–30 (photo, line drawing, partial rubbings).

Leigudun, Suizhou HuB, tomb no. 1 (1978): 4? sets *yongzhong*★ (12/11/12/10), 1 *bo*★, 3 sets *niuzhong*★ (6/6/7) [ZENG HOU YI].

> *Wenwu* 1979 (7): 1–24. Tone measurements: Wang Xiang 1981; *Shanghai Bowuguan Jikan* 2 (1982): 89–92; Tan and Feng 1988. First group of *yongzhong* (lower tier and the first and third set on the middle tier of the bell-rack in tomb no. 1, 33 pieces): photos, *Wenwu* 1979 (7), figs. 17, 22, 23, and pls. 1 and 3.2; *Sui Xian Zeng Hou Yi-mu*, figs. 9, 10, 14–21. Second set of *yongzhong* on the middle tier, set of 12: photos, *Wenwu* 1979 (7), fig. 17, pl. 1; *Sui Xian Zeng Hou Yi-mu*, figs. 9 and 10; *Hubei Suizhou Leigudun chutu wenwu*, fig. 4. *Bo*, photo, *Sui Xian Zeng Hou Yi-mu*, ill. 22. *Niuzhong*, photo, *Sui Xian Zeng Hou Yi-mu*, pl. 12.
>
> Other musical instruments found: 32 *qing*★ (4 sets) [ZENG HOU YI], 12 *se*, 2 *qin*, 5 *sheng*, 2 flutes, 4 drums (different types), drum stand.

Leigudun, Suizhou HuB, tomb no. 2 (1981): 2 sets *yongzhong* (8/28).

> *Wenwu* 1985 (1): 16–36. Tone measurements: *Huangzhong* 1988 (4): 9–12. First set, set of 8: *Wenwu* 1985 (1); photos, pls. 2.1, 3.2, 4; drawing, p. 29, fig. 34; *Hubei Suizhou Leigudun chutu wenwu*, photo, fig. 66–67a. Second set, set of 28: *Wenwu* 1985 (1): 16–36; photos, pls. 2.1 and 3.1; drawing, p. 29, fig. 35; *Hubei Suizhou Leigudun chutu wenwu*, photo, fig. 66.
>
> Other musical instruments found: 12 *qing*, 1 drum stand.

Leijiashan, Dawu HuB (1979): 7 *yongzhong* (2 sets: 5/2?).

> *Jianghan Kaogu* 1980 (2): 95–96, 90; rubbing, fig. 2; *Kaogu* 1988 (4): 300–306, 313; blurred photo, p. 306, fig. 8.

Liangshuiping, Binyang GX (1973): 1 *yongzhong*.

> *Wenwu* 1978 (10): 93–96; photo, p. 95, fig. 14; rubbings, p. 96, figs. 9 and 10; *Guangxi chutu wenwu*, pl. 39 (photo).

Lianhua, Ningxiang HuN (1965): 1 *yongzhong*.

> *Wenwu* 1966 (4): 4–5; photo, p. 4, fig. 13.

Lijialou, Xinzheng HN (1923): 4 *bo*, 2 sets *yongzhong* (10/9).

Sun Haibo 1937 (photos); *Chine, trésors et splendeurs*, cat. no. 25 (photo of 1 *yongzhong*). Tone measurements (six *yongzhong* only): Huang Xiangpeng 1978–80, pt. 2, 139.

Liling HuN (location unclear) (year unknown): 1 *nao*.

Gao Zhixi 1984a, 29, pl. 7.1 (photo).

Linkesuo, Jing'an JX (1983): 1 *nao*.

*Kaogu* 1984 (4): 375 (photo); *Jiangxi Lishi Wenwu* 1983 (2): 12 (photo).

Linwu HuN (location unclear) (1962): 1 *yongzhong*.

Gao Zhixi 1984a, 30; photos, pls. 8.1 and 2.

Liugezhuang, Penglai SD (1976/77 or 1984): 9 *niuzhong* on rack.

*Kaogu* 1990 (1): 803–10; photo, pls. 1.1 and 3.3; drawings, p. 805, figs. 5 and 6.3.

Liujiacun, Fufeng ShX (1972): 1 *yongzhong*.

*Kaogu yu Wenwu* 1980 (4): 16; photo, p. 10, fig. 4.4 (blurred). Tone measurements: Jiang Dingsui 1984, 88.

Liujiadianzi, Yishui SD (1977): 6 *bo*, 4 sets *yongzhong* (9/7/3/1), 9 *niuzhong*\* [CHEN DASANGSHI].

*Wenwu* 1984 (9): 1–10. *Yongzhong*, no illustrations published for sets 1–3 (seen by the writer in 1986); fourth set, photo, pl. 2.6. *Niuzhong*, photo, p. 9, fig. 17 (blurred); rubbing, p. 6, fig. 8. *Bo*, photo, p. 9, fig. 18 (blurred).

Other instruments found: 1 *zheng*, 2 *chunyu*, many *qing*.

Liulige, Hui Xian HN, tomb no. 60 (1935–37): 4 large *bo*, 8 small *bo*, 8 *yongzhong*, 9 *niuzhong*.

*Shanbiaozhen yu Liulige*. *Yongzhong*, rubbings, pls. 72, 75.1–5. First set of *bo*, rubbings, pl. 73. Second set of *bo*, rubbings, pls. 73, 76. *Niuzhong*, rubbings, pls. 74, 75.6–8.

Other musical instruments found: 11 *qing*.

Liulige, Hui Xian HN, tomb no. 75 (1935–37): 4 *bo*, 8 *yongzhong*, 9 *niuzhong*.

*Shanbiaozhen yu Liulige*. *Yongzhong*, rubbings, pls. 96, 98. *Bo*, rubbings, pls. 94–95. *Niuzhong*, rubbings, pl. 64.

Other musical instruments found: 10 *qing*.

Liulige, Hui Xian HN, tomb no. 80 (1935–37): 4 *niuzhong*.

*Shanbiaozhen yu Liulige*. *Niuzhong*, pl. 97 (rubbing only).

Other kinds of bells found: 1 *duo*.

Liulige, Hui Xian HN, tomb *Jia* (1935–37): 4 large *bo*, 9 small *bo*, 8 *yongzhong*, 9 *niuzhong*.

*Shanbiaozhen yu Liulige*, pl. 115.1 (blurred photo showing all the bells and chimestones). First set of *bo*, photos, Guo Baojun 1981, pl. 75.1; Wang

Haiwen 1980, 73. Second set of *bo*, photos, Guo Baojun 1981, pls. 75.1 and 2; Wang Haiwen 1980, 73.

Other musical instruments found: 11 *qing*.

Liulin, Pi Xian JS, tomb no. 118 (1960): 1 pottery bell.
*Kaogu Xuebao* 1965 (2): 9–47; drawing, p. 41, fig. 33.

Liurongshan, Yangxin HuB (1974): 2 *nao*.
*Wenwu* 1981 (1): 93–94 (photos, rubbings). *Zhongguo Hubei chutu wenwu*, item 64 (photo of *nao* no. 1).

Liuzhou GX (location unclear) (year unknown): 1 *yongzhong*.
Mentioned by Jiang Tingyu 1989, 30 (no illustration published).

Longjingxie, Rong Xian GX (1976): 4 *yangjiao*-bells.
*Kaogu* 1984 (9): 798–806 (esp. 802–804); *Wenwu* 1984 (5): 66–69.

Ludian, Kunming YN (year unknown): bell(s?) (details unclear).
*Wenwu Cankao Ziliao* 1955 (6): 39.

Luhe, Lucheng SX, tomb no. 7 (1983): 4 *bo*, 2 sets *yongzhong* (8/8), 8 *niuzhong*.
*Wenwu* 1986 (6): 1–19. *Yongzhong*, photo, pl. 3.1; drawing, p. 10, fig. 21.1. *Bo*, photo, pl. 3.2; drawing, p. 10, fig. 21.2. *Niuzhong*, photo, pl. 3.3; drawing, p. 10, fig. 22.

Other musical instruments found: 10 *qing*.

Luobowan, Gui Xian GX (1976): 2 cylindrical bells, 1 *yangjiao*-bell.
*Wenwu* 1978 (9): 25–42, 54; *Guangxi Gui Xian Luobowan Han-mu*. *Yangjiao*-bell: photo, pl. 10.3; drawing, p. 29, fig. 26.1; rubbing, ibid., fig. 26.2. Cylindrical bells: photo, pl. 10.4, 5; drawing, p. 29, fig. 26.3; rubbings, ibid., fig. 26.4, 5. Tone measurements: pp. 125–40. *Guangxi chutu wenwu*, pl. 84 (photo of cylindrical bell); *Quanguo chutu wenwu zhenpinxuan*, cat. no. 239 (photo of *yangjiao-niuzhong*); *Zhongguo meishu quanji, Gongyi meishu-bian*, vol. 5, pl. 191.

Other musical instruments found: 2 bronze drums.

Luofang, Xinyu JX (1980): 1 *nao*.
*Wenwu* 1982 (9): 88–89; *Jiangxi Lishi Wenwu* 3 1980: 48–49 (blurred photo).

Luyu, Binyang GX (1970): 1 *yongzhong*.
*Wenwu* 1978 (10): 93–96, esp. 96; photo; p. 95, fig. 15.

Maba, Qujiang GD (1984): 1 *nao*.
*Guangdong Wenbo* 1985 (1): 69; photo, pl. 1.7. *Guangdong wenwu pucha cheng-guo tulu*, item 44 (photo, rubbings, drawings).

Malong, Xiangxiang HuN (1968): 1 *yongzhong*.
Gao Zhixi 1984a, 29, pl. 7.4 (photo); Gao Zhixi 1984c, 67.

Maolin, Jing Xian AH (1980s): 3 *yongzhong*.
Mentioned in *Wenwu Yanjiu* 4 (1988): 161–186 (no illustration published).

Matougang, Qingyuan GD, tomb no. 1 (1962): 5 *yongzhong*.

*Kaogu* 1963 (2): 57–61. First type of *yongzhong*, photos, pls. 1.4–9; rubbings, p. 39, figs. 8.2,3,5. Second type of *yongzhong*, photo, pl. 1.2.

Other kinds of bells found: 1 *zheng*.

Matougang, Qingyuan GD, tomb no. 2 (1963): 7 *yongzhong*.

*Kaogu* 1964 (3): 138–42; photos, pls. 8.1–9; rubbing, p. 140, fig. 3.

Mawangcun, Chang'an ShX, hoard no. 2 (1973): 10 *yongzhong* (1/1/2/2/4).

*Kaogu* 1974 (1): 1–5. First set (no. 22), photo, p. 3, fig. 7.4. Tone measurements: Jiang Dingsui 1984, 87. Second set (no. 23), photo, p. 3, fig. 7.5. Tone measurements: Jiang Dingsui 1984, 88. Third set (nos. 20–21), photo, p. 3, fig. 7.3 (no. 20). Tone measurements: Jiang Dingsui 1984, 89. Fourth set (nos. 18–19), photo, p. 3, fig. 7.2 (no. 19). Tone measurements: Jiang Dingsui 1984, 88. Fifth set (nos. 14–17), photo, p. 3, fig. 7.1 (no. 14). Tone measurements: Jiang Dingsui 1984, 88.

Maxiang, Heng Xian GX (year unknown): 1 *yongzhong*.

*Kaogu* 1984 (9): 798–806 (esp. 802–804).

Meicun, Boluo GD (1975): 7 *yongzhong*.

*Guangdong chutu xian-Qin wenwu*, 48–69; mentioned in *Kaogu Xuebao* 1984 (4): 413–14 (no photos published).

Miaodigou, Sanmenxia HN (1957): 1 pottery toy (bell?).

*Miaodigou yu Sanliqiao*, drawing, p. 54, fig. 36.1; *Jianming Zhongguo lishi tuce* 1:131 (incorrect drawing).

Miaodun, Donghai JS (1982): 9 *yongzhong*.

*Kaogu* 1986 (12): 1073–78; photo, p. 1075, fig. 5; drawing, ibid., fig. 4.

Miaoqiancun, Wanrong SX (1958): 9 *niuzhong*, 1 *yongzhong*.

*Niuzhong: Wenwu Cankao Ziliao* 1958 (12): 34–35 (photo, rubbing). *Yongzhong: Shanxi chutu wenwu*, cat. no. 92 (photo).

Other musical instruments found: 10 *qing*.

Muluocun, Liujiang GX (1986): 1 *yongzhong*.

*Wenwu* 1990 (1): 92–93 (photo).

Nanluo, Lintong ShX, hoard no. 1 (1976): 13 *yongzhong*.

*Wenwu* 1977 (8): 1–7, 73; photos, pls. 1.3,4; rubbings, p. 4, fig. 15. Tone measurements: Jiang Dingsui 1984, 87.

Nanluo, Lintong ShX, hoard no. 2 (1979): 1 *yongzhong*.

*Kaogu yu Wenwu* 1983 (3): 111; photo, fig. 1 (blurred).

Nanmendong, Luoding GD (1977): 6 *yongzhong*.

*Kaogu* 1983 (1): 43–48, 29. *Yongzhong*, photo, pl. 8.1; drawing, p. 44, fig. 2.2; partial rubbings, p. 45, fig. 3.16, p. 48, fig. 6.7; *Guangdong chutu xian-Qin wenwu*, 62, fig. 9.2 (photo).

Other kinds of bells found: 1 *zheng*.

Nanxiang, Heng Xian GX (year unknown): 1 *yongzhong*.
*Kaogu* 1984 (9): 798–806; photo, p. 804, fig. 8 right.

Nanya, Jian'ou FJ (1980s): 2 *nao*.
*Kaogu Xuebao* 1990 (4): 391–407; photo, pl. 1.5.

Nasangcun (a.k.a. Mei'ershan), Heng Xian GX (1958): 1 *yongzhong*.
*Wenwu* 1978 (10): 93–96; photo, p. 95, fig. 13; *Guangxi chutu wenwu*, pl. 38 (photo).

Nihequ, Lujiang AH (1973): 1 *nao*.
*Anhui Sheng Bowuguan-cang qingtongqi*, item 10 (photo, rubbings); *Chinesisches Kunsthandwerk der Provinz Anhui aus drei Jahrtausenden*, 50–51 (cat. no. 7, photo).

Paotaishan, Luanping HB (1978): 3 ornate *ling*, 1 *niuzhong*.
*Wenwu Ziliao Congkan* 7 (1983): 67–74; photo, p. 72, fig. 13.

Pengjiaqiao, Pingxiang JX (1962): 2 *yongzhong*.
*Kaogu* 1963 (8): 417; photos, fig. 3.

Pengshan, Lianping GD (1978): 1 *yongzhong*, 1 *chunyu*.
*Guangdong chutu xian-Qin wenwu*, 230–233, cat. no. 59 (photo); *Wenbo Tong-xun* (Guangdong Sheng Bowuguan) 3 (1978): 14 (photo).

Pingliangtai, Huaiyang HN (year unknown): 5 bells (type uncertain).
Cao Guicen 1987, 63.

Pingru, Xiangxiang HuN (1982): 1 *yongzhong*.
Gao Zhixi 1984a, 29–30; photo, pl. 10.3.

Puducun, Chang'an ShX (1954): 1 set *yongzhong* (3 pieces).
*Kaogu Xuebao* 1957 (1): 75–86, pl. 2; *Kaogu Xuebao* 1956 (3): 123; photo, pl. 10; *Xin Zhongguo de kaogu shouhuo*, pl. 38.2 (photo). Tone measurements: Jiang Dingsui 1984, 87.

Putuo, Xilin GX (1966–72): 2 *yangjiao*-bells.
*Wenwu* 1978 (9): 43–51; *Guangxi chutu wenwu*, pl. 95 (photo).
Other musical instruments found· 4 bronze drums.

Qiangjiacun, Fufeng ShX, YI (1974): 1 *yongzhong*★ [SHI CHENG].
*Wenwu* 1975 (8): 57–62; *Shaanxi chutu Shang Zhou qingtongqi* 3:110–111; photo, pl. 107. Tone measurements: Jiang Dingsui 1984, 89.

Qianshan AH (location unclear) (year unknown): 1 *nao*.
Chen Mengjia 1955–56, pt. 5, 125, pl. 11 left; *Anhui Sheng Bowuguan-cang qingtongqi*, item 11 (photo).

Qiaodang, Ningxiang HuN (1975): 1 *yongzhong*.
*Wenwu* 1983 (10): 72–74; photo, p. 73, fig. 4.

Qijiacun, Fufeng ShX, hoard no. 1 (1960): 2 sets *yongzhong* (8★/8★).
First set [ZUO], *Fufeng Qijiacun qingtongqiqun*, pls. 24–30; *Shaanxi chutu Shang Zhou qingtongqi*, vol. 2, pls. 156–163 (photos, rubbings). Tone measurements:

Jiang Dingsui 1984, 90. Second set [ZHONG YI], *Fufeng Qijiacun qingtongqiqun*, pls. 32–39; *Shaanxi chutu Shang Zhou qingtongqi*, vol. 2, pls. 142–150 (photos, rubbings). Tone measurements: Jiang Dingsui 1984, 90.

Qijiacun, Fufeng ShX, hoard no. 2 (1966): 2 *yongzhong*.
*Kaogu yu Wenwu* 1980 (4): 16 (no illustrations published). Tone measurements of one specimen (T0120): Jiang Dingsui 1984, 88.

Qin Shihuangling [tomb of the First Emperor of Qin], Lintong ShX (1976): 1 *niuzhong*★ [YUEFU].
*Kaogu yu Wenwu* 1982 (4): 92–94 (drawings); photos, *Sensei-shō Hakubutsukan*, 26; Wu Zhao 1983, 25.

Qingfengcun, He Xian GX (1972): 1 *yongzhong*.
*Guangxi Wenwu* 1986 (4) (not seen); mentioned in Jiang Tingyu 1989, 29–30.

Qingjiang, Wuning JX (1982): 1 *yongzhong* (?).
*Jiangxi Lishi Wenwu* 1983 (3): 10 (blurred photo).

Qingshan, Gaochun JS (1974): 2 *yongzhong*, 2 *goudiao*.
*Wenwu Ziliao Congkan* 5 (1981): 108–109. *Yongzhong*, photo, pls. 9.4 and 5; rubbing, p. 109, fig. 6 left. *Goudiao*, photo, pl. 9.1.

Qiqiao, Gaochun JS (1980s): 1 *goudiao*.
*Wenwu* 1990 (9): 39 (no illustration published).

Qizhen, Fufeng ShX, hoard no. 1 (1966): 2 *yongzhong*★ [NING; YONGXIANG].
*Wenwu* 1972 (7): 9–12; *Shaanxi chutu Shang Zhou qingtongqi* 3:70–71. Ning-*yongzhong*, *Shaanxi chutu Shang Zhou qingtongqi*, vol. 3, pl. 60 (photo, rubbing). Tone measurements: Jiang Dingsui 1984, 90. Yongxiang-*yongzhong*, *Shaanxi chutu Shang Zhou qingtongqi*, vol. 3, pl. 61 (photo, rubbing). Tone measurements: Jiang Dingsui 1984, 89.

Qizhen, Fufeng ShX, hoard no. 2 (pre-1949): 1 *yongzhong*.
*Kaogu yu Wenwu* 1980 (4): 16; photo, p. 10, fig. 4.3. Tone measurements: Jiang Dingsui 1984, 89 (= T0026).

Quankoucun, Hengyang HuN (1979): 1 *nao*.
*Wenwu* 1985 (6): 83 (photo, partial rubbing); Gao Zhixi 1984c, 60.

Qucun, Quwo SX, tomb no. 7092 (1980s): 1 *yongzhong*.
Seen at the Beijing University Field Station in 1991 (report under preparation).

Rujiazhuang, Baoji ShX, tomb no. 1 (1974–75): 3 *yongzhong*.
*Baoji Yu-guo mudi* 1: 271–359; drawings, p. 282, fig. 193; vol. 2, pl. 155.1 (photo); *Wenwu* 1976 (4): 34–36; *Shaanxi chutu Shang Zhou qingtongqi* 4:68 (photo). Tone measurements: Jiang Dingsui 1984, 87.

Sanguandian, Lingyuan LN (1978): 6 *niuzhong*.
*Kaogu* 1985 (2): 108–111, 154; photo, pls. 1.10–13.

Sanji, Pingshan HB, tomb no. 1 (1974–78): 14 *niuzhong*.
 *Wenwu* 1979 (1): 1–31; *Chūzan ōkoku bunbutsuten*, cat. no. 3.
 Other musical instruments found: 13 *qing*.

Sanlian, Yin Xian ZJ (1974): 1 *yongzhong*.
 *Wenwu* 1985 (4): 91 (no illustration published).

Sanmudi, Ningxiang HuN (1973): 1 *nao*.
 Gao Zhixi 1984a, 129; English translation, 284; photo, fig. 61.4; *Konan-shō Hakubutsukan*, pl. 29.

Sanpu, Zhuzhou HuN (year unknown): 1 *nao*.
 Unpublished; exhibited by the Hunan Provincial Museum at the Shanghai Museum in 1990.

Shanbiaozhen, Ji Xian HN, tomb no. 1 (1935): 2 sets *bo* (5/9).
 *Shanbiaozhen yu Liulige*, pt. 1. First set of *bo*, photos, pls. 2–4; drawings, pp. 5–7; rubbings, pls. 36–37. Second set of *bo*, photos, pls. 2, 5–7; rubbings, pls. 38–39.
 Other musical instruments found: 10 *qing*.

Shangcunling, Sanmenxia HN, tomb no. 1052 (1956–57): 9 *niuzhong*.
 *Shangcunling Guo-guo mudi*, 22, pls. 38.1–3 (photo).
 Other kinds of bells found: 1 *zheng*.

Shangguocun, Wenxi SX (1970s): 2 sets of 8 *niuzhong* each.
 Unpublished; cf. *Shanxi chutu wenwu*, nos. 64–69.

Shangkuangcun, Yantai SD (1969): 1 *yongzhong*.
 *Wenwu* 1972 (5): 8–9; *Kaogu* 1983 (4): 289–92; photo, pl. 1.3.

Shangmacun, Houma SX, tomb no. 13 (1961): 9 *niuzhong*.
 *Kaogu* 1963 (5): 229–45; photo, pl. 3.8; partial rubbing, p. 238, fig. 11.7. Tone measurements: Huang Xiangpeng 1978–80, pt. 2, 142.
 Other musical instruments found: 10 *qing*.

Shangmacun, Houma SX, tomb no. 1004 (1973–1986): 9 *bo*.
 *Wenwu* 1989 (6): 1–21, 50; drawing, p. 9, fig. 11.3.

Shanqian Gongshe, Qingjiang JX (1979): 1 *nao*.
 *Jiangxi Lishi Wenwu* 1981 (3): 36–37 (photo).

Shaogou, Luoyang HN, tomb no. 21 (1950s): 6 *ling* (1 set, bronze *mingqi*).
 *Luoyang Shaogou Han-mu*, 183–86; drawing, p. 183, figs. 83.10–12.

Shaogou, Luoyang HN, tomb no. 123 (1950s): 6 *ling* (1 set, bronze *mingqi*).
 *Luoyang Shaogou Han-mu*, 183–86; photo, pl. 52; drawing, p. 183, fig. 83.9.

Shenze, Pan'an ZJ (1986): 1 *nao*.
 *Kaogu* 1987 (8): 727 (photo).

Shiguzhaishan, Ningxiang HuN (1959): 5 *nao* (not a set).
 *Wenwu* 1960 (10): 57–58; *Wenwu* 1966 (4): 2; *Hunan-sheng wenwu tulu*, 11;

*Zhongguo gu qingtongqi-xuan*, no. 23; *Chūgoku Jinmin Kyōwakoku kodai seidō-kiten*, no. 23 (depictions of first "Elephant *nao*" only). Gao Zhixi 1984b, 129; English translation, 279–84; photos, figs. 59, 60.1 and 2 (all 5 objects).

Shijiahe, Tianmen HuB (year unknown): Neolithic pottery bell.
  Mentioned in Feng 1988b, 3.

Shizhaishan, Jinning YN, tomb no. 6 (1954): 6 beehive-shaped bells, *yangjiao*-bells (number unreported).
  *Yunnan Jinning Shizhaishan gumuqun fajue baogao* 1:80–81, 2:63–65 (beehive-shaped bells); 1:16 (*yangjiao*-bells).

Shoufeng, He Xian GX, tomb no. 1 (1982): 18 bronze *ling* (bell *mingqi*).
  *Kaogu yu Wenwu* 1984 (4): 9–12; photo, pl. 2.4.

Shuanggudui, Fuyang AH (1977): 5 *bo*, 9 *yongzhong* (all ceramic *mingqi*).
  *Wenwu* 1978 (8): 12–31.
  Other *mingqi* musical instruments found: 2 sets *qing* (10/10).

Songshan, Zhaoqing GD (1972): 6 *yongzhong*.
  *Wenwu* 1974 (11); 69–79; *Guangdong chutu xian-Qin wenwu*, 266–67, 113, cat. no. 83 (photo, drawing); rubbing, p. 63, fig. 12.

Songxi, Gaochun JS (1974): 8 *goudiao*.
  *Wenwu Ziliao Congkan* 5 (1981): 108–9 (no illustrations published).

Subutun, Qingzhou (formerly Yidu SD), tomb no. 8 (1986): 3 *nao*.
  *Hai Dai Kaogu* 1 (1989): 254–274; photo, pl. 10.3; drawing, fig. 15.1; rubbing, fig. 12.10.
  Other musical instruments found: 1 *qing*.

Sunjiagou, Ningcheng LN (1982): 2 *niuzhong*.
  *Wenwu Ziliao Congkan* 9 (1985): 33–35; photo, p. 34, fig. 29.

Supan, Nanning GX (1940s): 1 *yongzhong*.
  *Wenwu* 1978 (10): 93–96; photo, p. 95, fig. 12.

Taigongmiao, Baoji ShX (1978): 3 *bo*★, 5 *yongzhong*★ [QIN GONG].
  *Wenwu* 1978 (11): 1–5. *Yongzhong*, photo, pl. 1; line drawing, p. 2, figs. 3, 4; rubbings, p. 2, figs. 1, 2; p. 5, figs. 8–10. Tone measurements (approximate): Ma Chengyuan 1981, 139. *Bo*, photo, pl. 2. Additional photos in *Higashi Ajia Bunmei-no genryūten*, cat. nos. 45–46.

Taihe JX (location unclear) (1970s): 1 *nao*.
  *Jiangxi Lishi Wenwu* 3 (1980): 50 (photo).

Tangdongcun, Jiangning JS (1974): 1 *nao*.
  *Wenwu* 1975 (8): 87–88; Gao Zhixi 1984b, 130; English translation, 284; photo, fig. 63.2.

Tangjiashan, Fanchang AH (1979): 1 *yongzhong*.
  *Wenwu* 1982 (12): 47–49; photo, pl. 5.4.

Taosi, Xiangfen SX (1983): Neolithic "bells" (1 metal, 2 pottery).
*Kaogu* 1984 (12): 1069–71, 1068; photos, pls. 3.2–4; drawing, p. 1069, fig. 1.

Tian'eshan, Zixing HuN (1983): 1 *nao*.
*Hunan Kaogu Jikan* 3 (1986): 26–30 (photo, line drawing, partial rubbings).

Tianjingwang, Ju Xian SD (1963): 3 *bo*, 6 *zhong* (type uncertain).
*Wenwu* 1972 (5): 11 (no illustrations published).

Tianxingguan, Jiangling HuB (1978): 4 *niuzhong*.
*Kaogu Xuebao* 1982 (1): 71–116; photos, pls. 19.9, 20.1; drawing, p. 96, fig. 19.
  Other musical instruments found: many *qing*, 6 *sheng*, 4 *se*, 2 drums of different sizes. Bell-rack has slots for 22 bells.

Touba, Zhuzhou HuN (1972): 1 *nao*.
*Wenwu Ziliao Congkan* 5 (1981): 103–105; Gao Zhixi 1984b, 130, English translation, 288; photo, fig. 63.3; Gao Zhixi 1984c, 67.

Wangcun, Qingyang AH (year known): 4 *goudiao* (unusual type).
*Anhui Wenbo* 3 (1983): 86–87, 86 (photo).

Wangjiashan, Dantu JS (1985): 3 *chunyu* (chimed set?), 1 *goudiao*.
*Wenwu* 1987 (12): 24–37. *Chunyu*, photos, pls. 1, 4.2, p. 32, fig. 12; drawing, p. 27, fig. 5.1; rubbings, p. 31, figs. 10, 11. *Goudiao*, photo, p. 34, fig. 25; drawing, p. 27, fig. 5.4.

Wanjiaba, Chuxiong YN (1975): 6 *yangjiao*-bells.
*Wenwu* 1978 (10): 1–18; *Kaogu Xuebao* 1983 (3): 347–82.

Wanrong, SX (location unclear) (year known): large *zhong* (no details known).
Mizuhara (1984, 11) quotes *Shanxi Ribao*, 4 January, 1962 (not seen).

Weipocun, Binyang GX, tomb no. 1 (1977): 1 *yongzhong*.
*Kaogu* 1983 (2): 146–48; photo, pl. 6.1.

Weipocun, Binyang GX, tomb no. 2 (1979): 2 *yongzhong*.
*Kaogu* 1983 (2): 146–48; photos, pls. 6.2–3.

Weizhuang, Pingdingshan HN (year unknown): 3 *yongzhong*.
*Kaogu* 1988 (5): 466 (photo). Tone measurements: Fang Jianjun 1986 (aural approximations).

Wudaohezi, Lingyuan LN, tomb no. 1 (1987): 3 *niuzhong*-like bells.
*Wenwu* 1989 (2): 52–61; photos, pl. 8.1, p. 57, fig. 10.1; drawing, p. 59, fig. 16.2. (Similar bells found in other tombs at the same site.)

Wuhu AH (location unclear) (1980s): 4 *yongzhong*, 1 *nao*.
Mentioned in *Wenwu Yanjiu* 4 (1988): 161–186 (no illustration published).

Wujun Xicun, Fufeng ShX (1973): 1 *yongzhong*.
*Kaogu yu Wenwu* 1980 (4): 16–17; photo, p. 10, fig. 4.6 (blurred). Tone measurements: Jiang Dingsui 1984, 87 (inv. no. 73–584).

Wujun Xicun, Fufeng ShX, hoard no. 2 (1978): 2 pieces (at least one a bell).
  Luo Xizhang 1988, 46 (listed in table; no illustrations).

Wuxuan GX (location unclear) (1981): 1 *yongzhong*.
  Mentioned by Jiang Tingyu 1989, 30 (no illustration published).

Xiajiashan, Leiyang HuN (1980): 1 *nao*.
  *Wenwu* 1984 (7): 49; Gao Zhixi 1984b, 130; English translation, 287–88;
  photo, fig. 62.3.

Xian Zhuanwachang, Shangcai HN (1979): 13 *niuzhong*.
  *Zhongyuan Wenwu* 1990 (2): 93–94, 80; photo, p. 94, fig. 6.

Xiangbizui, Changsha HuN, tomb no. 1 (1978): bell fragments (ceramic *mingqi*).
  *Kaogu Xuebao* 1981 (1): 111–30 (no illustration published).

Xianggangshan, Guangzhou GD (1983): 14 *niuzhong*, 5 *yongzhong*, 8 *goudiao*★
  [NANYUE WEN DI].
  *Kaogu* 1984 (3): 222–30. *Niuzhong*, photo in archaeological context, pl. 2.2 (no
  detailed illustrations published; *yongzhong* unpublished). *Goudiao*, photo and
  rubbing, p. 227, fig. 3; *Quanguo chutu wenwu zhenpinxuan*, pls. 241–48 (photos).
    Other musical instruments found: 2 sets *qing* (8/10), 1 *zheng*.

Xiangtan HuN (location unclear) (1973): 1 *yongzhong*.
  Gao Zhixi 1984a, 30; photo, pl. 10.4.

Xiangtan HuN (location unclear) (1954): 1 *yongzhong*.
  Gao Zhixi 1984a, 30; photo, pl. 11.1.

Xianjiahu, Changsha HuN (1974–75): *niuzhong* (number unclear), 2 mallets (all
ceramic *mingqi*).
  *Wenwu* 1979 (3); 1–16; photos, p. 12, figs. 29 and 32.
    Other *mingqi* musical instruments found: 14 *qing* (2 sets).

Xianyang ShX (location unclear) (year unknown): 1 *niuzhong*.
  *Higashi Ajia bunmei-no genryūten*, cat. no. 67. (Several similar specimens seen at
  the Xianyang Municipal Museum in 1991, apparently unpublished.)

Xiao'emeishan, Zhangqiu SD (year unknown): 4 *yongzhong*, 22 *goudiao*-shaped
objects.
  *Weuwu* 1989 (6): 67–72. *Yongzhong*: photo, p. 66, fig. 1; rubbing, ibid., figs.
  2. *Goudiao*-shaped objects: drawings, p. 67, figs. 3.1 and 2.

Xiaonanzhuang, Wen Xian HN (1968): 3 *nao*.
  *Wenwu* 1975 (2): 88–91 (photo); *Henan chutu Shang Zhou qingtongqi* 1:272
  (photo). Tone measurements: Huang Xiangpeng 1978–80, pt. 2, 135.

Xiaotianxi, Fuling SC, tomb no. 1 (1972): 14 *niuzhong*.
  *Wenwu* 1974 (5): 61–80; photos, pls. 1, 2.4; *The great Bronze Age of China*,
  287–89, 315; *Shisen-shō bunbutsuten*, 28–29 (cat. no. 40).
    Other kinds of bells found: 1 *zheng*, 1 pseudo-*yongzhong*.

Xiasi, Xichuan HN, tomb no. 10 (1978): 9 *niuzhong*★ (name of donor effaced).
*Kaogu* 1981 (2): 119–27; photo, pl. 6.1; rubbing, p. 123, fig. 5. Tone measurements (approximate): ibid., 125.

Other musical instruments found: 13 *qing*, 2 panpipes.

Xiasi, Xichuan HN, tomb no. 2 (1978): 26 *yongzhong*★ [WANGSUN GAO], 8 *bo* [?].
*Wenwu* 1980 (10): 13–20; Zhao Shigang 1986, photos, p. 48, fig. 3, pls. 3.1–3, 5; drawing, p. 49, fig. 4; rubbing, p. 47, fig. 1, p. 48, fig. 2; *Son of Heaven*, 60–62, cat. no. 9 (photos). Tone measurements: Zhao Shigang 1986.

Other musical instruments found: remains of *qin* [?], 13 *qing*.

Xiasi, Xichuan HN, tomb no. 10 (1978): 9 *niuzhong* [★LÜ WANG (?) (inscription unpublished)].
*Wenwu* 1980 (10): 13–20 (no illustrations published).

Other musical instruments found: 13 *qing*.

Xibeicun, Yangxin SD (1988): 5 *bo*, 9 *niuzhong*.
*Kaogu* 1990 (3): 218–222, 285; blurred photo, p. 221, fig. 5; partial rubbing, ibid., fig. 4.

Other musical instruments found: 13 *qing*.

Xibeigang, Anyang HN, tomb no. 1083 (1935): 1 enlarged set *nao* (3 + 1).
*Kaogu Xuebao* 7 (1954): 18, pls. 52–54; Chia 1980, 3, 4 (photos) and 6 (drawing). Tone measurements: Chia 1980, 14–15.

Xigaoquan, Baoji ShX (1978): 1 *yongzhong*.
*Wenwu* 1980 (9): 1–9; photo, pl. 1.1.

Xijiao (Western Suburbs), Anyang HN, tomb no. 8 (1957): 3 *nao*.
*Wenwu Cankao Ziliao* 1958 (12): 31; photo, inside back cover, fig. 12; *Kaogu* 1963 (4): 215–16, 220.

Xijiao (Western Suburbs), Luoyang HN (1962): 9 bronze *ling* of 4 different types (1★), 1 iron *ling*.
*Kaogu Xuebao* 1963 (2): 1–58, esp. pp. 27, 31, 34; drawings, p. 27, figs. 22.21–24.

Other musical instruments found: drum (pottery *mingqi*); figurines of performers.

Ximennei (Inside the West Gate), Shou Xian AH (Cai Hou Tomb) (1955): 8 *bo*★, 12 *yongzhong*★, 9 *niuzhong*★ [CAI HOU], bell fragments★.
*Shou Xian Cai Hou-mu*, 10. *Yongzhong, Shou Xian Cai Hou-mu*; photos, pls. 18, 20; rubbings, pls. 22–23; *Chūka Jinmin Kyōwakoku shutsudo bunbutsuten*, cat. no. 1–4 (photos). *Bo, Shou Xian Cai Hou-mu*; photos, pls. 19.1 and 21.1; rubbings, pls. 44–51; *Anhui Sheng Bowuguan-cang qingtongqi*, item 78 (photo). Tone measurements: Li Chunyi 1973, 18 (A-tones of two pieces only). *Niuzhong, Shou Xian Cai Hou-mu*; photos, pls. 19.2, 21.2; rubbings, pls. 52–59; *Anhui Sheng Bowuguan-cang qingtongqi*, item 77 (photo); *Chinesisches Kunst-*

*handwerk der Provinz Anhui aus drei Jahrtausenden*, 51 (cat. no. 8, photo). Tone measurements: Li Chunyi 1973, 16 (A-tones only).

Other kinds of bells found: 1 *chunyu*, 1 *zheng*.

Xinglongcun, Zhuzhou HuN (1988): 1 *nao*.
*Hunan Sheng Bowuguan Wenji* 1 (1991): 137–139; photo, back cover; drawing, p. 139, fig. 3.1; rubbing, p. 138, fig. 1.

Xinhua, Zhijiang HuB (1973): 1 typologically abnormal bell★ [JING].
*Wenwu* 1974 (6): 86 (photo); *Jianghan Kaogu* 1980 (2): 55–59; rubbing, p. 55, fig. 1; *Wenwu* 1980 (10): 31–41; photo, pl. 3.4.

Xinhuicun, Fengcheng JX (1985): 1 *nao*.
*Jiangxi Lishi Wenwu* 1985 (1): 12; photo, front cover.

Xinshi, Deqing ZJ (1976): 1 *yongzhong* (proto-porcelain *mingqi*).
*Wenwu* 1985 (4): 91 (no illustration published).

Xujiafan, Yuhang ZJ (1963): 1 *nao*.
*Kaogu* 1965 (5): 256; Gao Zhixi 1984b, 130; English translation, 284; photo, fig. 62.4.[5]

Ya'erzhou, Guangji HuB (1984): 23 *yongzhong* (6 sets), 2 *goudiao*.
*Jianghan Kaogu* 1984 (4): 38–47. *Yongzhong*, first set, photos, p. 43, pls. 1.3,4; drawings, p. 39, fig. 2; rubbings, p. 39, fig. 3, p. 40, fig. 11.[6] Second set, photos, p. 42, pls. 1.2,5,6; rubbings, p. 40, figs. 4, 10.[7] Third set, photo, p. 43, pl. 2.1; drawing, p. 41, fig. 5; rubbings, p. 41, fig. 6 upper left, lower left and right.[8] Fourth set, photo, p. 43, pl. 2.2.[9] Fifth set (H. 32, 23.2, and 20 [frgm.] cm), photos, p. 44, pls. 2.3, 4, and p. 44, pl. 2.5; drawing, p. 45, fig. 7; rubbings, p. 41, fig. 6 lower right, p. 45, fig. 8.[10] *Goudiao*, photo, p. 44, pl. 2.6; drawing, p. 45, fig. 9.

Yan Xiadu, Yi Xian HB, tomb no. 16 (1964): 2 sets *bo* (4/6), 2 sets *yongzhong* (8/8), 9 *niuzhong* (all pottery *mingqi*).
*Kaogu Xuebao* 1965 (2): 79–102; photos, pl. 8.4 and pls. 9.1 and 2; drawings, p. 96, fig. 18.

Other *mingqi* musical instruments found: 15 *qing*.

Yancheng, Wujin JS (1958): 7 *goudiao*.
*Wenwu* 1959 (4): 5 (photo); *Jiangsu chutu wenwu*, pl. 94 (photo); *Dongnan Wenhua* 1985 (4/5): 78–91; drawings, p. 83, fig. 3.3.

Yangcun, Huangshan AH (1982): 1 *yongzhong*.
*Kaogu* 1988 (5): 465 (very blurred photo).

---

5. Gao inexplicably writes "Tianjiafan" instead of "Xujiafan."
6. In the original report, this set is designated as Type A Ia.
7. In the original report, this set is designated as Type A Ib.
8. In the original report, this set is designated as Type A II.
9. In the original report, this bell is designated as Type A III.
10. In the original report, these bells are designated as Type B I and B II.

Yangjia, Gongcheng GX (1971): 2 *yongzhong*.
    *Kaogu* 1973 (1): 30–34, 41; photo, pl. 12.4; rubbings, p. 31, figs. 2.1 and 2; *Guangxi chutu wenwu*, pl. 40 (photo).

Yangjiacun, Mei Xian ShX (1985): 10 *yongzhong* belonging to three sets (4★/4/2) ★[MAI], 3 *bo*.
    *Wenbo* 1987 (2): 17–25. First set of *yongzhong*, photos, pls. 1.1 and 2; rubbing, p. 18.1; drawing, p. 21, figs. 2.1, 2.2. Second set (MAI-*yongzhong*), photos, pls. 1.3 and 4 and 2.1 and 2; rubbings, pp. 18–20; drawings, p. 22: 3–5, 7. Third set of *yongzhong*, photos, pls. 2.3 and 4, 3.1 and 2; rubbings, p. 22, nos. 10–12; drawings, p. 21, figs. 2.6, 8–10. *Bo*, photos, p. 22, fig. 3, pls. 3.3 and 4; drawing, p. 23, fig. 4; rubbing, p. 24.

Yangmei, Liuyang HuN (1978): 9 *niuzhong*.
    *Wenwu Ziliao Congkan* 5 (1981): 103–105. *Niuzhong*, photo, pl. 8.4; rubbing, p. 104, fig. 3.
    Other kinds of bells found: 1 *duo*.

Yangshan, Linqu SD (1963): 5 *bo*, 5 *niuzhong*.
    *Wenwu* 1972 (5): 13; mentioned in Ma Chengyuan 1981, 142, table 1 (no illustrations published).

Yangze, Jian'ou FJ (1978): 1 *nao*.
    *Wenwu* 1980 (11): 95; Gao Zhixi 1984b, 130; English translation, 287; photo, fig. 63.1; *Kaogu Xuebao* 1990 (4): 391–407; photo, pl. 1.4.

Yilijiecun, Zhijiang HuN (1980): 4 *yongzhong*.
    *Hunan Kaogu Jikan* 4 (1987): 179–180; photo, p. 179, fig. 1; rubbings, ibid., fig. 2.

Yingmin, He Xian GX (1979): 1 *bo*.
    *Kaogu yu Wenwu* 1982 (4): 62 (drawing).

Yinxu, Anyang HN, tomb no. 5 ("Fu Hao") (1976): 5 *nao*.
    *Yinxu Fu Hao-mu*, Beijing (Wenwu), 1976, 100–101 (drawing); photo, pl. 62.1.
    Other musical instruments found: 5 *qing* (2 sets).

Yinxu, Anyang HN, Western Area tomb no. 699 (1969–77): 3 *nao*.
    *Kaogu Xuebao* 1979 (1): 97–98, pl. 14.1 (photo).

Yongheping, Changyang HuB (1971): 1 *yongzhong*.
    *Kaogu* 1986 (4): 370; photo, fig. 1.2.

Yongningbao, Hongdong SX (1980): 1 *yongzhong*.
    *Wenwu* 1987 (2): 1–16, esp. 6–7; drawing, p. 7, fig. 9.

Youzhencun, Zhuzhou HuN (1985): 1 *nao*.
    *Hunan Kaogu Jikan* 4 (1987): 172 (photo).

Yuanlongpo, Wuming GX, tomb no. 264 (1986): 1 *yongzhong* fragment.
    *Wenwu* 1988 (12): 1–13 (no illustration provided).

Yueshanpu, Ningxiang HuN (1983): 1 *nao*.
  *Wenwu* 1986 (2): 44–45 (photo).

Yulongshan, Xinyu JX (1962): 1 *nao*.
  *Kaogu* 1963 (8): 416–18, 422, esp. 416–17 (photo, rubbings); Gao Zhixi 1984b, 130; English translation, 288; photo, fig. 63.3.[11]

Yushugou, Yongdeng GS (1980): 3 pairs of *ling*.
  *Kaogu yu Wenwu* 1981 (4): 34–36; photo, pl. 6.3.

Zangjiazhuang, Zhucheng SD (1970): 7 *bo*★, 9 *niuzhong*★ [JU GONGZI CHAO ZI].
  *Wenwu* 1972 (5): 14; *Wenwu* 1987 (12): 47–56. Bo, *Wenwu* 1972 (5): 14; photo, pl. 5.4; rubbing, p. 17, fig. 27; *Wenwu* 1987 (12); photo, p. 48, fig. 2; drawing, p. 47, fig. 1; rubbing, p. 50, fig. 6, inscription rubbing and transcription, p. 49, figs. 4–5. *Niuzhong, Wenwu* 1987 (12); photo, p. 48, fig. 3, and p. 54, fig. 15; drawing, p. 50, fig. 8; inscription rubbing, p. 51, fig. 9.
  Other musical instruments found: 13 *qing*.

Zengjiashan, Xiushui JX (1964): 7 *niuzhong*.
  *Kaogu* 1986 (1): 22–27, 11; photo, pl. 4.2; rubbing, p. 25, fig. 5; *Wenwu* 1990 (7): 32–35 (photo).

Zhangjiapo, Chang'an ShX, tomb no. 163 (1982): 2 *yongzhong*★ (+1 frgm.) [XING SHU].
  *Kaogu* 1986 (1): 22–27, 11; photo, pl. 4.2; rubbing, p. 25, fig. 5; *Wenwu* 1990 (7): 32–35 (photo).
  Other musical instruments found: several *qing* (5+).

Zhengxingcun, Xuancheng AH (1981): 1 *yongzhong* or *zheng* (unusual type).
  *Xuanzhou Wenwu* 1 (1983): 56 (blurred photo); *Xuanzhou Wenwu* 3/4 (1986): 61 (photo); *Wenwu* 1991 (8): 96; photo, fig. 4.

Zhi Huai Gongdi (Huai River Dyke Building Site), Shou Xian AH (1950s?): 3 *niuzhong*.
  Mentioned in Ma Chengyuan 1981, 142, table 1.

Zhiyang Xigang, Pingdingshan HN (1980s): 2 *niuzhong*.
  Mentioned in *Pingdingshan Wenwu* 4 (1986): 11–14 (no illustrations published).

Zhongdong, Pingjiang HuN (1980s): 1 *yongzhong*.
  *Kaogu* 1990 (12): 1145 (photo).

Zhongshan, Guanyang GX (1976): 1 *nao*.
  *Wenwu* 1978 (10): 93 (photo); *Guangxi chutu wenwu*, 93 (photo); Gao Zhixi 1984b, 130; English translation, 288; photo, fig. 62.1.

Zhoujiahe, Qian Xian ShX (1978): 1 *yongzhong*.
  *Kaogu yu Wenwu* 1981 (1): 11; photo, pl. 4.5.

---

11. Gao misprints "Yulongshan" as "Zhulongshan."

Zhuanchangba, Huili SC (1977): 6 beehive-shaped bells.

*Kaogu* 1982 (2): 216–17 (rubbings, photo).

Zhuangbai, Fufeng Shx, hoard no. 1 (1976): 21 *yongzhong* belonging to 6 sets (1*/4* + 3*/6*/3/2/2*), 7 proto-*niuzhong* ("chimed *ling*").

*Wenwu* 1978 (3): 1–18; *Shaanxi chutu Shang Zhou qingtongqi* 2 (1980): 77–108. *Yongzhong*, first set [First XING], *Shaanxi chutu Shang Zhou qingtongqi*, vol. 2, pl. 54 (photo and rubbing); *Chūgoku Sensei-shō Hōkei–shi Shūgen bunbutsuten*, 103 (cat. no. 29). Tone measurements: Jiang Dingsui 1984, 88. Second set [Second XING and "Type IV"], *Shaanxi chutu Shang Zhou qingtongqi* 2:55–58, 65–67 (photos and rubbings). Tone measurements: Jiang Dingsui 1984, 89. Third set [Third XING], *Shaanxi chutu Shang Zhou qingtongqi*, vol. 2, pls. 59–64 (photos and rubbings). Tone measurements: Jiang Dingsui 1984, 89. Fourth set of *yongzhong* ["Type V"], *Shaanxi chutu Shang Zhou qingtongqi*, vol. 2, pls. 68–70 (photos). Tone measurements: Jiang Dingsui 1984, 88. Fifth set of *yongzhong* ["Type VI"], *Shaanxi chutu Shang Zhou qingtongqi*, vol. 2, pls. 71–72 (photos). Tone measurements: Jiang Dingsui 1984, 88. Sixth set of *yongzhong* ["Type VII"; enigmatic inscription], *Shaanxi chutu Shang Zhou qingtongqi*, vol. 2, pls. 73–74 (photos and rubbings). Tone measurements: Jiang Dingsui 1984, 88. Proto-*niuzhong* ["chimed *ling*"], *Shaanxi chutu Shang Zhou qingtongqi*, vol. 2, pl. 75; *Chūgoku Sensei-shō Hōkei-shi Shūgen bunbutsuten*, 102–103 (cat. 32).

Zhuangli-Xi, Teng Xian SD (1984): 4 *bo* (* [TENG SIMA MAO] inscription unpublished), 9 *niuzhong*.

*Zhongguo kaoguxue nianjian* 1984, 121 (no illustrations published).

Other musical instruments found: 11 *qing* (excavated in 1978).

Zhuyuangou, Baoji Shx, tomb no. 7 (1980–81): set of 3 *yongzhong*.

*Baoji Yu-guo mudi* 1:92–128; drawing, p. 97, fig. 74; vol. 2, color pl. 12.2, pl. 43.2 (photos).

Zhuyuangou, Baoji Shx, tomb no. 13 (1980–81): single *nao*.

*Baoji Yu-guo mudi* 1:45–92; drawing and rubbing, p. 49, fig. 35; vol. 2, pl. 15.1 (photo).

Zifangshan, Xuzhou JS, tomb no. 3 (or no. 2?)[12] (1977): 10 *ling* (bronze *mingqi niuzhong*).

*Wenwu Ziliao Congkan* 4 (1981): 59–69; photo, p. 67, fig. 32.

Zixing County HuN (location unclear) (year unknown): 1 *bo*.

Gao Zhixi 1984a, 64; photo, p. 67; Gao Zhixi 1984c, 30; photo, pl. 8.4.

Zoumashan, Daye HuB (1972): 2 *yongzhong*.

*Wenwu Ziliao Congkan* 5 (1981): 203–205; drawings, rubbings, p. 204, fig. 2.

Zuiziqiancun, Haiyang SD, tomb no. 1 (1978): 2 *bo*, 5 *yongzhong*.

*Wenwu* 1985 (3): 12–19. *Yongzhong*, photos, p. 16, figs. 21–25; rubbing, p. 17, fig. 27. *Bo*, photos, p. 16, figs. 19, 20; rubbings, p. 17, fig. 28.

---

12. The text of the report says that the bells are from tomb no. 3, whereas the photo caption assigns them to tomb no. 2.

# A Comprehensive, Typologically Arranged
# List of Chinese Musical Bells[1]

## THE EARLIEST CLAPPER–BELLS (*LING*)[2]

Dadunzi (no details reported as yet).

Erlitou, exact locus of excavation unreported (H 14.7 [? more likely, 9.8] cm)

Erlitou Area V, tomb no. 4 (H 8.5 cm) (see fig. 55)

Erlitou Area IX, tomb no. 4 (H 8.2 cm)

Erlitou Area VI, tomb no. 11 (H 7.7 cm)

*Related unprovenienced specimens*

Dr. Paul Singer collection, Summit, N.J. (H 9 cm)[3]

Present location unknown (allegedly from Luoyang) (H 13 cm)[4]

## SHANG DYNASTY (ANYANG PERIOD) *NAO* FROM NORTH CHINA

I. *Unornamented specimens*

Dasikongcun tomb no. 51, set of 3 ★ (inscription still unpublished) (anomalous proportions)

Xiaonanzhuang, set of 3 (H 20.5, 17.0, 13.5 cm)

Xijiao (Anyang) tomb no. 8, set of 3

Yinxu tomb no. 5, enlarged set of 5 two inscribed ★ (YA GONG) (H 14.4, 11.5, 11.7, 9.8, 7.7 cm) (see fig. 56)

---

1. For discussion of typology, see Chapters 4 and 5 and Appendix 3. In this list, an asterisk indicates the presence of an inscription; the donor's name or another conventional designation is given in brackets.

2. Neolithic bells and clapper-bells from post-Erlitou periods are not included in this list; for a partial enumeration, see the notes to Chapter 4.

3. Fontein and Wu 1973, 29, cat. no. 1.

4. White 1934, pl. 177 fig. 515.

*Unprovenienced specimens (selection)*

Museum of Kyōto University (*ex* C. T. Loo collection, allegedly from a set of 3)[5]

Present location unknown, set of 3 ★ (indecipherable) (H 19.2, 16.6, 14.4 cm)[6]

Present location unknown, set of 3 ★ (?/ZHONG) (probably from Anyang)[7]

Present location unknown, set of 3 ★ (YA- ?)[8]

Present location unknown, set of 3 (probably from Anyang) ★ (indecipherable)[9]

Present location unknown ★ (indecipherable) (H 18.7 cm)[10]

Present location unknown ★ (YUYIZHENG)[11]

Present location unknown, set of 3 (H 10.2, 9.6, 8 cm)[12]

Richard C. Bull collection, Pennsylvania (H 12 cm) (anomalous decor)[13]

## II. *Ornamented specimens*

### A. *With mask ornamentation in raised lines*

*Unprovenienced specimens*

National Palace Museum, Taibei[14]

National Palace Museum, Taibei ★ (YA-WAN FU JI) (H 15.8 cm) (perhaps from Anyang)[15]

### B. *With mask ornamentation in full relief*

Dasikongcun tomb no. 1, set of 3 ★ (GU) (H 17.5, 14.8, 12.2 cm)

Dasikongcun tomb no. 312, set of 3 ★ (YA-?-MU PENG) (H 18–13.9 cm)

Hui Xian, set of 3 (no details published)

Jiazhuang tomb no. 269, set of 3 ★ (ZHONG) (no details published)

Subutun tomb no. 8, set of 3 (H 21–15 cm)

Yinxu Western Area tomb no. 699, set of 3 (H 21, 18, 14.3 cm)

Xibeigang tomb no. 1083, enlarged set of 4 (H 17.6, 16.6, 12.7, 12.5 cm) (see fig. 57)

Zhuyuangou tomb no. 13, 1 *nao* (H 19.5 cm)

*Unprovenienced specimens (selection)*

Ashmolean Museum, Oxford (H 16.5 cm)[16]

Japanese private collection, set of 3 ★ (indecipherable) (H 18.3, 15.2, 13.7 cm)[17]

Lüshun Museum (H 18.2 cm)[18]

Metropolitan Museum of Art (with a possibly forged inscription)[19]

---

5. Umehara 1940, pl. 28 lower left.
6. Rong Geng 1941 2:929; Hayashi 1984 2:389, *shō* 5–7.
7. Rong Geng 1941 2:930.   8. Ibid. 2:390, *shō* 10.
9. Hayashi 1984 2:390–91, *shō* 17–19.   10. Ibid. 2:390, *shō* 10.
11. Ibid. 2:391, *shō* 28.   12. Ibid. 2:391, *shō* 21–23.
13. Ibid., *shō* 20.
14. *Gugong tongqi tulu* 2:435, pl. *xia*-484. Hayashi 1984 2:392, *shō* 29.
15. Rong Geng 1941 2:927.   16. Helen Loveday, personal communication.
17. Hayashi 1984 2:389, *shō* 1.   18. Ibid. 2:390, *shō* 12.
19. Kane 1974–75, 89, fig. 23.

Shandong Provincial Museum, Jinan ★ (SHOU)[20]
Shanghai Museum ★ (YA-CHOU)[21]
Present location unknown ★ (YA-?/YOU)[22]
Present location unknown (allegedly from Anyang; repaired) ★
   (indecipherable)[23]
Present location unknown (possibly from Anyang) ★ (indecipherable)[24]
Present location unknown (possibly from the Anyang area) ★ (YA-TAI)[25]

Daguo (number of bells and stylistic position unclear)


SHANG AND WESTERN ZHOU *NAO* FROM SOUTH CHINA

I. *Earliest specimens, with no* xuan *and predominantly raised-line volute ornaments*

   Liurongshan, first *nao* (H 27 cm) (see fig. 60)
   Liurongshan, second *nao* (H 24 cm [fragmentary]) (see fig. 62)
   Qianshan (H 41.5 cm [fragmentary])
   Tangdongcun (H 46 cm) (see fig. 25)
   Xujiafan (H 29 cm) (see fig. 61)
   Jinhua (H 28.5 cm)
   Huangmasai (H 39 cm) (anomalous execution of decoration)
      *Unprovenienced specimens*
   Museum of Far Eastern Antiquities, Stockholm (*ex* collection of King Gustaf VI
      Adolf of Sweden) (H 35 cm) (similar to first Liurongshan specimen)[26]
   Metropolitan Museum of Art, New York (Rogers Fund) (H 29.5 cm) (similar
      to Xujiafan specimen)[27]
   Not extant (*ex* Song Imperial collection) (similar to the preceding)[28]
   Not extant (*ex* Song Imperial collection) (similar to Tangdongcun specimen)[29]
   Not extant (*ex* Song Imperial collection) (similar to Qianshan specimen)[30]
   Museum of Far Eastern Antiquities, Stockholm (H 51 cm) (see fig. 62)[31]

II. *Specimens with* xuan *and flat surface with sunken-line volute ornaments*

   Caoloucun (H 51.4 cm)
   Changxing Middle School (fragment, H 28.5 cm)


20. Seen by the author in 1986. Inscription in Luo Zhenyu 1936, 18.7.1.
21. Ma Chengyuan 1981, pl. 23.1.
22. Rong Geng 1941 2:925; Hayashi 1984 2:390, *shō* 13.
23. Rong Geng 1941 2:927.          24. Hayashi 1984 2:389, *shō* 2.
25. Ibid. 2:391, *shō* 26.
26. Palmgren 1948, pl. 11; see also Hayashi 1984 2:381, *shō* 12.
27. *The Great Bronze Age of China*, 124.     28. *Bogutulu* 26:46a/b.
29. Ibid. 26:45a/b.                 30. Ibid. 26:43b.
31. Karlgren 1949, pl. 37.

Sanmudi (H 66.3 cm) (see fig. 64)

Sanpu (unusual tiger decor)

Yangze (H 76.3 cm) (see fig. 65)

    *Unprovenienced specimens*

Formerly Kleijkamp collection (H 77.8 cm) (similar to Sanmudi specimen)[32]

Wacker collection, New York (H 76.5) (similar to Sanmudi specimen)[33]

Portland Art Museum (transitional to group III) (H 50.2 cm)[34]

Shanghai Museum (transitional to group IV)[35]

Not extant (*ex* Song Imperial collection) (similar to Sanmudi specimen)[36]

Not extant (*ex* Song Imperial collection) (similar to Yangze specimen)[37]

Ogawa collection, Japan; enigmatic inscription (possibly forged) (transitional to group IV)[38]

Dr. Paul Singer collection, Summit, N.J.[39]

III. *Large specimens with* xuan, *molded mask-derived decoration motif*

Baijiacun (H 44.5 cm)

Beifengtan, first *nao* (H 84 cm [fragmentary]) (sculptural tigers inside)

Beifengtan, second *nao* (H 89 cm)

Chenjiawan (H 71.8 cm)

Feijiahe (a.k.a. Binhu) (H 74 cm)

Gaochong (H 48 cm)

Goutouba (H 44 cm)

Nihequ (H 49.5 cm) (see fig. 59)

Shiguzhaishan, first *nao* (H 66.7 cm)

Shiguzhaishan, 2 "tiger *nao*" (not a set) (H 70, 69.5 cm)

Shiguzhaishan, first "elephant *nao*" (H 70 cm)

Shiguzhaishan, second "elephant *nao*" (H 40 cm [fragmentary])

Xinhuicun (H 56 cm)

Yueshanpu (H 103.5 cm) (see fig. 58)

    *Unprovenienced specimens*

Palace Museum, Beijing (*ex* von Lochow collection) (H 64.5 cm)[40]

Palace Museum, Beijing (H 68.9 cm [fragmentary])[41]

Shanghai Museum (H 66 cm)[42]

32. Kane 1974–75, 89, fig. 27.

33. Chen Mengjia 1955–1956, pt. 5:125, pl. 12 right.

34. Kane 1974–75, 89, fig. 26; Hayashi 1984 2:380, *shō* 6.

35. Ma Chengyuan 1981, pl. 21.1.　　　　36. *Bogutulu* 26:41a/b.

37. Ibid. 26:42a.

38. Umehara 1940, pl. 20.5; Hayashi 1984 2:381, *shō* 13.

39. Unpublished.　　　　40. Kane 1974–75, 89, fig. 25.

41. *Gugong Bowuyuan Yuankan* 1 (1958), front cover.

42. *Wenwu* 1959 (10):35., photo, p. 33, fig. 3.

Royal Ontario Museum, Toronto (H 67 cm)[43]

Not extant (*ex* Song Imperial collection) (3 separate pieces)[44]

IV. *Specimens featuring the standard* zhong *decoration scheme*

A. *With vertical lines in center of* zheng

Banqiao (H 43.5 cm)

Liling (H 29.8 cm) (see fig. 66)

*Unprovenienced specimens*

Hunan Provincial Museum, Changsha, inv. no. Yin(8)4:14 (H 34.4 cm)[45]

Hunan Provincial Museum, Changsha, inv. no. Yin(8)4:5 (H 42.8 cm)[46]

National Museum, Copenhagen (H 34.5 cm)[47]

Japanese private collection (H 38.5 cm)[48]

B. *With tongue-shaped motif in center of* zheng

Touba (H 34.5 cm)

Xiajiashan (H 32 cm)

Zhongshan (H 36 cm) (see fig. 67)

Xinglongcun (H 42.3 cm) (anomalous decor)

*Unprovenienced specimens*

Hunan Provincial Museum, Changsha, inv. no. Yin(8)4:2 (H 35.8 cm)[49]

Art Institute of Chicago (*ex* Buckingham collection) (ornament of "eyebrow-shaped" snakes)[50]

Tenri Sankōkan, Tenri (H 34.9 cm)[51]

Not extant (*ex* Song Imperial collection) (ornament as on the Chicago piece)[52]

Hunan Provincial Museum, Changsha (H 52.7 cm) (anomalous tiger decor)[53]

Hunan Provincial Museum, Changsha, inv. no. Yin(8)4:71 (H 25.5 cm) (anomalous number and distribution of *mei*; Eastern Zhou regional piece?)[54]

C. *With flat central* zheng *panel*

Changhe (H 42 cm)

Dengjiatiancun (H 40.2 cm)

Huangzhu (H 40.5 cm) (see fig. 68)

Kewang Damiaoxia (H 40.8 cm)

---

43. Chen Mengjia 1955–1956, pt. 5:125, pl. 12 left.
44. *Bogutulu* 26:37a/b, 40a/b, 47a/b.
45. Gao Zhixi 1984a, 30; no illustration published.
46. Gao Zhixi 1984a, fig. 2.3.   47. Hayashi 1984 2:381, *shō* 15.
48. Ibid., *shō* 20.   49. Gao Zhixi 1984a, pl. 9.4 (photo).
50. Chen Mengjia 1955–56, pt. 5, pl. 13 left; Kane 1974–75, 89, fig. 91; Hayashi 1984 2:381, *shō* 18.
51. Hayashi 1984 2:381, *shō* 17; *Yayoi-no seidōki*, cat. no. 21.
52. *Bogutulu* 23:14a/b.
53. Gao Zhixi 1984a, 30, very blurred photo, pl. 10.1.
54. Photo: Gao Zhixi 1984a, pl. 9.1.

Lanshi (H 32 cm)

Linkesuo (H 46 cm)

Maba (H 37.5 cm)

Qianshan Gongshe (H 50 cm)

Quankoucun (H 43.9 cm)

Shenze (H 27 cm [fragmentary])

Taihe (H 55 cm)

Tian'eshan (H 38 cm)

Youzhencun (H 39.5 cm)

Yulongshan (H 51 cm)

*Unprovenienced specimens*

Hunan Provincial Museum, Changsha, inv. no. Yin(8)4:16 (H 32.9 cm)[55]

Hunan Provincial Museum, Changsha, inv. no. Yin(8)4:6 (H 35.1 cm)[56]

Hunan Provincial Museum, Changsha, inv. no. Yin(8)4:9 (H 40.6 cm)[57]

Japanese private collection (H 47.8 cm)[58]

McAlpin Collection (H 41 cm)[59]

Hunan Provincial Museum, Changsha, inv. no. Yin(8)4:19 (H 36.7 cm) (note "eyebrow-shaped" ornament)[60]

D. *With decoration in faint raised lines*[61]

Beitang (H 36 cm) [?]

Jiashan (H 35 cm) [?]

Luofang (H 36.9 cm) [?]

*Unprovenienced specimens*

Hunan Provincial Museum, Changsha, inv. no. Yin(8)4:4 (H 38.8 cm)[62]

Hunan Provincial Museum, Changsha, inv. no. Yin(8)4:7 (H 43.9 cm)[63]

Hunan Provincial Museum, Changsha, inv. no. Yin(8)4:79 (H 43.9 cm) [?][64]

Hunan Provincial Museum, Changsha, inv. no. Yin(8)4:17 (H 32.3 cm) [?][65]

Hunan Provincial Museum, Changsha, inv. no. Yin(8)4:84 (H 47.4 cm) [?][66]

Hunan Provincial Museum, Changsha, inv. no. Yin(8)4:19 (H 36.7 cm) [?][67]

Private collection, New York (H 31.5 cm)[68]

Arthur M. Sackler Gallery, Washington, D.C. (H 32.6 cm) (see fig. 70)[69]

55. Gao Zhixi 1984a, 32, fig. 2.4.
56. Gao Zhixi 1984a, pl. 9.3.
57. Gao Zhixi 1984a, 32, fig. 2.5.
58. Hayashi 1984 2:381, *shō* 21.
59. Chen Mengjia 1955–56, pt. 5, pl. 13 right.
60. Gao Zhixi 1984a, 32, fig. 2.6 (blurred photo).
61. The published photos of all provenienced and some of the unprovenienced pieces listed are so blurred that their affiliation with this type is not completely certain.
62. Gao Zhixi 1984a, photo, fig. 3.
63. Ibid., pl. 10.2.
64. Ibid., fig. 2.2.
65. Ibid., pl. 9.2.
66. Ibid., fig. 2.1.
67. Ibid., fig. 2.6.
68. Chen Mengjia 1955–56, pt. 5, pl. 14.
69. Hayashi 1984 2:382, *shō* 26.

Zhang Naiji collection (H 50.8 cm)[70]

E. *With simplified hatched ornaments, studded* zhuan
Nanya, set of 2 (H 38.2, 32 cm)

## EARLY *YONGZHONG*
## (WESTERN ZHOU THROUGH EARLY SPRINGS AND AUTUMNS PERIOD)

I. *Earliest types, ca. mid–Western Zhou*

A. *Like southern* nao *IV-C, but with* wo

*Specimens of south Chinese provenience*
Gaotun (H 48.7 cm)
Hongjiaqiao, set of 2 (H 48, 45.4 cm)
Huaibaoshicun, 3 bells (not one set) (H 29.5, 29, 26 cm)
Pingru (H. 45.3 cm) (see fig. 69)

*Specimens from north China*
Beiqiao, first *yongzhong* (H 39.8 cm)
Mawangcun, set of 2 (H 45, 43.5 cm)[71]
Qucun tomb no. 7092
Yangjiacun, third set, set of 4
Zhuangbai hoard no. 1, fifth set, set of 2 (H 37.5, 36.5 cm)[72]

*Unprovenienced specimens*
Hunan Provincial Museum, Changsha, inv. no. Yin(8)4:15 (H 31.4 cm)[73]
Hunan Provincial Museum, Changsha, inv. no. Yin(8)4:80 (H 45.8 cm)[74]
Hunan Provincial Museum, Changsha, inv. no. Dong(8)1:56 (H 50.2 cm)[75]
Japanese private collection (H 33 cm)[76]

B. *Like southern* nao *IV-D, but with* wo

*Specimens of south Chinese provenience*
Binyang (H 41 cm)
Chang'anxiang (H 44 cm)

*Specimens from Shaanxi*
Beiqiao, second *yongzhong* (H 39.8 cm)
Guozhen (H 22.4 cm)

---

70. Chen Mengjia 1955–56, pt. 5, pl. 15 left.
71. In the original report, they are designated as the fourth set of *yongzhong* (nos. 18–19).
72. In *Shaanxi chutu Shang Zhou qingtongqi*, vol. 2, this set of uninscribed bells is labeled as "Type VI."
73. Gao Zhixi 1984a, 31, photo, pl. 11.3.
74. Ibid., p. 31, fig. 1.2.
75. Ibid., fig. 1.3.
76. Hayashi 1984 2:382, *shō* 29.

Mawangcun hoard no. 2, 3 pieces (possibly from 2 sets) (H 46.5, 44, 29.3 cm)[77]

Qijiacun hoard no. 2, set of 2 (1 H 60 cm)

Qizhen hoard no. 2 (H 50 cm)

Zhuangbai hoard no. 1 * (FIRST XING) (H 48 cm) (see fig. 19)

Zhuangbai hoard no. 1, fourth set (H 47, 41.5, 38 cm)[78]

*Unprovenienced specimens*

Sen'oku Hakkokan (Sumitomo collection), Kyōto (H 39.1 cm)[79]

British Museum, London (H 45 cm)[80]

C. *With studded* zhuan

*Specimens of south Chinese provenience*

Beiliu (H 29.5 cm)

Chengtan (H 44.3 cm) (see fig. 71)

Datang (H 34.5 cm)

Dujiacun (H 44.8 cm)

Jishui, set (?) of 3 (H 43, 32, 30.5 cm)

Lianhua (H 33.5 cm)

Malong (H 46.3 cm)

Pengjiaqiao, set of 2 (H 29, 26 cm)

Qiaodang (H 38.5 cm)

Qingjiang (H 20 cm)

Sanlian (no illustration published)

Xiangtan, 2 separate pieces (H 46.7, 39.1 cm)

*Specimens from north China*

Dingjiagou hoard no. 1, first set (H 37.5, 33.5 cm)

Dongjucun * (enigmatic inscription) (H 27 cm)

Liujiacun (H 26.5 cm)

Mawangcun tomb no. 2, set of 4 (H 54, 51.3, 48.5, 46 cm)[81]

Puducun, set of 3 (H. 48.5, 44, 38 cm) (see fig. 72)

Rujiazhuang tomb no. 1, set of 3 (H 31.7, 30.5, 23.3 cm) (typologically some-what heterogeneous)

Weizhuang, set of 3 (H 41.7–25.8 cm)

Yangjiacun, first set, set of 2 (H ca. 50 cm)

77. In the original report, these pieces constitute the second and third set (nos. 23, 20–21) among the ten *yongzhong* found in the hoard.

78. In *Shaanxi chutu Shang Zhou qingtongqi*, vol. 2, these three bells are designated as "Type V."

79. *Gakki*, cat. no. 3.

80. Rawson 1987, 83, cat no. 28.

81. In the original report, this is designated as the fifth set of *yongzhong* (nos. 14–17).

Zhuangbai hoard no. 1, sixth set ★ (enigmatic inscription),[82] set of 2
   (H 48, 45.5 cm)
Zhuyuangou tomb no. 7, set of 3 (H 34, 33, 28.8 cm)
   *Unprovenienced specimens*
★FIRST ZHA–*yongzhong* (dispersed set):
   1 Sen'oku Hakkokan (Sumitomo collection), Kyōto (H 44.9 cm)[83]
   1 Palace Museum, Beijing[84]
Museum of Fine Arts, Boston[85]
Hunan Provincial Museum, Changsha, inv. no. Yin(8)4:85 (H 42.2 cm)[86]
Hunan Provincial Museum, Changsha, inv. no. Yin(8)4:69 (H 36.3 cm)[87]
Japanese private collection (H 43.7 cm)[88]

II. *Later Western Zhou and early Springs and Autumns period* yongzhong *from north China*
   A. *With raised-line* zhuan, *volutes in* gu
   Baijiacun ★ (WUSI HU) (H 28 cm)
   Haosihe ★ (NI) set of 4 (H 59, 55.5, 53.5, 50.5 cm)
   Hongxing Commune ★ (YING HOU) (H 26 cm) (see also Unprovenienced
      Specimens)
   Qiangjiacun hoard no. 1 ★ (SHI CHENG) (H 76.5 cm) (see fig. 73)
   Qizhen hoard no. 1 ★ (YONGXIANG) (H 19 cm)
   Xigaoquan tomb no. 1 (H 23 cm)
   Zhangjiapo tomb no. 163 ★ (XING SHU), 3 pieces (part of larger set?) (largest,
      H 37.5 cm)

      *Unprovenienced specimens*
   Sen'oku Hakkokan (Sumitomo collection), Kyōto ★ (SECOND ZHA)
      (H 25.1 cm)[89]
   Sen'oku Hakkokan (Sumitomo collection), Kyōto ★ (CHU GONG JIA?), 3 pieces
      (H 53.2, 44.1, 36.7 cm) (no. 2 stylistically heterogeneous)[90]
   Sen'oku Hakkokan (Sumitomo collection), Kyōto ★ (JI HOU) (H 26.8 cm)
      (allegedly from Shouguang, Shandong; possibly forged)[91]

---

82. As grouped in *Shaanxi chutu Shang Zhou qingtongqi*, vol. 2, this set of bells is labeled as "Type VII."
83. *Gakki*, cat. no. 4; cf. also Rong Geng 1941, vol. 2, pl. 953; Chen Mengjia 1955–56, pt. 6:120.
84. This bell remains unpublished.
85. Chen Mengjia 1955–56, pt. 5, pl. 15 right; Hayashi 1984 2:382, *shō* 25.
86. Gao Zhixi 1984a, 31, photo, fig. 1.1.    87. Ibid., no illustration.
88. Hayashi 1984 2:382, *shō* 24.    89. Sen'oku Hakkokan, *Gakki*, cat. no. 5.
90. Sen'oku Hakkokan, *Gakki*, cat. nos. 10–12; cf. also Rong Geng 1941, vol. 2, pls. 945–46. Further photos in Mase 1986, 88.
91. Sen'oku Hakkokan, *Gakki*, cat. no. 8; cf. also Rong Geng 1941, vol. 2, pl. 951.

Shaanxi Provincial Museum, Xi'an ★ (XIAN) (H 49 cm)[92]

Shodō Hakubutsukan, Tōkyō, ★ (YING HOU) (see also under Hongxing)[93]

B. *With pair of L-shaped downward-facing dragons on gu*

Baozigou ★ (NANGONG HU) (H 54 cm) (see fig. 33)

Lijialou, 2 sets (10 and 9 pieces) (fig. 76)

Qijiacun hoard no. 1, first set ★ (ZUO), set of 8 (H 52–21 cm)

Qijiacun hoard no. 1, second set ★ (ZHONG YI), set of 8 (H 49–22.5 cm) (see fig. 18)

Qizhen hoard no. 1 ★ (NING) (H 54 cm) (see also unprovenienced specimens)

Taigongmiao, 5 pieces of 1 set ★ (QIN GONG) (H 48–27.6 cm) (fig. 111)

Yangjiacun hoard no. 1, second set, 4 bells ★ (MAI) (see also unprovenienced pieces)

Zhoujiahe (H 48.4 cm)

Zhuangbai hoard no. 1, second set ★ (SECOND XING, i.e., sets II/IV), 7 pieces extant (H 64.6–28.0 cm)[94]

Zhuangbai hoard no. 1, third set ★ (THIRD XING), 6 pieces extant (H 70.0–24.5 cm) (see fig. 74).[95]

*Unprovenienced specimens*

Dispersed sets

★ GUO SHU LÜ–*yongzhong* (allegedly excavated in Chang'an [Shaanxi]; seven pieces known through rubbings)[96]

    1 Shodō Hakubutsukan, Tōkyō (H 60 cm)

    1 Palace Museum, Beijing

    1 Shanghai Museum (H 53.1 cm)

    1 Sen'oku Hakkokan (Sumitomo collection), Kyōto (H 36 cm)

    1 Shandong Provincial Museum, Jinan (unpublished)

★ LIANGQI–*yongzhong* (allegedly discovered in 1940 at Rencun, Fufeng [Shaanxi])

    3 Shanghai Museum (H 55.4, 53.5, 38.1 cm)[97]

    1 Nanjing Municipal Museum[98]

92. *Qingtongqi Tushi*, 120.

93. Nakamura 1934; *Wenwu* 1977 (8):27–28 (photo, rubbing).

94. As grouped in *Shaanxi chutu Shang Zhou qingtongqi*, vol. 2, the four larger bells are labeled as "Type II" and the three smaller ones, inscribed with an abbreviated version of the text, as "Type IV."

95. As grouped in *Shaanxi chutu Shang Zhou qingtongqi*, vol. 2, this set of bells is labeled as "Type III."

96. Yoshimoto 1986, 76–78, photos of the first four. Cf. also: Sen'oku Hakkokan, *Gakki*, cat. no. 6, Rong Geng 1941, vol. 2, pl. 947 (same piece); for the Shanghai Museum piece, cf. *Shanghai Bowuguan Zhongguo qingtongqi chenlie*, 22.

97. One of them is depicted in *Shanghai Bowuguan-cang Shang Zhou qingtongqi* 1:160, 2:58f, and another in *Bronzi dell'antica Cina*, 130–31 (cat. no. 46).

98. *Nanjing Shi Bowuguan*, 6 (photo).

1 Musée Guimet, Paris (H 48.5 cm)[99]

★ KE–*yongzhong* (allegedly unearthed in 1890 at Rencun, Fufeng [Shaanxi]; 6 pieces known through rubbings)
    1 Fujii Yūrinkan, Kyōto (H 54.5 cm)[100]
    1 Shandong Provincial Museum, Jinan (*ex* Shandong Provincial Library)[101]
    2 Shanghai Museum (one H 38.3 cm)[102]

★ NING–*yongzhong* (see also Qizhen hoard no. 1)[103]
    1 Shanghai Museum (H 69.5 cm)
    1 Shodō Hakubutsukan, Tōkyō (H 67 cm)
    1 Sen'oku Hakkokan (Sumitomo collection), Kyōto (H 65 cm)

★ RUI GONG–*yongzhong*
    1 National Palace Museum, Taibei[104]
    1 Kurokawa Kobunka Kenkyūjo, Nishinomiya (H 34 cm)[105]

SHIFU–*yongzhong*
    2 Palace Museum, Beijing[106]
    1 Hunan Provincial Museum, Changsha[107]

★ XI ZHONG–*yongzhong* (6 pieces known through rubbings)
    1 Sen'oku Hakkokan (Sumitomo collection), Kyōto (H 40 cm)[108]
    1 Asian Art Museum, San Francisco (*ex* Brundage collection)[109]
    1 Shanghai Museum[110]

Cleveland Museum of Art (*ex* Ellsworth collection, New York) ★ (MAI) (H 65.1 cm) (see also Yangjiacun hoard no. 1)[111]

Japanese private collection ★ (LUKANG) (H 23.2 cm)[112]

National Palace Museum, Taibei ★ (HU) (better known as "Zongzhou-*zhong*")[113]

Tianjin Museum (H 32 cm) ★ (SHU LÜ YUFU)[114]

Sen'oku Hakkokan (Sumitomo collection), Kyōto[115]

---

99. Élisséeff 1947 (photos).      100. *Yūrinkan seika*, pl. 4.
101. *Wenwu Cankao Ziliao* 1951 (8):105–06; no illustration published.
102. One of these is published in *Jadequell und Wolkenmeer*, 96–97 (cat. no. 29) (with B-tone bird), another one in *Bronzi dell'antica Cina*, 128–29 (cat. no. 45).
103. Matsui 1984. Photos, pp. 62–64.
104. *Gugong tongqi tulu*, vol. 2, *shang* 239; also in Rong Geng 1941 1:498, 2:952.
105. Hayashi 1984 2:386, *shō* 565.
106. Seen by the writer in 1986; no illustration published. Inscription rubbings of three pieces in Guo Moruo (1958:–/124–126/128).
107. *Wenwu* 1991 (5):86–87. Photo: pl. 7.1; rubbings.
108. Sen'oku Hakkokan, *Gakki*, cat. no. 9; Rong Geng 1941, vol. 2, pl. 949.
109. Lefebvre d'Argencé 1966, pl. 37.
110. *Wenwu Cankao Ziliao* 1957 (2):81 (no illustrations published).
111. Ellsworth 1987, vol. 3, pl. II; partial rubbing.
112. Hayashi 1984 2:386, *shō* 53.
113. *Gugong tongqi tulu*, vol. 2, *shang* 238; also in Rong Geng 1941 1:497, 2:948.
114. *Wenwu* 1964 (9):35, photos, pls. 5.3, 4, rubbing, p. 36, fig. 5, lower middle and left.
115. Hayashi 1984 2:386, *shō* 57.

Formerly Morse Collection, New York (*ex* van Heusden collection) ★ (ZHENG XING SHU) (H 25 cm) (see fig. 76)[116]
Present location unknown ★ (RUO GONG)[117]
Present location unknown, set of 9 (allegedly excavated at Qufu) ★ (LU BEI)[118]
Not extant (*ex* Song Imperial collection) ★ (ZOU)[119]

EARLY *BO* (SHANG THROUGH FIRST HALF OF SPRINGS AND AUTUMNS PERIOD)

I. *With bird-flanges*

Huangjing (H 32.6 cm)
Yingmin (H 38.5 cm)
Zixing (H 49.5 cm)

*Unprovenienced specimens*

Palace Museum, Beijing (H 27.1 cm)[120]
Hunan Provincial Museum, Changsha (H 37.2 cm)[121]
Hunan Provincial Museum, Changsha (H 38.1 cm)[122]
Museum of Hengyang (Hunan) (H 39 cm) (see fig. 78)[123]
Japanese private collection[124]
Fujii Yūrinkan, Kyōto (H 41.5 cm)[125]
Dr. Paul Singer collection, Summit, N.J. (H 43.5 cm)[126]
Arthur M. Sackler Gallery, Washington, D.C. (H 31.3 cm) (see fig. 77)[127]

II. *With tiger-flanges*

*Unprovenienced specimens*

Palace Museum, Beijing (H 45 cm)[128]
Hunan Provincial Museum, Changsha (H 35 cm [fragmentary])[129]
Fujii Yūrinkan, Kyōto[130]
Sen'oku Hakkokan (Sumitomo collection), Kyōto (H 43.9 cm)[131]

116. *Spirit and ritual*, 34; Hayashi 1984 2:386, *shō* 58.
117. Line drawing in Guo Moruo 1958 (*Tu*-222).
118. Wu Shijian 1910.
119. *Kaogutu* (j. 7.2a–4b) depicts five, *Bogutulu* (22: 27b–32a) three pieces; Guo Moruo 1958, 212/61/79.
120. *Wenwu* 1960 (10):58–59.      121. Gao Zhixi 1984a, 30, photo, p. 31.6.
122. Gao Zhixi 1984a, 31, fig. 5 (blurred photo).
123. *Wenwu* 1980 (11):95–96, pl. 8.3.      124. Hayashi 1980, fig. 71.
125. Kane 1974–75, 87, fig. 19; Hayashi 1980, fig. 73.
126. Kane 1974–75, 87, fig. 18.
127. Rong Geng 1941 2:943 (unrestored state); *Art from ritual*, cat. no. 30; Bagley 1987, 537–51 (cat. no. 104).
128. Wang Haiwen 1980, 95; *Kokyū Hakubutsukan*, 69; Hayashi 1980, fig. 68.
129. Gao Zhixi 1984c, pl. 8.3 (photo).      130. Hayashi 1980, fig. 69.
131. *Gakki*, 16; Hayashi 1980, fig. 66.

Shanghai Museum (H 42 cm)[132]
Arthur M. Sackler Gallery, Washington, D.C. (H 38.5 cm) (see fig. 79)[133]
Not extant (*ex* Song Imperial collection)[134]

III. *With lateral flanges joined to suspension device*

Taigongmiao, set of 3 ★ (QIN GONG I) (H 75–64 cm) (see fig. 81)
Yangjiacun hoard no. 1, set of 3 (H 63.5, 57.5, 51.5 cm) (see fig. 80)

*Unprovenienced specimens*

Tianjin Museum ★ (KE) (H 63.5 cm) (allegedly excavated at Rencun, Qishan [Shaanxi])[135]

IV. *With standard* zhong *decoration scheme*

Lijialou, set of 4 (see fig. 82)

*Unprovenienced specimens*

Not extant (*ex* Song Imperial collection) ★ (QIN GONG II)[136]

EARLY *NIUZHONG* (LATE WESTERN ZHOU THROUGH FIRST HALF OF SPRINGS AND AUTUMNS PERIOD)

I. *With decoration in one central panel*

Bajiaolou, 2 (1 H ca. 14 cm)
Guanyang Gucheng, set of 4 (H 25.6–14.7 cm)
Jishiliang, set of 5 (largest, H 14.4 cm)
Liujiadianzi, set of 9 ★ (CHEN DASANGSHI) (largest, H ca. 20 cm)
Shangguocun, 2 sets of 8
Shangcunling, set of 9 (H 23.5–13.4 cm)
Zhuangbai hoard no. 1, set of 7 (H 14.4–9.5 cm)

*Unprovenienced specimens*

National Palace Museum, Taibei (H 21.2 cm)[137]
Present location unknown (H 18.25 cm)[138]

132. *Shanghai Bowuguan-cang qingtongqi*, 63; *Chūgoku Jinmin Kyōwakoku kodai seidōkiten*, cat. no. 45; *Zhongguo gu qingtongqi-xuan*, 46; *The great Bronze Age of China*, 245, photos, pp. 232–33 (cat. no. 58); *Shanghai Bowuguan Zhongguo qingtongqi chenlie*, 22; *Bronzi dell'antica Cina*, 132–33 (cat. no. 47).
133. Rong Geng 1941 2:944; Kane 1974–75, fig. 21; *Art from ritual*, cat. no. 471.
134. *Bogutulu*, 25:13a/b.   135. *Wenwu* 1972 (6):14, pl. 6 (photo).
136. Guo Moruo 1958, 238/289–91/250. Shirakawa, *Kinbun Tsūshaku* 34:1–28. The wood-block illustration of this bell was confused at an early time with that of the Shu Yi–*bo* from Linzi (Shandong), but Shirakawa has convincingly established that the object depicted in the traditional catalogs is indeed the Qin Gong II–*bo*.
137. Hayashi 1984 2:387, *shō* 66.
138. Rong Geng 1941, vol. 2, pl. 968; Hayashi 1980, 48, pl. 81.

II. *With the standard* zhong *decoration scheme*

      Daxin (H 16.7 cm)

        *Unprovenienced specimens*

      Dispersed set (perhaps from Jincun?)

          1 British Museum, London (Seligman Bequest) (H 17 cm)[139]

          3 present location unknown (H 24.8–19.7 cm)[140]

      Art Institute of Chicago (H 34.8 cm) (see fig. 83)

      British Museum, London (*ex* Seligman collection) (H 14 cm)[141]

      National Palace Museum, Taibei, partial set of 3 (H 21.8, 18.5, 14 cm)[142]

      National Palace Museum, Taibei * (ZHU DAZAI)[143]

      Present location unknown[144]

## MUSICAL BELLS FROM LATE SPRINGS AND AUTUMNS THROUGH HAN

I. *Northern stylistic group*

    A. *Late sixth-century style, with mask-shaped ornament composed of small snakes in* gu

        *Unprovenienced specimens*

        * LÜ-*yongzhong*, dispersed set of 13 (allegedly excavated in Ronghe [present-day Wanrong], Shanxi) (reported H 43.9–25.6 cm) (see fig. 100)

          10 Shanghai Museum[145]

          1 British Museum, London (*ex* Eumorfopoulos collection) (H 30.5 cm)[146]

          1 National Palace Museum, Taibei[147]

          1 present location unknown (formerly Fei collection, Wujin)

        Sen'oku Hakkokan (Sumitomo collection), 1 *yongzhong* (H. 32.9 cm)[148]

        Present location unknown (*ex* Yamanaka collection, Ōsaka), 1 *yongzhong*[149]

        Shanghai Museum, 1 *yongzhong* (H 29.4 cm)[150]

        Kunstindustriemuseet, Copenhagen, 1 *bo* (H 21.6 cm)[151]

        Musée Cernuschi, Paris, 1 *niuzhong* (H 24.1 cm)[152]

139. Rawson 1980, 125, fig. 96.       140. White 1934, pl. 172 (no. 507).

141. Hayashi 1984 2:387, *shō* 65. Rawson 1980, 125, fig. 96 right.

142. No. 1: *Gugong tongqi tulu* 1:172, 2:232, pl. *shang* 245. No. 2: 1:295, 2:429, pl. *xia* 474–75; also in Rong Geng 1941 2:966.

143. *Gugong tongqi tulu* 1:170, 2: 227–28, pl. *shang* 240–41; also in Rong Geng 1941 2:965.

144. Rong Geng 1941 2:967.

145. One of them is depicted in *Shanghai Bowuguan-cang Shang Zhou qingtongqi* 1:80, 2:80.

146. Yetts 1929 1:29–43 and 2:43–49; Watson 1962, pl. 69b; Rawson 1987, 87 (cat. no. 33).

147. *Gugong tongqi tulu*, vol. 2, *xia* 463.     148. *Gakki*, no. 13.

149. Umehara 1961, vol. 4, pl. 351; Weber 1973, 226–27.

150. *Ancient Chinese bronzes*, cat. no. 46.

151. Weber 1973, 210–15; photo, p. 213. The inscription on this piece is probably forged.

152. Ibid., 218–21.

Tenri Sankōkan, Tenri, 1 *niuzhong* (H 30 cm)[153]
Present location unknown (*ex* Burnet collection), 1 *niuzhong* (H 24.1 cm)[154]

B. *Fifth-century style, with banked dragon ornaments in* gu

Fenshuiling tomb no. 14, 2 *yongzhong*
Fenshuiling tomb no. 25, set of 5 *yongzhong* (H 35–25 cm)
Fenshuiling tomb no. 269, set of 9 *yongzhong*
Fenshuiling tomb no. 270, set of 8 *yongzhong*
Liulige tomb no. 60, set of 8 *yongzhong*
Liulige tomb no. 75, set of 8 *yongzhong* (see fig. 88)
Luhe tomb no. 7, 2 8-part sets of *yongzhong* (1 set, H. 30.5–14 cm) (see fig. 85)
Xiao'emeishan, set of 4 *yongzhong* (largest, H 74.4 cm)

Changlelu, set of 4 *bo* (H ca. 40–28 cm)
Fenshuiling tomb no. 25, set of 4 *bo* (H 43–32 cm)
Houchuan tomb no. 2040, set of 9 *bo*
Jinshengcun tomb no 251, first set of *bo*, set of 5 (H 41+?–35.8 cm)
Jinshengcun tomb no. 251, second set of *bo*, set of 14 (H 29.6–11.3 cm)
Liulige tomb *jia*, first set of *bo*
Liulige tomb no. 60, first set of *bo*, set of 4
Liulige tomb no. 75, set of 4 *bo*
Luhe tomb no. 7, set of 4 *bo* (H 29–22.4 cm) (see fig. 86)
Shanbiaozhen, first set of *bo*, set of 4
Shangmacun tomb no. 1004, set of 9 *bo* (H 31–17 cm)

Liulige tomb *jia*, second set of *bo* (special type), set of 9
Liulige tomb no. 60, second set of *bo* (special type), set of 8
Shanbiaozhen tomb no. 1, second set of *bo* (special type), set of 9

Changlelu, set of 9 *niuzhong* (H ca. 28–13 cm)
Dadian tomb no. 1, set of 9 *niuzhong* (H 24.2–14.9 cm)
Dadian tomb no. 2, set of 9 *niuzhong* ★ (JU SHU ZHONG ZI PING) (H 26–13 cm)
Fenshuiling tomb no. 14, set of 8 *niuzhong*
Fenshuiling tomb no. 25, set of 9 *niuzhong* (H 28.5–16 cm)
Fenshuiling tomb no. 269, set of 9 *niuzhong*
Fenshuiling tomb no. 270, set of 9 *niuzhong* (H 16.2–30.5 cm)
Jinpingshan, set of 9 *niuzhong*
Liulige tomb no. 60, set of 9 *niuzhong*
Liulige tomb no. 75, 4 *niuzhong*
Liulige tomb no. 80, set of 9 *niuzhong*

153. *Yayoi-no seidōki*, cat. no. 19.
154. Watson 1962, pl. 69c; Weber 1973, 216–17. Weber mistakenly asserts that this bell is now in the British Museum.

Luhe tomb no. 7, set of 8 *niuzhong* (H 15–9 cm) (see fig. 87)

Miaoqiancun, set of 9 *niuzhong* (H 30–14 cm)

Shangmacun tomb no. 13, set of 9 *niuzhong* (H 37–20 cm)

   *Unprovenienced specimens*

Dispersed set of *yongzhong*, 6 pieces documented[155]

   1 Asian Art Museum, San Francisco (*ex* Brundage collection) (H 63 cm)

   1 Art Institute, Minneapolis (*ex* Pillsbury collection) (H 58.4 cm)

   1 Nelson Gallery, Kansas City (H 57.2 cm)

   1 Falk collection, New York (H 34.3 cm)

   1 British Museum, London (H 28.2 cm)[156]

   1 Eguchi collection, Ōsaka (H 22.6 cm)

Dispersed set of *bo*, 5 pieces documented (see fig. 84)[157]

   2 Arthur M. Sackler Museum, Cambridge, Mass. (H 67.1, 49 cm)

   1 Rijksmuseum, Amsterdam (H 59.2 cm)

   1 British Museum (*ex* Stoclet collection, Brussels) (H 54 cm)[158]

   1 formerly Staatliche Museen Berlin (destroyed?) (H 36.1 cm)

Dispersed set of *bo*, 2 bells documented[159]

   1 Asian Art Museum, San Francisco (*ex* Brundage collection)

   1 Art Institute, Minneapolis (*ex* Pillsbury collection)

Dispersed set of *bo* (3 pieces documented)[160]

   1 Freer Gallery, Washington, D.C. (H 66.4 cm)

   1 Art Institute of Chicago (*ex* Buckingham collection) (H 62.2 cm)

   1 Arthur M. Sackler Museum, Cambridge, Mass. (H 54.9 cm)

Dispersed set of *bo* (4 pieces documented)[161]

   1 Art Institute, Minneapolis (*ex* Pillsbury collection) (H 26 cm)

   1 St. Louis Art Museum (H 26 cm.)

   1 Museum of Eastern Art, Oxford (H 15.2 cm)

   1 Los Angeles County Museum of Art (H 17.4 cm)[162]

Arthur M. Sackler Museum, Cambridge, Mass. (*ex* Winthrop collection), 1 *bo* (H 66 cm)[163]

Royal Ontario Museum, Toronto, 1 *bo* (H 25.2 cm)[164]

---

155. See Weber 1973, 300–311, for references to five of the six pieces.
156. Watson 1963, pl. 41b.
157. Weber 1973, 48–67; for more references, see Weber, nn. to p. 38.
158. Also in Rawson 1987, 89 (cat. no. 35).
159. Weber 1973, 312–17 (*q.v.* for further references).
160. Ibid., 254–60 (*q.v.* for further references).
161. The first three are ibid., 242–43.      162. *Ancient ritual bronzes of China*, cat. no. 42.
163. Weber 1973, 238–41.      164. Ibid., 244–50.

Museum of Far Eastern Antiquities, Stockholm (*ex* Hultmark collection), 1 *bo* (H 66 cm)[165]

Arthur M. Sackler Gallery, Washington, D.C. (*ex* C. T. Loo collection), 1 *bo* (H 38.1 cm)[166]

Arthur M. Sackler Gallery, Washington, D.C. (*ex* Holmes collection), 1 *bo* (H 19.3 cm)[167]

Arthur M. Sackler Gallery, Washington, D.C., 1 *bo* (H 41.8 cm)[168]

Palace of St. Michael and St. George, Corfù (Greece), (*ex* Manos collection), 1 *bo* (H 34 cm)[169]

Dispersed set of *bo* (allegedly from Jincun; similar to Changlelu bells) (H 49.5–36.6 cm)[170]

> 1 Arthur M. Sackler Gallery, Washington, D.C. (H 36.6 cm)[171]
> 1 Sano Bijutsukan, Shizuoka[172]

c. *Mid- to late Warring States period style, with ornament in wide receding panel*

Zangjiazhuang, set of 7 *bo* ★ (JU GONGSUN CHAO ZI)

Jincun tomb no. 7, set of 14 *niuzhong* ★ (BIAO) (H 32–12.6 cm) (now dispersed) (see fig. 89)[173]

Sanji, set of 14 *niuzhong*

Xianggangshan, set of 14 *niuzhong*

Zangjiazhuang, set of 9 *niuzhong* ★ (JU GONGSUN CHAO ZI) (see fig. 90)

> *Unprovenienced specimens*

Fujita Bijutsukan, Ōsaka, 1 *niuzhong*[174]

National Palace Museum, Taibei, 1 *bo*[175]

Royal Ontario Museum, Toronto, set of 9 *niuzhong* (H 26.7–13.3 cm) (allegedly from Jincun)[176]

Present location unknown, set of 3 *niuzhong* (H 22.4–20.3 cm) (allegedly from Jincun)[177]

165. Sirén 1929, pl. 106; *Bulletin of the Museum of Far Eastern Antiquities* 6 (1934), pl. 27; Karlgren 1948, pl. 36 (partial rubbing and drawing, pp. 18–19); Karlgren 1961, pl. 39; Umehara 1961 1:3, pl. 195; Weber 1973, 292–99 (restored).
166. Weber 1973, 232–37 (*q.v.* for further references).
167. Ibid., 262–67 (*q.v.* for further references).
168. *Art from ritual*, cat. no. 62.
169. *Wenwu Tiandi* 1985 (2):62–63. Photo: inside back cover.
170. White 1934, pl. 176A.
171. *Art from ritual*, cat. no. 64.
172. Hayashi Minao, personal communication, 1988.
173. Twelve pieces are now in the Sen'oku Hakkokan and two in the Royal Ontario Museum.
174. Sahara 1984, 86, fig. 17.
175. *Gugong tongqi tulu* 2:237, pl. *shang* 250.
176. White 1934, pl. 171. no. 506.
177. Ibid., pl. 176 right, no. 503.

Present location unknown, 1 *niuzhong* (H 32 cm), and fragments of 2 others (allegedly from Jincun)[178]

Present location unknown (H 12.7 cm) (allegedly from Jincun)[179]

Present location unknown, 1 *niuzhong* (H 16.5 cm) (allegedly from Jincun)[180]

Present location unknown, 1 *niuzhong* (H 30.5 cm) (allegedly from Jincun)[181]

Present location unknown, 2 *niuzhong* (H. 31.8, 29.2 cm) (allegedly from Jincun)[182]

Present location unknown, 2 *niuzhong* (H. 31.5, 16 [fragment] cm; unornamented) (allegedly from Jincun)[183]

D. *Qin and Han type, with inlaid or gilded decoration*

Qin Shihuangling, 1 *niuzhong* ★ (YUEFU) (H 13.3 cm) (see fig. 91)

Xianyang, *niuzhong* (number uncertain)

   *Unprovenienced specimens*

Sen'oku Hakkokan (Sumitomo collection), Kyōto, 1 *niuzhong* (H 23.1 cm)[184]

II. *Southern stylistic group*

A. *Sixth to fifth century style, with decoration pattern of relieved hooks*

Jiulidun, set of 4 *yongzhong*

Leigudun tomb no. 1 ★ (ZENG HOU YI) (45 *yongzhong* belonging to at least 3 sets) (see figs. 1, 11)

Leigudun tomb no. 2, 28 *yongzhong*. First group, 8 pieces; second group, 20 pieces (see fig. 95)

Xiasi tomb no. 2, set of 26 *yongzhong* ★ (WANGSUN GAO) (H 122.0–24.9 cm) (see fig. 21)

Ximennei, 12-part set of *yongzhong* ★ (CAI HOU) (H 79–48 cm) (see fig. 26)

Beishanding, set of 5 *bo* ★ (SHENLIU) (H 31.8–23.3 cm)

Chengqiao tomb no. 2, set of 5 *bo* (H 21.5–19 cm)

Leigudun tomb no. 1, 1 *bo* ★ (CHU WANG XIONG ZHANG) (see fig. 20)

Ximennei, set of 8 *bo* ★ (CAI HOU) (H 40.5–28.5 cm) (see fig. 27)

Beishanding, set of 7 *niuzhong* ★ (SHENLIU) (H 25–14.5 cm)

Chengqiao tomb no. 2, set of 7 *niuzhong* ★ (ZHESHANG) (H 27–17.5 cm)

Ximennei, set of 9 *niuzhong* (H 28–16.5 cm) (see fig. 28)

Xinhua ★ (JING) (H 38 cm) (morphologically abnormal bell)

178. Ibid., pl. 174, no. 510.
179. Ibid., pl. 175 right, no. 511.
180. Ibid., pl. 175 left, no. 512.
181. Ibid., pl. 173 right, no. 504.
182. Ibid., pl. 170 left, no. 509.
183. Ibid., pl. 173 left (photo), no. 508.
184. Sen'oku Hakkokan, *Gakki*, 39, pl. 67.

*Unprovenienced specimens*

★ ZHEJIAN-*yongzhong*, dispersed set of 11 (or more)
   1 Palace Museum, Beijing[185]
   1 Shanghai Museum (H 28.8 cm)[186]
   2 National Palace Museum, Taibei[187]
Asian Art Museum, San Francisco (*ex* Brundage collection) ★ (WANGSUN YIZHE)[188]
Shanghai Museum, 1 *yongzhong* ★ (ZHU GONG LE) (H 50.5 cm)[189]
Shanghai Museum, 1 *yongzhong* ★ (ZHU GONG KENG), 4 pieces documented
   (1 H 38.2 cm) (see fig. 92)[190]
Shanghai Museum, 1 *yongzhong* ★ (ZHU GONG HUA) (H 36 cm)[191]
Shanghai Museum, 1 *yongzhong* (allegedly from Jincun)[192]

Museum of Chinese History, Beijing (on loan from Shanghai Museum), 1 *bo* ★
   (LING) (H 67 cm)[193]
National Palace Museum, Taibei, 1 *bo*[194]
National Palace Museum, Taibei, 1 *bo* ★ (XIONG YUAN) (H 32 cm)[195]
Not extant (*ex* Song Imperial collection), set of 6 *bo* ★ (SONG GONG)[196]

Palace Museum, Beijing, 1 *niuzhong* ★ (YU WANGZI JIONG?)[197]
Japanese private collection, 1 *niuzhong* ★ (CHU WANG GAN)[198]
Shanghai Museum, 1 *niuzhong* (H 22.5 cm) ★ (CHOU? -ER) (4 pieces known
   through rubbings)[199]
Shanghai Museum, partial set of 3 *niuzhong* ★ (ZI ZHANG) (1 H 21.3 cm) (7 pieces
   known through rubbings)[200]

B. *Sixth to fifth century style, with flat dragon-bands*
   Hougudui, set of 8 *bo* ★ (FAN ZI)

185. No illustration published.
186. *Shanghai Bowuguan-cang Shang Zhou qingtongqi* 1:77, 2:74; Ma Chengyuan 1979.
187. *Gugong tongqi tulu*, vol. 2, *shang* 240 and *xia* 464. The latter piece also in Rong Geng 1941, vol. 2, pl. 957.
188. Rong Geng 1941 2:502.
189. *Shanghai Bowuguan-cang Shang Zhou qingtongqi* 1:83, 2:84f.
190. Ibid. 1:81, 2:81 (one specimen only).
191. Ibid. 1:82, 2:82; also in Rong Geng 1941, vol. 2, pl. 954.
192. *Ancient Chinese bronzes*, cat. no. 47.
193. Rong Geng 1941 1:509; photo, 2:969; *Shanghai Bowuguan-cang qingtongqi* 1:85, 2:88–89.
194. Rong Geng 1941, vol. 2, pl. 974; *Gugong tongqi tulu* 2:238, pl. *shang* 251.
195. Rong Geng 1941, vol. 2, fig. 971; *Gugong tongqi tulu* 2:425–27, pl. *xia* 470–72.
196. *Bogutulu*, 22:32b–42b.
197. Yang Yinliu 1980 vol. 1, pl. 21 (photo); Zhao Shigang 1987 (bell-face rubbing).
198. Rong Geng 1941 2:964.
199. *Shanghai Bowuguan-cang qingtongqi* 1:79, 2:78f.
200. Rong Geng 1941 2:963; *Shanghai Bowuguan-cang qingtongqi* 1:84, 2:86f.

Chengqiao tomb no. 1, set of 9 *niuzhong* ★ (GONGWU ZANGSUN) (H 22.5–14.5 cm)

Hougudui, set of 9 *niuzhong* ★ (FAN ZI)

Jiuxian, incomplete set of 6 *niuzhong* ★ (inscription deliberately effaced) (H 23.9–13.7 cm)

Leigudun tomb no. 1, 19 *niuzhong* ★ (ZENG HOU YI) (unornamented)

Xian Zhuanwachang, set of 13 *niuzhong* (no size measurements; wt. 1250–250 g)

Xiasi tomb no. 1, set of 9 *niuzhong* ★ (donor's name effaced) (H 21.1–11.5 cm) (see fig. 93)

    *Unprovenienced specimens*

★ ZHEDIAO-*niuzhong* (dispersed set) (see fig. 94)

      1 Palace Museum, Beijing[201]

      8 Tōhata collection, Hyōgo[202]

      2 Sen'oku Hakkokan (Sumitomo collection), Kyōto (H 25.7, 18.6 cm)[203]

      1 Shandong Provincial Museum[204]

      1 Shanghai Museum (H 25.3 cm)[205]

C. *Warring States period style, with decomposed dragon-derived ornaments*

Changtaiguan tomb no. 1, set of 13 *niuzhong*, 1 ★ (JINGLI) (H 30.2–12.9 cm) (see fig. 102)[206]

Tianxingguan, 4 *niuzhong* (upper portion unornamented) (see fig. 96)

Xiaotianxi tomb no. 1, set of 14 *niuzhong* (gilded) (see fig. 97)

Yangmei, set of 9 *niuzhong*

    *Unprovenienced specimens*

Royal Ontario Museum, Toronto, set of 7 *niuzhong* (allegedly from Jincun)[207]

*MINGQI* BELLS (WARRING STATES THROUGH SIX DYNASTIES)

I. *Warring States period*

    Changtaiguan tomb no. 2, set of 13 wooden *niuzhong* (H 11–23 cm)

    Chongxian tomb no. 1, 4 pottery *yongzhong* (H 27–25.3 cm)

    Huanghu, 2 miniature *goudiao*-like bells (H 8, 4.5 cm)

    Huangjiashan, 45+ pottery *mingqi* bells: 13 *yongzhong* (largest, H 43.2 cm), 3 *niuzhong* (1 fragment, H 14.6 cm), 12 *goudiao* (largest, H 44.7 cm), 2 *chunyu* (1

---

201. No photo published.
202. Asahara 1988b (photos). Tone measurements in Takahashi 1988.
203. *Gakki*, cat. nos. 14–15. Tone measurements in Takahashi 1988.
204. *Wenwu Cankao Ziliao* 1951 (8):105–06. No photo published.
205. Rong Geng 1941 2:963; *Shanghai Bowuguan-cang qingtongqi* 1:78, 2:76f.
206. Only the first of these bells is inscribed; it may not have belonged originally with the other twelve.
207. White 1934, pl. 170 right (no. 505).

H 44.9 cm), 11 globular bells [?] (1 H 7.9 cm)

Xinshi, 1 ceramic *mingqi yongzhong*

Yan Xiadu tomb no. 16, 5 sets of *mingqi* bells: 2 sets of *bo*, of 4 and 6 pieces, respectively (H 51.7–59.8 cm and 39.2–45.7 cm), 2 sets of *yongzhong* of 8 pieces each (H 46.3–54.8 cm and 40.1–45.9 cm), and 1 set of 9 *niuzhong* (H 14.7–23 cm)

> *Unprovenienced specimens*

Museum of Fine Arts, Boston, 3 ceramic *mingqi* bells: 1 *chunyu*, 1 *goudiao*, 1 *niuzhong*[208]

Art Institute of Chicago (*ex* Yamanaka collection), ceramic *mingqi zheng*[209]

Ningbo Antiquities Preservation Commission, ceramic *mingqi yongzhong* (H 33.8 cm) (allegedly from Shaoxing)[210]

Asian Art Museum, San Francisco (*ex* Brundage collection), ceramic *mingqi chunyu*[211]

Seattle Art Museum, ceramic *mingqi yongzhong* (H 33 cm)[212]

Shanghai Museum, pottery *mingqi niuzhong*[213]

Shanghai Museum, ceramic *mingqi chunyu*[214]

II. *Han and later periods*

Beidongshan, set of 3 bronze *mingqi niuzhong*

Changsha tomb no. 401, set of 7 lead *ling* (*mingqi*)

Dazhongyingcun, 12 ceramic *mingqi* chime-bells (H 8 cm) (see fig. 98)

Jishan, set of 9 gilt bronze *mingqi niuzhong* (H 6.4–10.4 cm), and set of 4 bronze *mingqi yongzhong*

Shaogou tomb no. 21, set of 6 *ling* (*mingqi* bells) (largest, H 5 cm)

Shaogou tomb no. 123, set of 6 *ling* (*mingqi* bells) (largest, H 5.5 cm)

Shoufeng tomb no. 1, set of 18 bronze *ling* (*mingqi*) (H 2.5–3.5 cm)

Shuanggudui, ceramic *mingqi* bells: set of 5 *bo* (H 16–18 cm), set of 9 *yongzhong* (H 13.5–16.5 cm)

Xiangbizui tomb no. 1, fragments of an undetermined number of ceramic chime-bell *mingqi*

Xianjiahu, undetermined number of pottery *mingqi niuzhong*

Xijiao (Luoyang), 9 bronze *ling* of 4 different types; 1 iron *ling* (*mingqi* bells)

Zifangshan, set of 10 bronze *ling* (*mingqi* bells) (H 5 cm)

208. Umehara 1938, 392–401; pl. 87 (photos).
209. Ibid., pl. 89 (photo); Hochstadter 1952, pl. 20, fig. 80.
210. *Kaogu* 1965 (5):256; photo, pl. 10.8.
211. *Ice and green clouds*, 38–39, cat. no. 6.
212. Hochstadter 1952, photo, pl. 26, fig. 104; *Ice and green clouds*, 40–41, cat. no. 7.
213. *Jadequell und Wolkenmeer*, 104–05, cat. no. 36.
214. *Wenwu* 1985 (8):70 (no illustrations published).

REGIONAL MUSICAL BELL–TYPES

I. *Eastern regional type*

> Ezhuangqu Huayuan, set of 9 *yongzhong*
> Liujiadianzi, 20 *yongzhong*: first set, 1 piece; second set, 7 pieces; third set, 3 pieces; fourth set, 5 pieces
> Miaodun, set of 9 *yongzhong*
> Shangkuangcun, 1 *yongzhong*
> Zuiziqiancun tomb no. 1, set of 5 *yongzhong* (H 31.5–24 cm)
> Dadian tomb no. 1, 1 *bo* (H 38.5 cm)
> Fenghuangling, set of 9 *bo* (H 37.5–17 cm)
> Liujiadianzi, set of 6 *bo*
> Xibeicun, set of 4 *bo* (H 32.5–24 cm)
> Zuiziqiancun, 2 *bo* (H 43.5, 40 cm) (see fig. 146)
> Fenghuangling, set of 9 *niuzhong* (H 24.6–13.1 cm)
> Liugezhuang, set of 9 *niuzhong* (H 24.3–14 cm)
> Xibeicun, set of 9 *niuzhong* (H 28–ca. 15 cm)
>
>> *Unprovenienced specimens (all* bo *)*
> National Palace Museum, Taibei[215]
> National Palace Museum, Taibei[216]

II. Yongzhong *of a widespread type, probably of south Chinese origin, with ornamented central* zheng *portion*

> Beiqishan, set of 2 (H 34.5, 31 cm)
> Dingjiagou, set of 2 (H 34.5, 31 cm)
> Guanyang Gucheng (H 45.5 cm)
> Huashan, 5 single *yongzhong*
> Leijiashan, 7 *yongzhong*, 1 set of 5 + 2 (H 38–25 cm)
> Linwu (H 46.5 cm) (see fig. 148)
> Mawangcun hoard no. 2 (H 42 cm)
> Nanluo hoard no. 1, set of 13 (H ca. 40–30 cm)
> Wujun Xicun
> Yongningbao tomb no. SW-11 (H 36.6 cm) (see fig. 147)
> Zhongdong (H 38 cm)
>
>> *Unprovenienced specimens*
> Hunan Provinical Museum, 2 pieces[217]

215. *Gugong tongqi tulu* 2:430, pl. *xia*, 476.
216. *Gugong tongqi tulu* 2:237, 239, pl. *shang*, 250, 252.
217. Gao Zhixi 1984b, 31; photos, pl. 11.2 and 4 (one H 47.5 cm).

Shaanxi Provincial Museum (allegedly from Rencun, Fufeng [Shaanxi]) (H 34 cm)[218]

III. *Far southern* yongzhong *(Western Zhou–mid Springs and Autumns)*

Cenxi
Huahu (H 35 cm)
Liangshuiping (H 45 cm)
Nasangcun (H 68.5 cm) (see fig. 152)
Pengshan (H 49.5 cm)

IV. *Southeastern regional* yongzhong *type*

A. *Finds from the Lower Yangzi region*

Qingshan, 2 *yongzhong* (H 31.2, 30 cm)
Tangjiashan (H 23 cm)
Ya'erzhou, 23 *yongzhong* (5 sets): first set, 6 pieces (H 52.2–38.1 [fragment] cm) (see fig. 149); second set, 8 pieces (H 39.3 [fragment]–22.8 cm); third set, 5 pieces (H 24.7–21.5 cm); fourth set, 1 piece (H 21.1 cm); fifth set, 3 pieces (with shoulder flanges) (H 32, 23.2, and 20 [fragment] cm) (see fig. 150)
Yangcun (H 43 cm)
Zoumashan, 2 bells (larger, H 25.8 cm)

B. *Finds from the far southern region*

Guishuwo, 6 pieces (H 50.5–38.1 cm)
Hengshan
Liuzhou
Luyu (H 41.3 cm)
Matougang tomb no. 1, first set, 5 pieces (H 38.5, 28.8 [fragment], 33.6, 29.1, 26.3 [fragment] cm)
Matougang, tomb no. 1, second type (with shoulder flanges)
Matougang tomb no. 2, 7 pieces (H 17.2, 17.2 [fragment], 17.8, 28.6, 24.4, 21.4, 17.8 cm)
Meicun, 7 pieces
Muluocun (H 27.8 cm) (with shoulder flanges)
Nanmendong, 6 pieces (H 37.5, 32.5, 27.5, 25.9, 23.1, 19.5 cm) (see fig. 153)
Nanxiang (H 26 cm)
Qingfengcun
Songshan, 6 pieces (H 56.5–35.5 cm)
Supan (H 26.3 [fragment] cm)
Weipocun

218. *Kaogu yu Wenwu* 1980 (4):15, photo, p. 10, fig. 4.5, rubbing, p. 15, fig. 10.

Wuxuan
Yangjia (H 45 cm)
Yilijiecun, set of 4 (largest, H 44 cm)
Yuanlongpo (fragment)

*Unprovenienced specimens*
Dazhongsi Museum, Beijing (anomalous decor)[219]
Hunan Provincial Museum, set of 4[220]
Shanghai Museum (H 105 cm)[221]
Present location unknown[222]
Present location unknown. "Zhù Hou Qiu–*yongzhong*" (inscription forged)[223]
Not extant (*ex* Song Imperial collection)[224]

V. Goudiao

Goutoushan, set of 2 *goudiao* ★ (PEI'ER) (H 45, 40 cm)
Guangde, 9 pieces (H 45.9–31.3, 42.6–27, 39 cm)
Qingshan, 2 *goudiao* (H 39 and 30 cm)
Qiqiao
Songxi, set of 8 (H 21.5–60 cm)
Xianggangshan, set of 8 *goudiao* ★ (NANYUE WEN DI) (largest, H 53.5 cm)
Wangcun, set of four (early type)
Ya'erzhou, 2 *goudiao* (H 22.1, 25.2 cm)
Yancheng, set of 7 (H 17.1–34.8) (see fig. 30)

Xiao'emeishan, 22 (2 sets) enigmatic *goudiao*-shaped objects (H 34–15.6 cm)
*Unprovenienced specimens*
Present location unknown ★ (GUFENG) (allegedly from Changshu [Jiangsu])[225]
★ QICI-*goudiao*, dispersed set of 2 or more (allegedly found with a set of 10 uninscribed pieces at Wukang, now Deqing [Zhejiang])
1 present location unknown (H 27.2 cm)[226]
1 Palace Museum, Beijing (H ca. 50 cm)[227]
Dr. Paul Singer collection, Summit, N. J.[228]

VI. *Beehive-shaped bells*

Dabona, 1 piece (decorated with angular spirals)
Futulongcun, set of 6 (decorated with round spirals)

219. Unpublished (seen in 1990).
220. Unpublished (seen in 1990).
221. *Zhongguo gu qingtongqi-xuan*, pl. 47.
222. Rong Geng 1941, vol. 2, pl. 958.
223. Shirakawa, *Kinbun Tsūshaku* 39:496–97.
224. *Bogutulu* 23:32a–34b.
225. Guo Moruo 1958, *Daxi*, –/158/157; Shirakawa, *Kinbun Tsūshaku* 40:614–16.
226. Rong Geng 1941 2:936 (rubbing).
227. Unpublished.
228. Unpublished.

Jiancun, set of 3 (decorated with cranes and tigers)

Shizhaishan, 6 pieces (decorated with dragons)

Zhuanchangba, 6 pieces (decorated with snakes) (see fig. 155)

VII. *Northern types*

A. *Upper Xiajiadian and contemporary cultures of the northeast*

Paotaishan tomb no. 6, 1 *niuzhong*

Sanguandian, 6 *niuzhong*

Sunjiagou tomb no. 7371, 2 *niuzhong* (see fig. 157)

Wudaohezi tomb no. 1, 3 *niuzhong* (largest, H 16 cm)

B. *Shajing Culture*

Yushugou, two sets of 3 *niuzhong* (largest, H 13 cm; smallest, H 7 cm)

# Bells from the Zhou Peripheries

Highly distinctive types of bells have been excavated in the peripheral areas sur-rounding the various polities of the Zhou realm. These bells were the products of regional bronze-casting traditions, some of which had pre-Zhou roots (see Chapters 4 and 5). So far, little is known about their cultural context, though for the most part we may assume that we are dealing with populations orga-nized at the chiefdom level. Chinese scholars tend to identify such archaeolog-ical remains with various "barbarian" populations mentioned in the classical literature, but such identification is uncertain, especially for pre-Qin times.[1] The archaeological sequences in those parts of China are still full of gaps. The geographic boundaries of the various individual local cultures are for the most part undefined, and there is no consensus as to their number or nomenclature.[2]

Peripheral bells as discussed in this appendix are bell-types whose distribution is restricted to marginal areas and that differ morphologically and stylistically from the mainstream traditions discussed in Chapters 4 and 5. We shall here ignore bells that were imported into the border areas from the Zhou cultural

1. Ethnonyms that may be connected with finds of late Bronze Age bells are the following: The Eastern Yi 東夷 along the eastern seaboard in Shandong and northern Jiangsu, and the Huai Yi 淮夷 further to the south; the population of Wu 吳 and Yue 越 in the Lower Yangzi region; the Nine Yue 九越 further to the south, in Zhejiang, Jiangxi, Guangxi, and Guangdong (Huang Zhan-yue 1986; He and He 1986); the Three Miao 三苗, who dwelled adjacent to the state of Chu along the middle course of the Yangzi River (Yu Weichao 1985, 228–42); the Ba 巴 and Shu 蜀 in the Sichuan Basin (Tong Enzheng 1979; Xu Zhongshu 1959, 1982); the Kingdom of Dian 滇 in Yunnan and southern Sichuan, with its highly distinctive Bronze Age culture (Pirazzoli-t'Serstevens 1974); the Rong 戎 and Di 狄 on the western and northern peripheries and their successors in later Zhou times (Yu Weichao 1985, 180–92). For a brief demonstration in English of the methodology involved for convincing identification of archaeological remains with such ethnonyms, see Tong Enzheng 1982.

2. This is also a problem in Chinese Neolithic archaeology of the last decades, which has been overwhelmingly dedicated to the exact delineation of local cultural phases. Paradoxically, the situa-tion in the Bronze Age appears even less clear; one reason is that until recently the notion of local

core (identifiable as such by stylistic similarity to those of core origin). Although the provincial products are often quite different visually from their mainstream prototypes, their makers must have regarded the locally manufactured bells as, in essential respects, equivalent to imported items. Their noticeable idiosyncrasies, as well as variations among different local strains of bells, highlight the differences between Zhou civilization and surrounding cultures.

It is problematic to subsume all bells from outside the immediate influence of the mainstream bell-casting traditions under one heading and dub them "peripheral" with respect to a "central" Zhou Chinese civilization.[3] Such treatment runs the danger of failing to do proper justice to indigenous characteristics, and may obscure the fact that, in most respects, the peripheral cultures were as distinct from each other as they were from the Zhou. It may, however, be justified by expediency of presentation, for if one included each peripheral bell-type in a comprehensive account of the history of Chinese bells at the point where it branches off from the mainstream, the result might be confusing. The intrinsic interest of the peripheral bells lies mainly in the various ways in which they deviate from their prototypes. Moreover, as I argue in Chapter 5, there may actually be some historical reality to the idea of a non-Zhou periphery around a Zhou core, at least at the elite cultural level.

Let us, then, embark on a brief bell-reviewing tour of the border regions of the Zhou realm.

## The Eastern Seaboard

Stylistically, bells of the important eastern state of Qi by and large resemble those of the Eastern Zhou typological mainstream, though too few specimens have survived to allow defining the specific characteristics of Qi bells.[4] Bells

---

cultures contemporary to the Shang and Zhou dynasties but outside their sphere of political influence was politically more or less taboo in China. Yu Weichao (1987) has proposed that altogether there were nine principal cultural groupings coexisting in early China, from the Neolithic era into the Bronze Age and beyond.

3. At present, the use of "center" and "periphery" in the social sciences is associated with the World Systems theory of Immanuel Wallerstein and his school. The applicability of such theory to precapitalist stages of economic development has been discussed by Schneider 1977 (see also Wolf 1982); Rowlands 1987 discusses its usefulness in European and Middle Eastern archaeology.

4. The most famous extant Springs and Autumn period Qi bell is the Ling-*bo* in the Museum of Chinese History, Beijing (Rong Geng 1941 2:969); with its large relieved hooks, it seems to resemble specimens of the southern group, as defined in Chapter 5. Another set of eight *yongzhong* from Daifuguan, Linzi (Shandong), which I saw at Linzi in 1986, remains unpublished; these bells seem to represent an effort at deliberate archaism, which may have been a characteristic feature of sixth-century B.C. Qi bronzes (see So 1980a, 254). The *niuzhong* chime from Liugezhuang and the four *yongzhong* from Xiao'emeishan may also be products of Springs and Autumns period Qi workshops. The only Warring States Qi bells known are those from Zangjiazhuang (references in Appendix 1); they closely resemble contemporary northern pieces.

from the smaller states in the vicinity of Qi likewise tend to be similar to those from areas closer to the center of the Zhou realm. For instance, the Zhu Gong Keng–*yongzhong* (see fig. 92), though featuring ornaments similar to those on Eastern Zhou specimens of the southern group, was commissioned by a ruler of the non-Zhou statelet of Zhu 邾 (Xuan Gong 宣公, personal name Keng 牼, r. 573?–556).[5]

In addition to such mainstream specimens, excavations of Springs and Autumns period tombs along the eastern seaboard in Shandong and northern Jiangsu have brought to light sets of bells bearing ornamentation in a somewhat different style. The *bo* and *yongzhong* from Zuiziqiancun, Haiyang, close to the tip of the Shandong peninsula, are an interesting case in point (fig. 146).[6] Their somewhat crudely executed decoration looks stylistically conservative, featuring S-shaped two-headed dragons on the flat top and in the *zhuanjian* as well as a pair of crested bird-like animals in the *gu*; both motifs hark back to those seen on Western Zhou *yongzhong* (see figs. 18–19, 74, etc.). In some specimens the back face (verso) is less ornate than the front face (recto). The *bo* from this and other comparable contexts lack the elaborate sculptural suspension devices typical of mainstream Zhou specimens.[7] This distinctive group of bells must predate such specimens as the Zhu Gong Keng–*yongzhong*; they are probably no later than the seventh century. Interestingly, these bells from the eastern seaboard of China show similarities to the contemporary or somewhat later *yongzhong* of the Lower Yangzi region (see figs. 149–51), a connection recently highlighted by the discovery of two sets of *goudiao*-like bells from a Springs and Autumns period tomb at Xiao'emeishan, Zhangqiu (Shandong).

## South China
### The Middle Yangzi

After the important developments that took place in the Middle Yangzi region during the period contemporary with the late Shang and early Western Zhou (see Chapter 4), bell-making in that area appears to have remained stagnant. Single *yongzhong* of the three earliest types (see figs. 75 and 77–79) seem to have continued to be cast in the south during and beyond late Western Zhou times. Specimens of a fourth type of *yongzhong*, related but still somewhat enigmatic, have been found in the Middle Yangzi region as well as at a variety of locations in north China (figs. 110 and 111). Like other early southern *yongzhong*, they are

5. Reference in Appendix 2.
6. References in Appendix 1. For a list of typologically related specimens, see Appendix 2.
7. See the list in Appendix 2.

FIGURE 146. Rubbings of the two sides of a *bo* excavated in 1978 at Zuiziqiancun, Haiyang (Shandong). *Top*, top of the bell; *middle*, recto; *bottom*, verso. Early Springs and Autumns period.

decorated with abstract volute patterns in the *gu* and *zhuanjian*; uniquely, however, in bells of this fourth type, volute decoration also covers the central field of the *zheng*, which on other types of late Western Zhou *yongzhong* is a preferred location of inscriptions. As it is significantly more ornate, the fourth *yongzhong* type may on the whole postdate the three earlier types of southern *yongzhong*.[8]

The best archaeological information so far for specimens of this ornate type of *yongzhong* is from hoards and burial sites in north China, where some of them may have been manufactured.[9] The earliest securely datable specimen known is a single bell excavated from the late Western Zhou tomb no. SW-6 at Yong-

8. In the bell in figs. 148 and 149, the *zhuan* take the form of straight raised ridges, similar to such pieces as those in figs. 70 and 74; on some other, presumably early, specimens of this type, however, they are executed as rows of small studs (similar to the early *yongzhong* type illustrated in figs. 72 and 73).

9. According to the findings of Chapter 5, this should be true especially of the chimed *yongzhong* sets of this type (of up to thirteen pieces!) that have been found in Shaanxi (listed in Appendix 1); all southern finds are single bells. No inscribed specimens have been found of this type.

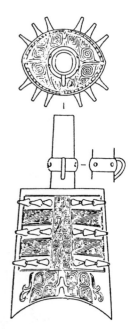

FIGURE 147. *Yongzhong* excavated in 1980 from tomb
no. SW-7 at Yongningbao, Hongdong (Shanxi). Early
part of late Western Zhou (mid-ninth century).

ningbao, Hongdong (Shanxi) (fig. 147).[10] Nevertheless, the geometrical ornamentation style characteristic for *yongzhong* of this type strongly suggests that
they originated in the Middle Yangzi region. Here they continued to be made in
the south well into Eastern Zhou times. The long and massive *mei* on specimens
like the one from Linwu (Hunan) (fig. 148),[11] resemble those on other mid–
Springs and Autumns period pieces (e.g., fig. 92). While this type of *yongzhong*
seems to have been of little influence on the further mainstream development of
Zhou musical bells, it is apparently ancestral to the distinctive Eastern Zhou
*yongzhong* types of the southeastern and far southern regions.

It appears that throughout the Western and early Eastern Zhou periods local
casters in the Middle Yangzi region never made bells in sets. Around the late
Springs and Autumns period the early bell-types were supplanted by mainstream chimes of bells with southern stylistic features. The chime-bell manufacturing industry in Chu during Eastern Zhou times is entirely of later northern
derivation; archaic-looking pieces did, however, linger on in the south (see
below).

10. References in Appendix 1. For a list of typologically related specimens, see Appendix 2. The
unquestionably Western Zhou date of the Yongningbao specimen (fig. 148) proves that, contrary to
Hayashi Minao (1980, 29; 1984 2:387; also in Wu Hung n.d.), all *yongzhong* with decorated central
*zheng* panels need not date to the Springs and Autumns period.
11. References in Appendix 1.

FIGURE 148. *Yongzhong* found in 1962 at Linwu (Hunan) (exact circumstances of excavation unknown). Local culture contemporary(?) with late Western Zhou.

## The Lower Yangzi

In the Lower Yangzi region, various kinds of bells have been found in Springs and Autumns period archaeological contexts. Their ornamentation style is to some degree comparable to those described in the preceding section. Most conspicuous among them are *yongzhong* featuring decoration in the center of the *zheng* panel, similar to earlier pieces (figs. 147 and 148). They are, however, different from mainstream bells in that the recto face is invariably ornamented with much greater care than the verso, which is often entirely unornamented. Some specimens show other morphological particularities: a reduced number of bosses (*mei*), or shoulder flanges (see fig. 150), which, though perhaps visually enhancing, almost certainly had an adverse acoustic effect. A large number of specimens (twenty-three pieces falling into six distinct groups) was found in the Yangzi River at Ya'erzhou, Guangji (Hubei).[12] On some of these, elegant dragon ornaments may be seen adorning the central panel of the *zheng* as well as the *gu*

12. Ibid. For a list of typologically related specimens, see Appendix 2. As the Ya'erzhou bells were hauled up from a depth of 10 m, the archaeological context of the discovery remains obscure. The report notes the possibility that they may have been looted pieces, which were being transported on a Japanese ship sunk near Ya'erzhou in the early 1940s (p. 47, n. 14); Mase Kazuyoshi has argued that this is likely for geological reasons (presentation to the Kinbun Kenkyūkai, Kyōto, February 1985). Even so, the provenience of these bells from somewhere along the Yangzi River (or further to the south in Guangdong or Guangxi) is virtually beyond doubt.

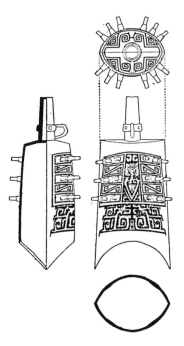

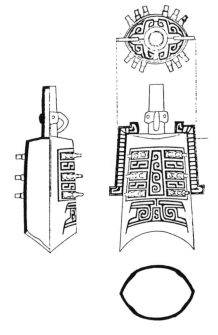

FIGURE 149. *Above, left: Yong-zhong* discovered in 1984 in the navigational channel of the Yang-zi River at Ya'erzhou, Guangji (Hubei). Local culture contemporary(?) with the early to middle Springs and Autumns period.

FIGURE 150. *Above, right: Yong-zhong* from Ya'erzhou (see fig. 149), shouldered type.

FIGURE 151. *Right:* One of three chimed *chunyu* excavated in 1985 at Wangjiashan, Dantu (Jiangsu). Local culture, turn of the fifth century B.C.

portion (fig. 149); on others, the ornaments are more abstract, resembling those on earlier bell-types from the Middle Yangzi region (fig. 150). Although such bells regularly form sets, the pieces within a set tend to differ in many details of ornamentation. Moreover, the casting is often of decidedly poor quality, suggesting that such bells may have been acoustically deficient. Their purpose may not have been primarily a musical one: they mainly served to show off their owners' material wealth and prestige. It is of interest that in just this area and time period there begin to appear appreciable numbers of high-fired pottery *mingqi*, which, likewise, were not acoustically viable.[13]

In addition to these *yongzhong*, Springs and Autumns period sites all along the eastern seaboard have also yielded some of the earliest known specimens of *chunyu* and *zheng* (see figs. 31 and 29). Throughout most of Eastern Zhou, those bells were used in non-musical functions (for example, as signal-giving instruments in warfare), but in eastern and southeastern China, they are sometimes excavated in association with musical bells.[14] What is more, casters in that area manufactured them as chimed sets. Large sets of *goudiao*, which are simply *zheng* turned into chime-bells, have been known for some time (see fig. 30);[15] recently, moreover, a graduated set of three *chunyu*, decorated according to the standard *zhong* decoration scheme and stylistically resembling the bells in figs. 146 and 149, has been reported from the early fifth century Wu tomb at Wangjiashan, Dantu (Jiangsu) (fig. 151).[16] Evidently attempting to liken this local bell-type to Western Zhou–type *yongzhong*, the casters of the Wangjiashan *chunyu* even fashioned bird-shaped B-tone markers, though bells of such a shape could never have emitted two distinct tones. *Goudiao*, on the other hand, though not featuring the standard *zhong* decoration scheme, seem to have been capable of functioning as two-tone bells. Though these bells are obviously far removed from mainstream Zhou musical bells in physical appearance, in manufacturing them, their patrons appear to have attempted to capture the spirit of Zhou bell music.

Around the end of the Springs and Autumns period, bells of the "southern group" locally supplanted these remarkable indigenous efforts at adapting the trappings of Zhou ritual music in the Lower Yangzi region; but *goudiao* as well as *yongzhong* decorated on only one side continued to be made in the far south.

13. It is actually not certain that their use was limited to funerary display, as was the case with later Han dynasty *mingqi*. Archaeological contexts for the Warring States "proto-porcelain" *mingqi* are so far unreported save for the site of Huangjiashan, Haiyan (Zhejiang), which may have been a manufacturing workshop.

14. Examples: Liujiadianzi, Yishui (Shandong), Ximen-nei, Shou Xian (Anhui), Zengjiashan, Xiushui (Jiangxi) (references in Appendix 1).

15. References in Appendix 1. For a comprehensive list of *goudiao*, see Appendix 2.

16. References in Appendix 1. These *chunyu* are so far unique; they are discussed in Falkenhausen 1989a.

In Western Zhou, the local populations in present-day Guangdong and Guangxi knew and sometimes imitated the standard *nao* and *yongzhong* types of the Middle Yangzi region. Old traditions persisted. The type of bell decoration first seen on middle Western Zhou specimens from the Middle Yangzi region (see fig. 71) still appears, insignificantly modified, on some mid–Springs and Autumns period *yongzhong*.[17] Other highly idiosyncratic local imitations of the more common Middle Yangzi bell-types may be exemplified by the *yongzhong* from Nasangcun, Heng Xian (fig. 152), which is probably contemporary with Western Zhou.[18] This poorly cast piece has a *wo*, but no *xuan* to speak of. The proportions of the resonating body are somewhat narrower than in bells of northern provenience. In what is obviously an elaboration on the studded *zhuan* of *yongzhong* of the type depicted in fig. 71, the *zhuan* are here marked as double rows of studs. The spaces between them are filled with narrow bands of sunken-line volutes; similar volute-bands also surround the entire *gu* portion. In the lateral portions of the *gu* on the recto face, we notice symmetrical snake-like motifs molded in high relief, a feature never otherwise encountered on *yongzhong*.[19] The decoration on the verso face is much simpler.

In the Warring States period, *yongzhong* from the Lower Yangzi region decorated only on one side became widespread in the far south. The *yongzhong* from Nanmendong, Luoding (Guangdong) (fig. 153), for instance, resemble the more abstract specimens from Ya'erzhou (see fig. 150).[20] Some bells of this type have been found in association with *zheng*. The set of eight large *goudiao* from the tomb of the king of Nanyue at Xianggangshan, Guangzhou (Guangdong), dated by inscription to the year 129 B.C., testify to the continued local production of such bells even after the end of the Zhou period.[21]

## The Southwest

### Central and Eastern Sichuan

Remarkable recent discoveries of an early Bronze Age culture at Sanxingdui, Guanghan (Sichuan), have so far yielded no evidence of musical instruments.[22] All bells found in the province date to the terminal Bronze Age. The inlaid

---

17. One good example for this tendency is the *yongzhong* from Pengshan, Lianping (Guangdong); references in Appendix 1.

18. References in Appendix 1. For a list of typologically related specimens, see Appendix 2.

19. There are some parallels for this on *nao* and *bo* from Hunan (compare Appendix 2).

20. References in Appendix 1. For a list of typologically related specimens, see Appendix 2. Extensive discussion in Jiang Tingyu 1989.

21. References in Appendix 1.

22. *Wenwu* 1987 (10):1–15; Bagley 1988.

FIGURE 152. *Yongzhong* excavated in 1958 at Nasangcun, Heng Xian (Guangxi). Local culture approximately contemporary with middle Western Zhou.

FIGURE 153. One of a set of five *yongzhong* excavated in 1962 from tomb no. 1 at Matougang, Qingyuan (Guangdong). *a*, recto; *b*, verso. Local culture contemporary with the Warring States period.

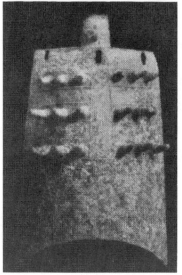

*a*

*b*

*niuzhong* from the tomb of a ruler of Ba at Xiaotianxi, Fuling (Sichuan) (see fig. 97), are almost certainly Chu imports from a time not long before the conquest of Sichuan by Qin in 316. An approximately contemporary local attempt at bell manufacture may be seen in the five bells, difficult to classify but provisionally termed *zheng*, from the tomb at Jiuliandun, Xindu (Sichuan) (fig. 154).[23] These bells are of bizarre shape, the rim being curved differently on each bell-face. The standard *zhong* decoration scheme has been reduced to varying numbers of crudely shaped *mei* haphazardly placed in a grid of raised lines. The shape of these objects may reflect that of imported bells (perhaps *zheng* of Chu manufacture), but one can hardly imagine them to have been acoustically feasible. The intention of creating at least the semblance of a chimed set of bells is, nevertheless, notable. Later during the Warring States and Han periods, *chunyu* of south Chinese derivation became the predominant bell-types in western Hunan and Sichuan. They sometimes come in large groups (of up to fifteen pieces),[24] but as far as we can know they were never manufactured as sets.

*The Far Southwest*

Further to the southwest, in the area of the Bronze Age culture of Dian, bells of highly distinctive beehive-shape were cast (fig. 155).[25] The earliest pieces may date to the third century or earlier, extending through the first century B.C.; their gorgeous decoration with geometric or animal patterns exemplify a representationalist aesthetics that sets them completely apart from Chinese bells. Nevertheless, the almond-shaped cross-section of these bells, as well as the curious coincidence of their metallic composition to that of contemporary mainstream Chinese chime-bells (see table 6), may indicate the presence of some sort of stimulus diffusion from China proper. Sets of up to six pieces have been found.

Another Southeast Asian type of bells, the sheep's horn–loop bells (*yangjiaoniuzhong* 羊角鈕鐘') (fig. 156), so called after their strangely shaped suspension devices, may also be in some roundabout way related to Chinese bell-making traditions.[26] Such bells do not seem to predate the second century B.C.

---

23. References in Appendix 1.

24. A group of fifteen *chunyu* was found at Xiongjiagang, Shimen (Hunan) (*Hunan Kaogu Jikan* 3 [1986]:261–63). Xiong Chuanxin (1983b, 43) argues persuasively against the idea of "*chunyu* chimes."

25. The illustrated specimen is that from Zhuanchangba, Huili (Sichuan); for a list of typologically related specimens, see Appendix 2.

26. Jiang Tingyu 1984 has collected virtually all the relevant evidence. The depicted specimen is from the Western Han tomb at Luobowan, Gui Xian (Guangxi) (references in Appendix 1).

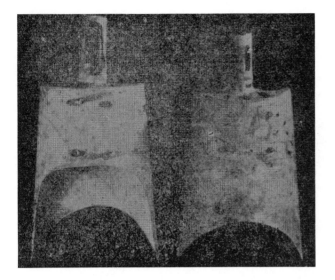

FIGURE 154. Two of five *zheng* excavated in 1980 at Jiuliandun, Xindu (Sichuan). Local culture approximately contemporary with the mid–Warring States period.

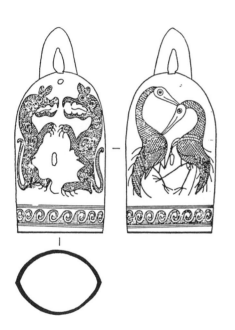

FIGURE 155. One of six beehive-shaped bells excavated in 1976 at Jiancun, Xiangyun (Yunnan). The drawing shows the two sides of the bell. Dian culture, third century B.C.

FIGURE 156. Sheep's horn–loop bell (*yangjiao-niuzhong*) excavated in 1976 at Luobowan, Gui Xian (Guangxi). The significance of the human head appearing in relief on the bell-face (see also fig. 152) is unknown. Local culture contemporary with the Western Han period.

FIGURE 157. Four of six *niuzhong* excavated in 1978 at Sanguandian, Lingyuan (Liaoning). Local culture contemporary with late Warring States.

and are more widespread than beehive-shaped bells, occurring in Yunnan, Guangxi, and Vietnam. They, too, have been found in sets of up to six.[27]

## The North

The distribution of bells along the northern fringes of the Zhou realm contrasts starkly with the profusion of distinctive bell types observed in the southern local cultures. Here, horse-bells are the only kinds of bells encountered with any frequency. A small number of tombs along the southern edge of the northern grasslands, however, have yielded groups of unornamented bells with loops of inverted U-shape, undoubtedly of local manufacture (fig. 157).[28] These bells are so small that we cannot be certain whether they are *ling* or *niuzhong*, but because clappers have not been found, and because there do seem to have been attempts at fashioning sets of bells of graduated sizes, they may be provisionally identified as *niuzhong* imitations.

27. Frequency measurements have been published for the set of six *yangjiao-niuzhong* from tomb no. 1 at Wanjiaba, Chuxiong (Yunnan) (*Kaogu Xuebao* 1983 [3]:376–77); no regularity is apparent in the tone distribution.

28. Such specimens are known from Upper Xiajiadian cultural contexts in the northeast, as well as from sites of the Shajing culture in Gansu. The depicted specimen is from Sunjiagou, Ningcheng (Liaoning). References in Appendix 1.

As chimed sets of bells are difficult to transport, they may not have been easily adaptable to the nomadic or seminomadic lifestyle of the northern neighbors of the Zhou. But this may not have been the only reason for their apparent unpopularity in the north. The cultural contrast between the inhabitants of China proper and their northern neighbors—as opposed to the similarity between China and areas further south—has often been noted; it has been fateful throughout much of the history of imperial China.[29] The virtual lack of Zhou-type musical instruments along the northern frontier bespeaks that area's generally low degree of acculturation to the ways of the Zhou. Ironically, from Han times onward, the folk musics of the various northern populations were adopted by the Chinese, as groups of performers were sent as gifts to the imperial court. These foreign musicians popularized various new forms of musical entertainment, decisively influencing the later history of Chinese music.[30]

29. Lattimore 1940; Barfield 1989.
30. Yang Yinliu 1980, 112 and passim.

# Tone Measurements

SOURCES OF TONE–MEASUREMENT DATA[1]

I. *Shang Dynasty* Nao

> ★Dasikongcun (tomb no. 315?), Anyang, HN, set of 3:
> Huang Xiangpeng 1978–80 2: 134.[2]
>
> ★Xiaonanzhuang, Wen Xian, HN, set of 3:
> Huang Xiangpeng 1978–80 1: 201 (A-tones only), 2:135 (A- and B-tones).
>
> ★Xibeigang tomb no. 1038, Anyang, HN (now Academia Sinica, Taibei), enlarged set of 4:
> Chia 1980, 14–15 (A-tones only).
>
> ★Anyang, HN (exact provenience not indicated), set of 3:
> Huang Xiangpeng 1978–80 1: 202 (A-tones only), 2: 134 (A- and B-tones).
>
> ★Palace Museum, Beijing (from Hui Xian, HN?), set of 3:
> Huang Xiangpeng 1978–80 1: 201 (A-tones only).

II. *Western Zhou* Yongzhong

> A. *Chimes of three or more pieces*
>
> ★Mawangcun, set no. V, 4 bells:
> Jiang Dingsui 1984, 88 (nos. 27–30).
>
> Nanluo hoard no. 1, 13 bells (11 broken):
> Jiang Dingsui 1984, 87 (nos. 4–16).
>
> ★NI–*yongzhong*, 4 bells (see Appendix 1, Haosihe):

---

1. For complete references, see Appendix 1. Entries marked with an asterisk are tabulated below in this appendix.

2. Huang labels these bells as "Ya Gong 亞弜" bells, which is probably wrong; the two known bells with that inscription form part of the enlarged set of five excavated from tomb no. 5 ("Fu Hao's tomb") at Yinxu, Anyang (Henan).

Jiang Dingsui 1984, 90 (nos. 82–85).
Puducun, set of 3:
    Jiang Dingsui 1984, 87 (nos. 17–19; repaired).
Rujiazhuang tomb no. 1, 3 bells:
    Jiang Dingsui 1984, 87 (nos. 20–21; repaired).
Weizhuang, set of 3:
    Fang Jianjun 1986 (aural approximations only).
\* SECOND XING–*yongzhong*, 7 bells (see Appendix 1, Zhuangbai hoard no. 1):
    Jiang Dingsui 1984, 89 (nos. 49–55).
\* THIRD XING–*yongzhong*, set of 6 (see Appendix 1, Zhuangbai hoard no. 1):
    Jiang Dingsui 1984, 89 (nos. 56–61).
\* ZHONG YI–*yongzhong*, 8 bells (see Appendix 1, Qijiacun hoard no. 1):
    Jiang Dingsui 1984, 90 (nos. 74–81).
\* Zhuangbai hoard no. 1, IV, 3 bells:
    Jiang Dingsui 1984, 88 (nos. 41–43).
\* Zhuyuangou tomb no. 7, set of 3:
    *Baoji Yu-guo mudi* 1:651–53.
\* ZUO–*yongzhong*, 8 bells (see Appendix 1, Qijiacun hoard no. 1):
    Jiang Dingsui 1984, 90 (nos. 66–73).

B. *Other measurements*

Beiqiao, 2 separate bells:
    Jiang Dingsui 1988, 88, 89 (nos. 32, 46).
CHU GONG JIA?–*yongzhong*, unprovenienced group of 3 late Western Zhou
*yongzhong* (2 from the same set; probably repaired) (see Appendix 2, Early
*yongzhong* II-A):
    Takahashi and Ueda 1986, 61.
Dongjucun, single bell:
    Jiang Dingsui 1984, 88 (no. 31).
GUO SHU LÜ–*yongzhong*, 1 unprovenienced bell from dispersed set, now in the
Sen'oku Hakkokan (Sumitomo Collection), Kyōto (see Appendix 2, Early
*yongzhong* II-B):
    Takahashi and Ueda 1986, 61.
Guozhen, single bell:
    Jiang Dingsui 1984, 88 (no. 26; broken).
Mawangcun I, single bell:
    Jiang Dingsui 1984, 87 (no. 1; broken).
Mawangcun II, single bell:
    Jiang Dingsui 1984, 88 (no. 25).
Mawangcun III, set of 2:
    Jiang Dingsui 1984, 89 (nos. 47, 48).
Mawangcun IV, set of 2:

Jiang Dingsui 1984, 88 (nos. 36, 37).

NANGONG HU–*yongzhong* (see Appendix 1, Baozigou):
Jiang Dingsui 1984, 90 (no. 87).

NING–*yongzhong*, single bell (see Appendix 1, Qizhen hoard no. 1):
Jiang Dingsui 1984, 89, 90 (no. 86).

Qijia (1 bell out of 2):
Jiang Dingsui 1984, 88 (no. 44).

Qizhen hoard no. 2, single bell:
Jiang Dingsui 1984, 89 (no. 46).

Wujun Xicun, single bell:
Jiang Dingsui 1984, 87 (no. 3).

XI ZHONG–*yongzhong*, 1 unprovenienced bell from dispersed set, now in the
Sen'oku Hakkokan (Sumitomo Collection), Kyōto (see Appendix 2, Early *yong-
zhong* II-B):
Takahashi and Ueda 1986, 61.

XIAN–*yongzhong*, unprovenienced single bell in the Shaanxi Provincial Museum
(see Appendix 2, Early *yongzhong* II-B):
Jiang Dingsui 1984, 88 (no. 39; broken).

FIRST XING–*yongzhong*, single bell (see Appendix 1, Zhuangbai hoard no. 1):
Jiang Dingsui 1984, 88 (no. 40).

YING HOU–*yongzhong*, single bell (see Appendix 1, Hongxing Commune):
Jiang Dingsui 1984, 88 (no. 38).

YONGXIANG–*yongzhong*, single bell (see Appendix 1, Qizhen hoard no. 1):
Jiang Dingsui 1984, 89 (no. 62).

FIRST ZHA–*yongzhong*, 1 unprovenienced bell from dispersed set, now in the
Sen'oku Hakkokan (Sumitomo Collection), Kyōto (see Appendix 2, Early *yong-
zhong* I-C):
Takahashi and Ueda 1986, 61.

SECOND ZHA–*yongzhong*, 1 unprovenienced bell, now in the Sen'oku Hakkokan
(Sumitomo Collection), Kyōto (see Appendix 2, Early *yongzhong* II-A):
Takahashi and Ueda 1986, 61.

Zhuangbai hoard no. 1, V:
Jiang Dingsui 1984, 88 (nos. 23–24).

Zhuangbai hoard no. 1, VI, 2 bells:
Jiang Dingsui 1984, 88 (nos. 34, 35).

Unprovenienced single mid–Western Zhou *yongzhong* in the Sen'oku Hakkokan
(Sumitomo Collection), Kyōto:
Takahashi and Ueda 1986, 61.

Unprovenienced single bell in the Shaanxi Provincial Museum (allegedly from
Rencun):

Jiang Dingsui 1984, 87 (no. 2).
Two unpublished bells in the Shaanxi Provincial Museum:
Jiang Dingsui 1984, 89 (nos. 63, 64).

III. *Eastern Zhou Chime-Bells* (yongzhong, bo, niuzhong*)*

★ BIAO-*niuzhong*, 14 *niuzhong* (see Appendix 1, Jincun tomb no. 7):
Tanabe in Hamada 1924 (A-tones only); Takahashi 1984, 1986 (A- and B-tones).

CAI HOU–*niuzhong*, 9 bells (see Appendix 1, Ximennei):
Li Chunyi 1973, 16 (A-tones only).

CAI HOU–*bo*, 8 bells (see Appendix 1, Ximennei):
Li Chunyi 1973, 18 (A-tones of 2 bells only).

Fenshuiling tomb no. 14, 8 *niuzhong*:
Li Chunyi 1973, 16 (A-tones of 7 bells only).

Houchuan tombs no. 2040 and 2041, sets of *bo*:
Measurements still unpublished; mentioned in Wang Shimin 1988, 17–18.

★ JINGLI-*niuzhong*, set of 13 (see Appendix 1, Changtaiguan tomb no. 1):
Yang Yinliu 1958 (A-tones only); Chen and Zheng 1980, 1985; Ma Chengyuan 1981, 140 (A- and B-tones).

Leigudun tomb no. 2, assemblage of 36 *yongzhong* (2 sets):
*Huangzhong* 1988 (4): 9–12.

★ Lijialou, second set of 10 *yongzhong*:
Huang Xiangpeng 1978–80 2: 139 (measurements on 6 bells only).

LÜ WANG–*niuzhong* (see Appendix 1, Xiasi tomb no. 10):
Tone measurements as yet unreported (mentioned in Tan Weisi 1988).

QIN GONG–*yongzhong*, 5 bells (see Appendix 1, Taigongmiao):
Ma Chengyuan 1981, 139 (aural approximations only).

★ Shangmacun tomb no. 13, 9 *niuzhong* (2 broken):
Huang Xiangpeng 1978–80 2: 142.

Xiasi tomb no. 1, set of 9 *niuzhong*:
*Kaogu* 1981 (2): 125 (nearest standard tone only).

Wangsun Gao–*yongzhong*, 26 bells (see Appendix 1; Xiasi tomb no. 2):
Zhao Shigang 1986 (2 sets of measurements).

★ ZENG HOU YI–bells (see Appendix 1, Leigudun tomb no. 1, assemblage of 65 bells (45 *yongzhong*, 1 *bo*, 19 *niuzhong*):
First set of measurements: Wang Xiang 1981; second set of measurements: *Shanghai Bowuguan Jikan* 2 (1982): 89–92; third set of measurements: Tan and Feng 1988, 41–44.

ZHEDIAO-*niuzhong*, unprovenienced set of a yet-undetermined number of bells (see Appendix 2, Musical bells II-B):
Takahashi 1988; 2 items also in Takahashi and Ueda 1986, 61.

Unprovenienced late Springs and Autumns period *yongzhong* in the Sen'oku
Hakkokan (Sumitomo Collection), Kyōto (see Appendix 2, Musical bells I-A):
    Takahashi and Ueda 1986, 61.
Shenliu-bells (2 *bo* from a set of 5, and 9 *niuzhong*):
    *Dongnan Wenhua* 1988 (3/4): 27.

## iv. *Lithophones*

Jinancheng, Jiangling, HuB (1970), 25 chimestones:
    *Kaogu* 1972 (3): 41–48, esp. p. 44. (Originally reported in *Wenwu* 1972 [1]:
    75; for color illustration, see *Wenhua Dageming Qijian chutu wenwu* 1: 74.)
*Shangmacun tomb no. 13, 7 chimestones (2 broken):
    Huang Xiangpeng 1978–80 2: 147.
*Sanmenxia (probably Houchuan tomb no. 2041), 9 chimestones:
    Huang Xiangpeng 1978–80 2: 147.
Xincun, Xun Xuan, HB (1933), various chimestones:
    Measured by Liu Fu (data unpublished; manuscript article mentioned in *Xun
    Xian Xincun*, 66).
Zhongzhou Daju, Luoyang, HN (1950s), 10 chimestones:
    Originally reported in *Wenwu* 1960 (4): 87; exact tone measurements so far
    unpublished (mentioned in Wang Shimin 1988, 18); aural approximations in
    Fang Jianjun 1989b.
Unprovenienced Shang dynasty set of 3 inscribed chimestones (allegedly from
Anyang) in the Palace Museum, Beijing:
    Huang Xiangpeng 1978–80 1:202.
Approximate aural tone data on several chimestones from prehistoric, Shang,
and Western Zhou times in Fang Jianjun 1989a.

### TONE-MEASUREMENT TABULATIONS

The published tone measurements for bells identified in the left column (e.g.,
*1A* means the A-tone of bell no. 1) have been converted into cent figures (center
column) with $C_0$ (16 Hz) as zero. The right column indicates the interval (in
cents) between the tone and the principal **do** of the respective chime, which is
marked in boldface.

*Late Shang chimes (see figs. 113, 114)*[3]

    Nao *from tomb no. 315? at Dasikong*

| | | |
|---|---|---|
| **1A** | **6147** | 0 |
| 1B | 6450 | 303 |

3. In each of the Shang chimes tabulated here, the lowest tone has arbitrarily been designated as
the principal **do** (see fig. 112).

| | | |
|---|---|---|
| 2A | 6775 | 628 |
| 2B | 6875 | 718 |
| 3A | 7035 | 888 |
| 3B | 7040 | 893 |

Nao *from Xiaonanzhuang*

| | | |
|---|---|---|
| **1A** | **6040** | **0** |
| 1B | 6232 | 192 |
| 2A | ? | |
| 2B | ? | |
| 3A | 6700 | 660 |
| 3B | 6897 | 857 |

Nao *from tomb no. 1038 at Xibeigang (A-tones only)*

| | | |
|---|---|---|
| **1A** | **6423** | **0** |
| 2A | 6723 | 300 |
| 3A | 7377 | 954 |
| 4A | 7354 | 931 |

Nao *from Anyang*

| | | |
|---|---|---|
| **1A** | **6932** | **0** |
| 1B | 7407 | 475 |
| 2A | 7055 | 123 |
| 2B | ? | |
| 3A | 7407? | 475 |
| 3B | 7910 | 978 |

*Palace Museum* nao *(A-tones only)*

| | | |
|---|---|---|
| **1A** | **6124** | **0** |
| 2A | 7475 | 351 |
| 3A | 6969 | 845 |

*Middle Western Zhou chimes of* yongzhong *(see fig. 115)*

*Mawangcun chime no. V*

| | | |
|---|---|---|
| 1A | 4408 | −411 |
| **2A** | **4819** | **0** |
| 3A | 5010 | 191 |
| 3B | 5339 | 520 |
| 4A | 5582 | 763 |
| 4B | 6002 | 1183 |

*Zhuangbai chime no. V*

| | | |
|---|---|---|
| 1A | 4472 | 305 |
| **1B** | **4775** | **0** |

|   |   |   |
|---|---|---|
| 2A | 4956 | 181 |
| 2B | 5292 | 517 |
| 3A | 5333 | 558 |
| 3B | 5696 | 921 |

## Yongzhong *chime from Zhuyuangou tomb no. 7*

|   |   |   |
|---|---|---|
| 1A | 5856 | −470 |
| 1B | 6209 | −117 |
| **2A** | **6326** | **0** |
| 2B | 6708 | 382 |
| 3A | 7131 | 805 |
| 3B | 7355 | 1029 |

## Late Western Zhou chimes of yongzhong

### Ni-yongzhong

|   |   |   |
|---|---|---|
| 1A | 4515 | −288 |
| **2A** | **4803** | **0** |
| 3A | 5226 | 423 |
| 3B | 5532 | 729 |
| 4A | 5742 | 939 |
| 4B | 6095 | 1293 |

### Second Xing–yongzhong[4]

|   |   |   |
|---|---|---|
| II-1A | 4290 | −300 |
| **II-2A** | **4590** | **0** |
| II-3A | 4972 | 382 |
| II-2B | 4982 | 392 |
| II-3B | 5290 | 700 |
| II-4A | 5470 | 880 |
| II-4B | 5815 | 1225 |
| IV-1A | 6217 | 1627 |
| IV-1B | 6541 | 1951 |
| IV-2A | 6729 | 2139 |
| IV-2B | 7060 | 2470 |
| IV-3A | 7459 | 2869 |
| IV-3B | 7766 | 3176 |

### Third Xing–yongzhong

|   |   |   |
|---|---|---|
| 1A | 4236 | −362 |
| **2A** | **4598** | **0** |

4. Because of their somewhat different inscriptions, the bells of this chime have been reported separately as Set II and Set IV.

| | | |
|---|---|---|
| 3A | 5038 | 440 |
| 3B | 5346 | 748 |
| 4A | 5425 | 827 |
| 4B | 5754 | 1156 |
| 5A | 6176 | 1578 |
| 5B | 6521 | 1923 |
| 6A | 6691 | 2093 |
| 6B | 7008 | 2410 |

*Zhong Yi*–yongzhong *(see fig. 116)*

| | | |
|---|---|---|
| 1A | 4380 | −320 |
| **2A** | **4700** | **0** |
| 1B | 4840 | 140 |
| 3A | 5065 | 365 |
| 3B | 5385 | 685 |
| 4A | 5549 | 849 |
| 4B | 5892 | 1192 |
| 5A | 6290 | 1590 |
| 5B | 6607 | 1907 |
| 6A | 6793 | 2093 |
| 6B | 7140 | 2440 |
| 7A | 7500 | 2800 |
| 7B | 7810 | 3110 |
| 8A | 7985 | 3285 |
| 8B | 8288 | 3588 |

*Zuo*-yongzhong

| | | |
|---|---|---|
| 1A | 4466 | −298 |
| **2A** | **4764** | **0** |
| 1B | 4862 | 98 |
| 3A | 5159 | 395 |
| 2B | 5164 | 400 |
| 3B | 5490 | 726 |
| 4A | 5667 | 903 |
| 4B | 5982 | 1218 |
| 5A | 6370 | 1606 |
| 5B | 6712 | 1948 |
| 6A | 6819 | 2055 |
| 6B | 7110 | 2346 |
| 7A | 7550 | 2786 |
| 7B | 7815 | 3051 |
| 8A | 8046 | 3282 |
| 8B | 8355 | 3591 |

*Springs and Autumns period chimes of musical bells*

   *Six* yongzhong *from Lijialou (perhaps part of set B; numbering provisional)*
   *(see fig. 117)*

| | | |
|---|---|---|
| (1)A | 3796 | −804 |
| (2)A | 4087 | −513 |
| (3)A | 4256 | −344 |
| (2)B | 4413 | −187 |
| **(4)A** | **4600** | **0** |
| (4)B | 4778 | 178 |
| (5)A | 4827 | 227 |
| (6)A | 4975 | 375 |
| (5)B | 5104 | 504 |
| (6)B | 5312 | 712 |

   *Lithophone from Shangmacun tomb no. 13 (see fig. 134)*

| | | |
|---|---|---|
| 1 | 5199 | −831 |
| 2 | 5530 | −500 |
| **4** | **6030** | **0** |
| 5 | 6220 | 190 |
| 7 | 7234 | 1204 |

   Niuzhong *from Shangmacun tomb no. 13 (see fig. 119)*

| | | |
|---|---|---|
| 1A | 4345 | −1697 |
| 4A | 5045 | −997 |
| 5A | 5235 | −807 |
| 4B | 5405 | −637 |
| 5B | 5550 | −492 |
| 6A | 5730 | −312 |
| **6B** | **6042** | **0** |
| 7A | 6260 | 218 |
| 8A | 6450 | 408 |
| 7B | 6620 | 578 |
| 8B | 6780 | 738 |
| 9A | 6950 | 908 |
| 9B | 7260 | 1218 |

*The Zeng bells (second set of measurements)*

   *Chime U3 + 4* (niuzhong) *(see fig. 122)*

| | | |
|---|---|---|
| **U3-7A** | **5377** | **0** |
| U2-6A | 5578 | 201 |
| U3-7B | 5725 | 348 |
| U3-6A | 5821 | 444 |
| U2-6B | 5923 | 546 |

| | | |
|---|---|---|
| U2-5A | 6065 | 688 |
| U3-6B | 6152 | 775 |
| U3-5A | 6235 | 858 |
| U2-5B | 6355 | 978 |
| U2-4A | 6462 | 1085 |
| U3-5B | 6543 | 1166 |
| U3-4A | 6700 | 1323 |
| U2-4B | 6775 | 1398 |
| U2-3A | 6783 | 1406 |
| U3-4B | 6919 | 1542 |
| U3-3A | 7021 | 1644 |
| U2-3B | 7117 | 1740 |
| U2-2A | 7288 | 1911 |
| U3-3B | 7348 | 1971 |
| U3-2A | 7503 | 2126 |
| U2-2B | 7584 | 2207 |
| U2-1A | 7691 | 2314 |
| U3-2B | 7761 | 2384 |
| U2-1B | 8018 | 2641 |
| U3-1A | 8120 | 2743 |
| U3-1B | 8419 | 3042 |

*Chime M1* (yongzhong) *(see fig. 120)*

| | | |
|---|---|---|
| 11A | 4859 | −981 |
| 10A | 5060 | −780 |
| 11B | 5182 | −658 |
| 9A | 5350 | −490 |
| 10B | 5464 | −376 |
| 8A | 5541 | −299 |
| 9B | 5736 | −104 |
| **7A** | **5840** | **0** |
| 8B | 5958 | 118 |
| 6A | 6048 | 208 |
| 7B | 6140 | 300 |
| 5A | 6238 | 398 |
| 6B | 6390 | 550 |
| 5B | 6562 | 722 |
| 4A | 6772 | 932 |
| 4B | 7084 | 1244 |
| 3A | 7260 | 1420 |
| 2A | 7513 | 1673 |
| 3B | 7581 | 1741 |

| | | |
|---|---|---|
| 2B | 7757 | 1917 |
| 1A | 8025 | 2185 |
| 1B | 8324 | 2484 |

*Chime M2 (yongzhong) (see fig. 120)*

| | | |
|---|---|---|
| 12A | 4884 | −1081 |
| 11A | 5137 | −828 |
| 12B | 5266 | −699 |
| 10A | 5387 | −578 |
| 9A | 5453 | −512 |
| 11B | 5553 | −412 |
| 8A | 5656 | −309 |
| 10B | 5812 | −153 |
| 9B | 5826 | −139 |
| **7A** | **5965** | **0** |
| 8B | 6073 | 108 |
| 6A | 6159 | 194 |
| 7B | 6254 | 289 |
| 5A | 6342 | 377 |
| 6B | 6478 | 513 |
| 5B | 6664 | 699 |
| 4A | 6849 | 884 |
| 4B | 7160 | 1195 |
| 3A | 7389 | 1424 |
| 2A | 7584 | 1619 |
| 3B | 7682 | 1717 |
| 2B | 7884 | 1919 |
| 1A | 8039 | 2074 |
| 1B | 8377 | 2412 |

*Chime M3 (yongzhong) (see fig. 121)*

| | | |
|---|---|---|
| 10A | 4268 | −506 |
| 9A | 4568 | −206 |
| 10B | 4682 | −92 |
| **8A** | **4774** | **0** |
| 9B | 4876 | 102 |
| 7A | 4950 | 176 |
| 8B | 5072 | 298 |
| 6A | 5150 | 376 |
| 7B | 5275 | 501 |
| 6B | 5458 | 684 |
| 5A | 5659 | 885 |

| | | |
|---|---|---|
| 5B | 5985 | 1211 |
| 4A | 6176 | 1402 |
| 3A | 6360 | 1586 |
| 4B | 6484 | 1710 |
| 2A | 6558 | 1784 |
| 3B | 6684 | 1910 |
| 1A | 6875 | 2101 |
| 2B | 6942 | 2168 |
| 1B | 7162 | 2388 |

### Chime L1 + 2 (yongzhong) (see fig. 121)

| | | |
|---|---|---|
| L1-1A | 2392 | 0 |
| L1-2A | 2462 | 70 |
| L2-10A | 2653 | 261 |
| L1-1B | 2702 | 310 |
| L1-2B | 2751 | 359 |
| L2-9A | 2755 | 363 |
| L2-10B | 2981 | 589 |
| L2-8A | 3117 | 725 |
| L2-9B | 3133 | 741 |
| L2-7A | 3201 | 809 |
| L2-8B | 3388 | 996 |
| L1-3A | 3442 | 1050 |
| L2-5A | 3587 | 1195 |
| L2-7B | 3689 | 1297 |
| L2-4A | 3763 | 1371 |
| L2-3B | 3889 | 1497 |
| L2-5B | 3897 | 1505 |
| L2-3A | 3955 | 1563 |
| L2-4B | 4094 | 1702 |
| L2-2A | 4171 | 1779 |
| L2-1A | 4277 | 1885 |
| L2-3B | 4371 | 1979 |
| L2-2B | 4568 | 2176 |
| L2-1B | 4639 | 2247 |

### Other Warring States period chimes

#### Lithophone from Sanmenxia (Houchuan tomb no. 2041?) (see fig. 135)

| | | |
|---|---|---|
| 1 | **4656** | 0 |
| 2 | 5029 | 373 |
| 3 | 5377 | 721 |
| 4 | no measurement | |

| | | |
|---|---|---|
| 5 | 6060 | 1404 |
| 6 | 6241 | 1585 |
| 7 | 6574 | 1918 |
| 8 | 6731 | 2075 |
| 9 | 7080 | 2424 |

Biao-niuzhong *(12 bells in the Sen'oku Hakkokan only, pitch measurements adjusted to 30° C standard room temperature) (see fig. 128)*

| | | |
|---|---|---|
| **S-1A** | **5372** | **0** |
| S-2A | 5573 | 201 |
| S-3A | 5751 | 379 |
| S-1B | 5772 | 400 |
| S-2B | 5878 | 506 |
| S-3B | 6066 | 694 |
| S-4A | 6226 | 854 |
| S-5A | 6464 | 1092 |
| S-4B | 6539 | 1167 |
| S-6A | 6677 | 1205 |
| S-5B | 6757 | 1385 |
| S-7A | 6951 | 1579 |
| S-6B | 6982 | 1610 |
| S-7B | 7269 | 1897 |
| S-8A | 7457 | 2085 |
| S-9A | 7627 | 2255 |
| S-8B | 7808 | 2436 |
| S-9B | 7938 | 2566 |
| S-10A | 7940 | 2568 |
| S-11A | 8142 | 2770 |
| S-10B | 8291 | 2919 |
| S-11B | 8455 | 3083 |
| S-12A | 8666 | 3284 |
| S-12B | 8955 | 3583 |

Jingli-niuzhong *(A-tones only) (see fig. 129)*

| | | |
|---|---|---|
| 1A | 5950 | −1140 |
| 2A | 6062 | −1028 |
| 3A | 6260 | −830 |
| 4A | 6576 | −514 |
| 5A | 6762 | −328 |
| 6A | 6960 | −130 |
| **7A** | **7090** | **0** |

| | | |
|---|---|---|
| 8A | 7274 | 184 |
| 9A | 7456 | 366 |
| 10A | 7804 | 714 |
| 11A | 7988 | 898 |
| 12A | 8157 | 1067 |
| 13A | 8610[?] | 1520 |

A-TONE.     One of the two tones on a TWO-TONE BELL, produced by striking the center of the bell-face near the SOUND-BOW.

B-TONE.     One of the two tones on a TWO-TONE BELL, produced by striking the side of the bell-face near the SOUND-BOW.

BELL-CHIME (*BIANZHONG* 編鐘). A tuned set of CHIME-BELLS.

*BO* 鎛.     One of the major classes of Chinese musical bells of the Zhou period (*see* bell classification at the beginning of Chapter 2).

CENT NOTATION. A logarithmic measuring unit for tonal intervals, which transforms the exponentially increasing frequency figures into a linear mathematical function. A value of 100 cents is assigned to each semitone.

CHIME.      A musical instrument (e.g., BELL-CHIME, LITHOPHONE) consisting of a set of tuned IDIOPHONES. (Some authors use *chime* synonymously with CHIMESTONE, a usage I avoid.)

CHIME-BELL. A bell manufactured as a component in a BELL-CHIME. Also known as MUSICAL BELL.

CHIMESTONE (*QING* 磬). A tuned slab of stone used with a musical function. Single large chimestones, which go back to the late third millennium B.C., are among the earliest known Chinese musical instruments. Most later chimestones function as components of LITHOPHONES.

CROTAL.     Hollow jingle in which a loose component (e.g., a pebble) produces a sound when the object is agitated. In ancient China, bronze crotals (*luan* 鑾) mainly functioned as parts of horse-and-chariot gear; they have no musical significance and were of no influence on the typological development of CHIME-BELLS.

*CHUNYU* 錞于. A class of bells (for the most part non-musical) manufactured in ancient China (*see* bell classification at the beginning of Chapter 2).

DUO 鐸. Hand-held clapper-bells (*see* bell classification at the beginning of Chapter 2).

FUNDAMENTAL. The most prominently audible PARTIAL of a bell; in ancient Chinese bells, the "nominal" tone of the bell.

GOUDIAO 句鑃. A class of musical bells developed out of the non-musical ZHENG along the southeastern coast of China during the late Springs and Autumns period (*see* bell classification at the beginning of Chapter 2).

GU 鼓. The "striking platform" close to the SOUND-BOW of a bell (*see* fig. 32).

HENG 衡. The top of the shank of a bell (*see* fig. 32).

HIGHER REGISTER. The higher-pitched part of a TONE DISTRIBUTION in a bell-chime, when it features an arrangement of tones different from (usually more regular than) that of the LOWER REGISTER.

IDIOPHONE. An object that, when struck or hit, emits a musically useable tone. In idiophones, the tone is produced by the vibrating substance itself, as opposed to other types of musical instruments, in which the tone is produced by the vibrations of enclosed air (aerophones), a membrane (membranophones), or a string (chordophones).

LING 鈴. Simple clapper-bells suspended from loops, typologically ancestral to all types of Chinese CHIME-BELLS (*see* bell classification at the beginning of Chapter 2).

LITHOPHONE (BIANQING 編磬). A musical instrument consisting of tuned slabs of stone (CHIMESTONES) suspended from a rack.

LOWER REGISTER. The lower-pitched part of a TONE DISTRIBUTION in a BELL-CHIME, when it features an arrangement of tones different from that of the HIGHER REGISTER.

LÜ 律. *See* PITCH STANDARD.

MAJOR-THIRD BELL. A TWO-TONE BELL in which the interval between the A-TONE and B-TONE is a major third (between 350 and 450 CENTS).

MEI 枚. The bosses on the faces of bells decorated according to the STANDARD ZHONG DECORATION SCHEME (*see* fig. 32).

MINOR-THIRD BELL. A TWO-TONE BELL in which the interval between the A-TONE and B-TONE is a minor third (between 250 and 350 CENTS).

"MUDDY" (ZHUO 濁). Prefix used in part of the Zeng inscriptions to lower a PITCH STANDARD by a semitone.

MUSICAL BELL. *See* CHIME-BELL.

NAO 鐃. The first chime-bells of China, manufactured from the late Shang onwards. *Nao* later developed into YONGZHONG (*see* bell classification at the beginning of Chapter 2).

NIU 鈕. The suspension loop of a bell.

NIUZHONG 鈕鐘 (LOOP-BELLS). One of the major classes of Eastern Zhou musical bells; virtually the only one still manufactured after mid–Warring States times (*see* bell classification at the beginning of Chapter 2).

NOTE (*YIN* 音). A constituent part of a musical system, related to other notes by certain defined intervals. Musical pieces consist of notes. In ancient Chinese musical theory, notes were moveable; they could be acoustically actualized as tones only when defined in reference to a PITCH STANDARD (*lü*). (For detailed discussion *see* Chapter 8.)

OCARINA (*XUN* 壎). A clay whistle. Ocarinas are among the oldest Chinese musical instruments, the earliest pieces dating back to Neolithic times.

PARTIAL. Acoustical constituent of a tone. When a bell is struck, many vibration patterns occur simultaneously, each pattern creating a partial; the most prominently audible partial is called the FUNDAMENTAL. The other partials ("overtones") also influence the timbre of the perceived tone.

PITCH STANDARD (*LÜ* 律). An acoustical measuring unit central to ancient Chinese musical theory, determining the pitch at which a musical piece was to be played. To be musically meaningful, tones had to be defined as NOTES in terms of one or another pitch standard. In later times, the concept of *lü* underwent considerable change; as a result, tones could simply be defined as *lü*, and the difference between the notes and the pitch standards became obliterated. (For detailed discussion *see* Chapter 8.)

RECTO (OF A BELL). The side of a bell facing the player.

SCALING. The process of designing and arranging several IDIOPHONES so that they come to constitute a tuned CHIME.

*SCHLAGTON.* The non-musical noise produced by the mallet hitting the bell surface.

SOUND-BOW. The vibrating rim of a bell.

STANDARD *ZHONG* DECORATION SCHEME. The characteristic pattern decorating almost all Zhou musical bells, featuring regularly arranged bosses (*MEI*) and ridges (*ZHUAN*) (*see* fig. 32).

TONE DISTRIBUTION. The distribution of playable tones (= potential NOTES) in a CHIME. Most chimes can emit only a selection of a few tones per octave, which often repeat regularly throughout several octaves; the scrutiny of tone distributions yields important clues to musical theory and practice in ancient China (*see* Chapter 7).

TWO-TONE BELL. A bell of almond-shaped cross-section that, depending on where it is struck, emits either of two distinct tones (A-TONE and B-TONE). In China, this TWO-TONE PHENOMENON was exploited musically from ca. 1000 B.C. onward.

TWO-TONE PHENOMENON. *See* TWO-TONE BELL.

VERSO (OF A BELL). The side of a bell facing away from the player.

*WO* 斡 (TRADITIONALLY, OFTEN *GAN* 幹). The suspension ring of a *YONGZHONG* (*see* fig. 32).

*WU* 舞. The flat top of a bell (*see* fig. 32).

*XIAN* 銑. The pointed spine of a bell of almond-shaped cross-section (*see* fig. 32).

*XUAN* 旋. The bulging horizontal ring around the shank of a bell (*see* fig. 32).

YONG 甬. The shank of a bell (*see* fig. 32).

YONGZHONG 甬鐘 (SHANK-BELLS). The principal class of musical bells of Western and most of Eastern Zhou China (*see* bell classification at the beginning of Chapter 2).

YU 于. The arch-shaped SOUND-BOW of some types of musical bells (*see* fig. 32).

ZHENG 鉦. (1) A class of bells (for the most part non-musical) manufactured in ancient China. *See* bell classification at the beginning of Chapter 2. (2) The upper part of the bell-face according to the STANDARD ZHONG DECORATION SCHEME. *See* fig. 32.

ZHONG 鐘. The most common and inclusive word for *bell* in classical and modern Chinese. More narrowly, this term sometimes refers particularly to CHIME-BELLS.

ZHUAN 篆. Ridges delimiting the ornamented panels (ZHENG [2], ZHUANJIAN, MEI) on the faces of bells decorated according to the STANDARD ZHONG DECORATION SCHEME (*see* fig. 32).

ZHUANJIAN 篆間. Ornamented rectangular panels delimited by ZHUAN, which separate rows of bosses (MEI) on the face of bells decorated according to the STANDARD ZHONG DECORATION SCHEME (*see* fig. 32).

**ABBREVIATIONS OF PROVINCIAL NAMES**

| | |
|---|---|
| AH | Anhui |
| FJ | Fujian |
| GD | Guangdong |
| GS | Gansu |
| GX | Guangxi |
| HB | Hebei |
| HN | Henan |
| HuB | Hubei |
| HuN | Hunan |
| NMG | Inner Mongolia |
| JS | Jiangsu |
| JX | Jiangxi |
| LN | Liaoning |
| SC | Sichuan |
| SD | Shandong |
| ShX | Shaanxi |
| SX | Shanxi |
| YN | Yunnan |
| ZJ | Zhejiang |

County seats and cities related to sites where bells have been discovered are indicated on maps 1 and 2.

## ANHUI PROVINCE (AH) 安徽

Chao Xian 巢縣
  Baizhadi 白閘地

Fanchang 繁昌
  Gao'an 高安
  Huanghu 黃滸
  Tangjiashan 湯家山

Feixi 肥西
  Dadunzi 大墩子

Fuyang 阜陽
  Shuanggudui 雙古堆

Guangde 廣德

Huangshan 黃山
  Yangcun 楊村

Jing Xian 涇縣
  Maolin 茂林

Lujiang 廬江
  Nihequ 泥河區

Qianshan 潛山

Qingyang 清陽
  Wangcun 汪村

Shou Xian 壽縣
  Chengqiang Xiufu Gongdi (City-Wall Repair Site) 城墻修復工地
  Ximennei (Inside the West Gate) 西門內
  Zhi Huai Gongdi (Huai River Dyke-Building Site) 治淮工地
  Zhujiaji 朱家集

Shucheng 舒城
  Jiulidun 九里墩

Wuhu 蕪湖

Xuancheng 宣城
  Zhengxingcun 正興村


## FUJIAN PROVINCE (FJ) 福建

Jian'ou 建甌
  Nanya 南雅
  Yangze 楊澤

GANSU PROVINCE (GS) 甘肅

Yongdeng 永登
  Yushugou 榆樹溝


GUANGDONG PROVINCE (GD) 廣東

Boluo 博羅
  Dalisanwucun 大瀝散屋村
  Meicun 梅村
Fogang 佛崗
  Kewang Damiaoxia 科旺大廟峽
Guangzhou 廣州
  Xianggangshan 象岡山
Huilai 惠來
  Huahu 華湖
Lianping 連平
  Pengshan 彭山
Luoding 羅定
  Nanmendong 南門洞
Qingyuan 慶遠
  Matougang 馬頭崗
Qujiang 曲江
  Maba 馬壩
Xingning 興寧
  Guishuwo 鬼樹窩
Zhaoqing 肇慶
  Songshan 松山


GUANGXI AUTONOMOUS REGION (GX) 廣西

Beiliu 北流
Binyang 賓陽
  Dabeimiao 大北廟
  Liangshuiping 涼水坪
  Luyu 簾圩
  Weipocun 韋坡村
Cenxi 岑溪
Gongcheng 恭城
  Yangjia 秧家

Guanyang 灌陽
  Zhongshan 鐘山
Gui Xian 貴縣
  Luobowan 羅泊灣
He Xian 賀縣
  Shoufeng 壽峰
  Qingfengcun 青風村
  Yingmin 英民
Heng Xian 橫縣
  Maxiang 馬鄉
  Nanxiang 南鄉
  Nasangcun 邢桑村
Liujiang 柳江
  Muluocun 木羅村
Liuzhou 柳州
  Hengshan 橫山
Nanning 南寧
  Supan 蘇盤
Pubei 浦北
  Dalingjiao 大嶺脚
Rong Xian 容縣
  Longjingxie 龍井坳
Wuming 武鳴
  Yuanlongpo 元龍坡
Wuxuan 武宣
Xilin 西林
  Putuo 普馱
Xincheng 忻城
  Datang 大塘


HEBEI PROVINCE (HB) 河北

Ci Xian 磁縣
  Dazhongyingcun 大冢營村
Luanping 灤平
  Paotaishan 炮臺山
Pingshan 平山
  Sanji 三汲

Shijiazhuang 石家莊
  Xiaoyancun 小沿村
Xinglong 興隆
Yi Xian 易縣
  Yan Xiadu 燕下都

## HENAN PROVINCE (HN) 河南

Anyang 安陽
  Dasikongcun 大司空村
  Jiazhuang 家莊
  Wuguancun 武官村
  Xibeigang 西北岡
  Xijiao (Western Suburbs) 西郊
  Yinxu 殷墟
Gushi 固始
  Hougudui 侯古堆
Huaiyang 淮陽
  Pingliangtai 平粮臺
Hui Xian 輝縣
  Liulige 玻璃閣
  Zhaogu 趙固
Ji Xian 汲縣
  Shanbiaozhen 山彪鎮
Luoyang 洛陽
  Changlelu 長樂路
  Jiefanglu 解放路
  Jincun 金村
  Shaogou 燒溝
Pingdingshan 平頂山
  Weizhuang 魏莊
  Zhiyang Xigang 滍陽西崗
Sanmenxia 三門峽
  Houchuan 後川
  Miaodigou 廟底溝
  Shangcunling 上村嶺
Shangcai 上蔡
  Xian Zhuanwachang 縣磚瓦廠
Wen Xian 溫縣
  Xiaonanzhuang 小南莊

Xichuan 淅川
  Xiasi 下寺
Xinyang 信陽
  Caipo 蔡坡
  Changtaiguan 長臺關
Xinye 新野
  Xiaoxiguan 小西關
Xinzheng 新鄭
  Lijialou 李家樓
Xun Xian 濬縣
  Xincun 新村
Yanshi 偃師
  Erlitou 二里頭
Ye Xian 葉縣
  Jiuxian 舊縣
Zhengzhou 鄭州
  Dahecun 大河村

## HUBEI PROVINCE (HUB) 湖北

Changyang 長陽
  Yongheping 永和坪
Dawu 大悟
  Leijiashan 雷家山
Daye 大冶
  Tonglüshan 銅綠山
  Zoumashan 走馬山
Echeng 鄂城
  Beizifan 北仔畈
  Wulipai 五里牌
Guangji 廣濟
  Ya'erzhou 鴨兒洲
Jiangling 江陵
  Gebeisi 葛陂寺
  Paimashan 拍馬山
  Tengdian 藤店
  Tianxingguan 天星關
  Wangshan 望山
  Yutaishan 雨臺山

Jingmen 荊門
  Baoshan 包山
Jingshan 京山
  Sujialong 蘇家壠
Suizhou 隨州
  Bajiaolou 八角樓
  Jishiliang 季氏梁
  Leigudun 擂鼓墩
  Lianyuzui 鰱魚嘴
  Xiongjialaowan 熊家老灣
  Zhoujiagang 周家崗
Tianmen 天門
  Shijiahe 石家河
Yangxin 陽新
  Liurongshan 劉榮山
Zaoyang 棗陽
  Duanying 段營
Zhijiang 枝江
  Xinhua 新華
Zhongxiang 鍾祥
  Huashan 華山
Zigui 秭歸
  Huaibaoshicun 懷抱石村

**HUNAN PROVINCE (HUN)** 湖南

Changde 常德
  Deshan 德山
Changsha 長沙
  Banqiao 板橋
  Liuchengqiao 瀏城橋
  Mawangdui 馬王堆
  Wulipai 五里牌
  Xiangbizui 象鼻嘴
  Xianjiahu 咸家湖
  Yangjiawan 楊家灣
Hengyang 衡陽
  Chang'anxiang 長安鄉
  Beitang 北塘
  Quankoucun 泉口村

Leiyang 耒陽
  Xiajiashan 夏家山
Liling 醴陵
Linli 臨澧
  Jiuli 九里
Linwu 臨武
Liuyang 瀏陽
  Baijiacun 栢嘉村
  Chengtan 澄潭
  Huangjing 黃荊
  Yangmei 楊梅
Ningxiang 寧鄉
  Beifengtan 北峰灘
  Chenjiawan 陳家灣
  Lianhua 蓮花
  Qiaodang 礄壋
  Sanmudi 三畝地
  Shiguzhaishan 師古寨山
  Yueshanpu 月山舖
Pingjiang 平江
  Zhongdong 鐘洞
Shaoshan Guanqu 韶山灌區
Wangcheng 望城
  Gaochong 高冲
Xiangtan 湘潭
  Gaotun 高屯
  Hongjiaqiao 洪家橋
Xiangxiang 湘鄉
  Goutouba 狗頭壩
  Huangmasai 黃馬塞
  Malong 馬龍
  Pingru 坪如
Ximen 西門
  Xiongjiagang 熊家崗
Xupu 漵浦
  Dajiangkou 大江口
Yiyang 益陽
  Yangwuling 楊舞嶺
Yueyang 岳陽
  Feijiahe 費家河

Zhijiang 芷江
　Yilijiecun 一里街村
Zhuzhou 株洲
　Huangzhu 黃竹
　Sanpu 傘鋪
　Touba 頭壩
　Xinglongcun 興隆村
　Youzhencun 油畇村
Zixing 資興
　Lanshi 蘭市
　Tian'eshan 天鵝山


INNER MONGOLIA (NMG) 內蒙古

Kalaxin Banner 喀喇沁旗
　Xishan 西山
Ningcheng (*see* Liaoning Province)


JIANGSU PROVINCE (JS) 江蘇

Dantu 丹徒
　Beishanding 北山頂
　Wangjiashan 王家山
Donghai 東海
　Miaodun 廟墩
Gaochun 高淳
　Qingshan 青山
　Qiqiao 柒橋
　Songxi 松溪
Jiangning 江寧
　Tangdongcun 塘東村
Lianyungang 連雲港
　Jinpingshan 錦屏山
Liyang 溧陽
Luhe 六合
　Chengqiao 程橋
Pi Xian 邳縣
　Dadunzi 大墩子
　Liulin 柳林

Wujiang 吳江
　Hengba 橫壩
Wujin 武進
　Yancheng 淹城
Xuzhou 徐州
　Beidongshan 北洞山
　Zifangshan 子房山


JIANGXI PROVINCE (JX) 江西

Fengcheng 豐城
　Xinhuicun 辛會村
Jing'an 靖安
　Linkesuo 林科所
Jishui 吉水
Pingxiang 萍鄉
　Dengjiatiancun 鄧家田村
　Pengjiaqiao 彭家橋
Qingjiang 清江
　Shanqian Commune 山前公社
Taihe 泰和
Wanzai 萬載
　Changhe 長和
Wuning 武寧
　Qingjiang 清江
Xinyu 新余
　Jiashan 家山
　Luofang 羅坊
　Yulongshan 玉龍山
Xiushui 修水
　Zengjiashan 曾家山


LIAONING PROVINCE (LN) 遼寧

Jianping 建平
　Kalaxinhe 喀喇沁河
Lingyuan 凌源
　Sanguandian 三官甸
　Wudaohezi 五道河子

Ningcheng (now in Inner Mongolia) 寧城
  Sunjiagou 孫家溝


## SHAANXI PROVINCE (SHX) 陝西

Baoji 寶鷄
  Guozhen 虢鎮
  Rujiazhuang 茹家莊
  Taigongmiao 太公廟
  Xigaoquan 西高泉
  Zhuyuangou 竹園溝
Chang'an 長安
  Puducun 普渡村
  Keshengzhuang 客省莊
  Mawangcun 馬王村
  Zhangjiapc 張家坡
Fengxiang 鳳翔
  Daxin 大辛
Fufeng 扶風
  Baijiacun 白家村
  Baozigou 豹子溝
  Beiqiao 北橋
  Beiqishan 北岐山
  Dongjucun 東渠村
  Guanwudiaozhuang 官務吊莊
  Huangdui 黃堆
  Liujiacun 劉家村
  Qiangjiacun 强家村
  Qijiacun 齊家村
  Qizhen 齊鎮
  Wujun Xicun 五郡西村
  Zhuangbai 莊白
Lantian 藍田
  Hongxing (Red Star) Commune 紅星公社
Lintong 臨潼
  Nanluo 南羅
  Qin Shihuangling 秦始皇陵
Mei Xian 眉縣
  Yangjiacun 楊家村

Qian Xian 乾縣
  Zhoujiahe 周家河
Wugong 武功
  Huilongcun 回龍村
Xianyang 咸陽
Yao Xian 耀縣
  Dingjiagou 丁家溝
Yongshou 永壽
  Haosihe 好時河


## SHANDONG PROVINCE (SD) 山東

Haiyang 海陽
  Guanyang Gucheng 觀陽古城
  Zuiziqiancun 嘴子前村
Huimin 惠民
  Daguo 大椁
Ju Xian 莒縣
  Tianjingwang 天景汪
Junan 莒南
  Dadian 大店
Linqu 臨朐
  Yangshan 楊善
Linyi 臨沂
  Ezhuangqu Huayuan 鵝莊區花園
  Fenghuangling 鳳凰嶺
Linzi 臨淄
  Daifuguan 大夫觀
  Heyatou 河崖頭
  Jishan 稷山
Penglai 蓬萊
  Liugezhuang 柳格莊
Qingzhou (formerly Yidu) 青州(益都)
  Subutun 蘇埠屯
Shouguang 壽光
  Yiduhoucheng 益都侯城
Teng Xian 滕縣
  Zhuangli-Xi 莊里西

Yangxin 陽信
　　Xibeicun 西北村
Yantai 煙臺
　　Shangkuangcun 上夼村
Yishui 沂水
　　Liujiadianzi 劉家店子
Zhangqiu 章丘
　　Xiao'emeishan 小峨眉山
Zhucheng 諸城
　　Zangjiazhuang 臧家莊

## SHANXI PROVINCE (SX) 山西

Changzhi 長治
　　Fenshuiling 分水嶺
Hongdong 洪洞
　　Yongningbao 永寧堡
Houma 侯馬
　　Shangmacun 上馬村
Lingshi 靈石
　　Jingjiecun 旌介村
Linyi 臨猗
　　Chengcun 程村
Lucheng 潞城
　　Luhe 潞河
Quwo 曲沃
　　Qucun 曲村
Shilou 石樓
　　Caojiayuan 曹家垣
Taiyuan 太原
　　Jinshengcun 金勝村
Wanrong 萬榮
　　Miaoqiancun 廟前村
Wenxi 聞喜
　　Nansongcun 南宋村
　　Shangguocun 上郭村
Xia Xian 夏縣
　　Dongxiafeng 東夏馮

Xiangfen 襄汾
　　Dagudui 大崮堆
　　Taosi 陶寺

## SICHUAN PROVINCE (SC) 四川

Fuling 涪陵
　　Xiaotianxi 小田溪
Huili 會理
　　Zhuanchangba 磚場壩
Xindu 新都
　　Jiuliandun 九聯墩

## YUNNAN PROVINCE (YN) 雲南

Chuxiong 楚雄
　　Wanjiaba 萬家壩
Jinning 晉寧
　　Shizhaishan 石寨山
Kunming 昆明
　　Ludian 魯店
Mouding 牟定
　　Futulongcun 福土龍村
Xiangyun 祥雲
　　Dabona 大波那
　　Jiancun 檢村

## ZHEJIANG PROVINCE (ZJ) 浙江

Changxing 長興
　　Caoloucun 草樓村
　　Changxing Middle School 長興中學
Deqing 德慶
　　Xinshi 新市
Haiyan 海鹽
　　Huangjiashan 黃家山
Jiangshan 江山
Jinhua 金華

Pan'an 盤安
  Shenze 深澤
Shaoxing 紹興
  Goutoushan 狗頭山
Xiaoshan 蕭山
  Dujiacun 杜家村
Yin Xian 鄞縣
  Sanlian 三聯
Yuhang 余杭
  Chongxian 崇賢
  Xujiafan 徐家畈

BIBLIOGRAPHY

*Classical Texts*

*Chu Ci* 楚辭 (Elegies of Chu), by Qu Yuan 屈原 (trad. dates 343?–ca. 315 B.C.) et al. EDI-
TION: *Chu Ci Buzhu* 楚辭補注, by Hong Xingzu 洪興祖 (1090–1155), with
*Soshi Sakuin* 楚辭索引, by Takeji Sadao 竹治貞夫, joint indexed edition, Kyōto:
Chūbun, 1964; reissued, 1979. TRANSLATION: Hawkes, David (Qu Yuan et al.),
*The Songs of the South*, Harmondsworth: Penguin, 1985.

*Chunqiu* 春秋 (The Springs and Autumns chronicle). Chronicle of the state of Lu, spanning
the years 722–468 B.C., allegedly edited by Kong Qiu 孔丘 (Confucius) (trad.
dates 552/551–479 B.C.). *Zuo Zhuan* 左傳 (Zuo commentary on the *Chunqiu*),
attributed to Zuoqiu Ming 左丘明 (probably fourth century B.C.). EDITIONS:
*Chunqiu Jingzhuan Yinde* 春秋經傳引得 (Combined concordances to the *Chunqiu*
chronicle and its three commentaries), Harvard-Yenching Institute Index Series,
supplement no. 11, Beijing, 1937; reprint, Taibei, 1966. 4 vols. (cited here as
"HYI edition"); commentary on *Zuo Zhuan* by Du Yu 杜預 (4th century A.D.)
and subcommentary by Kong Yingda 孔穎達 (A.D. 574–648) quoted from Ruan
Yuan's *Shisanjing Zhushu* (*see* Works of Premodern Scholarship, below). TRANS-
LATIONS: Legge, James, *The Ch'un Ts'ew with the Tso Chuen*, i.e., *The Chinese
Classics*, vol. 5, Oxford: Clarendon Press, 1872; reprint, Taibei: Southern Mate-
rials Center, 1983. Couvreur, Séraphin, *Tch'ouen-ts'iou et Tso-tchouan*, Ho Kien
Fou: Imprimerie de la Mission Catholique, 1914, 3 vols.

*Er Ya* 爾雅 (Dictionary of elegant expression), author(s) unknown, probably compiled at the
beginning of the Western Han dynasty. EDITION: *Er Ya Yinde* 爾雅引得 (Concordance to *Er Ya*), Harvard-Yenching Institute Index Series supplement no. 58,
Beijing, 1941; reprint, Taibei, 1966 (cited here as "HYI edition").

*Guan Zi* 管子 (Master Guan), Warring States period miscellany traditionally attributed to
Guan Zhong 管仲 (?–645 B.C.). EDITION: *Guan Zi*, with commentary by Fang

Xuanling 房玄齡 (A.D. 578–648), Guoxue Jiben Congshu edition, Shanghai: Shangwu, n.d.; reissued, Taibei, 1968. TRANSLATION (so far partial): Rickett, W. Allyn, *Guan Zi*, Princeton: Princeton University Press, 1985, vol. 1 (supersedes earlier edition).

*Guo Yu* 國語 (Narratives of the states), attributed to Zuoqiu Ming (cf. *Chunqiu*). EDITION: *Tiansheng Mingdao-ben Guo Yu* 天聖明道本國語, with commentary by Wei Zhao 韋昭 (A.D. 197–278), reissued after a Ming edition in 1800. PARTIAL TRANSLATION: Hart, James P., *The Philosophy of the Chou Yu*, Ph.D. diss., University of Washington, 1973; d'Hormon, André, *Guoyu: Propos sur les principautés*, edited and enlarged by Rémi Mathieu, Paris: Collège de France, Insititut des Hautes-Études Chinoises, 1985.

*Han Fei Zi* 韓非子 (Master Han Fei), by Han Fei 韓非 (ca. 280–233 B.C.). EDITION: *Han Fei Zi Yinde* 韓非子引得 (Index to the *Han Fei Zi*), Beijing: Zhonghua, 1982.

*Han Shu* 漢書 (Official history of the Western Han dynasty), by Ban Gu 班固 (A.D. 32–92) et al. EDITIONS: *Han Shu*, Beijing: Zhonghua, 1962, 20 vols.; *Han Shu Yiwenzhi* 漢書藝文志 (The Bibliographical Treatise of the *Han Shu*), indexed edition, Shanghai: Shangwu, 1954. PARTIAL TRANSLATION: Dubs, Homer H., *History of the Former Han Dynasty*, Baltimore: Waverley, 1938–1955, 3 vols.

*Huainan Zi* 淮南子 (Lord of Huainan), miscellany compiled under the direction of Liu An 劉安, Prince of Huainan (178?–122 B.C.). EDITION: *Huainan Zi*, with commentary by Gao You 高誘 (fl. A.D. 205–212), Sibu Congkan edition, Shanghai: Shangwu, 1927; reissued, Taibei, n.d.

*Li Ji* 禮記 (Notes on ritual; also known as *Xiao Dai Li Ji* 小戴禮記), allegedly compiled by Dai Sheng 戴聖 (Western Han dynasty), probably containing substantial pre-Qin portions. EDITION: *Li Ji Zhushu*, with commentary by Zheng Xuan 鄭玄 (A.D. 127–200) and Kong Yingda (cf. *Chunqiu*). Collation notes for each *juan* by Ruan Yuan 阮元 (1764–1849), Sibu Beiyao edition, Shanghai: Zhonghua, 1927; reissued, Taibei, n.d., 4 vols. TRANSLATION: Couvreur, Séraphin, *Li Ki, ou Mémoires sur les bienséances et cérémonies*, Ho Kien Fou: Imprimerie de la Mission Catholique, 1913.

*Lunyu* 論語 (The analects of Confucius), compiled by the followers of Confucius. EDITION: *Lun Yu Yinde* 論語引得 (Concordance to *Lun Yu*), Harvard-Yenching Institute Index Series, supplement no. 16, Beijing, 1940 (cited here as "HYI edition"). TRANSLATION: Lau, D. C., *Confucius, The Analects (Lun Yü)*, Harmondsworth: Penguin, 1979.

*Lüshi Chunqiu* 呂氏春秋 (Springs and autumns of Mr. Lü), compiled under the direction of Lü Buwei 呂不韋 (?–235 B.C.), preface dated 245 B.C. EDITION: *Lüshi Chunqiu*, with commentary by Gao You (cf. *Huainan Zi*), Sibu Congkan edition, Shanghai: Shangwu, 1927; reissued, Taibei, n.d. TRANSLATION: Wilhelm, Richard, *Frühling und Herbst des Lü-Bu-We*, Jena: Diederichs, 1928.

*Meng Zi* 孟子 (Master Meng), by Meng Ke 孟軻 (Mencius) (ca. 372–289 B.C.). EDITION: *Meng Zi Yinde* 孟子引得 (Concordance to *Meng Zi*), Harvard-Yenching Institute Index Series supplement no. 17, Beijing, 1941 (here cited as "HYI edition"). TRANSLATION: Lau, D. C., *Mencius*, Harmondsworth: Penguin Books, 1970.

*Mo Zi* 墨子 (Master Mo), by Mo Di 墨翟 (trad. dates: 468–376 B.C.) and others. EDITION: *Mo Zi Yinde* 墨子引得 (Concordance to *Mo Zi*), Harvard-Yenching Institute Index Series supplement no. 21, Beijing, 1937 (here cited as "HYI edition").

*Shen Zi* 慎子 (Master Shen), by Shen Dao 慎到 (ca. 360–ca. 285 B.C.). EDITION: Thompson, P. M., *The Shen Tzu Fragments*, London Oriental Series vol. 29, Oxford: Oxford University Press, 1979.

*Shi Ji* 史記 (Record of the historian), by Sima Tan 司馬談 (?–110 B.C.) and Sima Qian 司馬遷 (145 or 135–ca. 90 B.C.). EDITION: *Shi Ji*, Beijing: Zhonghua, 1959, 10 vols. TRANSLATION: Chavannes, Édouard, *Les Mémoires historiques de Se-ma Ts'ien*, Paris: Leroux, 1895–1905 and 1969, 6 vols.

*Shi Jing* 詩經 (Classic of poetry; also known as *Mao Shi* 毛詩 [The Odes as annotated by Mao Heng 毛亨 (2nd century B.C.)]), allegedly compiled by Confucius; poems ranging in date from Western Zhou through ca. 6th century. EDITION: *Mao Shi Yinde* 毛詩引得 (Concordance to the Mao version of *Shi Jing*), Harvard-Yenching Institute Index Series supplement no. 9, Beijing, 1936; reprint, Tōkyō 1962 (here cited as "HYI edition"). TRANSLATIONS: Karlgren, Bernhard, *The Book of Odes*, Stockholm: Museum of Far Eastern Antiquities, 1959 (contains amended text). Karlgren's philological commentary has been published as *Glosses on the Book of Odes*, Stockholm: Museum of Far Eastern Antiquities, 1964 (reprinted from *Bulletin of the Museum of Far Eastern Antiquities* 14 [1942]: 71–247; 16 [1944]: 25–169; 18 [1946]: 1–198). Waley, Arthur, *The Book of Songs*, 1937; reprint, New York: Grove, 1960.

*Shu Jing* 書經 (Classic of history; also known as *Shang Shu* 尚書 [Venerable documents from antiquity]), allegedly compiled by Confucius; documents in the *jinwen* (Modern Text) version ranging in date from Western Zhou through the Warring States period; the *guwen* (Old Text) version contains additional materials commonly regarded as Han forgeries. EDITION: *Shang Shu Tongjian* 尚書通檢 (Conspectus of *Shang Shu*), edited by Gu Jiegang 顧頡剛 (1893–1979), Beijing, 1936; reissued, Beijing: Shumu Wenxian, 1982. TRANSLATIONS: Karlgren, Bernhard, "The Book of Documents," *Bulletin of the Museum of Far Eastern Antiquities* 22 (1950): 1–82 (*jinwen* documents only); philological commentaries published as: *Glosses on the Book of Documents*, Stockholm: Museum of Far Eastern Antiquities, 1970 (reprinted from *Bulletin of the Museum of Far Eastern Antiquities* 20 [1948]: 39–315, and 21 [1949]: 63–206). Legge, James, *The Shoo King*, i.e., *The Chinese Classics*, vol. 3, Oxford: Clarendon Press, 1868 (various reprints); contains both *jinwen* and *guwen* documents.

*Shuowen Jiezi* 說文解字 (Explaining the graphs and analyzing the characters), by Xu Shen 許慎 (ca. 58–147 A.D.). EDITION: *Shuowen Jiezi-zhu* 說文解字注 (*Shuowen Jiezi* Annotated), by Duan Yucai 段玉裁 (1735–1815); indexed edition, Shanghai: Shanghai Guji, 1981 (cited here as "*Shuowen*").

*Wen Xuan* 文選 (Literary anthology), compiled by Xiao Tong 蕭統 (501–531). EDITION: *Wen Xuan Liu Chen Zhu* 文選六臣注 (The *Wen Xuan*, annotated by six princely subjects), with commentaries by six Tang dynasty scholars, Sibu Congkan edition, Shanghai: Shangwu, 1928.

*Xin Shu* 新書 (New writings), by Jia Yi 賈誼 (200–168 B.C.). EDITION: *Xin Shu*, with collation notes by Lu Wenchao 盧文紹 (1717–1796), Sibu Beiyao edition, Shanghai: Zhonghua, 1927; reissued, Taibei, n.d.

*Xun Zi* 荀子 (Master Xun), by Xun Kuang 荀況 (ca. 313–238 B.C.). EDITION: *Xun Zi Yinde* 荀子引得 (Concordance to *Xun Zi*), Harvard-Yenching Institute Index Series, supplement no. 22, Beijing, 1950 (cited here as "HYI edition"). TRANSLATION (so far partial): Knoblock, John, *Xunzi, A translation and study of the complete works*, Stanford, Calif.: Stanford University Press, 1988, vol. 1.

*Yan Zi Chunqiu* 晏子春秋 (Springs and autumns of Master Yan). Late pre-Qin miscellany, traditionally connected with Yan Ying 晏嬰 (?–500 B.C.). EDITION: *Yan Zi Chunqiu jishi* 晏子春秋集釋, ed. by Wu Zeyu 吳則虞 (20th century); reissued, Taibei: Dingwen, 1977. TRANSLATION: Holtzer, Peter, *Yen-tzu und das Yen-tzu Ch'un-ch'iu*, Frankfurt: Peter Lang, 1985.

*Yi Jing* 易經 (Classic of changes; also known as *Zhou Yi* 周易), divinatory manual with portions dating from Western(?) Zhou through Western Han times. EDITION: *Zhou Yi Yinde* 周易引得 (Concordance to the *Zhou Yi*), Harvard-Yenching Institute Index Series, supplement no. 10, Beijing, 1937 (cited here as "HYI edition"). TRANSLATION: Wilhelm, Richard, *I Ging*, Jena: Diederichs, 1923; new edition, Düsseldorf, 1973.

*Yi Li* 儀禮 (Ceremonial protocol), author(s) unknown, probably dating to the 3rd century B.C. EDITION: *Yi Li Zhengyi* 儀禮正義 (Rectified meaning of the *Yi Li*), with commentary by Zheng Xuan (cf. *Li Ji*) and subcommentary by Sun Yirang 孫詒讓 (1848–1908), Sibu Beiyao edition, Shanghai: Shangwu, 1927. TRANSLATION: Couvreur, Séraphin, *Cérémonial*, Hsien Hsien: Imprimerie de la Mission Catholique, 1916; 2d ed., 1928; new edition, Paris: Cathasia, 1951.

*Zhan'guo-ce* 戰國策 (Episodes from the Warring States), edited by Liu Xiang 劉向 (ca. 77–6 B.C.). EDITION: *Zhan'guo-ce jiaozhu* 戰國策校注 (Collated and annotated *Zhan'guo-ce*), by Bao Biao 鮑彪 (Song dynasty), with a commentary by Gao You (cf. *Huainan Zi*), Sibu Congkan edition, Shanghai: Shangwu, 1929. TRANSLATION: Crump, J. L., *Chan-kuo Ts'e*, revised 2d ed. (occasional series, no. 41), San Francisco: Chinese Materials and Research Aids Service Center, 1979.

*Zhou Li* 周禮 (The ritual system of the Zhou), author(s) unknown, probably dating to the

3rd century B.C. EDITION: *Zhou Li Zhengyi* 周禮正義 (Rectified meaning of the *Zhou Li*), with commentary by Zheng Xuan (cf. *Li Ji*) and subcommentary by Sun Yirang (cf. *Yi Li*), Sibu Beiyao edition, Shanghai: Zhonghua, 1927; reissued, Taibei, n.d., 6 vols. TRANSLATION: Biot, Édouard, *Le Tcheou-Li ou Rites des Tcheou*, Paris: Imprimerie Nationale, 1851, 3 vols; reprinted, Taibei, 1975.

*Zhuang Zi* 莊子 (Master Zhuang), by Zhuang Zhou 莊周 (ca. 369–286) et al. EDITION: *Zhuang Zi Yinde* 莊子引得 (Concordance to *Zhuang Zi*), Harvard-Yenching Institute Index Series, supplement no. 20, Beijing, 1936 (cited here as "HYI edition"). TRANSLATIONS: Watson, Burton, *The Complete Works of Chuang Tzu*, New York: Columbia University Press, 1968; Graham, Angus C., *Chuang Tzû, The Inner Chapters*, London: George Allen & Unwin, 1981.

*Zuo Zhuan*. See *Chunqiu*.


## Works of Premodern Scholarship

Cheng Yaotian 程瑤田 (1725–1814). *Kaogong chuangwu xiaoji* 考工創物小記 (Short records on the objects manufactured by the [Zhou] royal artisans). In *Huang Qing jingjie* 皇清經解 (Imperial Qing edition of the Chinese Classics and their commentaries), vols. 125–26 (j. 537–38).

Dai Zhen 戴震 (1724–1777). *Kaogongji-tu* 考工記圖 (Illustrations on the *Kaogongji*). In *Huang Qing jingjie* (Imperial Qing edition of the Chinese Classics and their commentaries), j. 132.

Liang Shizheng 梁詩正 (18th century), compiler. *Xi Qing gujian* 西清古鑑 (Bronzes in the Qing imperial collection in the Xi Qing Studio), compiled ca. 1751–1752. Edition, Shanghai: Hongwen, 1888. 24 vols.

Lü Dalin 呂大臨 (fl. 1092), compiler. *Kaogutu* 考古圖 (Illustrations for inquiring into antiquity). Edition by Huang Sheng 黃聖 (Qing dynasty), in *Sangutu* 三古圖, vols. 20–23.

Ruan Yuan 阮元 (1764–1849), compiler. *Shisanjing zhushu* 十三經注疏 (Annotations and commentaries on the Thirteen Classics). New edition in two volumes and an index volume, Beijing: Zhonghua, 1980.

Shen Gua 沈括 (1031–1095). *Xinjiaozheng Mengxi bitan* 新校正夢溪筆談 (The newly collated *Scribblings of Dreamy Brook [i.e., Shen Gua]*). Edited by Hu Daojing 胡道靜. Beijing: Zhonghua, 1959, reissued 1987.

Wang Fu 王黼 (fl. 12th century) et al., compilers. *Bogutulu* 博古圖錄 (a.k.a. *Xuanhe Bogutu* 宣和博古圖) (Catalog of antiques in the Song imperial collection), compiled ca. 1123. Edition by Wu Gonghong 吳恭鴻, 1603; reprint, Taibei: Yiwen Yinshuguan, n.d.

Wang Jie 王杰 (late 18th century) et al., compilers. *Xi Qing xujian* 西清續鑑 (Further bronzes in the Qing imperial collection on display in the Xi Qing Studio), compiled ca. 1793. 2 series: *Jiabian* 甲編, edition, Shanghai: Hanfenlou, 1911; *Yibian* 乙編, edition, Beijing: National Palace Museum, 1931. 20 vols. each.

Wang Yinzhi 王引之 (1766–1834). *Jingyi shuwen* 經義述聞 (Gleanings on the meaning of the Classics). In *Huang Qing jingjie* (Imperial Qing edition of the Chinese Classics and their commentaries), vols. 260–71 (j. 1781–1809).

Xue Shanggong 薛尚功 (13th century). *Lidai zhongding yiqi kuanzhi* 歷代鐘鼎彝器欵識 (Assessment of bells, tripods, and other ritual vessels from historical times). Edited by Yu Xingwu 于省吾. 4 vols., Gu Shu Liutongchu, 1935.

Zhao Jiucheng 趙九成 (fl. 1162), compiler. *Xu-Kaogutu* 續考古圖 (Sequel to *Kaogutu*). Edition, Suzhou: Taoshengfu, 1902; reprint, Taibei: Yiwen Yinshuguan, 1970.

Zheng Qiao 鄭樵 (1104–1162). *Tongzhi-lüe* 通志略 (The "Abbreviated Discussions" from the *Tongzhi* miscellanea). Sibu Beiyao edition, Shanghai: Shangwu, n.d.

*Works Cited by Title*

*Ancient Chinese bronzes in the collection of the Shanghai Museum.* 1983. Hong Kong: Hong Kong Museum of Art.

*Ancient ritual bronzes of China.* 1976. George Kuwayama. Los Angeles: Los Angeles County Museum of Art.

*Anhui Sheng Bowuguan-cang qingtongqi* (Bronzes in the collection of the Anhui Provincial Museum). 1987. Shanghai: Renmin Meishu.

*Art from ritual: Ancient Chinese bronze vessels from the Arthur M. Sackler Collections.* 1983. Dawn Ho Delbanco. Cambridge, Mass.: Fogg Museum.

*Arts of China I* (Neolithic cultures to Tang dynasty), *Recent discoveries.* 1968. Ed. Akiyama Terukazu et al. Tōkyō: Kōdansha. 1968.

*Baoji Yu-guo mudi* (The necropolis of the state of Yu at Baoji). 1988. Lu Liancheng and Hu Zhisheng. Beijing: Wenwu. 2 vols.

*Bronzi dell'antica Cina.* 1988. Milano: Electa.

*Chang'an Zhangjiapo Xi-Zhou tongqiqun* (The Western Zhou hoard of bronzes at Zhangjiapo, Chang'an). 1965. Beijing: Wenwu.

*Changsha fajue baogao* (Changsha excavation report). 1957. Beijing: Kexue.

*Changsha Mawangdui yihao Han-mu* (The Han dynasty tomb no. 1 at Mawangdui, Changsha). 1973. Beijing: Wenwu.

*Chine, Trésors et splendeurs.* 1986. Montreal: Palais de la Civilisation; Paris: Arthaud.

*Chinesisches Kunsthandwerk der Provinz Anhui aus drei Jahrtausenden.* 1988. Hannover: Niedersächsisches Landesmuseum, Völkerkunde-Abteilung.

*Chu wenhua kaogu dashiji* (A record of important events in the archaeology of Chu culture). 1984. Beijing: Wenwu.

*Chu wenwu zhanlan tulu* (Illustrated catalog of the exhibition of Chu cultural relics). 1954. Beijing: Wenwu.

*Chūgoku Konan-shō shutsudo bunbutsu* (Cultural relics excavated in Hunan province, China). 1985. Otsu; Shiga Kokusai Yūkō Shinzen Kyokai.

*Chūgoku Rekishi Hakubutsukan* (The Museum for Chinese History, Beijing). 1982. Tōkyō: Heibonsha.

*Chūgoku Sensei-shō Hōkei-shi Shūgen bunbutsuten* (Exhibition of cultural remains of Zhouyuan from Baoji municipality, Shaanxi province, China). 1988. Gifu: Gifu-shi Rekishi Hakubutsukan.

*Chūgoku tōyō-no bi* (The beauty of Chinese clay figures). 1985–86. Tōkyō: Tōkyō National Museum.

*Chūka Jinmin Kyōwakoku kodai seidōkiten* (Exhibition of ancient bronzes from the People's Republic of China). 1976. Tōkyō: Tōkyō National Museum.

*Chūka Jinmin Kyōwakoku shutsudo bunbutsuten* (Exhibition of cultural relics excavated in the People's Republic of China). 1973. Tōkyō et al.: Tōkyō National Museum.

*Chūka Jinmin Kyōwakoku shutsudo bunbutsuten* (Exhibition of cultural relics excavated in the People's Republic of China). 1977–78. Tōkyō et al.: Tōkyō National Museum.

*Chung'ang Kungnip Pangmulkwan* (The National Museum of Korea). 1978. Seoul.

*Chūzan ōkoku bunbutsuten* (Exhibition of cultural relics from the kingdom of Zhongshan). 1981. Tōkyō et al.: Tōkyō National Museum.

*Dai Kōga bunmei-no nagare (Santō-shō bunbutsuten)* (The flow of civilization along the great Yellow River [Exhibition of cultural relics from Shandong province]). 1986. Yamaguchi: Yamaguchi Prefectural Museum.

*Dian, Ein versunkenes Königreich in China.* 1987–88. Zürich et al.: Museum Rietberg et al.

*Dictionnaire français de la langue chinoise.* 1976. Compiled by the Institut Ricci. Taibei: Kuangchi.

*Fengxi fajue baogao* (Fengxi excavation report). 1962. Beijing: Wenwu.

*Fufeng Qijiacun qingtongqiqun* (The hoard of bronzes from Qijiacun, Fufeng). 1960. Beijing: Wenwu.

*Gakki.* 1982. Kyōto: Sen'oku Hakkokan.

*Gaocheng Taixi Shang-dai yizhi* (The Shang dynasty site at Taixi, Gaocheng). 1985. Beijing: Wenwu.

*Gongnong kaogu jichuzhishi* (Basic archaeological know-how for workers and peasants). 1978. Beijing: Wenwu.

*The great Bronze Age of China.* 1980. Ed. Wen Fong. New York: Metropolitan Museum of Art.

*Guangdong chutu xian-Qin wenwu* (Pre-Qin cultural relics excavated in Guangdong). 1984. Hong Kong: Zhongwen Daxue Wenwuguan.

*Guangdong wenwu pucha chengguo tulu* (Pictorial record of the results of the cultural relics survey of Guangdong province). 1990. Guangzhou: Guangdong Keji.

*Guangxi chutu wenwu* (Cultural relics excavated in Guangxi). 1978. Beijing: Wenwu.

*Guangxi Gui Xian Luobowan Han-mu* (The Han tombs at Luobowan, Gui Xian [Guangxi]). 1988. Beijing: Wenwu.

*Guangzhou Han-mu* (The Han tombs of Guangzhou). 1981. 2 vols. Beijing: Wenwu.

*Gugong tongqi tulu* (Album of bronzes in the National Palace Museum). 1958. 2 vols. Taibei: National Palace Museum.

*Henan chutu Shang Zhou qingtongqi* (Shang and Zhou bronzes excavated in Henan). Vol. 1, 1981. Beijing: Wenwu. Subsequent volumes never published.

*Henan Xinyang Chu-mu chutu wenwu tulu* (Illustrated catalog of cultural relics excavated in the Chu tomb at Xinyang, Henan). 1959. Zhengzhou: Henan Renmin.

*Higashi Ajia bunmei-no genryūten* (Exhibition on the origins of East Asian civilization). 1989. Toyama: Toyama Shi Taiiku Bunka Sentā.

*Houjiazhuang* ([The site of] Houjiazhuang). In *Zhongguo kaogu baogaoji* (Collection of archaeological reports from China). No. 3, *Houjiazhuang.* Gao Quxun et al. Taibei: Academia Sinica, Institute of History and Philology. v.2 (1962 [two fascicles]), v.3 (1965), v.4 (1967), v.5 (1970), v.6 (1968).

*Hubei Suizhou Leigudun chutu wenwu* (Cultural relics excavated at Leigudun, Suizhou [Hubei]). 1984. Hong Kong: Zhongguo Wenwu Zhanlanguan.

*Hui Xian fajue baogao.* 1956. Guo Baojun. Beijing: Kexue.

*Hunan-sheng wenwu tulu* (Illustrated catalogue of cultural relics from Hunan province). 1964. Changsha: Hunan Renmin.

*Ice and green clouds: Traditions of Chinese celadon.* 1987. Mino Yutaka and Katherine R. Tsiang. Indianapolis: Indianapolis Museum of Art/Indiana University Press.

*Jadequell und Wolkenmeer: 5000 Jahre chinesischer Kunst aus dem Museum von Shanghai.* 1988. Hamburg: Museum für Kunst und Gewerbe.

*Jiangling Yutaishan Chu-mu* (The Chu tombs at Yutaishan, Jiangling). 1984. Beijing: Wenwu).

*Jiangsu chutu wenwu* (Cultural relics excavated in Jiangsu). 1963. Beijing: Wenwu.

*Jianming Zhongguo lishi tuce* (Brief atlas of Chinese history). Vol. 1, *Yuanshi shehui* (Primitive society). 1978. Tianjin: Renmin Meishu.

*Kōga bunmeiten* (Exhibition on the Yellow River civilization). 1986. Tōkyō: Tōkyō National Museum.

*Kokyū Hakubutsukan* (The Palace Museum, Beijing). 1975. Tōkyō: Kōdansha.

*Konan-shō Hakubutsukan* (The Hunan Provincial Museum). 1981. Tōkyō: Kōdansha.

*Linyi Fenghuangling Dong-Zhou-mu* (The Eastern Zhou tombs at Fenghuangling, Linyi [Shandong]). 1987. Jinan: Qilu Shushe.

*Luoyang Shaogou Han-mu* (The Han tombs at Shaogou, Luoyang). 1959. Beijing: Kexue.

*Luoyang Zhongzhou-lu (Xi gongduan)* ([Excavations along] Zhongzhou Road, Luoyang

[Western Section]). 1959. Su Bingqi et al. Beijing: Kexue.

*Miaodigou yu Sanliqiao* ([The sites of] Miaodigou and Sanliqiao). 1959. Beijing: Kexue.

*Nanjing Shi Bowuguan* (The Municipal Museum of Nanjing). 1987. Beijing: Wenwu.

*The new Grove dictionary of music and musicians.* 1980. Ed. Stanley Sadie. 20 vols. London: Macmillan; New York: Grove's Dictionaries of Music et al.

*Qingtongqi tushi* (Illustrations and explanations of bronzes [in the Shaanxi Provincial Museum]). 1960. Beijing: Wenwu.

*Quanguo chutu wenwu zhenpinxuan* (Selection of valuable excavated cultural relics from the entire country). 1987. Beijing: Wenwu.

*The quest for eternity.* 1987. Los Angeles: Chronicle Books and Los Angeles County Museum of Art.

*Sainan rekishi bunbutsu* (Historical relics from Jinan). 1985. Wakayama.

*Sensei-shō Hakubutsukan* (The Shaanxi Provincial Museum). 1982. Tōkyō: Kōdansha.

*Shaanxi chutu Shang Zhou qingtongqi* (Shang and Zhou bronzes excavated in Shaanxi). 1980–84. 4 vols. Beijing: Wenwu.

*Shanbiaozhen yu Liulige* ([The sites of] Shanbiaozhen and Liulige). 1959. Guo Baojun. Beijing: Kexue.

*Shandong wenwu xuanji* (A selection of cultural relics from Shandong). 1959. Beijing: Wenwu.

*Shangcunling Guo-guo mudi* (The cemetery of the state of Guo at Shangcunling). 1959. Lin Shoujin et al. Beijing: Kexue.

*Shanghai Bowuguan-cang qingtongqi* (Bronzes in the collection of the Shanghai Museum). 1964. 2 vols. Beijing: Wenwu.

*Shanghai Bowuguan Zhongguo qingtongqi chenlie* (The bronzes display at the Shanghai Museum). N.d. (ca. 1987). Shanghai.

*Shanxi chutu wenwu* (Cultural relics excavated in Shanxi). 1980. Taiyuan: Shanxi Sheng Wenwu Gongzuo Weiyuanhui.

*Shou Xian Cai Hou-mu* (The tomb of the marquis of Cai at Shou Xian). 1956. Beijing: Kexue.

*Shuihudi Qin-mu zhujian* (The bamboo slips from the Qin tombs at Shuihudi). 1978. Beijing: Wenwu.

*Son of Heaven.* 1988. Robert L. Thorp. Seattle: Son of Heaven Press.

*Spirit and ritual: The Morse Collection of ancient Chinese art.* 1982. Robert L. Thorp and Virginia Bower. New York: Metropolitan Museum of Art.

*Sui Xian Zeng Hou Yi-mu* (The tomb of Marquis Yi of Zeng at Sui Xian). 1980. Beijing: Wenwu.

*Tonglüshan: Zhongguo gu kuangye yizhi* (Tonglüshan, an ancient mining site in China). 1980. Beijing: Wenwu.

*Unearthing China's past.* 1973. Jan Fontein and Wu Tung. Boston: Museum of Fine Arts.

*Wenhua Dageming qijian chutu wenwu*, vol. 1 (Cultural relics excavated during the Cultural Revolution). 1972. Beijing: Wenwu.

*Wenwu kaogu gongzuo sanshinian* (Thirty years of work on cultural relics and archaeology). 1979. Beijing: Wenwu.

*Wenwu yu kaogu lunji* (Essays on cultural relics and archaeology [presented on the 30th anniversary of Cultural Relics Publishing House]). 1986. Beijing: Wenwu.

*Wusheng chutu wenwu zhanlan tulu* (Illustrated catalogue of the exhibition of cultural relics excavated in five provinces). 1959. Beijing: Wenwu.

*Xiaotun* ([The site of] Xiaotun). 1970 (vol. 1, 2 fascicles) and 1980 (vol. 5, 2 fascicles). No. 2 of *Zhongguo kaogu baogaoji*, by Shi Zhangru et al. Taibei: Academica Sinica, Institute of History and Philology. Part I, 3d Ser. (Archaeological Reports).

*Xin chutu jinwen fenyu jianmu* (Simplified catalogue of newly excavated bronze inscriptions ordered according to geographical provenience). 1983 Beijing: Zhonghua.

*Xin Zhongguo de kaogu faxian he yanjiu* (Archaeological discoveries and studies in New China). 1984. Beijing: Wenwu.

*Xin Zhongguo de kaogu shouhuo* (The achievements of archaeology in New China). 1961. Beijing: Wenwu.

*Xinyang Chu-mu* (The Chu tombs at Xinyang). 1986. Beijing: Wenwu.

*Xun Xian Xincun* ([The site of] Xincun, Xun Xian). 1964. Guo Baojun. Beijing: Kexue.

*Yayoi-no seidōki: Dōtaku, Dōriki* (Yayoi bronzes: Dōtaku bells, bronze implements). 1975. Tōkyō: Tenri Gallery.

*Yinan gu huaxiangshi-mu fajue baogao* (Excavation report on the ancient tomb with pictorial stone reliefs at Yinan). 1956. Beijing[?]: Wenhuabu Wenwu Guanliju.

*Yinxu fajue baogao 1958–1961* (Report on excavation at the Waste of Yin). 1987. Beijing: Wenwu.

*Yinxu Fu Hao-mu* (The tomb of Fu Hao [or Fu Zi] at Yinxu). 1976. Beijing: Wenwu.

*Yinyue yanjiu wenxuan* (Selected studies on music). 1985. 2 vols. Beijing: Wenhua Yishu.

*Yunnan Jinning Shizhaishan gumuqun fajue baogao* (Excavation report on the ancient cemetery at Shizhaishan, Jinning [Yunnan]). 1959. 2 vols. Beijing: Wenwu.

*Yūrinkan seika* (Masterworks from the Fujii Yūrinkan). 1985. Kyōto: Fujii Seiseikai.

*Zeng Hou Yi-mu* (The tombs of Marquis Yi of Zeng). 1989. 2 vols. Beijing: Wenwu.

*Zhan'guo Zeng Hou Yi-mu chutu wenwu tu'an-xuan* (A selection of ornaments on the relics excavated from the Warring States period tomb of Marquis Yi of Zeng). ca. 1984. Wuhan: Changjiang Wenyi.

*Zhongguo gudai duliangheng tuji* (Atlas of ancient Chinese length, volume, and weight measurements). 1984. Beijing: Wenwu.

*Zhongguo gudai yejin* (Ancient Chinese metallurgy). 1978. Beijing: Wenwu.

*Zhongguo gudai yueqi* (Ancient Chinese musical instruments). 1983. Beijing: Wenwu.

*Zhongguo gujin diming dacidian* (Comprehensive dictionary of ancient and modern Chinese geographical names). [1931] 1981. ed. Zang Lihe et al. Shanghai: Shangwu.

*Zhongguo gu qingtongqi-xuan* (A selection of ancient Chinese bronzes). 1976. Beijing: Wenwu.

*Zhongguo Hubei chutu wenwu* (Cultural relics excavated in Hubei, China). 1988. Wuhan: Hubei Huabaoshe.

*Zhongguo kaoguxue nianjian 1984* (Annual of Chinese archaeology). 1985. Beijing: Wenwu.

*Zhongguo kaoguxue nianjian 1985.* 1986. Beijing: Wenwu.

*Zhongguo kaoguxue nianjian 1986.* 1987. Beijing: Wenwu.

*Zhongguo kaoguxue nianjian 1987.* 1988. Beijing: Wenwu.

*Zhongguo kaoguxue nianjian 1988.* 1989. Beijing: Wenwu.

*Zhongguo kaoguxue yanjiu I* (Studies in Chinese archaeology in commemoration of the fiftieth anniversary of the start of Professor Xia Nai's career in archaeology). 1986. Beijing: Wenwu.

*Zhongguo kaoguxue yanjiu II.* 1986. Beijing: Kexue.

*Zhongguo kaoguxue yanjiu lunji* (Collected essays in the study of Chinese archaeology). 1987. Xi'an: San Qin.

*Zhongguo kaoguxue-zhong tan-shisi niandai shujuji 1965–1981* (A collection of radiocarbon dates collected in Chinese archaeology). 1983. Beijing: Wenwu.

*Zhongguo meishu quanji, Gongyi meishu-bian* (Complete compendium of Chinese art, Applied arts section). 1985. Vols. 4 and 5: *Qingtongqi I–II* (Bronzes I–II), ed. Li Xueqin. Beijing: Wenwu.

*Zhongguo yinyue cidian* (Dictionary of Chinese music). 1984. Beijing: Renmin Yinyue Chu-banshe.


*Works Cited by Author*

van Aalst, J. A. 1884. *Chinese music.* Shanghai: Imperial Maritime Customs Series, vol. 6. Reprint, New York: Paragon, 1964.

An Jiayao. 1987. "Zhongguo zaoqi de tongling" (The early bronze clapper-bells of China). *Zhongguo Lishi Bowuguan Guankan* 10: 35–38, 59.

Anonymous. 1984. "Zeng Hou Yi bianzhong fuzhi chenggong" (The successful completion of the replication of Zeng Hou Yi's chime-bells). *Jianghan Kaogu* 1984 (4): 90.

Appadurai, Arjun. 1986. "Introduction: Commodities and the politics of value." In *The social life of things: Commodities in cultural perspective*, ed. A. Appadurai, 3–63. Cambridge: Cambridge University Press.

Asahara Tatsurō. 1984. "Sen-Shin jidai-no ongaku riron" (Musical theory of the pre-Qin period). Unpublished handout. Kyōto: Kinbun Kenkyūkai.

———. 1985. "Zokuhei tangen" (On the origin of the weapons of Shu). *Koshi Shunjū* 2:23–52.

———. 1987. "Sen-Shin jidai-no shōritsu to sanpunson'eki-hō" (The tone pitches of the pre-Qin period and the Pythagorean tuning method). *Tōhō Gakuhō* 59 (1987): 63–123.

———. 1988a. "Shibo dōseiji-to sono on'in" (Some remarks on the Chinese characters with dual phonetic determinatives). *Kangoshi-no shomondai* (Some problems in the history of the Chinese language), ed. Ōzaki Yūjirō and Hirata Shōji, 1–22. Kyōto: Kyōto Daigaku Jinbunkagaku Kenkyūjo.

———. 1988b. "Sōhin-yori: Shatō-shō" (From the collections: the Zhediao-bells). *Sen'oku Hakkokan Kiyō* 5: 17–41.

Austin, J. L. 1967. *How to do things with words*. Cambridge: Harvard University Press.

Bagley, Robert W. 1977. "P'an-lung-ch'eng: A Shang city in Hupei." *Artibus Asiae* 39 (3/4): 165–219.

———. 1980a. "The appearance and growth of regional bronze-using cultures." In *The great Bronze Age of China*, ed. Wen Fong, 109–33. New York: Metropolitan Museum of Art.

———. 1980b. "Transformation of the bronze art in later Western Zhou." In *The great Bronze Age of China*, 191–213.

———. 1987. *Shang ritual bronzes in the Arthur M. Sackler Collections*. Vol. 1 of *Ancient Chinese bronzes in the Arthur M. Sackler Collections*. Cambridge: Harvard University Press.

———. 1988. "Sacrificial pits of the Shang period at Sanxingdui in Guanghan county, Sichuan province." *Arts Asiatiques* 43: 78–86.

Barfield, Thomas J. 1989. *The perilous frontier: Nomadic empires and China*. Cambridge, Mass.: B. Blackwell.

Barnard, Noel. 1961. *Bronze casting and bronze alloys in ancient China*. Monumenta Serica Monographs, no. 14. Canberra: Australian National University and Monumenta Serica.

———. 1978. "The nature of the Ch'in 'Reform of the Script' as reflected in archaeological documents excavated under conditions of control." In *Ancient China: Studies in early civilization*, ed. David Roy and Tsuen-hsuin Tsien, 181–213. Hong Kong: Chinese University Press.

———. 1987. "The entry of cire-perdue investment casting, and certain other metallurgical techniques (mainly metal-working) into south China and their progress northwards." Paper presented at Conference on Ancient Chinese and Southeast Asian Bronze Cultures, Kioloa, N.S.W., February 1988 (pre-print No. 15).

Barnard, Noel, and Cheung Kwong-yue (Zhang Guangyu). 1978. *Zhong Ri Ou Mei Ao Niu suojian suota suomo mingwen huibian* (Collection of inscriptions seen, rubbed, and copied in China, Japan, Europe, America, Australia, and New Zealand). 8 vols.

Taibei: Yiwen Yinshuguan.

Barnard, Noel, and Satō Tamotsu. 1975. *Metallurgical remains of ancient China*. Tōkyō: Nichiōsha.

Becker, Babette W. 1957. *Music in the life of ancient China: From 1400 B.C. to 300 B.C.* Ph.D. diss., University of Chicago.

Bilsky, Lester James. 1975. *The state religion of ancient China*. Asian Folklore and Social Life Monographs, vols. 70 and 71. Taibei: Orient Cultural Service.

Biot, Édouard. 1851. *See* Classical Texts: *Zhou Li*.

Bodde, Derk. 1975. *Festivals in classical China*. Princeton and Hong Kong: Princeton University Press and Hong Kong University Press.

———. 1986. "The state and empire of Ch'in." In *The Cambridge History of China*. Vol. 1, *The Ch'in and Han empires*, ed. Denis Twitchett and Michael Loewe, 20–102. Cambridge: Cambridge University Press.

Boltz, Judith M. n.d. *Northern and southern variations on the song of dynastic legitimacy*. Unpublished paper, University of California, Berkeley.

Broman, Sven. 1961. "Studies on the *Chou Li*." *Bulletin of the Museum of Far Eastern Antiquities* 33:1–88.

Cai Yonghua. 1986. "Suizang mingqi guankui" (Observations on funerary *mingqi*). *Kaogu yu Wenwu* 1986 (2): 74–78.

Cao Guicen. 1987. "Huaiyang Chu-mu lunshu" (On the Chu tombs at Huaiyang). In *Chu wenhua yanjiu lunji* (Collected essays on Chu culture), vol. 1, ed. Gu Tiefu, 60–70. Wuhan: Jingchu.

Carr, Michael. 1985. "Personation of the dead in ancient China." *Computational Analysis of Asian & African Languages* 24:1–107.

Carroll, Thomas D. 1963. "The origin, development and diffusion of musical scales: An index to cultural contacts." In *Proceedings of the Second Conference of the International Association of Historians of Asia*. Taibei, 149–73.

Chang Kwang-chih (Zhang Guangzhi). 1975. "Ancient trade as economy or as ecology." In *Ancient civilization and trade*, ed. C. C. Lamberg-Karlovsky and Jeremy Sabloff, 211–24. Albuquerque: University of New Mexico Press.

———. 1976. *Early Chinese civilization: An anthropological perspective*. Cambridge: Harvard University Press.

———. 1977. *The archaeology of ancient China*. 3d ed. New Haven: Yale University Press.

———. 1980. *Shang civilization*. New Haven: Yale University Press.

———. 1981a. "The animal in Shang and Chou bronze art." *Harvard Journal of Asiatic Studies* 41 (2): 527–54.

———. 1981b. "Archaeology and Chinese historiography." *World Archaeology* 13 (2): 156–69.

———. 1983. *Art, myth, and ritual: The path to political authority in ancient China*. Cambridge:

Harvard University Press.

———. 1986. *The archaeology of ancient China*. 4th ed. New Haven: Yale University Press.

Chang Kwang-chih, ed. 1986. *Studies of Shang archaeology*. New Haven: Yale University Press.

Chang Renxia. 1954. "Yin-Zhou shiqing xiaoji" (Brief note on Shang and Zhou musical stones). In *Zhongguo gudian yishu*, 17–31. Shanghai: Shanghai Chuban Gongsi.

———. 1978. "Guqing" (Ancient musical stones). *Wenwu* 1978 (7): 77–78.

Chavannes, Édouard. 1895–1910. *See* Classical Texts above: *Shi Ji*.

———. 1898. "Des rapports de la musique grecque avec la musique chinoise." In *Les Mémoires historiques de Se-ma Ts'ien*. Trans. E. Chavannes. Vol. 3: 630–45, Paris: Leroux.

Chen Cheng-Yih (Cheng Zhenyi). 1987. "The generation of chromatic scales in the Chinese bronze set-bells of the -5th century." In *Science and technology in Chinese civilization*, ed. Chen Cheng-yih. Singapore: World Scientific.

Chen Fangmei. 1987. "The stylistic development of Shang and Zhou bronze bells." In *Style in the East Asian tradition*, ed. Rosemary Scott and Graham Hutt, 19–37. Colloquies on Art and Archaeology in Asia, No. 14, London: School of Oriental and African Studies, Percival David Foundation of Chinese Art.

Chen Mengjia. 1936. "Shang-dai de shenhua yu wushu" (Mythology and shamanism in the Shang dynasty). *Yanjing Xuebao* 20: 485–576.

———. 1938. "Wuxing zhi qiyuan" (The origin of the Five Phases). *Yanjing Xuebao* 24: 35–54.

———. 1941. "She yu jiao" (Shooting rituals and suburban sacrifices). *Qinghua Xuebao* 13 (1): 115–62.

———. 1949. "'Liu Guo jinian-biao' kaozheng" (Philological interpretation of the "Chronological table of the Six States" [of the Warring States period, in Sima Qian's *Shi Ji*]). *Yanjing Xuebao* 36: 97–140 and 37: 159–202.

———. 1955–1956. "Xi Zhou tongqi duandai" (Chronology of Western Zhou bronzes). *Kaogu Xuebao* (9): 137–76; (10): 69-142; 1956 (1): 65–114; 1956 (2): 85–94; 1956 (3): 105–27; 1956 (4): 85–122 [series incomplete].

———. 1956a. "Shou Xian Cai Hou mu tongqi" (Bronzes from the tomb of the marquis of Cai at Shou Xian). *Kaogu Xuebao* 1956 (2): 95–123.

———. 1963. "Cai-qi san ji" (Three points on the Cai bronzes). *Kaogu* 1963 (7): 361, 381–84.

———. 1964a. "Song Dasheng bianzhong kaoshu" (Remarks on the Dasheng chime-bells of the Song dynasty). *Wenwu* 1964 (2): 51–53.

———. 1964b. "Zhan'guo duliangheng lüeshuo" (Abbreviated explanations of the metrological systems of the Warring States). *Kaogu* 1964 (6): 312–14.

Chen Pan. 1969. *"Chunqiu Dashibiao: Lieguo juexing ji cunmiebiao" zhuanyi* (Critical annotations on the "Tabulation of the ranks and clans, existence and annihilation of the various states" in [Gu Donggao's] *Tabulation of important events in the Springs and Autumns period.* 7 vols. Academia Sinica, Institute of History and Philology Monograph No. 52. Taibei: Academia Sinica; reissued in 3 vols., 1988.

——. 1970. *Bujianyu "Chunqiu Dashibiao" zhi Chunqiu fangguo-gao* (Notes on the marginal polities not discussed in [Gu Donggao's] *Tabulation of important events in the Springs and Autumns period.* Institute of History and Philology Monograph No. 59. Taibei: Academia Sinica.

Chen Peifen. 1982. "Pan-*you*, Zou-*ding* ji Liangqi-*zhong* mingwen quanshi" (Interpretation of the inscriptions of the Pan-*you*, Zou-*ding*, and Liangqi-*yongzhong*). *Shanghai Bowuguan Jikan* 2: 15–25.

Chen Pengxin. 1988. "Hubei Jiangling Zhan'guo Chu-mu chutu lüguan" (The pitch-pipes unearthed in a Warring States period Chu tomb at Jiangling, Hubei). *Yueqi* 1988 (1): 15–16.

Chen Qiyou. 1962a. "Huangzhong guanchang-kao" (On the length of the HUANGZHONG pitch pipe). *Zhonghua Wenshi Luncong* 1: 183–88.

——. 1962b. "Shi'er lüguan zhi chang-kao" (On the length of the twelve *lü* pitch pipes). *Zhonghua Wenshi Luncong* 2: 235–40.

Chen Tong and Zheng Darui. 1980. "Gu bianzhong de shengxue texing." *Shengxue Xuebao* 1980 (5): 161–71. Translated as "Acoustical properties of chime-bells." *Chinese Journal of Acoustics* 4 (1985): 1–9.

——. 1983a "Acoustic properties of chime-bells." Paper presented at the 11th International Congress of Acoustics, Toulouse.

——. 1983b. "Flexural vibration of truncated elliptical cone [*sic*] and Chinese chime bells." *Chinese Journal of Acoustics* 2 (1983): 32–39.

——. 1985. "Jingli-bianzhong de shengpin-pu" (Frequency tables for the Jingli-bells). *Kexue Tongbao* 25 (1980.11): 527–28.

Chen Xingcan. 1990. "Zhongguo shiqian yueqi chulun" (An initial analysis of Chinese prehistoric musical instruments). *Zhongyuan Wenwu* 1990 (2): 29–36.

Chen Yingshi. 1983. "Lunzheng Zhongguo gudai de chunlü lilun" (On the pure tuning theory of Chinese antiquity). *Zhongyang Yinyue Xueyuan Xuebao* 1983 (1): 34–39.

Chen Zhenyu. 1988a. "Woguo xian-Qin qingtongzhong de fenqu tansuo" (An examination of the geographical distribution of pre-Qin bronze bells in our country). Paper prepared for the International Exchange Activities of Ancient Chinese Science and Technology and Culture Symposium on the Chime-bells of Marquis Yi of Zeng [*sic*]. Wuhan. Now published in *Hunan Wenwu* 3 (1988): 17–36.

——. 1988b. "Woguo xian-Qin shiqing chuxi" (An initial analysis of pre-Qin lithophones in our country). Paper prepared for the International Exchange Activities of Ancient Chinese Science and Technology and Culture Symposium on the

Chime-bells of Marquis Yi of Zeng. Wuhan.

Chen Zhenyu and Liang Zhu. 1985. "Shilun Zeng-guo yu Zeng-Chu guanxi" (Hypothetical remarks on the state of Zeng and its relationship with Chu). *Kaogu yu Wenwu* 1985 (6): 85–96.

Chia, Sylvia Shih-heng (Jia Shiheng). 1980. "The four clapper-bells in the Academia Sinica collection." *Dongwu Daxue Zhongguo Yishushi Jikan* 10: 1–37.

Chmielewski, Janusz. 1957. "Remarques sur le problème des mots disyllabiques en chinois archaïque." *Mélanges de l'Institut des Hautes Études Chinoises* 1: 423–45.

Chou Wen-chung (Zhou Wenzhong). 1976. "Chinese historiography and music: Some observations." *Musical Quarterly* 62 (2): 218–40.

Condominas, G. 1952. "Le lithophone préhistorique de Ndut Lieng Krak." *Bulletin de l'École Française d'Extrême-Orient* 45 (2): 359–92.

Courant, Marcel. 1922. "Essai historique sur la musique classique des Chinois." In *Encyclopédie de la musique & Dictionnaire du Conservatoire* 1 (V): 77–241. Paris: Delagrave.

Couvreur, Séraphin. 1913. *See* Classical Texts above: *Li Ji.*

———. 1914. *See* Classical Texts above: *Chunqiu.*

———. 1916. *See* Classical Texts above: *Yi Li.*

Creel, Herrlee Glessner. 1970. *The origins of statecraft in China.* Vol. 1 of *The Western Chou empire.* Chicago: University of Chicago Press.

Cui Xian. 1988. "Zeng Hou Yi bianzhong gongtiao guanxi qianxi" (A superficial analysis of the tuning with respect to **do** of the chime-bells of Marquis Yi of Zeng). *Huangzhong* 1988 (4): 47–57. Special issue for the International Exchange Activities of Ancient Chinese Science and Technology and Culture Symposium on the Chime-bells of Marquis Yi of Zeng. Wuhan, 1988.

Dai Nianzu. 1980. "Gudai bianzhong fayin de wuli texing" (Physical characteristics of sound production in ancient chime bells). *Baike Zhishi* 1980 (8): 68–71.

———. 1981. "Zhongguo de bianzhong ji qi zai kexueshi-shang de yiyi" (China's chime-bells and their importance for the history of science). *Ziran Bianzheng-fa Tongxun* 1981 (1): 65.

———. 1983. "Acoustics." In *Ancient China's technology and science*, ed. Chinese Academy of Sciences, Institute of the History of the Natural Sciences, 139–51. Beijing: Foreign Languages Press. Originally published in Chinese by Zhongguo Qingnian Chubanshe, 1978.

———. 1986. "Zhongguo de zhong ji qi zai wenhuashishang de yiyi" (The bells of China and their cultural-historical significance)." In *Yazhou wenming luncong* (Articles on Asian civilization), ed. Huang Shengzhang, 101–20. Chengdu: Sichuan Renmin.

DeWoskin, Kenneth J. 1982. *A song for one or two: Music and the concept of art in early China.*

Ann Arbor: University of Michigan Center for Chinese Studies.

———. 1983. "Early Chinese music and the origins of aesthetic terminology." In *Theories of the arts in China*, ed. Susan Bush and Christian Murck, 187–214. Princeton: Princeton University Press.

———. 1985. "The sound and science of archaic Chinese bells." Paper read at the 195th meeting of the American Oriental Society, Ann Arbor, Mich.

———. 1987. "Comment on 'The bronze chime bells of the Marquis of Zeng: Babylonian biophysics in ancient China' by E. G. McClain." *Journal of Social and Biological Structures* 10:329–41.

———. 1988. "The Chinese *xun*: Globular flutes from the neolithic to the Bronze Age, 6000–1000 B.C." In *The archaeology of early music cultures: Third international meeting of the ICTM Study Group on Music Archaeology*, ed. Ellen Hickmann and David W. Hughes, 249–64. Orpheus: Schriftenreihe zu Grundfragen der Musik vol. 51. Bonn: Verlag für systematische Musikwissenschaft.

Dien, Albert E. 1987. "Chinese beliefs in the afterworld." In *The quest for eternity*, 1–16.

Dien, Albert E., Jeffrey K. Riegel, and Nancy T. Price, eds. 1985. *Chinese archaeological abstracts*. Vols. 2–4. Monumenta Archaeologica 9–11. Los Angeles: UCLA Institute of Archaeology.

Doty, Darrel Paul. 1982. *The bronze inscriptions of Ch'i*. Ph.D. diss., University of Washington.

Douglas, Mary T. 1967. "Primitive rationing: A study in controlled exchange." In *Themes in economic anthropology*, ed. Raymond Firth, 119–47. London: Tavistock.

———. 1982. "Goods as a system of communication." In *In the active voice*, 16–33. London: Routledge & Kegan Paul.

Douglas, Mary T., and Baron Isherwood. 1981. *The world of goods*. New York: Basic Books.

Du Naisong. 1976. "Cong lieding zhidu kan 'Keji fuli' de fandongxing" (The reactionary nature of "overcoming the self and restoring the rites," seen from the perspective of the sumptuary rules governing the use of sets of tripods). *Kaogu* 1976 (1): 17–21.

———. 1987. "Tan Jiangsu diqu Shang Zhou qingtongqi de fengge yu tezheng" (Remarks on the style and characteristics of Shang and Zhou bronze vessels from the Jiangsu region). *Kaogu* 1987 (2): 169–74.

Dubs, Homer H. See Classical Texts: *Han Shu*.

———. 1958. "The archaic royal Jou religion." *T'oung Pao* 46: 217–59.

Eberhard, Wolfram. 1933. "Beiträge zur kosmologischen Spekulation Chinas in der Han-Zeit." *Baessler-Archiv* 16: 1–100.

Élisséeff, Vadime. 1947. "Une cloche chinoise." *Bulletin des Musées de France* 12 (3): 11–16.

Ellsworth, Robert H. 1987. *Later Chinese painting and calligraphy, 1800–1950*. 3 vols. New York: Random House.

Elman, Benjamin. 1984. *From philosophy to philology: Intellectual and social aspects of change in Late Imperial China*. Harvard East Asia Monographs, No. 110. Cambridge: Harvard University Press.

Fairbank, Wilma. 1972. "Piece-mold craftsmanship and Shang bronze design." In *Adventures in retrieval*, 181–201. Harvard-Yenching Institute Studies 28. Cambridge: Harvard University Press.

von Falkenhausen, Lothar A. 1985. "The bells of Zeng and the development of ancient Chinese music: An overview." Unpublished paper.

———. 1988. *Ritual music in Bronze Age China: An archaeological perspective*. Ph.D. diss., Harvard University. Ann Arbor, Mich.: University Microfilms.

———. 1989a. "'Shikin-no onsei': Tō-Shū jidai-no shun, taku, dō, taku-ni tsuite" (Some Eastern Zhou bells used for signal-giving in warfare). *Sen'oku Hakkokan Kiyō* 6: 3–26.

———. 1989b. "*Niuzhong* chime-bells of Eastern Zhou China." *Arts Asiatiques* 44: 68–83.

Fang Jianjun. 1986. "Weizhuang bianzhong de niandai ji qi yinjie jiegou" (The dating and the scale structure of the chime-bells from Weizhuang). *Pingdingshan Wenwu* 4 (1986): 36–37.

———. 1989a. "Shang-dai qing he Xi-Zhou qing" (Shang dynasty chimestones versus Western Zhou chimestones). *Wenbo* 1989 (3): 36–45.

———. 1989b. "Luoyang Zhongzhou Daju chutu bianqing shitan" (Preliminary examination of the lithophone from Zhongzhou Daju, Luoyang). *Kaogu* 1989 (9): 834–38.

———. 1990. "Xian-Qin wenzi suo fanying de shi'erlü mingcheng" (The names of the twelve *lü* as reflected in the pre-Qin epigraphic records). *Zhongyang Yinyue Xueyuan Xuebao* 1990 (4): 76–79.

Fang Yousheng. 1981. "Youguan Zeng Hou Yi de jige wenti" (Some problems concerning Marquis Yi of Zeng). *Wuhan Daxue Xuebao: Shehui Kexue-ban* 1981 (6): 45–49.

Feng Guangsheng. 1982. "Jinlai woguo yinyue kaogu de zhuyao shouhuo" (Recent principal achievements in musical archaeology in our motherland). *Jianghan Kaogu* 1982 (1): 72–75, 71.

———. 1988a. "Zeng Hou Yi bianzhong ruogan wenti qianlun" (A superficial discussion of some problems regarding the chime-bells of Marquis Yi of Zeng). Paper prepared for the International Exchange Activities of Ancient Chinese Science and Technology and Culture Symposium on the Chime-bells of Marquis Yi of Zeng. Wuhan.

———. 1988b. "Bianzhong suyuan" (Tracing the origin of chime-bells). Paper prepared for the International Exchange Activities of Ancient Chinese Science and Technology and Culture Symposium on the Chime-bells of Marquis Yi of Zeng. Wuhan.

Feng Jiexuan. 1984. "Lun Zheng Wei zhi yin" (On the music of Zheng and Wei). *Yinyue Yanjiu* 1984 (1): 64–84.

Feng Shi. 1986. "Zeng Hou Yi bianzhong de suowei 'biangong' wenti" (The problem of the so-called 'reduced *gong*' in the [inscriptions of] the Zeng Hou Yi chime bells). *Kaogu* 1986 (7): 632–38.

Feng Wenci. 1985. "Lüelun woguo dangqian lüzhi wenti" (Abbreviated discussion of the problem of our motherland's present intonation systems). *Yinyue Yanjiu* 1985 (3): 61–67.

Fokker, A. D. 1971. "Acoustical analysis of a peal of thirteen Chinese bells." *Verhandelingen der Koninklijke Nederlandse Akademie van Wetenschappen*, Series B: 74 (3): 257–62.

Franklin, Ursula M., John Berthrong and Alan Chan. 1985. "Metallurgy, cosmology, knowledge: The Chinese experience." *Journal of Chinese Philosophy* 12 (4): 333–70.

Gao Hongxiang. 1988. "Zeng Hou Yi zhongqing bianpei jishu" (The technology of orchestrating the bell-chimes and lithophones of Marquis Yi of Zeng). *Huangzhong* 1988 (4): 85–95.

Gao Ming. 1981. "Zhongyuan diqu Dong-Zhou shidai qingtong liqi yanjiu" (Studies on the Eastern Zhou ceremonial bronze vessels from the Central Plains). *Kaogu yu Wenwu* 1981 (2): 68–82, (3): 84–103, and 1981 (4): 82–91.

Gao Zhixi. 1984a. "Hunan Sheng Bowuguan-cang Xi-Zhou qingtong yueqi" (Western Zhou bronze musical instruments in the collection of the Hunan Provincial Museum). *Hunan Kaogu Jikan* 2: 29–34.

———. 1984b. "Zhongguo nanfang chutu Shang-Zhou tongnao gailun." *Hunan Kaogu Jikan* 2: 128–35. *Translated as* "An introduction to Shang and Chou bronze *nao* excavated in south China." In *Studies of Shang Archaeology*, 275–99. *See* Chang Kwang-chih, ed. 1986.

———. 1984c. "Hunan chutu de Xi-Zhou tongqi" (Western Zhou bronze vessels excavated in Hunan). *Jianghan Kaogu* 1984 (3): 59–68.

———. 1986. "Lun Shang-Zhou tongbo" (On the bronze *bo* of the Shang and Zhou dynasties). *Hunan Kaogu Jikan* 3: 209–14, 109.

Gettens, Rutherford J. 1969. *The Freer Chinese bronzes*. Vol. 2. *Technical studies*. Washington: Smithsonian Institution, Publication 4706.

Girard-Geslan, Maud. 1986. "La tombe à linceul de jade du roi de Nanyue à Canton." *Arts Asiatiques* 41 (1986): 96–103.

Graham, Angus C. 1981. *See* Classical texts above: *Zhuang Zi*.

———. 1986a. *Yin-Yang and the nature of correlative thinking*. Institute of East Asian Philosophies Monograph Series, No. 6. Singapore: University of Singapore.

———. 1986b. *Studies in Chinese philosophy and philosophical literature*. Singapore: Institute of

East Asian Philosophies.

———. 1989. *Disputers of the Tao.* LaSalle, Ill.: Open Court.

Granet, Marcel. 1959. *Danses et légendes de la Chine ancienne.* 2 vols. Paris: Presses Universitaires de France.

———. [1929] 1968. *La civilisation chinoise.* Paris: Albin Michel.

———. [1934] 1968. *La pensée chinoise.* Paris: Albin Michel.

Gu Tiefu. 1958. "Youguan Xinyang Chu-mu de jige wenti" (Some problems concerning the Chu tombs at Xinyang). *Wenwu Cankao Ziliao* 1958 (1): 6–8.

———. 1979. "Xinyang yihao Chu-mu de diwang yu renwu" (The location of tomb no. 1 at Xinyang and the identity of its owner). *Gugong Bowuyuan Yuankan* 1979 (2): 76–80.

———. 1980. "Sui Xian Zeng Hou Yi-mu wu sui-jie" (Why the tomb of Marquis Yi at Sui Xian does not have a causeway). *Kaogu yu Wenwu* 1980 (1): 86–87, 79.

———. 1981. "Cong Sui Xian Zeng Hou Yi-mu kan fengjian zhidu-xia de xixun wenti" (The problem of human sacrifice under the feudalist system as perceived from the tomb of Marquis Yi at Sui Xian). *Jianghan Kaogu* 1981 (1): 3–13.

———. 1985. "Guanyu Henan Xichuan Chu-mu de ruogan cankao yijian" (On the Chu tombs at Xichuan [Henan]: Some opinions for the record). *Gugong Bowuyuan Yuankan* 1985 (3): 79–90.

Guan Hongye and Luo Baoyuan. 1983. "Yong chuantong shilafa fuzhi Zeng Hou Yi daxing yongzhong de yanjiu" (A study on replicating a large *yongzhong* of Marquis Yi of Zeng using traditional lost-wax casting technique). *Jianghan Kaogu* 1983 (2): 85–89, 84.

Guo Baojun. 1963. *Zhongguo qingtongqishidai* (The Chinese Bronze Age). Beijing: Sanlian. Reissued 1978.

———. 1981. *Shang Zhou tongqiqun zonghe yanjiu* (Comprehensive researches on the bronze assemblages of the Shang and Zhou dynasties). Beijing: Wenwu.

Guo Dewei. 1983. "Chu-mu fenlei wenti tantao" (Inquiries into the problem of the classification of Chu tombs). *Kaogu* 1983 (3): 149–59.

Guo Moruo. 1958. *Liang Zhou jinwenci daxi tulu kaoshi* (A great framework for bronze inscriptions from the Western and Eastern Zhou dynasties, with illustrations and philological interpretations). 2d enlarged ed. 8 vols. Beijing: Kexue.

Hamada Kōsaku. 1924. "Shin-shi kusō henshō" (Chime-bells formerly in the collection of Chen Jieqi). *Sen'oku Seishō Besshū.* Kyōto. Privately published with English translation.

Harich-Schneider, Eta. 1955. "The earliest sources of Chinese music and their survival in Japan." *Monumenta Nipponica* 11: 195–213.

Hart, James P. 1973. *See* Classical Texts above: *Guo Yu.*

Hawkes, David. 1985. *See* Classical Texts above: *Chu Ci.*

Hayashi Minao. 1961–62. "Sen'goku jidai-no gazōbun" (The pictorial scenes of the Warring States period). *Kōkogaku Zasshi* 47 (3): 27–49, 47 (4): 20–48, 48 (1): 1–21.

———. 1964. "In Shū seidō iki-no meishō to yōto" (Nomenclature and usage of Shang and Zhou ritual bronzes). *Tōhō Gakuhō* 34: 199–298.

———. 1976. *Kandai-no bunbutsu* (Cultural remains of the Han dynasty). Kyōto: Research Institute for Humanistic Studies.

———. 1980. "In Sei-Shū jidai-no chihōkei seidōki" (Regional-style bronzes of the Shang and Zhou periods). *Kōkogaku Memoir* 1980: 17–58.

———. 1981. "In Sei-Shū jidai reiki-no ruibetsu to yōhō" (Classification and usage of Shang and Western Zhou ritual vessels). *Tōhō Gakuhō* 53: 1–108.

———. 1984. *In Shū jidai seidōki-no kenkyū* (Studies on Shang and Zhou bronzes). Part 1 of *In Shū seidōki sōran* (Conspectus of Shang and Zhou bronzes). 2 vols. Tōkyō: Yoshikawa Kōbunkan.

———. 1986. *In Shū jidai seidōki monyō-no kenkyū* (Studies on the ornamentation of Shang and Zhou bronzes). Part 2 of *In Shū seidōki sōran*. Tōkyō: Yoshikawa Kōbunkan.

———. 1988. *Shunjū Sen'goku jidai seidōki-no kenkyū* (Studies on Springs and Autumns and Warring States period bronzes). Part 3 of *In Shū seidōki sōran*. Tōkyō: Yoshikawa Kōbunkan.

He Hao. 1988. "Cong Zeng-qi kan Sui-shi" (A look at the history of Sui from the perspective of the Zeng vessels). *Jianghan Kaogu* 1988 (3): 52–55.

He Jisheng and He Jiejun. 1986. "Gudai Yuezu de qingtong wenhua" (The bronze culture of the ancient Yue tribes). *Hunan Kaogu Jikan* 3: 215–39.

Henderson, John. 1984. *The development and decline of Chinese cosmology.* New York: Columbia University Press.

Hirase Takao. 1988. "Bianzhong de zhizuo yu Sanfen Sunyifa" (The manufacture of chime-bells and the "Method of Subtracting and Adding a Third"). Paper prepared for the International Exchange Activities of Ancient Chinese Science and Technology and Culture Symposium on the Chime-bells of Marquis Yi of Zeng, Wuhan.

Hochstadter, Walter. 1952. "Pottery and stonewares of Shang, Chou and Han." *Bulletin of the Museum of Far Eastern Antiquities* 24: 81–108.

Holtzer, Peter. *See* Classical Texts: *Yan Zi Chunqiu.*

d'Hormon, André. *See* Classical Texts: *Guo Yu.*

Hornbostel, Erich M. von, and Curt Sachs. 1914. "Systematik der Musikinstrumente—Ein Versuch." *Zeitschrift für Ethnologie* 46: 552–90.

Hosler, Dorothy. 1988. "Ancient West Mexican metallurgy: South and Central American origins and West Mexican transformations." *American Anthropologist* 90: 832–55.

Houtsma, Adrianus J. M., and Thomas D. Rossing. 1987. "Effects of signal envelope on the pitch of short complex tones." *Journal of the Acoustical Society of America* 81 (2): 439–44.

Hsu Cho-yun (Xu Zhuoyun). 1965. *Ancient China in transition: An analysis of social mobility, 722–222 B.C.* Stanford: Stanford University Press.

Hsu Cho-yun and Katheryn M. Linduff. 1988. *Western Chou civilization.* New Haven: Yale University Press. Originally published in Chinese by Hsü as *Xi-Zhou-shi.* Taibei: Lianjing, 1984.

Hu Jiaxi et al. 1981. "Caiyong guochan youji guixiangjiao fanzhi Zeng Hou Yi-mu bian-zhong moju qude chenggong" (The success achieved in making casting molds of the bells of Marquis Yi of Zeng using silicone rubber produced in China). *Jianghan Kaogu* 1981 (1): 42–45.

Hua Jueming. 1981. "Zeng Hou Yi bianzhong ji sunju gouti de yezhu jishu" (The metallur-gical technology of the bells and bell-rack supporting caryatids of Marquis Yi of Zeng). *Jianghan Kaogu* 1981 (1): 17–18.

Hua Jueming et al. 1986. *Zhongguo yezhushi lunji* (Collection of essays on the history of Chinese metallurgy). Beijing: Wenwu.

Hua Jueming and Guo Dewei. 1979. "Zeng Hou Yi-mu qingtongqiqun de zhuhan jishu he shilafa" (The casting and soldering technologies used for the assemblage of bronzes from the tomb of Marquis Yi of Zeng and the lost-wax casting method). *Wenwu* 1979 (7): 46–48, 45. For English abstract, see Dien, Riegel, and Price 1985, vol. 2: 770–72.

Hua Jueming and Jia Yunfu. 1983. "Xian-Qin bianzhong sheji chuangzuo de tantao." *Ziran Kexueshi Yanjiu* 1983 (1): 72–82. Also published in *Zhongguo yezhushi lunji. See* Hua Jeming et al. 1986. For an English version, see "A research on the Chinese ancient chime bells: Its history, casting process, design and calculation." *Historia Scientiarum* 23 (1982): 63–79.

Huang Ranwei [Wong Yin-wai]. 1978. *Yin Zhou qingtongqi shangxi mingwen yanjiu* (Studies on the inscriptions on Shang and Zhou bronzes documenting the conferral of rewards). Hong Kong: Longmen.

Huang Shengzhang. 1978. "Xi-Zhou Wei jiazu jiaocang tongqiqun chubu yanjiu" (Prelimi-nary studies on the Western Zhou hoard of Wei family bronzes). *Shehui Kexue Zhanxian* 1978 (3): 194–206.

Huang Xiangpeng. 1978–80 "Xinshiqi- he qingtongqishidai de yi-zhi yinxiang ziliao yu woguo yinjie fazhanshi wenti" (The presently known tonal material from the neolithic and the Bronze Age and the problem of the developmental history of tonal scales in our motherland). *Yinyue Luncong*, n.s. 1: 184–206 and 3: 127–61.

———. 1979a. "Xian-Qin yinyue wenhua de guanghui chuangzao—Zeng Hou Yi-mu de gu yueqi" (The ancient musical instruments from Marquis Yi of Zeng's tomb— A glorious achievement of pre-Qin musical culture). *Wenwu* 1979 (7): 32–39. For an English abstract, see Dien, Riegel, and Price 1985, 2: 765–69.

———. 1979b. "Liangqiansibainian-qian de yizuo dixia yinyue baoku" (A musical treasure-trove from 2400 years ago). *Wenyi Yanjiu* 1979 (1): 93–96.

———. 1979c. "Shi *Chushang*—Cong Zeng Hou zhong de diaoshi yanjiu guankui Chu wenhua wenti" (Interpretation of *Chushang*—Studies regarding the problem of Chu culture in the light of the modal patterns in the bells of the Marquis of Zeng). *Wenyi Yanjiu* 1979 (2): 72–81. For an English translation, *see* Shen Sinyan. "'Chu Shang' Elucidated." *Chinese Music* 3[1980](1): 20–24 and (3): 56–60.

———. 1980. "The mystery of dual-pitch systems in Chinese *bian-zhong*." *Chinese Music* 3 (3): 51–52.

———. 1981. "Zeng Hou Yi zhong qing mingwen yuexue tixi chutan" (Preliminary investigations into the musicological system of the inscriptions on the bells and musical stones of Marquis Yi of Zeng). *Yinyue Yanjiu* 1981 (1): 22–53.

———. 1982. "Xian-Qin bianzhong yinjie jiegou de duandai yanjiu" (Studies on the periodization of the structure of tonal scales in pre-Qin chime bells)." *Jianghan Kaogu* 1982 (2): 7–12.

———. 1983a. "Fuzhi Zeng Hou Yi–*zhong* de tiaolü wenti" (Tuning problems in replicating the bells of Marquis Yi of Zeng). *Jianghan Kaogu* 1983 (2): 81–84.

———. 1983b. "Zhongguo gudai lüxue—Yizhong juyou minzu wenhua tedian de kexue yichan" (The science of tuning in ancient China—A scientific heritage possessing ethnic culture characteristics). *Yinyue Yanjiu* 1983 (4): 111–18.

———. 1983c. "Zhong qing fuyuan de yanjiu chengguo" (Research results achieved in replicating bells and lithophones). *Renmin Yinyue* 1983 (3): 38–39, 50.

———. 1983d. "Yinyue kaoguxue zai minzu yinyue xingtai yanjiuzhong de zuoyong"(The usefulness of musical archaeology in the study of ethnomusicological patterns). *Renmin Yinyue* 1983 (8): 37–40.

———. 1988. "Junzhong-kao—Zeng Hou Yi-mu wuxuanqi yanjiu" (On the 'bell-adjuster'—A study of the five-stringed musical instrument from the tomb of Marquis Yi of Zeng). Paper prepared for the International Exchange Activities of Ancient Chinese Science and Technology and Culture Symposium on the Chime-bells of Marquis Yi of Zeng, Wuhan.

———. 1989. "Wuyang Jiahu gudi de ceyin yanjiu" (Studies on the tone measurements of the bone flute from Jiahu, Wuyang [Henan]). *Wenwu* 1989 (1): 15–17.

Huang Xiquan. 1988. "Zeng Hou Yi bianzhong jieming zhuici *zha* [?] yu *bian* [?] de shidu wenti" (The problem of how to understand the terms *zha* [?] and *bian* [?], which indicate octavic equivalents in the chime-bells of Marquis Yi of Zeng). Paper prepared for the International Exchange Activities of Ancient Chinese Science and Technology and Culture Symposium on the Chime-bells of Marquis Yi of Zeng. Wuhan.

Huang Zhanyue. 1986. "Lun liang-Guang chutu de xian-Qin qingtongqi" (On the pre-Qin bronzes excavated in Guangxi and Guangdong). *Kaogu Xuebao* 1986 (4): 409–34.

Hubei Sheng Bowuguan (Hubei Provincial Museum). 1981. "Jing duo xueke yanjiu, Zeng Hou Yi bianzhong fuzhi yi jiben chenggong" (As a result of multidisciplinary study, the replication of the chime-bells of Marquis Yi of Zeng has already basically succeeded). *Jianghan Kaogu* 1981 (1): 14–16, 30.

————. 1988. *Zeng Hou Yi zhong qing guyueqi ziliaomulu* (A list of published works on the bells, lithophones, and other ancient musical instruments of Marquis Yi of Zeng). Compiled for the International Exchange Activities of Ancient Chinese Science and Technology and Culture Symposium on the Chime-bells of Marquis Yi of Zeng, Wuhan.

Hubei Sheng Bowuguan, Zhongguo Kexueyuan Wuhan Wuli Yanjiusuo (Hubei Provincial Museum and Wuhan Institute of Physics, Chinese Academy of Sciences). 1984. "Zhan'guo Zeng Hou Yi bianqing de fuyuan ji xiangguan wenti de yanjiu" (Studies on the replication of the Warring States period lithophone of Marquis Yi of Zeng and related problems). *Wenwu* 1984 (5): 60–65. A somewhat fuller version of the same paper, titled "Zhan'guo Zeng Hou Yi bianqing de fuzhi ji qi xiangguan wenti de yanjiu," was prepared for the International Exchange Activities of Ancient Chinese Science and Technology and Culture Symposium on the Chime-bells of Marquis Yi of Zeng, Wuhan, 1988.

Ito Michiharu. 1987. *Chūgoku kodai kokka-no shihai kōzō* (The government structure of the ancient Chinese state). Tōkyō: Chūō Kōron.

Jia Jun. 1981. "*Shi Jing* yinyue chutan" (Preliminary remarks on the music of the *Shi Jing*). *Yinyue Yanjiu* 1981 (1): 95–103.

Jia Longsheng et al. 1981. "Yong jiguang quanxi jishu yanjiu Zeng Hou Yi bianzhong de zhendong moshi" (Study of the vibration modes of the chime-bells of Marquis Yi of Zeng, using laser optical holography technology). *Jianghan Kaogu* 1981 (1): 19–24. Also (published in *Zhongguo yezhushi lunji*.) *See* Hua Jueming et al., 1986, 208–210.

Jia Yunfu and Chen Zhonghang. 1988. "Zeng Hou Yi bianzhong texing de yanjiu" (A study of the peculiar features of the chime-bells of Marquis Yi of Zeng). Paper prepared for the International Exchange Activities of Ancient Chinese Science and Technology and Culture Symposium on the Chime-bells of Marquis Yi of Zeng, Wuhan.

Jiang Dingsui. 1984. "Shilun Shaanxi chutu de Xi-Zhou zhong" (A preliminary consideration of the Western Zhou bells excavated in Shaanxi). *Kaogu yu Wenwu* 1984 (5): 86–100.

Jiang Kongyang. 1979. "Yinyang Wuxing yu Chunqiu shidai de yinyue meixue sixiang" (*Yinyang Wuxing* and ideas on musical aesthetics during the Springs and Autumns period). *Shehui Kexue Zhanxian* 1979 (3): 58–67 and (4): 60–67.

————. 1984. "Tan xian-Qin shidai de 'Li-Yue' zhidu" (On the Ritual/Music system of the pre-Qin period). *Fudan Xuebao* 1984 (2): 32–37.

Jiang Langchan. 1988. "Zeng Hou Yi-mu gu yueqi yanjiu" (A study of the ancient musical instruments from the tomb of Marquis Yi of Zeng). *Huangzhong* 1988 (4): 73–84.

Jiang Tingyu. 1984. "Yangjiaoniuzhong chulun" (Preliminary discussion of the "sheep's horn–loop" bells). *Wenwu* 1984 (5): 66–69.

———. 1989. "Lüelun Lingnan qingtong yongzhong" (A superficial discussion of bronze *yongzhong* from the Lingnan area). *Jiangxi Wenwu* 1989 (1): 22–30.

Jiang Wujian. 1988. "Zeng Hou Yi-mu de yueqi he yuedui" (The musical instruments and the orchestra in the tomb of Marquis Yi of Zeng). Paper prepared for the International Exchange Activities of Ancient Chinese Science and Technology and Culture Symposium on the Chime-bells of Marquis Yi of Zeng, Wuhan.

Kane, Virginia. 1974–75. "The independent bronze industries in the south of China contemporary with the Shang and Western Chou dynasties." *Archives of Asian Art* 28: 77–107.

———. 1982–83. "Aspects of Western Zhou appointment inscriptions: The charge, the gifts, and the response." *Early China* 8: 14–28.

Karlbeck, Orvar. 1935. "Anyang moulds." *Bulletin of the Museum of Far Eastern Antiquities* 7: 39–60.

Karlgren, Bernhard. 1926. "On the authenticity and nature of the Tso Chuan." *Göteborgs Högskolas Årsskrift* 32. Göteborg: Elander.

———. 1931. "The early history of the Chou Li and Tso Chuan texts." *Bulletin of the Museum of Far Eastern Antiquities* 3: 1–59.

———. 1935. "Yin and Chou in Chinese bronzes." *Bulletin of the Museum of Far Eastern Antiquities* 8: 9–154.

———. 1936. "On the script of the Chou dynasty." *Bulletin of the Museum of Far Eastern Antiquities* 8: 155–78.

———. 1941. "Huai and Han." *Bulletin of the Museum of Far Eastern Antiquities* 13: 1–125.

———. 1948. "Bronzes in the Hellström Collection." *Bulletin of the Museum of Far Eastern Antiquities* 20: 1–38.

———. 1949. "Some bronzes in the Museum of Far Eastern Antiquities." *Bulletin of the Museum of Far Eastern Antiquities* 21: 1–26.

———. 1950. *See* Classical Texts above: *Shu Jing.*

———. 1959. *See* Classical Texts above: *Shi Jing.*

———. 1961. "Miscellaneous notes on some bronzes." *Bulletin of the Museum of Far Eastern Antiquities* 33: 91–102.

———. 1964. *See* Classical Texts above: *Shi Jing.*

———. 1970. *See* Classical Texts above: *Shu Jing.*

Kawahara Shūjō. 1985. "Chūgoku shōritsu shōshi" (A short history of Chinese intonation systems). In *Shin hatsugen Chūgoku kagakushi shiryō-no kenkyū*. Vol. 2, *Ronbun-hen*, 463–504. Kyōto: Jinbun Kagaku Kenkyūjo.

Keightley, David N. 1969. *Public works in ancient China*. Ph.D. diss., Columbia University.

———. 1970. "The temple artisans of ancient China: Part one: The *kung* and *to-kung* of Shang." Unpublished paper.

———. 1978a. *Sources of Shang history*. Berkeley and Los Angeles: University of California Press.

———. 1978b. "The religious commitment: Shang theology and the genesis of Chinese political culture." *History of Religions* 17:211–25.

———. 1981. "The giver and the gift: The Western Chou as social polity." Unpublished paper.

———. 1987. "Archaeology and mentality: The making of China." *Renditions* 18: 91–128.

Keightley, David N., ed. 1983. *The origins of Chinese civilization*. Berkeley and Los Angeles: University of California Press.

Keiya Yoshinobu. 1978. *Tō Dōwa 'Jōko on'inhyō-kō' saku'in* (Index to Dong Tonghe's '*Shang-gu yinyunbiao-gao* [Draft table of archaic phonetic sounds]'). Taibei: Haiwen. Originally published in 1969.

Keyser, Barbara W. 1979. "Decor replication in two late Chou bronze *chien*." *Ars Orientalis* 11: 127–62.

Kipp, Rita S., and Edward M. Schortman. 1989. "The political impact of trade in chief-doms." *American Anthropologist* 91 (2): 370–85.

Knoblock, John. 1988. *See* Classical Texts above: *Xun Zi*.

Kondo Mitsuo. 1955. "Tai Shin-no *Kōkōki-zu*-ni tsuite—Kagaku shisōshiteki kōsatsu" (On Dai Zhen's *Kaogongji-tu*—An enquiry into his scientific thought). *Tōhōgaku* 1955 (11): 1–22.

Kopytoff, Igor. 1986. "The cultural biography of things: Commoditization as process." In *The social life of things: Commodities in cultural perspective*, ed. Arjun Appadurai, 64–91. Cambridge: Cambridge University Press.

Kroeber, Alfred L. 1940. "Stimulus diffusion." *American Anthropologist* 42 (1): 1–20.

Kubler, George. 1962. *The shape of time*. New Haven: Yale University Press.

Kunst, Jaap. [1948] 1974. *Ethnomusicology: A study of its nature, its problems, methods, and repre-sentative personalities to which is added a bibliography*. Den Haag: Martinus Nijhoff.

Kurihara Keisuke. 1978. *Chūgoku kodai gakuron-no kenkyū* (Studies on the musical theory of ancient China). Tōkyō: Daitō Bunka Daigaku, Tōyō Kenkyūjo.

Kuttner, Fritz A. 1953. "The musical significance of archaic Chinese jades of the *pi* disk type." *Artibus Asiae* 16: 25–50.

———. 1958. "A 'Pythagorean' tone system in China—Antedating the Greek achieve-ments." *Bericht über den 7. Musikwissenschaftlichen Kongreß*, 174–76. Köln, 1958.

———. 1967. "Zur Entwicklung des Musikbegriffes in Chinas Frühgeschichte." In *Festschrift für Walter Wiora*, 536–44. Kassel: Bärenreiter. For an English translation, see "The development of the concept of music in China's early history." *Asian Music* 1[1979](2): 12–21.

———. 1968. "Acoustical-mathematical knowledge: Migration from West Asia to East China before 1000 B.C." In *A survey of Persian art, from prehistoric times to the present*, ed. Arthur U. Pope and Phyllis Ackerman. Vol. 15, temporary fascicle. Proceedings, 4th International Congress of Iranian Art and Archaeology, New York and Washington, 1960. Section 103: *Various influences of Persian art in the art of the Far East*, vol. 1, 3220–226. London et al.: Asia Institute of Pahlavi University, Oxford University Press, Meiji Shōbō.

Laloy, L. 1909. *La musique chinoise*. Paris: Laurens.

———. 1914. "Houaï-nân Tzè et la musique." *T'oung Pao* 15: 501–30.

Lattimore, Owen. 1940. *The Inner Asian frontiers of China*. New York: American Geographical Society.

Lau, D. C. *See* Classical Texts: *Lunyu, Meng Zi*.

Lee Yuan-yuan. 1980a. "The music of the Zenghou *zhong*." *Chinese Music* 3 (1): 3–15.

———. 1980b. "Music theory suggested by *Zenghou zhong* and its inscriptions." *Chinese Music* 3 (3): 61–67.

Lefebvre d'Argencé, René-Yvon. 1977. *Bronze vessels of ancient China in the Avery Brundage Collection*. San Francisco: Asian Art Museum of San Francisco.

Legge, James. *See* Classical Texts: *Shu Jing, Zuo Zhuan*.

Lehr, André. 1971. "Een Chinees klokkenspel uit de 6de eeuw voor Christus." *Klok en Klepel* 14: 6–15.

———. 1976. *Leerboek der campanologie*. Asten: Nationaal Beiaardmuseum.

———. 1984. "Tweetonige Chinese spelklokken?" *Klok en Klepel* 33: 29–35.

———. 1985. *Klokken en klokkenspelen in het oude China tijdens de Shang- en Chou-dynastie*. Asten: Athanasius Kircher-Stichting.

———. 1987a. *A sound of bells in the National Carillon Museum*. Asten: Nationaal Beiaardmuseum.

———. 1987b. *The designing of swinging bells and carillon bells in the past and present*. Asten: Athanasius Kircher Foundation.

———. 1988. "The tuning of the bells of Marquis Yi." *Acustica* 67: 144–48.

———. N.d. a. "Some notes on Chinese lithophones of the Chou dynasty." Manuscript.

———. N.d. b. "Arithmetic and historical truth." Comments on McClain 1985. Manuscript.

Levis, J. H. 1936. *Foundations of Chinese musical art*. Peiping [Beijing]: Henri Vetch.

Li Chengyu. 1983. "Zeng Hou Yi bianqing de chubu yanjiu" (Preliminary studies on the lithophone of Marquis Yi of Zeng). *Yinyue Yanjiu* 1983 (1): 86–93.

———. 1984. "Qingju bianlie bianzheng—Zeng Hou Yi bianqing yanjiu zhi er" (Discussion of the arrangement of the musical stones on their rack: Studies on the lithophone of Marquis Yi of Zeng no. 2). *Zhongyang Yinyue Xueyuan Xuebao* 1984 (3): 32–37.

Li Chi (Li Ji), ed. 1964–73. *Gu qiwu yanjiu zhuankan* (Monographs on the study of ancient artifacts). 5 vols. Taibei: Academia Sinica.

Li Chunyi. 1957a. *Woguo yuanshi shidaiqi yinyue shitan* (Hypothetical investigations into the music of the primitive age of our motherland). Beijing: Yinyue Chubanshe.

———. 1957b. "Guanyu Yin zhong de yanjiu" (Regarding the study of Shang bells). *Kaogu Xuebao* 1957 (3): 41–50. Also published in *Yinyue Jianshe Wenji* 2 (1959): 536–49 under the title "Guanyu Yin-Zhou zhong de ruogan yanjiu."

———. 1963. "Shilun Chunqiu shidai Yinyang Wuxing xuepai de yinyue sixiang" (Preliminary discussion of the musical thought of the *Yinyang Wuxing* school of the Springs and Autumns period). *Wenshi* 1963 (3): 1–16.

———. 1964a. *Zhongguo gudai yinyue shigao* (Draft history of ancient Chinese music). 2d ed. Beijing: Yinyue Chubanshe. A previous ed. was published in 1958.

———. 1964b. "Yuanshishidai he Shang-dai de taoxun" (Ocarinas from the primitive age and the Shang dynasty). *Kaogu Xuebao* 1964 (1): 51–54.

———. 1965. "*Guan Zi*: 'Wuxing-pian' yinlü sixiang yanjiu" (Study of the musicological thought in *Guan Zi*: "Wuxing-pian"). *Zhonghua Wenshi Luncong* 6: 57–82.

———. 1973. "Guanyu gezhong, xingzhong, ji Cai Hou-bianzhong" (On singing bells, marching bells, and the Cai Hou chime-bells). *Wenwu* (7) (1973): 15–19.

———. 1981. "Zeng Hou Yi bianzhong mingwen kaocha" (Enquiry into the chime-bell inscriptions of Marquis Yi of Zeng). *Yinyue Yanjiu* 1981 (1): 54–67.

———. 1983. "Zeng Hou Yi bianqing mingwen chuyan" (Initial study on the lithophone inscriptions of Marquis Yi of Zeng). *Yinyue Yishu* 1983 (1): 8–24.

———. 1985. "Zeng Hou Yi mu bianzhong de bianci he yuexuan" (The sequence and hanging of the chime-bells of Marquis Yi of Zeng). *Yinyue Yanjiu* 1985 (2): 62–70.

———. 1986a. "Guanyu zhengque fenxi yinyue kaogu cailiao de yixie wenti" (On correctly analyzing some problems concerning the materials of musical archaeology). *Yinyue Yanjiu* 1986 (1): 8–10.

———. 1986b. "Guanyu Shaanxi diqu de yinyue kaogu" (On the musical archaeology of the Shaanxi region). *Zhongguo Yinyuexue* 1986 (2): 46–54.

———. 1990. "Zhongyuan diqu Xi-Zhou bianzhong de zuhe" (The scaling of Western Zhou bell-chimes from the Central Plains area). *Wenwu Tiandi* 1990 (5): 22–25.

Li Feng. 1988. "Huanghe liuyu Xi-Zhou muzang chutu qingtongqi de fenqi yu niandai" (The periodization and dating of the bronzes excavated from Western Zhou tombs in the Huanghe river system). *Kaogu Xuebao* 1988 (4): 383–419.

Li Jinghua and Hua Jueming. 1985. "Bianzhong de zhongmi, zhongsui xinkao" (A new analysis of the *mi* and *sui* portions of chime-bells). In *Kejishi Wenji*. Vol. 13: 40–46. Shanghai: Shanghai Kexue Jishu. Also published in *Zhongguo yezhushi lunji*. See Hua Jueming et al. 1986.

Li Ling. 1979. "Chunqiu Qin-qi shitan" (Preliminary remarks on the Qin bronzes of the Springs and Autumns period). *Kaogu* 1979 (6): 515–21.

———. 1981. "'Chu Shu zhi sun Peng' jiujing shi shui?" (Who after all was 'Peng, Chu descendant in the junior line'?). *Zhongyuan Wenwu* 1981 (4): 36–37.

———. 1986. "Chu-guo tongqi mingwen biannian huishi" (Comprehensive explanations of the bronze inscriptions from the state of Chu, placed in chronological order). *Gu Wenzi Yanjiu* 13: 353–97.

Li Xiandeng. 1986. "Zeng-guo tongqi de chubu fenxi" (A preliminary analysis of the bronzes of the state of Zeng). *Zhongguo Lishi Bowuguan Guankan* 9: 45–49.

Li Xiaoding, Zhou Fagao, and Zhang Risheng, eds. 1977. *Jinwen gulin fulu* (Postscripts to *Jinwen gulin*). Hong Kong: Chinese University Press. Reprinted in 4 vols. Taibei, n.d.; *see* Zhou Fagao et al. 1974.

Li Xueqin. 1979. "Xi-Zhou zhongqi qingtongqi de zhongyao biaochi—Zhouyuan Zhuangbai, Qijia liangchu qingtongqi jiaocang de zonghe yanjiu" (An important yardstick for Western Zhou middle period bronzes—A comprehensive study of the bronze hoards found at Zhuangbai and Qijia). *Zhongguo Lishi Bowuguan Guankan* 1: 29–36.

———. 1980a. "Lun Han Huai jian de Chunqiu qingtongqi" (On some bronzes from the area between the Han and Huai rivers). *Wenwu* 1980 (1): 54–58.

———. 1980b. "Qin-guo wenwu de xin renshi" (New insights into Qin antiquities). *Wenwu* 1980 (9): 25–31.

———. 1984. "Dong Zhou wangdu yu Jincun gumu" (The Eastern Zhou royal capital and the tombs of Jincun). *Heluo Chunqiu* 1984 (1): 23–29.

———. 1985. *Eastern Zhou and Qin Civilizations*. Trans. K. C. Chang. New Haven: Yale University Press.

———. 1986. "Han-dai qingtongqi de jige wenti" (Some problems concerning Han bronzes). *Wenwu Yanjiu* (1986) 2: 101–6.

———. 1987. "Kaogu faxian yu gudai xingshi zhidu" (Archaeological discoveries and the kinship system of antiquity). *Kaogu* 1987 (3): 253–57, 241.

Li Zhiwei. 1984. "Zeng Hou Yi-mu bianzhong ji zun, zunzuo zhuzao fangfa xintan" (A new investigation into the casting technique of the chime-bells, the *zun* and the *zun* stand from the tomb of Marquis Yi of Zeng). In *Chushi luncong (Chuji)* (Essays on Chu history [Initial collection]), ed. Zhang Zhengming, 73–92. Wuhan: Hubei Renmin.

Li Zhongda, Hua Jueming, and Zhang Hongli. 1982. "Shang Zhou qingtongqi hejinchengfen de kaocha—jianlun 'Zhongding zhi Qi' de xingcheng" (Investigation into the alloy composition of Shang and Zhou bronzes—a comprehensive consideration of the formation of the 'formulae for bells and tripods'). In *Zhongguo yezhushi lunji*, ed. Hua Jueming et al., 149–165. Beijing: Wenwu, 1986. Originally published in *Xibei Daxue Xuebao, Ziran Kexue-ban* 1982 (2).

Lian Shaoming. 1983. "'Shi Qiang–*pan*' mingwen yanjiu" (Studies on the Shi Qiang–*pan* inscription). *Gu Wenzi Yanjiu* 8: 31–38.

Liang Jingjin. 1978. "Guangxi chutu de qingtongqi" (Bronzes excavated in Guangxi). *Wenwu* 1978 (10): 93–96.

Liang Shuquan and Zhang Gannan. 1950. "The chemical composition of some early Chinese bronzes." *Zhongguo Huaxuehui Huikan* 17 (1): 9–17 [not seen].

Liao Yongmin. 1957. "Zhengzhou-shi faxian de yichu Shang-dai juzhu yu zhuzao tongqi yizhi jianjie" (Brief report on a Shang dynasty dwelling and bronze-casting site at Zhengzhou [Henan]). *Wenwu Cankao Ziliao* 1957 (6): 73–74.

Lin Rui et al. 1981. "Dui Zeng Hou Yi bianzhong jiegou de tantao" (Discussion on the structure of the chime-bells of Marquis Yi of Zeng). *Jianghan Kaogu* 1981 (1): 25–30. Also published in *Zhongguo yezhushi lunji*, ed. Hua Jueming et al., 211–16. Beijing: Wenwu, 1986.

Liu Binhui. 1984. "Chu-guo youming tongqi biannian gaishu" (Comprehensive discussion on the chronology of inscribed Chu bronzes). *Gu Wenzi Yanjiu* 8: 331–72.

———. 1985a. "Suizhou Leigudun erhao-mu qingtongqi chulun" (Preliminary discussion of the bronzes found in tomb no. 2 at Leigudun, Suizhou). *Wenwu* 1985 (1): 37–39.

———. 1985b. "Chu-guo qingtong liqi chubu yanjiu" (Preliminary steps to the study of Chu ritual bronze vessels). *Zhongguo Kaoguxuehui disici nianhui (1983) lunwenji*, 108–122.

———. 1988. "Zeng Hou Yi-mu qingtong liqi chubu yanjiu" (An initial study of the bronze ritual vessels from the tomb of Marquis Yi of Zeng). *Hubei Sheng Kaoguxuehui Lunwen Xuanji* 1: 133–42.

Liu Fu. 1932. "Tiantan suocang bianzhong bianqing" (The chime-bells and lithophone kept at the Altar of Heaven). *Guoli Beijing Daxue Guoxue Jikan* 3 (2): 183–84.

———. 1934. "*Lüshi Chunqiu* 'Guyue-pian' huangzhong jiejie" (The pitch of HUANGZHONG according to *Lüshi Chunqiu* 'Guyue-pian'). " *Wenxue* (Shanghai), 2 (6): 993–1001.

———. n.d. "Gugong suocang yueqi yinlü ceyan-lu" (Record of tone measurements taken on musical instruments kept in the former Imperial Palace). Unpublished paper [not seen].

Liu Jie. 1958. *Gushi kaocun* (On remnants of ancient history). Beijing: Renmin.

Liu Shi-yue. 1988. "Neolithic bone flutes from Hemudu, China." In *The archaeology of early music cultures: Third international meeting of the ICTM Study Group on Music Archaeology*, ed. Ellen Hickmann and David W. Hughes, 51–54. Orpheus:

Schriftenreihe zu Grundfragen der Musik, vol. 51. Bonn: Verlag für systematische Musikwissenschaft.

Liu Xing. 1985. "Dongnan diqu qingtongqi fenqi" (The chronology of bronzes from the southeastern area). *Kaogu yu Wenwu* 1985 (5): 90–101.

Liu Yu. 1986. "Lü Qi bianzhong de chongxin yanjiu" (A re-study of the Lü Qi chime-bells). *Gu Wenzi Yanjiu* 12: 257–66.

Lu Benshan. 1985. "Tonglüshan Chunqiu zaoqi de liantong jishu" (The early Springs and Autumns period copper-smelting technology at Tonglüshan). *Kejishi Wenji* 13: 11–23.

Lü Ji. 1978. "Cong yuanshi shizushehui dao Yindai de jizhong taoxun—tansuo woguo wusheng yinjie de xingcheng niandai" (Some ocarinas dating from the primitive clan society to the Shang dynasty—an inquiry into the formation date of our country's pentatonic scale). *Wenwu* 1978 (10): 54–61.

Lü Linlan. 1983. "Changsha Mawangdui yihao Han-mu chutu shi'er lüguan kaoshi" (Interpretation of the twelve pitch-pipes excavated from the Han dynasty tomb no. 1 at Mawangdui). *Yinyue Yanjiu* 1983 (3): 71–76.

Lü Wenhui. 1985. *Shi Kuang, Gu xiaoshuo jiyi* (Shi Kuang, Collected fragments of an ancient novel). Shanghai: Shanghai Guji.

Luo Xizhang. 1980. "Fufeng chutu de Shang Zhou qingtongqi" (Shang and Zhou bronzes excavated at Fufeng). *Kaogu yu Wenwu* 1980 (4): 6–22, 53.

———. 1988. "Zhouyuan qingtongqi jiaocang ji youguan wenti de tantao" (A discussion of hoards of bronzes from Zhouyuan and related problems). *Kaogu yu Wenwu* 1988 (2): 40–47.

Luo Xunzhang. 1984. "Liujiadianzi Chunqiu mu suokao" (Trivial notes on the Springs and Autumns period tomb at Liujiadianzi). *Wenwu* 1984 (9): 11–13.

Luo Zhenyu. 1936. *Sandai jijin wencun* (Epigraphic remains on auspicious bronzes from the Three Dynasties). 20 vols. Shanghai: privately published. New ed., 3 vols., Beijing: Zhonghua, 1983.

Ma Chengyuan. 1964. "Ji Shanghai Bowuguan xin shouji de qingtongqi" (Notes on some newly collected bronzes in the Shanghai Museum). *Wenwu* 1964 (7): 10–19.

———. 1979. "Guanyu Miaosheng-*xu* he Zhejian-*zhong* de jidian yijian" (Some points of view on the Miaosheng-*xu* and the Zhejian-*yongzhong*). *Kaogu* 1979 (1): 60–65.

———. 1981. "Shang Zhou qingtong shuangyinzhong." *Kaogu Xuebao* 1981 (1): 131–46. For an English translation, see Shen Sin-yan, trans., "Ancient Chinese two-pitched bronze bells." *Chinese Music* 3 (1980) [4]: 81–86, 4 (1981) [1]: 18–20 and (2): 31–36.

Ma Chengyuan and Pan Jianming. 1981. "Xinmang Wuyi lüguan dui huangzhong shi'erlü yanjiu" (Study of a WUYI *lü* pitch-pipe from the Wang Mang period, and its position within the twelve *lü* starting from HUANGZHONG). *Shanghai Bowuguan*

*Guankan* 1: 1–9. For an English translation, by Liu Charng-ming, see *Chinese Music* 4 (1981) [3]: 53–57.

Maa Dah-You and Chen Tong. 1987. "Chinese musical instruments of prechristian era [sic]." Paper read at the 12th International Congress for Acoustics, Toronto.

Mackenzie, Colin. 1987. "The evolution of southern bronze styles in China during the Eastern Zhou period." *Bulletin of the Oriental Ceramic Society of Hong Kong* 7: 31–48.

Major, John S. 1978. "Research priorities in the study of Chu religion." *History of Religions* 17: 226–43.

Maspero, Henri. [1927] 1965. *La Chine antique.* Vol. 71 of *Annales du Musée Guimet.* Paris: Maisonneuve. New ed., Paris: Presses Universitaires de France.

———. 1933. "Le mot *ming.*" *Journal Asiatique* 223: 249–96.

———. 1950. "La crise religieuse des Royaumes Combattants." *Mélanges posthumes*, 1: 37–47. Publications du Musée Guimet, Bibliothèque de diffusion t. 57. Paris: Civilisations du Sud.

———. 1954. "Contribution à l'étude de la société chinoise à la fin des Chang et au début des Tcheou." *Bulletin de l'École Française d'Extrême-Orient* 46: 335–402.

Matsui Yoshinori. 1984. "Sōhin-yori: Seijin Jinnei-shō" (From the collections: The Jingren Renning-*zhong*). *Sen'oku Hakkokan Kiyō* 1: 50–64.

Matsumaru Michio, ed. 1980. *Sei-Shū seidōki to sono kokka* (Western Zhou bronzes and the Western Zhou state). Tōkyō: Tōkyō Daigaku Shuppansha.

Mauss, Marcel. [1923–24] 1950. "Essai sur le don. Forme et raison de l'échange dans les sociétés archaïques." In *Société et anthropologie*, 143–279. Paris: Presses Universitaires de France. Originally published in *L'Année Sociologique.*

McClain, Ernest G. 1985a. "The bronze chime bells of the Marquis of Zeng: Babylonian biophysics in ancient China." *Journal of Social and Biological Structures.* 8: 147–73. *See* DeWoskin 1987; Lehr n. d. b; Renfrew 1986b.

———. 1985b. "Some personal observations of Chinese bells with special attention to interiors." Manuscript.

Merriam, Alan P. 1960. "Ethnomusicology: Discussion and definition of the field." *Ethnomusicology* 4: 107–14.

———. 1964. *The anthropology of music.* Evanston: Northwestern University Press.

Miao Tianrui. 1983. *Lüxue* (The science of tuning). Beijing: Renmin Yinyue Chubanshe. First published in 1965 with a foreword by Yang Yinliu not contained in this edition.

Miyamoto Kazuo. 1985. "Shichigoku buki-kō: ka, geki, bō-wo chūshin-ni shite" (The weapons of the Seven States [of the Warring States period], focusing on the *ge, qi,* and *mao*). *Koshi Shunjū* 2: 75–109.

Mizuhara Ikō. 1965. "Chūgoku kodai ongaku shisō kenkyū" (Studies on the musicological thought of ancient China). *Tōyō Ongaku Kenkyū* 10: 207–31.

————. 1984. *Chūgoku ongaku kankei chokyū ronbun mokuroku* (A bibliography of works and articles related to Chinese music). Kyōto: Hōyū Shoten.

Mochii Yasutaka. 1980. "Sei Shū jidai-no Seishū jūdō kōbō-ni tsuite" (On the bronze manufacture at Chengzhou during the Western Zhou period). In *Sei-Shu seidōki to sono kokka*, ed. Michio Matsumaru, 185–240. Tōkyō: Tōkyō Daigaku Shuppansha, 1980.

Montelius, Oscar. 1903. *Die älteren Kulturperioden im Orient und in Europa*. Part 1 of *Die Methode*. Stockholm: by author; Berlin: Ascher.

Morohashi Tetsuji. 1956. *Dai Kan-Wa jiten* (Great Chinese-Japanese character dictionary). 13 vols. Tōkyō: Taishūkan.

Moseley, K. P., and Immanuel Wallerstein. 1978. "Pre-Capitalist social structures." *Annual Review of Sociology* 4: 259–90.

Mu Haiting and Zhu Jieyuan. 1983. "Xin faxian de Xi-Zhou wangshi zhongqi Wusi Hu-zhong-kao" (On a recently discovered important Western Zhou royal bronze: the Wusi Hu-*yongzhong*). *Renwen Zazhi* 1983 (2): 118–121.

Needham, Joseph. 1961. *Science and civilisation in China*. Vol. 1. Cambridge: Cambridge University Press.

————. 1980. "The evolution of iron and steel technology in East and Southeast Asia." In *The coming of the age of iron*, ed. Theodore A. Wertime and James D. Muhly, 507–41. New Haven: Yale University Press.

Needham, Joseph, with Kenneth G. Robinson. 1962. "Sound (Acoustics)." In *Science and civilisation in China*. Vol. 4 (I):126–228. Cambridge: Cambridge University Press.

Needham, Rodney. 1967. "Percussion and transition." *Man* n.s. 2 (4): 606–14.

Okamura Hidenori. 1985. "Shin bunka-no hennen" (The chronology of the Qin culture). *Koshi Shunjū* 2: 53–74.

————. 1986a. "Go-Etsu izen-no seidōki" (Bronzes from Southeast China predating the Wu and Yue kingdoms). *Koshi Shunjū* 3: 63–89.

————. 1986b. "Henshō-no sekkei to kōzō [Hyō-shi henshō-wo chūshin-ni]" (The design and structure of chime-bells, with emphasis on the Biao-*niuzhong*). *Sen'oku Hakkokan Kiyō* 3: 33–49.

Okura Takahiko. 1965. "I-i-no fu—*Saden* no Ka-I kannen" (The vagaries of the meaning of Yi—the concept of Xia versus Yi in *Zuo Zhuan*). In *Chūgoku kodaishi kenkyū* (Studies on ancient Chinese history), vol. 2: 153–188. Tōkyō: Furukawa Kobunkan. Also published in Okura's *Chūgoku kodai seiji shisō kenkyū* (Studies on the political history of ancient China), 131–61. Tōkyō: Aoki Shoten, 1970.

Palmgren, Nils. 1948. *Selected Chinese antiquities from the collection of Gustaf Adolf, Crown Prince of Sweden*. Stockholm: Generalstabens Litografiska Anstalts Förlag.

Pan Jianming. 1980. "Guanyu cong yuanshi shehui taoxun tansuo woguo wusheng yinjie xingcheng niandai de shangque" (Disputing that the formation date of our country's pentatonic scale can be inferred from ocarinas dating to the primitive society). *Yinyue Yishu* 1980 (1): 53–59.

———. 1981. "Sui Xian gumu chutu yueqi" (Musical instruments from the ancient tomb at Sui Xian). *Yinyue Yishu* 1981 (3): 87–88.

———. 1982. "Zeng Hou Yi bianzhong yinlü yanjiu" (Studies on the intonation of the chime-bells of Marquis Yi of Zeng). *Shanghai Bowuguan Jikan* 2: 93–115.

Peng Hao. 1982. "Chu muzang-zhi chulun" (Preliminary discussion on the Chu burial system). *Zhongguo Kaoguxuehui di'erci nianhui (1980) lunwenji*, 33–40.

Peng Xiancheng. 1988. "Gu yuedui chutan" (An initial examination of ancient orchestras). *Huangzhong* 1988 (4): 96–102.

Pian, Rulan Chao. 1967. *Song dynasty musical sources and their interpretation.* Harvard Yenching Institute Monograph Series no. 16, Cambridge: Harvard University Press.

Picken, Laurence D. 1957. "The music of Far Eastern Asia." In *New Oxford History of Music.* Vol. 1: 83–190. Oxford: Oxford University Press.

———. 1969. "The musical implications of line-sharing in the Book of Songs (*Shih ching*)." *Journal of the American Oriental Society* 89 (2): 408–10.

———. 1977. "The shapes of the *Shi Jing* song texts and their musical implications." *Musica Asiatica* 1: 85–109.

Pirazzoli-t'Serstevens, Michelle. 1974. *La civilisation du royaume de Dian à l'époque Han.* Paris: École Française d'Extrême-Orient.

Pratt, Keith. 1986. "The evidence for music in the Shang dynasty: A reappraisal." *Bulletin of the British Association for Chinese Studies.* September 1986: 22–50.

Price, Sir Percival. 1983. *Bells and man.* Oxford: Oxford University Press.

Qian Boquan. 1984. "Guanyu Zeng Hou Yi-mu Chu-boming de shangque" (A proposal regarding the inscription of the Chu *bo* found in the tomb of Marquis Yi of Zeng). *Jianghan Kaogu* 1984 (4): 93–94.

Qiao Shizhi. 1983. "Jiantan Dong-Zhou shiqi Jin-guo de yinyue" (A simplified discussion of the music of the Jin state during the Eastern Zhou period). *Shanxi Wenwu* 1983 (2): 33–36, 69.

Qiu Qiongsun. 1964. *Lidai yuezhi lüzhi jiaoshi* (Collated exegeses of the intonation systems in use through the history of [Imperial] China). Vol. 1. Beijing: Zhonghua Shuju. Vol. 2 was never published.

Qiu Xigui. 1979. "Tantan Sui Xian Zeng Hou Yi-mu de wenzi ziliao" (On the epigraphic materials from the tomb of Marquis Yi of Zeng). *Wenwu* 1979 (7): 25–33.

Qiu Xigui and Li Jiahao. 1981. "Zeng Hou Yi-mu mingwen shiwen shuoming" (Explanation of the transcriptions of the inscriptions from Marquis Yi of Zeng's tomb). *Yinyue Yanjiu* 1981 (1): 17–21. Also in Rao and Zeng, 1985: 149–55. For an English abstract, *see* Dien, Riegel, and Price 1985, vol. 2: 760–764.

―――. 1988. "Tan Zeng Hou Yi-mu zhong qing mingwen-zhong de jige zi" (On some characters in the bell and lithophone inscriptions from the tomb of Marquis Yi of Zeng). Paper prepared for the International Exchange Activities of Ancient Chinese Science and Technology and Culture Symposium on the Chime-bells of Marquis Yi of Zeng, Wuhan.

Rao Yu-an, Edward C. Carterette, and Wu Yu-kui. 1987. "A comparison of the musical scales of the ancient Chinese bronze bell ensemble and the modern bamboo flute." *Perception & Psychophysics* 41 (6): 547–62.

Rao Zongyi. 1988a. "Zeng Hou Yi zhonglü yu Babilun tianwenxue" (The pitches of the bells of Marquis Yi of Zeng and Babylonian astronomy). *Yinyue Yishu* 1988 (2) [not seen].

―――. 1988b. "Gushishang tianwen yu yuelü guanxi zhi tantao—Zeng Hou Yi zhonglü yu Babilun tianwenxue wuguan shelun" (A discussion of the relationship between astronomy and musical temperament in ancient history—arguing that the temperament of Marquis Yi of Zeng has nothing to do with Babylonian astronomy). Paper prepared for the International Exchange Activities of Ancient Chinese Science and Technology and Culture Symposium on the Chime-bells of Marquis Yi of Zeng. Wuhan. Possibly identical with the preceding item.

Rao Zongyi and Zeng Xiantong. 1985. *Sui Xian Zeng Hou Yi-mu zhongqing mingci yanjiu* (Studies on the characters inscribed on the bells and musical stones from the tomb of Marquis Yi of Zeng at Sui Xian). Hong Kong: Chinese University Press.

Rawson, Jessica. 1980. *Ancient China, art and archaeology.* London: British Museum.

―――. 1987. *Chinese bronzes, art and ritual.* London: British Museum.

―――. 1988. "A bronze casting revolution in the Western Zhou and its impact on provincial industries." In *The beginning of the use of metals and alloys,* ed. Robert Maddin, 228–38. Cambridge, Mass.: MIT Press.

Renfrew, Colin. 1984. *Approaches to social archaeology.* Cambridge: Harvard University Press.

―――. 1986a. "Varna and the emergence of wealth in prehistoric Europe." In *The social life of things: Commodities in cultural perspective,* ed. Arjun Appadurai, 141–68. Cambridge: Cambridge University Press.

―――. 1986b. "Comment on 'The structure of ancient wisdom'" (McClain 1985). *Journal of Social and Biological Structures* 8: 1–4.

―――. 1986c. "Introduction: Peer polity interaction and socio-political change." In *Peer polity interaction and socio-political change,* ed. C. Renfrew and John F. Cherry, 1–18. Cambridge: Cambridge University Press.

Rickett, W. Allyn. 1985. *See* Classical Texts above: *Guan Zi.*

Robinson, Kenneth G. 1954. "New thoughts on ancient Chinese music." *Annual of the*

Chinese Society of Singapore, 30–33.

Rong Geng. 1927. "Yin-Zhou liyueqi kaolüe" (Abbreviated discussion on ritual and musical instruments of the Shang and Zhou periods). *Yanjing Xuebao* 1: 83–142.

———. 1941. *Shang Zhou yiqi tongkao* (Comprehensive analysis of Shang and Zhou ritual vessels). Beijing: Harvard-Yenching Institute.

Rong Geng and Zhang Weichi. 1958. *Yin Zhou qingtongqi tonglun* (Comprehensive discussion of Shang and Zhou bronzes). Beijing: Kexue.

Rossing, Thomas D. 1984. "The acoustics of bells." *American Scientist* 72 (5): 440–47.

———. 1986. "Acoustics of oriental gongs and bells." Paper read at the 112th meeting of the Acoustical Society of America, Anaheim, Calif., Dec. 8–12.

———. 1987. "Chinese bells." *Carillon News* (Spring 1987): 4.

———. 1989a. "Acoustical comparison of ancient Chinese bells with Western bells." Manuscript.

———. 1989b. "Acoustics of eastern and western bells, old and new." *Journal of the Acoustical Society of Japan* 10 (5): 241–52. English edition.

Rossing, Thomas D., ed. 1984. *Acoustics of bells*. New York: Van Nostrand Reinhold.

Rossing, Thomas D., and N. H. Fletcher. 1983. "Nonlinear vibrations in plates and gongs." *Journal of the Acoustical Society of America* 73 (1): 345–51.

Rossing, Thomas D., D. Scott Hampton, Bernard E. Richardson, H. John Sathoff, and André Lehr. 1988. "Vibrational modes of Chinese two-tone bells." *Journal of the Acoustical Society of America* 83 (1): 369–73.

Rossing, Thomas D., and Adrianus J. M. Houtsma. 1986. "Effects of signal envelope on the pitch of short sinusoidal tones." *Journal of the Acoustical Society of America* 7 (6): 1926–32.

Rossing, Thomas D., and Robert Perrin. 1987 "Vibrations of bells." *Applied Acoustics* 20: 41–70.

Rossing, Thomas D., and Zhou Hong-fan. 1989. "Sound spectra of ancient Chinese bells in the Shanghai Museum." Paper presented at the 117th meeting of the Acoustical Society of America, Syracuse, N.Y.

Rostoker, William, Bennet Bronson, and James Dvorak. 1984. "The cast iron bells of China." *Technology and Culture* 25 (4): 750–67.

Rowlands, Michael J. 1987. "Centre and periphery: A review of a concept." In *Centre and Periphery in the Ancient World*, ed. Michael J. Rowlands et al., 1–11. Cambridge: Cambridge University Press.

Sachs, Curt. 1929. *Geist und Werden der Musikinstrumente*. Berlin: Reimer.

———. 1940. *The history of musical instruments*. New York: Norton.

Sahara Yasuo. 1984. "Sōhin-yori: Hyōshi henshō" (From the collections: The Biao chime-bells). *Sen'oku Hakkokan Kiyō* 1:65–93.

Sahlins, Marshall. 1972. *Stone Age economics*. New York: Aldine.

Schaeffner, André. 1951. "Une importante découverte archéologique: Le lithophone de Ndut Lieng Krak (Vietnam)." *Revue de Musicologie*, n.s. 33: 1–19.

Schneider, Albrecht, and Hartmut Stoltz. 1988. "Notes on the acoustics of ancient Chinese bell chimes." In *The archaeology of early music cultures: Third international meeting of the ICTM Study Group on Music Archaeology*, ed. Ellen Hickmann and David W. Hughes, 265–72. Orpheus: Schriftenreihe zu Grundfragen der Musik vol. 51. Bonn: Verlag für systematische Musikwissenschaft.

Schneider, Jane. 1977. "Was there a pre-Capitalist world system?" *Peasant Studies* 6: 20–29.

Schwartz, Benjamin. 1985. *The world of thought in ancient China*. Cambridge: Harvard University Press (Belknap Press).

Shaughnessy, Edward L. 1983–85. "The date of the 'Duo You *ding*' and its significance." *Early China* 9/10: 55–69.

———. 1991. *Sources of Western Zhou history*. Berkeley: University of California Press.

Shen Sinyan. 1986–87. "The acoustics of the bian-zhong bell chimes of China." *Chinese Music* 9 (3): 53–57; (4): 73–78; 10 (1): 10–19.

———. 1987. "Acoustics of ancient Chinese bells." *Scientific American*, April 1987: 104–10.

Sheng Dongling. 1983. "Xi-Zhou tongqi mingwenzhong de renming ji qi dui duandai de yiyi" (Personal names in Western Zhou bronze inscriptions and their significance for dating). *Wenshi* 17: 27–64.

Shi Zhangru. 1955. "Yin-dai de zhutong gongyi" (The bronze casting industry of the Shang dynasty). *Zhongyang Yanjiuyuan Jikan* 26: 95–129.

———. 1965. "Shang Zhou yiqi mingwen buwei lilüe" (Brief examples of the placing of inscriptions on Shang and Zhou ritual vessels). Vol. 2 of *Xian-Qin-shi yanjiu lunji*. Dalu Zazhi Shixue Congshu ser. 1, vol. 3: 181–201. Taibei: Dalu Zazhi-she.

Shirakawa Shizuka. 1962–1984. *Kinbun tsūshaku* (Comprehensive interpretation of bronze inscriptions). *Hakutsuru Bijitsukan-shi* (Hakutsuru Museum Journal). Vols. 1–56. Kōbe: Hakutsuru Bijutsukan. Further volumes to appear in the future.

Si Weizhi. 1947. "Liang Zhou jinwen suojian zhiguan-kao" (On the offices seen in Western and Eastern Zhou bronze inscriptions). *Zhongguo Wenhua Yanjiu Huikan* 7: 1–25.

Sima Qian. *See* Classical Texts: *Shi Ji*.

Sirén, Osvald. 1929. *A history of early Chinese art*. Vol. 1, *The pre-historic and pre-Han periods*. London: Ernest Benn.

So, Jenny F. S. 1980a. "New departures in bronze designs: The Spring and Autumn period." In *The Great Bronze Age of China*, ed. Wen Fong, 249–320. New York: Metropolitan Museum of Art.

———. 1980b. "The inlaid bronzes of the Warring States period." In *The Great Bronze Age* of China, 303–20.

———. 1982. *Bronze styles of the Eastern Zhou period*. Ph. D. diss., Harvard University.

Soper, Alexander. 1964. "The tomb of the Marquis of Ts'ai." *Oriental Art* 10: 153–57.

Spear, Nathaniel. 1978. *A treasury of archaeological bells*. New York: Hastings House.

Stickney, John. 1982. "The sound of music from a lost world." *Discover*, May 1982: 57–59.

Su Bingqi. 1984. *Su Bingqi kaoguxue lunshu xuanji* (Selected essays on archaeology by Su Bingqi). Beijing: Wenwu.

Sun Changshu. 1978. "Qin Gong ji Wang Ji zhong, bo mingwen kaoshi" (Interpretation of the Qin Gong and Royal Ji–*yongzhong* and -*bo* inscriptions). *Jilin Shifan Daxue Xuebao* 1978 (4): 14–23.

Sun Haibo. 1937. *Xinzheng yiqi* (Ceremonial vessels from Xinzheng). Kaifeng: Henan Tong-zhiguan.

Takahashi Junji. 1984. "Hyō-shi henshō onkō sokutei" (Pitch frequency measurements on the Biao chime-bells). *Sen'oku Hakkokan Kiyō* 1: 94–110.

———. 1986. "Hyō-shi henshō-ni okeru *pitch* to *size*-no kankei" (The relationship between pitch and size in the Biao chime-bells). *Sen'oku Hakkokan Kiyō* 3: 50–59.

———. 1988. "Shatō-shō-no onkō sokutei" (Pitch measurements on the Zhediao-bells) and "Shatō-shō-no kōsaku" (The structure of the Zhediao-bells). *Sen'oku Hakkokan Kiyō* 5: 42–49.

———. 1989. "Size-frequency relation and tonal system in a set of ancient Chinese bells: *Piao-shi bianzhong*." *Journal of the Acoustical Society of Japan*. English ed. 10 (5): 299–303.

Takahashi Junji and Ueda Kōzō. 1986. "Sen-Shin jidai-no shō-no onkō sokutei" (Pitch frequency measurements on some pre-Qin bells). *Sen'oku Hakkokan Kiyō* 3: 60–61.

Tambiah, Stanley J. 1985. *Culture, thought, and social action*. Cambridge: Harvard University Press.

Tan Danjiong. 1977. *Xinzheng tongqi* (Bronzes from Xinzheng). Guoli Lishi Bowuguan Lishi Wenwu Congkan, vol. 3.2. Taibei: Guoli Bianyiguan.

Tan Weisi. 1988a. "Jiangling Yutaishan 21-hao Chu-mu lüguan qiantan" (Superficial discussion of the pitch tubes from tomb No. 21 at Yutaishan, Jiangling [Hubei]). *Wenwu* 1988 (5): 39–42.

———. 1988b. "Chu-guo yueqi chulun—guanyu yueqi zhizao de ruogan wenti" (An initial discussion of the musical instruments of Chu—some problems relating to the manufacture of musical instruments). Paper prepared for the International Exchange Activities of Ancient Chinese Science and Technology and Culture Symposium on the Chime-bells of Marquis Yi of Zeng. Wuhan.

Tan Weisi and Feng Guangsheng. 1981. "Guanyu Zeng Hou Yi-mu bianzhong yinyue xing-tai de qianjian—jianyu Wang Xiang tongzhi shangque" (A shallow opinion regarding the musical functionability of the chime-bells from the tomb of

Marquis Yi of Zeng—challenging the view of Comrade Wang Xiang). *Yinyue Yanjiu* 1981 (1): 79–87.

———. 1988. "Zeng Hou Yi bianzhong de faxian yu yanjiu" (The discovery and study of the chime-bells of Marquis Yi of Zeng). Paper prepared for the International Exchange Activities of Ancient Chinese Science and Technology and Culture Symposium on the Chime-bells of Marquis Yi of Zeng, Wuhan.

Tan Weisi, Shu Zhimei, and Guo Dewei. 1980. "Sui Xian Zeng Hou Yi-mu fajue de zhuyao shouhuo" (Main results from the excavations of the tomb of Marquis Yi of Zeng at Sui Xian). *Zhongguo Kaoguxuehui diyici nianhui* [1979] *lunwenji*, 225–28.

Tanaka Tan. 1980. "Sen-Shin jidai kūjitsu kenchiku josetsu" (Introduction to the architecture of pre-Qin palace buildings). *Tōhō Gakuhō* 52: 123–98.

Tang Chi. 1979. "Jingzhan de jiyi, qiwei de zaoxing—ping Sui Xian Zeng Hou Yi-mu chutu de qingtongqi" (Wondrous craftsmanship, rare shapes—evaluating the bronzes unearthed from the tomb of Marquis Yi of Zeng at Sui Xian). *Zhongguo Meishu* 1979 (1): 63–66.

Tang Lan. 1933. "Gu yueqi xiaoji" (Short remarks on ancient musical instruments). *Yanjing Xuebao* 14: 59–101.

———. 1978. "Lüelun Wei-shi jiazu jiaocang tongqi de zhongyao yiyi" (Abbreviated discussion on the important significance of the bronzes from the Wei family's hoard). *Wenwu* 1978 (3): 19–24, 42.

Tang Wenxing. 1981. "Xichuan Xiasi yihao-mu qingtongqi de zhuzao jishu" (The casting technique of the bronzes from tomb no. 1 at Xiasi, Xichuan). *Kaogu* 1981 (2): 174–76.

Thompson, P. M. 1979. *See* Classical texts above: *Shen Zi*.

Thorp, Robert L. 1981–82. "The Sui Xian tomb: Re-thinking the fifth century." *Artibus Asiae* 43: 67–110.

Thote, Alain. 1985. *Une tombe princière du cinquième siècle avant notre ère (tombe no. 1 de Leigudun): Recherches anthropologiques et historiques.* Ph.D. diss., Université de Paris 7.

———. 1986. "Une tombe princière du cinquième siècle avant notre ère." *Comptes rendus de l'Académie des Inscriptions et Belles-lettres* 1986: 393–413.

———. 1987. "Une sculpture chinoise en bronze du Ve siècle avant notre ère: essai d'interprétation." *Arts Asiatiques* 42: 45–58.

Tian Changhu. 1985. "Cong xiandai shiyan poxi Zhongguo gudai qingtong zhuzao de kexue chengjiu" (The scientific success of ancient Chinese bronze casting as seen from the perspecive of modern experimentation). *Kejishi Wenji* 13 (1985): 24–34.

Tian Haifeng. 1990. "Youguan Zeng Hou Yi bianzhong de jige wenti" (Some problems concerning the chime-bells of Marquis Yi of Zeng). *Wenbo* 1990 (3): 30–36.

Tian Xingnong and Luo Zhongru. 1981. "'Duo You-*ding*'de faxian ji qi mingwen shishi"

(The discovery of the Duo You–*ding* and a preliminary interpretation of its inscription). *Renwen Zazhi* 1981 (4): 115–18.

Tong Enzheng. 1979. *Gudai de Ba Shu* (Ba and Shu in antiquity). Chengdu: Sichuan Renmin.

———. 1982. "Slate cist graves and megalithic chamber tombs in southwest China: Archaeological, historical, and ethnographical approaches to the identification of early ethnic groups." *Journal of Anthropological Archaeology* 1: 266–74.

Tong Kin-woon (Tang Jianhuan). 1983–84. "Shang musical instruments." *Asian Music* 14 (2): 17–182; 15 (1): 103–84; and 15 (2): 68–143.

Tong Shibu. 1981. "Zeng Hou Yi-mu bianqing fuzhi chenggong" (The results of replicating the lithophone from the tomb of Marquis Yi of Zeng). *Yueqi* 1981 (6) [not seen].

Tong Zhongliang. 1984. "Zeng Hou Yi bianzhong de sandu yinxi" (The tonal system based on thirds in the chime-bells of Marquis Yi of Zeng). *Renmin Yinyue* 1984 (5): 38–43 and (6): 38–40.

———. 1988. "Baizhong tanxun—Leigudun yi-, erhao mu chutu bianzhong de bijiao" (Examining the hundred bells—a comparison of the chime-bells from tombs no. 1 and 2 at Leigudun). *Huangzhong* 1988 (4): 1–8.

Tong Zhongliang and Zheng Rongda. 1988. "Jing-Chu min'ge sandu chongdie yu chunlü yinsu—jianlun Hubei minjian yinyue yu Zeng Hou Yi bianzhong yinyue de bijiao" (Elements of overlaying of thirds and pure tuning in the folksongs of Chu, and a discussion on comparing the folk music of Hubei with the music of the chime-bells of Marquis Yi of Zeng). *Huangzhong* 1988 (4): 57–65.

Umehara Sueji. 1927. *Dōtaku-no kenkyū* (Studies on dōtaku bells). 2 vols. Tōkyō: Tai-Okayama.

———. 1936a. *Rakuyō Kinson kobo shuei* (Collected masterpieces from the ancient tombs at Jincun, Luoyang). Kyōto: Kobayashi.

———. 1936b. *Sengokushiki dōki-no kenkyū* (Studies on Warring States style bronzes). Research Reports of the Kyōto Institute of the Academy of Oriental Culture, vol. 7. Kyōto: Tōhō Bunka Gakuin Kyōto Kenkyūjo.

———. 1938. *Shina kōkogaku ronkō* (Essays on Chinese archaeology). Tōkyō: Kōbundō.

———. 1940. *Tōa kōkogaku ronkō* (Essays on East Asian archaeology). Vol. 1. Kyōto: Hoshino.

———. 1959–64. *Nihon shūcho Shina kodō seika* (Masterpieces of ancient Chinese bronzes in Japanese collections). 6 vols. Osaka: Yamanaka Shōkai.

Vandermeersch, Léon. 1977–80. *Wang Dao ou La voie royale: Recherches sur l'esprit des institutions de la Chine archaïque.* Vol. 1, "Structures cultuelles et structures familiales." Vol. 2, "Structures politiques: Les rites." Publications de l'École Française d'Extrême-Orient, vol. 113. Paris: Maisonneuve.

Veblen, Thorstein. 1899. *The Theory of the leisure class*. New York: Macmillan. Various reprints.

Wagner, Donald. 1987. "The dating of the Chu graves of Changsha: The earliest iron artifacts in China?" *Acta Orientalia* 48: 111–56.

Wang Entian. 1985. "Henan Gushi 'Gouwu Furen-mu'" (The 'tomb of the Lady of Wu' at Gushi, Henan). *Zhonyuan Wenwu* 1985 (2): 59–62, 64.

Wang Fei. 1986. "Yongding zhidu xingshuai yiyi" (The significance of the rise and fall of the sumptuary system involving the use of the *ding* tripod). *Wenbo* 1986 (6): 29–33.

Wang Guowei (1877–1927). 1916. *Gu liqi lüeshuo* (Abbreviated explanations of old ceremonial vessels). In *Xuetang Congke*. Luo Zhenyu. Vol. 11, item 4. Shanghai: by author.

————.1927a. *Guantang jilin* (Collected works of Wang Guowei). Reprinted Taibei: Shijie Shuju.

————.1927b. *Sandai Qin Han jinwen zhulu-biao* (Bibliographic tables on bronze inscriptions of the Three Dynasties, Qin, and Han). Reprinted Taibei: Yiwen Yinshuguan, 1969.

Wang Haiwen. 1980. "Yuezhong zongshu" (Comprehensive remarks on musical bells). *Gugong Bowuyuan Yuankan* 1980 (4): 73–79.

Wang Qingyuan. 1988. "Zeng Hou Yi bianzhong yu Xingshan tixi minge de dinglü jiegou" (The tuning structures of the chime-bells of Marquis Yi of Zeng and of the folk songs of the Xingshan system). *Huangzhong* 1988 (4): 66–72.

Wang Shimin. 1983. "Xi-Zhou Chunqiu jinwen-zhong de zhuhou juecheng" (The rank designations of feudal lords in Western Zhou and Springs and Autumns period bronze inscriptions). *Lishi Yanjiu* 1983 (3): 3–17.

————. 1986a. "Guanyu Xi-Zhou Chunqiu gaoji guizu liqi zhidu de yixie kanfa" (Some ideas on the sumptuary system governing the ritual vessels of high aristocrats during the Western Zhou and Springs and Autumns periods). *Wenwu yu Kaogu Lunji*, 158–66.

————. 1986b. "Xi Zhou ji Chunqiu Zhan'guo shidai bianzhong mingwen de pailie xingshi" (Types of inscription arrangement on Western Zhou as well as Springs and Autumns and Warring States periods chime-bells). In *Zhongguo Kaoguxue Yanjiu* 2: 106–120.

————. 1988. "Chunqiu Zhan'guo zangzhizhong yueqi he liqi de zuhe zhuangkuang" (The assemblages of musical instruments and ritual vessels in the funerary system of the Springs and Autumns and Warring States periods). Paper prepared for the International Exchange Activities of Ancient Chinese Science and Technology and Culture Symposium on the Chime-bells of Marquis Yi of Zeng. Wuhan.

Wang Wenyao. 1984. "Zeng Hou Yi-zhong mingwen zhi guanjian" (My humble opinion on the inscriptions on the bells of Marquis Yi of Zeng). *Guwenzi Yanjiu* 9: 391–406.

Wang Xiang. 1981. "Zeng Hou Yi-mu bianzhong yinlü de tantao" (An inquiry into the tones and pitches of the bells from the tomb of Marquis Yi of Zeng). *Yinyue Yanjiu* 1981 (1): 68–78.

Wang Yuzhu et al. 1981. "Xichuan gu bianzhong de zhendong moshi yu jiegou fenxi" (Analysis of the vibration modes and structure of the ancient chime-bells from Xichuan). Paper read at the XVIth International Conference for the History of Science [not seen].

Wang Yuzhu, An Zhixin, Tan Weisi, and Hua Jueming. 1988. "Qingtong bianzhong shengpu yu shuangyin" (The sound spectra in bronze bell-chimes and the two-tone phenomenon). *Kaogu* 1988 (8): 757–65.

Watson, Burton. 1968. *See* Classical Texts above: *Zhuang Zi.*

———. 1962. *Early Chinese literature.* New York: Columbia University Press.

Watson, James L. 1977. "Hereditary tenancy and corporate landlordism in traditional China: A case study." *Modern Asian Studies* 11:161–82.

———. 1982. "Chinese kinship reconsidered: Anthropological perspectives on historical research." With comment by Denis Twitchett. *China Quarterly* 92: 589–627.

———. 1986. "Anthropological overview: The development of Chinese descent groups." In *Kinship organization in late imperial China, 1000–1940,* ed. Patricia M. Ebrey and J. L. Watson, 274–92. Berkeley and Los Angeles: University of California Press.

Watson, William. 1962. *Ancient Chinese bronzes.* London: Faber & Faber.

Weber, Charles D. 1968. *Chinese pictorial bronze vessels of the late Chou period.* Ascona: Artibus Asiae. Originally published in *Artibus Asiae,* vols. 28–30.

Weber, George W. 1973. *The ornaments of late Chou bronzes.* New Brunswick, N.J.: Rutgers University Press.

Wei Junyun. 1985. "Yitan Sanfen Sunyi-fa" (More on the "Pythagorean" tuning system). *Yinyue Yanjiu* 1985 (3): 68–70.

Wells, Peter S. 1980. *Culture contact and culture change: Early Iron Age Central Europe and the Mediterranean world.* Cambridge: Cambridge University Press.

Wen Tingjing. 1934–35. "Zhejian-*zhong*-shi" (Interpretation of the Zhejian-*yongzhong* [inscription]). *Zhongshan Daxue Wenshi Yanjiusuo Yuekan* 3 (2): 63–65.

White, Lynn, Jr. 1962. "The act of invention: Causes, contexts, continuities, and consequences." *Technology and Culture* 3 (4): 486–500.

White, William Charles. 1934. *Tombs of old Lo-yang.* Shanghai: Kelly and Walsh.

Williams, Edward V. 1985. *The bells of Russia.* Princeton: Princeton University Press.

Wolf, Eric. 1982. *Europe and the people without history.* Berkeley and Los Angeles: University of California Press.

Wu Dacheng. 1896. *Kezhai jigulu* (Records of antiques collected by Kezhai [Wu Dacheng]). Privately published. N. p. Reissued Shanghai: Hanfenlou, 1930.

Wu Houpin et al. 1981. "Yong xiandai rongmo zhuzao gongyi fuzhi Zeng Hou Yi bian-zhong" (Replicating the chime-bells of Marquis Yi of Zeng using modern smelting mold casting technology). *Jianghan Kaogu* 1981 (1): 46–51.

Wu Hung (Wu Hong). 1988. "From temple to tomb: Ancient Chinese art and religion in transition." *Early China* 13: 78–115.

———. N.d. "Straight-handled bronze bells of Shang and Western Zhou." Manuscript.

Wu Laiming. 1986. "'Liu Qi,' Shang Zhou qingtongqi huaxue chengfen ji qi yanbian de yanjiu" (The 'Six Balances': Studies on the chemical composition of Shang and Zhou bronzes and its change over time). *Wenwu* 1986 (11): 76–84.

Wu Nanxun. 1964. *Lüxue huitong* (Digest of tuning studies). Beijing: Kexue Chubanshe.

Wu Shijian. 1910. *Jiuzhong jingshe jinshi bowei* (Antiquarian remarks in appreciation of a set of nine bells). Privately published.

Wu Shiqian. 1980. "Qin Gong-zhong kaoshi" (Interpretation of the Qin Gong bells). *Sichuan Daxue Xuebao* 1980 (2): 103–08.

———. 1981. "Wei-shi jiazu tongqiqun niandai chutan" (Preliminary enquiry into the chronology of the assemblage of bronzes of the Wei lineage). *Guwenzi Yanjiu* 5: 97–138.

———. 1984. "Wangzi Wu-*ding*, Wangsun Gao-*zhong* mingwen kaoshi" (Interpretation of the inscriptions of the Wangzi Wu-*ding* and the Wangsun Gao-*yongzhong*). *Guwenzi Yanjiu* 9: 275–94.

Wu Zhao. 1980 "Ye tan 'Chusheng' de diaoshi wenti—Du 'Shi *Chushang*' yiwen-hou de ji-dian yijian" (An alternative view of the problem of modes in "Chu music"—some criticisms after reading the article "Interpretation of *Chushang*"). *Wenyi Yanjiu* 1980 (2): 76–85. *See* Huang Xiangpeng, 1979c.

———. 1983. *Zhongguo gudai yueqi* (Ancient Chinese musical instruments). Beijing: Wenwu, 1983.

Wu Zhao and Liu Dongsheng. 1983. *Zhogguo yinyue shilüe* (Abbreviated history of Chinese music). Beijing: Renmin Yinyue Chubanshe.

Wu Zhenfeng. 1980. "Xin chutu Qin Gong zhongming kaoshi yu youguan wenti" (Interpretation of the inscription on the newly excavated Qin Gong bell and related problems). *Kaogu yu Wenwu* 1980 (1): 88–92, 61.

Xia Mailing. 1984. "Kaogu suojian Shang-dai de yuewu" (Music and dance of the Shang dynasty as perceived through archaeological materials). *Zhongyuan Wenwu* 1984 (4): 76–80.

Xiao Menglong. 1986. "Shilun Jiangnan Wu-guo qingtongqi" (A preliminary discussion of Wu bronzes from south of the Yangzi river). *Dongnan Wenhua* 2: 96–108.

Xiong Chuanxin. 1981. "Hunan chutu de gudai chunyu zongshu" (Comprehensive discussion of ancient *chunyu* excavated in Hunan). *Kaogu yu Wenwu* 1981 (4): 36–42.

———. 1982. "Woguo gudai chunyu gailun" (Introductory remarks on the ancient *chunyu* of our motherland). *Zhongguo Kaoguxuehui di'erci nianhui (1980) lunwenji*, 80–89.

———. 1983a. "Hunan faxian de gudai Ba-ren yiwu" (Relics of the ancient Ba population discovered in Hunan). *Wenwu Ziliao Congkan* 7 (1983): 30–33.

———. 1983b. "Ji Xiang-xi xin faxian de huniu chunyu" (Notes on *chunyu* with tiger-shaped loops newly discovered in western Hunan). *Jianghan Kaogu* 1983 (2): 38–43.

Xu Dingsui. 1988. "Leigudun erhao mu bianzhong ji qi yinlü ceshi" (The chime-bells from tomb no. 2 at Leigudun and the measurements of their tone-pitches). *Huang-zhong* 1988 (4): 9–12.

Xu Xuexian, Feng Guangsheng, and Chu Meijuan. 1982. "Sui Xian Zeng Hou Yi-mu fuzhi bianqing shengyin shicheng chutan" (A preliminary investigation into the sound duration of the replicated lithophones from the tomb of Marquis Yi at Sui Xian). *Zhongguo Kexueyuan Wuhan Wuli Yanjiusuo Jikan*, 1982 (1) [not seen].

Xu Xuexian, Feng Guangsheng, and Zhang Baocheng. 1983. "Bianqing yin'gao de jisuan" (The calculation of lithophone pitch). *Shengxue Jinzhan* 1983 (2) [not seen].

Xu Zhongshu. 1936. "Jinwen guci shili" (Examples of auspicious words in bronze inscriptions). *Zhongyang Yanjiuyuan Lishi Yuyan Yanjiusuo Jikan* 6 (1): 1–44.

———. 1959. "Ba-Shu wenhua chulun" (A preliminary discussion of the Ba-Shu culture). *Sichuan Daxue Xuebao* 1959 (2): 21–44.

———. 1982. *Lun Ba-Shu wenhua* (On the Ba-Shu culture). Chengdu: Sichuan Renmin.

Xu Zhongshu, ed. 1984. *Yin Zhou jinwen jilu* (Collected records on Shang and Zhou bronze inscriptions). Chengdu: Sichuan Renmin.

Xu Zhongshu and Tang Jiahong. 1981. "Gudai Chu-Shu de guanxi" (The relations between Chu and Shu in antiquity). *Wenwu* 1981 (6): 17–25.

Xue Zongming. 1981–83. *Zhongguo yinyueshi* (History of Chinese music). 2 vols. Taibei: Taiwan Shangwu Yinshuguan.

Yang Kuan. 1982. *Zhongguo gudai yetie jishu fazhanshi* (History of the development of ancient Chinese siderurgical technology). Shanghai: Shanghai Renmin.

———. 1984. "Xi-Zhou zhongyang zhengquan jigou poxi" (The power structure of the central administration in Western Zhou). *Lishi Yanjiu* 1984 (1): 78–91.

Yang Kuangmin. 1988. "Zeng Hou Yi bianzhong yinlie ji qita" (The succession of tones on the chime-bells of Marquis Yi of Zeng, and other things). *Huangzhong* 1988 (4): 39–46.

Yang Yinliu. 1944. *Zhongguo yinyue shigang* (Outline history of Chinese music). Chongqing. Several reprints.

———. 1959a. "Ruhe duidai wusheng yinjie yu qisheng yinjie tongshi cunzai de lishi chuan-tong." *Yinyue Yanjiu* 3: 2–10. Also in *Yinyue Jianshe Wenji* 3: 464–77. For a German translation, see Gerd Schönfelder, trans. "Zur gleichzeitigen Existenz pentatonischer und heptatonischer Leitern in der chinesischen Musik." *Beiträge zur*

*Musikwissenschaft* 6 (1964) 1: 43–52.

———. 1959b. "Xinyang chutu Chunqiu bianzhong de yinlü." *Yinyue Yanjiu* 1959 (1): 77–80. For a German translation, see Gerd Schönfelder, trans. "Die Tonskalen des in Xinyang ausgegrabenen Glockenspiels aus der Frühlings- und Herbstperiode." *Beiträge zur Musikwissenschaft* 7 (1965) 2: 123–27.

———. 1979. "Guanlü bian'e" (The debate on the standard pitch pipes). *Wenyi Yanjiu* 1979 (4): 78–82.

———. 1980. *Zhongguo gudai yinyue shigao* (Draft history of ancient Chinese music). 2 vols. Beijing: Renmin Yinyue Chubanshe. Vol. 1 formerly published as two volumes. Beijing: Renmin Yinyue Chubanshe, 1964 and 1966.

———. 1982. "Sanlü-kao" (On the three intonations). *Yinyue Yanjiu* 1982 (1): 30–39.

Yang Yubin. 1985. *Henan kaogu* (The archaeology of Henan province). Zhengzhou: Zhongzhou Guji.

Ye Xuexian et al. 1981. "Huaxue chengfen, zuzhi, rechuli dui bianzhong shengxue texing de yingxiang" (The influence of chemical particles, alloy composition, and heat adjustment on the acoustical properties of chime-bells). *Jianghan Kaogu* 1981 (1): 31–41.

Yetts, W. Perceval. 1929. *The George Eumorfopoulos Collection: Catalogue of the Chinese and Corean bronzes, sculpture, jade, jewelry, and miscellaneous objects.* Vols. 1 and 2. London: Benn Ltd.

Yin Weizhang and Cao Shuqin. 1986. "Changjiang liuyu zaoqi yongzhong de xingtaixue fenxi" (Typological analysis of early *yongzhong* excavated in the Yangzi River basin). *Wenwu yu kaogu lunji*, 261–70.

Yin Zhiyi. 1977. "Shandong Yidu Subutun mudi he 'Yachou' tongqi" (The cemetery at Subutun, Yidu [Shandong] and the 'Yachou' bronzes). *Kaogu Xuebao* 1977 (2): 22–33.

Ying Youqin and Sun Keren. 1988." Zeng Hou Yi bianqing 'jianyin' xinjie yu bianlie yanjiu" (A new explanation of the "intermediary notes" among the chimestones of Marquis Yi of Zeng, and a study of their arrangement). Paper prepared for the International Exchange Activities of Ancient Chinese Science and Technology and Culture Symposium on the Chime-bells of Marquis Yi of Zeng, Wuhan.

Yoshimoto Michimasa. 1986. "Sōhin-yori: Kaku Shuku Ryo-shō" (From the collections: The Guo Shu Lü–*yongzhong*)." *Sen'oku Hakkokan Kiyō* 3: 62–78.

Young, Bell N. 1980. "Theory." In *The New Grove*. vol. 4: 260–62. Under entry "China."

Yu Shuji. 1988. "Gu bianzhong de yinpin texing" (The tone-vibration characteristics of ancient chime-bells). *Huangzhong* 1988 (4): 31–38.

Yu Weichao. 1980a. "Han-dai zhuhouwang yu liehou-mu de xingzhi fenxi—Jiantan 'Zhouzhi,' 'Hanzhi' yu 'Jinzhi' de sanjieduanxing" (Analysis of the layout of the tombs of feudal kings and princes of the Han dynasty—The three-stage succession of the Zhou, Han, and Jin sumptuary systems). *Zhongguo Kaogu Xuehui Diyici (1979) Nianhui Lunwenji*, 332–37. Also in Yu Weichao 1985, 117–24.

———. 1985. *Xian-Qin, liang Han kaoguxue lunji* (Collected essays on the archaeology of the pre-Qin and Han periods). Beijing: Wenwu.

———. 1987. "Zaoqi Zhongguo de si da lianmeng jituan" (The four great alliance-groups of early China). Paper presented at the XIᵉ Congrès de l'Union des Sciences Préhistoriques et Protohistoriques, Mainz.

Yu Weichao and Gao Ming. 1973. "Qin Shihuang tongyi duliangheng he wenzi de lishi gongji" (The historical achievement of Qin Shihuang's unification of the weights and measures, and of the writing system). *Wenwu* 1973 (12): 6–13.

———. 1978–79. "Zhoudai yongding zhidu yanjiu" (Studies on the sumptuary system governing the use of the *ding*-tripod in the Zhou dynasty). *Beijing Daxue Xuebao: Shehui Kexue-ban* 1978 (1): 84–98; (2): 84–97; and 1979 (1): 83–96. Also in Yu Weichao 1985, 62–114.

Yu Xingwu. 1957. *Shang Zhou jinwen luyi* (Record of bronze inscriptions remaining from the Shang and Zhou dynasties). Beijing: Kexue.

Yule, Paul, and Martin Bemmann. 1987. "Klangsteine aus Orissa—Die frühesten Musikinstrumente Indiens?" Manuscript article.

Zaccagnini, Carlo. 1987. "Aspects of ceremonial exchange in the Near East during the late second millennium B.C." In *Centre and periphery in the ancient world*, ed. Michael J. Rowlands et al., 57–65. Cambridge: Cambridge University Press.

Zeng Hou Yi Bianzhong Fuzhi Yanjiuzu (Study Group on the Replication of Marquis Yi of Zeng's Bell-Chime). 1983. "Zeng Hou Yi bianzhong fuzhi yanjiu-zhong de kexue jishu gongzuo" (Scientific and technological work done during the research in connection with the replication of the Zeng Hou Yi chime-bells). *Wenwu* 1983 (8): 55–60.

Zeng Shaomin and Li Qin. 1980. "Zeng-guo he Zeng-guo tongqi zongkao" (Comprehensive study on the state of Zeng and its bronzes). *Jianghan Kaogu* 1980 (1): 69–84.

Zhang Changshou. 1987. "Taosi yizhi de faxian he Xia wenhua de tansuo" (The discovery of the site of Taosi and the enquiry into the Xia culture). *Wenwu yu Kaogu Lunji*, 110–13.

Zhang Huaimin. 1988. "Zeng Hou Yi bianzhong meixue jiazhi chutan" (An initial discussion of the aesthetic value of the chime-bells of Marquis Yi of Zeng). Paper prepared for the International Exchange Activities of Ancient Chinese Science and Technology and Culture Symposium on the Chime-bells of Marquis Yi of Zeng, Wuhan.

Zhang Jian. 1980. "Cong Henan Xichuan Chunqiu Chu-mu de fajue tan dui Chu wenhua de renshi" (The information on the Chu culture obtained through the excavation of the Springs and Autumns period Chu tomb at Xichuan, Henan). *Wenwu* 1980 (10): 21–26.

Zhang Tian'en. 1980. "Dui 'Qin Gong-*zhong* kaoshi'-zhong de youguan wenti de yixie kanfa" (Some points of contention about problems concerning the article 'Interpretation of the Qin Gong-bells' [by Wu Shiqian]). *Sichuan Daxue Xuebao* 1980 (4): 93–100.

Zhang Yachu. 1985. "Xichuan Xiasi erhao-mu de muzhu, niandai yu yihao-mu bianzhong de mingcheng wenti" (The problems concerning the identity of the owner, as well as the date, of tomb no. 2 at Xiasi, Xichuan, and the naming of the bells from tomb no. 1). *Wenwu* 1985 (4): 54–58.

Zhang Zhenxin. 1979. "Zeng Hou Yi bianzhong liangjia jiegou yu zhongju tongren" (The structure of the chime-bell rack of Marquis Yi of Zeng, and its bronze caryatids). *Wenwu* 1979 (7): 49–50.

———. 1980. "Guanyu zhongju tongren de tantao" (A discussion of the bronze caryatids of the bell rack). *Zhongguo Lishi Bowuguan Guankan* 2: 35–38.

Zhao Congcang. 1988. "Jieshao yizu qingtong zhong, ling" (Introducing a group of *zhong* and *ling* bells). *Wenbo* 1988 (3): 83–85.

Zhao Shigang. 1983. "Xinyang Changtaiguan yihao-mu de niandai yu guobie" (The date and state affiliation of tomb no. 1 at Changtaiguan, Xinyang). *Kaogu yu Wenwu* 1983 (4): 56–59.

———. 1986 "Xichuan Xiasi Chu-mu Wangsun Gao-*zhong* de fenxi" (Analysis of the Wangsun Gao bells from the Chu tombs at Xiasi, Xichuan). *Jianghan Kaogu* 1986 (3): 45–57.

———. 1987. "Xu Wangzi Jiong[?] yu Xu jun shixi" (Xu Wangzi Jiong[?] and his position in the genealogy of the Xu rulers). *Huaxia Kaogu* 1: 194–201.

———. 1988. "Zeng Hou Yi zhong yu Chu zhong" (The bells of Marquis Yi of Zeng as compared with Chu bells). Paper prepared for the International Exchange Activities of Ancient Chinese Science and Technology and Culture Symposium on the Chime-bells of Marquis Yi of Zeng, Wuhan.

Zheng Rongda. 1988. "Shitan xian-Qin shuangyinbianzhong de sheji gouxiang" (A tentative approach to the design ideas underlying pre-Qin two-tone chime-bells). *Huangzhong* 1988 (4): 13–30.

Zheng Zuxiang. 1983. "Handai guchuiyue de qiyuan ji qi leixing" (The origins and types of the fife-and-drum music of the Han dynasty). *Zhongyang Yinyue Xueyuan Xuebao* 1983 (4): 57–59.

Zhong Hui. 1983. "Zeng Hou Yi bianzhong fuzhi yanjiu chengguo jiandinghui shuyao" (Protocol of the conference assessing the result of the studies concerning the replication of the chime-bells of Marquis Yi of Zeng). *Jianghan Kaogu* 1983 (2): 90–92, 43.

Zhongyang Yinyue Xueyuan Minzu Yinyue Yanjiusuo Diaochazu (Investigation team of the Institute for Folk Music, Central Conservatory of Music). 1958. "Xinyang Zhan'guo Chu-mu chutu yueqi chubu diaocha-ji" (Notes on the preliminary investigations of the musical instruments excavated from the Chu tomb at Xinyang). *Wenwu Cankao Ziliao* 1958 (1): 15–23.

Zhou Fagao, ed. 1982. *Jinwen gulin-bu* (Supplement to *Jinwen gulin*). 8 vols. Academia Sinica Institute for History and Philology Monograph no. 77. Taibei: Academia Sinica.

Zhou Fagao, with Zhang Risheng, Xu Zhiyi, and Lin Jieming, compilers. 1974. *Jinwen gulin* (Collected comments on bronze inscriptions). 16 vols. Hong Kong: Chinese University Press.

Zhu Dexi. 1979. "Jingli Quluan-jie" (Explanation of the Chu datings and regionalisms in Eastern Zhou bronze inscriptions). *Fangyan* 1979 (4): 33.

Zhuang Benli. 1960. "Zhongguo yinlü-zhi yanjiu" (Studies on Chinese notes and pitches). *Zhongguo Yinyueshi Lunji*, vol. 2, ed. Dai Cuilun. Taibei: Zhonghua Wenhua Chuban Shiyeshe [not seen].

———. 1963. *Zhongguo gudai zhi paixiao* (Ancient Chinese panflutes). Monographs of the Institute of Ethnology, no. 4. Taibei: Academia Sinica.

———. 1966. "Guqing yanjiu zhi yi (Guoli Lishi Bowuguan-cang Zhou-qing)" (Studies on ancient musical stones, part one: The Zhou dynasty musical stones in the collection of National Museum of History). *Zhongyang Yanjiuyuan Minzuxue Yanjiusuo Jikan* 22 (1): 97–137. With extensive English summary.

———. 1972. "Xun de lishi yu bijiao zhi yanjiu" (The history and comparative study of ocarinas). *Zhongyang Yanjiuyuan Minzuxue Yanjiusuo Jikan* 33: 177–253.

Zou Heng. 1980. *Xia Shang Zhou kaoguxue lunwenji* (Essays on the archaeology of the Xia, Shang, and Zhou dynasties). Beijing: Wenwu.

# INDEX

A-tone. *See* two-tone phenomenon

acoustics, 17, 76–80; and alloys, 102, 107; deficiencies in, 96, 118, 381; in inscriptions, 123; and ornamentation, 125, 145, 174, 189; and preservation, 222–23; and shape, 76–80, 85–91, 118, 119, 120, 136n16; and technology, 108, 114, 115, 154, 264–67. *See also* tones; two-tone phenomenon

African bells, 118

almond-shaped cross-section, 117–18, 119n64, 136n18, 154, 169, 384; earliest examples of, 130, 157

amplitude. *See* pitch

ancestral cult: changes in, 47, 51, 52, 55; and inscriptions, 40, 43, 280; role of bells in, 24–28

ancestral spirits, 56–57, 59, 61, 124; impersonators of, 25–26, 28

anhemitonic pentatonic gamut, 233, 236. *See also* pentatonicity

Anlu (Hubei), 5n16

antinodes, 77, 80–84, 120–21

Anyang, bells found at, 350–51; tone data on, 229, 388, 393. *See also particular bells and sites*

Anyang period bells, 103, 134–38, 157, 159, 160, 168, 200, 349–51; ornamentation on, 137, 145; tone data on, *230, 231, 233. See also particular bells and sites*

appearance of bells, 99–100, 102, 125, 259. *See also* ornamentation

archery contests, 29, *31*, 52

Art Institute, Minneapolis, bell in, 364

Art Institute of Chicago, bells in, *175*, 353, 362, 364, 369. *See also particular bells*

Arthur M. Sackler Gallery, bells in, 354, 360, 361, 365

Arthur M. Sackler Museum, bell in, 364

Asahara Tatsurō, 201, 259, *261*, 306, 308n58

Ashmolean Museum, Oxford, bell in, 104, 350

Asian Art Museum, San Francisco, bells in, 359, 364, 367, 369

assemblages of bells, 176–77, 199–201, 202–5

auspicious metals (*jijin*), 99

B-tone. *See* two-tone phenomenon

Ba, 374n1

Ba, ruler of, *188*, 189, 384

Bagley, Robert W., 112n42, 139, 169n, 170

Baijiacun, Fufeng (Shaanxi), 325, 357

Baijiacun, Liuyang (Hunan), 325, 352

Baizhadi, Chao Xian (Anhui), 325

Baizifan, Echeng (Hubei), 55n64

Bajiaolou, Suizhou (Hubei), 325, 361

Balázs, Étienne, 96

Bali, 324

Ban Chiang culture, 118

Banqiao, Changsha (Hunan), 325, 353

banquets, 29, 52, 54, 64, 318

*bao* (precious, preserve), 98

Baoji, 109n38, 162

Baoshan, Jingmen (Hubei), 55n64, *71*

Baoshi-*zhong*, 49

Hongjiaqiao, Xiangtan (Hunan), 157n69, 331, 355
Hongxing Commune, Lantian (Shaanxi), 58n80, 331, 357
horse-bells, 386
Houchuan, Sanmenxia (Henan), 176, 331, 363, 391, 392, 399–400
Hougudui, Gushi (Henan), 34, 62n100, 222, 332, 367, 368; assemblages at, 176; bell-racks from, 207n24; mallets from, 210n30
Houma (Shanxi), 56n68, 65, 110, 179
Hu Daoying, 76n
*hu* vessels, 29, *212. See also particular vessels*
Hu-*yongzhong*, 44, 45, 101n21, 167n26, 359
Hua Jueming, 112, *113*
Huahu, Huilai (Guangdong), 332, 371
Huai style, 185
Huai Yi (ethnic group), 374n1
Huaibaoshicun, Zigui (Hebei), 332, 355
Huaibiaoshan, Zigui (Hubei), 157n69
*Huainan Zi*, 3n8, 118n61, 206n21; on pitch standards, 290n21, 298, 299n37, 300
Huan Gong, 321n39
Huan Zi Meng Jiang–*hu*, 57
Huang, state of, 6n18
Huang Xiangpeng, 119n64, 228n4, 229n5, 264, 265, 284n
Huangdui, Fufeng (Shaanxi), 332
Huanghu, Fanchang (Anhui), 332, 368
Huangjiashan, Haiyan (Zhejiang), 177, 332, 368, 381n13
Huangjing, Liuyang (Hunan), 332, 360
Huangmasai, Xiangxiang (Hunan), 149n55, 332, 351

HUANGZHONG (name of pitch standard): and pitch-pipes, 311, 314–15; and pitch standards, 299, 300, 313, 314, 317; and regional music, 318; and Spiral of Fifths, 302, *303*
Huangzhu, Zhuzhou (Hunan), 151, *152*, 154, 155, 332, 353
Huanzi Meng Jiang–*hu*, 204n11
Huashan, Zhongxiang (Hubei), 332, 369–70
Hui Xian (Henan), 332, 350
Huilongcun, Wugong (Shaanxi), 332
human figures, 29, *30, 31*, 62, *212. See also* ornamentation
Hunan Provincial Museum, bells in, 149n52, 353, 354, 355, 357, 359, 360, 370, 372

idiophones, 67, 78; defined, 403. *See also* bell-chimes; chime-bells; lithophones
Indian lithophones, 201n4
inlaid bells, 189, 209n28, 366, 382, 384
inscriptions, 13, 41, 42, 70, 74, 135, 168n33, *203*, 256n22; and ancestral cult, 27; casting of, 111n41; on Chu bells, 185; dating by, 130, 167, 172; and donors, 14, 39; evidence from, 98–102; and musical theory, 123, 291, 293, 310, 312; onomatopoeia in, 123, 199; poetic devices in, 40; and political power, 59; tone-naming, 5n16, 214, 215, 245, 280–83, 282, 288–89, 310; Western Zhou, 162n9, 164, 165, 167; on Zhediao–*niuzhong*, 259, 261. *See also* Cai inscriptions; Zeng inscriptions
intonation: problem of, 276–79. *See also* tones

investiture, 40, 56–57, 58–59. *See also* gift-giving
iron, 24, 107–8, 114

jade, 201n5, 202, 216, 217
Japanese bells, 159n2
Japanese court music, 324
Java, 324
Ji clan, 44, 49–51, 318
Ji Hou–*yongzhong*, 208n27, 357
Jia Yi, 33, 39
Jia Yunfu, *113*
Jiahu, Wuyang (Henan), 265n31
*jian* vessel, *31*
Jiancun, Xiangyun (Yunnan), 332, 373
Jiangshan (Zhejiang), 333
Jiashan, Xinyu (Jiangxi), 333, 354
Jiazhuang, Anyang (Henan), 142n33, 333, 350
Jiefanglu, Luoyang (Henan), 176, 333
Jin, Dao Gong of, 60n90
Jin, Ping Gong of, 118
Jin, Tang Shu of, 56n70
Jin, Wei Jiang of, 60n90
Jin, state of, 49, 60–61, 182, 289
Jin dynasty, 190
Jin foundries, 65, 110, 179, *182*
Jinancheng, Jiangling (Hubei), 269, *270*, 392
Jincun, Luoyang (Henan), *184*, 185, 333, 362, 365, 366, 367, 391; tone data from, 256, *257*
Jing-*zhong*, 49, 345, 366
Jingjiecun, Lingshi (Shanxi), 138n26
jingles, 104
Jingli-*niuzhong*, 49, 207, 209, 210, 222, 326, 368; ornamentation on, 189; proportions of, 90, 94; tones of,

89, 92n43, 92–93; and pitch-
pipes, 311; and pitch standards, 301, 309; and scaling,
118, 119n64, 120, 276, 277,
278; and Spiral of Fifths,
304, 306; and tonal accuracy, 96, 118, 276, 323; and
tones, 218, 219, 227n1; and
Zeng bells, 249, 255
Matougang, Qingyuan
(Guangdong), 336, 337, 371,
*383*
Mawangcun, Chang'an
(Shaanxi), 337, 355, 356,
369–70; tone data from,
388, 389
Mawangcun chimes, *232, 233,
234*, 237, 238, 278, 393
Mawangdui, Changsha
(Hunan), 312, *313*
Maxiang, Heng Xian (Guangxi), 337
measurement standards, 315–
16, 317–18, 319n34
*mei* ornamentation: on *bo*, 174;
defined, 73, 75, 403; on
northern bells, 179;
periodization by, 157n69; in
Sichuan, 384; on southern
bells, 148, 151, 353, 378,
379; on Zeng bells, 187,
296
Meicun, Boluo (Guangdong),
337, 371
Mei'ershan (Nasangcun),
Heng Xian (Guangxi), 338
melodies, 53, 267, 283, 287,
312, 314, 324. *See also* folk
music
Mencius, 32, 53–54, 216, 322
metal alloys, 99–108, 115,
130, 132, 265. *See also particular metals*
Metropolitan Museum of Art,
bells in, 350, 351
Mexican bells, 132
Miao, Three (ethnic group),
374n1

Miaodigou, Sanmenxia
(Henan), 132n6, 337
Miaodun, Donghai (Jiangsu),
337, 369
Miaoqiancun, Wanrong
(Shanxi), 35, 174n47, 337,
364
*mingqi* bells, 102, 114n46, 159,
259, 325, 368–69; bronze,
340, 348; ceramic, 177, 329,
332, 341, 343; and decline of
bell-chimes, 322, 323; geographical distribution of,
180–81; gilt bronze, 177,
333; Han, 108, 190; lead,
326; pottery, 327, 344, 345,
381; proto-porcelain, 345,
381n13; wooden, 207n24,
327. *See also* lithophones;
musical instruments; ritual
vessels
minor-third bells, 234–36,
238–39, 241, 246, 247–49,
256, 310; defined, 233, 403;
and major-third bells, 264.
*See also* major-third bells
minor thirds, 266, 277, 307.
*See also* major thirds
mirrors, 103
modes, 77, 78, 267n, 276. *See
also* tones
Mohists, 322
Montelius, Oscar, 130n
Morse Collection, New York,
bell in, 360
mountain cults, 139
mouth-organs, 9, *10, 36*, 53,
119n64, 311n5; in texts, 215,
217
"muddy" (*zhuo*) pitch standards, 289n16, 290, 300,
317; defined, 287, 403; and
hexatonic sets, 288, 296,
297, 299, 304, 305, 308; and
tone definitions, 291, 293,
295
Muluocun, Liujiang (Guangxi), 337, 371

Musée Cernuschi, Paris, bell
in, 362
Musée Guimet, Paris, bell in,
359
Museum of Chinese History,
Beijing, bell in, 367
Museum of Eastern Art, Oxford, bell in, 364
Museum of Far Eastern Antiquities, Stockholm, bells in,
148, 351, 365
Museum of Fine Arts, Boston,
bells in, 357, 369
Museum of Hengyang
(Hunan), bell in, 360
music, 1–5; history of, 226–
27; and political power, 319.
*See also* folk music; musical
theory; popular music; ritual
music
musical bells, 402, 403. *See
also* chime-bells
musical instruments: at Anyang, 136; bells as, 14; and
correlative cosmology, 4–5,
101; and decline of bells,
323; earliest, 132; melodic,
275, 277; as *mingqi*, 55n64,
119n64, 332; in orchestras,
160, 215–17, 266; and social
order, 1; tones of, 226,
229n5, 265, 267; tuning
of, 314; Western Zhou,
159n4; in Zeng tomb, 7,
9, 53
musical notation system, 19
musical stones. *See* chimestones; lithophones
musical theory: and bells, 16,
18–19, 314; and decline of
bells, 320, 323; earliest
sources on, 3, 4; and
measurement standards,
315; and pitch, 226–27; and
pitch-pipes, 310–14; and
ritual, 23; and tones, 217,
267, 324; in Zeng inscriptions, 9, 12, 280–309

Designer:      Nola Burger
Compositor:    Asco Trade Typesetting Ltd.
Text:          10/13 Bembo
Display:       Bembo
Printer:       Thomson-Shore, Inc.
Binder:        Thomson-Shore, Inc.